T5-CRL-010

Paradox 4:
The Complete Reference

Carole Boggs Matthews
and
Patricia Shepard

Osborne **McGraw-Hill**

Berkeley New York St. Louis San Francisco
Auckland Bogotá Hamburg London Madrid
Mexico City Milan Montreal New Delhi Panama City
Paris São Paulo Singapore Sydney
Tokyo Toronto

This book is dedicated to Marty Matthews and Dick Shepard for their encouragement and support on those dark days before the dawn.

Osborne **McGraw-Hill**
2600 Tenth Street
Berkeley, California 94710
U.S.A.

For information on translations and book distributors outside of the U.S.A., write to Osborne **McGraw-Hill** at the above address.

Paradox 4:   The Complete Reference

Copyright © 1993 by Martin S. Matthews and Carol Boggs Matthews. All rights reserved. Printed in the United States of America. Except as permitted under the Copyright Act of 1976, no part of this publication may be reproduced or distributed in any form or by any means, or stored in a database or retrieval system, without the prior written permission of the publisher, with the exception that the program listings may be entered, stored, and executed in a computer system, but they may not be reproduced for publication.

1234567890 DOC 99876543

ISBN 0-07-881794-3

Information has been obtained by Osborne **McGraw-Hill** from sources believed to be reliable. However, because of the possibility of human or mechanical error by our sources, Osborne **McGraw-Hill**, or others, Osborne **McGraw-Hill** does not guarantee the accuracy, adequacy, or completeness of any information and is not responsible for any errors or omissions or the results obtained from use of such information.

Contents

Part I
The Paradox Environment

1
Introducing Paradox   3

2
Database Basics   31

Part II
Creating and Modifying

3
Creating and Editing a
Database   69

Acknowledgments

As with any book, many people contribute to creating a quality product. There are several people who deserve to be recognized for their parts in producing *Paradox 4: The Complete Reference.*

Ed Hartmann, owner of Database Consulting Services, contributed much to the programming content of the book. He wrote Chapter 13, "Summary of PAL Functions and Commands," and contributed much to Chapter 15, "Using Paradox SQL Link." Ed's technical expertise in these areas is greatly appreciated as well as his responsiveness to our tight deadlines. Karen Quick, Systems Engineer at Novell, Inc., supported Ed during his work on the Paradox SQL Link by providing access to the Novell SQL database server. P. T. Ong, software engineer and expert in SQL, provided technical editing of the chapter. Their contributions are greatly appreciated.

From Borland, Nan Borreson, Manager of Publishing Relations, and Administrative Assistant, Karen Giles, helped by responding to our continuous needs for information, beta copies, and documentation. They were very helpful and responsive—so very important when trying to write a book under deadlines.

From Borland, Technical Editor, Rick Elliott, performed the technical review of the book and kept us honest by verifying the accuracy of the book. His efforts are greatly appreciated.

Robin Rowe, of Rowe Software, soon to be a new neighbor in Washington, also gave valuable feedback on the book.

The excellent team from Osborne **McGraw-Hill** responsible for producing the book deserves a hearty round of applause. They pushed forward with good humor and expertise, supporting us in our efforts to write a quality book. A very big thanks to Bill Pollock, Acquisitions Editor; Vicki Van Ausdall, Associate Editor; Judith Brown, Project Editor; and Ann Spivack, Copy Editor, and all the others on the team.

Introduction

Paradox 4 is a comprehensive database management system developed by Borland International. It is said to be a paradox in database systems, since it combines full database power with ease of use. This provides you with a tool to increase productivity and make better decisions in your business or profession.

About This Book

If you have purchased Paradox 4 or are contemplating buying it to use in your business, *Paradox 4: The Complete Reference* is for you. As a reference book, it can help you learn how to use the features of Paradox 4 to solve business problems, it can serve as a quick learning tool, or simply as a reminder for how to perform a function. *Paradox 4: The Complete Reference* will help you whether you're a new user of Paradox or a somewhat experienced user who now wants to develop more advanced skills or get some new ideas on how to apply the program. If you are new to Version 4, *Paradox 4: The Complete Reference* can help you get oriented quickly to the new features.

Instructions in the book are generally presented with a step-by-step technique, explaining not only what you should do, but also why, and what the implications of each procedure are. Icons (see "Conventions" below) mark tips, notes, and cautionary tidbits, which are scattered throughout the book to emphasize certain subjects. Shortcut keys and mouse actions, also marked with icons, are identified when appropriate, so that you can learn how to accomplish a task the most convenient or quickest way. As you work with the examples, you will be able to compare the screens on your monitor with reproductions of the screen throughout the book, so that you will always be firmly anchored in the program.

Paradox 4: The Complete Reference supplements Borland's own documentation, by continuing where that documentation leaves off. Whereas the Borland documentation presents you with several manuals covering each of the major parts of Paradox, *Paradox 4: The Complete Reference* consolidates this information into one comprehensive reference book. *Paradox 4: The Complete Reference* covers Paradox thoroughly and efficiently by presenting what you need to know to use the product effectively in one easy-to-use book.

How This Book Is Organized

The organization of *Paradox 4: The Complete Reference* provides both flexibility and ease of use in learning the program. The book is primarily organized by operation or task, for example, creating a table or printing a report. Then, indexes organized by command name, like Chapter 13 on PAL commands and Appendix D on Paradox commands, supplement this task-oriented organization. You can find what you need by finding either the command name or the operation you want to accomplish.

The book is divided into six parts. Part I, "The Paradox Environment," introduces databases and Paradox 4. If you are new to Paradox, you will want to read these chapters; if you are an experienced user of Paradox, you still will find it worthwhile scanning these chapters since they provide an overview of Paradox's environment, and also a grounding in terminology and concepts that are used in the rest of the book.

Chapter 1, "Introducing Paradox," defines databases and then describes Paradox features, first from a generic viewpoint and then from the viewpoint of the particular capabilities of Paradox 4. It discusses the concepts of relational databases in order to put the product in perspective with other packages. (Relational databases are discussed further in Chapter 3.)

Chapter 1 also describes the basic elements of the Paradox 4 environment. It includes a detailed description of the menus and screens and how Paradox 4 uses the keyboard. Submenus, error messages, and prompts are discussed. Common database terminology, such as columns, rows, fields, and queries, are explained, as are Paradox-specific terms such as tables, forms, images, scripts, and objects.

Chapter 2, "Database Basics," provides a reference for all the housekeeping and basic functions that must be performed in a computer environment. Such activities as using Help, bringing up Paradox and exiting, setting up directories, working with disk files, naming objects, and backing up are discussed. This chapter also covers renaming, copying, and deleting files.

Chapters 3, 4, and 5 comprise Part II, "Creating and Modifying," which describes how a database is created and maintained. Chapter 3, "Creating and Editing a Database," describes how to design and then create a database—that is, one or more tables. Defining columns or fields and field types is covered, as are alternate ways to view the table structure. Then the basics of entering data into the table are discussed. (Chapter 4 also describes how to edit data in a table using the Editor.) Chapter 3 also covers moving the cursor, adding information to a record, inserting and deleting records, undoing editing changes, and using the field editor to change data.

The Paradox Editor, which has been expanded to include text editing in Version 4, is covered in Chapter 4, "Using the Editor." Using the Editor to enter or change Memo fields (a new addition to Version 4) or any text file is discussed. Primarily, however, the Editor is used to create and edit PAL scripts, which are discussed in Chapter 12.

Chapter 5, "Modifying the Database," discusses how to add a new table or change the table structure (restructure) in a database. Adding or deleting a field to or from an existing table, changing the field type, or renaming a field are described. In addition, the chapter addresses how to sort data in a single field and then in multiple fields. Finally, creating and using secondary indexes is covered here.

Chapters 6, 7, 8, and 9 make up Part III, "Querying and Reporting." Chapter 6, "Querying a Database," describes querying a single table versus querying more than one table, which includes such tasks as selecting fields, specifying a sort order, and entering the query criteria. Key fields used to link data in more than one table are described. Also included are calculating values, querying a group of records, defining and querying a set of records, and applying inclusive links to display all records in linked tables. Chapter 6 also covers saving and retrieving queries.

In Chapter 7, "Creating and Using Forms," you learn how to use a standard or preferred form to enter, edit, or view data, as well as how to use a custom form for one or multiple tables. Designing the custom form, creating it for one or more tables, merging forms for multiple tables, and then using the form to enter, edit, and view information are covered. When dealing with multiple tables, master tables and linked detail tables are discussed.

Using the standard free-form or tabular report format is described in Chapter 8, "Creating and Using Reports." In a discussion of custom reports, you learn how to add page or report headers, insert and delete fields from the report, change the page layout, group and summarize data, and combine multiple tables in a report. Creating form letters and mailing labels are also described.

Chapter 9, "Working with the Image Menu and Graphs," covers how to alter the information displayed on the screen and how to create lines and markers graphs, bar graphs, pie charts, plus seven other types of graphs.

Part IV, "Scripts and Programming," consists of chapters 10 through 13. Chapter 10, "Creating and Using Scripts," addresses how to create scripts (PAL programs or macros) by recording frequently used keystrokes and then saving and using them. The chapter covers how to create a script without knowing PAL. Chapter 10 also includes how to execute a script repeatedly, how to edit a script, and how to save it.

In Chapter 11, "Using the Application Workshop," you learn how to install the Workshop and then how to use it to create an application. This includes selecting tables to be used in the application, creating and editing application menus and submenus, defining menu commands and actions, and changing a menu or action.

Chapter 12, "Using PAL," assumes you have some programming experience in the discussion of the PAL programming language. It describes some of the newer, more complex commands available in Version 4, such as SHOWPULLDOWN and

GETEVENT. The chapter covers how to use such facilities of PAL as the PAL menu and the PAL Debugger. Concepts and basic features of the language are discussed, such as event driven programming, new pull-down menus and dialog box commands, and the PAL layered environment. You also learn how to enter commands and expressions, and how to use variables, arrays, and dynamic arrays.

Each PAL command, its syntax, a short description, an example when needed, and helpful hints about the command are listed in Chapter 13, "Summary of PAL Functions and Commands." Particularly useful is a list of the commands by category, which is at the end of the chapter. If you are not sure which command to use, you can look it up by category, for example, Financial, Input/Output, or Date and Time.

In Part V, "Tools and Networking," Chapter 14, "Using Paradox Tools," describes the comprehensive Tools menu and its options, QuerySpeed, ExportImport, Info, Net, and More. The chapter describes how to enter passwords, establish access with Lock and PreventLock, provide protection of a network, export and import files, plus other features. (The Tools options to rename, copy and delete tables, forms, reports, scripts, and graphs are covered in Chapter 2.)

Chapter 15, "Using Paradox SQL Link," describes how to use the Paradox SQL Link to connect to one or more SQL database servers. It defines SQL (Structured Query Language) and then describes how to install an SQL link, connect to a server, query a remote table, and create and use a remote table. Paradox's unique SQL commands are summarized in the chapter.

Part VI, "Appendixes," includes Appendix A, "Installing Paradox," Appendix B, "Customizing Paradox," Appendix C, "ASCII and Extended ASCII Character Sets," and Appendix D, "Command Index." Particularly useful is the Paradox command index in Appendix D. It is a table of Paradox menu paths with a cross-reference to where the path is discussed in the book.

Finally, you will find a pull-out command card at the back of the book with all of the shortcut keys and key combinations that can be used in each mode in Paradox.

Equipment You Will Need

To run Paradox 4, you must have at least 2MB of RAM. Although more memory is not required, additional extended memory provides benefits in performance.

A hard disk is required, and you need 5MB of disk space to install Paradox 4 without the optional programs, or 5.5MB with the optional software. You also need to maintain free disk space of about three times the size of the largest table you will be using. Paradox uses the space to create several temporary tables when you are working with the program, particularly during queries.

You will need a monitor with an adapter, and to display graphics, you need a CGA, EGA, VGA, 8514, 3270, ATT, TandyT1000, or Hercules monitor with adapter.

You will make best use of Paradox 4 with a mouse. Paradox supports any mouse compatible with Microsoft's or Logitech's bus or serial mice, or IBM's PS/2 mouse.

Conventions

Paradox 4: The Complete Reference uses several conventions designed to make the book easier for you to use. These are as follows:

- **Bold** type is used when you are instructed to type text from the keyboard.

- Keys on the keyboard that are commands are presented in small capital letters; for example, RIGHT ARROW and ENTER.

- When you are expected to enter a command, you will be told to press the key(s). If you are to enter text or date, you will be told to type.

- Menu paths are indicated by menu option names separated by slashes, such as **T**ools/**M**ore/**D**irectory.

- Some Menu options contain a boldface letter, for example, **S**cripts. This indicates that the *S* is a *hot key,* and that pressing it will invoke the menu as if you selected the menu option with the mouse or keyboard.

- Icons mark paragraphs that emphasize tips, notes, cautions, shortcut keys, and mouse actions, for example:

This icon advises you about how to use shortcut keys to accomplish a task without using the system of menus and submenus.

This icon advises you about how to use your mouse to accomplish a task without using the menus and submenus.

This icon advises the reader about a useful tip

This icon advises the reader about notes which emphasizes information or expands on it.

This icon warns the user about potentially harmful actions.

Part *I*

The Paradox
Environment

Chapter *1*

Introducing Paradox

The name "Paradox" is a tribute to the modern trend in database development. Database software has always been thought to be *either* easy to use and limited in capability, *or* comprehensive in capability and therefore hard to use. Paradox is both easy to use and comprehensive in capability–a *paradox* in database software.

Database programs vary greatly in capability and capacity. On the one extreme are mainframe computer databases that require complete staffs to manage and use them; on the other are limited database programs that allow simple uses, such as name and address listings, that one person would use, perhaps for addressing Christmas cards or tracking golf teams. Paradox is much more than a limited, single-use database. It offers many of the features of a larger and more sophisticated database on a mainframe, but without the staff requirements. In many ways the large mainframe and microcomputer databases are approaching each other in capabilities. When you consider the availability of remote database systems to a Paradox user, through the Paradox SQL Link, for instance, the transition from micro to mainframe is really made.

This chapter explains the concepts of databases and some of their more common features, including searching and sorting, editing, and reporting. Then the chapter explains the basic elements of the Paradox environment, such as screens and menus, working with multiple tables, and using the mouse. In addition to common database terminology, specific terms unique to Paradox are covered. Some of the new features in Paradox 4 are described. Finally, the chapter gives a brief overview of each of the Main menu options.

Database Concepts

A database program's job is to help organize lists and files of items. Almost any list or table of data, such as lists of names, inventory items, accounting data, customer or vendor information, and so on, can be entered into a database. Information is placed into a database so that it can be quickly and easily retrieved and arranged. Once you have entered data into a database, you can rearrange and report on it as needed to see or analyze the desired data.

Most database programs offer organizational possibilities that are unavailable with nonautomated files. As Figure 1-1 illustrates, Paradox is centered around a database itself, called a *table* in Paradox. The most basic functions to Paradox, or any database, are data entry and editing–to enter data and then correct or modify it until you can trust it to give you the information you need. The next layer of functions involves retrieving information–the prime reason for having a database in the first place.

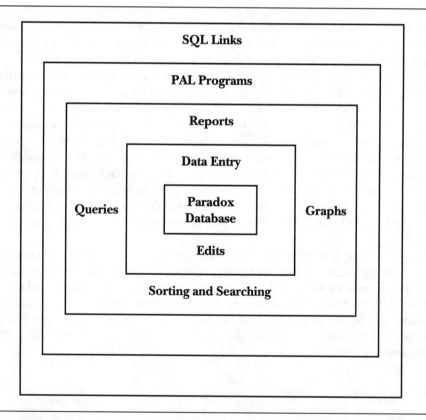

Figure 1-1. *Paradox functions are centered around the core of the system, the database*

Retrieving information in turn involves sorting and searching the database for specific information, running queries to answer questions about the data, and then printing reports or graphs showing the relationships of the data. If you want to explore the farthest reaches of Paradox, you can also use PAL (Paradox Application Language) to program your own application to use the functions of Paradox. Or, using the Paradox SQL Link, you can use Paradox commands to interface with remote databases.

Searching and Sorting

Software-based databases offer an ability to arrange data, search it for specific information, report on it in a variety of ways, and update and correct the data so that large amounts of information can be managed quickly at reasonable cost.

Data within files can be arranged by sorting the records in many ways, using such criteria as name, city, state or ZIP, product type, size of sale or purchase, and so on. The data to be sorted can be a subset of the entire database, and it is possible to view and sort only selected records within the database.

A database can be easily searched for specific data. Some databases allow search and replace capabilities where one value is replaced with another throughout the entire database or a selected subset. Searches need not be made for exact matches of a specific criteria. "Somewhat like" searches, that is, searches where the exact criteria are uncertain or unknown, can also be performed. You can select values within ranges as well. For example, perhaps you want to find all sales over a certain dollar amount. If you want a faster search to be available on a certain table, perhaps to link it up with another table, you can instruct the database programs to build an index of the table. An *index* identifies a field of data, such as Last Name, which can be used to sort and retrieve data quickly. Sorting and searching is discussed in detail in Chapter 5.

Editing

Editing changes are easily and efficiently made within databases. It is a relatively simple matter to locate and update out-of-date records quickly. At the same time, obsolete records can be saved to a backup file, and then later deleted from the file. Both the editing techniques of inserting new characters between existing ones and overtyping characters so that original characters are overwritten with new ones are usually supported. Editing a database is covered in Chapter 3.

Some database systems, like Paradox, also have a text editor as a separate tool, as opposed to the database editor. These can be used for creating and editing text data, such as memos or notes about a particular database item. You can also create any text file, such as a PAL program, using the Paradox Editor. Text editing is discussed in Chapter 4.

Reporting

Databases allow you to generate reports from information contained in the database. In reporting, most databases allow you to create either tabular, one-line lists of data using selected data from records, or reports showing more information from each record than the one-line list allows (called *free-form* reports). Figure 1-2 shows an example of a simple telephone list. Figure 1-3 shows an example of a free-form report created using Paradox.

Many database programs, including Paradox, can also generate graphs based on raw or calculated values. These graphs provide instant visual feedback on the contents of the data. Retrieving information from several database sources to compile one report is a feature of many databases, including Paradox. Figure 1-4 shows an example of a graph created with Paradox.

```
1/09/92                        FESTIVAL '92 MERCHANT NAMELIST                              Page   1
No.   Company / First Name  Last Name    Address Line 1 / Line 2    City      ST  ZIP   Phone 1/2   Typ/Auc89-91
----  --------------------  ---------    -----------------------    ----      --  ---   ---------   ------------
AREA: A

  1   Adventure Northwest Byline         P.O. Box 1111              Auburn    WA  98002  555-1234   SERVICE
      Carole              Ormaye                                                          555-5432

  2   Alaska Adventures                  P.O. Box 5555              Seattle   WA  98168  555-1234   Service
      James A.            Jobson         Only mention Soroptimist                                  Y

  3   Alaska State Tree Search           8324 Sanford Drive         Oak Harbor WA 98277  555-1246   SERVICE
      John and Sally      Samualson                                                      525-9094

  4   Albert C. Gabel                    2115 Sequal                Langley   WA  98260  555-2857   Construct
      Albert & Sara       Gabel                                                                     Y

  5   Alexander and Sedro                P.O. Box 100               Clinton   WA  98236  555-1234   Retail
                                                                                                    Y

  6   Allied Services                    5000 View Lane             Langley   WA  98260             SERVICE
      Alice               Berg

  7   Alpine Inns                        405 Highway 20             Leavnworth WA 98826  (509)      TOUR-INN
                                                                                         555-3784

  8   American Assoc. Of Pest Controllers 6256 Central Ave          Clinton   WA  98236  555-1536   Service
      Richard Weeder                                                                     555-0987

  9   Anderson Printing Works            P.O. Box 22                Anacortes WA  98221  555-8569   SERVICE
      Trudy               Anderson

 10   Andrew Stauffer Enterprises        P.O. Box 6                 Langley   WA  98260  555-1271   Service
      Andrew              Stauffer

 11   Andy Huffer                        8111 SeaSide Drive         Clinton   WA  98236  555-1234   PROF

 12   Andy's Auto Repair                 7500 Caulter Bay           Clinton   WA  98236  555-1234   Service
      Andy                Cacus                                                                     Y

 13   Ann Prichard                       5300 Harbor Ave            Freeland  WA  98249  555-1374   Prof
                                                                                                    Y   Y

 14   Annie Steven's                     P.O. Box 8800              Langley   WA  98260  555-1769   RETAIL
      Donna               Vasolet        1001 S. 8th                                                Y   Y

 15   Anthony's Port                     456 Army Way               Edmonds   WA  98020  555-1357   TOUR-REST
      Susan               McDowell

 16   Audrey Beener                      2777 Sully Drive           Clinton   WA  98236  555-1278   PROF

 17   Clean Carpets                      1818 Langley Way           Langley   WA  98260  555-1357
      Rick and Shirley    Rosa                                                                      Y

 18   Investigations Galore              6400 Center Street         Clinton   WA  98236  555-7171   SERVICE
      Dick                McMellon                                                                  Y

 19   Kinsky Construction                3500 W. Sweet Lane         Clinton   WA  98236  555-1234   Construct
      Art                 Kincaid                                                        555-7654

 20   Seko Enterprises                   P.O. Box 666               Freeland  WA  98249  555-7654

 21   Steve Construction                 2685 Westlet Way           Clinton   WA  98236  555-1357   Construct
      Steve               Smith
```

Figure 1-2.   *Tabular type of report*

```
4/02/92          Customer List for Auction        Page    1


    Code: A
       Company: Clean Carpets
         Fname: Rick and Shirley
         Lname: Rosa
      Address1: 1818 Langley Way
      Address2:
          City: Langley        ST: WA    ZIP: 98260

        Phone1: 555-1357       Phone2:
          Type:

         Auc90:       Cou91:        Auc92:        Auc93: Y


    Code: A
       Company: Kinsky Construction
         Fname: Art
         Lname: Kincaid
      Address1: 3500 W. Sweet Lane
      Address2:
          City: Clinton        ST: WA    ZIP: 98236

        Phone1: 555-1234       Phone2: 555-7654
          Type: Construct

         Auc90:       Cou91:        Auc92:        Auc93:


    Code: A
       Company: Investigations Galore
         Fname: Dick
         Lname: McMellon
      Address1: 6400 Center Street
      Address2:
          City: Clinton        ST: WA    ZIP: 98236

        Phone1: 555-7171       Phone2:
          Type: SERVICE

         Auc90: Y     Cou91:        Auc92:        Auc93:
```

Figure 1-3.   *Free-form type of report*

Entering Data

When entering data into a database, you can create an input form that closely resembles the paper forms on which you collect the data. For example, when entering billing information, you may create an entry screen that has the same data elements in the same order as the original purchase order. This ability to provide a close relationship between different forms with related data allows for greater ease in data entry because you do not have to search the source document for the next data to be entered into the computer. When entering data, it is also possible to specify certain tests, called *validation* or *valchecks*, to be applied to the data so that fewer entry mistakes are made. For example, your database can be designed to make sure that all digits of a telephone number are entered, or to make sure that the customer ID is not omitted from a new customer's record.

More complex forms, such as those in Paradox, allow you to create multiple pages per form to enter one record, multiple record forms to enter more than one record

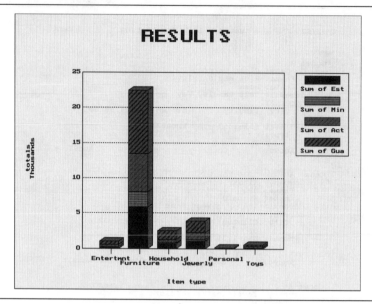

Figure 1-4.   *Example of a Paradox graph*

per page of a form, and multiple table or database forms to enter data into several tables at once. Chapter 3 discusses how to create a database.

Queries

A *query* is made when you are seeking information about the data contained in the database. You specify what information you want to see, and the program searches the database (or databases) to present the answer to you. The nature of queries is usually broader than a search for one record. An example of a query might be, which salesmen earned commissions for Product A in Houston? Or, which items in your inventory are approaching the point at which you must reorder? Chapter 6 shows how to use queries in Paradox.

Networking

Networking allows users to share database files with other users, but networking data also raises problems when two or more users want the same data. The use of passwords and the ability to lock records while changes are being made to them are two commonly used measures to prevent data from being erroneously and disastrously modified.

SQL Link in Paradox provides a way to connect a Paradox-based system with remote SQL database servers. This allows remote users to access mainframe or remote micro-based databases using Paradox commands. Paradox tools are available even though the user is based on a separate and distant computer.

Programming with Databases

Many database systems provide programming languages so that a user can create custom applications, such as an inventory system or an order entry system. These custom applications provide an environment where the user doesn't have to know how to use Paradox to use the application.

PAL (Paradox Application Language) allows you to create a complex application or to simply create shorter ways to perform common tasks without using Paradox menus. For example, you can record the keystrokes needed to print a report or run a query, and then replay them by pressing only one or two keystrokes. Chapters 12 and 13 address using PAL.

Elements of a Paradox Database

As shown in Figure 1-5, a *database* is a collection of lists or *tables* containing information about a category of data. Paradox considers databases and tables to be closely related, but slightly different. For instance, one table may be a collection of names and addresses or inventory items; a database is one or more of these tables that are related to each other in some way, as you'll see shortly.

Paradox is a relational database. *Relational* databases allow you to retrieve data from several different tables, thereby showing complete information without having to duplicate data. For example, one table might contain a customer's name and address, a second might have the customer's purchase orders, a third might list current billing information, while a fourth might have an analysis of products purchased by the customers. All four tables are customer related, yet each has its own peculiarities and is in some way unique from the other tables. Only one field, perhaps the customer ID number, may be common to the tables. Yet, in this example, all four tables comprise the customer database. The retrieved data remains stored in four separate files, but is viewed together through the power of the relational database program. Later, you will see more clearly how this is done in Paradox.

Table Structures

In a table, *records* contain all information about one entity or item in the database. For example, one record in a table might list one customer's name and address, while another record in a second table might contain that customer's purchase orders. A record contains *fields,* individual data items, which actually hold the data element. For example, a customer's record might include several fields, such as Business

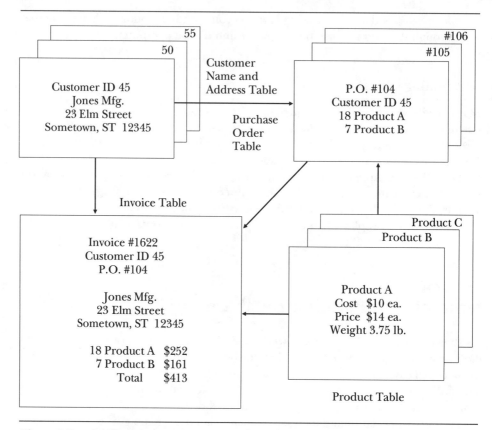

Figure 1-5.   *A billing database in Paradox showing the close relationship between tables and databases*

Name, Street Address, City, State, and ZIP. Figure 1-6 shows this record and field relationship.

Tables may have several smaller data files or tables attached to them. All "attachments" to a table are called *objects*. Paradox allows you to attach several different types of objects, such as tables, forms, reports, graphs, and scripts, to your tables.

Tables may have their own *report formats* or report specifications, which define the fields and the order in which they appear on a report. For example, when you want a printed report from the Customer table, you may choose to print mailing labels, name lists (perhaps in several different sequences), or perhaps a customer record "dump," where all information contained in a table about one record is printed. You may have other table related specifications as well as an ability to build graphs—perhaps of performances of salespeople—with an ongoing, continuously updated, visual graph. In addition, if you perform one action frequently (for example, monthly searches for specific data, or sorting and printing special reports), you can capture

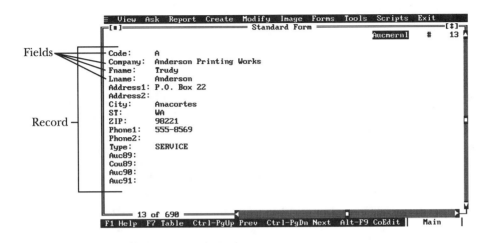

Fields

Record

Figure 1-6. *Form image of a record showing record and field relationship*

the keystrokes in a macro (called a *script*) needed to do the task. Thereafter, you would simply press a combination of keys to activate that captured script.

Paradox Capacities

In Paradox a table may contain as many as 262 million characters. An additional 64MB can be contained within a single memo field, which is a field containing comments or text. However, the memo field characters are stored in two files: up to a *fixed* 240 characters are stored within the table itself and the remaining *overflow* characters are stored in a separate file attached to the table. The overflow memo file is identified by its .MB extension. The 64MB size limitation can be increased to 256MB per memo with some adjustments in Paradox.

A table may have up to 255 fields of data and each field may contain 255 characters per field, except for memo fields. The types of data contained in fields are described in Chapter 3.

Each table can have up to 15 forms and reports attached to it.

Up to 24 tables can be included in a single query; that is, a query can retrieve information from 24 tables in order to answer one query. Although this isn't a limitation since complex queries are usually solved better piece by piece than as one huge query.

Table Images

When viewing a table on the screen, you may see information contained in the table displayed in one of two ways. As a *form image* or *view,* you can see information pertaining to one record only. In Figure 1-6, you see one customer's name and address data on a form image. Paradox automatically creates one standard form per table on which to display data. You can change the standard form and create others. Forms can be created to view several records at a time, even from different tables.

Table images show data about many customers displayed in columns and rows, as seen in Figure 1-7. *Columns* show only one type of information in vertical listings. For example, the first column in Figure 1-7 contains only the record number, the second column contains a code, the third column the company name, and so on. A row of data is a horizontal display of information for one record. For example, on Figure 1-7, record 3 contains information about one company, Investigations Galore. The information displayed in a row is restricted because of the screen size. Consequently, fewer fields of data can be seen (unless you move the screen image to display the unseen fields or reduce the size of the fields seen on the screen—both of which Paradox allows).

Table view is the default display when you first see the table on the screen. A *default* is the assumed option Paradox uses until you change it. For example, you can change the table view to form view.

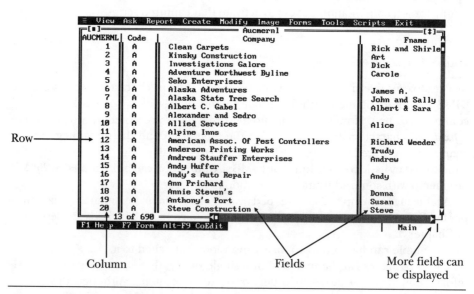

Figure 1-7.   *Screen showing a table image of the table*

Paradox Desktop and Windows

Paradox uses the concept of a *desktop* to interface with its users. When you retrieve database tables from disk and place them onto the Paradox workspace, you are placing them "on the desktop." When you retrieve several tables from disk, you will place them in a stack on the desktop. The most recently retrieved table is placed on the top of the stack, and is the active window. You can easily change the active window with several available commands.

Active Windows

You can tell that a window is *active* when the window border is highlighted, when mouse tools are displayed (described more fully shortly), and the cursor is evident in the table. On the other hand, inactive tables have dull borders, no mouse tools, and no cursor. Figure 1-8 shows a comparison of active and inactive tables.

Window Displays

When multiple tables are placed on the desktop, the tables are shown in a *cascaded* display by default, as shown in Figure 1-9. The tables are shown in a stack, with the active window on top, hiding the rest of the tables. A cascaded display allows you to

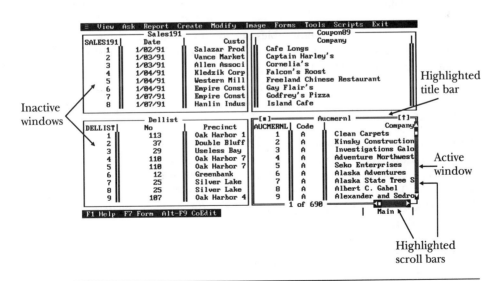

Figure 1-8.   *Lower-right window is the active window in this tiled display of tables*

Inactive
stacked
windows

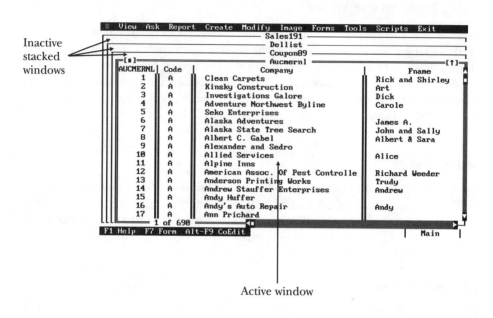

Active window

Figure 1-9.   *Screen showing cascaded display of tables*

see a fuller image of the tables, allowing a complete form to be shown, as compared to the tiled view.

When you want to see several tables at one time, you may display them as *tiled* windows, or with smaller windows shown side by side, as in Figure 1-8. Tiled displays can show you some of several tables.

Paradox Modes

Paradox is organized into *modes*, which are basically levels of menus and submenus. When you move from one menu to another, you may be entering a different mode as well. The uppermost mode is the Main mode, which includes the System, View, Ask, Image, Tools, Scripts, and Exit options. Each of the other options, Report, Create, Modify, and Forms, represents another mode and has its own system of menus and screen displays.

A mode indicator, on the right of the status bar, indicates which mode you are in, as seen here in Report mode:

Anytime you are in a mode other than Main mode and wish to exit, you must first complete or cancel the operation you are performing. You will then be returned to Main mode. The following shows an example of a **R**eport mode menu that allows you to **D**o-It!, or **C**ancel and then exit.

```
≡ Field  TableBand  Group  Output  Setting  DO-IT!  Cancel
```

Paradox 4's Screens and Menus

Screens and menus in Paradox provide you with needed information. Screens offer certain status information, such as record counts and warning messages, to enable you to track your progress. Menus provide the interface to Paradox's programs and allow you to give directions to Paradox by selecting menu options.

When you first bring up Paradox 4 on your screen, you will see the screen shown in Figure 1-10. This screen contains four parts: the Main menu, the desktop, the message area at the bottom of the screen (not shown), and the speedbar, which contains key and mouse reminders such as F1 (Help). If a menu is displayed, the name of the menu option is also displayed. (The message window is not shown in Figure 1-10 because it only appears when a message is displayed.)

To display the Main menu and move the cursor to it, you must press F10 first.

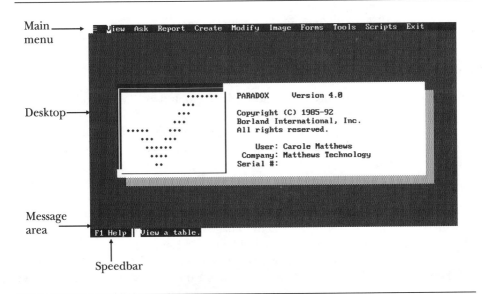

Figure 1-10.   *Main menu shown when Paradox is first loaded*

Selecting Menu Options

You tell Paradox which actions to take by selecting options or commands from the menu at the top of the screen. Choosing an option may cause an action to take place immediately, or it may lead to another menu or dialog box (which allows you to provide additional information to Paradox). When a menu option has an arrow tip to the right of it, as shown in the following illustration, you will be shown another menu. An option followed by dots indicates a dialog box will be displayed.

You can choose an available option in three ways:

- After pressing F10 to move the cursor from the desktop to the menu, you can use the LEFT ARROW or RIGHT ARROW keys to move to the option. Once it is highlighted, press ENTER.

- You can type the first or highlighted letter of the option you want when the menu is displayed.

- You can click on the menu option with the mouse.

Using Mouse Screen Tools

The Paradox screen contains several mouse driven tools that allow you to manipulate windows within Paradox, as shown in Figure 1-11.

The *Close box* at the top left of the window closes a window. When you click on this icon with the mouse, Paradox will cancel the actions in the active window and remove it from the screen.

The *Maximize/Restore* icon at the top right of the window allows you to toggle between maximizing the size of a screen and restoring it to its previous size. If the active image is already maximized and you click on the icon, the image will be returned to the previous size. If the active image has not been maximized when you click on the icon, the size of the image will be maximized.

The *vertical* and *horizontal scroll bars* at the bottom and right side of the window can be used to scroll through a table. Clicking on the upward or downward arrows on the scroll bars will cause the image in the window to move up or down by one line. If you click and hold the arrows, the image moves continuously up or down.

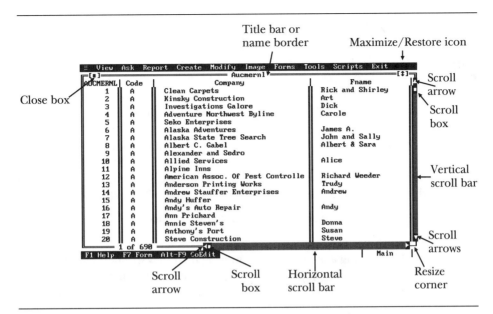

Figure 1-11. *Mouse tools enhance your ability to work with screens*

The rectangular *scroll box* at the right of the screen places the image relatively within the table. For example, in Figure 1-11, the scroll box is shown all the way at the top, indicating that you are viewing the beginning of the table. If the scroll box is in the middle of the scroll bar, you will see the middle part of the table; if at the bottom, you'll see the end of the table.

The *Resize corner* at the bottom right of the screen resizes a window. When you click on the Resize corner of an active window, you can drag the corner, changing the size of the window as you drag the mouse, as shown here:

The *top border* (title bar) at the top of the window performs two functions: if you click on it and then drag it, the window will move on the screen, or if you simply double-click on the Border icon, the window, if not already maximized in size, will become so.

An inactive window will become active if you click anywhere within it.

Features of Paradox 4

Enhancements to Paradox 4 have been made in three areas: modifications seen by end users, internal changes such as speed enhancements, and PAL programming enhancements for application programmers. This book focuses on the changes visible to end users and the PAL programming enhancements.

- A *new user interface* features windows. You can move the windows on the screen, resize them, or switch from window to window, all using either a keyboard or a mouse. You can view most objects in separate, stacked windows. Vertical and horizontal scroll bars on a window may be used to scroll quickly through a table.

- *Pull-down menus* are featured with pop-up dialog boxes.

- *Mouse functions* may be used for several purposes, such as moving the cursor to a field, selecting a menu option, entering field view so a field can be edited, resizing a column or window, moving a column or window to a different position, or maximizing or closing a window.

- You can choose to retain the *Paradox 3.5 user interface* or to move on to the *version 4 user interface*. This allows applications written for 3.5 to operate correctly.

- A new *System menu* has been added which includes many options for working with the screen display, such as rearranging and resizing windows, switching between versions 3.5 and 4 interfaces, using cascading or tiled displays of windows, or choosing between 43- or 50-line video display modes. This menu is also where you can access the Custom Configuration Program for custom changes to Paradox, or the Paradox Application Workshop (previously called the Personal Programmer) for guided application programming.

- *Memo fields,* a new field type, allow you to enter text of virtually any length. You can query memo fields, report on them, sort them on the fixed part of a memo field, and use them to store binary data (*BLOB* fields). A new text editor is included that offers the extensive editing capabilities of cut and paste, search and replace, and block operations.

- Using windows, you can now *design a form or report* with a table image showing at the same time.

- Paradox 4 has *enhanced support of secondary indexes,* while it continues its support of primary and secondary indexes. Tables can be sorted by any column. If the column is not an indexed one, Paradox will build a secondary index automatically. You can select multiple fields to be a secondary index, or you can create indexes that ignore uppercase and lowercase letters while sorting or group them separately. More than one secondary index can exist for a table.

- The *Report Previewer* has been enhanced to allow scrolling up, down, left, and right through an image of a report displayed on the screen as it will be printed on paper. You can search for text within a report.

- There is now *PostScript printer* support.

- *Networking options* are available on whether to restart queries to a table when other users are editing it, or to provide the user with an answer to the query regardless of the changes. The user can choose whether speed or accuracy is more important.

- *Faster response times* in Paradox 4 are available because of improvements to memory management, query and sort algorithms, network performance, and other internal programming areas.

- PAL programs *run faster* because of new and improved programming techniques.

Paradox Main Menu Options

The Main menu is displayed when you press F10 and the cursor is moved to the **View** option. If the Main menu is already displayed, only the cursor is moved. The Paradox Main menu commands are as follows:

- *System* provides tools for manipulating the display of screens and windows, gaining access to Paradox utilities, and so on.

- *View* places a table on the desktop where the data can be changed or modified.

- *Ask* provides a way for you to query a table.

- *Report* allows you to design or modify a report.

- *Modify* allows you to modify a database, its structure (the order and type of data), and the sequence of the data.

- *Image* adjusts how the data is displayed on the screen. It can also be used for creating graphs.

- *Forms* provides a way to design or change a form, such as an input form used for data entry.

- *Tools* provides miscellaneous tools for manipulating tables and objects, and for setting system defaults.

- *Scripts* allows you to create PAL programs, simple scripts, or complex applications.

- *Exit* leaves Paradox.

These menu options are explained more thoroughly in the coming chapters. However, a brief explanation of each is offered here, in order to orient you to the many functions performed by each of the options.

The System Option

The System submenu, the first option on the Main menu, is displayed as three horizontal dashes. You choose the System menu by pressing ALT-SPACEBAR or by clicking on the icon with the mouse. The System submenu offers commands that apply to a screen or window, rather than to a database or task being performed. The System submenu is always available to you in Paradox, regardless of which mode you are in. A summary of the System submenu commands is shown in Table 1-1. The menu is pictured here:

View Option

Choosing the View option displays a dialog box, as shown in Figure 1-12, which allows you to identify and then retrieve a table from disk. You may either type in the path and name of the table you wish to retrieve, or you may simply press ENTER and Paradox will display a list of tables in the default directory. To view a list of tables in another directory, you must type in a new path and press ENTER again.

As mentioned earlier, Paradox tables are first displayed in table view. To switch to a form view, use **I**mage/**P**ickform, or press F7 (Form View Toggle).

Ask Option

The **A**sk option allows you to query a table, or ask it questions. Choosing the **A**sk option displays a dialog box, as shown in Figure 1-13. This figure shows the query image, where the criteria are specified after a table has been identified as the query source. You may specify the search criteria for your query as well as the fields you want to see in answer to your query. You may also search for values within the table or create new values based on the table's fields. Chapter 6 explains the **A**sk option in detail.

System Command	Description	Function Key Command	Mouse Command
Next	Moves bottom window to the top	CTRL-F4	Click on bottom inactive window
Maximize/Restore	Toggles between increase to maximum size and restore previous size	SHIFT-F5	Click on the Maximize/Restore icon
Size/Move	Resizes active window to maximum size or moves active window. Use arrow keys only to move. Use SHIFT- arrow keys to resize	CTRL-F5	Click on Resize corner or click on top of border and drag to move window
Close	Closes the active window. May cancel task	CTRL-F8	Click on Close box
Window	Lists windows on desktop. Can choose the active window		
Interface	Switches from Paradox 4 to Paradox 3.5 user interfaces		
Desktop	Displays a menu of options to redraw, tile, cascade, or empty the screen windows, or display query windows		
Video	Displays a menu of video modes		
Editor	Loads the text editor for a new or existing file		

Table 1-1. System Options with Function Key and Mouse Commands

System Command	Description	Function Key Command	Mouse Command
Utilities	Displays a menu for choosing the Custom Configuration Program, or Paradox Application Workshop		
About	Displays Paradox version number and copyright information		

Table 1-1. *System Options with Function Key and Mouse Commands* (continued)

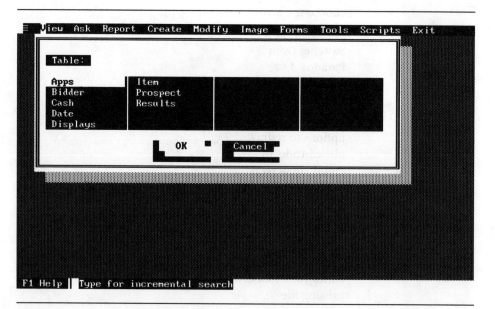

Figure 1-12. *Dialog box displayed when you choose the View option*

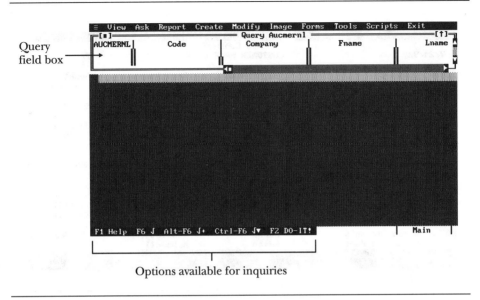

Query field box

Options available for inquiries

Figure 1-13. *Dialog box displayed when you choose the Ask option*

Report Option

The **R**eport option is used to create and print reports from one or more tables. The submenu looks like this:

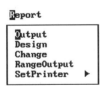

Within the **R**eport option are two modes, each with its own menus and screens. (Chapter 8 will explain these features in detail.) The **R**eport Designer mode allows you to create and change report specifications. You enter this mode with the **D**esign or **C**hange options. The output of the **R**eport Designer mode is a Paradox object, a report specification, attached to the table. The Report object is identified by the extension .R?? where ?? is a sequential number assigned to the report.

The second mode, **R**eport Previewer, lets you preview or view the report by displaying it on the screen. Once displayed, you can scroll back and forth through the report, viewing it before you print it to disk or on paper. You cannot edit the report in this mode. The **R**eport Previewer mode is entered by selecting it as the output medium from the **R**eport/**O**utput or **R**eport/**R**angeOutput options from the

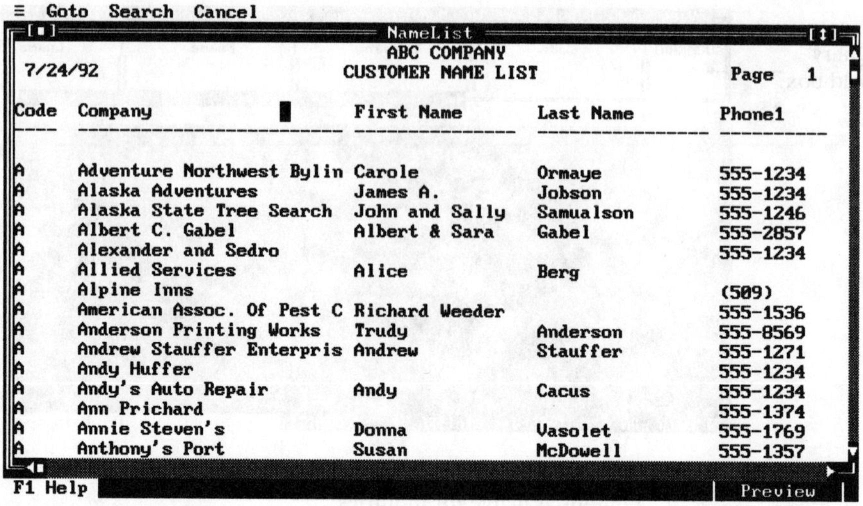

```
 ≡  Goto  Search  Cancel
╔[■]══════════════════════════NameList════════════════════════[↕]╗
║                         ABC COMPANY                             ▲
║   7/24/92              CUSTOMER NAME LIST          Page    1     ▓
║                                                                 ║
║ Code  Company            ▮     First Name    Last Name    Phone1║
║ ────  ──────────────────────   ──────────────  ──────────  ─────║
║                                                                 ║
║ A     Adventure Northwest Bylin Carole         Ormaye      555-1234
║ A     Alaska Adventures          James A.       Jobson      555-1234
║ A     Alaska State Tree Search   John and Sally Samualson   555-1246
║ A     Albert C. Gabel            Albert & Sara  Gabel       555-2857
║ A     Alexander and Sedro                                   555-1234
║ A     Allied Services            Alice          Berg
║ A     Alpine Inns                                           (509)
║ A     American Assoc. Of Pest C  Richard Weeder             555-1536
║ A     Anderson Printing Works    Trudy          Anderson    555-8569
║ A     Andrew Stauffer Enterpris  Andrew         Stauffer    555-1271
║ A     Andy Huffer                                           555-1234
║ A     Andy's Auto Repair         Andy           Cacus       555-1234
║ A     Ann Prichard                                          555-1374
║ A     Annie Steven's             Donna          Vasolet     555-1769
║ A     Anthony's Port             Susan          McDowell    555-1357  ▼
║ ◄▮                                                          ►
╚ F1 Help                                            │ Preview  │
```

Figure 1-14.   *Before printing a report, you can view it onscreen in the Report*
Previewer mode

Main menu, as well as from the **O**utput option on the **R**eport Designer menu. The
Report Previewer image is not a Paradox object: it is temporary. Figure 1-14 shows
an image of a report printed to the screen with **R**eport Previewer. SetPrinter is used
to change printers.

Create Option

The **C**reate option is used to create new tables for a database. When you choose this
option, you will be asked to name the table, and you will then be asked to identify
the fields to be contained within the new table. Figure 1-15 shows an example of a
new table being built using Create. Chapter 3 addresses the Create option in more
detail.

Modify Option

The **M**odify command is used for several purposes, all of which have to do with
changing a table in some way. The **M**odify submenu is shown here:

With the **M**odify option, you can **S**ort a table, **E**dit the data within it, or **C**oEdit on a network or as a single user. (It is not necessary to be in a network to use **C**oEdit. See Chapter 3 for other differences between the two options.) You may enter data into one table with **M**odify/**D**ataEntry or into multiple tables with **M**odify/**M**ulti-Entry. You may also rebuild a table, perhaps by adding or deleting fields with the **R**estructure option. Finally, you may build an index for speedier access to information within a table with the **I**ndex option. Chapter 5 discusses the **M**odify option in more detail.

Most of the Edit mode, CoEdit mode, DataEntry mode, MultiEntry, Restructure, and Index options are separate modes with separate menus and screens.

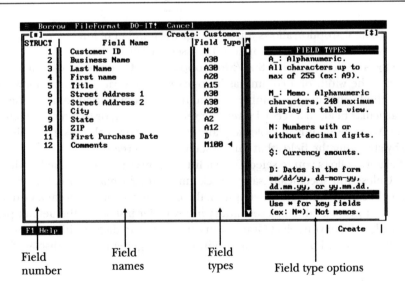

Figure 1-15. *New table created using the Create option*

Image Option

The Image option, covered in Chapter 9, provides several choices for changing the image on the screen without modifying the data in a table. When viewing a table in table view, the options offered on the submenu differ from those seen in form view, as shown here:

When viewing a table with form view, the submenu options will be Format, Zoom, PickForm, and KeepSet, as shown here:

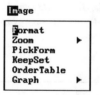

The TableSize option allows you to change the number of lines seen on the screen in table view. This is the same option discussed earlier in the System submenu and mouse tools sections, with the Size/Move option. The ColumnSize option allows you to change the width of a column as it appears in table view. Format allows you to change the formatting on number or date fields. Zoom is used to move the cursor to a particular field, to a record given the record number, or to a record containing a value. Move, used only in table view, allows you to move columns in a table image, thereby changing the fields that can be seen on the screen.

PickForm allows you to select from a list of forms that are attached to the active table. Unless you specifically save the ColumnSize, Format, Move, and PickForm changes by selecting the KeepSet option, the changes will be temporary. OrderTable allows you to view a table in a secondary index order instead of the default primary index order. When you select Graph, you can create and display either a new custom graph or a standard bar graph that can instantly be generated and displayed.

Forms Option

The Forms submenu, shown in the following illustration, offers two options, Design and Change. Design allows you to design a new form to be used for entering data into a table. Change is used to alter a previously created form. Forms are objects attached to a table; they are discussed in Chapter 7.

Tools Option

The **Tools** option allows you to work with the table, rather than its data, as a file. It has two menus: the first, displayed when you choose **Tools**, is shown here:

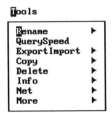

You can **R**ename a table, form, report, script, or graph. You are offered a choice of which you want to rename. QuerySpeed, when used with a specific query, analyzes the query and determines whether a secondary index would speed up the results. ExportImport allows you to import a foreign database or file into Paradox, or to export a Paradox table to another database system or format. You can import or export from and to Quattro or Quattro Pro; Lotus 1-2-3 or Symphony; Reflex; dBASE II, III, III PLUS, and IV; PFS:File; VisiCalc; and ASCII files.

The **C**opy option copies a table, form, report, script, graph, or table family. It creates a backup, or duplicates an object that can be used as a starting point for creating a similar, but new object. The **D**elete option deletes a table, form, report, script, or QuerySpeed secondary index as well as a **K**eepSet setting, ValCheck, or Graph. The Info option provides information about a table and many of the objects, such as reports, forms, and scripts. This option allows you to see what objects are attached to a table **F**amily; the structure of a table (fields and field types); the files in a directory, including object files (**I**nventory); **W**ho is using the network at any time; how many **L**ocks are being used on a table; and which secondary indexes now exist (**T**ableIndex).

The **N**et option can be used to change the current network options, such as locking and preventing a lock on records while an update is being performed, setting up a private directory where temporary files connected with networking can be accessed, obtaining the name of a user who may have locked an object, or forcing a query or report to be displayed regardless of the changes occurring to the table or objects due to active processes.

Selecting **M**ore from the first menu displays a second menu, shown in the following illustration, which includes **A**dd, **M**ultiAdd, **F**ormAdd, **S**ubtract, **E**mpty, **P**rotect, **D**irectory, and **T**oDOS:

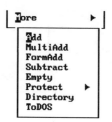

Add allows you to add records from one table to another. (The tables do not have to be structured identically to do this.) **MultiAdd** adds the records from one table to two or more tables at a time. **FormAdd** is a specialized tool which allows you to add records from one table to another when the two tables are separate and unrelated, such as when you are consolidating databases created within two branches of a business. **Subtract** deletes duplicate records from one table if they are found in another. For instance, to delete obsolete records from a master file, you might create a backup file from the records, and then delete them from the master file.

Empty can be used to remove all data records from a table, while keeping the table's structure intact. The **Protect** option protects your tables and scripts from being changed or even accessed by others by allowing you to set a password for access. The **Directory** option can be used to change the current directory for a single session. Finally, **ToDOS** is used to temporarily exit Paradox and go to DOS in order to perform some DOS tasks. When you are finished, you can return to Paradox by typing **exit**.

The **Tools** option is discussed further in Chapter 14.

Scripts Option

The **Scripts** option provides a way to capture frequently used keystrokes and "play" them back with a simple command (also called macros). For instance, if you select records from a table and then print a report on a daily basis, you could record each of the keystrokes involved in this process to a *script*, which can later be recalled. (You cannot use the mouse to record commands.) When you choose the **Scripts** option, the following menu is displayed:

Play activates an existing script when you type in the script name. **BeginRecord** records keystrokes. You choose the command, give the new script a name, and Paradox begins recording keystrokes until you signal to stop. **QuerySave** records queries. You may have complex or commonly used queries that can be recorded, named, and saved as scripts. **S**howPlay allows you to view the progress of each of the recorded keystrokes. Requesting **P**lay allows you to see only the end result. On the other hand, **S**howPlay lets you see what is happening as it occurs within a script. **R**epeatPlay replays the same script a specified number of times. Finally, **E**ditor allows you to create or change a script, using a comprehensive editor which has many of the capabilities of a word processor. Scripts are covered in Chapter 10.

Exit Option

Exit is the recommended way to leave Paradox and it is the only way to leave Paradox without potentially losing or corrupting data. When you choose this option you will be asked if you really want to leave, and then you will be returned to DOS. The **E**xit submenu is shown here:

Although Borland considers data loss to be the highest priority problem, erroneous procedures, such as illegal exits from Paradox, may cause them. In particular, if the computer is turned off while Paradox is up and running, either accidentally, or by loss of power, or by rebooting the computer while Paradox is running, you risk losing or corrupting data.

Chapter 2

Database Basics

This chapter addresses the "housekeeping" functions that must be performed in working with Paradox. Housekeeping functions deal with maintaining your Paradox files and with interfaces you commonly have with MS-DOS; for example, bringing up Paradox and closing it down; canceling actions; setting up and removing directories; working with disk files to copy, delete, or rename them; and using the Help feature.

Bringing Up Paradox 4

When you install Paradox 4, as instructed in Appendix A, you copy the files into a directory, most likely \PDOX40. To run Paradox, you must first be in that directory. Then you simply type **paradox** and press ENTER.

Follow these steps to run Paradox:

1. Change the directory by typing **cd** *directory name* and pressing ENTER.

2. Type **paradox**, as shown here, and press ENTER.

```
C:\>
C:\>cd \pdox40

C:\PDOX40>paradox
```

You may want to modify the AUTOEXEC.BAT file to include Paradox. Then you will not have to change directories before running Paradox. Appendix A tells how to do that.

Leaving Paradox

Although leaving Paradox is simple to do, it is important to do it correctly. If you leave Paradox without using the appropriate procedure, for instance just by turning off the computer, you may lose data, damage tables, or end up with temporary files and tables cluttering your disk. Paradox needs to know when you are leaving so that it can perform its own housekeeping functions, including saving tables and getting rid of temporary tables.

Follow these steps when leaving Paradox:

1. If you are not already in Main mode, return to that screen.

2. Bring up the Main menu by pressing F10 (Main menu).

3. Type **E** for **E**xit.

4. Type **Y** for **Y**es, as shown here:

Canceling an Action or Closing a Window

You can use one of several methods in Paradox to cancel an action or command, or to close a window. Which technique you use will depend on the mode and command you are attempting to cancel. The following list gives several ways to cancel an action from the menus:

- Choose **C**ancel from the active menu when you are not in the Main mode. Or click on the Cancel button to cancel any dialog boxes.

- Choose System/**C**lose by moving the cursor to the System option. (This does not cancel actions when in **E**dit or **C**oEdit mode.)

- Choose **U**ndo from a menu, such as the **E**dit menu, to cancel edits or new records.

To use your mouse to cancel an action:

- Click on **C**ancel from the active menu when you are not in the Main mode. Or click on the Cancel button to cancel any dialog boxes.

- Click on the Close box of the current window. Or click on System/**C**lose.

- Click on a higher level menu bar or window.

- Click on **U**ndo from a menu, such as the **E**dit menu, to cancel edits or new records.

To use shortcut keys to cancel an action:

- Press ESC to cancel Main mode operations, escape from pull-down menus, or remove a dialog box from the screen.

- Press CTRL-F8 (Close) to cancel or close an operation. (This will not cancel actions in **E**dit or **C**oEdit.)

- Choose System/**C**lose by pressing ALT-SPACEBAR to move the cursor to the System menu and then choose **C**lose. (This will not cancel actions in **E**dit or **C**oEdit.)

- Press CTRL-U (Undo) to cancel edits or new records.

- Press CTRL-BREAK to interrupt an action and return to a previous screen.

Be sure not to turn off your computer while a CTRL-BREAK is being processed by Paradox.

Working with Directories

When installing Paradox, using Appendix A guidelines, you learned about creating directories to organize your data files. You can install the program files in one directory and establish another directory for your data files. You will probably have several directories to contain your data files since directories provide an excellent way to organize your files on disk.

When Paradox is searching for a table or file, it looks in one of four directories:

- The directory where the program files are stored, most likely \PDOX40

- The directory you choose to be the permanent default in the Custom Configuration Program

- The temporary directory you set in **T**ools/**M**ore/**D**irectory that will be active for this session only

- A directory you type in when prompted for a table or filename

Setting a Permanent Default Directory

It is helpful to choose one directory that will contain your most frequently used tables as the "permanent" working default. It is permanent only in the sense that the default will remain in effect until it is changed. (Exiting Paradox and then running it again later will not remove the default. Other types of defaults can be set to exist just for the duration of one session.)

 Setting a working default relieves you from specifying the directory path each time you enter Paradox.

You set the default working directory in the Custom Configuration Program (CCP), which is available from System/Utilities.

Follow these steps to set the "permanent" directory default:

1. Choose System/**U**tilities/**C**ustom.

2. If prompted to do so, choose your monitor type, Black & White (B&W) or Color. You may not be asked to do this if you have already set this option. The menu shown in Figure 2-1 will be displayed.

3. Choose **S**tandard Settings. The Standard Settings dialog box shown in Figure 2-2 will be displayed.

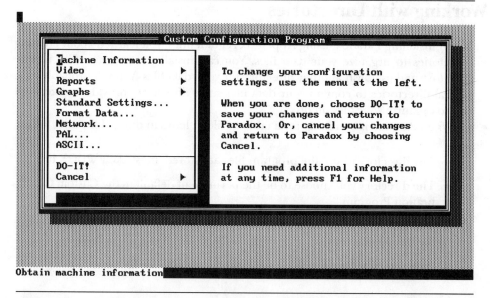

Figure 2-1. *The Custom Configuration Program menu offers options for changing the desktop environment*

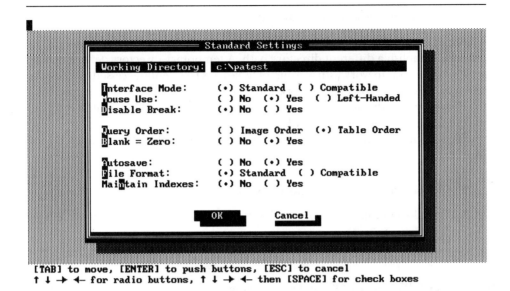

```
                        Standard Settings
 Working Directory:   c:\patest

 Interface Mode:      (•) Standard    ( ) Compatible
 Mouse Use:           ( ) No  (•) Yes   ( ) Left-Handed
 Disable Break:       (•) No  ( ) Yes

 Query Order:         ( ) Image Order  (•) Table Order
 Blank = Zero:        ( ) No  (•) Yes

 Autosave:            ( ) No  (•) Yes
 File Format:         (•) Standard    ( ) Compatible
 Maintain Indexes:    (•) No  ( ) Yes


              OK            Cancel
```

[TAB] to move, [ENTER] to push buttons, [ESC] to cancel
↑ ↓ → ← for radio buttons, ↑ ↓ → ← then [SPACE] for check boxes

Figure 2-2. *The Standard Settings dialog box allows you to enter a permanent default directory name*

4. Type the path and directory name of the permanent working directory.

5. Choose OK from the Standard Settings dialog box.

6. Choose **D**o-It! from the Custom Configuration Program menu.

7. Choose HardDisk to save changes to the directory where the Paradox program files are stored.

HardDisk can be specified for either a stand-alone computer system or a network workstation. When you specify HardDisk, Paradox writes the configuration file to the directory where Paradox is located, usually \PDOX40. Network allows you to specify a path for storing the configuration file.

After a short pause while the new setting is saved on disk, the screen will be restored to its original display. Paradox automatically reloads its programs with the new settings.

You can also start the Custom Configuration Program (or any script) directly from DOS by typing **paradox custom** from the Paradox program directory. From within Paradox, you can start the CCP by choosing **S**cripts/**P**lay and typing the path and then **custom**. Chapter 10 deals with scripts.

Setting a Temporary Directory Default

A temporary directory default establishes a directory path for one session only, or until you establish a different directory path. A temporary directory default may be set when you want to work with a group of tables less frequently accessed. Setting the temporary default allows you to work with the tables and files without respecifying the directory path during one session. Upon leaving Paradox this default is replaced with the directory setting in the CCP.

You set the temporary default from the **T**ools/**M**ore/**D**irectory options on the Main menu. Follow these steps:

1. Choose **T**ools/**M**ore/**D**irectory to set the default.

2. Type the complete path to the directory you want, as shown in Figure 2-3.

3. Choose OK.

Working with Tables in Other Directories

You can work with tables in directories other than the default working directory simply by typing in a path when prompted for a table name. If you know the table name, you can type that as well. If not, press ENTER and Paradox will list the tables in the directory so you can choose the one you want.

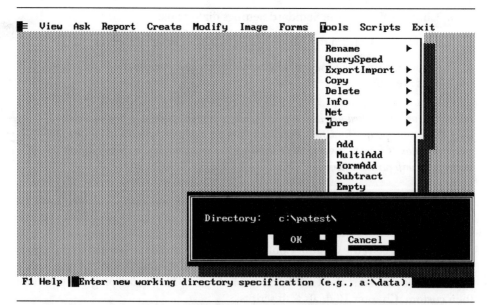

Figure 2-3.   *Use Tools/More/Directory to set a temporary directory default*

Follow these steps to type your own path:

1. When prompted for the table name, type the path for the directory where the file is located. Include the drive, directory (or directories if needed), and the filename if you know it; for example C:*directory name**filename.*

2. If you do not know the filename, press ENTER after typing the path, and Paradox will list the tables.

3. Choose the file you want by moving the cursor to it and pressing ENTER, or click on it with the mouse, or type the name and press ENTER.

Paradox-Created Directories

Paradox creates directories to store some of its own files. You can change some of the directory names during installation. Here are some of the files and directories created by Paradox:

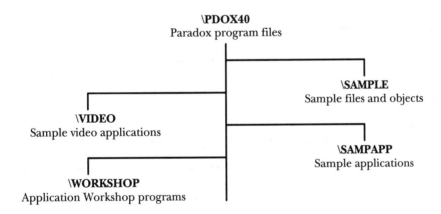

\PDOX40
Paradox program files

\SAMPLE
Sample files and objects

\VIDEO
Sample video applications

\SAMPAPP
Sample applications

\WORKSHOP
Application Workshop programs

Creating a New Directory

To create a new directory from within Paradox, access DOS from the **Tools/More** options. (You might want to do this while creating a new table, when you don't want to leave Paradox to use DOS.)

Follow these steps to create a new directory:

1. Choose **Tools/More/ToDOS** to access DOS. If you want a directory off the root directory, type **cd**\ to return to the root directory.

2. Type **md** and then type the name of the new directory. Press ENTER.

3. Type **exit** to return to Paradox, as shown here:

```
C:\PATEST>cd\
C:\>md \cust
C:\>exit
```

 Press CTRL-O as a shortcut for **T**ools/**M**ore/**T**oDOS. If you need more memory, use ALT-O (DOS Big) to suspend Paradox while you are using DOS. Paradox will be unloaded, using about 100K instead of the 420K of memory normally used. However, leaving Paradox to go to DOS, and returning to Paradox when you are finished with DOS takes somewhat longer.

 While in DOS, do not rename, copy, or delete any Paradox files or objects, or load any RAM-resident programs, or Paradox files and programs may be corrupted.

Removing a Directory

To remove a directory that you no longer need, use the DOS command REMOVE DIRECTORY, which is shortened to RD. All files in the directory, as well as any subdirectories, must be deleted before the directory itself can be removed.

To remove a directory, follow these steps:

1. From within Paradox, access DOS by typing **T**ools/**M**ore/**T**oDOS.

2. Change to the directory you want to remove by typing **cd**\ *directory name* and pressing ENTER.

3. List the files in the directory by typing **dir**.

4. Type **copy** *filename path\filename* to copy a file into another directory and press ENTER. If you don't want to copy any of the files but simply want to delete them, skip this step and go to step 5.

5. Type **del** *filename* to delete a file (but not a Paradox file) and press ENTER.

6. When all files are gone from the directory, return to the root directory by typing **cd**\.

7. Now type **rd** *directory name* and press ENTER to remove the directory.

8. Return to Paradox by typing **exit** and pressing ENTER.

To keep Paradox files and programs intact while in DOS do not rename, copy, or delete any active Paradox tables or objects, or load any RAM-resident programs. The system will crash if critical pointers within the system are corrupted.

Working with Files

You'll recall from Chapter 1 that tables may have objects attached to them, such as report formats, indexes, and so on. A table and all of its objects are called a *family*. Although these family objects look like individual files to DOS, to Paradox they are not; objects are tied to one table. Without that table, objects have no basis. On the other hand, as DOS files, these same objects do not have these ties to each other outside of Paradox. If you try to use DOS utilities to maintain these objects, you run the risk of damaging Paradox's ability to use its files. Consequently, to maintain the Paradox objects, including renaming objects, copying, or deleting them, you must use the Paradox utilities under **T**ools.

Types of Files

Basically there are six types of files that you may find in Paradox: database files (tables), objects, temporary tables, Paradox program files, text, and memo files.

Database Files, Called Tables

Tables are the standard database data files you create in Paradox, and the reason you are using the program. The commands and screens in Paradox deal primarily with being able to create, edit, and report on these types of files.

Files as Objects

Objects that are attached to tables either support the tables or provide some useful service to you. These types of objects may be report specifications, indexes, and so on. They are used by Paradox to support the database table; for example, to report information, provide sort and search indexes, or hold graph settings.

Objects are identified by name. If they are attached to a table, they will always have the same name as the table with a unique identifying extension. Table 2-1 contains a list of objects and their extensions. You seldom need to be concerned with family objects. Paradox manages the tasks of naming, copying, deleting, and finding them, and other requirements needed to perform a task.

Some objects, such as graphs, are not attached to tables. You provide a name for these objects but allow Paradox to provide the extension. Some files, such as scripts,

Objects	Paradox File Extensions
Tables	.DB
Forms	.F or .F??
Reports	.R or .R??
Scripts	.SC (not an object)
Graph settings	.G
Memos for a single table	.MB
Image settings	.SET
Validity checks	.VAL
Primary index	.PX
Secondary index	.X**
Secondary index	.Y**
Network locks	.LCK

? The question marks represent a number between 1 and 15.

* Each asterisk represents a letter or a hexadecimal digit.

Table 2-1.   *Objects Can Be Identified by Their Filename Extension*

are not considered to be objects at all. They are not tied specifically to one table, but are functions performed on tables.

Temporary Tables

Paradox creates temporary tables during certain operations. A list of temporary filenames is shown in Table 2-2. Some of the tables exist until they are overwritten with new data, and all are deleted at the end of the session. You will be warned before Paradox overwrites an existing temporary table. Paradox deletes temporary tables when you change the directory using **Tools/More/Directory** and **Tools/Net/Set-Private**, and when you issue a RESET command in PAL.

PAL is the Paradox Application Language. It is discussed in Chapters 12 and 13.

Filename	Description
Answer	Query results from Ask
Changed	Backup of changed records from **Ask, C**hangeTo (not Fast) or **T**ools/**M**ore/**A**dd, Updates
Crosstab	Crosstab results from **T**ools/**G**raph/**C**rosstab, or ALT-X
Deleted	Backup of deleted records from **Ask, D**elete (not Fast)
Entry	Newly inserted records from **M**odify/**D**ataEntry, **M**odify/**M**ultiEntry
Keyviol	Duplicate key records from **M**odify/**R**estructure, **M**odify/**D**ataEntry, **M**odify/**M**ultiEntry, **T**ools/**M**ore/**A**dd (NewEntries), or **T**ools/**M**ore/**M**ultiAdd
Family	Reports and forms for a table from **T**ools/**I**nfo/**F**amily
Inserted	Inserted records from **Ask, I**nsert (not Fast)
List	List of tables, scripts, and files in a directory from **T**ools/**I**nfo/**I**nventory List of paradox network users from **T**ools/**I**nfo/**W**ho List of locks of tables and family in a network from **T**ools/**I**nfo/**L**ock List of Keyviol tables from **T**ools/**M**ore/**F**ormAdd
Password	Auxiliary passwords from **T**ools/**M**ore/**P**rotect/**P**assword/**T**able
Problems	Records in danger of being lost or damaged in importing or restructuring from **T**ools/**E**xportImport/**I**mport or **M**odify/**R**estructure
Struct	Table definitions from **C**reate, **M**odify/**R**estructure, **T**ools/**I**nfo/**S**tructure or **T**ools/**I**nfo/**T**ableIndex

Table 2-2.   Paradox Temporary Tables

Some of the tables are created so that you can correct problems in another table; for example, the Keyviol table is created when duplicate keys are created, and the Problems table is created for several reasons including a possible loss of data while restructuring a table. You can edit and access one of these tables until it is overwritten or deleted by Paradox.

*To ensure that a temporary file is saved you must rename it using **Tools/Rename**.*

Paradox creates other temporary tables that are invisible to you. Paradox uses them internally and then erases them. You cannot use the names of these files since Paradox might use the same name for a temporary table, and even delete it. These files will only be seen by you when Paradox has been unable to delete them, such as after a power failure or an illegal exit from Paradox.

Do not use any of these names for your files since Paradox may delete them: Chantemp, Kvtemp, Resttemp, Deltemp, Passtemp, Sortques, Instemp, and Probtemp.

Paradox Program Files

The program files, stored on the hard disk in a directory, usually \PDOX40, contain the program code that provides the screens and commands comprising Paradox. It is not necessary or even desirable to do anything with them, other than to know they exist and where they are.

Text Files

Text files are ASCII files that can be used for scripts or PAL programming. You can edit, print, and maintain these files. Chapter 4 discusses text files, and Chapter 10 covers script files.

Memo Files

A memo file, discussed in Chapter 10, is created when a memo field overflows its allocated capacity up to 240 characters. A separate file is then established with the extension .MB to store within a table all overflow characters contained in the memo fields. Memo fields are used for collecting notes about a record, such as about an employee, inventory item, accounts payable or receivables account, and so on.

Naming Tables and Objects

You must supply the names of tables and some objects, such as scripts, graphs, secondary indexes, and text files. The names must follow these rules:

- The names can contain up to eight alphanumeric characters plus a three-character extension (which Paradox supplies in most cases), and they can be in upper- or lowercase.

- Names must follow the DOS rules for naming files—that is, the name cannot contain spaces or characters in the IBM extended character set.

- Names cannot have the same name as another object of the same type; for example, two graph settings with the same name cannot be attached to the same table.

- Names cannot have an extension since Paradox supplies one (except for some text files for which you supply an extension).

- Each name should be descriptive and mean something to you.

Renaming Tables and Objects

Tools/Rename changes the name of a table and any of its attached objects, or other objects such as graphs or scripts. You can change an individual object or a family of objects. The most common use of Tools/Rename is to change the name of the temporary file, Answer, which is created as the result of a query. Answer is then renamed in order to protect the data from being overwritten by the next query. Rename is also a way to move files from one directory to another.

Choosing Tools/Rename causes a menu to be displayed from which you specify the objects you want to rename: Table, Form, Report, Script, or Graph, as shown in Figure 2-4.

Figure 2-4.   *The Tools/Rename menu allows specific objects to be renamed*

Follow these steps to rename an object:

1. Choose **T**ools/**R**ename.

2. Choose from the options **T**able, **F**orm, **R**eport, **S**cript, or **G**raph.

3. Type the table name (or the name of the graph or script).

4. Follow the instructions according to the option chosen.

Tools/Rename/Table

Table renames a table and all of its attached objects. The table's family is renamed according to the new name. For attached objects, the eight-character name will be changed, but the extension will remain the same—that is, the official DOS names are changed but the Paradox descriptions remain the same.

 Rename will move a table and its family to a new directory or drive if you type a new path in addition to the name.

To rename a table, follow these instructions:

1. Select the **T**able option.

2. When prompted, type the name of the table to be renamed.

3. Type the new name when prompted. If the name already exists, you will be warned to cancel the command or retype a new name.

Tools/Rename/Form

Form renames a form by changing its extension only; the DOS eight-character name remains the same as the family table name (but the Paradox description can be changed in **F**orms/**C**hange).

The extension consists of .F?? where ? stands for a number from 1 to 15. **T**ools/**R**ename allows you to change only the number part of the extension, for example, you can change .F12 to .F15. The number you use to rename the form can be a number you have already used or a new number. If the number is currently used by another form; that form will be overwritten by the renamed form. You will be given a chance to prevent this if you do not want the current form replaced by the renamed one.

To rename a form, follow these instructions:

1. Select the **F**orm option.

2. When prompted, type the name of the table containing the form to be renamed, or select it from the list box. You will then be shown a list of form numbers and descriptions.

3. Select the form from the list, as shown in the example in Figure 2-5. You will be shown another list of used and unused form numbers from which to choose. If a number is not in use, its description is "Unused."

4. Choose a number from the list to be the new number. If that number is in use, you will be asked if you want to replace the selected form or to cancel the rename operation.

Tools/Rename/Report

Report renames a report by changing the number of the extension only; the DOS eight-character name remains the same as the family table name (but the Paradox description can be changed in **R**eport/**C**hange).

The extension consists of .R?? where ? stands for a number from 1 to 15. **T**ools/**R**ename allows you to change only the numeric part of the extension, for example, .R2 to .R3. The number you use to rename the report can be a number you have already used, or it can be a new number. If the number is currently used by another report, that report will be overwritten by the renamed report. You will be given a chance

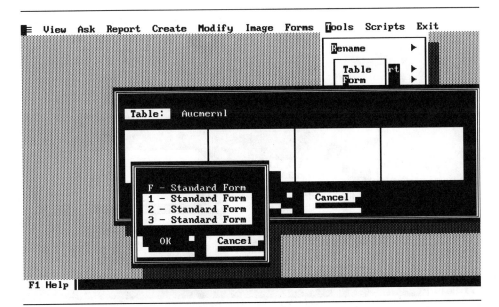

Figure 2-5. *Paradox lists the forms available to be renamed, copied, or deleted*

to prevent this if you do not want the current report replaced with the renamed one. The number being replaced will then become an available number, or unused.

To rename a report, follow these instructions:

1. Select the **R**eport option.

2. When prompted, type the name of the table containing the report to be renamed, or select it from the list box. You will then be shown a list of report numbers and descriptions.

3. Select the report from the list. You will be shown a second list of used and unused report numbers to be used to rename the report, as shown in Figure 2-6. If a number is not in use, the list describes it as "Unused."

4. Choose a report number from the list to be the new number. If the number is in use, you will be asked if you want to replace the selected report or to cancel the rename operation.

Tools/Rename/Script

Script renames the eight-character name of a script file but leaves the extension, .SC, unchanged. **R**ename/**S**cript can be used to move a script to another drive or directory by typing a path in addition to the name.

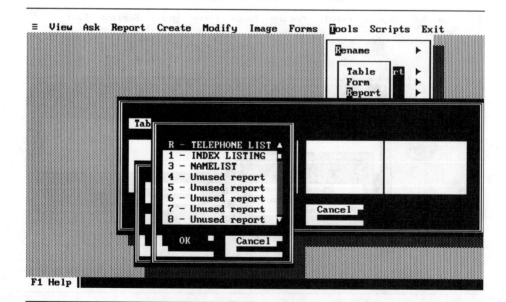

Figure 2-6. *When renaming reports, Paradox lists the choices of numbers available for the rename operation. You must select one of these*

To rename a script, type in the new name when prompted. If the name exists already, you will be warned and can cancel the command or retype a new name.

Tools/Rename/Graph

Graph renames the eight-character name of a graph setting file, not a graph image file. The extension, .G, is unchanged. **R**ename/**G**raph can be used to move a graph setting file to another drive or directory by typing a path in addition to the filename.

To rename a graph setting file, type in the new name when prompted. If the name exists already, you will be warned and can cancel the command or retype a new one.

Copying Objects

You will want to copy tables and objects for several reasons. You may want to back up your files, or to create a test copy of your database with which to experiment. **T**ools/**C**opy copies objects individually, or together as a family. When you choose **T**ools/**C**opy, another menu is displayed with the copy options **T**able, **F**orm, **R**eport, **S**cript, **J**ustFamily, and **G**raph, as shown in Figure 2-7.

Always use Tools/Copy to back up or copy Paradox objects rather than the DOS COPY command. Using the DOS command endangers Paradox's ability to manage and work with its files since DOS does not know of the internal linkages between files, tables, and

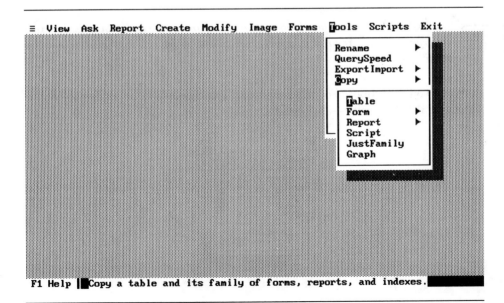

*Figure 2-7.   Menu shown when you use **T**ools/**C**opy*

objects within Paradox that must be maintained and preserved. Objects copied using DOS may show as "corrupt" on the menu.

Tools/Copy/Table

Table copies a table and all of its attached objects. The table's family is copied according to the new name. For attached objects, the eight-character name will be changed, but the extension will remain the same. In other words, the official DOS names are changed; the Paradox descriptions and the descriptive names you have entered remain the same.

To copy a table, follow these steps:

1. Choose **Tools/Copy/Table** from the menu.

2. Type or select from a list box the name of the table to be copied.

3. Type the filename of the copy when prompted. If the name exists already, you will be warned and can cancel the command or retype a new name.

Tools/Copy/Form

Form copies a form, either to the same table or to a different one. Changing the form number creates a copy of a form that can then be modified as desired within the same table. If copying to a different table, the filename and possibly the extension number will change.

 Use Tools/Copy/Form to quickly bring up a copy of an existing form that is similar to one you want to create. You can modify the copy quickly to get what you want, rather than starting from scratch.

When you first choose **Form**, a menu with two choices will be displayed—Same-Table and DifferentTable—as shown here:

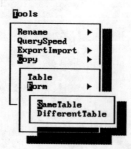

SameTable SameTable copies the form to another form with a different extension. When you first choose SameTable, you will be asked for the table name. Follow these steps:

1. Type the table name or select it from a list box. You will then be shown a list of existing form numbers and descriptions.

2. Choose a form number to be copied. A list of unused and used numbers will be displayed, as shown in Figure 2-8. If a number is not in use, the list describes it as "Unused."

3. Choose a number from the list to be the new number. If the number is in use, you will be asked if you want to overwrite the form with that number or cancel the copy operation.

DifferentTable DifferentTable copies the form to another table. When you first choose DifferentTable, you will be asked for the table name containing the form to be copied. Follow these steps:

1. Type the table name or select it from a list box. A list of existing forms will appear.

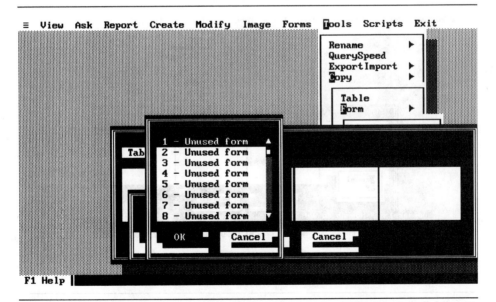

Figure 2-8. *When copying a form number, Paradox provides a list of used and unused numbers from which to choose*

2. Choose the form you wish to copy. You will then be asked for the destination table name.

3. Choose the target table name. If the table has different field names and types, you will be warned. (If the table structures are different, extra fields not matching the new table will be deleted from the report.) You can either choose to continue the copy process by selecting OK or choose to cancel, as shown in Figure 2-9.

4. Type the number of the copy.

Tools/Copy/Report

Report copies a table by changing its extension only; the DOS eight-character name remains the same as the family table. Changing the report number creates a copy of a report that can be modified any way you like.

 *Use **Tools/Copy/Report** to quickly bring up a copy of a report that is similar to one you want to create. You can modify the copy quickly into the form you want, rather than starting from scratch.*

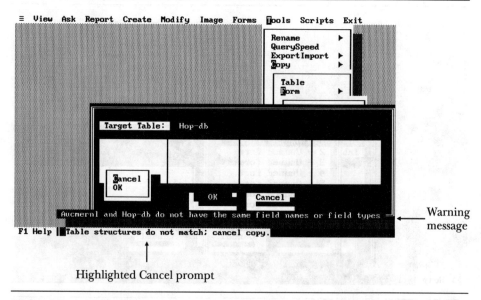

Figure 2-9. *A warning message appears when you attempt to copy to a table with a different structure*

When you first choose **R**eport, a menu with two choices will be displayed: SameTable and DifferentTable.

SameTable   SameTable copies the report to another report with a different extension. When you first choose **S**ameTable, you will be asked for the table name. Follow these steps:

1. Type the table name or select it from a list box. You will then be shown a list of existing report numbers and descriptions.

2. Choose a report number to be copied. A list of unused and used numbers is displayed. If a number is not in use, the list describes it as unused.

3. Choose a number from the list to be the new number. If the number is in use, you will be asked if you want to overwrite the report currently occupying the used number or cancel the copy operation.

DifferentTable   DifferentTable copies the report to another table. When you first choose **D**ifferentTable, you will be asked for the table name containing the report to be copied. Follow these steps:

1. Type the table name or select it from the list box. A list of existing reports will appear.

2. Choose the report to be copied. You will then be asked for the destination table name.

3. Choose the target table name. If the table has different field names and types, you will be warned. You can either choose to continue the copy process or cancel it.

    You will then be shown a list of report numbers and descriptions. If a number is not in use, the list describes it as unused.

4. Choose a number from the list to be the new number. If the number is in use, you will be asked if you want to overwrite the report currently occupying that number or cancel the copy operation.

Tools/Copy/Script

Script copies a script, changing the eight-character name and leaving the extension, .SC, unchanged. You can then modify the script copy to suit your purposes.

To copy a script, type in the name of the script to be copied, or select it from the list box. Then type in the name of the copy when prompted. Press ENTER or choose OK to initiate the copy.

Tools/Copy/JustFamily

JustFamily copies all objects belonging to a table, without copying the table itself. This is most useful when you've used a query to select records from a table into an Answer table, and now want to use some of the reports or forms with the new table. You can rename Answer and copy JustFamily to the new file to have the complete capabilities of the original table.

    You will first be asked for the table containing the family of objects to be copied. Then you will be asked for a target table name. The destination table must already exist for the JustFamily objects to be attached to it. Any objects being copied will overwrite objects of the same type and name. Objects with differing names will remain unaffected. If the structures of the tables differ, you will be warned. (If the table structures are different, extra fields not matching the new table may be deleted.) You can choose to continue the copy operation or to cancel it.

Tools/Copy/Graph

Graph copies the graph setting file that contains the setting and defaults for the graph, not the graph image file containing the graph printed to a file. The copy can be used to create another graph while retaining the original setting file.

    To copy a graph setting file, type in the name of the file to be copied. Then, when prompted, type in the name of the copy. If the name exists already, you will be warned and can cancel the command or retype a new name.

You must use the DOS COPY command to copy graph images printed to a file.

Deleting Objects

Deleting objects removes objects individually or as a family. Use **Delete** to erase a table, form, report, script, query-speedup index, a setting file, a validity check file, or a graph settings file. As shown in Figure 2-10, when you choose **Tools/Delete** you are shown another menu with the types of objects or files you can delete: **Table**, **Form**, **Report**, **Script**, **Index**, **KeepSet**, **ValCheck**, and **Graph**.

Tools/Delete/Table

Table deletes a table and all of its attached objects. All objects and files associated with the table are deleted.

*Always use **Tools/Delete/Table** cautiously since everything associated with a table will be deleted.*

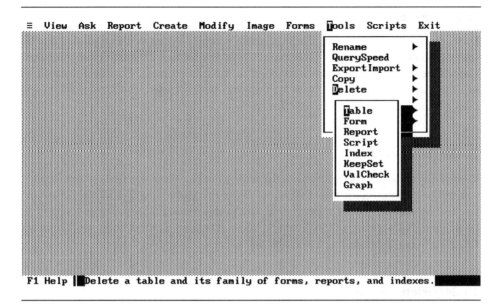

Figure 2-10. *Menu shown when you choose **T**ools/**D**elete*

To delete a table and its objects, type the name of the table to be deleted or select it from a list box. Paradox will ask if you want to continue. Respond with Cancel or OK.

Paradox warns you before deleting a table, as shown in the following illustration. If you respond by selecting Cancel, the table is not deleted. If you respond by choosing OK, the delete proceeds.

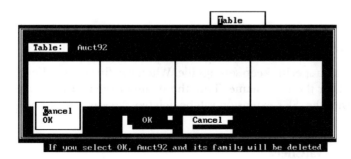

Tools/Delete/Form

Form deletes a specific form from the table's family. When you first choose Form, you will be prompted for the table name. Type the name or select it from a list box. You will be shown a list of forms attached to the named table. Choose a form to be deleted. No warning will be given. When it has been deleted, the form number will then become unused and available for use.

Tools/Delete/Report

Report deletes a specific report from the table's family. When you first choose Report, you will be prompted for the table name. Type the name or select it from a list box. You will be shown a list of reports attached to the named table. Choose a report to be deleted. No warning will be given. When it has been deleted, the report number will then become unused and available for use.

Tools/Delete/Script

Script deletes a specific script. When you first choose Script, you will be prompted for the table name. Type the name or select it from a list box. The named file with the .SC extension will be deleted. No warning will be given.

Tools/Delete/Index

Index deletes all secondary indexes. When you first choose Index, you will be prompted for the table name. Type the name or select it from a list box. All secondary indexes with the .X?? or .Y?? extensions will be deleted. No warning will be given.

 Be doubly warned that Paradox deletes all secondary indexes with the Tools/Delete/Index option.

Tools/Delete/KeepSet

KeepSet deletes a specific keep settings file. When you first choose KeepSet, you will be prompted for the table name. Type the name or select it from a list box. The named file with the .SET extension will be deleted. No warning will be given.

Tools/Delete/ValCheck

ValCheck deletes a specific validity check file. When you first choose ValCheck, you will be prompted for the table name. Type the name or select it from a list box. The named file with the .VAL extension will be deleted. No warning will be given.

Tools/Delete/Graph

Graph deletes the graph setting file (with the .G extension), not the graph image file. To delete a graph setting file, type in the name of the table file. The file with the .G extension will be deleted. No warning will be given.

To delete the graph image file, use the DOS DEL command.

Backing Up Data

Backing up data consists of creating copies of your tables and other files in order to protect yourself from losing data in case of disk failures. Although hard disk failures are rare, they can be disastrous since all data on a failed disk can be lost. Backing up files onto floppy diskettes or a tape drive is the only safe way to protect against this potential catastrophe.

Any tables or files that you want to keep should be backed up periodically. How often depends on the volume of changes being made to the file. The more changes, the more frequently you need to back up the data. If you would have to spend more than an hour reconstructing a file by updating it with current changes, you should back up the file.

To back up your Paradox tables, follow these steps:

1. Choose **T**ools/**C**opy/**T**able from the menu.

2. Type or select from a list box the name of the table to be copied.

3. Type the filename of the copy when prompted. If the name exists already, you will be warned and can cancel the command or retype a new name.

Saving Files to Disk

While you are working with your tables, they are stored on the desktop in your computer's memory. If you have been changing or editing a table, the copy in memory may not be the same as the one on disk. To update the copy on disk and preserve the changes, you must occasionally save the table to your hard disk. Paradox helps with this task by automatically saving your data to disk each time you press F2 (Do-It!) or exit from Paradox.

To protect against power surges or fluctuations, press F2 (Do-It!) frequently, to force Paradox to save the active table in memory to disk.

Paradox can periodically save data to disk to minimize data loss in the event of a system crash or power outage. To select automatic saves to disk, choose System/Utilities/Custom/Standard settings, and select the Autosave option by pressing TAB and RIGHT ARROW or by clicking on the Autosave Yes option.

Setting Automatic Disk Save

Paradox automatically saves files to a temporary disk file periodically during edit or data entry sessions. This is done whether or not the Autosave option is set. The frequency of automatic saves can be increased by using the Autosave option. Autosave causes Paradox to save updates to a temporary file not only periodically, but also when a pause of computer activity is sensed.

Since it doesn't affect performance or response time, you can turn the automatic save feature on or off, as you wish. The only effect will be the extra saves to the temporary file when you pause in entering or editing data.

You still must press Do-It! to save changes to the table itself.

The Autosave option in the System/Utilities/Custom/Standard Settings menu will have a dot next to Yes if the automatic save option has been selected, as shown in Figure 2-11. If the dot is next to No, the automatic save option has not been selected.

To turn the automatic save on or off, follow these steps:

1. Choose System/Utilities/Custom/Standard Settings to display the dialog box containing the automatic save option.

2. Move the cursor to Autosave.

3. To turn on the automatic save option if there is no dot next to Yes, click on the Yes box or press the RIGHT ARROW to insert a dot. Similarly, to turn the option off, press the LEFT ARROW or click on the No box.

When you choose Do-It! from the CCP Main menu, the automatic save setting will take effect.

Using Help

Help in Paradox is available online when you need to review a command or see a summary of a subject. Help is not meant to replace Paradox manuals or documentation; it is only a supplement.

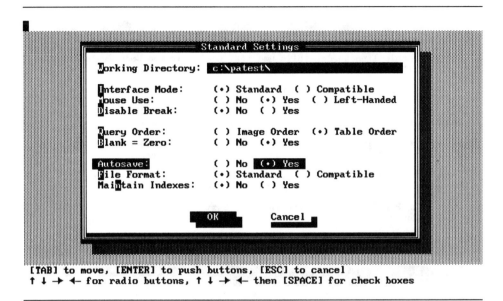

Figure 2-11.   *When the Autosave option has a dot on Yes, it indicates that Paradox will automatically save files to disk periodically*

First Level of Help Screens

Several levels of help are available in Paradox. The first level is the immediate help displayed when you press F1 at any time. This help screen is *context sensitive*, which means the help offered is related to the subject or command currently active on the screen. As you change your actions in Paradox, the help offered changes as well. The help screen that appears when you press F1 while in the Main mode is shown in Figure 2-12.

A menu at the top of the screen lists other subjects on which you can get help. In Figure 2-12 these subjects are **B**asics, **G**ettingAround, **K**eys, **M**enuChoices, **I**ndex, **S**cripts/PAL, and **P**aradox. **B**asics shows basic terminology and concepts of Paradox 4. **G**ettingAround displays keys used to move between menus, within and between tables, within the help system, and with Zoom. **K**eys displays the function key commands, arrow keys, and special keys. **M**enuChoices lists an overview of the Main menu options. **I**ndex gives tips on how to use the index in the help system. **S**cripts/PAL displays definitions and overviews of using scripts and PAL. Finally, **P**aradox returns to whatever you were doing before calling for help. Each of these options has its own screens and menus.

As you change your actions, the first level help menu changes to include choices related to your actions.

To use the first level help screens, follow these steps:

1. Press F1 from any screen in the system.

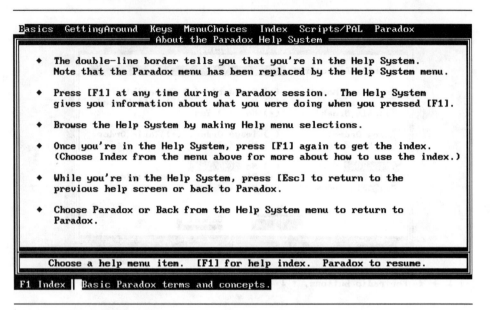

Basics GettingAround Keys MenuChoices Index Scripts/PAL Paradox
═══════════════ About the Paradox Help System ═══════════════

◆ The double-line border tells you that you're in the Help System.
   Note that the Paradox menu has been replaced by the Help System menu.

◆ Press [F1] at any time during a Paradox session. The Help System
   gives you information about what you were doing when you pressed [F1].

◆ Browse the Help System by making Help menu selections.

◆ Once you're in the Help System, press [F1] again to get the index.
   (Choose Index from the menu above for more about how to use the index.)

◆ While you're in the Help System, press [Esc] to return to the
   previous help screen or back to Paradox.

◆ Choose Paradox or Back from the Help System menu to return to
   Paradox.

Choose a help menu item.   [F1] for help index.   Paradox to resume.

F1 Index ‖ Basic Paradox terms and concepts.

Figure 2-12.   *You obtain the first level of help by pressing F1*

2. Select an option from the menu to see additional information.

3. When finished, press ESC to return to a previous help menu or choose **P**aradox
   from the menu bar to leave the help system.

Second Level of Help Screens

The first level of help only provides information on the current command or subject.
If you press F1 a second time, you'll get another level of help: the help index. The
help index provides a complete list of subjects that have help screens available. Figure
2-13 shows the help index displayed from the Main menu.

Two types of entries are listed. If a subject contains a bullet (•) in front of the
entry, it has a help screen specifically about it. If a subject has no bullet, it is a grouping
of other subjects.

To display and use the help index, follow these steps:

1. Press F1, F1 for the help index.

2. Find the subject you want by pressing UP ARROW, DOWN ARROW, PGUP, and PGDN
   (to see the next or previous subject) and press ENTER.

3. When finished, press ESC or choose **P**aradox from the menu bar to leave the
   help screen.

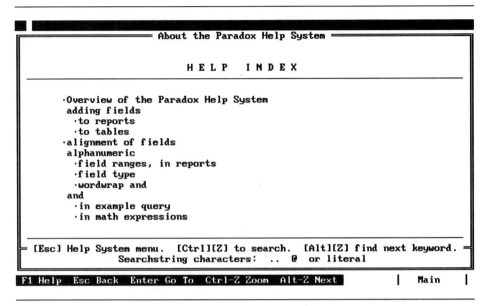

Figure 2-13. *First screen of the help index*

Help System Special Keys

You can use special keys to move around and view information in the help system regardless of whether you are in the first or second level. The following list tells you how to use these special keys:

Key	Function
F1	Displays help screen on current context
F1, F1	Displays index of help subjects
ESC	Returns to previous screen or menu
P	Returns to Paradox, or beeps (when available on menu)
UP ARROW	Moves up a line in the help index
DOWN ARROW	Moves down a line in the help index
PGUP	Displays previous help index screen
PGDN	Displays next help index screen
CTRL-Z	Finds a specific value
ALT-Z	Finds the next occurrence of a value
ENTER	Chooses current entry

Leaving the Help System

When you leave the help system you are returned to the screen you were using before you asked for help. You can leave the help system in one of three ways:

- You can press ESC until you leave the system. Depending on where you are in the help system, you may need to press it more than once.

- You can click on or select **P**aradox from the menu option. (When it is available you can type **P**.)

- You can press F2 (Do-It!) to leave.

About the Paradox Option

Choosing System/**A**bout displays the release number and copyright information for Paradox. Use this to verify which version of Paradox is loaded.

Working with Windows

You'll recall from Chapter 1 that windows are arranged in a stack with the top of the stack visible on the screen, and the other windows in a stack under it. Paradox offers several options from the System menu for displaying the stack of windows, as shown in Figure 2-14.

Since the System menu is available throughout the Paradox system, you can always access these options for refreshing the screen, viewing the files in Cascade or Tile modes (more on these shortly), emptying the desktop, or bringing query windows to the top of the stack.

In addition the Paradox System menu offers options for rearranging, resizing, or moving from one window to the next. These are useful if you have opened multiple tables or forms, or if you are querying a table and have both the Query form and the Answer table displayed. You can open a report when other windows are on the desktop; however, you cannot move to other windows until you close the report.

Maximizing/Restoring a Window

Each window can be expanded to its maximum size. This can make viewing and working in the window easier. When you are done with your work in the current window, you can restore it to its original size and go to another window.

Follow these steps to maximize the window:

1. Press ALT-SPACEBAR to go to the System menu.

2. Choose **Maximize/Restore**. The window expands to its maximum size.

With your mouse, click on the **Maximize/Restore** icon (the up arrow) in the upper-right corner of the window. Or you can double-click on the window title bar. The icon becomes a two-pointed arrow when the window is maximized.

To restore the window to its original size, follow these steps:

1. Press ALT-SPACEBAR.

2. Choose **Maximize/Restore**.

With your mouse, click on the **Maximize/Restore** icon (the two-pointed arrow) in the upper-right corner of the window or double-click on the window title bar. The icon becomes an up arrow when the window is restored to its original size.

Moving a Window

It is sometimes convenient to move the current window to a different position so you can see other windows or portions of other windows that are opened.

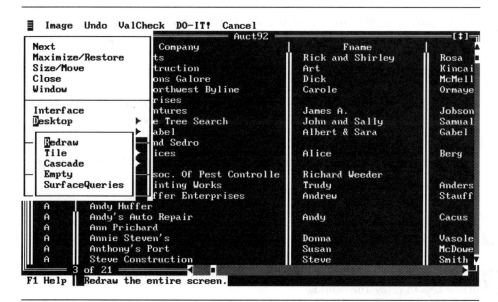

Figure 2-14. *You have a variety of ways in which to display a stack of windows, as this menu shows*

To move the window, follow these steps:

1. Press ALT-SPACEBAR to go to the System menu and choose Size/Move. A prompt with instructions is displayed at the bottom of the screen, as shown in the following illustration.

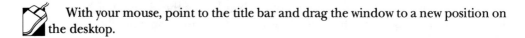

2. Press any of the arrow keys to move the window to a new position on the desktop.

3. Press ENTER when done.

 With your mouse, point to the title bar and drag the window to a new position on the desktop.

 To use shortcut keys, press CTRL-F5 and then use the arrow keys to move the window.

Sizing a Window

It is helpful to be able to control the size of the window beyond using the Maximize/Restore function. You can use the Size/Move option to change the window to any size you want.

To adjust window size precisely, follow these steps:

1. Press ALT-SPACEBAR to go to the System menu and choose Size/Move. The prompt is shown at the bottom of the desktop with instructions for using the arrow keys.

2. Press SHIFT and any of the arrow keys to change the size of the current window.

3. Press ENTER when done.

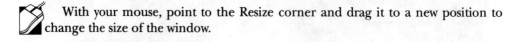 With your mouse, point to the Resize corner and drag it to a new position to change the size of the window.

To use shortcut keys, press CTRL-F5 and then use the SHIFT key with any of the arrow keys to resize the window.

Moving from One Window to Another

Often you may want to work in a different window while you have the current window open. The quickest way to do this is to use either the shortcut keys or the mouse; however, if you are not sure of the files that have been opened, you can use the System/Window menu to display the list of files—tables, queries, forms, reports, and so on—currently open on the desktop.

To list files on the desktop, follow these steps:

1. Press ALT-SPACEBAR to go to the System menu and choose Window. A list of the files currently displayed appears, as shown in Figure 2-15.

2. Move the cursor to the file you want and press ENTER.

 Use CTRL-F4 as a shortcut to move to the next window.

You can press either F3 (Up Image) or F4 (Down Image) to move among queries and tables. These keys cannot be used, however, to go to a form that is open. Press CTRL-F4 to move to a form or other nontable object.

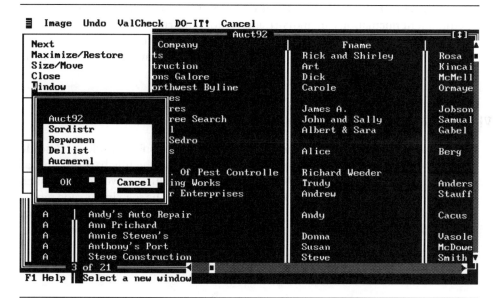

Figure 2-15.   *System/Window menu showing the list of files that are open*

With your mouse, click on the window that you want to make active. You may have to rearrange the window display in order to see windows that have been stacked below the current window.

Displaying the Next Window

Next displays the bottom-most window on the stack, which may not be the actual "next" window on the stack. In other words, the bottom-most window is activated and brought to the top of the stack. The current window is deactivated and placed under the newly activated window.

To move the bottom-most window to the top of the stack, choose System/**N**ext.

    The shortcut keys CTRL-F4 are the same as the System/**N**ext option.

    The Next option cannot be used while a window is specific to a mode, such as Edit, CoEdit, Report Designer, or Form Designer modes.

Redrawing a Window

You use System/**D**esktop/**R**edraw to refresh a window when it has been interrupted by equipment fluctuations, memory-resident programs running at the same time as Paradox, or other events that cause the screen to be corrupted.

To redraw the window, choose System/**D**esktop/**R**edraw. The screen will be refreshed immediately.

Viewing Windows in Cascade Mode

Paradox uses the **C**ascade mode as the default when it displays windows. **C**ascade mode shows the windows one on top of the other with just the title bars showing, as shown in Figure 2-16. The top window is not maximized, although you can see much of it—more than in the **T**ile mode. Query windows cannot be seen in **C**ascade mode.

Cascading can be used when you have opened tables in operating modes that display windows in maximized size, such as **E**dit, where the title bars are not showing.

To display a window in **C**ascade mode choose System/**D**esktop/**C**ascade. The screen will be refreshed in **C**ascade mode.

Viewing Windows in Tile Mode

An example of windows displayed in a tiled pattern is shown in Figure 2-17. Every window in the stack appears onscreen, which means each looks very small and frequently you can only see a portion of the data in the window. This mode is useful

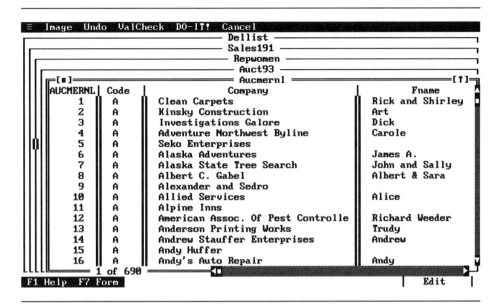

Figure 2-16. *This cascaded display of a stack of windows is the default mode*

```
≡  Image  Undo  ValCheck  DO-IT!  Cancel
┌─ Aucmernl ──────────────────┐  ┌─ Dellist ──────────────┐
│AUCMERNL│ Code        Company │  │DELLIST│    No      Precinct│
│    1  │ A   Clean Carpets    │  │   1  │   113    Oak Harbor 1│
│    2  │ A   Kinsky Construction│ │   2  │    37    Double Bluff│
│    3  │ A   Investigations Galo│ │   3  │    29    Useless Bay│
│    4  │ A   Adventure Northwest│ │   4  │   110    Oak Harbor 7│
│    5  │ A   Seko Enterprises  │  └────────────────────────┘
│    6  │ A   Alaska Adventures │  ┌─ Repwomen ─────────────┐
│    7  │ A   Alaska State Tree S│  │  First      Last       │
│    8  │ A   Albert C. Gabel   │  │  Vicky    Burton     Vic│
└──────────────────────────────┘  │  Ginny    Barr       Gin│
┌[■]═══ Auct93 ═══════[↑]┐  │  Edna     Bunsom     Edn│
│AUCT93      First          │  │  Joan     Caldweld   Joa│
│   1  │ Brauw       Abua   │  │  Jerry    Clark      Jin│
│   2  │ David & Jan Alld   │  └────────────────────────┘
│   3  │ Dick & Kathy Ambr  │  ┌─ Sales191 ─────────────┐
│   4  │ Arland & Cecelia Ande│ │SALES191│   Date    Custo│
│   5  │ Linda       Ande   │  │   1  │ 1/02/91  Salazar Prod│
│   6  │ Russ & Joanne Ande │  │   2  │ 1/03/91  Vance Market│
│   7  │ Tom & Mary Jane Andr│  │   3  │ 1/03/91  Allen Associ│
│   8  │ Bob & Bo    Arnd   │  │   4  │ 1/04/91  Kledzik Corp│
│   9  │ Tom & Sally Baen   │  │   5  │ 1/04/91  Western Mill│
└═══ 9 of 286 ═══════════┘  └────────────────────────┘
F1 Help  F7 Form                      |   Edit   |
```

Figure 2-17. *A tiled display of windows shows a small part of each window*

when you are creating a form or table in one window with an example of another shown in a separate tiled window.

To display a window in **Tile** mode choose System/**Desktop**/**Tile**. The screen will be refreshed in **Tile** mode.

Emptying the Desktop

When you empty the desktop all windows are closed and operations canceled. Be sure that you want to do this because you can lose data if you have not saved your work prior to using the **Empty** command.

To empty the desktop, choose System/**Desktop**/**Empty**.

 The shortcut keys ALT-F8 are the same as choosing System/**Desktop**/**Empty**.

Bringing Queries to the Top of the Stack

Query forms are stacked one on top of the other. When you want to see which queries are on the desktop, choose System/**Desktop**/**SurfaceQueries**. The bottom-most query on the stack will be placed on the top.

Part *II*

Creating and Modifying

Chapter **3**

Creating and Editing a Database

This chapter discusses designing a database, and presents the procedures for creating tables. To create a table you must define columns—which consist of a name and field type, and have the option of designating key fields—and enter information in the table. This chapter also covers editing information using both Edit and Field View modes, adding and deleting records, and undoing editing changes.

Designing a Database

To briefly review the elements of a database as described in Chapter 1, a database may be one or several tables. A *table* is a file that contains information entered in columns (*fields*) and rows (*records*). Each column (field) contains a similar detail for every individual or item in the table. For example, one field would contain only last names, another field only first names, and so on. Each row (record) contains all of the information pertaining to one individual or item.

Some Guidelines for Planning

Before planning the tables, list the questions that you want the database to answer. What kind of information do you need? For example, suppose your business sells office furniture. You might want to know what products you sell, their cost, selling price, and the amount on hand; orders from customers, their names, addresses, and telephone numbers; employees' names, hire dates, and what products they sold, and so on.

The next step is to structure your tables using these questions as a guide. Divide the data that will answer these questions into tables that relate, or can be linked, to each other. This process of organizing data and putting only related information in a table is called *normalization*. The primary goal of normalizing a database is to eliminate duplication of data in tables.

Use the following as a guide for designing your database:

- Be complete, but do not include too much information in one table.

- Avoid duplicating information in tables. Because Paradox can link information from several tables, you can add a field that contains unique information and use it as a link to other tables. For example, in an Orders table, instead of entering a customer's full name and address, use an ID number for the individual. Then in the table of customer names include a field that contains an ID number for each customer. This field can then be used to link the information from the two tables. Types of links are discussed later in this section.

- Think of all the related information that you want in one table and plan a field (column) for each item. For example, in planning a table containing a list of names and addresses, use separate fields for the last names and first names. This will allow you to select or sort the list on the basis of the last name. Or place the city, state, and ZIP code, each in separate fields so the records can be sorted by ZIP, by city, or by state.

- Enter only the information that you currently are keeping in files. More information can always be added later as the need arises. Paradox allows you to easily restructure the table when you need to add fields, as described in Chapter 5.

- Use table and field names that indicate the information that is stored in them.

- Create a data directory to store the table or tables. This keeps the tables separate from the Paradox system files.

If you plan to link tables later to display data in reports or in query Answer tables, or to link them in forms used to add or edit records, then it is important to understand the types of database relationships that exist between normalized tables.

- **One-to-one** relationships exist when a record in one table corresponds directly to details in another table. For example, you might create a Customer table that shows only the customer ID number and the last and first names. Then in a Maillist table, include the customer ID number and detailed information about the customer–company name, address, phone number, and so on. One record in the Customer table relates to only one record in the Maillist table.

By placing in both tables a common field that contains identical values and is unique to each record (such as Customer ID), you will be able to link the tables. Names and addresses are not necessarily unique, but an ID number can be. By structuring the tables so that this ID field is a keyed field, Paradox prevents duplication of records, even when names may be the same.

- **One-to-many** relationships exist when one record in a table relates to several records in another table. An example might be the relationship between the Customer table and the Sales table. One customer ID may be entered in several sales records. The records in the Customer table will contain information about the customers such as names, addresses, phone numbers; the Sales table will contain details of each sale; and a common field, Customer ID for example, will be placed in both tables that link the two.

  In a one-to-many relationship such as this, the linking Customer ID field will be keyed in the Customer table, thus preventing duplicate values from being entered. It will not be the keyed field in the Sales table, allowing duplicate customer ID numbers to be entered there. This eliminates duplicating name and address information about the customer (with the exception of the ID number) in every sales record. It is required that the fields that link the tables be the same in both tables–the field types must be the same and the values in the fields (the ID numbers for example) must be an exact match.

- **Many-to-one** relationships are demonstrated by an Orders table that contains many orders for the same customer. This is significant when creating forms that link the tables. If the Orders table is the master table in a form and the Customer table is the detail table with the linking field being the Customer ID field, as you move through the form from record to record, you can see many records in the master Orders table that are linked to one record in the detail Customer table. The Customer ID field is keyed in the Customer table, but it is not keyed in the Orders table. Master and detail tables are discussed in Chapter 7.

- **Many-to-many** relationships exist when several records in one table can relate to several records in another table. For example, a many-to-many relationship exists between an Employee table and a Sales table if the Sales table shows records of sales by employee A of a desk and a filing cabinet, and also shows desks sold by employee A and employee B.

  Another example of a many-to-many relationship is that of records of class enrollments–many students take many classes. One table can contain records of the classes being offered with names, times, instructors, and course ID numbers which are keyed fields, thereby avoiding duplication. Another table can contain records of students with names, addresses, and student IDs, also in a keyed field. A third table can contain records of students (identified by ID number) who have enrolled in each course (identified by course ID number). The Student ID and Course ID fields will not be keyed in this table, thereby allowing duplication of records. By linking the three tables through the course ID and student ID numbers, you can display data from all three tables–for example, you could display the names of all courses and the last name of each student enrolled in every course. Or, perhaps more realistically, you could display the name of one student and show all courses in which that individual is enrolled, or show the name of one course and the names of all students who have enrolled in that course. By structuring the tables in this fashion, you have eliminated duplication of information, thereby taking up less disk space and making the data much more flexible for displaying through querying or in reports.

Examples of Tables

Three examples of tables are shown in Figure 3-1. Several fields in the Clients table and the Order table are not showing because they extend beyond the screen image.

Creating a Table

When you create a table, you first give it a name and then define the columns. To define columns type a name and assign a field type for each one. If you like, you can

```
≡  View  Ask  Report  Create  Modify  Image  Forms  Tools  Scripts  Exit
```
```
─────────────────────────── Clients ───────────────────────────
CLIENTS│    Client ID  │      Last Name     │     First Name    │      C
   1   ║     101       ║  Brown             ║  Barbara          ║  Thir
   2   ║     103       ║  Davis             ║  Don              ║  Mast
   3   ║     104       ║  Adams             ║  Alice            ║  Asso
─────────────────────────── Prodinv ───────────────────────────
PRODINV│Product #  │         Item        │  Units on hand  │  Cost per unit
   1   ║   124     ║  Telephone console  ║       2         ║    225.00
   2   ║   125     ║  Conference table   ║       3         ║    750.00
   3   ║   156     ║  Filing cabinet, 4 drawe ║  7          ║    100.00
   4   ║   157     ║  Filing cabinet, 2 drawe ║  20         ║    100.00
┌─[■]────────────────────────── Order ──────────────────────────[↑]═
│ORDER │   Order #  │    Date    │  Client ID  │  Product #  │  Quantity  │
│   1  ║   2202     ║  2/12/92   ║     101     ║     123     ║      2     ║   *
│   2  ║   2201     ║  2/01/92   ║     103     ║     123     ║      1     ║   *
│   3  ║   2203     ║  3/05/92   ║     103     ║     156     ║      4     ║   *
│   4  ║   2205     ║  4/03/92   ║     107     ║     176     ║      2     ║   *
│L  5  ║   2208     ║  4/10/92   ║     108     ║     124     ║      1     ║   *
│   6  ║   2207     ║  4/06/92   ║     109     ║     115     ║      2     ║   *
│   7  ║   2211     ║  5/01/92   ║     112     ║     157     ║      1     ║   *
│   8  ║   2212     ║  5/01/92   ║     112     ║     126     ║      1     ║   *
│   9  ║   2217     ║  5/01/92   ║     112     ║     231     ║      6     ║   *
│  10  ║   2218     ║  5/01/92   ║     112     ║     156     ║      1     ║   *
F1 Help  F7 Form  Alt-F9 CoEdit                           │  Main  │
```

Figure 3-1.   *Examples of tables*

also designate a column as a *key field,* which is a field used by Paradox to sort tables, to find records within tables, and to link tables. Key fields are discussed later in this chapter.

Naming the Table

Standard DOS conventions are used for naming Paradox files—that is, table names consist of one to eight characters without spaces. In addition, the name must be unique, and cannot be used more than once in the directory in which you are working. In your table names you may use numbers, letters, and some characters such as $ and _, but do not add an extension. Paradox adds the extension .DB automatically to the filename.

The Main menu must be displayed as shown in the following illustration:

≡ ▌iew Ask Report Create Modify Image Forms Tools Scripts Exit

To name the table, follow these steps:

1. Choose Create from the Main menu.

2. Type the name of the table at the prompt and press ENTER. The image for defining the columns is displayed as shown in Figure 3-2.

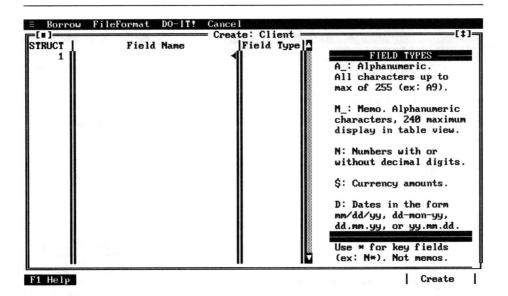

Figure 3-2.   *Table structure image*

Defining Columns

Figure 3-3 shows an example of the table structure image containing column names and field types. This is the way the image looks when you have defined all columns.

The numbers in the Struct column are entered automatically as the names are typed. The column names are typed in the Field Name area of the image. You can enter up to 25 characters and insert spaces, but the name cannot start with a space. Names must be unique (you cannot use the same name more than once in the same table). Any characters can be used in the field name except the number sign, #. It is not a good idea, however, to use parentheses, ( ), double quotes, " ", brackets, [ ], braces, { }, and the combination of a hyphen and the right angle bracket, ->. These characters are used frequently in expressions and PAL programming, and errors could occur if field names containing these same characters are also used in expressions and programming commands. When the table is viewed later, the columns will be displayed in the table (from left to right) in the order in which the names are typed.

The Field Type specifies the kind of information stored in a column and is assigned by typing the letter representing the type.

Field Types and Assignment Letters

By assigning field types, you can control the type of data and the way it is entered in a field. For example, if a field is a *currency* field, by default the numbers entered in

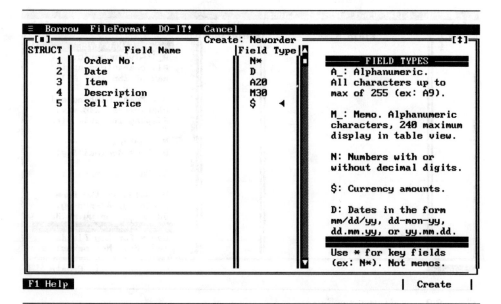

Figure 3-3.   Column names and field types shown in the Neworder table

that column will be rounded to two decimal places. The following are the choices of field types and a description of each.

Alphanumeric   Type **A** followed by a number to designate an *alphanumeric* column and to specify the number of characters that may be entered in the column. For example, **A2** could be used if the column contains only the two-character abbreviations for states. The column width is limited to 255 characters. Any characters can be included in this column—letters, numbers, or symbols. If numbers are stored in this type of column, they cannot be calculated.

Number   Type **N** to designate a *number* column. Up to 15 digits, including decimals, may be entered, but commas cannot be entered. Numbers with more than 15 digits are rounded and stored as a scientific notation. Negative numbers are shown preceded by a minus sign. You can calculate numbers in this type of column. Decimal digits in numeric fields are displayed only when explicitly entered.

Currency   Type **$** to designate a *currency* column. This column is used for currency amounts, and can be calculated. The default display rounds the amounts to two decimal places. Negative numbers are shown in parentheses.

Date   Type **D** to designate a *date* column. Any valid date can be entered. For example, an error message would be displayed if a leap year date that didn't exist were entered. Numbers in a date column can be calculated.

Date format choices are as follows:

Format	Example
mm/dd/yy	1/01/92
dd-mon-yy	1-Jan-92
dd.mm.yy	1.01.92
yy.mm.dd	92.01.1

The default format for dates is mm/dd/yy. The displayed format can be changed in Edit mode by choosing Image/Format from the Edit menu. This is discussed in Chapter 5. The default format is determined when Paradox is installed and can be changed by reinstalling or by playing the Custom Script. The Custom Script is used to go to the Custom Configuration Program where you can change the formats to suit your needs. The Custom Configuration Program is discussed in Chapter 2 and Appendix B.

Memo   Type **M** to designate a memo field. Memo fields are similar to alphanumeric fields; however, they are of variable length and can be up to 64MB in size. Examples of data in memo fields are descriptions of products, personnel information about employees, or detailed information about situations pertaining to customers. When you assign Memo as a field type, enter the number of initial characters—up to 240—that will be displayed in the table. The remaining characters are stored in a separate memo file ending with the extension .MB. A memo field cannot be a key field and "Required"the only validity check that is allowed. (Validity checks are covered later in this chapter.) DataEntry and editing in memo fields can only be done by using the Editor and is discussed in Chapter 4.

Short Number   Type **S** to designate a short number field. These are number fields that are used by application developers and are intended to be used when the table is very large and it is important to conserve space. Short number fields require less disk space than regular number fields. These fields can contain only integers between –32,767 and 32,767.

Binary   Type **B** to designate a binary field. These fields are of variable length and are used to store Binary Large OBjects (BLOBs). Values in a binary field can only be viewed or edited by using an editor of your own that can be accessed through the Paradox Custom Configuration Program. This is discussed in Appendix B. A binary field cannot be a key field.

Unknown   You cannot assign this field type—Paradox assigns this field type automatically to data that is brought in to a table from a compatible program. You can then use the **B**orrow command, discussed later in this chapter, to transfer this field to a new table.

Key Fields

Type an asterisk (*) after the letter for the field type to designate it as a key field. As mentioned earlier in this chapter, a key field is used by Paradox to sort data automatically in a table, and to link to other tables. It must be the first field in the table. While designating a key field is optional, there are several advantages to doing so:

- Because each value entered in a key field must be unique, you have the ability to extract specific information. For example, if you designate a field that stores product ID numbers as a key field, that field could be used as a link to other tables. You could enter the product ID number in a sales table and not have to enter columns that describe the product. The description could be entered in a products table. When you query the tables, the key field could link and display the information about the product whose ID number is entered in a particular sale as well as the information about the sale.

- All data in the table will be automatically sorted according to the values in the key field.

- A primary index, which sorts data and facilitates queries, will be created automatically on that field. For example, if a column that stores product ID numbers is designated as a key field, Paradox will create a primary index on that field. This means that as records are entered in the table, they will be sorted automatically in the order of the product ID number. By creating an index, a specific record can be quickly located. The index is a separate file, with the extension .PX, created by Paradox. It can be compared to an index in a book that lists topics alphabetically and specifies the pages where these topics are located so that they may be easily found.

Multi-Field Keys

Generally, only one field is defined as a key field; however, you can designate a *multi-field key* or *concatenated key* by typing an asterisk (*) following the letter, for more than one field type. These fields must be the first consecutive fields in the table. You would use this if you had duplicate values in the *primary* key field (the first field). The values in the other key fields could be used to establish the uniqueness of the records.

For example, assume you have a table containing last names, first names, and addresses. It is very likely that you will have more than one record with the same last name, and possibly have more than one record with the same last name and same first name. However, the possibility of having more than one record with the same last name, same first name, and same address is remote. Therefore, define the last name, first name, and address fields as key fields (remember that they must be the first three fields in the table). When you save the data, the records will be sorted automatically in alphabetical order by last name, then first name, and finally by the address.

Figure 3-4 shows how a multi-field key would look in the table structure image. Figure 3-5 shows the Names table as the data was entered. Notice the duplication of data in the first three fields. Figure 3-6 shows how the records were rearranged as the result of using multi-field keys.

*If there is duplication of values in key fields—either in single field keys or in multi-field keys—Paradox stores the data in a temporary Keyviol table. This is true if the data was added to the keyed table through **Tools/More/Add**, through **Modify/DataEntry**, or if the table already containing duplicate values was restructured and the keys added. The data that is stored temporarily in the Keyviol table can be edited and moved into the table for which it was intended. Key violation tables are discussed later in this chapter. Neither **Edit** nor **CoEdit** produce Keyviol tables; however, if there is a key violation in CoEdit mode, Paradox displays a message indicating that a duplicate key exists and allows you to edit the data to resolve the violation.*

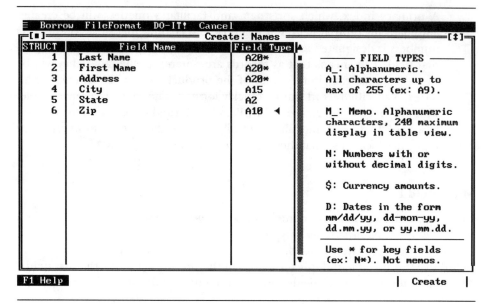

Figure 3-4.   *Table structure for defining multi-field keys*

```
≡  Image  Undo  ValCheck  KeepEntry  DO-IT!  Cancel
┌[■]══════════════════ Data Entry: Names ══════════════════[‡]┐
│ENTRY │Last Name│First Name│    Address    │  City  │State│   Zip   │▲
│   1  ║ Brown   │ Barry    │1501 North Fifth║ Seattle│ WA  │ 98199  │▒
│   2  ║ Green   │ Gladys   │1501 North Fifth║ Seattle│ WA  │ 98199  │
│   3  ║ Brown   │ Beverly  │1501 North Fifth║ Seattle│ WA  │ 98199  │
│   4  ║ Green   │ Gladys   │999 N. E. 8th  ║ Bellevue│ WA  │ 98009  │
│   5  ║         │          │              ◄║        │     │         │
│      ║         │          │               ║        │     │         │
│      ║         │          │               ║        │     │         │
│      ║         │          │               ║        │     │         │
│      ║         │          │               ║        │     │         │
│      ║         │          │               ║        │     │         │
│      ║         │          │               ║        │     │         │
│      ║         │          │               ║        │     │         │
│      ║         │          │               ║        │     │         │
│    ══ 5 of 5 ══║         ║◄█            ║         █║         █║▼
│F1 Help  F7 Form                                    │ DataEntry │
```

Figure 3-5.   *Example of data as it is entered in the table*

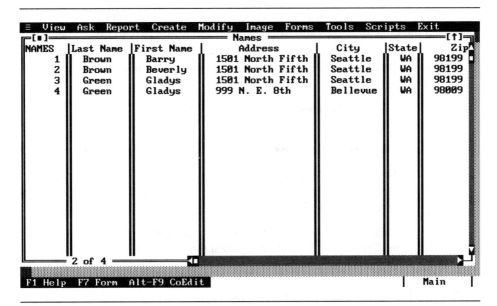

Figure 3-6.   *Result of using multi-field keys*

Naming Columns and Assigning Field Types

An example of a table structure was shown in Figure 3-3 earlier in this chapter. To name columns and assign field types, follow these steps:

1. Type the name of the first column. (In Figure 3-3 it is Order No.)

2. Press LEFT ARROW or ENTER to move to the Field Type area, and type the letter representing the field type. If you want to designate a key field, also type * following the field type.

3. Press ENTER to move to the next line.

4. Repeat these steps for the remaining column names.

5. When all columns have been defined, press F2 (Do-It!) to save the structure and return to the Main menu, or press F10 (Menu) to move to the menu and then choose **Do-It!**. If you change your mind, you can choose **C**ancel.

Borrowing Fields

A convenient way to enter field names in a table is to borrow them from another table. For example, assume a table consisting of names, addresses, and phone numbers exists. You want to create a new table that records sales and includes the names and phone numbers of customers. You can borrow the fields for the customer data from the table of names and insert it in the sales table. To do this:

1. Choose **C**reate from the Main menu, type a name for the new table, and press ENTER.

2. Enter any new field names and move the cursor to the position where you want to insert fields from another table.

3. Press F10 (Menu) to go to the **C**reate menu at the top of the screen.

4. Choose **B**orrow. A prompt is displayed asking for the name of the table to borrow from. If you press ENTER, a list of the existing table names in the current directory will be displayed.

5. Type the table name, or choose the table name from the list and press ENTER. All field names from the table will be inserted at the cursor position in the new table.

6. Edit the field names if needed. Delete the fields you do not want to use.

7. Press F2 (Do-It!) or click on **D**o-It! to save.

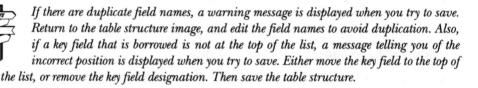 *If there are duplicate field names, a warning message is displayed when you try to save. Return to the table structure image, and edit the field names to avoid duplication. Also, if a key field that is borrowed is not at the top of the list, a message telling you of the incorrect position is displayed when you try to save. Either move the key field to the top of the list, or remove the key field designation. Then save the table structure.*

Entering Data

The **D**ataEntry command, as well as the **E**dit and **C**oEdit commands in the **M**odify menu can all be used to enter new data in a table. The **M**ultiEntry command, which can be used to enter data in one table and transfer that data to two or more tables at the same time, will not be covered here. It is covered in Chapter 6. Data may also be entered by using a form, which is covered in Chapter 7. Entering data in a memo field is covered in Chapter 4.

Using the DataEntry Command

The **D**ataEntry command is recommended for entering several records simultaneously in a single table. When you first select the **D**ataEntry command, the desktop shows a blank table named Entry. This table has the same structure as the table that will receive the entries, and it provides a temporary storage for data. When the **D**ataEntry session is over and you press F2, the data is transferred to the actual table.

Because the records entered prior to the current **D**ataEntry session are not displayed, the chance of inadvertently deleting stored information is eliminated. (When **E**dit or **C**oEdit are used, records that have been entered previously will be displayed and that information can be edited.) The records are numbered beginning with 1; however, when these records are added to the previous records, they will be renumbered and saved in the order in which they are added to the existing file, unless a key field has been assigned. If a key field has been assigned, the records will be merged into the file in the key field order.

Figure 3-7 shows the Clients table containing data that has been entered.

To enter data using the **D**ataEntry command, follow these steps:

1. Choose **M**odify/**D**ataEntry from the Main menu. A dialog box appears asking for the name of table to be used, as shown here:

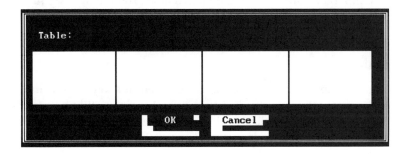

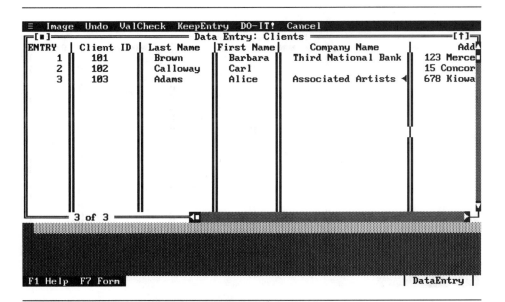

Figure 3-7.   *Clients table showing data entry*

2. Type the table name and press ENTER; or press ENTER to see the list of table names, move the cursor to the table you want, and press ENTER again. The blank table is displayed as shown in Figure 3-8.

3. Type the value in the first field (Client ID number, 101, in Figure 3-9), and press ENTER to move to the next field.

4. Continue to type the data for the fields and press ENTER. If you don't want to enter data in a field, press ENTER to go to the next field. When you press ENTER for the last field, the cursor will move to the next record.

5. Repeat these steps for all remaining records.

6. When done, press F2 (Do-It!) to save the records in the named table; or press F10 (Menu) to display the menu, and choose **Do-It!**. This merges the data from the temporary Entry table to the named table. You will then see the table with the new records, as shown in Figure 3-7 earlier in this chapter.

Key Violations

Key violations occur when duplicate data is entered in a key field or in multi-field keys. Paradox stores the data that has caused the key violation in a temporary table named Keyviol. This table is displayed on the screen when you save (press F2) the entries currently being made in a table. Figure 3-9 shows an example of a Keyviol table.

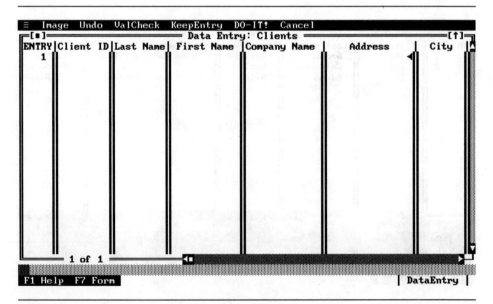

Figure 3-8.   *Blank Entry table for Clients*

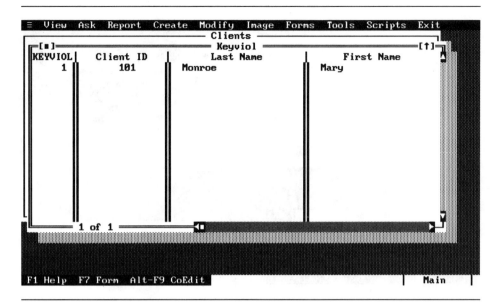

Figure 3-9. *Keyviol table*

Edit the data in the Keyviol table to eliminate the duplications and transfer the entries to the table for which it was intended using **T**ools/**M**ore/**A**dd. The steps for doing this are as follows:

1. Edit the data in the Keyviol table and then press F2 (Do-It!) to save the edit.

2. Choose **T**ools/**M**ore/**A**dd from the Main menu.

3. Press ENTER and choose Keyviol as the *source* table from the list that is displayed. See an example of this in Figure 3-10.

4. Press ENTER and choose the *target* table from the list that is displayed.

5. Choose **U**pdate. An example of the Update prompt is shown in Figure 3-11.

6. You can now press ALT-F8 (ClearAll) to clear the screen of the tables.

The entries in the Keyviol table will remain there until they are replaced by subsequent data during the current session, or until you exit Paradox. Changing directories will also delete temporary tables like Keyviol.

Using the DataEntry Menu

When you are entering data using the **D**ataEntry command, you have several options available to you. To activate the **D**ataEntry menu from the desktop when you are

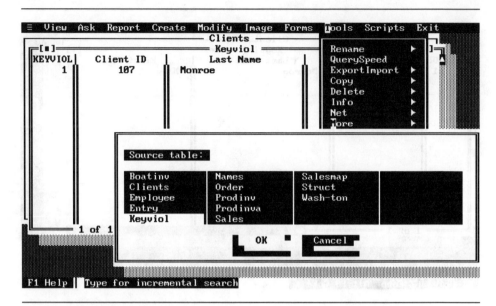

Figure 3-10.   *Prompt asking for source table*

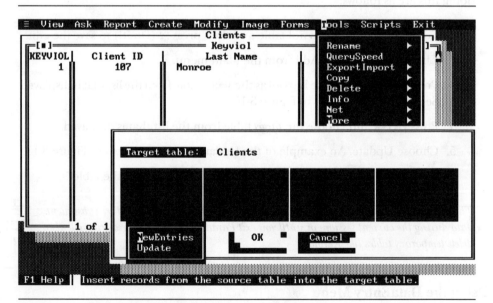

Figure 3-11.   *Update prompt*

entering data in a table, press F10 (Menu), or click on it with the mouse. Explanations of the options are listed here.

Image

Use the **I**mage option to rearrange or change the way information is displayed in the desktop. You can change the number of records showing in a table; change the column width; change the format for data in a specific column; use **Z**oom, which allows you to enter values to search for; move a column to a new location; or select a form for showing the image. For example, this option can be used to change the vertical size of a table, as shown in Figure 3-12. To do this, follow these steps:

1. Choose **M**odify/**D**ataEntry, and choose the table.

2. Press F10 to move the cursor to the **D**ataEntry menu and choose Image/TableSize.

3. Press UP ARROW or DOWN ARROW to resize the table, then press ENTER (as directed at the top of the screen). The result can look like the table shown in Figure 3-12. (To change the size horizontally, use the mouse or System/**S**ize/Move command.)

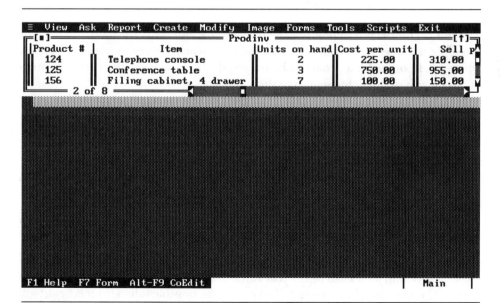

Figure 3-12.   Example of a reduced table size

Undo

You can reverse the last changes, one edit at a time, with the **U**ndo option. When you first choose **U**ndo, the last change is reversed. The next time, it reverses the second to the last change, and so on. CTRL-U is the shortcut key used for this function. This is discussed further in the later sections, "Editing Data" and "Undoing Edits."

ValCheck

Validity checks automatically determine if the values for a field type you have chosen are valid. Position the cursor in the field you want to check and choose ValCheck. Two options are available: **D**efine and **C**lear.

    Define is used to set validity checks for a field. Options in this menu are

LowValue   Use the LowValue option to set a minimum value for a field. For example, in a date field, you can type **TODAY**, which is a reserved word that will specify that no date earlier than today's date can be entered. Alphanumeric values are acceptable. To use this option, choose it, type the value, and press ENTER.

HighValue   Use the **H**ighValue option to set a maximum value for a field. For example, you can set a value that cannot be exceeded, such as a credit limit. The reserved word TODAY can also be used in this option to specify that no date later than today's date be entered. Again, alphanumeric values can be used. To use this option, choose it, type the value, and press ENTER.

Default   The **D**efault option sets the value that is entered if the field is blank. For example, if you set the default at 5, in any field that is blank, Paradox will automatically enter a 5. In order for a default to be triggered, you must move the cursor through it. To use this option, choose it, type the value, and press ENTER.

TableLookup   The TableLookup option ensures that some or all of the values you enter in one table correctly exist in another table. This requires that field values already exist in the first field in another table, and the lookup field is the same type as the current field—the field names do not have to be the same. To use this option, choose it, enter the name of the lookup table, and press ENTER. The following two choices are available:

- *JustCurrentField* checks values in the current field against values in the lookup table and can be used to fill in lookup values. Two options are available:

   PrivateLookup checks values but prevents access to the lookup table. No lookup values can be filled in automatically in the target table. If the values do not match, a message, "Not one of the possible values for this field," will be displayed. You can then correct the value or leave the field blank.

HelpAndFill browses (allows you to move the cursor) through the lookup table and is used to automatically copy the lookup values into the current table. Press F1 to display the lookup table in the desktop. You can use **Z**oom and Zoom **N**ext to search for values in the lookup table. When you find the values, you can press ESC to return to the current table without filling in the values, or you can press F2 (Do-It!) to fill in the current value in the first field of the lookup table into the table you are editing.

- *AllCorrespondingFields* is similar to JustCurrentField, except that in addition to checking values in the first field, it also automatically fills in values from corresponding fields. These fields must have identical names and field types in both tables. Two choices are available:

  FillNoHelp prevents browsing in the lookup table. Values can be filled in from corresponding fields in the lookup table, but you cannot move the cursor to look at the data in the lookup table.

  HelpAndFill browses (allows you to move the cursor) through data in the lookup table. Help is available by pressing F1 to display the lookup table in the desktop. The other functions are also the same as in the **HelpAndFill** choice in the JustCurrentField menu.

Picture   This option sets up the required format for the values so that all entries will be consistent. For example, the picture format for a social security number would be ### - ## - ###. This would require that the number entered has three digits, a hyphen, two digits, a hyphen, and three digits. The **P**icture prompt is shown in Figure 3-13.

Here are some other characters or symbols that can be used in the picture format:

Character	Represents
#	Numeric digit
?	Alphabet character, A through Z or a through z
&	Letter and converts to uppercase
@	Any character
!	Any character and converts all letters to uppercase
*	Repetition counts. Enter a number following the asterisk or any of the symbols listed above.
;	Take literally (show as is) any character that follows
[]	Optional items—you may choose to enter values or not. You must always have both a left and a right bracket.
{}	Grouping operator that displays choices for an entry. You must always have both a left and a right brace.
,	Alternative values

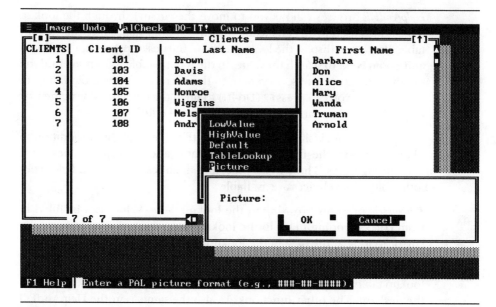

Figure 3-13.   *Picture prompt*

Some examples of picture formats are as follows:

Format	Data
[(###)]### - ####	Phone number with optional area code. The brackets indicate that entering the area code is optional.
&?????	An alphabet character in uppercase followed by five alphabet characters, either in upper- or lowercase
&*?	Alphabet string of any length, with the first letter capitalized
&*10?	Alphabet string of ten characters with the first letter capitalized
#####[- ####]	A five- or nine-digit ZIP code. The last four digits are optional.
;#@@@	A number sign would be inserted automatically followed by three characters of any type—number, symbols, or letters.
{Yes,No}	The letter *Y* or *N* would be entered and converted to Yes or No.

Required   The **R**equired option indicates whether or not a field can remain blank. For example, if you are using product ID numbers to identify each product and want to make sure that each product has a number, Set **R**equired to **Yes**. Then Paradox will not allow a product to be entered in a table without an ID number (as long as the cursor is in the required field). **R**equired is the only validity check that is allowed in a memo field.

Auto   The Auto option is chosen if you want Paradox to move the cursor to the next field when the validity check is okay. The options in this menu are: **F**illed, **P**icture, and **L**ookup.

- *Filled* will allow Paradox to move the cursor to the next field when the current field has the number of characters in it that are allowed.

- *Picture* is chosen if the field has a **P**icture specification. When the data in the field is valid, the cursor will move automatically to the next field.

- *Lookup* is chosen if a **L**ookup specification has been set for the field. When the **L**ookup is complete, the cursor will move to the next field.

The second option when using ValCheck—**C**lear—is used to remove the validity checks that have been set in the current table. The choices are **F**ield and **A**ll. Use **F**ield to remove the validity check from the field in which your cursor is located. Use **A**ll to remove all validity checks from the current table.

KeepEntry

Use **K**eepEntry to save new data in the Entry table, the temporary table where data is stored during data entry, without merging it to the table that was specified. This is useful on a network where the table is locked and, therefore, unable to receive the new data. You can save the Entry table, then use **T**ools/**R**ename to rename Entry so that the data will not be lost. Later, when the target table is no longer locked, you can use **T**ools/**M**ore/**A**dd to merge these records into it. If you choose not to use KeepEntry, you can choose **C**ancel to end the session and lose the data; or wait for the table to be unlocked, and then press F2 (Do-It!) to save the data.

Do-It!

The **D**o-It! option saves the edits and returns to the main desktop. This ends the edit session. F2 is the shortcut key used for this option, or click on it with the mouse.

Cancel

End the edit session with **C**ancel. It also undoes all changes to the images on the desktop and returns you to the main desktop.

The Paradox Help screen can always be accessed from any menu by pressing F1.

Using the Edit Command to Enter New Data

The **E**dit command can also be used to enter new data into an existing table. These new records can be added at the beginning, end, or within a table. The previous records will be displayed, instead of the blank table, which appears when the **D**ataEntry command is used. You can use the **M**odify/**E**dit menu; or you can use View and choose the name you want to display the table, then press F9 (Edit) to go to **E**dit mode.

If you are working on a network, you can choose **M**odify/**C**oEdit to enter new data. This procedure is the same as using the **M**odify/**E**dit menu except that it allows two or more users to enter or edit data in a table at the same time. When this menu is used, Paradox automatically locks the record that is being added or edited, thus preventing other network users from accessing that particular record. Additional information about using the **C**oEdit command is discussed later in this chapter in the "Editing Data" section, and locking and unlocking is covered further in Chapter 14.

To edit a table, follow these steps:

1. From the Main menu choose **M**odify/**E**dit. The prompt asking for a table name will be displayed.

2. Type the name of the table and press ENTER, or press ENTER to display the list of table names and choose the table name. The table containing previously entered data will be displayed.

Cursor Movement in a Table

The following are keys used to move the cursor within a table:

LEFT/RIGHT ARROW	Move from field to field
UP/DOWN ARROW	Move from record to record
HOME	Move to the first record in the table
END	Move to the last record in the table
CTRL-HOME	Move to the beginning of the record
CTRL-END	Move to the end of the record
INSERT	Inserts a new row where data can be entered
ENTER	Moves to the next field

Adding New Records

To add new records to a table using the **Modify/Edit** command, find the location in the file where you want to add records, press the appropriate commands discussed next, and enter the data. The records will be physically entered in the location shown on the screen. If the file has a key field, the records will be automatically arranged in order based on the key field.

Adding a Record at the End of the Table

In order to add records at the end of a table, move the cursor to the last record in the file and press DOWN ARROW. A blank row will be displayed and data can be entered. To do this, follow these steps:

1. Press END to move the cursor to the last record in the table, and press DOWN ARROW to go to the next line. A blank line will be displayed.

2. Enter the data in each appropriate column.

Adding a Record at the Beginning of the Table

If a record is to be added at the beginning of the table, move the cursor to the first record, press INSERT to create a new blank record, and enter the data. To do this, follow these steps:

1. Press HOME to move the cursor to the first record.

2. Press INSERT to insert a blank row.

3. Enter the information for that record.

Adding a Record Within the Table

In order to insert records between two existing records, move the cursor to the record that should follow the record to be entered, press INSERT, and enter data. To do this, follow these steps:

1. Move the cursor to the record just behind the record that is to be inserted.

2. Press INSERT to insert a blank row.

3. Enter the data for the new record.

Ending an Edit Session When New Records Have Been Added

The procedure for ending an edit session when new records have been added is the same as in other editing functions. Follow these steps:

1. Press F2 (Do-It!) to save the edits; or press F10 (Menu) to display the **Edit** menu, and choose **Do-It!**.

2. Press F8 (Clear) to clear the current image from the desktop. This is optional depending on what your next task is going to be.

 To end an edit session using the mouse:

1. Click on **Do-It!** to save.

2. Click on the Close box at the left end of the title bar to clear the current image from the desktop.

Editing Data

To edit data in a table, you can use either the **Modify/Edit** menu or the **Modify/CoEdit** menu. The **Edit** command is intended for individual users; the **CoEdit** command is for network users. Individual users can also use **CoEdit** (covered later in this chapter). The Editor window is used when you edit memo fields and is discussed in Chapter 4.

You can display the table that is to be edited by choosing **Modify/Edit** and selecting the table to be edited; or by choosing View from the Main menu, selecting the table, and pressing F9 (Edit) to change to **Edit** mode.

To choose **View** and then change to **Edit** mode when the table is displayed, follow these steps:

1. From the Main menu, choose **View** to display the prompt asking for a table.

2. Type the table name and press ENTER, or press ENTER to display the list of table names and choose the table.

3. Press F9 (Edit) to change to **Edit** mode. The screen now displays "Edit" in the lower-right corner. Your screen should resemble Figure 3-14.

Using Edit Mode

You can use the **Edit** command to add new records, to change existing data, or to add data in a field.

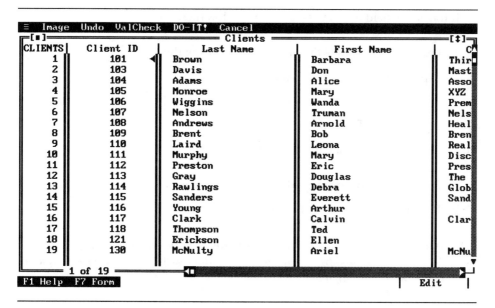

Figure 3-14.   *Clients table in Edit mode*

Editing Actions

The following lists the keys and their functions that can be used in Edit mode. The keys for moving the cursor were listed previously in this chapter.

BACKSPACE	Deletes the character to the left of the cursor
CTRL-BACKSPACE	Deletes the current field
DELETE	Deletes the current record
CTRL-U	Undoes the last change
F3(Image Up), or F4(Image Down)	Moves the cursor from one table to another

Editing Data in a Field

Edit data either by replacing several characters or deleting all characters in the fields and replacing with new data.

To replace several characters in a field, follow these steps:

1. Press BACKSPACE to delete those characters.

2. Type new characters in their place.

If the entire field needs to be changed, follow these steps:

1. Press CTRL-BACKSPACE to delete the contents of the field.

2. Type the new characters in the field.

Deleting an Entire Record

To delete a record from a table, follow these steps:

1. Move the cursor to any field in the record to be deleted.

2. Press DELETE to remove the entire record.

 When you delete a record, you can free up or recover the space that was used for the record. To do this choose Modify/Restructure from the Main menu, choose the table from which you deleted the records, and press F2 (Do-It!).

Adding Information at the End of a Field

To add characters to the end of a field follow these steps:

1. Move the cursor to the field in the record to be changed.

2. Type the new data.

Using Field View Mode

The Field View mode is used to edit characters within a field entry. It is activated by pressing ALT-F5 or CTRL-F and turned off by pressing ENTER or F2 (Do-It!). When the mode is active, the cursor is displayed as a box with a flashing underscore (Insert mode) or a flashing box (Typeover mode). When the mode is ended and the normal Edit mode is active, the cursor returns to normal display. INSERT acts as a toggle between the Insert and Typeover modes while you are in the Field Editing mode. The cursor tells you which mode you are in, as described next.

 If you are using a mouse, you can double-click on the field to go to Field View mode. Double-click again to return to normal Edit mode.

Inserting Characters

Use Insert mode to add characters to a field. Insert mode is the default editing mode and means that existing characters will move automatically to the right as new characters are typed in. Insert mode inserts the new characters within the existing ones.

1. Move the cursor to the field to be changed.

2. Press ALT-F5 or CTRL-F to change to Field View mode. Notice the change in the cursor display. The cursor is now a box and the underscore character is flashing.

3. Move the cursor to the character following those to be inserted.

4. Type the new characters.

5. Press ENTER or F2 (Do-It!) to leave the Field View mode and return to normal **E**dit mode.

You must leave the Field View mode in order to move the cursor to another field.

Typing Over Characters

Use Typeover mode to change characters within a field using the Field View mode. Typeover mode allows you to "type over" existing characters with new characters, and thus automatically delete the old characters.

1. Move the cursor to the field to be changed.

2. Press ALT-F5 or CTRL-F to change to Field View mode. The cursor is now displayed in a box and is flashing.

3. Move the cursor over the characters to be replaced.

4. Press INSERT to change to Typeover mode. The cursor box is now a flashing box.

5. Type over the existing characters.

6. Press ENTER or F2 (Do-It!) to leave field view mode and return to normal **E**dit mode.

Undoing Edits

You can easily reverse or undo your last action by pressing CTRL-U or choosing **U**ndo from the **E**dit menu. You can undo a sequence of edits, not just the last one. If you repeat the **U**ndo function, the next to last edit will be reversed, then the edit just preceding the next to last will be reversed, and so on. You cannot be in Field View mode when you use **U**ndo. Your cursor can be positioned in any field when using this command.

To reverse the last edit press CTRL-U.

Saving Edits

When you have finished editing a file, you must save the changes and return to Main mode. Press F2 (Do-It!), which will save the edits and leave Edit mode. The word "Edit" is no longer displayed in the lower-right corner of the screen.

 With the mouse, click on **Do**-It! to save your edits and return to Main mode.

Displaying More Than One Table

Several tables can be displayed on the desktop at once and edited. The tables are displayed in a stacked configuration, with the most recent table displayed on top of the preceding one. An example is shown in Figure 3-15. Additional tables are displayed from the **Modify/Edit** command, or from the **View** menu. If you are currently in **Edit** mode, you must leave it before adding other tables to the desktop. Once additional tables are displayed, use the Up Image key (F3) or the Down Image key (F4) to move from one table to the next. Then edits can be made in the current table.

```
 ≡  View  Ask  Report  Create  Modify  Image  Forms  Tools  Scripts  Exit
┌──────────────────────────── Clients ───────────────────────────┐
│CLIENTS│   Client ID  │      Last Name  │    First Name     │      │Thi
│   1   ║     101      │  Brown          │  Barbara          │      │Mas
│   2   ║     103      │  Davis          │  Don              │      │Ass
│   3   ║     104      │  Adams          │  Alice            │      │XYZ
│   4   ║     105      │  Monroe         │  Mary             │      │
┌─[■]─────────────────────── Prodinv ════════════════════════[↑]═╗
│PRODINV│Product #  │        Item         │Units on hand│Cost per unit│ ▲
│   1   ║   124     │  Telephone console  │      2      │    225.00    │ █
│   2   ║   125     │  Conference table   │      3      │    750.00    │ █
│   3   ║   156     │  Filing cabinet, 4 drawer │  7   │    100.00    │
│   4   ║   157     │  Filing cabinet, 2 drawer │ 20   │    100.00    │
│   5   ║   176     │  Computer desk      │     10      │    200.00    │
│   6   ║   200     │  Credenza           │      4      │    155.00    │
│   7   ║   231     │  Office chair, stackable │ 30   │     15.00    │
│   8   ║   232     │  Office chair, with arms │ 25   │     20.00    │ ▼
╚════ 2 of 8 ═════════════◄■►════════════════════════════════►═╝

 F1 Help  F7 Form  Alt-F9 CoEdit                              │  Main  │
```

Figure 3-15.   *Paradox desktop showing Clients table and the Prodinv table*

To display an additional table press F10 (Menu) to display the Main menu, choose **M**odify/**E**dit, select the table name, and press ENTER. Or choose **V**iew, select the table name, and press ENTER. Now two tables are displayed in the desktop, as shown in Figure 3-15.

Moving from One Image to Another

Now that more than one table is shown in the desktop, press either F3 (Up Image) or F4 (Down Image) to move to the table where you want to make changes. Use the usual edit functions to make changes.

Changing the Display of Tables

The way the tables are arranged on the screen can be changed easily. You can be in either Main mode or **E**dit or **C**oEdit mode. In either mode, press F10. You will go to the Main menu if you are viewing, or to the **E**dit or **C**oEdit menu if you are editing. Then choose **I**mage.

Changing the Size of a Table

You can change the number of records displayed in a table by increasing or decreasing the height of the table. To do this, follow these steps:

1. Move to the table you want and press F10 to go to the menu.

2. Choose **I**mage/**T**ableSize. A message at the top of the screen appears instructing you how to resize the table.

3. Press UP ARROW or DOWN ARROW to move the lower edge of the table to a new position.

4. Press ENTER when done.

Changing a Column Width

By adjusting the width of a column, you can display more fields in each record. To do this, follow these steps:

1. Move to the table you want to change and press F10 (Menu) to go to the menu.

2. Choose **I**mage/**C**olumnSize. A message is displayed at the top of the screen instructing you to go to the column you want.

3. Move the cursor to the column you want to resize and press ENTER. The message at the top of the screen now changes and instructs you how to resize the column.

4. Press LEFT ARROW or RIGHT ARROW to change the column size.

5. Press ENTER when done.

Keeping the Changes to the Table and Columns

If the table is cleared from the screen, the next time you view it the size will return to the original size unless you save the changes. To do this, follow these steps:

1. Press F10 (Menu) to move to the menu.

2. Choose Image/KeepSet.

Using the Mouse to Change the Table Display

If you are using a mouse, the table size, column width, and the position of the table on the screen can be changed quickly and easily.

 To change the size of the table, follow these steps:

1. Point to the Resize corner in the lower-right corner of the table.

2. Hold down the left mouse button and drag the icon up and down or left and right to change the height and width of the table.

3. Release the left mouse button.

 To change the width of a column, follow these steps:

1. Point to the vertical line to the right of the column you want to resize.

2. Hold down the left mouse button and drag the line to a different position. Be sure all of the data you want to display is showing.

3. Release the left mouse button.

 To move the table to a new position, follow these steps:

1. Point to the title bar at the top of the table.

2. Hold down the left mouse button and drag the table to a different position on the screen.

3. Release the left mouse button.

 To scroll the screen to the right or left in a table, do one of the following:

- Point and click with the left mouse button on the left or right arrows in the horizontal scroll bar at the bottom of the table.

or

- Point to and drag the box in the horizontal scroll bar to the left or right.

 To scroll the screen up or down in a table, do one of the following:

- Point and click with the left mouse button on the up or down arrows in the vertical scroll bar at the right of the table.

or

- Point to and drag the box in the vertical scroll bar up or down.

Using Shortcuts

In addition to using some of the shortcut keys already discussed, such as F2 (Do-It!), or CTRL-U to choose Undo, Paradox provides the following commands that can be used in **Edit** mode:

- *Ditto command* (CTRL-D)   This copies a field value entered in the previous record to the same field in the next record.
- *Zoom command* (CTRL-Z)   This quickly locates a particular value.
- *Zoom Next command* (ALT-Z)   This moves to repeated occurrences of the same value.

Ditto Command

Enter the value in a specific field, then move the cursor to the same field in the following record and press CTRL-D. Use this to enter duplicate values in the same column. For example, use this command if you need to enter the name of a state in several consecutive records.

Zoom Command

To locate a specific value, move the cursor to the field that contains the value for which you're searching. Press CTRL-Z to display the prompt asking for the value, as shown in the following illustration. Type the value and press ENTER. The cursor will move immediately to that value.

To search for a value, follow these steps:

1. Move the cursor to the field containing the desired value.

2. Press CTRL-Z (Zoom) to display the Zoom prompt.

3. Type the value for which you are searching.

4. Press ENTER, or click on OK if you are using a mouse.

Zoom Next Command

Use Zoom Next to search for subsequent occurrences of the same value. Be sure your cursor is in the field in which you are locating the value, and press ALT-Z.

To Use Wildcard Characters in Zoom

You can use Paradox wildcard characters, @ and .., to enter patterns for a search. The @ operator represents one character. For example, if you want to search for all clients living in states starting with an *A*, press CTRL-Z to display the Zoom prompt, type **A@**, and press ENTER (or click on OK) to search. Press ALT-Z (Zoom Next) to find subsequent values.

The .. operator is used to search for more than one character. For example, to search for all cities beginning with the letter *S*, at the Zoom prompt, type **S..**, and press ENTER (or click on OK) to search. Press ALT-Z (Zoom Next) to find subsequent values.

These same wildcard characters are used in querying tables and will be discussed further in Chapter 6.

Zoom and Zoom Next are case-sensitive searches unless you use wildcards, in which case they become case insensitive.

Clearing the Desktop

Multiple tables can be displayed in the desktop at one time; however, if you are no longer editing data in a table, you may want to remove it so the screen is not cluttered. Or you may want to clear the desktop of all tables and display others. The F8 and ALT-F8 keys are used to perform these functions. Paradox will not permit a table to be cleared when **E**dit mode is used. Press F2 (Do-It!) to save the edits, or choose **C**ancel from the **E**dit menu; then you can clear the tables.

- Press F8 (Clear) if you want to remove one table from the desktop but continue to edit remaining tables. F8 clears the current worksheet.

- Press ALT-F8 (ClearAll) to clear the desktop of all tables.

- Press ALT-SPACEBAR to go to the System menu, and choose **D**esktop/**E**mpty.

 Click on the Close box at the left end of the title bar to clear the current worksheet.

Using the Edit Menu

When you are in **E**dit mode, press F10 (Menu) to go to the **E**dit menu. The options in this menu are the same as those in the **D**ataEntry menu discussed earlier in this chapter, except the **K**eepEntry option is not available. Also, the **I**mage option in the **E**dit menu contains a choice, **K**eepSet, that allows you to keep any changes you made to the screen image—table size, column width, and so on. This choice is not in the **I**mage option in the **D**ataEntry menu. Refer to the earlier section, "Using the DataEntry Menu," for further information about the options.

Using CoEdit Mode

CoEdit mode is intended to be used by network users; however, the editing procedures are the same in **C**oEdit mode as they are in **E**dit mode, and individual users can use either one.

To go to **C**oEdit mode, follow these steps:

1. Choose **M**odify/**C**oEdit from the Main menu.

2. Choose the table you want to coedit. The word "CoEdit" is displayed in the lower-right corner of the screen, as shown in Figure 3-16.

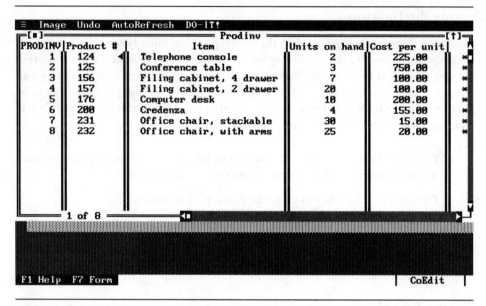

Figure 3-16. Screen showing CoEdit mode

*If you used **View** to display the table, you can go to CoEdit mode from the Paradox desktop by pressing ALT-F9 (CoEdit).*

You can also click on ALT-F9 in the speedbar to go to **C**oEdit mode.

The advantage to individual users of using the **C**oEdit menu is that if there is a key violation—that is, if the key field in a new record conflicts with that in an old record—the user can choose whether or not to keep the old values in the non-key fields. If there is a key violation, the "Key exists" message is displayed, as shown in Figure 3-17. This allows the user to confirm and remove the record that is a duplicate—press ALT-L (LockToggle) to do this. The other choice is to press ALT-K (KeyViol), which allows you to edit the entry and then add it to the table.

*When you are in **Edit** mode and there is a key violation, the new values in non-key fields automatically replace the old values. There is no warning of this—the "Key exists" message is not displayed in **Edit** mode.*

If you are using **C**oEdit on a network, Paradox automatically locks the record you are using, thus preventing others on the network from editing that particular record. Other users can, however, edit other records in the same table. A record is automat-

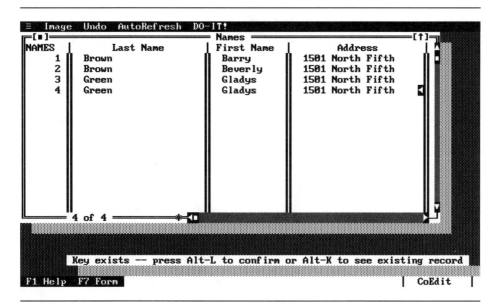

Figure 3-17.   *"Key exists" message*

ically unlocked when you move the cursor to another record, or when you press F2 (Do-It!), which ends the editing.

When other users are working on the same table as you, you can see which record is locked by looking at the status message at the top of the screen. A statement is displayed saying "Coediting" followed by the table name.

As other users make changes to a record, you will see those changes on the screen. The changes may not be shown immediately, depending upon the number of other users working at the same time and where they are working. If you wish to speed up the display of changes, press ALT-R (Refresh) to immediately update the records. You may also change the intervals (in seconds) that Paradox automatically updates records by choosing AutoRefresh from the CoEdit menu.

Editing Data on a Network

If you are on a network and choose Modify/Edit, a *full lock* is placed on the table in which you are working, preventing other users from working on that table. CoEdit, on the other hand, places a *prevent full lock* on that table, preventing others from gaining exclusive rights to the table. Prevent full lock will allow others to query the table or perform other procedures that do not require exclusive use of the table.

Chapter *4*

Using the Editor

The Paradox Editor has been enhanced in Version 4. In previous versions the Editor was used primarily for editing scripts, but it has been expanded to include text editing. You can access the Editor from any point in the program—except memo fields—by pressing ALT-E or by choosing **U**tilities/**E**ditor from the System menu. In memo fields, press ALT-F5 or CTRL-F to display the Editor screen and menu.

You'll see how to use the Editor in memo fields later in this chapter. Using the Editor to edit scripts will be covered in Chapter 10.

Creating a New File in the Text Editor

The Editor can be used to write memos, notes, letters, or any other ASCII text files that you may need. You can create, print, edit, and save these files. You can also insert a text file in any field in a table, as long as it meets the requirements of the field.

Creating the File

To create a new file, access the Editor from the Paradox desktop, choose New, and then type a filename using standard DOS naming conventions—that is, one to eight characters with no spaces. The file is created in ASCII format.

From any point on the Paradox desktop, follow these steps:

1. Press ALT-SPACEBAR or click on the System menu.

2. Choose **E**ditor. A menu appears, as shown in Figure 4-1.

3. Choose **N**ew. A dialog box asks for a filename, as shown here:

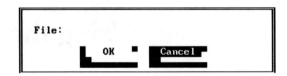

4. Type a filename and press ENTER. You are now in the Editor. The filename and path appear in the title bar, as shown in Figure 4-2.

 To use shortcut keys, from any point on the Paradox desktop, follow these steps:

1. Press ALT-E. A menu is shown with the choices **N**ew and **O**pen, as shown here:

2. Choose **N**ew, type a filename, and press ENTER to go to the Editor window.

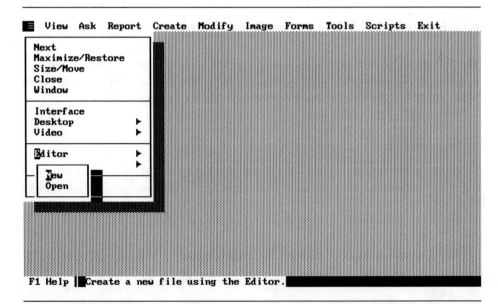

Figure 4-1. *Editor menu*

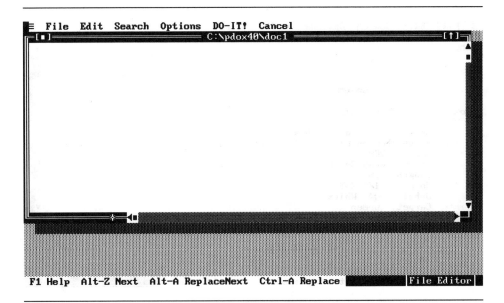

Figure 4-2.   *Paradox Editor window*

Entering Text

You enter text by simply typing it, as you would enter text in any text editor. Figure 4-3 gives an example of how typed-in text appears. This figure shows a list that was indented using **O**ptions/AutoIndent. (The default for AutoIndent is off.) When you type text, the default is to have WordWrap on, allowing text to wrap at the end of each line; however, you can turn WordWrap off if you like. With WordWrap on, press ENTER to end paragraphs and to insert blank lines. You can also press SPACEBAR and TAB to indent and insert spaces.

To correct errors as you type, press BACKSPACE to delete characters to the left, or DELETE to delete the character at the cursor position. Other editing functions will be covered later in this chapter.

Cursor Movements in the Editor Window

As you enter text, you may want to move the cursor around in the file. Cursor movements are controlled with the following keys:

Key	Movement
LEFT ARROW	Left one character
RIGHT ARROW	Right one character
UP ARROW	Up one line

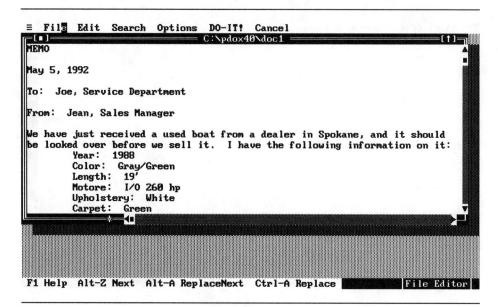

Figure 4-3.   *Editor window showing text set up using AutoIndent*

Key	Movement
DOWN ARROW	Down one line
CTRL-LEFT ARROW	Left one word
CTRL-RIGHT ARROW	Right one word
HOME	To beginning (first character) of the line
END	To end (last character) of the line
PGUP	Up one window
PGDN	Down one window
CTRL-PGUP	To beginning (first character) of the file
CTRL-PGDN	To end (last character) of the file

Saving the File

A text file is typed into desktop memory. Periodically you need to save it to disk. A file is saved to disk by choosing **File/Save** from the **Editor** menu. This saves the file and leaves the text in the Editor window. You can also save by pressing F2 (Do-It!) or clicking on **Do-It!** with the mouse. Using **Do-It!** saves the edits, ends the Editor session, and returns you to the Main menu.

To save the file and remain in the Editor:

- Press F10 to go to the **E**ditor menu and choose **F**ile/**S**ave.

To save the file and end the Editor session:

- Press F2 (Do-It!) or click on **D**o-It! with the mouse.

Printing the File

When you print the text file, it will print as shown on the screen.
To print:

- Press F10 to go to the **E**ditor menu and choose **F**ile/**P**rint.

- If you are using a laser printer, you may have to press Form Feed (an option on the printer—not an Editor command) to eject the paper.

Using Options

Choose **O**ptions from the **E**ditor menu if you want to use the AutoIndent feature, turn off **W**ordWrap, or turn on **C**aseSensitive.

AutoIndent

AutoIndent allows you to repeat in consecutive lines indents that have been entered by pressing either TAB or SPACEBAR. If you use TAB, the indent will be equivalent to eight spaces.
To turn on **A**utoIndent, follow these steps:

1. Press F10 to go to the **E**ditor menu and choose **O**ptions/**A**utoIndent. A menu showing two choices—**S**et and **C**lear—is displayed as shown here:

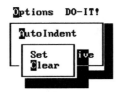

2. Choose **S**et to turn on AutoIndent.

To use **A**utoIndent, follow these steps:

1. Press TAB or SPACEBAR to indent the amount you want.

2. Type the text for the first line and press ENTER. Your cursor is now on the line beneath its previous location and is indented the same amount as the previous line.

    Repeat as many times as you want. Refer back to Figure 4-3 to see an example of text that has been entered using AutoIndent. The list of items—Year, Color, Length, and so on—have all been entered using AutoIndent.

WordWrap

As mentioned earlier in this chapter, **WordWrap** is turned on as the default, but if you want to turn it off, you can. WordWrap automatically ends a line at the right margin; the text that follows is entered on the next line. When you use WordWrap you do not have to press ENTER at the ends of lines in a paragraph. You do need to press ENTER to end a paragraph, to end short lines, or to insert blank lines. If WordWrap is turned off, then you must press ENTER at the end of each line.

To turn off **WordWrap**, follow these steps:

1. Press F10 to go to the **Editor** menu and choose **Options/WordWrap**. A menu showing the options **Set** and **Clear** is displayed, as shown here:

2. Choose **Clear** to turn off **WordWrap**. You are returned to the Editor window.

3. When you type text, press ENTER at the end of each line to go to the next line.

To turn on **WordWrap**, follow these steps:

1. Press F10 to go to the **Editor** menu and choose **Options/WordWrap**.

2. Choose **Set**.

CaseSensitive

You can specify whether or not searches in the Editor are case sensitive. If **CaseSensitive** is turned on, Paradox will only locate values where uppercase and lowercase characters are an exact match with the values entered in the Search dialog box. To set case sensitivity:

1. Press F10 to go to the Editor menu and choose **O**ptions/**C**aseSensitive. A menu with the options **S**et and **C**lear is displayed.

2. Choose either **S**et to turn case sensitivity on, or **C**lear to turn it off.

Closing a File

Closing a file clears the text from the Editor window, but you remain in the Editor session and can create or edit other files.

There are several ways to close a file. You can use any of these methods:

- Press ALT-SPACEBAR to go to the System menu, or click on the System menu and then choose **C**lose.

- Click on the Close box in the upper-left corner of the Editor window.

- Press CTRL-F8 (Close).

Opening a Text File

Once you have created a file, you can retrieve it, edit it, and save it again. Multiple files can be opened and edited during an Editor session.

To open a text file, follow these steps:

1. Press ALT-E from any point in Paradox (if you are in a memo field, press ALT-F5 or CTRL-F), or choose **U**tilities/**E**ditor from the System menu.

2. Choose **O**pen. A dialog box appears asking for the filename.

3. Type the filename you want and press ENTER, or press ENTER to display a list of files as shown in Figure 4-4.

4. To choose from the list, move the cursor to the file you want to open and press ENTER. The text is now displayed in the Editor window.

Working with Editor Windows

If you open multiple files displaying several Editor windows including the Clipboard window (which is discussed later in this chapter), you can rearrange, resize, or move

Figure 4-4. *Example of a list of files that can be opened in the Editor*

from one window to another on the desktop. You can use the mouse or the shortcut keys to perform these tasks quickly. However, the System menu is available in the Editor windows as it is in other areas of Paradox, and can be used to **M**aximize/**Re**store, **S**ize/**M**ove, or display a list windows. You can then choose the file you want from the list.

The procedures for working with Editor windows are the same that you use to work with any other Paradox windows. (Refer back to Chapter 2 for a review of these procedures.)

Editing Text

Editing text simply means changing existing text. Cursor movements for moving around in the Editor window were covered earlier in this chapter in the "Cursor Movements in the Editor Window" section. Once you are positioned in the text, you can insert or delete characters as needed. In addition to using BACKSPACE and DELETE to remove single characters, you can also use Overwrite mode (press INSERT) to type over existing text with new characters.

Selecting Text

Many edits require that you first *select* (or highlight) a block of text. Then you can delete it, copy it, cut and paste to move it, or save it.

The following is a list of keys that may be used to select text:

Key	Selects
SHIFT-LEFT ARROW	One character to the left
SHIFT-RIGHT ARROW	One character to the right
SHIFT-HOME	From cursor to the beginning of the line
SHIFT-END	From cursor to the end of the line
SHIFT-CTRL-LEFT ARROW	One word to the left
SHIFT-CTRL-RIGHT ARROW	One word to the right
SHIFT-UP ARROW	One line up
SHIFT-DOWN ARROW	One line down
SHIFT-PGUP	From cursor to the top of the window
SHIFT-PGDN	From cursor to the bottom of the window
SHIFT-CTRL-PGUP	From cursor to the top of the file
SHIFT-CTRL-PGDN	From cursor to the end of the file

 Select varying amounts of text using the mouse with these methods:

- *Select a block* by pointing to the beginning of the block, holding down the left or right button, moving the pointer to the end of the block, and releasing the button. The block will be highlighted.

- *Select a line* by double-clicking on the line.

- *Deselect a block* by clicking the mouse button. This will remove the highlighting without deleting it and reposition the cursor to wherever you were pointing when you clicked the button.

If you press any key—other than a function key or a direction key—when text is selected (highlighted), the selected block will be cut and placed on the Clipboard, and the key you pressed will replace the selected block in the text.

Editing with Shortcut Keys

The following are shortcut keys that you can use to cut, paste, or delete single characters or blocks of text.

Key	Edit Action
INSERT	Toggle between Insert and Overwrite modes
DELETE	Delete permanently the character the cursor is on, or delete a selected block of text
ALT-D	Delete a word

Key	Edit Action
CTRL-T*	Delete from the cursor position to the end of the word, including spaces and punctuation that follow the word
CTRL-Y*	Delete the line the cursor is on
CTRL-INSERT	Copy selected text to the Clipboard
SHIFT-DELETE	Cut the selected text and move it to the Clipboard
SHIFT-INSERT	Paste the selected text from the Clipboard into the text at the cursor position

*In the preceding table, the keys with a * have different functions in other Paradox areas. CTRL-T is used in the Debugger to begin the process of tracing in a script. CTRL-Y is used in the Report Designer to delete text from the cursor position to the end of the line.*

Using XCut

Use the **E**dit/**X**Cut option to remove a block of text from the file and move it to the Clipboard.

When a block of text is moved to the Clipboard window, it is automatically selected or highlighted. When the next block of text is moved to the Clipboard, it replaces this text unless the highlighting has been removed or deselected. *Deselect* means to remove the highlighting from previously selected or highlighted text.

To deselect in the Clipboard window, press one of the arrow keys, or click the mouse button at any point in the window. When the text in the Clipboard is deselected, then the next block of text that is moved to the Clipboard is inserted at the cursor position. Follow these steps to remove a block of text:

1. Select the text to be cut.

2. Press F10 from the **E**ditor menu and choose **E**dit/**X**Cut. This removes the selected block of text and places it on the Clipboard.

To use shortcut keys, select a block of text and press SHIFT-DELETE to cut the block and place it in the Clipboard.

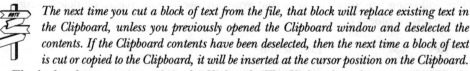

The next time you cut a block of text from the file, that block will replace existing text in the Clipboard, unless you previously opened the Clipboard window and deselected the contents. If the Clipboard contents have been deselected, then the next time a block of text is cut or copied to the Clipboard, it will be inserted at the cursor position on the Clipboard. The deselected text remains as is in the Clipboard. (The Clipboard, at this point, contains the previously selected text plus the new text that has been cut.)

Copying

The **Edit/C**opy option will leave a selected block of text in its original position and place a copy of it on the Clipboard.

To copy text onto the Clipboard, follow these steps:

1. Select the block of text.

2. Press F10 to go to the **Editor** menu and choose **Edit/C**opy.

 To use shortcut keys, select the block of text and press CTRL-INSERT to copy it to the Clipboard.

The next time you copy a block of text to the Clipboard, that block will replace existing text that is on the Clipboard, unless you have previously opened the Clipboard window and deselected the contents. If the Clipboard contents have been deselected, then the next time a block of text in the Editor window is cut or copied to the Clipboard, it will be inserted at the cursor position on the Clipboard.

Using the ShowClipboard Option

The **S**howClipboard option opens the Clipboard and allows you to view and edit the current contents. You use most of the same editing functions to edit text in the Clipboard window that you use in the Editor window; however, you cannot cut and paste or save text in the Clipboard.

To show the Clipboard window, press F10 to go to the **Editor** menu and choose **Edit/S**howClipboard.

As shown in Figure 4-5, the Clipboard displays the block of text that was copied from the DOC1 file. Edit the text, if you like.

To leave the Clipboard window and go to another Editor file window, press ALT-SPACEBAR and choose **W**indow.

 To use shortcut keys, press CTRL-F4 (WinNext) to move to the next window on the desktop.

 To use your mouse, click at any position in the Editor window, or click on the System menu and choose **W**indow.

To close the Clipboard window, press ALT-SPACEBAR to go to the System menu and choose **C**lose.

 Click on the Close box with the mouse to close the Clipboard window.

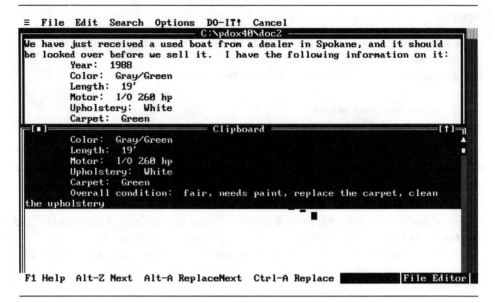

≡ File Edit Search Options DO-IT! Cancel
```
═══════════════════════ C:\pdox40\doc2 ═══════════════════════
We have just received a used boat from a dealer in Spokane, and it should
be looked over before we sell it.  I have the following information on it:
        Year:   1988
        Color:  Gray/Green
        Length: 19'
        Motor:  I/O 260 hp
        Upholstery:  White
        Carpet:  Green
┌[■]══════════════════════ Clipboard ════════════════════════[↑]┐
        Color:  Gray/Green
        Length: 19'
        Motor:  I/O 260 hp
        Upholstery:  White
        Carpet:  Green
        Overall condition:  fair, needs paint, replace the carpet, clean
the upholstery


F1 Help  Alt-Z Next  Alt-A ReplaceNext  Ctrl-A Replace ████████ │File Editor│
```

Figure 4-5.   *Clipboard window showing a block of text*

Pasting

Use the **E**dit/**P**aste option to insert the *selected* contents of the Clipboard into a file in the Editor or into a memo field. If the text in the Clipboard is not selected, you will not be able to *paste* it in a file.

To paste a block of text, follow these steps:

1. Move the cursor to the position where you want to insert the text.

2. Press F10 to go to the **E**ditor menu and choose **E**dit/**P**aste.

 To use shortcut keys, press SHIFT-INSERT to paste the block from the Clipboard into the text at the cursor position.

 If no text is inserted when you press SHIFT-INSERT, the contents of the Clipboard have not been selected. To select the contents quickly, press CTRL-INSERT—you don't have to be in the Clipboard window. Then you can press SHIFT-INSERT to paste the text at the cursor position.

Erasing

If you erase a block of text, it will be removed permanently from the file. It will not be stored in the Clipboard.

To erase text using the menu, follow these steps:

1. Select the block of text you wish to erase.

2. Press F10 to go to the **E**ditor menu and choose **E**dit/**E**rase.

   After selecting the block of text, press the DELETE key to remove it.

Using Goto

The **G**oto option allows you to move the cursor immediately to a specified line.

To use **G**oto, follow these steps:

1. Press F10 to go to the **E**ditor menu and choose **E**dit/**G**oto. A dialog box like the one shown here asks you to enter a line number:

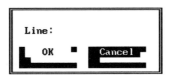

2. Type the line number you want and press ENTER to go to that line.

Using the Location Option

When the Location option is chosen, numbers are shown in the lower border of the Editor window indicating the line and column position of the cursor.

To show cursor position numbers:

• Press F10 to go to the **E**ditor menu and choose **E**dit/**L**ocation.

The numbers indicating the position of the cursor are shown in the lower-left border, as displayed in Figure 4-6.

The line and column numbers are shown only for the current cursor position. When the cursor is moved, the numbers are removed from the border.

Using the Search Menu

The **Search** menu allows you to locate a value or string of characters, move to the next occurrence of the value, replace a value or string with a new value or string, or replace all occurrences of the value. **Search** is not case sensitive, nor does it look for whole words only.

Using Find

The **Search/Find** option is used to locate a value or string. You can use it to search from the cursor position to the end of the file.

To use **Search/Find**, follow these steps:

1. Press F10 to go to the **Editor** menu and choose **Search/Find**. A Find dialog box, like the one shown in Figure 4-7, allows you to enter the value or string.

2. Type the value or string. (The word *Year* has been entered in Figure 4-7.)

3. Press ENTER, or choose OK if you are using a mouse, to locate the first occurrence of the value.

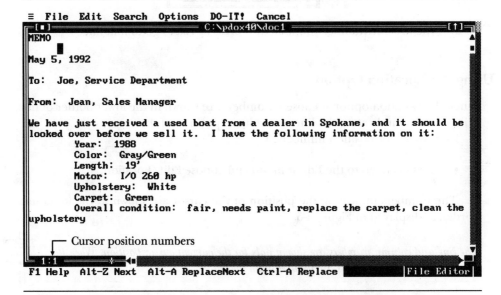

Figure 4-6.   *Editor window showing the line and column position numbers*

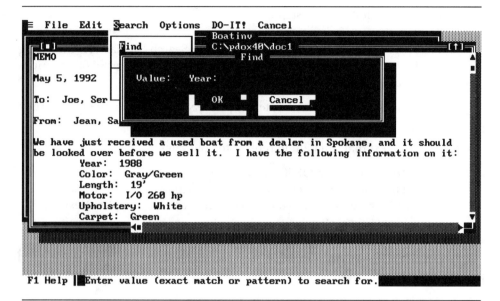

Figure 4-7. *Find dialog box*

To use shortcut keys, press CTRL-Z (Zoom) to display the dialog box, enter the value, and press ENTER.

Using Next

The **Search/Next** option is used to find the next occurrence of the value that you previously used **Find** or **Replace** to locate. Your cursor must be located in front of the next value to locate, otherwise you will see a message telling you the value cannot be found.

To use **Search/Next**, follow one of these methods:

- Press F10 to go to the **Editor** menu and choose **Search/Next.**

To use shortcut keys, press ALT-Z to use **Z**oomNext.

Using Replace

The **R**eplace option allows you to locate and replace an existing value with a new value. You are limited to 80 characters in the text box and 80 characters for the replacement. The function can be used from the cursor position to the end of the file, or it can be used within a selected block of text.

To use **Replace**, follow these steps:

1. Press F10 to go to the **Editor** menu and choose **Search/Replace**. A Find dialog box for locating the value will be displayed, as shown in Figure 4-8. A previous **Search** or **Replace** value may be showing.

2. Enter the value you want to locate and press ENTER. A Replacement dialog box is displayed, as shown in Figure 4-9.

3. Type the text that you want to replace the old value.

4. Press ENTER, or choose OK if you are using a mouse. The cursor moves to the right of the value, but does not replace it. A prompt displayed in the lower-right corner of the desktop tells you "To continue, use Alt-A ReplaceNext or Alt-Z Next" as shown here:

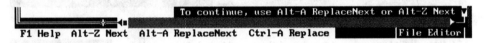

5. At this point you may do one of the following:

   - Edit the text.
   - Press CTRL-A to replace.
   - Press ALT-A to replace and search for the next occurrence of the text.
   - Press ALT-Z to skip the replacement and go to the next occurrence of the text.

Using ChangeToEnd

The **ChangeToEnd** option allows you to replace all occurrences of a value with a new value. You can use this function from the cursor position to the end of the file. As in the **Replace** option, you are limited to 80 characters for both the value to locate and the replacement value.

To use **ChangeToEnd**, follow these steps:

1. Press F10 to go to the **Editor** menu and choose **Search/ChangeToEnd**. A Zoom dialog box displays, asking you to enter the value to be replaced.

2. Enter the value and press ENTER or choose OK if you are using a mouse. Another dialog box asking for the replacement value is displayed.

3. Type the replacement value and press ENTER or choose OK. A menu lets you choose between **No** and **Yes**, as shown in Figure 4-10.

4. Choose **Yes** to go ahead with the global replacement; choose **No** if you want to cancel the replacement.

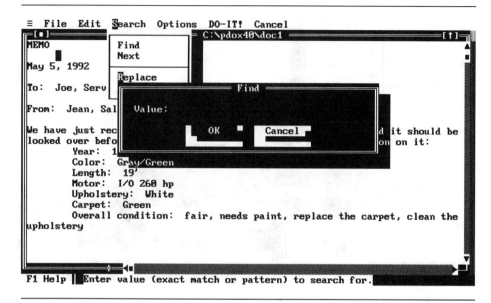

Figure 4-8. *Replace/Find dialog box*

Be sure that you are aware of the outcome of the global replacement. In the example shown here, the phrase the boat *would replace all occurrences of the word* it, *including the* it *in the word* condition *(which would result in* condthe boation*). To avoid this, enter a space before and after the string in both the Zoom box and the Replacement box.*

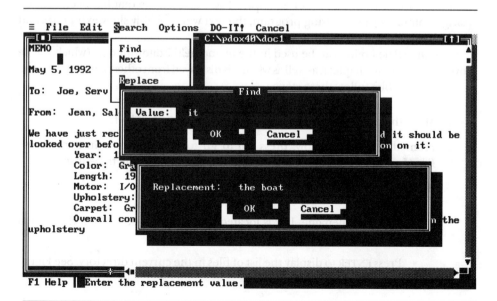

Figure 4-9. *Replacement dialog box*

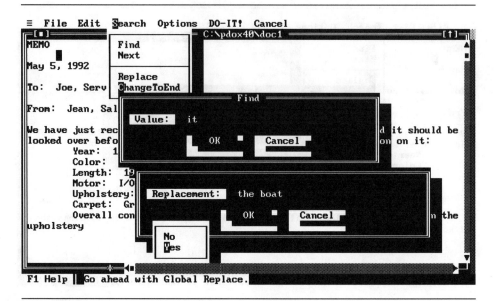

Figure 4-10.   *ChangeToEnd option and dialog boxes*

Using InsertFile

You use the InsertFile option to insert an ASCII file into another file. You can insert files with a format other than an ASCII format; however, you may get strange characters when you do this. For example, if you insert a file that has been created using another word processing program, the text will probably show extra lines and symbols, which would make it unusable.

The InsertFile option can be used in the memo field Editor window (which will be covered later in this chapter), as well as when it is displayed from other points in Paradox.

To insert a file, follow these steps:

1. Move the cursor to the point where you want to insert the file.

2. From the Editor window, press F10 to go to the Editor menu and choose File/InsertFile. You are prompted for the name of the file to be inserted.

3. At this point, follow either of these steps:

    • Type the filename. If it is located in a directory other than the default directory, type the path name.

    • Press ENTER to display the list of files in the current directory. See Figure 4-11.

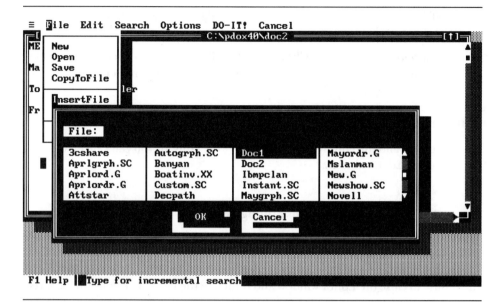

Figure 4-11.   *Dialog box asking for the filename and the box showing the list of files*

4. If you typed the filename, press ENTER; choose OK if you are using a mouse. If you displayed the list of files, move the cursor to the file you want, or select it with the mouse; and press ENTER or choose OK.

The InsertFile option copies the file into the current window. The original file remains intact.

Using WriteBlock

WriteBlock allows you to save a block of text as a separate file or to send a block of text to another file. You must select the text you wish to write.

To use **WriteBlock**, follow these steps:

1. Open the file in the Editor window.

2. Select a portion of the text.

3. Press F10 to go to the **Editor** menu and choose **File/WriteBlock**. A dialog box asking for a filename is displayed.

4. Type a new filename or type the name of an existing file, and press ENTER. If you enter the name of an existing file, a prompt at the bottom of the desktop

tells you that the file exists and a menu displays the choices **C**ancel or **R**eplace, as shown in Figure 4-12.

5. Respond to the prompt. Choose **R**eplace if you want to overwrite an existing file, or choose **C**ancel and then give the block a different filename.

Ending the Editing Session

You can either end the editing session by saving the edits, or you can cancel the edits, and leave the Editor window.

Saving the Edits and Ending the Editing Session

When you save and end the editing session, you leave the Editor window and return to the Main menu.

To save edits and end the editing session, press F2 (Do-It!) or click on **D**o-It! with the mouse to close the Editor window and return to the table. The edits will be saved.

 *If you want to save the edits but remain in the Editor window, choose **File/Save** from the Editor menu.*

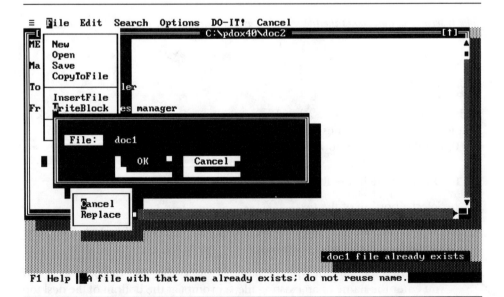

Figure 4-12. *Prompt asking for confirmation that you want to overwrite a file*

Canceling the Editing Session

Canceling the editing session leaves the Editor window and does not save your edits. You are returned to the Main menu.

To cancel the session without saving, do one of the following:

- Press F10 to go to the **E**ditor menu and choose **C**ancel/**Y**es. (If you choose **N**o, you will return to the Editor window.)

- Click on the Close box.

Entering and Editing Text in a Memo Field

Because a memo field is a variable length field, you can use the Editor window to enter text, as well as to edit the data in it. The purpose of this field, as mentioned in Chapter 3, is to store notes about the records. Descriptions of products, notes about employees, information about customers that may be useful to sales staff, explanations of currency amounts are some of the ideas for information that can be stored in memo fields.

Entering Text in a Memo Field

To go to the Editor window from a memo field, press ALT-F5 or CTRL-F (Field View) or double-click using the mouse. You cannot press ALT-E, which is used in other positions in Paradox, to go to the Editor window from a memo field.

To enter text in the memo field, follow these steps:

1. Display the table containing the memo field on the Paradox desktop. You can use either **V**iew or **E**dit to do this.

2. Move the cursor to the memo field and press ALT-F5 or CTRL-F (or if using the mouse, double-click in the field) to display the Editor window, as shown in Figure 4-13.

The table name and the memo field name are shown at the top of the Editor window.

3. Press F9 or ALT-F9 to go to **E**dit or **Co**Edit mode, if you are not already there. Check the lower-right corner of the desktop to see which mode you are in.

4. Enter the text that is to be in the memo field.

The number of characters that will be displayed when you view the table is determined by the number of characters entered for the memo field when the table was created. For example,

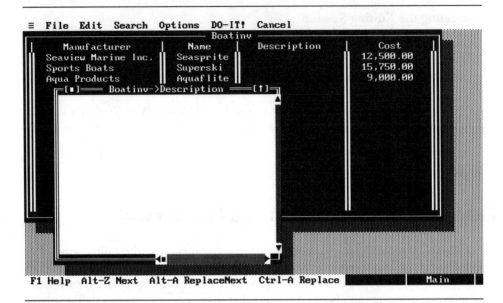

Figure 4-13. *Editor window from a memo field*

if you specified M15 as the field type, the first 15 characters you enter in the Editor window will be displayed in the memo field when you view the table.

5. Make any edits you like using the options discussed in this chapter.

6. Press F2 (Do-It!) to save and return to the table. The first characters of the text now appear in the memo field.

7. Press F2 (Do-It!) to save the table, or perform other editing functions in the table.

Editing Text in a Memo Field

The process of editing text in a memo field is similar to entering text anywhere else. Press ALT-F5 or CTRL-F or double-click with the mouse to go to the Editor window and edit the text.

The Editor window can also be accessed from form view. This will be discussed in Chapter 7.

To edit in a memo field, follow these steps:

1. Display the table on the desktop and move the cursor to the memo field.

2. Press ALT-F5 or CTRL-F or double-click with the mouse to go to the Editor window. All of the text that is in the field is displayed—not just the first characters that are shown when you view the table.

3. Use the editing functions discussed earlier in this chapter to make any changes.

Inserting a File into a Memo Field

You can open any file in the memo field Editor window just as you do in any other Editor windows. When you press F2 (Do-It!) to save, the text will be inserted in the memo field and the initial characters will be displayed in the table. You can also paste blocks of text from the Clipboard into the memo field Editor window and then save it in the memo field.

To insert a file, follow these steps:

1. Move the cursor to the memo field that is to receive the file.

2. Press ALT-F5 or CTRL-F, or double-click with the mouse. The memo field Editor window is displayed.

3. Press F10 to go to the **Editor** menu and choose **File/InsertFile**.

4. Type the filename and press ENTER; or press ENTER to display the list of files, select the file you want, and press ENTER again. The file is now displayed in the Editor window for the memo field, as shown in Figure 4-14.

5. Edit the text if you want to change it before saving it in the memo field. (In the examples shown in Figure 4-15, all text except information about the boat has been deleted.)

6. Press F2 (Do-It!) or click on **Do**-It! to save and return to the memo field. The text from the Editor window has been inserted in the table, as shown in Figure 4-16.

7. At this point, you could enter or edit text in other fields, then save the edits, and go on to other Paradox functions.

Parent/Child Windows

Because the memo field Editor window is dependent upon the table, Paradox refers to the table view as the *parent window* and refers to the memo window as the *child window*. If you close the table view (parent window), the memo window (child window) closes automatically. You can keep the Editor window open (without ending the Editor session) and toggle between the table view and the Editor window. This is convenient because it allows you to edit all memos in a table without having to enter field view for each memo.

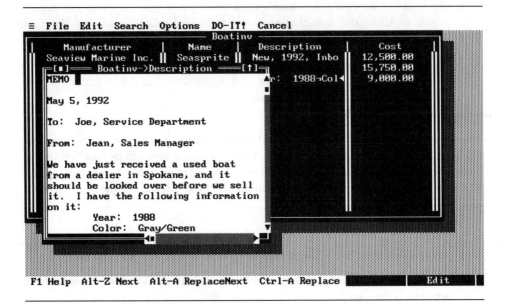

Figure 4-14. *Memo field Editor window showing an inserted file*

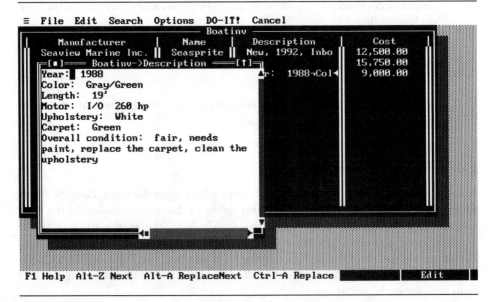

Figure 4-15. *Edited text that is to be stored in the memo field*

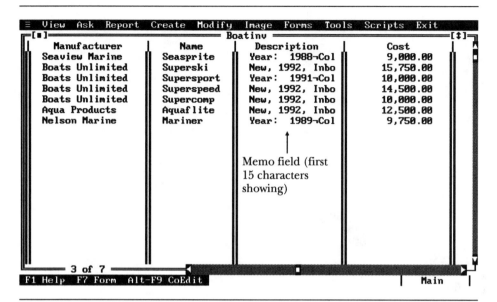

Figure 4-16. *Text in the memo field in a table*

 To use shortcut keys to toggle between table view and the Editor window:

- Press ALT-F5 or CTRL-F to move from one to the other.

 To toggle between table view and the Editor window with the mouse:

- Click on the table view window or click on the Editor window.

When you are finished editing, choose **D**o-It! to save and end the editing session as previously discussed in this chapter.

Chapter 5

Modifying the Database

In this chapter you will learn how to change the structure of the database. As discussed in Chapter 3, a table should be kept as simple as possible; however, as you work with the database, you may find that more information should be included in a table. This can be done quite easily using the **M**odify menu to restructure the table. *Restructuring* involves changing, adding, or deleting fields in a table.

This chapter also discusses changing the order of records in a table by sorting data in single and multiple fields, as well as sorting records on a network.

In addition, creating and using secondary indexes is covered. You use secondary indexes in a table that has a primary index to sort records on the basis of data in non-keyed fields.

Finally, using the **I**mage menu to change the format for date, numeric, and currency fields in the database is discussed here. Format changes are in effect for the current session only unless you use **I**mage/**K**eepSet to make the changes permanent.

Restructuring Tables

The **M**odify/**R**estructure menu is used to restructure tables. This process can include adding fields, deleting fields, changing the field type, changing the number of characters that can be entered in an alphanumeric field, renaming fields, adding or removing key field designations, and changing the order of the fields in a table.

The process of restructuring is very similar to creating the table. The temporary Struct table is displayed and can be edited. As in other editing procedures, once the changes have been made, you save them by pressing F2 (Do-It!) or clicking on **D**o-It! with the mouse.

Once you have made changes to the table, Paradox protects the data that is stored in the table. For example, if you reduce the number of characters in an alphanumeric field, you will be warned that there may be data lost as a result of the change. You can then make a decision about the change—whether to keep it or not. In any situation, if there is a chance that data can be lost as a result of the change, a warning will be displayed.

Adding a Field

After working with a table for a period of time, you may find that you need other information in it. For example, in Chapter 3, the table containing client names and addresses did not include the clients' telephone numbers, but it would be very easy to add a field for this data to the table.

A field can be added at the end of the table, or it can be inserted above or between existing fields.

To add a field, follow these steps:

1. Choose **M**odify/**R**estructure from the Main menu.

2. Choose the table that you want to edit. A Restructure table image is displayed, as shown in Figure 5-1.

3. Move the cursor to the field that is to follow the new field and press INSERT; you can also move the cursor to the end of the list of field names and press DOWN ARROW.

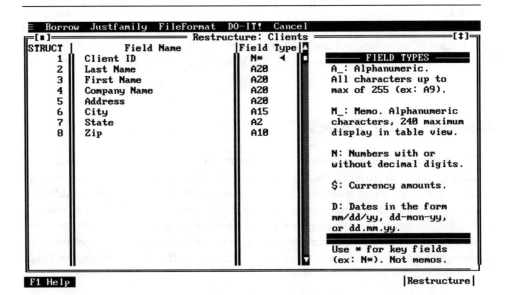

Figure 5-1.   *xample of the Restructure table image*

4. Enter the field name and designate a type (and size, if necessary) as you did when you created the table.

5. Press F2 (Do-It!), or click on **Do-It!** with the mouse, to save the change.

Deleting a Field

When you delete a field, data that is stored in the field will be permanently lost. The field also will be removed from related Paradox objects such as forms, reports, validity checks, indexes, and settings. Fields that are based on calculations or summaries of the deleted field will also be deleted.

To delete a field, follow these steps:

1. Choose **M**odify/**R**estructure from the Main menu, and choose the table you want to display in the Restructure table image.

2. Move the cursor to the field to be deleted and press DELETE.

3. Press F2 (Do-It!), or click on **Do-It!** with the mouse, to save the change.
   A warning message will be displayed at the bottom of the image if the deleted field contains records. Figure 5-2 shows an example. The message gives the name of the field and reads "Please confirm deletion of (*name*) field." Also, a menu is displayed with the choices **D**elete and **O**ops.

4. Choose **D**elete to remove the field and all data in it. Choose **O**ops to return to the Restructure table image, and reenter the field name and field type to save the data.

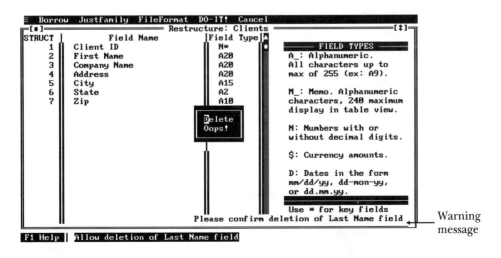

Figure 5-2. *Warning message cautions against loss of data*

*To recover data from a field you have mistakenly designated to be deleted, choose **O**ops from the menu. You can then type the field name and field type to save the data. The field and its data will be restored. Or choose **C**ancel to abandon any changes you have made and return the table to its original condition.*

Changing the Field Type

You can change a field type from numeric, currency, or date to an alphanumeric field without any problem, because the alphanumeric field can contain any type of data. The only risk is in not setting the specified number of characters to a high enough number. If you have more characters in your data than the specified number of characters allows for, you could lose data.

If this happens, Paradox will display a warning message, and you can edit the data to prevent its loss. When you change the field type from alphanumeric to a date or a numeric field, the data that does not fit the field type is stored in a temporary table named Problems. You can then edit the Problems table and use **T**ools/**M**ore/**A**dd to add the data to the original table. Or use **T**ools/**R**ename to save the data in a new table to prevent data loss.

Changing a Field to Alphanumeric

You may want to change a numeric field to alphanumeric if you want to include letters in the field. For example, if your business decides to change "Order Numbers" to include letters, the field type would have to be alphanumeric.

To change a numeric field to alphanumeric, follow these steps:

1. Choose **M**odify/**R**estructure from the Main menu, and choose the table to be displayed in the Restructure table image.

2. Move the cursor to the Field Type column, delete the original specification, and type the new field type.

3. Press F2 (Do-It!), or click on **D**o-It! with the mouse, to save the change.
   If there is a possibility of losing data, a message will be displayed, "Possible data loss for *field*."

4. If this message appears, choose one of the following from the menu at the top of the screen:

   - *Trimming* shortens the field and cuts off remaining data that doesn't fit. The data that is cut off will be lost permanently.

   - *No-Trimming* shortens the field, but data that would be cut off is stored temporarily in a Problems table. If you choose this option, edit the data to fit and then choose **T**ools/**M**ore/**A**dd to add the data to the table. Or use **T**ools/**R**ename to give the Problems table a valid table name.

- *Oops* returns you to the Restructure table image where you can increase the size of the field to accommodate the data that would otherwise be lost.

Changing a Field to a Date Field

Again, when you change the field type to a date field, Paradox stores the data that isn't a date value in the Problems table, which can then be edited or renamed. If the field that is to be changed to a date field is alphanumeric, any record that does not contain a valid date in this field will be stored in the Problems table. If the field that is to be changed to a date field is a numeric field, *all* records will be stored in the Problems table, since there is no possibility of a valid date being in the field before it was changed.

Paradox allows any valid dates between January 1, 100 and December 31, 9999 to be entered in date fields. An invalid date would be a date that doesn't exist—for example, a non-leap year date such as February 29, 1991.

Changing the Number of Characters in a Field

You can easily change the number of characters stored in an alphanumeric field or the number of characters initially displayed in a memo field, by editing the number in the Field Type column in the Restructure table image.

To change the number of characters in a field, follow these steps:

1. Choose **Modify/Restructure** from the Main menu, and choose the table that you want to change.

2. Move the cursor so that it follows the number of characters (in Figure 5-2, for example, it's A20 for First Name) and press BACKSPACE to delete the numbers.

3. Type in new numbers and press F2 (Do-It!), or click on **Do**-It! with the mouse, to save.

If there is a chance of losing data, a warning message will be displayed. You can then choose to accept the loss or return to the Restructure table image and change the number of characters to prevent data loss.

Renaming a Field

Renaming a field is simply a matter of editing the field name. To do this, follow these steps:

1. Use **Modify/Restructure** to display the table in the Restructure table image.

2. Move the cursor to the field name and press CTRL-BACKSPACE to erase the field name.

Do not press the DELETE key, as this will delete the entire field.

3. Type in a new name and press F2 (Do-It!), or click on **Do**-It! with the mouse, to save the change.

Moving a Field

A field may be moved from one position to another, and all data stored in the field will be moved automatically the next time you view the table. Do this when you want to see the data displayed differently on the screen, or if you need to move a field to the beginning of the list so that you can designate it as a key field.

To change the position of a field, follow these steps:

1. Choose **Modify/Restructure** from the Main menu and choose the table you want.

2. Press INSERT to insert a blank line at the position where you want to move the field.

3. Type the field name. Be sure it exactly matches the field to be moved. After typing the field name, press TAB or ENTER. Paradox then automatically copies the field type in the new position. If the field doesn't appear in the new position, check to be sure you spelled the field name exactly as it was typed originally. When done correctly, the field name in the old position will be deleted automatically.

4. Press F2 (Do-It!), or click on **Do**-It! with the mouse, to save the change.

Changing the Key Field Designation

You can either remove or add a key field designation to an existing field. You might do this if you want the file in a different sequence, or want to link to a file requiring a new or different key designation. Remember that key fields must be the first fields in the table, so this may require moving a field.

When a field is designated as a key, Paradox examines the data and if duplicate key values are found, Paradox stores the duplicate records in the temporary Keyviol table. This was discussed in Chapter 3. Refer to that chapter for information on editing and transferring the data from the Keyviol table to the actual table for which it was intended.

Removing a Key Field Designation

Removing the key field designation allows you to make another field the key field or to have no key field in the table.

To remove the designation making the field a key field, follow these steps:

1. Choose **M**odify/**R**estructure from the Main menu and choose the table you want.

2. Move the cursor to the asterisk (*) following the field type specification and delete it.

3. Press F2 (Do-It!), or click on **D**o-It! with the mouse, to save the change.

Adding a Key Field Designation

Any field that is to be a key field must be moved to the top of the list of field names, if it is not already there. Then you simply flag the field as a key field with an asterisk.

To designate a key field, follow these steps:

1. Choose **M**odify/**R**estructure from the Main menu and choose the table you want.

2. If necessary, move the field that is to be designated as a key to the top of the list of names.

3. Type an asterisk (*) following the field type designation.

4. Press F2 (Do-It!), or click on **D**o-It! with the mouse, to save the change.

If there is a key violation (as explained in Chapter 3), the Keyviol table will be displayed automatically.

Using the Restructure Menu

The **R**estructure menu is accessed by pressing F10 from the Restructure table image or by clicking on it with the mouse. This menu is available during the Restructure function. You already used the Restructure menu when you pressed F2 (Do-It!), or clicked on **D**o-It! with the mouse, to save. You'll be given these choices in the Restructure menu:

- *Borrow* allows you to borrow the structure from another table. This is the same as using **B**orrow to create a table, as discussed in Chapter 3. Use the **B**orrow option when you want two tables to be similar or the same.

- *JustFamily* brings objects associated with the table, such as forms and reports, up to date with the table. When you press F2 (Do-It!), or click on **D**o-It! with the mouse, to save a restructured table, these objects are automatically restructured.

If you have used the DOS COPY command to back up a Paradox table and associated family members, Paradox may treat these files as obsolete. If this happens, go to the **M***odify/***R***estructure menu and choose* **J***ustFamily/OK to resynchronize the table and the family members. This takes less time than restructuring the actual table.*

- *FileFormat* can be used to save the table in a file format compatible with earlier Paradox versions. Two choices are available: *Standard*, which is the default and saves the tables in a standard Paradox 4 format; and *Compatible*, which allows you to save the table in a format compatible with an earlier Paradox version.

- *Do-It!* saves the changes.

If you have deleted records from a table, you can use **M***odify/***R***estructure/***D***o-It! to free up the spaces left in a table after deleting records.*

- *Cancel* cancels the restructuring changes to the table and returns you to the Main menu.

Restructuring Tables on a Network

The procedures for changing the structure of tables are the same on a network as in single-user databases; however, the tables that are being restructured and their related objects (forms, reports, scripts, graphs, indexes, and so on) automatically have a full lock placed on them. (A *full lock* gives the user exclusive use of the table.) If the table that you want to restructure is being used when you choose **M**odify/**R**estructure, you won't be able to access it until the other user has closed the table.

Sorting Data

The **S**ort option, located in the **M**odify menu, is used to rearrange data. The data that is sorted can be saved in the same table or in a new table. If you sort a table that contains a key field, then you *must* save the sort in a new table. The default sort order is in ascending order, but you can specify descending order.

Sorting a Field

When you sort data in a table, the table can either be on the desktop when you choose Modify/Sort, or, from an empty desktop, you can choose Modify/Sort and select the table for the sort.

To sort records in the table on the basis of one field, follow these steps:

1. Choose **Modify/Sort** from the Main menu. If the table is already on the desktop, you may have to press F10 to go to the Main menu.

2. Type the table name and press ENTER. Or press ENTER to display the list of table names, choose the one you want, and press ENTER again. As shown in Figure 5-3, the box displayed below the prompt for the table will give you the choice of saving the sort output to the same table or to a new table.

3. Choose either **New** or **Same**. If you choose **New**, you must type a new table name for the sorted data and press ENTER. If you choose **Same**, the data in the existing file will be sorted. A Sort Questionnaire, like the one shown in Figure 5-4, is now on the desktop.

4. Move the cursor to the field that is to be sorted and type **1**. This tells Paradox to sort this field in ascending order. If you want the sort to be in descending order, type **1D**. (You do not have to type an **A** to specify ascending, because it is the default.)

5. Press F2 (Do-It!), or click on **Do-It!** with the mouse, to sort the records in the table on the basis of the field that you designated.

Sorting Two Fields

More than one field can be sorted at a time. For example, in a list of names and addresses, you could sort the cities in alphabetical order, and then sort the last names in each city in alphabetical order. Or you could sort the ZIP codes in descending order, and then the last names in each ZIP code area in ascending order. To sort more than one field, follow these steps:

1. Choose **Modify/Sort** from the Main menu.

2. Type the name of the table and press ENTER. Or press ENTER to display a list of tables, choose the one you want, and press ENTER again. You will see the prompt asking if you want to save to the same table or to a new table.

3. Choose either **Same** or **New** (if you choose **New**, type a table name and press ENTER). The Sort Questionnaire is now displayed.

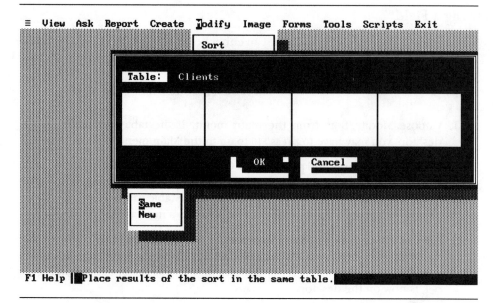

Figure 5-3.   *Menu for choosing the same table or a new table*

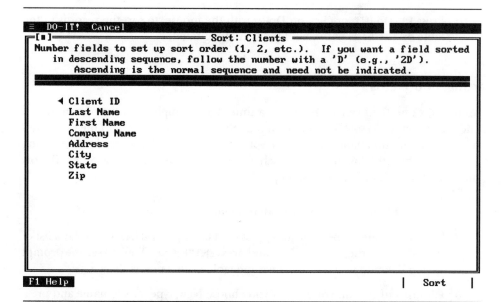

Figure 5-4.   *Example of the Sort Questionnaire*

4. Move the cursor to the first field you wish to sort and type **1**. Type **1D** if you want the sort to be in descending order.

5. Move the cursor to the second field to sort and type **2**. Type **2D** if you want a descending sort order. See the example of the Sort Questionnaire in Figure 5-5. In this example, the field to be sorted first is the City field. The Last Name field is to be sorted next in ascending order.

6. Press F2 (Do-It!), or click on **Do-It!** with the mouse, to sort. See Figure 5-6, which shows an example of the output that results from sorting two fields. The cities are in alphabetical order and the last names in each city are in alphabetical order.

Sorting a Table That Contains a Key Field

Occasionally you will want to sort a table in a different order than the order the key field produces. The key field automatically determines the sort order in a table, and this cannot be changed unless you remove the key field designation. Therefore, if you wish to display data from the table in a different order, you must create a new

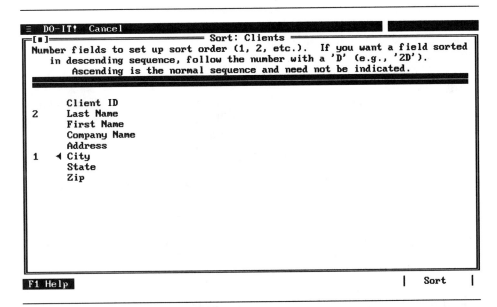

Figure 5-5.   Sorting two fields at the same time

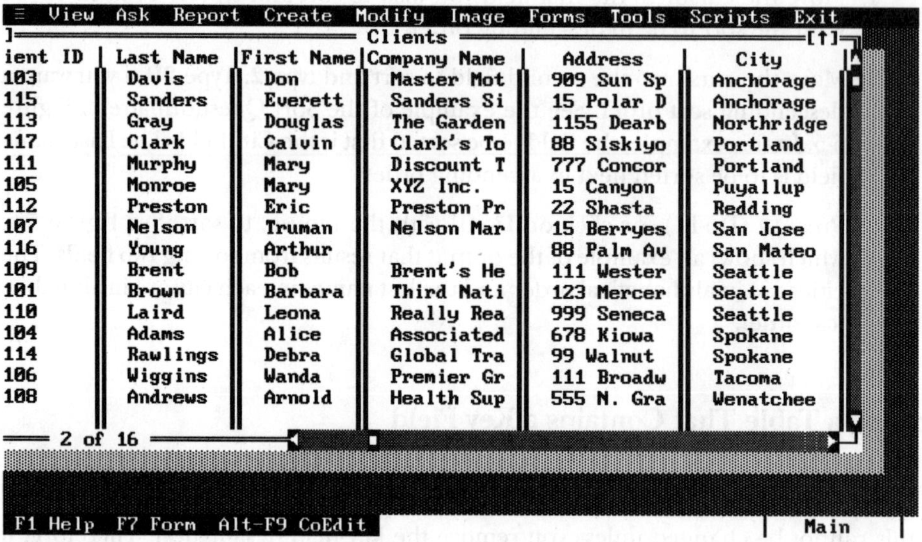

```
☰   View  Ask  Report  Create  Modify  Image  Forms  Tools  Scripts  Exit
]══════════════════════════════ Clients ═══════════════════════════[↑]═
ient ID │  Last Name │First Name│Company Name│   Address   │    City
103          Davis       Don       Master Mot   909 Sun Sp   Anchorage
115          Sanders     Everett   Sanders Si   15 Polar D   Anchorage
113          Gray        Douglas   The Garden   1155 Dearb   Northridge
117          Clark       Calvin    Clark's To   88 Siskiyo   Portland
111          Murphy      Mary      Discount T   777 Concor   Portland
105          Monroe      Mary      XYZ Inc.     15 Canyon    Puyallup
112          Preston     Eric      Preston Pr   22 Shasta    Redding
107          Nelson      Truman    Nelson Mar   15 Berryes   San Jose
116          Young       Arthur                 88 Palm Av   San Mateo
109          Brent       Bob       Brent's He   111 Wester   Seattle
101          Brown       Barbara   Third Nati   123 Mercer   Seattle
110          Laird       Leona     Really Rea   999 Seneca   Seattle
104          Adams       Alice     Associated   678 Kiowa    Spokane
114          Rawlings    Debra     Global Tra   99 Walnut    Spokane
106          Wiggins     Wanda     Premier Gr   111 Broadw   Tacoma
108          Andrews     Arnold    Health Sup   555 N. Gra   Wenatchee

═══ 2 of 16 ═══        ◄        ■                              ►

F1 Help  F7 Form  Alt-F9 CoEdit                           │  Main  │
```

Figure 5-6.   *Output from sorting two fields, both in ascending order*

table or use a secondary index. (Secondary indexes are discussed later in the chapter.) Paradox prompts you to enter a new table name during the sort. To sort a table with a key field, follow these steps:

1. Choose **M**odify/**S**ort from the Main menu.

2. Choose the table containing a key field that you want to sort. When you press ENTER to choose the table, a prompt will be displayed asking for a new table name. An example of this prompt is shown in Figure 5-7.

3. Type the new table name and press ENTER. You will see the Sort Questionnaire.

4. Type the sort instructions for the fields you want to sort. Type the field numbers followed by a **D** for descending if you want the sort to be in descending order. (Ascending is the default—you may type an **A** but it is not necessary.)

5. Press F2 (Do-It!), or click on **D**o-It! with the mouse, to sort and save to a new table. The new table will be on the desktop, as shown in Figure 5-8.

Using the System Menu in the Sort Questionnaire

The System menu is available in the Sort Questionnaire just as it is available in other menus. However, there are some restrictions on the choices available in this environ-

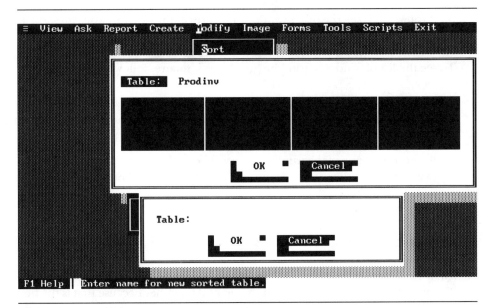

Figure 5-7.   *A dialog box prompts you for a new table name*

≡ View Ask Report · Create Modify Image Forms Tools Scripts Exit

PRODINVA	Product #	Item	Units on han	Cost per
1	176	Computer desk	10	200.00
2	125	Conference table	3	750.00
3	200	Credenza	4	155.00
4	115	Desk, 30 x 45	15	175.00
5	123	Desk, 30 x 60	5	250.00
6	157	Filing cabinet, 2 drawer	20	100.00
7	156	Filing cabinet, 4 drawer	7	150.00
8	126	Folding table, 30 x 72	12	35.00
9	231	Office chair, stackable	30	15.00
10	232	Office chair, with arms	25	20.00
11	124	Telephone console	2	225.00

11 of 11

F1 Help F7 Form Alt-F9 CoEdit   Main

Figure 5-8.   *New table with the sort output from a table containing a key field*

ment. If you want to see the other windows that are on the desktop, you can see a list of those windows, but you cannot leave the Sort Questionnaire and go to one of those. You must first exit the Sort Questionnaire to go to another window.

To see the list of windows from the Sort Questionnaire, follow these steps:

1. Press ALT-SPACEBAR or click on the System menu and choose **W**indow. A list of the tables that are on the desktop is displayed. Figure 5-9 shows how the screen appears at this point.

2. If you choose one of the windows, you will hear a beep, but you will not be able to go to the window. Instead, you will be returned to the Sort Questionnaire.

Adding a Secondary Index

You may routinely sort a table on the basis of two fields. For example, the Clients table automatically displays the records by client ID number because that is the field that is the primary index; however, you may also frequently want to see these names displayed in ZIP code order. To do this you can create a *secondary index* that will quickly display the names in an order other than that given by the primary index. A secondary index is used with tables that already have a primary index—that is a *keyed* field.

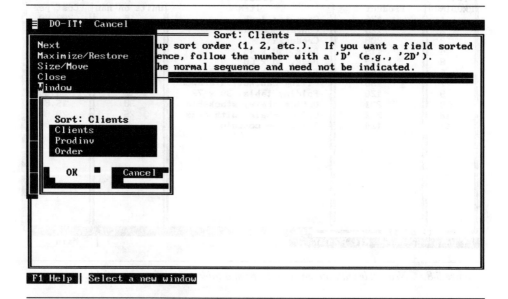

Figure 5-9.   *List of windows on the desktop*

There are four ways to create a secondary index:

- Use the **Modify/Index** menu.

- Use the **Image/OrderTable**, which will be covered in Chapter 9.

- Use the **Tools/QuerySpeed** menu, which will be covered in Chapter 14.

- Use ALT-S, which will be discussed later in this chapter.

Using the Modify/Index Menu to Add a Secondary Index

Using the **Modify/Index** menu to create a secondary index provides you with the most control in creating a secondary index. You can choose the table using this menu, and then in the Secondary Index Questionnaire, type a name for the secondary index (if you want more than one field to be included in the index), and number the fields that are to be used in the index. If you are only using one field for the index, the name of the field will automatically become the name of the secondary index—there is no need to type the name in the Questionnaire. Using the **Modify/Index** menu is the only way you can create an index based on more than one field.

To use the **Modify/Index** menu to add a secondary index, follow these steps:

1. From the Main menu choose **Modify/Index**.

2. Type the name of the table you want to use, and press ENTER; or press ENTER to display the list of tables, choose the table you want, and press ENTER again. A Secondary Index Questionnaire is displayed as shown in Figure 5-10.

3. Type a name for the secondary index if you want to use a name other than the first field name, and press ENTER to go to the next line.

When you create a multi-field index, Paradox sets up two indexes: one index is created using the field name of the first field you choose; another index is created with the new name that you enter for the secondary index.

If you want to create an index based on a single field other than the key field, you do not need to type a name. When you type 1 in front of the field name, that field name will become the name of the secondary index. The primary index is not affected.

4. At the **Maintained** option, you may type either **Y** for **Yes** or **N** for **No**. Yes is the default response, and will instruct Paradox to automatically update the secondary index when data is edited, added to, or deleted from the table. This happens when F2 is pressed to save the changes during an editing session. This updating may take some time, which is why you may choose **No** as the response. To update a non-maintained index, you can use either the **Modify/Restructure** menu to restructure the table, rebuild the index using **Modify/Index**, or

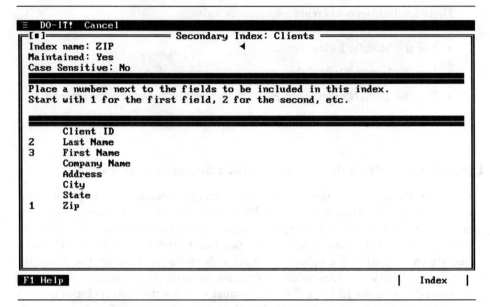

```
≡   DO-IT!   Cancel
┌─[■]─────────────── Secondary Index: Clients ══════════
│ Index name: ZIP                           ◄
│ Maintained: Yes
│ Case Sensitive: No
│
│ Place a number next to the fields to be included in this index.
│ Start with 1 for the first field, 2 for the second, etc.
│
│
│         Client ID
│    2    Last Name
│    3    First Name
│         Company Name
│         Address
│         City
│         State
│    1    Zip
│
│
│
│
│
 F1 Help                                        |   Index   |
```

Figure 5-10.   Example of the Secondary Index Questionnaire

update through PAL (Paradox Application Language). Zooms, locates, and queries no longer update non-maintained secondary indexes.

ALT-S does not give you any access to non-maintained secondary indexes.

Another suggestion for updating is to create a script that updates all your secondary indexes when you start up Paradox.

5. The default for the **Case Sensitive** option is **No**, which means values will be sorted without regard to case, and searches will also be case insensitive—that is, you would not have to match the case exactly to locate values. If you like, you may type **Y** to choose **Yes**. **Yes** sorts the values on the same basis for the sort order that is used in the primary index, and searches for data in the field based on case.

The search referred to here is the search Paradox performs when the index is used to sort data. When **Case Sensitive** is set to **Yes**, the data is searched for and displayed in an order that may be different from the order displayed when **Case Sensitive** is set to **No**.

6. Move the cursor to the field that is the first sort field, and type **1**. Continue typing numbers, **2, 3**, and so on for other fields that will be "tie-breakers" for the sorting.

7. When finished press F2 (**Do**-It!) or click on **Do**-It! with the mouse to save.

Using the Secondary Index

The advantage of using the secondary index is faster zooms, locates, or queries. This has always been true; however, in Paradox 4, you can now view your data in secondary index order without having to sort the data. Since this happens primarily in RAM, it is much quicker than sorting, which happens on disk. The ALT-S key is used to quickly sort the view of the data in the table on the basis of a secondary index.

To view data in secondary index order, follow these steps:

1. Display the table that contains the secondary index. You cannot be in **E**dit mode when you use the secondary index, but you can be in **C**oEdit mode.

2. Move the cursor to the field that has the 1 in front of it.

3. Press ALT-S. A menu of indexes for the table is displayed, as shown in Figure 5-11. According to the dialog box, three secondary indexes (CompNames, ZIP, and ZIP code) exist for this table.

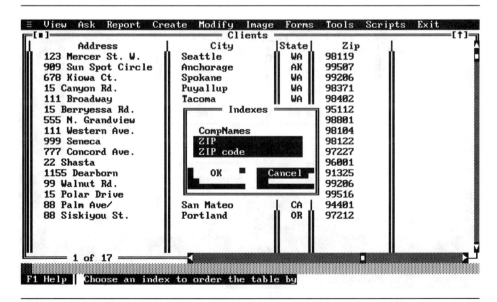

Figure 5-11.   *A list of secondary indexes*

4. Move the cursor to the index you want, and press ENTER or choose OK. The table view will be sorted automatically on the basis of the secondary index.

Using ALT-S to Build an Index

ALT-S allows you to use an index that you have already created, or to create a single-field secondary index without using the **M**odify/**I**ndex command. Using ALT-S to create an index limits the basis for the index to one field. If you want a secondary index based on more than one field, use the **M**odify/**I**ndex menu discussed earlier in this chapter.

To use ALT-S to access or create a secondary index, follow these steps:

1. Display the table in the desktop.

2. Move the cursor to the field that is to be used to build the secondary index.

3. Press ALT-S. An Indexes box is displayed showing the field name.

4. Press ENTER to display the Option box showing the choices **C**ancel or OK.

5. Move the cursor to OK. As shown in Figure 5-12, a message is displayed at the bottom of the screen, "Build index (may take some time)."

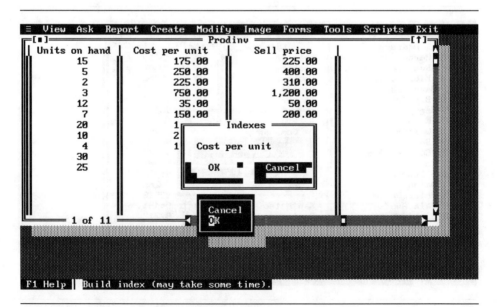

Figure 5-12. *An options box for creating a secondary index using ALT-S*

6. Press ENTER to begin building the index. The data will be sorted on the basis of the new index.

After using ALT-S to build a secondary index, use that index in the same way any other secondary index is used.

Changing the Format for a Field

As you work with the tables in your database, you may wish to display the data in a format different from the default format provided by Paradox. Format changes may be made to date fields, to numeric fields, or to currency fields. Alphanumeric fields and short number fields have only one format, and therefore, cannot be changed.

Use the Image/Format menu to change the format of a field. Any changes are temporary and the data will return to its original format the next time you look at the table. However, if you want to change the format permanently, use the Image/KeepSet menu to save the change.

Changing the Date Format

One of the most common format changes that may be made is to the display of the date. The default date format is MM/DD/YY (if you have installed Paradox using the United States country group), which displays the date as, for example, 3/15/92. Other choices for the date format were discussed in Chapter 3, and are given again here:

Format	Example
dd-mon-yy	15-Mar-92
dd.mm.yy	15.03.92
yy.mm.dd	92.03.15

To change the date format, follow these steps:

1. Use the View menu to display the table containing the date field that you want to change.

2. Press F10 to go to the Main menu; from there choose Image/Format. The cursor changes and a message, telling you to point to the field you want to format, is displayed, as shown here:

```
Move to the field you want to reformat, then press ↵...
```

3. Move the cursor to the date field and press ENTER. A menu showing the date format options is displayed, as shown in Figure 5-13. As you move the cursor from one option to another, a message is displayed in the status bar describing each format.

4. Move the cursor to the option you want and press ENTER. All of the entries in the date field are changed immediately to the new format.

Saving the Format Change Permanently

If you do not save the format change, the next time you view the table with the date format change, the date will appear in the original default format. Use **Image/KeepSet** if you want to save the change permanently.

To make the format change permanent, follow these steps:

1. Press F10 from the table to go to the Main menu.

2. Choose **Image/KeepSet**.

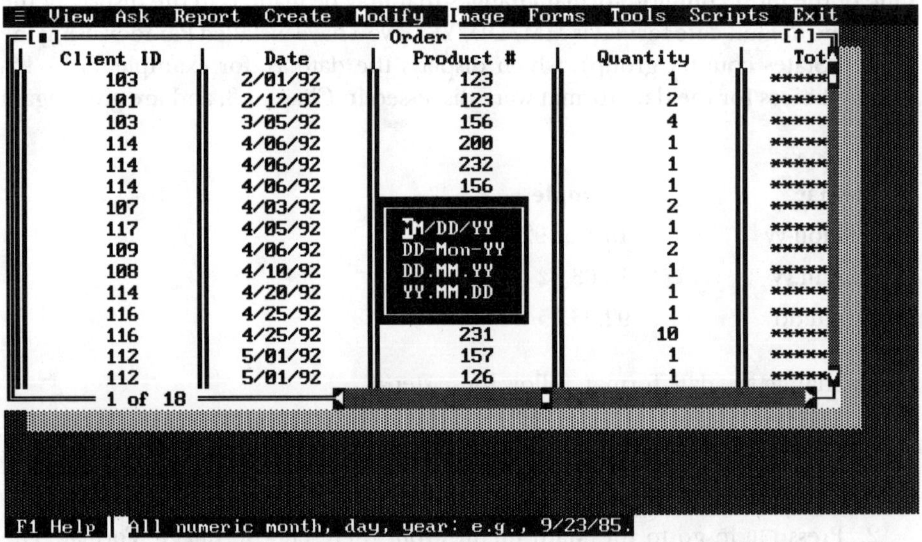

```
≡  View  Ask  Report  Create  Modify  Image  Forms  Tools  Scripts  Exit
┌[■]════════════════════════ Order ═══════════════════════════[↑]┐
║   Client ID    │      Date      │    Product #   │    Quantity    │  Tot▲
║        103     │    2/01/92     │      123       │       1        │ ******■
║        101     │    2/12/92     │      123       │       2        │ ******
║        103     │    3/05/92     │      156       │       4        │ ******
║        114     │    4/06/92     │      200       │       1        │ ******
║        114     │    4/06/92     │      232       │       1        │ ******
║        114     │    4/06/92     │      156       │       1        │ ******
║        107     │    4/03/92     │                │       2        │ ******
║        117     │    4/05/92     │ ▓M/DD/YY       │       1        │ ******
║        109     │    4/06/92     │ DD-Mon-YY      │       2        │ ******
║        108     │    4/10/92     │ DD.MM.YY       │       1        │ ******
║        114     │    4/20/92     │ YY.MM.DD       │       1        │ ******
║        116     │    4/25/92     │                │       1        │ ******
║        116     │    4/25/92     │      231       │      10        │ ******
║        112     │    5/01/92     │      157       │       1        │ ******
║        112     │    5/01/92     │      126       │       1        │ ******▼
└═══ 1 of 18 ═══════════════◄═══════════════■════════════════════►┘

F1 Help ║ All numeric month, day, year: e.g., 9/23/85.
```

Figure 5-13. *Menu showing date format options*

Changing the Format in Numeric or in Currency Fields

The process of changing numeric or currency format is similar to changing the date format—the Image/Format menu is also used for this task. When you change the format in a numeric or currency field, you may choose to change the number of digits following a decimal, use commas to separate groups of digits, display negative numbers in parentheses, or use scientific notation.

To change the format in numeric or in currency fields, follow these steps:

1. Use View to display the table containing the fields you want to change.

2. Press F10 to go to the Main menu and choose Image/Format. The message is displayed at the top of the screen instructing you to move the cursor to the field you want.

3. Move the cursor to the field to be changed and press ENTER. A menu of options is displayed. As you move the cursor from one option to the next, a description of the formatting is displayed and a description of each is shown in the status bar at the bottom of the screen. You'll be given these choices:

   • *General* aligns all numbers at the right in the column.

   • *Fixed* allows you to assign the number of digits following the decimal. You may assign up to 15 digits.

   • *Comma* inserts commas between three-digit groups and shows negative numbers in parentheses. You can also enter the number of digits following a decimal in this format.

   • *Scientific* shows numbers in scientific notation. The display in the status bar shows examples of these notations—x.xxE+xx or x,xxE=xx. Also, you can assign the number of digits following a decimal in this format.

4. Choose the type of format you want. As shown in Figure 5-14, a prompt asks for the number of decimal places you prefer. You can either type a new number (for decimal places) or leave 2, as shown in Figure 5-14, and choose OK or press ENTER. The format of the data in the field changes immediately.

Saving the Format Changes Permanently

The format changes will be in effect only during the current session unless you use Image/KeepSet to save the changes permanently. If you do not save the changes, the next time you display the table, the format for the field will be returned to the format that was used originally.

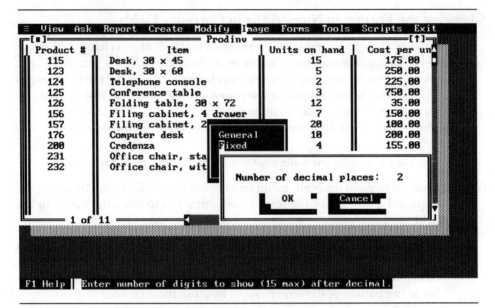

Figure 5-14.   *A dialog box lets you enter the number of decimal places you wish to use*

To save the change permanently, follow these steps:

1. Press F10 to go to the Main menu.

2. Choose **I**mage/**K**eepSet.

Part **III**

Querying and Reporting

Chapter *6*

Querying a Database

This chapter discusses the process of obtaining information from a database. It shows you how to request data from a single table and also from multiple tables. In addition, you'll see how to select specific fields and records, and how to perform calculations. Also, you'll learn the process of entering data in more than one table at a time using MultiEntry, which requires query forms to set up the tables used for this command.

The purpose of having a database is to store information that answers questions—about products, about services, about customers or clients, or about sales. *Querying* a database is the process of asking questions and obtaining answers from the stored information. The **Ask** menu is used to perform the various query functions.

You can query one table or several tables. You can specify that only selected fields be displayed in the answer, you can specify only selected records, and you can perform calculations. You can also use querying to change information in a field, delete records, add new records, or locate records in a table.

Paradox provides a function called *Query-by-example* (QBE) that allows you to query a table or tables by entering an example of the result you want. Then Paradox determines how to perform the query and displays the results.

When you perform a query, you use a *query form.* In this form you tell Paradox which fields and records you want to obtain information from. You can use several query forms at once if you want to obtain information from multiple tables. The result of using several query forms is a *query statement.* You can save the query statement using **Scripts/QuerySave.** The result of the query is usually displayed in a temporary Answer table. This table may be saved using **Tools/Rename** to give the Answer table a different name. *Operators* are symbols used in query forms to specify or define conditions that control the output of the query.

Operators Used in Query Forms

When entering criteria for a query, you type the value that you want to find. For example, if you want to display names of clients living in a certain ZIP code area, type the ZIP code number in the ZIP code field. The value in the query form must exactly match the value in the field you are querying. You can also specify criteria using operators that tell Paradox to search for data that is greater or less than a specific value, using wildcard operators that represent one or several characters or using special operators that tell Paradox to search for data that is similar to other data or that does not match other data.

Table 6-1 lists the operators that can be entered in a field and tells how to use them. To use these operators, move the cursor so it follows the checkmark in the field you want, and then type the operator followed by the value associated with it. If you do not want to display the data from a field that contains an operator, do not enter a checkmark in that field.

Category	Operator	What It Does
Reserved words and symbols	√	Displays field in answer table, suppresses duplicates, and sorts in ascending order
	√+	Displays field and includes duplicate values
	√▼	Displays field with values in descending order
	G	Specifies a group for set operators
	CALC	Calculates new field
	INSERT	Inserts new record with specified values
	DELETE	Removes selected records from the table
	CHANGETO	Changes values in selected records
	FAST	Performs an INSERT, DELETE, or CHANGETO query without generating an Inserted, Deleted, or Changed table
	FIND	Locates selected records in a table

Table 6-1. *Operators Used in Query Forms*

Category	Operator	What It Does
	SET	Defines selected records as a set for comparisons
Arithmetic operators	+	Adds or concatenates
	−	Subtracts
	*	Multiplies
	/	Divides
	()	Groups operators in a query expression
Comparison operators	=	Equal to (optional). You can just type the value that specifies the criteria without the equal sign; type **CA** in the state field to search for customers living in California
	>*n*	Requests values greater than *n* in the field
	<*n*	Requests values less than *n* in the field
	>=*n*	Requests values greater than or equal to *n*
	<=*n*	Requests values less than or equal to *n*
Wildcard operators	..	Fills in characters in a general search; type **A..** in a state field to locate all states beginning with *A*
	@	Finds a single character; type **9810@** to locate all ZIP codes beginning with 9810
Special operators	LIKE	Finds similar words; type **LIKE Jonson** to locate Johnson, Johanson, and so on
	NOT	Finds words that do not match; type **NOT Seattle** to show all cities in a field except Seattle
	BLANK	Gives no value
	TODAY	Gives today's date; this will ask for only those records for the current date

Table 6-1. *Operators Used in Query Forms* (continued)

Category	Operator	What It Does
	OR	Specifies OR conditions in a field; type **WA OR AK** to ask just for those records from Washington or Alaska
	,	Specifies AND conditions; type **Seattle,98101** to ask for records with Seattle addresses located in ZIP code area 98101
	AS	Specifies name of field in the Answer table; type **AS Custname** to change the field name from *Last name* to *Custname* in the Answer table
	!	Displays all records in a field regardless of matches
Summary operators	AVERAGE	Averages the values
	COUNT	Counts number of unique values
	MAX	Gives highest value
	MIN	Gives lowest value
	SUM	Totals the values
	ALL	Calculates a summary based on all values in group, including duplicates
	UNIQUE	Calculates a summary based on unique values in group only
Set comparison operators	ONLY	Displays records that match only members of the defined set
	NO	Displays records that match no members of the defined set
	EVERY	Displays records that match all members of the defined set
	EXACTLY	Displays records that match all members of the defined set and no others

Table 6-1. *Operators Used in Query Forms* (continued)

Querying a Single Table

When you query a single table, choose **Ask** from the Main menu, enter the name of the table containing the information you want, and then fill in the query form to display that information in an Answer table.

To query a single table, follow these steps:

1. Choose **Ask** from the Main menu. A dialog box appears that asks for the table name.

2. Type the table name and press ENTER; or press ENTER to display the list of tables, move the cursor to the table you want, and press ENTER again. You should see a query form like the one shown here:

```
  ┌[■]────────────────────── Query Clients ═══════════════════[↑]┐
  │CLIENTS│Client ID│Last Name│First Name│Company Name│Address│City│State│Zip │
  │       │         │         │          │            │       │    │     │    │
```

You now can place checkmarks in the fields that you want to be displayed in the answer. The speedbar at the bottom of the screen shows the keys that can be used in the query form. They are

F1 Help   F6 √   ALT-F6 √+   CTRL-F6 √▼   F2 Do-It!

You can change the size and placement of the query form on the desktop the same way you change other Paradox objects using either the mouse or the Image menu. However, you cannot use Image/KeepSet to save the changes.

Selecting Fields

If you want to display all entries in just the selected fields in your answer, place a checkmark in the fields that you want. Pressing F6 (Checkmark) enters the checkmark.

Follow these steps to display all entries in selected fields:

1. Move the cursor to the field you want.

2. Press F6 to insert a checkmark.

3. Repeat for every field you want displayed in the answer. The following illustration shows an example of selected (checkmarked) fields that will display the first names, last names, and cities for each person in the Clients table.

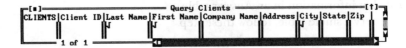

 To remove a checkmark, move the cursor to the field and press F6 (Checkmark) again. This toggles the checkmark off and on.

4. When done, press F2 (Do-It!) to perform the query. The result of the query is displayed in an Answer table like the one shown in Figure 6-1.

Clearing the Answer Table and the Query Form

If you want to change the query, but use the same table for the new query, clear the Answer table by pressing F8 (Clear Image). The query form remains on the desktop, and new specifications can be entered for a different query. If you want to perform a query on a different table, press ALT-F8 (Clear All) to clear the desktop. The desktop does *not* have to be cleared before you perform another query.

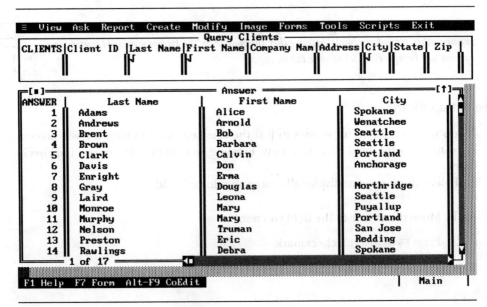

Figure 6-1.   *Example of an Answer table*

Click on the Close box in both the Answer table and the query form to clear them from the desktop.

Displaying All Fields in Selected Records

To display all fields in just those records that meet a certain criteria, place a checkmark in every field by pressing F6 (Checkmark) in the leftmost field. You can also enter a statement that specifies the criteria to be met. If you don't enter a specific criterion, then all fields in all records will be displayed in the Answer table. You can enter criteria in one field or in several fields, as you'll see shortly. Entering criteria in several fields creates a logical AND query—that is, you ask Paradox to match criterion *x and* criterion *y.*

When entering values as criteria, be careful to match spelling and case. If the criteria does not exactly match the values in the field, the query will fail.

Matching Criteria in One Field

You can show all fields in records that match criteria in one field. Enter one criterion in the query form, and place checkmarks in all fields so that all fields in each record that match that criterion will be displayed.

To select records that match the criterion and display all fields in those records, follow these steps:

1. Choose **A**sk from the Main menu, and select a table for the query.

2. With the cursor in the leftmost column, press F6 (Checkmark). A checkmark is placed in all fields in the query form for the table.

3. Move the cursor to the field where a criterion is to be entered; type the criterion for the query after the checkmark. The following shows *WA* entered in the State column. This criterion tells Paradox to display all records of clients living in Washington. The criterion must exactly match the data in the field. Other operators that can be entered to specify certain criteria are shown in Table 6-1; these will be discussed further later in this chapter.

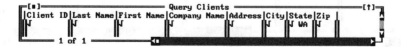

To remove all checkmarks, move the cursor to the leftmost field and press F6 (Checkmark). This toggles all checkmarks off and on.

4. When finished, press F2 (Do-It!) to display the Answer table. Figure 6-2 shows the Answer table for this example.

5. Press ALT-F8 (Clear All) or click on the Close box to clear the Answer table and the query form.

Matching More Than One Criterion

Criteria can be entered in several fields. For example, you may want to know the names of all boats manufactured by Boats Unlimited that cost more than $10,000.

Follow these steps to search for records that include both Boats Unlimited and an amount greater than $10,000:

1. Choose **Ask** from the Main menu and choose the table you want. The query form is displayed.

2. Enter the criteria in the appropriate fields. For example, enter **>10000** under the Cost field. (When entering the dollar amount, do not type the dollar sign or the comma.) Then enter **Boats Unlimited** in the Manufacturer field.

3. Press F2 (Do-It!) when done to display the Answer table.

```
≡  View  Ask  Report  Create  Modify  Image  Forms  Tools  Scripts  Exit
=[■]=========================== Answer ===========================[↑]=
 Last Name |First Name| Company Name |    Address    |    City    |State
  Brown     Barbara    Third Nation   123 Mercer St.   Seattle     WA
  Adams     Alice      Associated A   678 Kiowa Ct.    Spokane     WA
  Monroe    Mary       XYZ Inc.       15 Canyon Rd.    Puyallup    WA
  Wiggins   Wanda      Premier Grap   111 Broadway     Tacoma      WA
  Andrews   Arnold     Health Suppl   555 N. Grandvie  Wenatchee   WA
  Brent     Bob        Brent's Heat   111 Western Ave  Seattle     WA
  Laird     Leona      Really Real    999 Seneca       Seattle     WA
  Rawlings  Debra      Global Trave   99 Walnut Rd.    Spokane     WA

==== 6 of 8 ====
 F1 Help  F7 Form  Alt-F9 CoEdit                              Main
```

Figure 6-2.   *Answer table showing only clients who live in Washington*

You do not have to enter a checkmark in the fields that contain criteria unless you want the information from that field to be in the Answer table. See Figure 6-3 for an example of the query form and the resulting Answer table.

The values from the checkmarked fields that are displayed are based upon two criteria—Boats Unlimited and amounts greater than $10,000.

Displaying Duplicate Values in Fields

To display duplicate values in a field, press ALT-F6 (CheckPlus) rather than just F6 (Checkmark). When a field is selected using just the checkmark, no duplicate values in the field are displayed in the answer. For example, if one boat manufacturer supplied a dealer with more than one boat, when you search for the manufacturer's name, it would appear only once in the Answer table if a checkmark was placed in the Manufacturer field. To display the manufacturer's name more than once in the Answer table, in the query form move the cursor to the Manufacturer field and press ALT-F6 (CheckPlus). The answers would not be sorted, but records containing duplicate manufacturer's names would appear. Figure 6-4 shows an example of this.

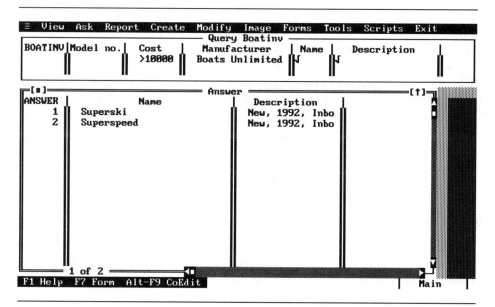

Figure 6-3.   *Query form with more than one criterion and the resulting Answer table*

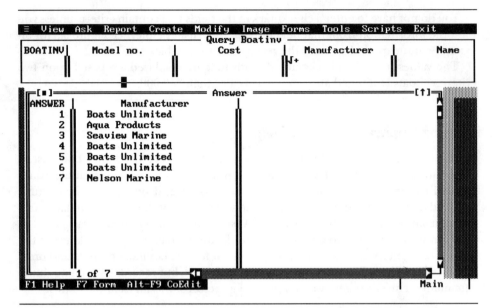

Figure 6-4.   *Answer table showing duplicate records*

Displaying Values in a Field in Descending Order

To reverse the sort order and display the results in descending order—that is, alphabetically from Z to A, dates from latest to earliest, or numbers from highest to lowest—press CTRL-F6 (CheckDescending) in the selected field.

The field containing CheckDescending must be to the left of other fields that you want to include in the Answer table because records in the Answer table are sorted from left to right. That is, the records will be sorted on values in the first field, then—if a "tiebreaker" is needed—on values in the next field to the right, and so on.

Figure 6-5 shows an example of products listed from the most expensive to the least expensive. Duplicate records will not be displayed.

Using Comparison Operators

The comparison operators are =, >, <, >=, and <=. To enter any of them, move the cursor to the field you want, press F6 (Checkmark), type the operator followed by a value, and then press F2 (Do-It!) to display the Answer table showing the result.

The = Operator

The = operator is optional. When you use the = operator, the values that appear in the Answer table exactly match the value you entered after the = in the query form.

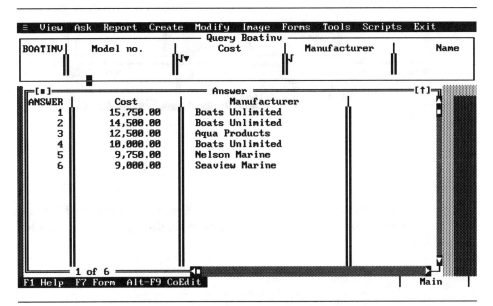

Figure 6-5. *Answer table showing cost of boats displayed in descending order*

The = operator is the only one that you can use without actually typing the symbol; you can enter the value without entering = and the result of the query will be the same. To save time, most users do not enter the equal sign. See the example in the following illustration. The = operator was not entered in the operation illustrated by this screen, yet the result was the same as if it had been entered in front of 16915.

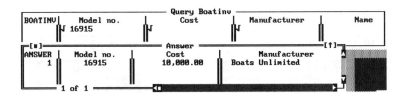

The > Operator

You use the > operator to ask for values that are greater than the value entered following the operator. The following illustration shows the > operator requesting values that are greater than $10,000. You do not enter dollar signs or commas in currency values used with the operator.

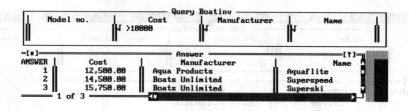

The < Operator

You use the < operator to ask for values that are less than the value entered after the operator. The operator used for the following example displays values that are less than $10,000.

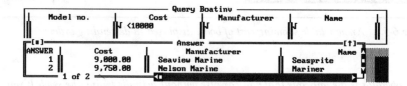

The >= Operator

You use the >= operator to ask for values that are equal to or greater than a specified value. The following illustration shows an example using the >= operator, which in this case displays values that are both equal to and greater than $10,000.

```
                        Query Boatinv
BOATINV   Model no.  |      Cost     |  Manufacturer  |     Name
   ||                |N >=10000      |N               |N
=[■]                     Answer                          =[↑]=
ANSWER        Cost        Manufacturer                Name
   1       10,000.00   Boats Unlimited        Supercomp
   2       10,000.00   Boats Unlimited        Supersport
   3       12,500.00   Aqua Products          Aquaflite
   4       14,500.00   Boats Unlimited        Superspeed
   5       15,750.00   Boats Unlimited        Superski
         1 of 5
```

The <= Operator

You use the <= operator to ask for values that are equal to or less than a specified value. The following illustration shows the result of the querying asking for values of $10,000 or less.

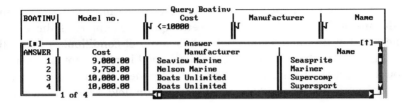

Using Wildcard Operators

The wildcard operators are .. and @. You use the dots .. when looking for any number of unknown characters in a value. You use the at symbol @ to look for one unknown character in a value.

The .. Operator

To use the dots (..) in a query, move the cursor to the field you want, press F6 (Checkmark), and type any one of the following configurations:

- **B..n** in a *name* field to ask for all names beginning with *B* and ending with *n*.
- **B..** in a *name* field to ask for all names beginning with *B*.
- **..son** in a *name* field to ask for all names ending with *son*.

You can use this operator in any field. If you used it in a date field, you might type **5/../92** to ask for all dates in May, 1992.

To use the at (@) symbol, type **981@@** in a ZIP code field to ask for all five-digit ZIP codes beginning with 981. This shows an example of the results:

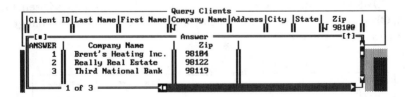

*You might also use @ to limit the characters when searching for values. For example, instead of using .. in B..n, you could enter **B@@@n**. This would locate Brown, but not Berentson or Baldwin.*

In memo fields, you probably would use .. rather than @. For example, use .. to ask for all records in which the memo fields start with the same phrase. If the phrase began the memo, you could enter **Concerning..** for example. If the text were somewhere within the memo you might enter **..overall condition..**, or something similar. At the end of the text, you might enter something like **..not recommended.** Here you see the query form and Answer table using the .. operator in a memo field. To look for 1992 boats, type **..1992..** in the Description field, which is a memo field.

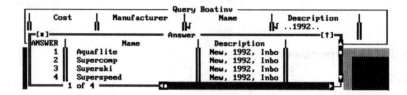

Using Special Operators

The special operators are LIKE, NOT, BLANK, TODAY, OR, comma (,), AS, and exclamation point (!).

The operators in this section are shown in uppercase; however, when you enter them in a query form, you can type them in either uppercase or lowercase. Uppercase is used in this book simply to separate them from other text.

The LIKE Operator

You use LIKE to ask for values similar to your criterion. For example, perhaps you do not know the exact spelling of a name. Type the operator, **LIKE**, followed by characters that are similar to the value you want to display in the Answer table; for example, **LIKE Olson** typed in the *Last name* field may show last names Olsen, Olson, Ohlson, Ohlsen. If you don't get the result you want, you may have to change some of the characters in the value.

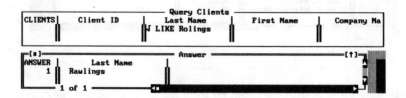

You cannot use the LIKE operator in a memo field.

The NOT Operator

NOT is used to show all values except for the one entered with the operator. Move the cursor to the field, press F6 (Checkmark), type **NOT** and the value, then press F2 (Do-It!) to perform the query. The following illustration shows the NOT operator that could be used to show all cities except Seattle. To enter it, type **NOT Seattle** in the City field, as shown here:

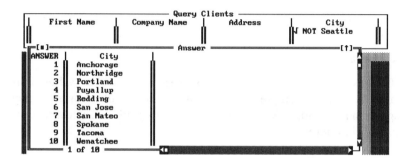

*You can also use NOT with a pattern (containing wildcard characters). For example, in a state field, type **NOT A@**. Records with the state Alaska, Alabama, Arizona, and Arkansas would not be shown in the Answer table.*

The BLANK Operator

You use BLANK to display records that contain blank fields. To display a list of the clients who are not associated with a company (the Company field in those records is blank), move the cursor to the Company field, type **BLANK** following the check-mark, as shown in the following illustration, and press F2 (Do-It!).

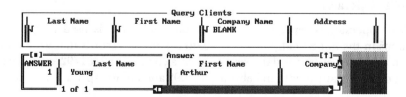

The TODAY Operator

You use TODAY to locate records that contain only the current date. You can enter checkmarks in any other fields that you want to display in the Answer table, as shown here:

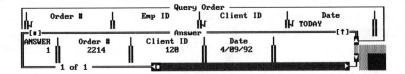

The OR Operator

You use OR to specify an either/or condition—ask for either one value or another in the same field. For example, if you want to ask for all records of clients in Anchorage or in Portland, move the cursor to the City field, and type **Anchorage OR Portland**, as shown here:

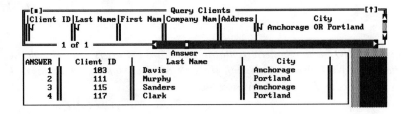

*You can specify more than two conditions in a field. In the example just shown, for instance, you could type **Anchorage OR Portland OR Seattle** to ask for records from all three cities.*

The AND Operator

The AND operator is represented by the comma (,) and is used to specify two conditions in the same field. For example, to ask for all records that were entered between two dates, enter the dates separated by a comma—**>2/01/92,<4/01/92**—to look for dates that are later than February 1, 1992 and before April 1, 1992, as shown here:

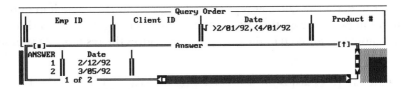

If you enter conditions that contain a comma, such as numbers, currency amounts, or dates that use commas rather than a slash or hyphen, then enclose the condition in quotations marks—">March 5, 1992,<August 5, 1992".

The AS Operator

You use AS to change the name of the field in the Answer table. This does not change the field name in the original table. For example, from a product inventory table of office items, say you want to ask for all fields mentioning desks. In the original table, *Product #* was used as the name of a field. You could use AS to change this field name to *Model No.* in the Answer table, as shown here:

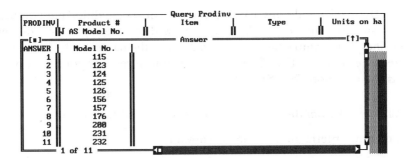

Using OR Conditions in Different Fields

You can enter OR conditions in two different fields; however, they must be entered on separate lines in the query form. You can enter up to 64 lines in one query form. Assume you wanted to find clients who live in either Washington or Oregon or in the ZIP code area 99507 in Anchorage.

In order to enter the OR that represents Oregon, you must type it in quotation marks to distinguish it from the OR operator. The following illustration shows how the values should be entered in the query form and gives the resulting Answer table.

```
                          ┌──── Query Clients ────┐
│Last Name │First Nam│Company Nam│Address │City │    State    │    Zip    │
│┆         ┆         ┆           ┆        ┆     ┆N WA OR "OR" │N          │
│┆         ┆         ┆           ┆        ┆     ┆N            │N 99587    │
┌─[■]─                         ─── Answer ───                        ─[↑]─┐
│ANSWER │      Last Name │State│    Zip    │                              ▲
│     1 │ Adams          │ WA  │  99206    │                              █
│     2 │ Andrews        │ WA  │  98801    │                              █
│     3 │ Brent          │ WA  │  98104    │                              █
│     4 │ Brown          │ WA  │  98119    │                              █
│     5 │ Clark          │ OR  │  97212    │                              █
│     6 │ Davis          │ AK  │  99587    │                              █
│     7 │ Laird          │ WA  │  98122    │                              █
│     8 │ Monroe         │ WA  │  98371    │                              █
│     9 │ Murphy         │ OR  │  97227    │                              █
│    10 │ Rawlings       │ WA  │  99206    │                              ▼
│    11 │ Wiggins        │ WA  │  98402    │                              ▼
└──── 1 of 11 ────        ◄□               □                           ►──┘
```

When performing this type of query, place a checkmark on each line of the applicable fields in the query form in order to produce the desired results. Note the two checkmarks in the Last Name, State, and ZIP fields in the previous illustration.

Using AND and OR Conditions in One Query

To use AND and OR conditions in one query, each query condition must be entered on a separate line. The OR condition is expressed by entering the conditions on separate lines. For example say you wanted to know the names of the boats that are grey/green *and* cost less than $9000 *or* are manufactured by Sports Boat or Aqua Products and cost more than $10,000:

1. Choose **Ask** from the Main menu and select the table you want.

2. Enter the criteria. In the example shown here:

   - Press F6 (Checkmark) and type **<=9000** in the Cost field.

   - Press F6 and type **>10000** on the second line in the Cost field.

   - Move the cursor to the first line in the Manufacturer field and press F6 to place a checkmark.

   - Move the cursor to the second line in the Manufacturer field, press F6 and type **Boats Unlimited OR Aqua Products**.

   - Place checkmarks on both lines in the Name field.

   - Move the cursor to the first line in the Description field, press F6 and type **..grey/green..**

- Place a checkmark on the second line in the Description field.

3. When done, press F2 (Do-It!) to display the Answer table.

The following illustration shows the query form and the Answer table for this query. You don't see the color in the memo field, but if you move the cursor to that field in the Answer table and press ALT-F5 or CTRL-F to go to the Editor window, you would see the colors listed.

```
┌──────────────────────── Query Boatinv ────────────────────────┐
│BO│          Cost          │          Manufacturer          │  Description  │
│ √│ <=9000                 │                                │ ..Grey/Green..│
│ √│ >10000                 │ √ Boats Unlimited OR Aqua Products │ √         [↑]│
│=[■]══════════════════════ Answer ═══════════════════════════════════════│
│ANSWER│          Cost       │          Manufacturer       │   Description  │ ▲
│    1 │       9,000.00      │ Seaview Marine              │ Year:  1988¬Col│
│    2 │      12,500.00      │ Aqua Products              │ New, 1992, Inbo│
│    3 │      14,500.00      │ Boats Unlimited            │ New, 1992, Inbo│
│    4 │      15,750.00      │ Boats Unlimited            │ New, 1992, Inbo│
│                                                                          │ ▼
│═══════ 1 of  4 ═══════════◄■                                         ►│
```

Using Quotation Marks and Backslashes

As discussed previously, you use quotation marks to enclose values that contain commas so that the AND operator may be used. You also need to enclose in quotation marks other values that contain commas in order for the query to be performed accurately. For example, to ask about Fred Foster, Jr., in the query form type **"Fred Foster, Jr."** following the checkmark in the field.

If you use a reserved word or any alphanumeric value that contains a punctuation mark, that value must be enclosed in quotation marks. The reserved words and symbols are listed in Table 6-1.

Quotation marks must also enclose values that contain double quotations marks (" "), and a backslash must precede the quotations marks. For example, if you want information about Fred "Downtown" Brown, enter the value as **"Fred \"Downtown\" Brown"**.

If the value contains a backslash, then precede the backslash with a second backslash. For example, to locate a filename, C:\FILE.DOC, type **"c:\\file.doc"**.

Saving the Answer Table

You can save the result of your query by using **Tools/Rename** to save the Answer table. For example, if you frequently need information on just those clients living in Washington, instead of querying for this information repeatedly, perform the query once and save the Answer table as a separate table. You can then access that table whenever you need the information.

You can also simply view the table in secondary index order, with an index on State. However, if you need to report on selected records, you still need to do the query first.

To save the *Answer table* when it is active, follow these steps:

1. Choose **T**ools/**R**ename/**T**able.

2. Type **answer** and press ENTER; or press ENTER to display a list of tables, choose Answer, and press ENTER again. A dialog box for the new name is displayed, as shown in Figure 6-6.

3. Type the new name and press ENTER. The Answer table now appears with the new name.

4. When finished, press ALT-F8 (Clear All) to clear the desktop of the table and the query form, or click on the Close boxes in the windows.

You can use **V***iew to display this table later, or choose* **M***odify/***E***dit or CoEdit as you would to edit other tables.*

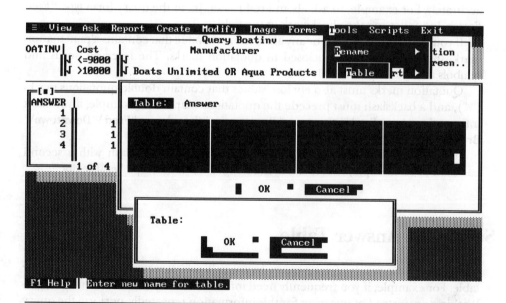

Figure 6-6. *Dialog box asking for a name for the Answer table*

Querying Multiple Tables

When querying more than one table, fill out query forms for each table, and use *example elements* to link the tables. The process of filling out the query form is similar to that for a single table. The difference is including the example elements. When you query more than one table, the tables must be linked by a common field. Then the example elements are entered on those fields. For example, in the tables used here, the Order table includes the Employee ID number that is also in the Employee table, the Client ID number that is in the Client table, and the Product # that is in the Prodinv table. These fields are the links that get information from the tables. When you enter an example element in the field, you must press F5 (Example Element), type the example, and then press ENTER, SPACEBAR, or F5 again to end the example element (it's a toggle). The example must consist of alphabet characters or digits, and cannot contain spaces. The element can be anything—*xyz, 567,* or a date.

The characters used in example elements do not have to match any value. They are merely placeholders and tell Paradox that if there is a value in the field, then it should be linked to records in another table with the same value in a corresponding field (for which you have typed a matching example element in the query form).

You cannot use an example element in a memo or a BLOB field.

Querying Two Tables

When querying two tables, the tables must have a field in common. In the following example, each table contains the Client ID field. The query gives the names of the customers who placed orders with each employee. Figure 6-7 shows the query forms and the examples entered in each that produce the desired result. The two tables that will produce the correct information are the Order table and the Clients table.

To query two tables, follow these steps:

1. Choose **Ask** from the Main menu, and choose the first table. Either type in the table name or choose it from the list of tables.

2. Choose **Ask** again from the Main menu and choose the second table. Two query forms are now displayed on the desktop.

3. Press F6 (Checkmark) to place a checkmark in the fields you want.

4. For the fields that link the two tables, enter an example element in both fields. Press F5 (Example Element), type an example element, and press ENTER or SPACEBAR to end the example.

When using an example element, the characters will be highlighted.

```
 ≡  View  Ask  Report  Create  Modify  Image  Forms  Tools  Scripts  Exit
┌──────────────────────────── Query Order ────────────────────────────────┐
│ORDER  │      Order #      │      Emp ID      │     Client ID     │   Date   │
│       │                   │∎√       │∎√ abc   │          │
└───────────────────────────────────────────────────────────────────────────┘
┌──────────────────────────── Query Clients ──────────────────────────────┐
│CLIENTS│     Client ID     │     Last Name     │    First Name     │Company Na│
│       │∎ abc    │∎√       │∎√       │          │
└───────────────────────────────────────────────────────────────────────────┘
┌─[∎]══════════════════════════ = Answer ═══════════════════════════[↑]─┐
│ANSWER │    Client ID    │    Emp ID    │      Last Name      │  First N│
│   1   │      101        │     772      │ Brown               │ Barbara  ∎│
│   2   │      103        │     580      │ Davis               │ Don      │
│   3   │      107        │     612      │ Nelson              │ Truman   │
│   4   │      108        │     882      │ Andrews             │ Arnold   │
│   5   │      109        │     580      │ Brent               │ Bob      │
│   6   │      112        │     882      │ Preston             │ Eric     │
│   7   │      114        │     456      │ Rawlings            │ Debra    │
│   8   │      116        │     580      │ Young               │ Arthur   │
│   9   │      117        │     882      │ Clark               │ Calvin   │
│  10   │      121        │     456      │ Erickson            │ Ellen    │
├───────────────────────────────────────────────────────────────────────────┤
│F1 Help   F7 Form   Alt-F9 CoEdit                          │   Main       │
└───────────────────────────────────────────────────────────────────────────┘
```

Figure 6-7.   *Answer table showing the results of linking and querying two tables*

5. Press F2 (Do-It!) to perform the query.

6. When done, press ALT-F8 to clear the images from the desktop. It is a good idea to keep the desktop as free from clutter as possible.

Querying Additional Tables

You can link up to 24 tables. If Paradox cannot perform the query, a prompt, "Query appears to ask two unrelated questions," will be displayed. Correct your queries—check to see that conditions are entered accurately; check spelling where an exact match is required; check position of operators, or that operators are included when needed. Then press F2 (Do-It!) to try again. Be sure that every query form on the desktop is intended for the current query.

 *You can bring all of the current queries to the top of the desktop by choosing **Desktop/Surface Queries** from the System menu.*

Using Conditions in a Query

You can enter the same conditions when querying multiple tables that you used in querying single tables. The difference in querying multiple tables is primarily that of remembering to enter example elements to link the tables. Often when a query performed on several tables is unsuccessful, it is because characters that are intended to be example elements have not been entered by pressing F5 (Example Element) before typing. Remember, literal characters are taken to be exact search conditions; example elements link tables.

Using AS to Change a Field Name

You use AS to change a field name in the Answer table, perhaps to avoid duplicate field names. For example, assume that in addition to displaying the customer name, you also want to display the name of the employee who took the order. The AS condition is used to change the Last Name field in the Employee table to EName, and it is also used in the Clients table to change the Last Name field to CName. This will produce results that are more easily identified than if the Last Name field were used for both columns.

To use AS, follow these steps:

1. Select **Ask** from the Main menu, and choose the tables you want.

2. Enter the checkmarks and the example element in the appropriate fields in the new query form. To enter the example element, press F5 (Example Element), type any characters—**abc** for example—and press ENTER or SPACEBAR to end the example element.

If you are entering an example in more than one field, the value must be different in each field, as shown in Figure 6-8. The example element in the Emp ID field is different from the one in Client ID.

3. Enter the AS condition in the field where you want to change the field name. Leave the other query forms as is, if you want to display the same information.

4. Press F2 (Do-It!) to display the Answer table. See the example in Figure 6-8.

You can press CTRL-R to rotate the fields in the Answer table in a new order that makes sense to you.

Using AND Conditions

Use AND conditions to display information that meets several requirements (not either/or requirements). The operator for AND is the comma (,) which is used when

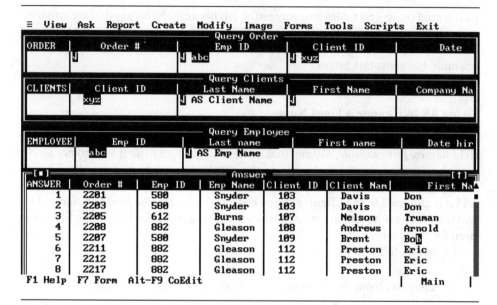

≡ View Ask Report Create Modify Image Forms Tools Scripts Exit

ORDER	Order #	Emp ID	Client ID	Date
	√	√ abc	√ xyz	

Query Clients

CLIENTS	Client ID	Last Name	First Name	Company Na
	xyz	√ AS Client Name	√	

Query Employee

EMPLOYEE	Emp ID	Last name	First name	Date hir
	abc	√ AS Emp Name		

Answer

ANSWER	Order #	Emp ID	Emp Name	Client ID	Client Nam	First Na
1	2201	580	Snyder	103	Davis	Don
2	2203	580	Snyder	103	Davis	Don
3	2205	612	Burns	107	Nelson	Truman
4	2208	882	Gleason	108	Andrews	Arnold
5	2207	580	Snyder	109	Brent	Bob
6	2211	882	Gleason	112	Preston	Eric
7	2212	882	Gleason	112	Preston	Eric
8	2217	882	Gleason	112	Preston	Eric

F1 Help   F7 Form   Alt-F9 CoEdit   Main

Figure 6-8. *Query forms and Answer table showing employee names and client names*

you specify an AND condition in a single field. See Table 6-1 for examples of operators.

All entries in an AND condition are on one line. If they are on two lines, an error message will be displayed, unless you have accidentally or intentionally made an OR condition. Checkmarks are placed in all fields that contain the information that you want displayed in the Answer table. Example elements must be entered in the fields that will link the data—remember to press F5, type the example, and press ENTER or SPACEBAR to end the example element.

Figure 6-9 shows an example of query forms that ask for the client's last name, the product name, and the sales rep for orders that consist of only one item and that were placed after April 1, 1992.

Conditions are entered in the Quantity field to specify one order, and in the Date field to ask for orders placed after March 15, 1992. The Last name field in Employee table is renamed Name, using the AS operator.

The columns in the example shown in Figure 6-9 were rotated from their previous position so the fields that are to be used in the query are all showing on the screen. Also, additional fields are not shown on the screen in this example.

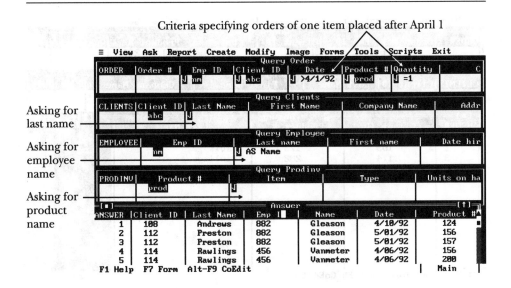

Figure 6-9.   *Using AND conditions in querying multiple tables*

Using OR Conditions

You can specify an OR condition in one field or you can specify an OR condition in two fields, just as you did previously when querying one table.

Assume you want to see the names of clients who order desks or who ordered credenzas. Figure 6-10 shows the query forms and the Answer table for this.

If you want to use an OR condition in two fields, then the conditions must be entered on two lines, as shown in Figure 6-11. When entering conditions in two lines, be sure to place checkmarks in the same fields in both lines, and then enter different example elements in the same field. If you don't place checkmarks in the same fields, a message "Query appears to ask two unrelated questions" will be displayed. In Figure 6-11 two different example elements are entered in the Client ID field. This query shows clients who ordered products numbered 123 or 200; and it shows clients who ordered products valued over $500.

Using Example Elements in Selections

Example elements can be used in selection criteria as well as in linking tables. They can be used in ranges, in arithmetic expressions, and with LIKE or NOT. Remember to press F5 (Example Element), type the element, and then press ENTER or SPACEBAR to leave the example element. Figure 6-12 shows a query that tells which boats cost less than a Supersport. Note that Supersport is not an example element; Amt is the example element. The first line tells Paradox to look up the cost of Supersport, then

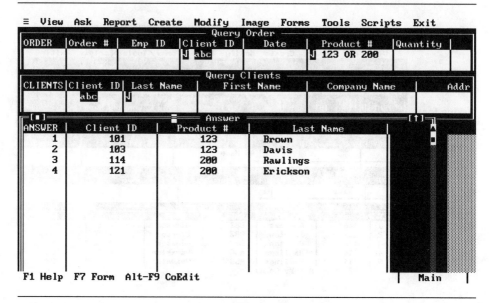

Figure 6-10.   *Examples of using an OR condition in one field*

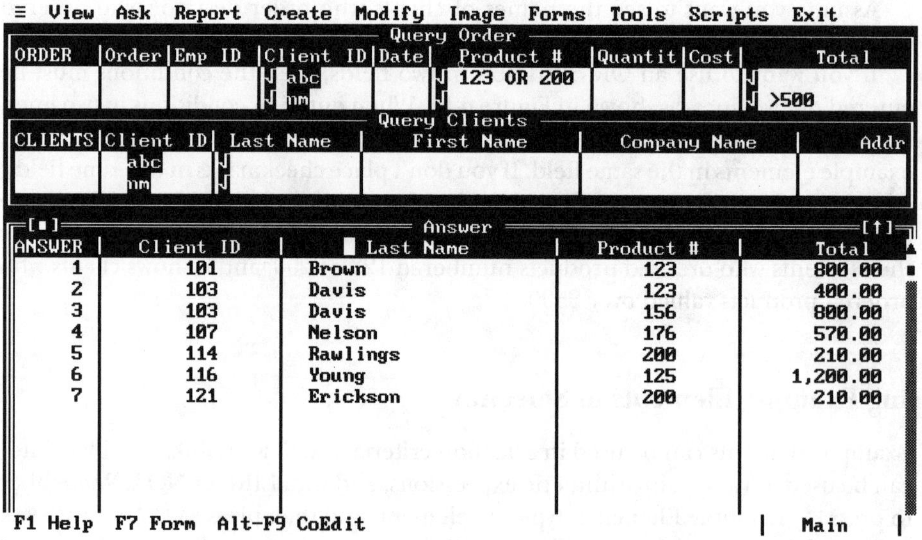

Figure 6-11.   *Example of using an OR condition in two fields*

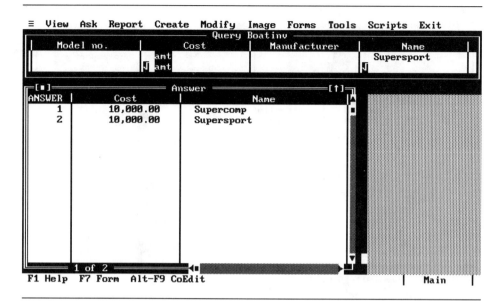

```
 ≡  View  Ask  Report  Create  Modify  Image  Forms  Tools  Scripts  Exit
┌──────────────────────────── Query Boatinv ──────────────────────────────┐
│   Model no.      │      Cost      │    Manufacturer   │      Name         │
│                  │           amt  │                   │   Supersport      │
│                  │ ⅃ amt          │                   │ ⅃                 │
└──────────────────┴────────────────┴───────────────────┴───────────────────┘
┌─[■]══════════════════════ Answer ═══════════════[↑]─┐
│ANSWER │     Cost     │        Name         │         │
│    1  │  10,000.00   │  Supercomp          │   ■     │
│    2  │  10,000.00   │  Supersport         │         │
│       │              │                     │         │
│       │              │                     │         │
│       │              │                     │         │
│       │              │                     │         │
│       │              │                     │   ▼     │
│══ 1 of 2 ═════════════════════◄■▓▓▓▓▓▓▓▓▓▓▓▓▓▓▓►▓ ▓  │
 F1 Help   F7 Form   Alt-F9 CoEdit              │   Main   │
```

Figure 6-12.   *Using an example element to enter a selection criterion*

the second line tells Paradox to find and display names of boats that cost the same as a Supersport.

Using an Example Element in a Range

You can use an example in a range. Figure 6-13 shows how to enter a query that displays the names and prices of boats costing less than a Supersport. Again the query consists of two lines: the first line finds the cost of Supersport, and the second finds and displays the price and the name of boats that cost less than Supersport.

Using an Example Element with LIKE and NOT

Special operators can be used in combination with example elements. The example in Figure 6-14 displays a query form that finds the names of all clients who do NOT live in the same state as a client whose name is LIKE Wigins.

Using the Inclusion Operator

The previous examples of querying multiple tables have shown queries that are called *exclusive links*—that is, data in one table must match data in another table in order to be displayed in the Answer table. There may be times when you want to display records that *don't* match in addition to the data specified in the query. These queries

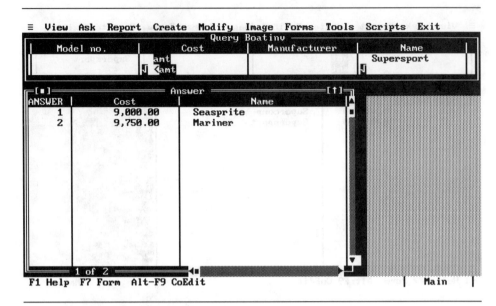

Figure 6-13.   *Using an example element in a range*

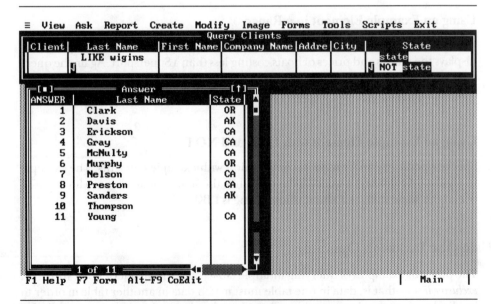

Figure 6-14.   *Using an example element with LIKE and NOT*

are called *inclusive links*. To do this, the inclusion operator—the exclamation point (!)—can be added following the example element in the field. For instance, say you wanted to see the names of all products, not just those that have been sold; you would set up query forms as shown in Figure 6-15. PROD is the example element in both query forms.

You can specify selection conditions when you use inclusive links, as shown in Figure 6-16. When you specify conditions and use the inclusion operator (!), the conditions with the inclusion operator are always processed first. The table containing the inclusion operator is called the *master* table. The results can be quite different depending upon the table that contains the inclusion operator. In Figure 6-16, the inclusion operator is in the Emp ID field in the Employee query form. In Figure 6-17, the inclusion operator is in the Emp ID field in the Order query form. Notice the different output. NM is the example element in both query forms.

Using Multiple Inclusive Links

The inclusion operator (!) also can be used to show all records in two linked tables, or multiple inclusion operators (also !) can be used in a query. Figure 6-18 shows how to use the inclusion operator to link two tables and show all records from the Clients table and the Order table.

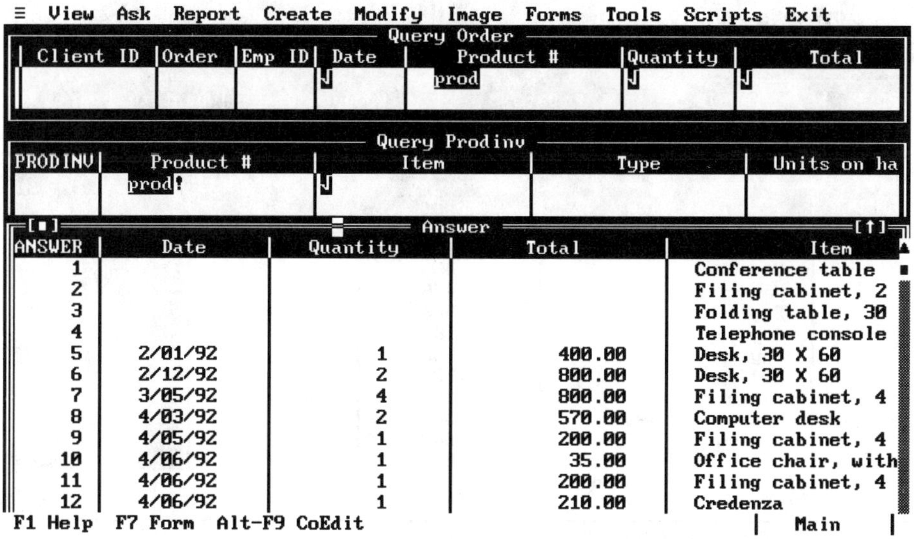

```
≡  View  Ask  Report  Create  Modify  Image  Forms  Tools  Scripts  Exit
                              ─── Query Order ───
│ Client ID │Order │Emp ID│ Date │      Product # │Quantity │      Total
│           │      │      │ ‖    │      prod       │ ‖       │ ‖

                            ─── Query Prodinv ───
│PRODINV│      Product # │      Item      │      Type      │      Units on ha
│       │      prod!     │ ‖    │         │                │
┌[■]─────────────────────────── Answer ───────────────────────────[↑]─┐
│ANSWER │      Date      │ Quantity │      Total      │           Item
│    1  │                │          │                 │ Conference table  ■
│    2  │                │          │                 │ Filing cabinet, 2
│    3  │                │          │                 │ Folding table, 30
│    4  │                │          │                 │ Telephone console
│    5  │ 2/01/92        │ 1        │      400.00     │ Desk, 30 X 60
│    6  │ 2/12/92        │ 2        │      800.00     │ Desk, 30 X 60
│    7  │ 3/05/92        │ 4        │      800.00     │ Filing cabinet, 4
│    8  │ 4/03/92        │ 2        │      570.00     │ Computer desk
│    9  │ 4/05/92        │ 1        │      200.00     │ Filing cabinet, 4
│   10  │ 4/06/92        │ 1        │       35.00     │ Office chair, with
│   11  │ 4/06/92        │ 1        │      200.00     │ Filing cabinet, 4
│   12  │ 4/06/92        │ 1        │      210.00     │ Credenza          ▲
 F1 Help  F7 Form  Alt-F9 CoEdit                    │    Main
```

Figure 6-15. *Using the inclusion operator*

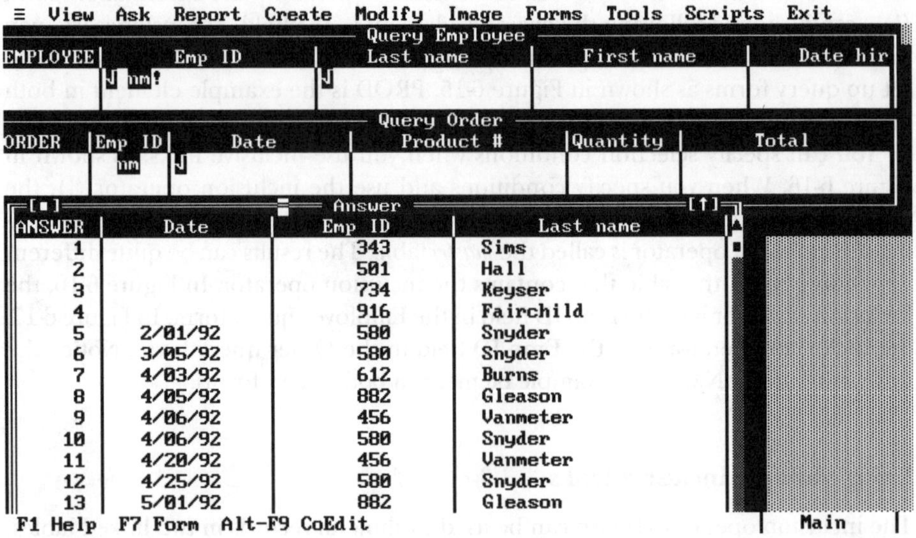

≡ View Ask Report Create Modify Image Forms Tools Scripts Exit
┌─────────────────────────── Query Employee ───────────────────────────┐
│EMPLOYEE│   Emp ID   │   Last name   │   First name   │   Date hir│
│   │ ⌐ nm!   │ ⌐   │   │   │
├─────────────────────────── Query Order ──────────────────────────────┤
│ORDER   │Emp ID│   Date   │   Product #   │ Quantity │   Total │
│   │ nm   │ ⌐   │   │   │   │
├─[■]──────────────────────── Answer ─────────────────────[↑]─┐
│ANSWER │   Date   │   Emp ID   │   Last name   │█▲│
│   1   │   │   343   │ Sims   │█ │
│   2   │   │   501   │ Hall   │▓ │
│   3   │   │   734   │ Keyser   │▓ │
│   4   │   │   916   │ Fairchild   │▓ │
│   5   │   2/01/92   │   580   │ Snyder   │▓ │
│   6   │   3/05/92   │   580   │ Snyder   │▓ │
│   7   │   4/03/92   │   612   │ Burns   │▓ │
│   8   │   4/05/92   │   882   │ Gleason   │▓ │
│   9   │   4/06/92   │   456   │ Vanmeter   │▓ │
│   10   │   4/06/92   │   580   │ Snyder   │▓ │
│   11   │   4/20/92   │   456   │ Vanmeter   │▓ │
│   12   │   4/25/92   │   580   │ Snyder   │▓ │
│   13   │   5/01/92   │   882   │ Gleason   │▓ │
 F1 Help   F7 Form Alt-F9 CoEdit   Main

Figure 6-16. *Specifying conditions with the inclusion operator in the query form for the Employee table*

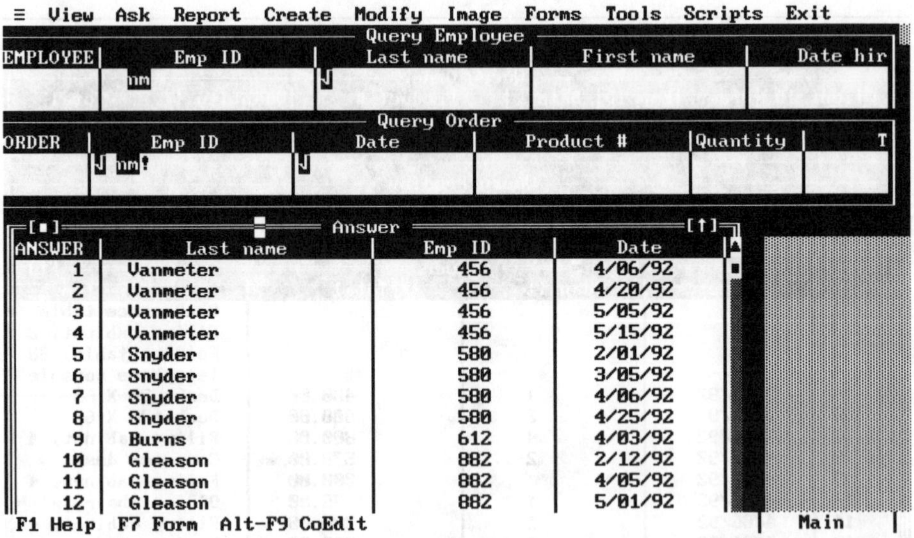

≡ View Ask Report Create Modify Image Forms Tools Scripts Exit
┌─────────────────────────── Query Employee ───────────────────────────┐
│EMPLOYEE│   Emp ID   │   Last name   │   First name   │   Date hir│
│   │ nm   │ ⌐   │   │   │
├─────────────────────────── Query Order ──────────────────────────────┤
│ORDER   │   Emp ID   │   Date   │   Product #   │ Quantity │   T│
│   │ ⌐ nm!   │ ⌐   │   │   │   │
├─[■]──────────────────────── Answer ─────────────────────[↑]─┐
│ANSWER │   Last name   │   Emp ID   │   Date   │█▲│
│   1   │ Vanmeter   │   456   │   4/06/92   │█ │
│   2   │ Vanmeter   │   456   │   4/20/92   │▓ │
│   3   │ Vanmeter   │   456   │   5/05/92   │▓ │
│   4   │ Vanmeter   │   456   │   5/15/92   │▓ │
│   5   │ Snyder   │   580   │   2/01/92   │▓ │
│   6   │ Snyder   │   580   │   3/05/92   │▓ │
│   7   │ Snyder   │   580   │   4/06/92   │▓ │
│   8   │ Snyder   │   580   │   4/25/92   │▓ │
│   9   │ Burns   │   612   │   4/03/92   │▓ │
│   10   │ Gleason   │   882   │   2/12/92   │▓ │
│   11   │ Gleason   │   882   │   4/05/92   │▓ │
│   12   │ Gleason   │   882   │   5/01/92   │▓ │
 F1 Help   F7 Form Alt-F9 CoEdit   Main

Figure 6-17. *Specifying conditions with the inclusion operator in the query form for the Order table*

```
 ≡  View  Ask  Report  Create  Modify  Image  Forms  Tools  Scripts  Exit
                          Query Clients
CLIENTS│    Client ID     │   Last Name    │   First Name    │ Company Na
        │ 123            │              │                 │
        │                │              │                 │

                          Query Order
│   Order #   │   Emp ID   │   Client ID   │   Product #   │   Quanti
│            │            │ 123          │             │

┌[■]──────────────────── Answer ────────────────────[↑]┐
ANSWER │       Last Name      │    rder #    │   Product #   │
     1 │ Adams                │              │               │
     2 │ Andrews              │              │               │
     3 │ Brent                │    2207      │     115       │
     4 │ Brown                │    2202      │     123       │
     5 │ Clark                │    2206      │     156       │
     6 │ Davis                │    2201      │     123       │
     7 │ Davis                │    2203      │     156       │
     8 │ Erickson             │    2213      │     200       │
     9 │ Erickson             │    2222      │     200       │
    10 │ Gray                 │              │               │
    11 │ Laird                │              │               │
 F1 Help   F7 Form   Alt-F9 CoEdit                          │   Main   │
```

Figure 6-18.   *Using the inclusion operator to show all records from two tables*

Figure 6-19 shows an example that uses more than one inclusion operator to link tables and show data based on conditions. This figure shows all clients, all orders, and all product types in each order.

Using the Inclusion Operator in Expressions

The inclusion operator (!) can be used in expressions. *Expressions* consist of characters and operators representing values or quantities. Figure 6-20 shows the inclusion operator in an expression that shows all orders that will reduce the amount of a specific product on hand by 50 percent or more.

>=.5 * amt!, AS Order Amount

This would be helpful in tracking inventory of various products. The values entered with the inclusion operator are example elements—F5 (Example Element) must be pressed before typing these values.

Using Calculations

Use the CALC reserved word to perform calculations on data stored in the various fields. You can use CALC to add, subtract, multiply, divide, or use the parentheses to

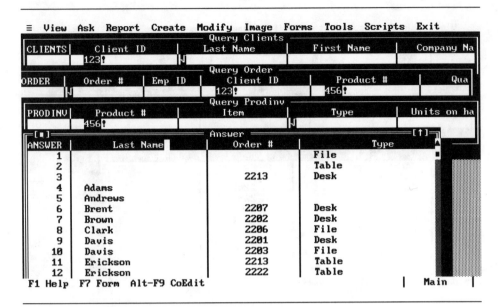

Figure 6-19.   *Using more than one inclusion operator*

≡ View Ask Report Create Modify Image Forms Tools Scripts Exit
┌─────────────────────────── Query Order ───────────────────────────┐
│ Order # │ Emp ID │ Client ID│   Product #   │   Quantity   │
│ ⌐   │   │   │ abc⌐   │ ⌐ >=.5 * amt⌐, AS Order │

┌─────────────────────────── Query Prodinv ─────────────────────────┐
│ PRODINV│ Product # │ Item   │ Type   │   Units on hand   │ Cos │
│   │ abc   │ ⌐   │   │ ⌐ amt, AS Product Amount │

┌─[■]──────────────────────────── Answer ────────────────────────[↑]─┐
│ ANSWER │ Order # │ Order Amount │   Item   │ Product Amount │
│   1   │ 2201   │   1   │   │   │
│   2   │ 2202   │   2   │   │   │
│   3   │ 2203   │   4   │ Filing cabinet, 4 drawer │   7   │
│   4   │ 2204   │   1   │   │   │
│   5   │ 2205   │   2   │   │   │
│   6   │ 2206   │   1   │   │   │
│   7   │ 2207   │   2   │   │   │
│   8   │ 2208   │   1   │ Telephone console │   2   │
│   9   │ 2209   │   1   │   │   │
│ 10   │ 2213   │   1   │   │   │
│ 11   │ 2214   │   1   │   │   │
│ F1 Help   F7 Form   Alt-F9 CoEdit   │   Main   │

Figure 6-20.   *Using an inclusion operator in an expression*

combine or group operations. When using the parentheses, multiplication and division are performed before addition and subtraction. You can also use CALC with COUNT to count records, with AVERAGE to calculate averages, and with MAX, MIN, and SUM to show a maximum value, minimum value, or a total value of groups of records. When using CALC, you also need to include an example element that can be used in the calculation expression. Figures 6-21 and 6-22 show examples of using CALC. In Figure 6-21, the Answer table shows the result of adding 20 percent to the cost of each boat in the Boatinv table—you might do this if you wanted to determine the selling price when cost is increased by 20 percent. Figure 6-22 uses two tables to show the total amount of all office products that have been sold (shown in the Order table) when a sales tax of 8.2 percent is added (shown in the Prodinv table). Notice that an example element is entered in each field that contains the CALC expression. AMT is the example element in Figure 6-21. Cost is the example element in Figure 6-22.

CALC will also be used later in this chapter in the section on grouping records.

Using Query Operations

Query operations use the following: INSERT, DELETE, CHANGETO, and FIND. From the query form, these operations insert new records into a table, delete records

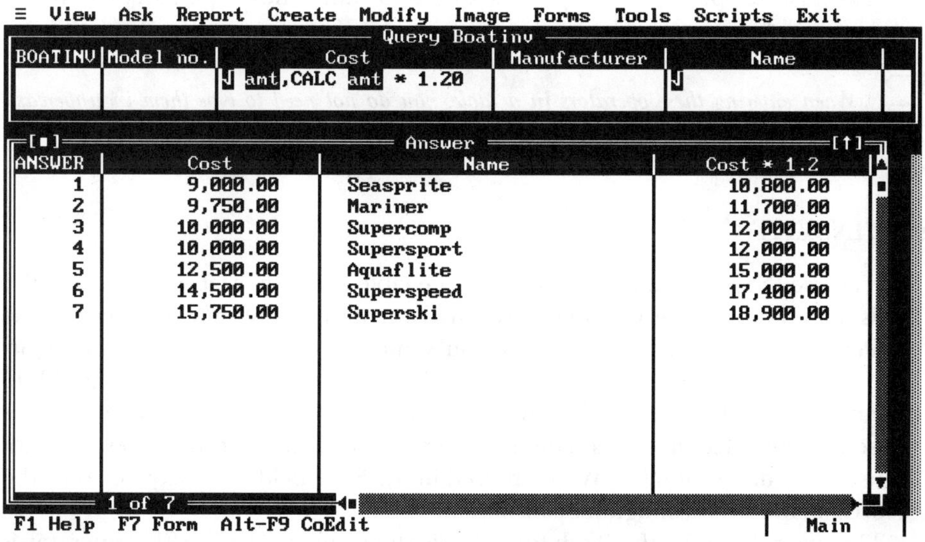

Figure 6-21.   *Using CALC to determine the selling price when 20 percent is added to the cost*

```
 ≡  View  Ask  Report  Create  Modify  Image  Forms  Tools  Scripts  Exit
┌──────────────────────────── Query Order ────────────────────────────
│ORDER  │Order # │ Emp ID │Date │ Product # │ Quantity │  Cost  │    Tota
│       │√       │        │     │√ prod     │√         │        │
│       │        │        │     │           │          │        │
└─────────────────────────────────────────────────────────────────────

┌─────────────────────── Query Prodinv ───────────────────────
│ │Product # │ Item │ Type │Units on ha│        Cost per unit        │
│ │ prod     │      │      │           │√ cost,CALC cost * 1.082 AS Total│
│ │          │      │      │           │                             │
┌[■]─────────────────────── Answer ──────────────────────────[↑]┐
│ANSWER │ Order # │ Product # │Quantity│ Cost per unit │   Total    │▲
│     1 │ 2201    │ 123       │ 1      │     250.00    │    270.50  │■
│     2 │ 2202    │ 123       │ 2      │     250.00    │    270.50  │
│     3 │ 2203    │ 156       │ 4      │     100.00    │    108.20  │█
│     4 │ 2204    │ 200       │ 1      │     155.00    │    167.71  │
│     5 │ 2205    │ 176       │ 2      │     200.00    │    216.40  │
│     6 │ 2206    │ 156       │ 1      │     100.00    │    108.20  │
│     7 │ 2207    │ 115       │ 2      │     175.00    │    189.35  │
│     8 │ 2208    │ 124       │ 1      │     225.00    │    243.45  │
│     9 │ 2209    │ 176       │ 1      │     200.00    │    216.40  │
│    10 │ 2213    │ 115       │ 1      │     175.00    │    189.35  │
│    11 │ 2213    │ 200       │ 1      │     155.00    │    167.71  │
│    12 │ 2214    │ 232       │ 1      │      20.00    │     21.64  │
 F1 Help  F7 Form  Alt-F9 CoEdit                      │   Main    │
```

Figure 6-22.   *Using two tables to show the result of adding a sales tax to the cost of the products that have been sold*

from a table, change values in a field, and locate and display all values that match an expression. The operator, FAST, can also be used with INSERT, DELETE, and CHANGETO to speed up the query. Using FAST with these operators eliminates generating a temporary table.

When entering these operators in a table, you do not need to type them in uppercase. Uppercase is used here to set them apart from other text.

Using INSERT

You can use INSERT to add records from one table to another table, even when the fields do not match. For example, if you had a mailing list of only those customers or clients who lived in Washington, and you wanted to insert the names of the clients from Washington listed in the Clients table into the Wash-ton table, you would do this using INSERT. Figure 6-23 shows the query form for the Clients table, which is the source table. Example elements are inserted in each field whose values you want to insert in a different table. WA is entered in the State field to specify that only the records including Washington be displayed.

The query form for the Wash-ton table is shown next. The INSERT operator is entered in the leftmost field, which is the name of the table. Example elements are

```
 ≡  View  Ask  Report  Create  Modify  Image  Forms  Tools  Scripts  Exit
                          Query Clients
 CLIENTS│Client ID│Last Name│First Name│Company│Address│ City │ State │ Zip  │
        │    1    │   ln    │   fn     │       │  ad   │  c   │ s,WA  │  z   │


                          Query Wash-ton
 WASH-TON│ Client ID │ Last Name│First Name│Address│    City,State,ZIP      │
 INSERT  │     1     │    ln    │   fn     │  ad   │ c + "," + s + " " + z  │
 ┌[■]─────────────────────────────Inserted───────────────────────────[↑]┐
 INSERTED│Client ID│ Last Name│First Name│     Address     │          Cit▲
    1    │   101   │  Brown   │ Barbara  │ 123 Mercer St.  │ Seattle,WA 9811■
    2    │   104   │  Adams   │ Alice    │ 678 Kiowa Ct.   │ Spokane,WA 9920▓
    3    │   105   │  Monroe  │ Mary     │ 15 Canyon Rd.   │ Puyallup,WA 983▓
    4    │   106   │  Wiggins │ Wanda    │ 111 Broadway    │ Tacoma,WA 98402▓
    5    │   108   │  Andrews │ Arnold   │ 555 N. Grandvi ▌ Wenatchee,WA 98▓
    6    │   109   │  Brent   │ Bob      │ 111 Western Av  │ Seattle,WA 9810▓
    7    │   110   │  Laird   │ Leona    │ 999 Seneca      │ Seattle,WA 9812▓
    8    │   114   │  Rawlings│ Debra    │ 99 Walnut Rd.   │ Spokane,WA 9920▓



 F1 Help  F7 Form  Alt-F9 CoEdit                          │   Main   │
```

Figure 6-23. *Using INSERT in a query form to insert records from one table into another*

entered in the Wash-ton table in each field that corresponds to the query form for the Clients table. In the City,State,ZIP field, an expression has to be entered that tells Paradox to combine the example elements from the City, the State, and the ZIP fields in the Clients table. The comma that is to be inserted following City, and the space following State have to be enclosed in quotation marks. When F2 (Do-It!) is pressed, the records are displayed in a temporary Inserted table.

If you want to undo the insertions, enter **DELETE** in place of INSERT in the query form for the table that is to receive the records (in Figure 6-23, it is the Wash-ton table); or choose **T**ools/**M**ore/**S**ubtract, and then choose the Inserted table as the source and the Wash-ton table as the target table.

When the records are inserted, the source table still will contain the records. Also, the records will remain in the Inserted table until you perform another insertion, which will replace the current records in the Inserted table. If you leave Paradox, the Inserted table will be deleted.

The table that receives the records will not be displayed unless you choose View to see it.

Example elements cannot be entered in memo fields. Use selection criteria that corresponds to values in the memo fields.

Using DELETE

A query form can be used to delete a group of records from a table. Assume clients in a certain city are served by a sales outlet in a different area and should no longer be included in a particular table. For example, in Figure 6-24, because Spokane clients are now served by their own outlet, all the records of clients living in Spokane are removed from the Wash-ton table. In the query form, the name of the city happens to be in a field that also contains the name of the state and the ZIP code; therefore, the city name must be followed by two dots.

When records are deleted they are shown in a Deleted table, which allows you to undo the deletions much like you undo insertions. If you want to reverse the deletion, enter **INSERT** in place of DELETE in the query form for the table that contains the records to be deleted, or choose **T**ools/**M**ore/**A**dd to restore the records. For example, choose the Deleted table as the source and the Wash-ton table as the target. The Deleted table is replaced with new records the next time this function is used. If you leave Paradox, the records are also removed from the table.

Use View to see the table from which the records have been deleted.

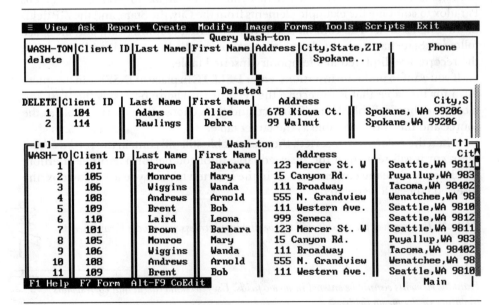

Figure 6-24.   *Using DELETE in a query form to remove records from a table*

Using CHANGETO

CHANGETO is used to change values in a field using a query form. Assume a business that you deal with changes their company name. For example, in Figure 6-25, the query form shows how to change the name of a boat manufacturer. The manufacturer, Sports Boats, changes its name to Boats Unlimited. Use CHANGETO to make the change throughout the table from the query form. This is similar to using a replace function in a text editor or word processing program; however, it is much more powerful because you can enter expressions, or you can make several changes at once.

As in other query operators, a temporary table shows the original records that were affected by the query, as they were *before* the query occurred. This is your backup. If changes that you don't want to make appear in the Changed table, delete the changed records from the queried table—in this example, Boatinv is the queried table. Then use **T**ools/**M**ore/**A**dd to return the original records from the Changed table back to the queried table.

Figure 6-26 shows how to use CHANGETO with an expression that calculates the cost when multiplied by 30 percent and changes the amount to the new calculated amount. An example element must be entered to do this—*cost* is entered as an example element in the Cost field, and then used again in the expression.

Use **V**iew if you want to see the tables that have been changed.

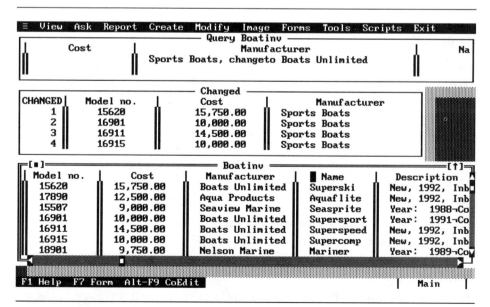

Figure 6-25.   *Using CHANGETO to change values in a table*

```
 ☰  View  Ask  Report  Create  Modify  Image  Forms  Tools  Scripts  Exit
                            ┌── Query Boatinv ──
 BOATINV│ Model no. │          Cost          │Manufacturer│      Name
        ║           ║   cost , changeto cost *1.30 ║            ║
 ────────────────────────── Changed ──────────────────────────
  Model no. │      Cost      │  Manufacturer  │    Name     │  Description
   15620    │   15,750.00    │ Boats Unlimited │ Superski    │ New, 1992, In
   17890    │   12,500.00    │ Aqua Products  │ Aquaflite   │ New, 1992, In
   15507    │    9,000.00    │ Seaview Marine │ Seasprite   │ Year:  1988¬C
   16901    │   10,000.00    │ Boats Unlimited │ Supersport  │ Year:  1991¬C
   16911    │   14,500.00    │ Boats Unlimited │ Superspeed  │ New, 1992, In
   16915    │   10,000.00    │ Boats Unlimited │ Supercomp   │ New, 1992, In
   18901    │    9,750.00    │ Nelson Marine  │ Mariner     │ Year:  1989¬C
 =[■]══════════════════════ Boatinv ══════════════════════[↑]═
 BOATINV│ Model no. │     Cost     │  Manufacturer  │    Name     │ De
    1   │  15620    │  20,475.00   │ Boats Unlimited │ Superski    │ New
    2   │  17890    │  16,250.00   │ Aqua Products  │ Aquaflite   │ New
    3   │  15507    │  11,700.00   │ Seaview Marine │ Seasprite   │ Yea
    4   │  16901    │  13,000.00   │ Boats Unlimited │ Supersport  │ Yea
    5   │  16911    │  18,850.00   │ Boats Unlimited │ Superspeed  │ New
    6   │  16915    │  13,000.00   │ Boats Unlimited │ Supercomp   │ New
    7   │  18901    │  12,675.00   │ Nelson Marine  │ Mariner     │ Yea
 ◄□                                                              ►
 F1 Help  F7 Form  Alt-F9 CoEdit                          │  Main
```

Figure 6-26.   *Using CHANGETO with a math expression*

You cannot use CHANGETO in a memo field.

Using FIND

The FIND operator is different from using CTRL-Z (Zoom) because it not only locates records on the basis of a value, but it also displays only those records. FIND also allows complex multifield searches with conditions, which Zoom cannot do. Figure 6-27 shows how to use FIND to locate all records of the sales made by one sales rep. Enter **FIND** in the leftmost field. When F2 is pressed to perform the query, the cursor will move to the first occurrence of the value to be located. You can then choose View/**A**nswer to display all records found. The Answer table is not displayed automatically.

In Figure 6-27, View/Answer was used to show the Answer table.

Using FAST

The FAST operator is used with INSERT, DELETE, or CHANGETO to perform the query without generating the temporary table associated with each. Type **FAST** in the leftmost column followed by the other operator you want to use. When you press

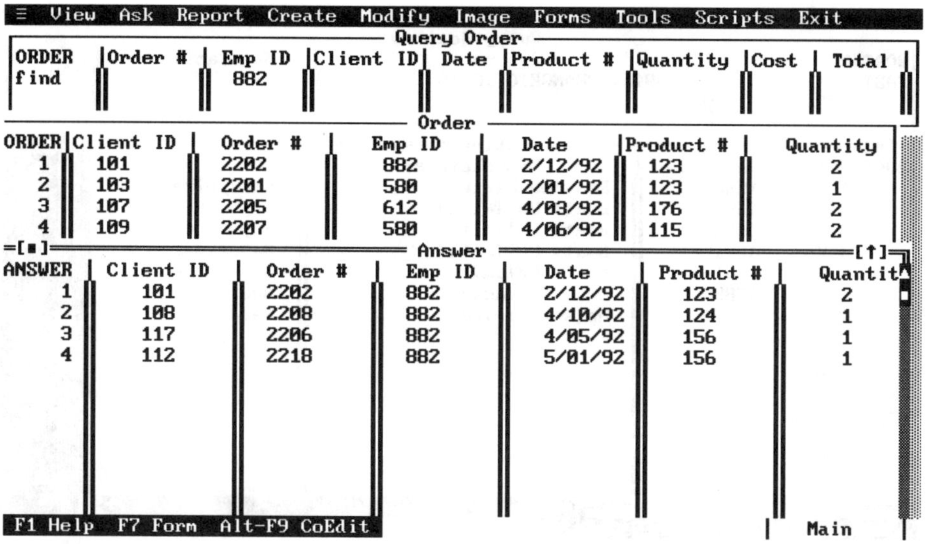

```
≡  View  Ask  Report  Create  Modify  Image  Forms  Tools  Scripts  Exit
                          ═══ Query Order ═══
ORDER  |Order # | Emp ID |Client ID| Date |Product # |Quantity |Cost | Total |
find            ||        882      ||       ||         ||        ||    ||      ||
                          ─── Order ───
ORDER|Client ID |  Order # |    Emp ID  |   Date   |Product # |  Quantity
  1  || 101     || 2202    || 882      || 2/12/92 || 123     ||    2
  2  || 103     || 2201    || 580      || 2/01/92 || 123     ||    1
  3  || 107     || 2205    || 612      || 4/03/92 || 176     ||    2
  4  || 109     || 2207    || 580      || 4/06/92 || 115     ||    2
=[■]══════════════════════ Answer ══════════════════════════[↑]═
ANSWER  | Client ID  |  Order # |  Emp ID  |  Date   | Product # | Quantit
   1    ||    101    || 2202    || 882     || 2/12/92 ||  123     ||   2
   2    ||    108    || 2208    || 882     || 4/10/92 ||  124     ||   1
   3    ||    117    || 2206    || 882     || 4/05/92 ||  156     ||   1
   4    ||    112    || 2210    || 882     || 5/01/92 ||  156     ||   1



 F1 Help  F7 Form  Alt-F9 CoEdit                          |  Main  |
```

Figure 6-27. *Using FIND to locate and show records*

F2 (Do-it!) to perform the query, you will not see the temporary table; however, if you go to the table upon which the query was performed, you will see the change. Figure 6-28 shows an example using the FAST operator with CHANGETO to change a model number in the Boatinv table. View was used in Figure 6-28 to place the Boatinv table on the desktop to display the results of the query operation. In this example, Model # 16915 was changed to 16916.

Grouping Records

Records can be grouped by AVERAGE, COUNT, MAX, MIN, or SUM, called *summary operators.* This is helpful in answering questions that cannot be answered by displaying separate records. These operators can be used to show, for example, how many boat manufacturers make boats that cost over a certain amount or between one amount and another; or how many manufacturers have supplied only one boat to the dealer.

When selecting records based on these groups, checkmarks are on the same line with the operator and indicate how records are to be grouped—based upon the values in the checkmarked field. The checkmarks also cause information from that field to display in the Answer table.

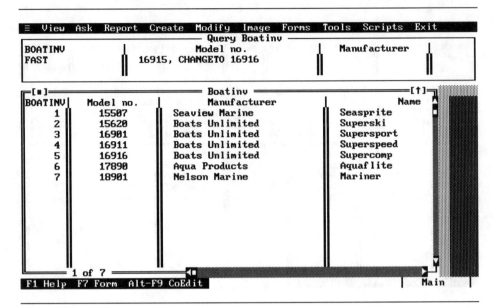

Figure 6-28.   *Using the FAST operator*

The AVERAGE Operator

The AVERAGE operator is used to display an average based on all values in a field; it can be used in number, date, and currency fields. Figure 6-29 shows the AVERAGE operator used to display the names of manufacturers that have new boats whose average price is between $10,000 and $15,000. A criterion specifying only new boats is in the memo field, Description.

The COUNT Operator

The COUNT operator is used to display the number of values and can be used in all fields except BLOB and memo fields. Any duplicate in the fields will be ignored; however, if you want to include duplicates, add the word **ALL** to the CALC statement in a query—for example, **CALC COUNT ALL**. Figure 6-30 shows the names of manufacturers who supplied only one boat to the dealer.

The MAX Operator

The MAX operator is used to show the record with the highest value and can be used in any field except a memo field. For example, use MAX to show any manufacturers with boats that sell for $10,000 or more, as shown in Figure 6-31.

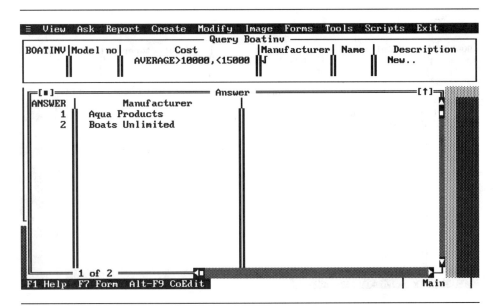

Figure 6-29.   *Using AVERAGE in a query*

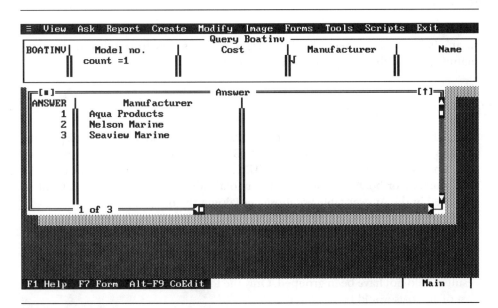

Figure 6-30.   *Using COUNT in a query*

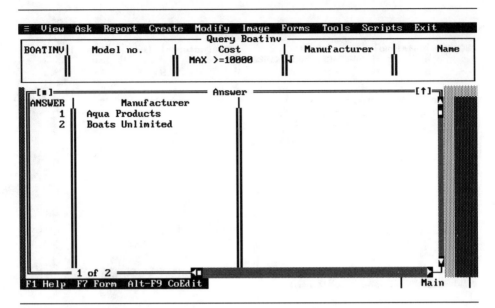

Figure 6-31.   Using MAX in a query

The MIN Operator

The MIN operator is used to show the record with the lowest value and can be used in any field except a memo field. Figure 6-32 shows how to use this to show any manufacturer with boats priced at $10,000 or less.

Using CALC and SUM

Calculations can be included with the CALC and SUM operators. To display the average cost of boats, enter **CALC AVERAGE** in the Cost field as shown in Figure 6-33. Enter **CALC COUNT** and **CALC SUM** as shown in Figure 6-34 to calculate the total number of boats in stock and their total value. The only fields that will be displayed in the Answer table are those containing the operators.

Figure 6-35 shows CALC COUNT and CALC SUM in a query that also indicates grouping based upon the manufacturer. Notice that a checkmark has been placed in the Manufacturer field, which will then display the results of the query grouped by manufacturer. If a checkmark had not been placed in the Manufacturer field, the results would not have been grouped. Only the total number of models and the total cost of all boats would be displayed.

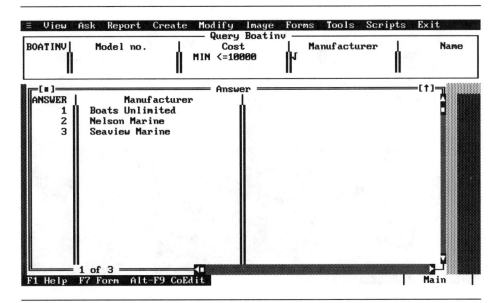

Figure 6-32.   *Using MIN in a query*

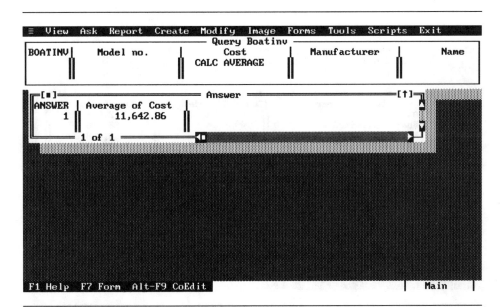

Figure 6-33.   *Using CALC AVERAGE in a query*

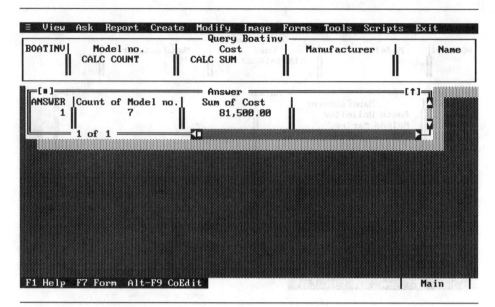

Figure 6-34.   *Using CALC with COUNT and with SUM*

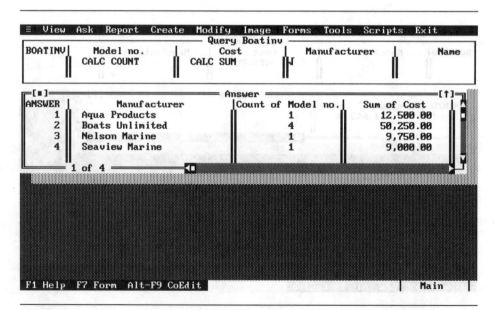

Figure 6-35.   *Using CALC with COUNT and with SUM showing results by groups*

Sets of Records

A *set* is a way of grouping records when you intend to ask questions about the group. The operators that are used for this are called *set comparison operators*. They are NO, ONLY, EVERY, and EXACTLY. You would use sets of records when you wanted to answer questions such as:

- Which clients did *not* order a specific product (use NO)

- Which products were ordered only by clients living in Alaska (use ONLY)

- Which employees took orders for every product (use EVERY)

- Which employees have taken orders from clients living in California and no other states (use EXACTLY)

You'll see how to use these set comparison operators shortly.

Figure 6-36 shows a new field named Type that has been added to the Prodinv table. This will be useful in providing answers in sets or groups of records because it creates categories for the various products that makes grouping them more logical.

```
≡  View  Ask  Report  Create  Modify  Image  Forms  Tools  Scripts  Exit
┌[■]══════════════════════════ Prodinv ══════════════════════════[‡]┐
│PRODINV│ Product # │          Item          │          Type        │█
│     1 ║   115     │ Desk, 30 x 45          │ Desk                 │▐
│     2 ║   123     │ Desk, 30 x 60          │ Desk                 │
│     3 ║   124     │ Telephone console      │ Table                │
│     4 ║   125     │ Conference table       │ Table                │
│     5 ║   126     │ Folding table, 30 x 72 │ Table                │
│     6 ║   156     │ Filing cabinet, 4 drawer│ File                │
│     7 ║   157     │ Filing cabinet, 2 drawer│ File                │
│     8 ║   176     │ Computer desk          │ Desk                 │
│     9 ║   200     │ Credenza               │ Table                │
│    10 ║   231     │ Office chair, stackable │ Chair               │
│    11 ║   232     │ Office chair, with arms │ Chair               │
│                                                                   │▼
║══ 1 of 11 ═══════════════◄▌                              ▐►═══════╝
 F1 Help  F7 Form  Alt-F9 CoEdit              │        Main        │
```

Figure 6-36.   *Prodinv table showing the added Type field*

Set Queries

A set query consists of one or more lines that define the set, and one or more lines that display records that meet comparisons to the set. The set may also include lines that show any related information that you may want to include.

In Figure 6-37, the "set" line shows an example element in the Product # field, and "chair" in the Type field defines the group of product numbers that is to be selected. The checkmark in the Client ID field in the Order table indicates the values to be displayed and "NO ccc" in the Product # field links the two tables. When the query is performed, Paradox searches the two tables and compares the records to the "set" defined in the Prodinv table, and displays them in the Answer table.

Defining a Set

When you define a set, type the reserved word **SET** in the leftmost field on every line that defines a set. Then enter example elements, instead of checkmarks, in the fields you wish to select. Lines in a set cannot contain checkmarks or summary operators (such as SUM, AVERAGE, and so on).

The NO Operator

As shown in Figure 6-37, a set query is entered that asks which clients bought no chairs. CCC is the example element that links the queries.

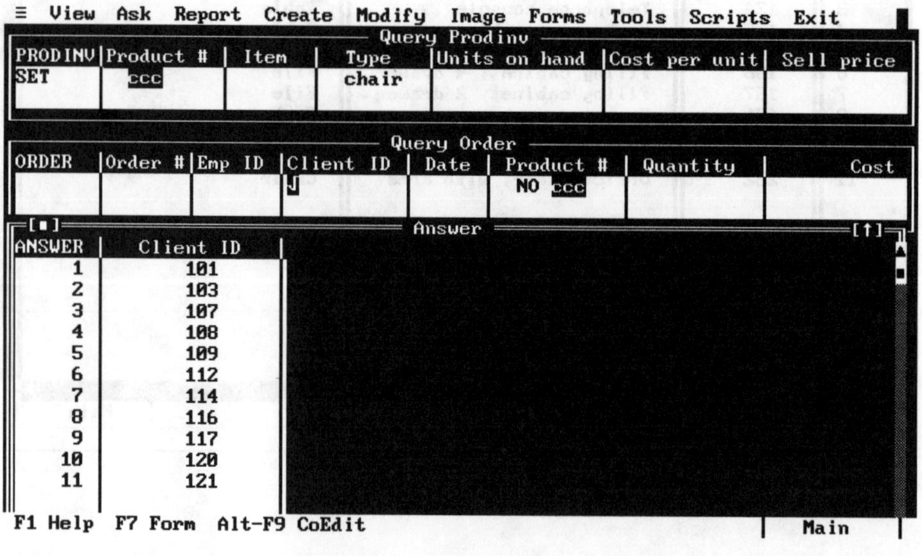

```
 ≡  View  Ask  Report  Create  Modify  Image  Forms  Tools  Scripts  Exit       ■
                            ─── Query Prodinv ───
 PRODINV│Product #│  Item  │  Type  │Units on hand│Cost per unit│ Sell price
 SET    │ ccc     │        │ chair  │             │             │

                            ─── Query Order ───
 ORDER  │Order #│Emp ID│Client ID│ Date │ Product # │ Quantity │        Cost
        │       │      │ √       │      │ NO ccc    │          │
 ┌─[■]════════════════════════════ Answer ═══════════════════════════[↑]═┐
 │ANSWER │   Client ID  │                                                ▲
 │     1 │       101    │                                                █
 │     2 │       103    │
 │     3 │       107    │
 │     4 │       108    │
 │     5 │       109    │
 │     6 │       112    │
 │     7 │       114    │
 │     8 │       116    │
 │     9 │       117    │
 │    10 │       120    │
 │    11 │       121    │
 F1 Help  F7 Form  Alt-F9 CoEdit                            │    Main    │
```

Figure 6-37.   *Set query using the NO operator*

The ONLY Operator

The ONLY operator is used in Figure 6-38 to show which clients ordered only a desk. The desks ordered by clients could be any one of the three types of desks. The query does not specify which desk is ordered. The query does mean that the clients ordered nothing other than a desk. Again, CCC is the example element.

The EVERY Operator

In Figure 6-39 the EVERY operator is used to show which clients ordered every type of filing cabinet. They may have also ordered other products; however, this query only determines that they did order filing cabinets.

The EXACTLY operator

The EXACTLY operator is actually a combination of ONLY and EVERY. The query in Figure 6-40 asks for the clients who ordered every type of filing cabinet and did not order any other product. In this particular query, no client matches the condition of the query, therefore the Answer table is empty.

Using the GroupBy Operator

Up to this point in set queries, the F6 (Checkmark) was pressed in the field that was to be used to group the records. This also displayed the values in that field in the

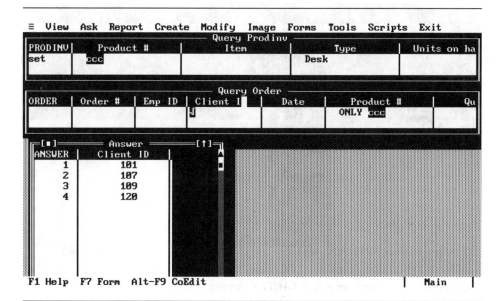

Figure 6-38. Set query using the ONLY operator

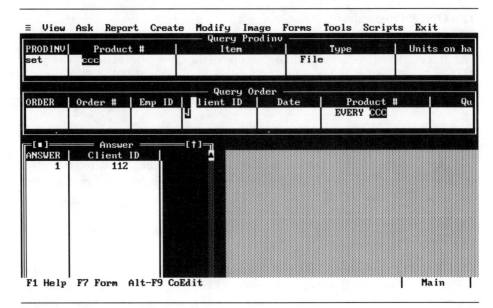

Figure 6-39.   *Set query using the EVERY operator*

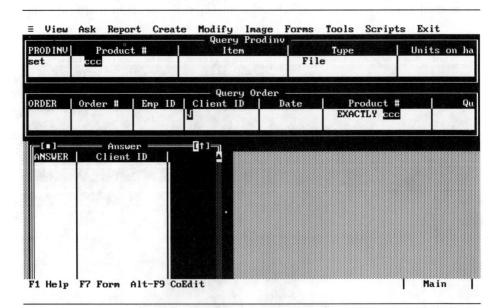

Figure 6-40.   *Set query using the EXACTLY operator*

Answer table. If you don't need to see the values in that field, press SHIFT-F6 (GroupBy) if you want to group records by the values in the field, but do not want the values displayed in the Answer table. When you do this, a *G* will be displayed in the field rather than a checkmark.

Using Scripts/QuerySave

As you can see, querying tables can become quite complex. If you find that you perform the same query frequently, Paradox allows you to save the queries, thereby eliminating the need to construct the query repeatedly. For example, the query that was just shown might be one that you would want to save.

To save a query statement, follow these steps:

1. Construct the query and use it to be sure it produces the results you want.

2. Press F10 to go to the Main menu.

3. Choose **S**cripts/**Q**uerySave. A dialog box asking for a script name is displayed, as shown in the following illustration:

4. Type a name using DOS naming conventions—eight characters or less and no spaces—and press ENTER.

At this point, it would be a good idea to test the saved query to see if it actually produces the results that you want.

To test the query, follow these steps:

1. Press ALT-F8 (Clear All) to clear the desktop of all windows, or click on the Close box in each window.

2. Choose **S**cripts/**P**lay from the Main menu.

3. Type the name of the script, or press ENTER to display the list, choose the script you want, and press ENTER. The query form will be displayed exactly as you created it.

4. Press F2 (Do-It!) to perform the query.

Using the MultiEntry Command

The MultiEntry command enables you to add the same data in two or more tables when you add data into one table. You would use this if you had two tables with some of the same field names. Query forms are used to set up the tables that are required for this command.

You must have the following in your database in order to use the MultiEntry command:

- A *source* table that is used to enter the new data, and contains the fields that correspond to fields in the target tables that will receive the data. The source table is created from the target tables shown in a query form and from the map using **Modify/MultiEntry/Setup**.

- Two or more *target* tables that receive the data entered in the source table. These tables must have some of the same fields that are in the source table.

- A predefined *map* specifies which fields in the target tables relate to fields in the source table.

Creating the Map and the Source Table

Before using **MultiEntry/Setup**, you must use **Ask** to show query forms for the tables that are to be the target tables. In these query forms, check the fields to be included in the source table. The two query forms with checkmarks in the fields are shown in Figure 6-41.

To create the map and source table, follow these steps:

1. After placing checkmarks in the query forms, press F10 to go to the Main menu and choose **Modify/MultiEntry/Setup**. A dialog box asking for a source table name appears, as shown in Figure 6-42. Sales is the source table name shown.

2. Type a name using DOS naming conventions and press ENTER. You are then asked to name the map table. Again refer to Figure 6-42 to see an example.

3. Type a name using DOS naming conventions and press ENTER. Salesmap is the map table name shown in Figure 6-43.

 The new table is stacked on the desktop. You can rearrange the table in order to see the others, as shown in Figure 6-43. Press F4 (Down Image) enough times to go to the source table, if it is not showing on the desktop.

4. When done, clear the desktop, if you like. This is not required.

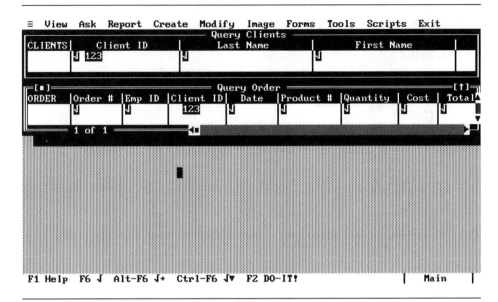

Figure 6-41.   *Query forms for the tables that are to be target tables*

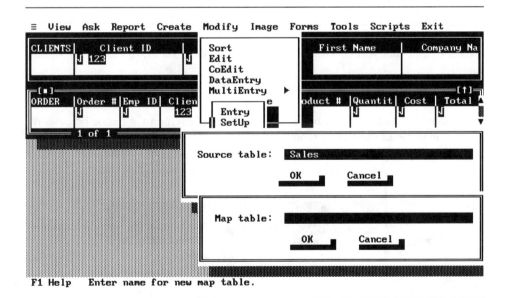

Figure 6-42.   *Source table and Map table dialog boxes*

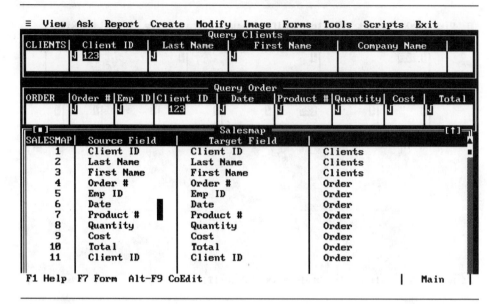

Figure 6-43. *Query forms and Salesmap*

Using MultiEntry to Enter Data in Multiple Tables

You can use **MultiEntry** to enter data in several tables. Once the source table and map have been created, the procedure for entering data is the same as for other tables, except that you choose **MultiEntry** rather than **DataEntry** from the **Modify** menu.

To use **MultiEntry** to do this, follow these steps:

1. Choose **Modify/MultiEntry/Entry** from the Main menu. A dialog box asks for the name of the source table, as shown here:

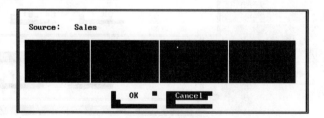

2. Type the source table name and press ENTER, or choose it from a list and press ENTER to display another dialog box. The dialog box shown here asks for the map table:

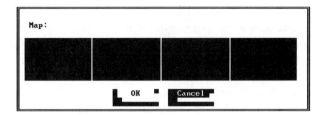

3. Type the map table name and press ENTER, or choose it from a list and press ENTER. The new table is displayed on the desktop as shown in Figure 6-44.

4. Enter the data as you would in any other table.

5. When finished, press F2 (Do-It!) to save. A message appears briefly telling you that data has been entered in the target tables. View these tables, if you like, to see the new data.

Using Queries on a Network

Paradox automatically places a prevent full lock on all tables being queried, which allows access to tables while others are viewing or even editing the records in the

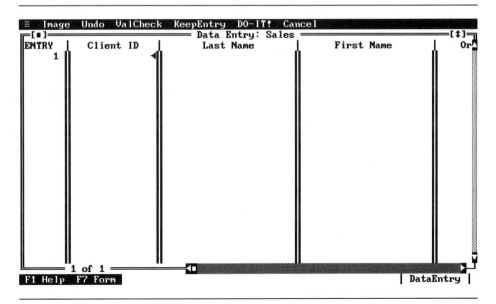

Figure 6-44.   *Source table used to enter data in multiple tables*

tables being queried. However, if another user has a full lock on a table, you cannot use that table in a query until their operation is complete and the full lock is released. The exceptions to this are if you are using INSERT, DELETE, and CHANGETO, which are query functions that change the information in tables. When you press F2 (Do-It!) to process a query with these functions, a full lock is placed on all of the tables that are used in the query.

If others are editing a table while you are performing a query, Paradox will try to use the most current information. If changes are made during the query, Paradox may restart the query. If this happens, a message will be displayed and you can press CTRL-BREAK to cancel the automatic restart.

You can use Tools/Net/Changes/Continue to instruct Paradox to base the queries on recent changes, but changes made during the current query process would not be used in the query. If you want this to be the default, use the Custom Configuration Program to make this change.

Chapter 7

Creating and Using Forms

This chapter shows how to use the standard form for entering or editing data in tables, as well as how to use **F**orms/**D**esign or **F**orms/**C**hange to custom design forms. The discussion of custom forms includes embedding forms for other tables, using calculated fields, drawing lines and borders, and designing a form that continues on to more than one page.

There are several advantages to using a form rather than a table for data entry:

- A form can show many fields on the screen at once, whereas a table will only show a few. This is convenient because data entry is easier if all fields are shown at the same time.

- A form can show one record at a time or several records at a time, whereas a table can only show many records.

- A form can contain calculated fields that are not part of the table.

- A form can contain wrapped fields.

- The information in a form can be arranged however it is most convenient for you to enter or edit data. In a table the information is arranged only in rows and columns.

- Data can be displayed from more than one table by embedding one form within another. Forms are automatically updated along with other objects related to a specific table. When the table is renamed, copied, or deleted, all

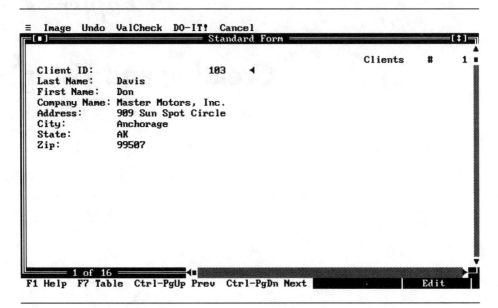

Figure 7-1.   *Standard or F form for a table*

the forms related to it are automatically renamed, copied, or deleted. Also, when the table is restructured, the fields in the forms are restructured as well.

Using the Standard Form

Paradox supplies a standard form, also called the *F form,* that can be used with any table. This form view is displayed by pressing F7 (Form Toggle) from the table that is active on the desktop. Each field in the table is shown on a separate line in the form, and up to 20 fields can be shown on a page in the form. If a table has more than 20 fields, each group of 20 fields will make up a page. The example in Figure 7-1 shows a standard form with eight fields.

A form view is referred to as a child window and can only be displayed when its corresponding table view is on the desktop. The table view is called the parent window. (You might remember child and parent windows from Chapter 4.) When you close the table view, the form view is automatically closed as well.

The F form is the *preferred form* for a table—that is, the form that will automatically be displayed when F7 (Form Toggle) is pressed. It is also the standard form that Paradox supplies. The appearance of this form can be changed using Forms/Change, if you like (you'll see how to do this shortly).

To display and use the standard form, follow these steps:

1. Choose either **V**iew or **M**odify/**E**dit or /**C**oEdit and display the table on the desktop.

2. Press F7 (Form Toggle) to display the form on the desktop.

You can arrange form views on the desktop the same way you arrange other windows using the System menu or the mouse to move, size, or maximize the window. Figure 7-1 shows a window that has been maximized.

3. You can then enter data in a new page or go back through the previous records and edit data. If you choose **V**iew to display the table, you will have to press F9 (Edit) or ALT-F9 (CoEdit) to go to an edit mode.

   Table 7-1 shows the keys that you use to move around in forms. These are the same keys you used to move around in a table view.

You can use the mouse in the scroll bars to scroll the screen up/down or right/left, click on a field, or click on the keys listed in the speedbar to perform the various actions shown there.

4. When done, press F2 (Do-It!) or click on **D**o-It! with the mouse to save the data entries.

5. After saving the edits, press F8 (Clear) to clear the desktop. Because the form view is the child window corresponding to the table, F8 clears both the form and the table—you do not have to use ALT-F8 (Clear All).

Designing a Custom Form for a Single Table

The Form Designer is used to custom design forms for tables that you don't want to follow the standard form. This allows you to enter the fields in whatever position you want in the form. You can enter new fields that calculate amounts based on other fields in the table. You can add borders and lines in the form, move fields to a more appropriate place, or design a form that looks like a printed copy of a form that employees are familiar with. You can also embed one form in another and edit or enter data in multiple tables. Each table can have up to 15 custom forms associated with it.

Figure 7-2 shows an example of a custom-designed form for the Clients table. This same form will be used later in this chapter when embedding forms is discussed.

Choosing the Table for the Form

In order to use the Form Designer, you must first choose the table that is to be the basis for the form.

Keys	Action
UP ARROW	Previous field (Left or Up), or previous record if on first field in form
DOWN ARROW	Next field (Right or Down), or next record if on last field in form
RIGHT ARROW	Previous field (Left or Up), or previous record if on first field in form
LEFT ARROW	Next field (Right or Down), or next record if on last field in form
CTRL-HOME	First field
CTRL-END	Last field
CTRL-PGUP	Same field of previous record
CTRL-PGDN	Same field of next record
HOME	First record
END	Last record
PGUP	Previous page or record
PGDN	Next page or record
INSERT	Insert new record
DELETE	Delete record

Table 7-1.   *Keys Used to Move Around in a Form*

To choose the table, follow these steps:

1. Choose **F**orms/**D**esign from the Main menu. A dialog box appears asking for a table name.

2. Type the table name for the form and press ENTER, or press ENTER to display a list of names, choose the one you want, and press ENTER. A list of forms, like the one shown in Figure 7-3, is displayed.

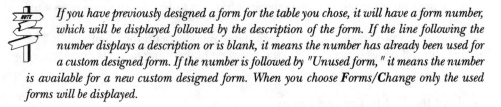

*If you have previously designed a form for the table you chose, it will have a form number, which will be displayed followed by the description of the form. If the line following the number displays a description or is blank, it means the number has already been used for a custom designed form. If the number is followed by "Unused form," it means the number is available for a new custom designed form. When you choose **Forms/Change** only the used forms will be displayed.*

3. Choose the number you want and press ENTER.

```
≡ Field  Area  Border  Page  Style  Multi  DO-IT!  Cancel
 [■]═══════════════Form Design: Clients.F1══════════════[‡]
                          OFFICE INTERIORS INC.
                            CLIENT LIST

Client ID _____  First Name _____  Last Name _____
                        Company_____
                        Address _____
                   City _____  State __  ZIP _____




 16, 9  1:1  ◄■                                                    ■
 F1 Help                                                       Form
```

Figure 7-2. *Custom designed form for Clients table*

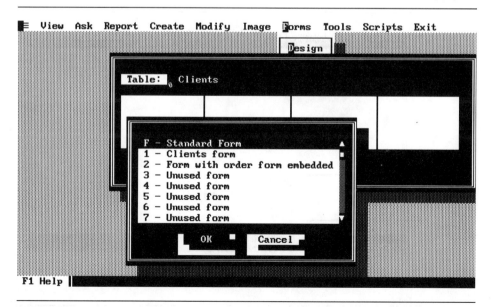

Figure 7-3. *List of available forms*

4. A dialog box for a description is displayed. You can enter a description and press ENTER, or bypass it by pressing ENTER without entering any information. The Form Design window is then displayed, as shown in Figure 7-4.

When the Form Design window is first displayed, the cursor is in the top-left corner of the window. The window frame at the bottom of the screen shown just above the status line indicates the cursor position as it is moved around in the window. The first two numbers—for example, 1, 1 in Figure 7-4—show the line number and the column number of the cursor position. The following numbers—1:1—show the page number and the total pages. When a field is placed, the status line shows the field name when the cursor is positioned in a field.

The Form Designer menu is at the top of the screen and can be accessed by clicking the option you want or by pressing F10 and then choosing the option you want.

The System menu can be accessed by clicking on it or by pressing ALT-SPACEBAR. The options available there are the same as in other windows. These were covered in Chapter 1.

If you choose System/Interface and switch to 3.5 compatibility, you'll lose any changes you make to the form during the current session.

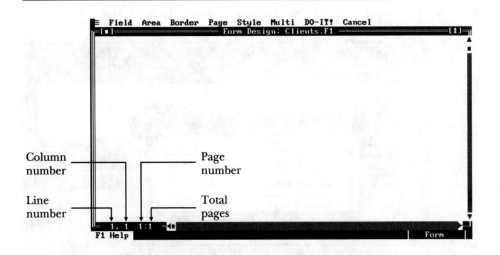

Figure 7-4.   *Form Design window*

Entering Text in the Form

You can enter text for labels, titles, or other comments in the form in much the same way you enter text in any editor. Move the cursor to the position where you want to enter characters and begin typing. Use the indicators at the bottom of the screen as a guide when placing text. You probably want to enter titles at the top of the form, and enter labels for the fields in the body of the form. The text that you enter is referred to as *literals*, meaning that anything typed on the screen will be printed exactly as it is shown—in other words, it does not represent anything other than the characters shown there.

You can toggle between Insert mode and Overwrite mode by pressing INSERT. Overwrite is the default.

Working with Fields

The major work in designing a form is placing the fields and formatting them so that entering and editing data is easier than if you were to enter it directly into the table. The Field option in the Form Designer menu is used here. The Form Designer menu is accessed by pressing F10 or clicking on the option that you want.

Placing Fields in the Form

You place fields in forms using the **Field/Place** menu, which has several functions. It can be used to insert the regular table fields in the form; to enter a field as DisplayOnly (which shows the values in fields but does not allow editing); to enter a calculated field (which inserts a new field based on calculations of values in existing fields or PAL functions and variables); or to enter the Record Number field (which is the leftmost field in a table and contains the number of each record in the table).

To place a field—either Regular, Calculated, or #Record—you first specify the position and the length of the field. Follow these steps:

1. After choosing **Field/Place** and the type of field you want, a prompt with instructions for placing the field is displayed at the top of the screen as shown in the following illustration. Move the cursor to the position where you want the field and press ENTER.

   Move to where you want the field to begin, then press ↵...

2. A line will be displayed representing the length of the field. Another prompt with instructions for adjusting the field size is displayed as shown in the following illustration. Press the arrow keys to reduce or lengthen the line. When the line is the length you want, press ENTER.

   You use → and ← to adjust the width of the field, then press ↵.

*The hyphenated line then becomes a line of underscores indicating that the field is placed. If the field is too small, asterisks will be displayed in place of the values when you view the form. You can then return to the Form Designer and adjust the width using **Field/Reformat**. This is discussed later in this chapter.*

Inserting Regular Fields   To insert a regular field in the form, choose **Field/Place/Regular**. A list displays the fields names that are in the table, as shown in Figure 7-5. Choose the field name you want and press ENTER. The prompt at the top of the screen instructs you to move the cursor to the position where you want the field inserted and press ENTER. Another prompt appears with instructions for adjusting the field width. Press the arrow keys to adjust the width of the field and press ENTER. You may want to enter text as a label in front of the field before doing this. Refer back to Figure 7-2 for an example of fields labeled in a form.

You can place a field in the form only once. When you place the next field, the list of field names will be displayed again; however, the field names that have already been placed will not be on the list.

*The placement of groups of fields can be changed using **Area/Move**, or the length of a field can be changed using **Field/Reformat**.*

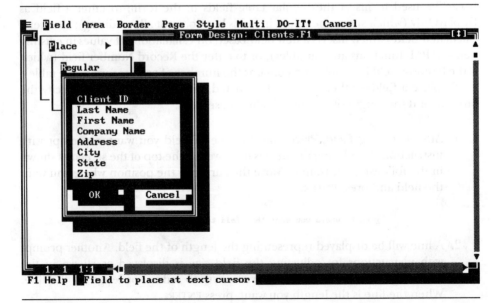

Figure 7-5.   *List of field names for the form*

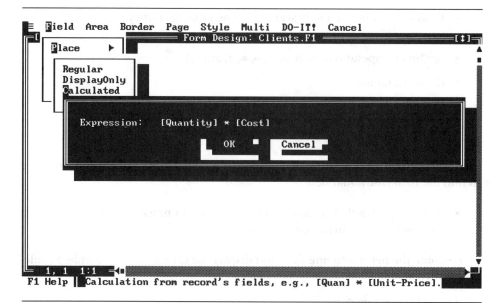

Figure 7-6. *Dialog box for entering an expression*

Using DisplayOnly DisplayOnly is used primarily in multitable forms when you want the same information from a field to be displayed on following pages. The value will be displayed, but can't be edited. Choose **Field/Place/DisplayOnly**. A list of fields is shown. Choose the one you want and then place the field as you would place any other field. While you can't modify the contents of the **DisplayOnly** field directly through the form, if the data changes due to some other process—a PAL script or editing the table in table view—the **DisplayOnly** field will reflect those changes when you next view the form.

Inserting Calculated Fields You can use the **Calculated** option to enter a new field based on calculations from other fields, or PAL functions and variables. To do this choose **Field/Place/Calculated** from the Form Designer menu. A dialog box like the one shown in Figure 7-6 asks you for the expression. Type the expression—up to 175 characters—and press ENTER. You then have to position the cursor to indicate the position for the field. If the calculated value does not fit in the space you've specified for the field, you may see one of two results: If the whole digits do not fit in the space, Paradox will display a row of asterisks; if the whole digits fit, but any decimal digits do not, Paradox will cut off the decimals that don't fit the field. When you place a PAL expression, the field will take up all the available space until you resize it.

You can enter any of the following in the expression:

- Field names enclosed in brackets [ ], typed exactly as they appear in the table structure

- Arithmetic operations such as +, −, *, /, and ()

- Constant values

- Variables

- Most of the PAL functions (refer to Chapter 13)

An example of an expression to multiply the quantity in an order by the unit price to find the total cost would be

- [*quantity*] * [*cost*]. The field names shown are in brackets and must be exact matches with the field names in the table.

To combine the fields into one field and display the values as, for example, Seattle, WA 98101:

- [*city*] + "," + [*state*] + [*zip*]

Inserting #Records   If you want to place in the form the number of the record—that is the number that identifies each record and is entered automatically in the leftmost column in the table—choose **Field/Place/#Re**cord. Then move the cursor to the position where you want the field, press ENTER, adjust the size of the field, and press ENTER again.

Saving the Form Design   Saving the design is similar to saving changes in other Paradox functions. Press F2 (Do-It!) or click on **Do-It!** with the mouse.

Erasing Fields

You can remove a field from the form if you like. Choose **Field/Erase** from the form menu. A message will be displayed at the top of the screen instructing you to move to the field. Press an arrow key to move to the field you want and press ENTER. The field will be deleted from the form. You can remove several fields at once by doing an **Area/Erase**.

Reformatting Fields

If you find that a field is too long—that it takes up more space than it should—you can shorten it; or if you find that the field is not long enough to show the values, you can lengthen it. To do this, choose **Field/Re**format from the **Form** menu, move the cursor to the field you want to adjust, and press ENTER. A prompt at the top of the screen instructs you to press the LEFT ARROW or RIGHT ARROW to adjust the width. When the line is the length you want, press ENTER.

Editing Calculations in Fields

Choose Field/CalcEdit from the Form Designer menu to edit any calculation expressions that have been entered. A prompt appears instructing you to choose the field you want to edit. Move the cursor to the field to be edited and press ENTER. The current expression is shown in a dialog box here:

You can edit the expression by pressing BACKSPACE to delete characters, or press CTRL-BACKSPACE to erase the entire value. You can also toggle between Insert mode and Overwrite mode by pressing INSERT. Edit the expression, and press ENTER or choose OK when finished. You can also move around as if you were in field view.

Using WordWrap in Fields

If you need enough space in the form for values to wrap to the next line, you can specify this for the field. Choose Field/WordWrap from the Form Designer menu, move the cursor to the field you want, and press ENTER. A dialog box appears asking for the number of lines you want for the field. Type the maximum number you could possibly want for that field (as shown here) and press ENTER:

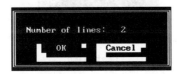

The number of lines must fit below the current line in the current maximized window. If a value is too long to be displayed in its entirety in the form field, you can press ALT-F5 or CTRL-F (Field View) to scroll through the remaining text. You also need to use Field View if you plan to edit memo fields.

Working with an Area

Areas are any selected sections of the form. Borders, fields, and literals can be included in an area; however, you must include all of a field—you cannot select just part of a field. You can move areas in the form window, or you can erase them. This allows you to work with several fields at once, moving them to a different position in the window, or deleting them.

Moving an Area

If you find that a portion of the form needs to be moved—perhaps the title is in the wrong place—use the **Area/Move** menu.

To move a portion of the form, follow these steps:

1. Choose **Area/Move** from the Form Designer menu. A message is displayed instructing you to move to one corner of the area that you want to move. Press any of the arrow keys to move to the new position and press ENTER.

2. Another message appears at the top of the screen instructing you to move to the diagonal corner. Press any of the arrow keys to move to the diagonal corner. A highlighted block will now appear on the screen that represents the area that is to be moved. When the block is the size that you think is correct, press ENTER.

3. A third message—this one instructing you to use the arrow keys to drag the area to a new position—appears at the top of the screen as shown in Figure 7-7. (You cannot use the mouse for this.) Press any of the arrow keys to move

```
Jse ↑ ↓ → ← to drag the area, then press ↵ .
[■]═════════════════ Form Design: Clients.F1 ═════════════[ ]

 OFFICE INTERIORS INC            ███████████████
 CLIENT LIST

 Client ID      _____

 First Name     _____    Last Name  _____

 Company        _____

 Address_____

 City, State and Zip    _____



 3,49   1:1
 F1 Help
```

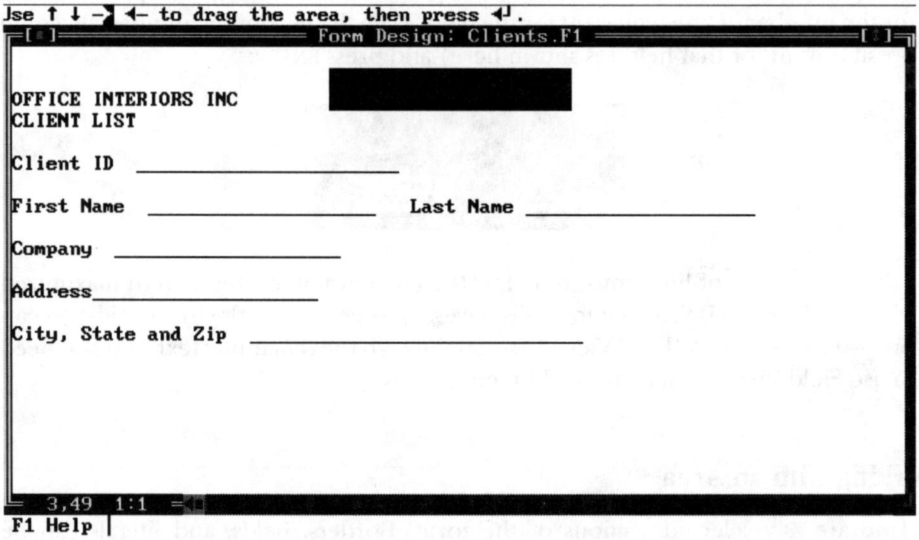

Figure 7-7.   Using Area/Move

the area and press ENTER. The highlighting disappears, which means the selected area of the form has been moved.

You cannot use Area/Move to move an embedded form. You have to use Multi/Ta-bles/Move to do this. Also, you cannot use Area/Move to move records in a multirecord area—use Multi/Records for this. When you choose Multi/Records/Adjust, the copies of the records are removed from the form. Then you are prompted to move the lower-right corner to a new size and shape (which determines the width and number of rows); you next designate the new copies you want. At least one copy is required.

Erasing an Area

The process of erasing or deleting an area allows you to remove several fields at once. Choose Area/Erase, move the cursor to the beginning of the area that you want to erase, and press ENTER. Then move the cursor diagonally to highlight the area and press ENTER to delete or erase the area.

When the area is erased, it is removed permanently from the form. This change exists only in the form—the fields remain in the table. Also you cannot use Area/Erase to remove an embedded form—use Multi/Tables/Remove instead.

Working with Borders

You can greatly enhance the appearance of your form and emphasize certain portions of it by adding borders or boxes, or by inserting lines that separate portions of the form. Using the **B**order menu, you can add borders, boxes, and lines that consist of single lines, double lines, or you can specify any other character of your choice for the border. You also use the **B**order menu to erase borders.

Adding a Single-Line or Double-Line Border

You can vary the use of lines in a form to call attention to specific parts of the form. To add single- or double-line borders, follow these steps:

1. Choose **B**order/**P**lace and then choose **S**ingle-line or **D**ouble-line. A message displayed at the top of the window instructs you to move to a corner and press ENTER.

2. Move the cursor to where you want one corner of the border and press ENTER.

You cannot intersect a field, but that is the only restriction on borders.

```
≣  Field   Area   Border   Page   Style   Multi   DO-IT!   Cancel
┌[■]══════════════════════ Form Design: Clients.F1 ═════════════════[↕]┐
│                                                                      ▲
│                                                                      ▓
│                    ┌───────────────────────────────┐                ▓
│                    │    OFFICE INTERIORS INC        │                ▓
│                    │    CLIENT LIST                 │                ▓
│                    └───────────────────────────────┘                ▓
│ Client ID  _____     First Name  _____     Last Name _____ │
│                                                                      │
│                         Company   _____                │
│                                                                      │
│                         Address   _____                │
│                                                                      │
│               City _____  State __  ZIP _____          │
│                                                                      │
│                                                                      │
│                                                                      │
│                                                                      │
│                                                                      │
│                                                                      │
│                                                                      ▼
├══ 5,56   1:1  ◄▊══════════════════════════════════════════════════▶█┤
│ F1 Help                                              │     Form       │
```

Figure 7-8.   *Drawing a border around the title*

3. Press any of the arrow keys to move diagonally to the opposite corner to form
    the border and press ENTER. The border is displayed in the form, as shown in
    the example in Figure 7-8.

If you place the border (represented by the highlighting) on top of text, the text will be deleted.

Adding a Border Made of Another Character

You can use any other keyboard character to form the lines of a border, or you can
enter ASCII codes to have some different characters make up the lines. Perhaps you
want a bullet, a shaded box, or Greek letters or symbols for the line, rather than
alphabet or numeric keyboard characters. To enter any of these ASCII codes in the
dialog box asking for a different character, press ALT and the numbers that represent
the characters entered on the number keypad at the right (from 128 to 254). Refer
to Appendix C for a list of the ASCII character set.

To form a border using characters, follow these steps:

1. Choose **B**order/**P**lace/**O**ther. A dialog box asking for the character is dis-
    played, as shown here:

2. Type the character or enter the ASCII code using ALT and the code number entered from the number keypad.

3. Press ENTER.

4. Press the arrow keys to move to the beginning of the border and press ENTER.

5. Press the arrow keys to draw the border diagonally and press ENTER.

Inserting a Horizontal or Vertical Line Border

You can use a horizontal or vertical line rather than an enclosed border if you like. Use the **B**order/**P**lace menu to enter a line separating parts of the form, as shown in the example in Figure 7-9. The line shown here consists of asterisks, but any character can be used for the line.

To create a horizontal or vertical line border within the form, follow these steps:

1. Choose **B**order/**P**lace, then choose **S**ingle-line, **D**ouble-line, or **O**ther.

```
≡ Field  Area  Border  Page  Style  Multi  DO-IT!  Cancel
═[■]════════════════ Form Design: Clients.F1 ═══════════════[↕]═
                ┌─────────────────────────────────┐         ▲
                │      OFFICE INTERIORS INC        │         ■
                │      CLIENT LIST                 │
                └─────────────────────────────────┘
Client ID  _____     First Name  _____     Last Name  _____

                       Company  _____

                       Address  _____

            City  _____  State  __  ZIP  _____
*****************************************************************************




                                                                           ▼
═ 13, 1  1:1  ◄■──────────────────────────────────────────────────■►
F1 Help                                              │   Form   │
```

Figure 7-9. *Inserting a line in a form*

2. If you chose **O**ther you have to enter a character and press ENTER.

3. Press any of the arrow keys to move to where you want the line to begin and press ENTER.

4. Press any the arrow keys to move *horizontally* or *vertically* (not diagonally) to where you want to end the line and press ENTER.

Erasing a Border

A border can be removed from the form as easily as it is inserted. From the Form Designer menu choose **B**order/**E**rase, move the cursor to one corner of the border and press ENTER, move the cursor to the diagonal corner to highlight all sides of the border, and press ENTER to remove it.

Inserting or Removing Pages

You can arrange the form in some other way and add pages if you like. A form can have as many as 15 pages. There is no limit, other than space, on the number of fields in a custom form. (In a standard form, Paradox breaks pages every 20 fields because the fields are placed vertically on the page and they would not fit otherwise.)

To add a page choose **P**age/**I**nsert from the Form Designer menu. A menu like this one appears, asking if you want to add a page after the current one or before the current one (choose whichever you prefer):

To remove a page, move the cursor to the page you want to remove and choose **P**age/**D**elete. A dialog box asks you to confirm the deletion. Choose OK. The page and all fields, labels, borders, and literals (text or characters) will be removed.

 After deleting the page, if you decide that you want to restore it, you can choose Cancel from the Form Designer menu if you haven't previously saved the form with the deletions.

Using the Style Menu

The Style menu contains options that allow you to change the screen colors in a form, change the display on a monochrome monitor, display field names in the form, and remove or show highlighting in a multirecord area.

Changing Colors in a Form

You may want to customize the colors in a form in order to enhance the display, make it easier to read, call attention to a specific area, and so on. You can change the colors either in areas or in borders. Text within a border is not affected by the color change.

To change colors, follow these steps:

1. Choose **S**tyle/**C**olor from the Form Designer menu, then choose:

   • *Area,* if you want to change the color in a specific area in the form.

   • *Border,* if you want to change the color of a border.

2. Once you've chosen **A**rea or **B**order, move the cursor to a corner of the area or border to be changed and press ENTER.

3. Move the cursor to the opposite corner—be sure the entire section is highlighted—and press ENTER. A color palette is now displayed in the upper-left corner as shown in Figure 7-10; you are prompted to press the arrow keys to change the colors in the section you have highlighted.

4. Select the colors you want by pressing the arrow keys—UP ARROW or DOWN ARROW for the background color; LEFT ARROW or RIGHT ARROW for the foreground colors. As the cursor moves through the color palette, the colors in

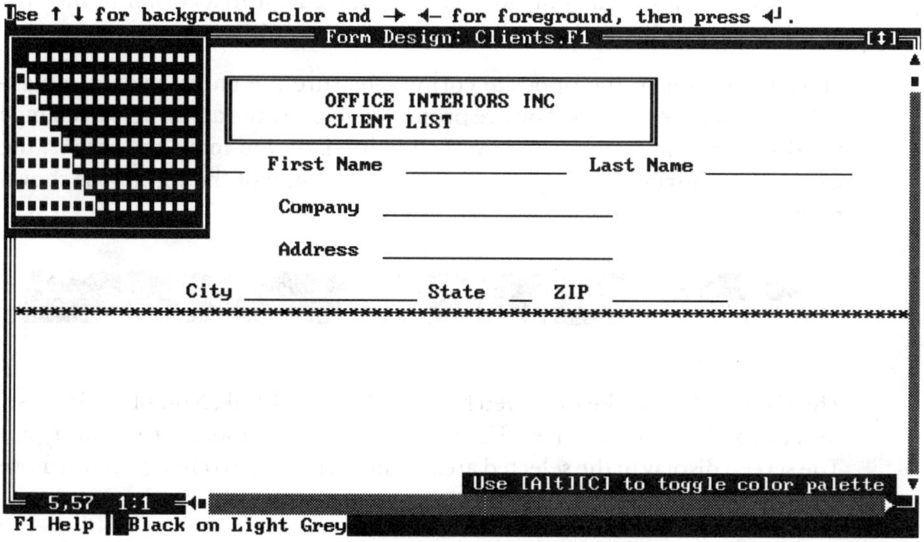

Figure 7-10. *Color palette*

the area or border change so you can see the effect you will get with different choices.

5. When you have the combination that looks best to you, press ENTER to set the colors.

 Press ALT-C to toggle the color palette off and on. You might do this if you need to see what you are doing and then want to return to the color palette.

 If you want the color palette to be displayed every time you design a form, you can use the Custom Configuration Program to set FormPalette on.

Choosing Monochrome from the Style Menu

The Style/Monochrome menu can be used with either a color monitor or a monochrome monitor. Use this menu to change the intensity of text or borders, to choose reverse or intense-reverse video, or to add blinking to borders, boxes, or lines.

To change the display, follow these steps:

1. Choose Style/Monochrome from the Form Designer menu, then choose:

   • *Area,* if you want to change the display in a specific area in the form.

   • *Border,* if you want to change the display in a border.

2. Once you've chosen **Area** or **Border**, move the cursor to a corner of the area or border to be changed and press ENTER.

3. Move the cursor to the opposite corner—be sure the entire section is highlighted—and press ENTER. You are prompted to press the arrow keys to change the display in the section you have highlighted. As you move the arrows, the name of the attribute is displayed in the bottom line of the window as shown here:

The choices that can be displayed here are Normal, Blink, Non-blink, Intense, Reverse, and Intense-reverse. (Use the arrow keys to choose the display type.) The screen display in the selected area of the form will also change as you move through the choices.

4. Move the arrow keys to choose the type of display you want and press ENTER.

Showing Field Names

The field names are always shown at the bottom of the window as you move the arrow key into that field in the form; however, you can also display all field names on the screen in their corresponding positions while you are designing the form. This can help you keep track of the fields that have been entered in the form, especially when you are working with a fairly large form.

To make field names show, choose **S**tyle/**F**ieldnames from the Form Designer menu, then choose **S**how. The field names will replace the hyphenated lines that are the default for the fields. The names will appear, as shown in Figure 7-11, while you are designing the form, but they will not show later when you view the form or use it to edit or enter data.

Choose **S**tyle/**F**ieldnames/**H**ide to stop the field names from showing on the form. The display will then return to the default: hyphenated lines representing the fields.

Using ShowHighlight

The default display for multirecord areas is to have the area highlighted in reverse video or in a contrasting color. Choose **S**tyle/**S**howHighlight/**H**ide to remove the highlighting from the multirecord areas. To turn it back on, choose **S**tyle/**S**howHighlight/**S**how.

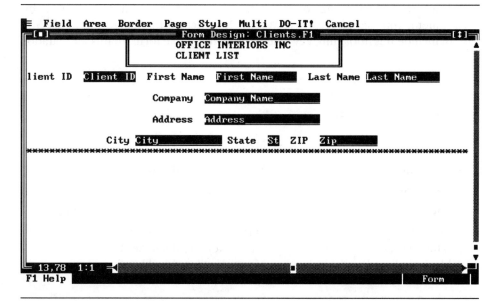

Figure 7-11. *Showing field names in a form*

Designing Multitable Forms

A multitable form can greatly enhance data entry by allowing you to use a single form to enter or edit data in more than one table. The multitable form consists of a *master table form*, which is the form for the table upon which the form is based, and *detail table forms*. The detail forms are *embedded* in the master form, and they may be either linked or unlinked. *Linked table forms* are those that relate to each other by having a common key field or fields. *Unlinked table forms* may have no particular relationship to each other, but are shown in the same form just to provide access to information in other tables.

Embedding Linked Tables

When combining linked tables in a form, think first of the relationship between tables. You should be aware of the types of relationships existing between tables: one-to-one, one-to-many, many-to-one, or many-to-many. Refer to Chapters 1 and 3 for a discussion of database relationships. Table 7-2 shows examples of how key fields in master and detail tables match for each type of relationship.

    This section discusses a multitable form based on a one-to-many relationship. The example tables used are the Clients table and the Order table, which show a one-to-many relationship—one customer to many orders. The Clients table will be used for the master form. The Order form will be the detail form that will be embedded in it. The tables are linked by a common field—*Client ID*. This linked field *must be the first key field* in the detail table (the Order table in this example). If the tables that you are planning to work with in a multitable form do not meet this requirement, you may have to use **Modify/Restructure** to change the fields. You cannot include this initial link key field in the Order table form. In this way Paradox

Link Type	Match
One-to-one	Master key 1 to detail key 1
One-to-many	Master key 1 to detail key 1, detail key 2
Many-to-one	Master key 1, master key 2 to detail key 1
Many-to-many (or the master table is not keyed)	Master key 1 to detail key 1 Master key 2 to detail key 2 Master key 3 to detail key 3

Table 7-2.   *Relational Database Keys and Matches*

ensures *referential integrity* by preventing the possibility of changing a linking key field in the detail table without also changing it in the master table.

If you include the linking field in the detail form, an error message appears, and you are prevented from embedding the form containing the duplicate field when you place the detail form in the master form. Figure 7-12 shows an example of this message.

When designing a multitable form, the first step is to design forms for each of the tables to be included in the multitable form. The second step is to display the master table form at the top of the form window, and then embed the detail table forms below the master form.

Designing the Forms

The forms can be any design that you choose; however, when you intend to have more than one form on a page be aware of the amount of space used by each form. Designing a multirecord form is discussed later in this chapter.

Follow these steps to design a form:

1. Choose **F**orms/**D**esign from the Main menu, and design the forms for each of the tables following the same procedures used for any other forms.

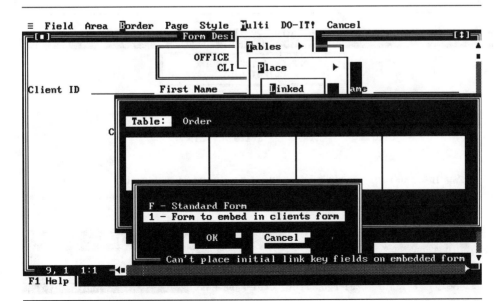

Figure 7-12.   *Error message when embedding a form containing an initial link key field*

2. Clear the screen of all images when you are done and have pressed F2 (Do-It!) to save the form.

Combining the Forms

The master form must be displayed first, then detail forms can be added. Figure 7-13 shows an example of a completed form as it will look when it is used for data entry. The master form shows the fields for the Clients table, and the detail form shows the fields for the Order table.

To combine forms, follow these steps:

1. Choose **F**orms/**C**hange from the Main menu.

2. Choose the table that is to be the master table and the form number that you want. Press ENTER to display the Description dialog box.

3. Press ENTER to bypass the description, or enter or edit the description if one is already displayed, and then press ENTER.

It is helpful to enter a description, because this will later be displayed in the menu of form numbers and can help you identify which form you want.

4. Maximize the window.

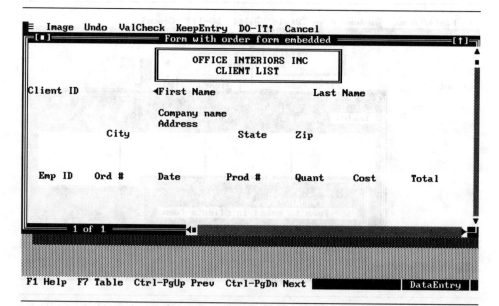

Figure 7-13.   *Completed multitabel form as it appears when used for data entry*

5. To embed the second form, choose **Multi/Tables/Place** from the Form Designer menu. A second menu is shown.

6. Choose **Linked**. The dialog box asking for the table name is shown. Choose the table that is to be the detail table and choose the form number to be used.

7. A menu of field names from the master table and a message appear at the bottom of the screen asking for the linking field name to be matched in the master table. Figure 7-14 shows an example of the list of field names. (In this case it would be Client ID.) Press ENTER to display the highlighted area, and to display the prompt at the top of the screen with instructions for placing the form.

8. Move the cursor to the position where the detail form is to be embedded. This is the same procedure you used to place fields. Press ENTER when you have selected a position to complete the embedding. A shaded area representing the embedded table is now shown in the master form.

9. Press F2 (Do-It!) or click on **Do-It!** to save. Figure 7-15 shows the completed form as it appears in the Form Design window.

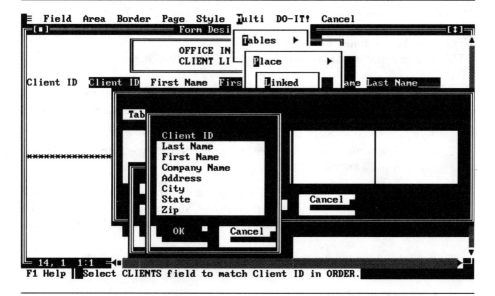

Figure 7-14.   List of names from the master form

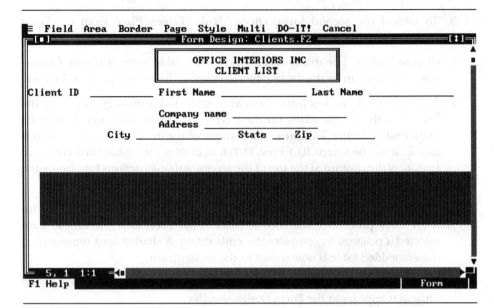

Figure 7-15.   *Completed form in the Form Design window*

Designing a Multirecord Form

In the previous example, the detail form on the Orders table could be designed to display multirecords. This would display several records together in one section of the form rather than in separate windows. This is necessary if you want to produce a form like the one shown in Figure 7-15. Forms with multirecords can be single forms or they can be combined with other forms.

To design a multirecord section in a form, follow these steps:

1. Choose **Forms/Design**, and then choose the table you want to use. In this example, the Order table is used because it can show several records for each client.

2. Choose an unused form number and press ENTER. Type a description if you like and press ENTER.

3. Place the fields in the form; an example is shown in Figure 7-16. The text identifying each field is entered on one line, and the actual field is placed on the line below. This makes it easier to display multiple records in the form.

To extend the fields downward to display multiple records, follow these steps:

1. Choose **Multi/Records/Define**.

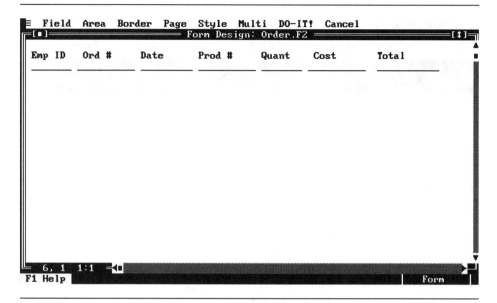

≡ Field Area Border Page Style Multi DO-IT! Cancel

Figure 7-16. *Placing fields in a multirecord form*

2. Move the cursor to the corner of the region you want to define and press ENTER. Look at the status line at the bottom of the window to determine the row where the cursor is located, as shown in Figure 7-17. In this example, the row and column numbers in the window frame show that the cursor is at the left in Row 2.

To avoid a cluttered look in the form, do not include the column titles when you are defining the multiple records. Select and copy only the fields. This eliminates duplicating the titles in each row of fields.

3. Move the cursor to the diagonal corner and press ENTER.

4. Press the DOWN ARROW to extend the region downward. If you go too far, press the UP ARROW. You may want to add only three or four rows for the multiple records.

5. Press ENTER to finish defining the region; Figure 7-17 shows an example.

6. Add a border around the multiple record area, if you like.

7. Press F2 (Do-It!) or click on **D**o-It! to save.

Removing Multirecords

If you decide to change the form and want to remove all the multirecords that are displayed, choose **M**ulti/**R**ecords/**R**emove from the Form Designer menu. Move the

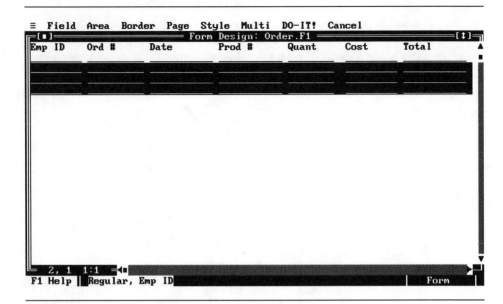

Figure 7-17.   *Defining the region for multiple records in a form*

cursor to the area of multiple records and press ENTER. The records will be deleted from the form. Fields, borders, and literals, including titles and labels, will remain in the form.

Adjusting a Multirecord Area

You can change the size and shape of the original records by using the Adjust option. To use the Adjust option, follow these steps:

1. Display the form in the Form Designer window and choose **M**ulti/**Re**-cords/**A**djust. The copies of the records are removed and the cursor is located at the original record. You are instructed to adjust that region.

2. Press the arrow keys to move the bottom-right corner to a new size and shape. The top-left corner remains in its original position. Press ENTER when the area is the size you want.

3. You are then asked to designate new copies. Press the DOWN ARROW to select the number of copies you want to add, or press the UP ARROW to select the number of copies to delete, and press ENTER.

*If you want to leave **M**ulti/**R**ecords/**A**djust without making copies, press ESC.*

Embedding a Form

When preparing to embed a detail form, be aware of the space available in the master form. Be sure you have sufficient room on the page for it. If you don't have enough room, change either the master form or the detail form, or both, if necessary, so that the information you want can be displayed on one page.

It is a good idea to design the detail table so that it is easy to read, and as small as possible. When designing the form, start at the upper-left corner of the screen and work down to your right. Don't worry about centering titles or headings, borders, and so on. You can adjust those later when you embed the detail form in the master form.

To embed the form, follow these steps:

1. Choose **F**orms/**C**hange from the Main menu.

2. Choose the table that is to be the master table and choose the form number that you want. At the Description dialog box, press ENTER or enter or edit a description.

3. Once the master form is on the desktop, choose **M**ulti/**T**ables/**P**lace/**L**inked.

4. Choose the detail table (the Order table in this example) and choose the form number containing the multiple records. Press ENTER to bypass the Description dialog box, or enter or edit information in it and then press ENTER.

5. The menu showing the field names in the master table is displayed. Choose the linking field in the master table that matches the key field in the detail table. (In this example Client ID is the field that links the tables.) Press ENTER to display a highlighted area that represents the detail form.

As discussed earlier in this chapter, the key field in the detail table cannot be placed in the detail form. There is no need for it because it already is placed in the master table form.

6. Move the cursor to set the embedded form at the position where you want it and press ENTER.

7. Press F2 (Do-It!) or click on **D**o-It! to save the form and clear the desktop.

*If you want to see the form containing the data, choose View from the Main menu, select the master table, choose **I**mage/**P**ickform, and choose the form number. Move the cursor through the data to see the change in the display. The cursor remains in the master table. Press F4 (Up Image) to go to the detail table. Press F3 (Down Image) to return to the master table.*

Embedding an Unlinked Form

When you combine unlinked tables, you should first design forms for each table you want to combine. Then display the master table form on the desktop using **F**orms/**C**hange from the Main menu. Forms that are added or embedded are detail forms.

To embed an unlinked table form in the master table form, follow these steps:

1. Choose **M**ulti/**T**ables/**P**lace/**U**nlinked.

2. Choose the table and the form number to be embedded, and press ENTER.

3. Position the form in the master form and press ENTER.

4. Press F2 (Do-It!) or click on **D**o-It! to save.

An unlinked form has no particular relation to the master form, but is used to merely display other information along with the information shown in the master form.

Removing an Embedded Form

If you are changing your tables, you may want to remove an embedded table from a form. You can use this procedure with either linked or unlinked tables.

To remove an embedded table, follow these steps:

1. Choose **F**orms/**C**hange from the Main menu; then choose the master table for the form.

2. Edit the description for the form if you like, and press ENTER.

3. In the Form Designer, choose **M**ulti/**T**ables/**R**emove. A prompt appears instructing you to point to the form you want to remove.

4. Move the cursor to the shaded area representing the form you want to remove and press ENTER.

5. A dialog box appears asking you to confirm.

6. Choose OK to remove the form.

Moving an Embedded Form

Moving an embedded form is very similar to removing a form. You can use this procedure with either linked or unlinked tables.

To move an embedded form, follow these steps:

1. Choose **F**orms/**C**hange from the Main menu, and choose the master table and form number that you want.

2. In the Form Designer window, choose **M**ulti/**T**ables/**M**ove.

3. Move the cursor to the form you want to move and press ENTER. The highlighting changes color.

4. Press the arrow keys to move the highlighted area to another position and press ENTER.

Using DisplayOnly

The **D**isplayOnly option allows you to determine whether all records that are displayed in the form can be edited or only viewed. **D**isplayOnly is used to protect data from being inadvertently changed during an edit session. You can use this option to specify whether the records are in the master form or in the detail forms that are embedded.

To use **D**isplayOnly, follow these steps:

1. Choose **F**orms/**C**hange from the Main menu and choose the master table you want.

2. In the Form Design window, choose **M**ulti/**T**ables/**D**isplayOnly. A second menu appears that asks you to choose **M**aster or **O**ther. If you choose **O**ther, you will have to move to the form to be changed.

3. Choose **Y**es to specify DisplayOnly, or **N**o which is the default and allows data to be edited.

Using Multitable Forms

You can use multitable forms the same way you use single table forms—choose the table that is to receive new data or that contains data that is to be edited, then choose the form you want, and edit or enter new data in the form. When you are done, save the entries and edits. They will be stored in the associated tables. The advantage in using multitable forms is that you can enter data or edit data in multiple tables during one editing session. The data in all tables associated with the forms in a multitable form will be changed, or new data will be added to the appropriate tables.

DataEntry Using a Multitable Form

To enter new records in multiple tables, use **Modify/DataEntry**. You can also use **Modify/Edit** or **Modify/CoEdit**, which will be covered next in this chapter.

To use **DataEntry** with the multitable form, follow these steps:

1. Choose **Modify/DataEntry** from the Main menu.

2. Choose the table used for the master table in the form. (Clients is shown in the example here.)

3. Choose **Image/Pickform**.

 If there is a validity check on a field, you may either have to enter a value in a field in the table that is shown on the desktop or remove the validity check, if you want to go to the DataEntry menu to choose Image/PickForm.

4. Choose the form you want. The blank form is displayed, as shown in the example in Figure 7-18.

5. Enter data in the master form section, pressing TAB to move from one field to the next.

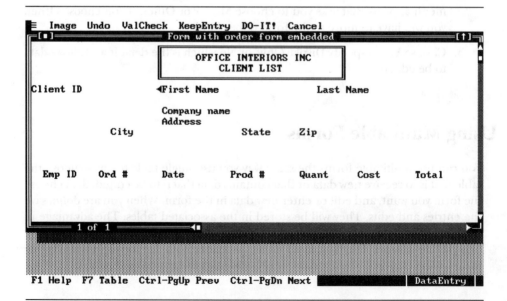

Figure 7-18.   The blank multitable form

6. Press F4 (Up Image) or use the mouse to move to the next detail section. Press F3 (Down Image) to go back to the master section or to the previous section. Enter data in all sections, as shown in the example in Figure 7-19.

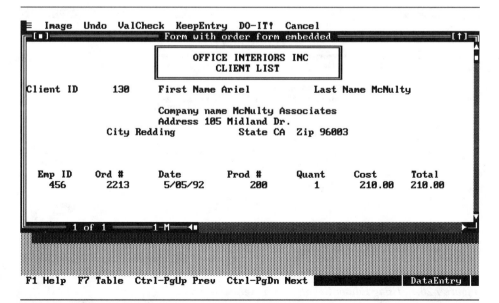

The window frame in Figure 7-19 shows 1-M to indicate a one-to-many link in this form.

There are some restrictions on data entry in a multitable form:

- You must enter the data in the link key in the master form before entering data in a detail form.

- If you have a one-to-one or a one-to-many link, you cannot delete a master record when there are values in the detail record that depend on it. If your form is a many-to-one or a many-to-many link, then you can make this deletion.

- If you have a one-to-one or a one-to-many link, entering or editing a value in a master field changes or enters values in the corresponding linked detail field unless a field has been formatted as DisplayOnly.

7. When all entries have been made in the current record, press DOWN ARROW, PGDN, or click on the speedbar to display a blank form, and then enter values for the next record.

```
≡  Image  Undo  ValCheck  KeepEntry  DO-IT!  Cancel
┌[■]════════════════ Form with order form embedded ════════════[↑]┐
│   ┌─────────────────────────────────────┐                       ▲
│   │         OFFICE INTERIORS INC         │                       ║
│   │             CLIENT LIST              │                       ║
│   └─────────────────────────────────────┘                       ║
│Client ID      130     First Name Ariel          Last Name McNulty║
│                                                                  ║
│                       Company name McNulty Associates            ║
│                       Address 105 Midland Dr.                    ║
│               City Redding              State CA  Zip 96003       ║
│                                                                  ║
│                                                                  ║
│   Emp ID    Ord #      Date       Prod #     Quant    Cost    Total║
│    456      2213     5/05/92       200        1      210.00  210.00║
│                                                                  ║
│                                                                  ║
└═══ 1 of 1 ═════1-M══◄■══════════════════════════════════════════►┘

 F1 Help   F7 Table   Ctrl-PgUp Prev   Ctrl-PgDn Next ▐           ▌ DataEntry ▌
```

Figure 7-19.   *Using a multitable form for DataEntry*

8. When done, press F2 (Do-It!) or click on **Do-It!** to save and clear the images from the desktop.

Editing and CoEditing Using a Multitable Form

When you use **M**odify/**E**dit or **M**odify/**C**oEdit in a multitable form, all previous records will be displayed. You can then either edit the data that is displayed, or you can add new records to the tables included in the form.

To use **M**odify/**E**dit or **M**odify/**C**oEdit, follow these steps:

1. Choose **M**odify/**E**dit or **M**odify/**C**oEdit from the Main menu, and choose the master table.

2. Choose **I**mage/**P**ickForm from the **E**dit or **C**oEdit menu, and choose the form number for the multitable form. The screen will show the values in the first record, as shown in Figure 7-20. Then edit and add records as discussed in the following sections.

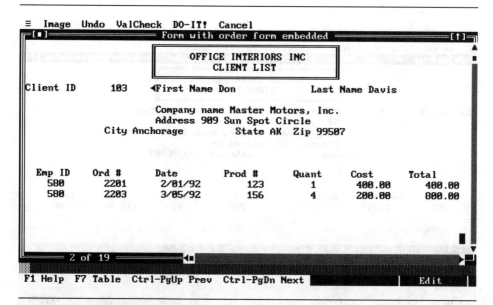

Figure 7-20.   Using Edit or CoEdit with a multitable form

Editing Records

You can go to any record and edit the data. Press F4 (Down Image) or use the mouse to move to the detail section of the form. Press F3 (Up Image) or use the mouse to move back to the previous section in the form. Press the DOWN ARROW, PGDN, or click on the speedbar to go to the next record. When finished, press F2 (Do-It!) or click on **Do-It!** to save the entries. Then press F8 or click on the close box to clear the screen.

Adding Records

To add new records, press END to go to the last record. Press DOWN ARROW, PGDN, or click on the speedbar to go to the next blank form. To insert a blank form between existing records, press INSERT. This is faster that going to the end of the records because less keystrokes are used, and it is also safer if you are working on a network. (Another user could enter a record that gets posted at the end of the table in the time it takes to press END, DOWN ARROW, and PGDN.)

After displaying the blank form, enter the values in the fields. When done, press F2 (Do-It!) or click on **Do-It!** to save the entries. Press F8 or click on the close box to clear the screen.

Using Forms on a Network

When you are designing a form, Paradox puts a *prevent full lock* on the table that is the basis for the form. This allows others nearly full use of that table. At the same time, a *full lock* is placed on the form so that others may not use it in any way while you are working on it. They can still work on the table associated with the form, however.

If the table is being used elsewhere on the network and has a full lock on it, you will have to wait until the full lock is removed before using the table for form design.

The owner of a table can restrict access to it. In that case, you would have to enter a password to use the table for form design.

Chapter 8

Creating and Using Reports

The purpose of a report is to display and print data from existing tables and to arrange the data so that the output is meaningful.

This chapter first covers using InstantReport to instantly produce a standard report based on data in a table. InstantReport is a quick and easy way to print the data contained in a table, and for many it may be the only type of report necessary. However, most of the chapter covers using the Report Designer to create, edit, and use custom reports that can be designed to meet specific needs. The reports discussed here include *tabular reports* that display the data in columns, and *free-form reports* that display the data at any position you choose and can be used to produce form letters, labels, checks, and so on. Reports can be based on data obtained from one table or from multiple tables, or a report can be based on a query.

Using InstantReport

You can use the standard Paradox report form, called the *R report*, by pressing ALT-F7 (InstantReport) to print a tabular report instantly. All data in the table is used for the report and formatted in columns, with the data from each field printed in separate columns. This report does not group records, calculate new fields, or calculate totals and subtotals. If a record contains more fields than will fit on a page, the extra fields print on additional pages. Depending upon the number of fields, the number of records, and the type of printer being used, the data may print on several pages.

In Paradox, the instant, or R, report can also be called the preferred or standard report. This is the report you get automatically when you press ALT-F7 (InstantReport). To use InstantReport, follow these steps:

1. Choose **View** from the Main menu, and then choose the table for the report.

2. Be sure your printer is turned on and that the table is on the desktop and current. Press ALT-F7 (InstantReport). The data is sent directly to the printer.

3. Clear the desktop or work with other Paradox functions.

Report Designer

The Report Designer is similar to the Form Designer in that you use it to design custom reports that fit specific needs. The layout or design of the report is called the *report specification* and is displayed in the Report Designer window when you choose **R**eport/**D**esign from the Main menu. This specification is saved as a part of the table's family of objects. You can design up to 15 different reports for each table. If the table structure changes, the report specifications also change automatically. For example, if you change a field type while restructuring the table, the field type automatically changes in the report too. If a field is deleted in a table, that field is automatically deleted in the report. Changing data in a table does not, however, change the report specification.

Up to 252 fields can be included in a report, and each field can be used 252 times. Also, any number of lookup tables can be linked to the master table in a report, and the fields in the lookup tables can be placed in the report in the same way the fields from the master table are placed. A *lookup table* is one containing data related to the master table, such as a Vendor table related to a master Inventory table. The two files are linked by key fields which are the same in both files. For example, a Vendor ID could be used as the key field linking the Vendor and Inventory tables.

Formats for Reports

As mentioned earlier, there are two types of report formats: tabular and free-form.

- A tabular format automatically places fields in horizontal rows in the report specification. When the report is printed, each column in the report will show data from one of the fields in the table. These fields can be moved, reformatted, or deleted. Figure 8-1 shows an example of a tabular report format.

- A free-form format initially places the fields vertically in the report specification, similar to the standard Paradox form. You can then place them at any location you want in the report. Free-form reports are generally used for form

```
≡  Goto  Search  Cancel
┌[■]════════════════════ Boat Inventory ═══════════════════[↕]┐
│                                                            ▲
│                                                            ■
│   7/07/92                  Boat Inventory           Page   │
│                                                            │
│                                                            │
│ Model no.  Cost              Manufacturer        Name      │
│ ───────── ───────────────── ─────────────────── ────────────
│   15507         9,000.00     Seaview Marine       Seasprite
│   15620        15,750.00     Boats Unlimited      Superski
│   16901        10,000.00     Boats Unlimited      Supersport
│   16911        14,500.00     Boats Unlimited      Superspeed
│   16916        10,000.00     Boats Unlimited      Supercomp
│   17890        12,500.00     Aqua Products        Aquaflite
│   18901         9,750.00     Nelson Marine        Mariner
│                                                            │
│                                                            │
│                                                            │
│                                                            ▼
│■◄■                                                        ■►■
│ F1 Help                                         │ Preview │
└────────────────────────────────────────────────────────────┘
```

Figure 8-1.   *Tabular report format*

letters, labels, invoices, purchase orders, checks, and so on. Figure 8-2 shows a free-form format report.

Basing Reports on Tables

You use reports to arrange and display data from a table, either on paper, on screen, or in a file, and you can base reports on one table or on multiple tables.

There are two ways to combine data from more than one table:

- You can prepare a report that consists of fields from a master table (refer to Chapter 7 for information about master tables in forms), and then, using the Field/Lookup option in the Report Designer, link the lookup tables to the master table.

- You can use the Ask option from the Main menu to query multiple tables. Then base the design of the report on the Answer table (described in Chapter 6).

Report Bands, Masks, and Literals

Reports are made up of several components, as shown in the tabular report in Figure 8-3. The main components are bands, field masks, and literals. An explanation of each follows.

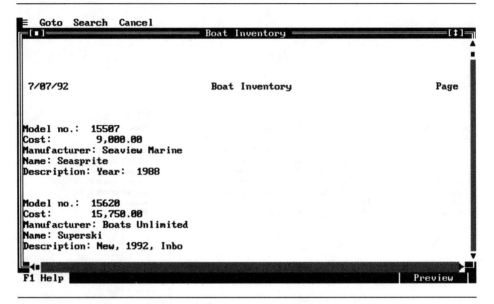

Figure 8-2. *Free-form report format*

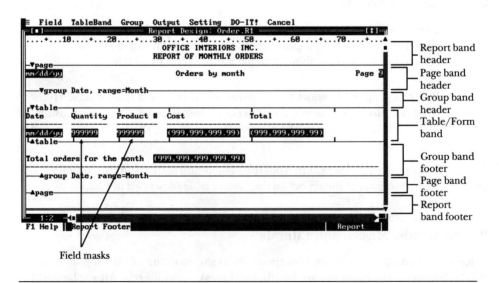

Figure 8-3. *Parts in a tabular report specification*

Bands

Bands are horizontal sections of the report separated by thin lines on screen. (They do not appear on the printed report.) Bands extend across the entire width of a report and are used to control the display of data in specific sections. There are several types of bands, depending on their location and the information they contain.

A *report band* is divided into two parts—one at the top and one at the bottom of the report. The top part is called the *report header*. It generally contains the title, and is printed only at the beginning of the report. The bottom part is called the *report footer* and is printed at the end of the report, but before the last page footer. Report footers may contain summaries or totals of all data in the report.

A *page band* is also divided into a top and bottom part; the *page header* is printed at the top of every page, right below the report header. Page headers often contain page numbers, dates, or subtitles that you want printed on every page. When you choose **R**eport/**D**esign or **R**eport/**C**hange, a dialog box will be displayed where you can enter a description of the report. This description will be entered as the title of the report in the page header. The *page footer* is printed at the bottom of every page before the report footer.

A *group band* is the next layer, and sits within the two halves of the page band layer. It contains a group of records with the band printed once for each group. In the example used in this chapter, records are grouped on the basis of sales for each month. You could also group sales by each sales rep; or in an inventory, group the items by manufacturer or type of product, for example. You can have up to 16 groups in a report. The top part of the group band is the *group header*, which is printed at the top of each group. The bottom part is the *group footer*, which prints at the bottom of each group, above the page band.

A *table band* or *form band* sits in the center of the report. (Tabular reports have a table band and free-form reports have a form band.) These bands contain the fields, labels, text, and data. In a table band, the fields are initially placed in columns. In a form band, the fields are initially placed vertically. In both types of bands, the fields can be moved or deleted.

Field Masks

Field masks represent the values in a field. They show the type and size of the field as it is defined in the table structure. For example, mm/dd/yy represents the date, and tells you that July 4, 1992 will be displayed as 07/04/92. Field masks are placed in the report at the position where the data is to be displayed when the report is printed. There are several types of field masks.

An *alphanumeric field mask* is displayed by a string of A's in the report at the position where the field is placed, as shown in the following illustration. You'll see the same number of A's as there are characters in the field; however, this can be shortened in the report by using **F**ield/**R**eformat. The field mask cannot be widened beyond the width set in the table structure.

```
Manufacturer
-------------------------
AAAAAAAAAAAAAAAAAAAAAAAAAA
```

A *memo field mask* is also displayed by a string of A's. Again, the number of A's is determined by the display width that was set for the memo field in the table structure. The size of the field mask can be changed—either shortened or widened—using Field/**R**eformat.

A *number* or *short field mask* displays a string of 9's in the report at the position of the field, as shown in the following illustration. If the field contains commas and decimals, those will show in the field mask display.

```
Model no.
---------
999999
table
```

A *currency field mask* is also represented by a string of 9's shown with commas and two decimal places and enclosed in parentheses.

A *date field mask* is shown in whatever date format is assigned to the date field that is being represented. For example, mm/dd/yy (shown in the following illustration) or dd-Mon-yy, would be used if one of these is the format used in the table structure for the date field.

```
mm/dd/yy
```

A *current time mask* is shown in the format used in a time field, as in the following illustration. For example, hh:mm pm would result in six o'clock p.m. printing as 6:00 pm.

```
hh:mm pm
```

Literals

Literals (also discussed in Chapter 7) refer to any unchanging text that is entered in the report, such as titles, field labels, or other comments or information.

Page breaks are entered only if needed. You can type the reserved word **PAGEBREAK** wherever you want a new page to start. For example, you can place each group on a new page (or on a free-form report, start each form on a new page) by typing **PAGEBREAK** at the top or bottom of the form band.

The word PAGEBREAK must always be entered in all caps; it must be alone on a separate line and must be at the left margin.

Page widths are also entered only if needed. Paradox automatically splits fields among several page widths if there are more fields than can be printed on one page width. A thick vertical line is displayed showing the page width. The default page width is 80 columns. When the report is printed, all pages in the first page width are printed, then all pages in the next page width are printed, and so on. Since pages don't print in page order, you paginate after printing. You can use **S**etting/**P**ageLayout in the Report Designer to change the page width specifications. You use this primarily in formatting for labels or when you want to print in landscape orientation.

Understanding Report Design

Understanding bands and their relations to each other is an integral part of designing a custom report. When a report is first displayed in the Report Designer window, the bands that are automatically included are report, page, and either a table band if you are using a tabular format, or a form band if you are using a free-form format. The table band and the form band contain the fields from the table you are using. No group bands are shown at this time. You add group bands depending on whether or not you want to group the records by any of the fields and on whatever basis you want to specify the grouping.

Designing the report can include any of the following:

- Entering literals—titles, lines, labels, headers and footers, or any other characters.

- Working with fields—inserting, erasing, moving, reformatting, changing the alignment of values, looking up.

- Working with columns—inserting, moving, resizing, erasing, copying, entering text.

- Working with groups—inserting, entering new fields, adding headings, sorting records, or changing the group specifications.

- Changing the settings that control display of group and table headers, that control the display of repeated values, that affect page layout, set margins, enter pauses, or select new printer ports.

These aspects of report design can be handled in any order. For example, you do not necessarily have to enter text in headers before moving fields. It is a good idea, however, to work with some general plan in mind. Perhaps enter the text in the report header first, then work in the page band, entering any text or fields that should go there, deleting or adding lines, and so on. After that add a group band, if you want to group data, then move or delete fields in the group, add summary fields and text. Finally add text in page and report footers, if you want.

Remember that this order is not required; if you change your mind after entering text or moving fields, you can always make changes to the report. Use the Report Previewer to see how the data will actually look when it is printed, then return to the Report Designer window and make any changes you want before saving the report. Even if you save the report, you can always choose **R**eport/**C**hange from the Main menu to change it later.

The main discussion about reports is in the following section on tabular reports; however, the concepts and menus generally apply to both tabular and free-form reports. The differences between the two types of reports is covered in the section, "Designing Free-Form Reports," later in this chapter.

Designing Tabular Reports Based on a Single Table

A custom designed report can be based on a single table, or it can be based on a master table and linked to one or more lookup tables. (This will be discussed later in this chapter.) The procedures are basically the same for both. Custom designing a report allows you to rearrange and adjust the placement of fields from the table upon which the report is based, so that when the report is printed, the data is presented in a format that may be more appropriate and easier to read than that used in Instant Report.

You can custom design up to 15 different reports for each table in your database. The **R**eport/**D**esign menu is used for this. When you choose **R**eport/**D**esign and then choose the name of the table that is to be the basis for the report, a list of report numbers is displayed. The numbers that are available are labeled "Unused report". The numbers that have been used will be followed by the description or by a blank if no description was entered.

As discussed previously, the report can be designed to display the data in columns, or it can be designed to display the data in free-form format. The advantage of using a free-form format is that you can rearrange the fields to eliminate or reduce spaces between fields. This can make the report more attractive and much easier to use, especially when data from one record will occupy more than one or two lines on the printed report. Tabular reports generally print one record on a single line. You'll see how to use free-form tables later in this chapter.

Choosing the Table and Type of Report

When you the select the table that is to be the basis for the report, you also have to select the type of report—tabular or free-form—that you want to use.

To tell Paradox which type of table you will use, follow these steps:

1. Choose **R**eport/**D**esign from the Main menu, and choose the table that is to be the basis for the report—either type the table name and press ENTER, or press ENTER to see the list of tables, move the highlight to the table you want, and press ENTER again.

2. Choose the report number you want from the displayed list, and press ENTER. The first report is the standard or R report. Choose another report, unless you want to change the standard report. If you have designed several reports, the numbers for those reports will show the description following them (or will be blank if you entered no descriptions).

3. A dialog box for the description is displayed. Type a description for the report, and press ENTER. The description that you type will become the text in the page header band, and it will also be displayed along with the list of numbers mentioned in step 2. If you do not want a description, press ENTER to bypass this dialog box. You'll find it convenient, however, to have the description displayed when you choose the report number later.

4. A menu appears that lets you choose the type of formatting for the report, as shown in Figure 8-4. Choose **T**abular and press ENTER or choose OK.

5. The Report Designer window appears on the desktop, as shown in Figure 8-5. The description entered earlier is now shown as the title in the Page Header section. This title will be printed at the top of every page. The page number and date are automatically provided in the page band. The band name is shown on the bottom left of the status bar.

Using the Report Designer Window

You use the Report Designer window to design a custom report. This window shows the placement of fields, the literals (titles, heading, lines, and any other text that you choose to enter), and the bands that define sections of the report. The menu in the Report Designer window is used to:

- Place and edit various field types

- Reformat, move, delete, or otherwise adjust columns

- Work with groups of records

- Specify the output for the report—printer, screen, or file

- Change the layout—margins, format, or print characteristics

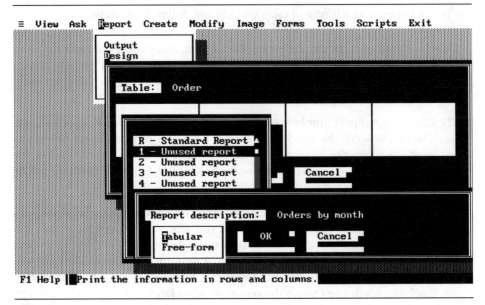

Figure 8-4. *Menu for choosing the type of report format*

 The Report Designer window and menu for free-form reports are slightly different from those for tabular reports. They are covered later in this chapter in the section, "Designing Free-Form Reports."

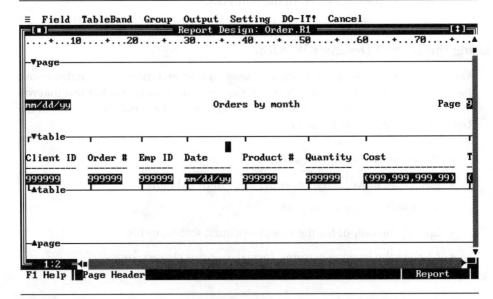

Figure 8-5. *Report Designer window*

The Report Designer window displays the fields that have been placed automatically in columns. As you move the cursor down through the report, the *band* and *field indicator* in the status bar names each part of the report—report header, page header, table band, page footer, report footer, and so on. Also, as the cursor moves onto a field, the field name is displayed in the status bar.

In the window frame, a *page width* display—1:2—shows the current page number and the total number of page widths in the report, as shown in the following illustration. The page width indicator tells the user, not how long the report is, but how wide it is.

You use the System menu in the Report Designer window the same way you use it in other Paradox windows. Refer to Chapter 2 for a discussion of the uses of the System menu.

Entering Literals

Literals refers to all characters that you type in the report. These may include titles, headings, text for summaries, lines of hyphens, or any other characters that may be appropriate for the report you are designing. Move the cursor to the position where you want to enter text, and begin typing. As you enter literals (or text), you may use the following keys to edit:

- BACKSPACE or DELETE to remove characters.

- CTRL-Y to delete a line from the cursor to the end of the line.

- INSERT to toggle between Insert mode and Overwrite mode.

- ENTER to insert a blank line. You must be in Insert mode to do this.

Figure 8-6 shows an example of entering text in a report. A title has been typed in the report header band with a blank line above and below the two lines of text. The title will print only at the top of the first page of the report.

Grouping Data

Grouping records in a report allows you to organize the display of the data on the basis of fields. For example, you might group records in a sales table by item number; or group based on ranges within fields. For example, grouping sales by month would display all records entered between the first and the end of the month. Or you might group specified numbers of records—blank lines will be entered between specified numbers of records so they can be read more easily.

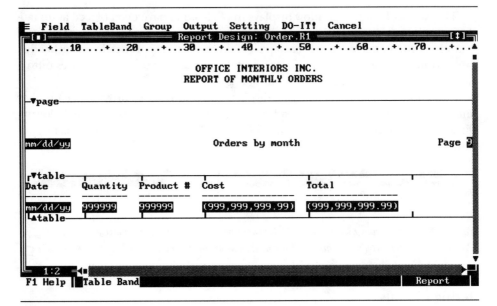

Figure 8-6.   *Text entered in a report design*

You can also summarize results of groups and enter amounts in new *summary* fields, which show the computed value of a group of records, such as total sales for each month.

The specification shown in Figure 8-7 groups the data by the months in which the orders were placed. In addition, a summary of the total amount of orders for each month is shown in the group footer. This requires placing a summary field in the group band (which you will learn how to do later in this chapter). Figure 8-8 shows an example of the output of this report as displayed in the Report Previewer. The data is grouped by months, showing the month, day, and year of each order.

To group data, follow these steps:

1. Choose **G**roup/**I**nsert from the Report Designer menu. Another menu, as displayed in the following illustration, is shown with **F**ield, **R**ange, or NumberRecords as the choices.

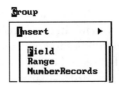

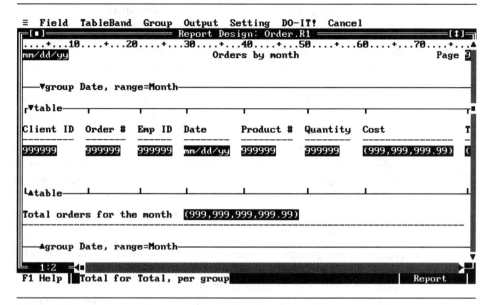

Figure 8-7.   *Report specification for grouping data*

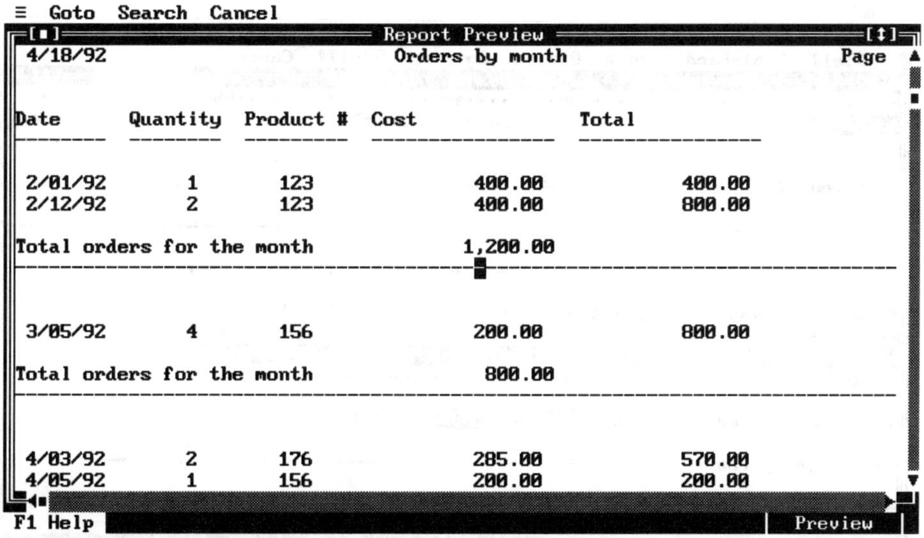

Figure 8-8.   *Output of the report grouping data shown in the Report Previewer*

- *Field* groups records on the basis of the same value in a field. The records will be sorted on the values in the group in ascending order.

- *Range* groups records on the basis of a range of values in a field. For example, in the report shown here, the range consists of all values in a given month. Other examples of ranges could be all amounts between values or between values in a ZIP code. After choosing Range, another dialog box appears asking you to specify the range. What this box asks depends upon the type of field upon which you are basing the range. If you choose an alphanumeric field type, it will ask how many characters to group on. A range size of 1 would group the records on the basis of the first character. If you entered 3, the records would be grouped on the basis of the first three characters. When you choose the date field, you will then be asked to choose whether the range depends on days, weeks, months, or years.

- *NumberRecords* groups records by a specific number of records. This makes the data easier to read by entering a blank line between every specified number of records automatically. You can use this choice in combination with other groupings by placing other groupings outside the NumberRecords group. For example, to display data in groups of five by month, place the NumberRecords group just above the table band. Then place the Range group just above the NumberRecords group. See an example in Figure 8-9.

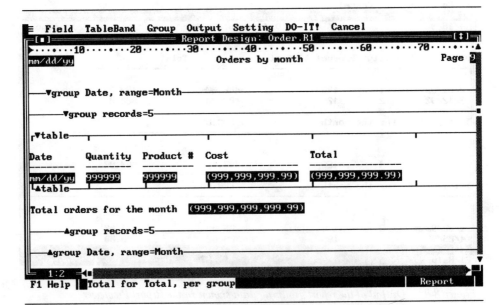

Figure 8-9.   *Example of a NumberRecords group within another group*

2. Choose the type of group you want. In this example, **R**ange is chosen to display records that fall within a certain range. The records in the group would all have the same month in the date field.

3. Depending upon the type of grouping chosen, a second menu appears. This displays a list of the fields in the table. *Date* is chosen as the basis for the group. Another list appears showing the date choices that are available—Day, Week, Month, or Year, as shown in Figure 8-10.

4. Choose appropriate responses in the submenus. (**M**onth is selected here.) You are then returned to the Report Designer window, and a prompt is displayed at the top of the screen asking you for the new position where you want to place the group.

5. Move the cursor within the page band or group band. A group band appears only if a group had been inserted previously. If the cursor is within the table band, an error message appears, as shown here:

```
 Cursor must be within the Page band or a Group band to insert a new
 group
   1:2  ◄■
```

6. When the cursor is at the correct position, press ENTER. A group band is now displayed, as shown in Figure 8-11.

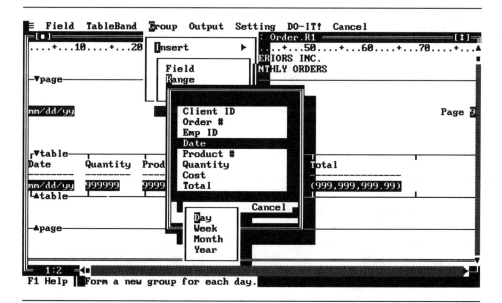

Figure 8-10.   *Grouping by date*

```
≡  Field  TableBand  Group  Output  Setting  DO-IT!  Cancel
[■]════════════════════ Report Design: Order.R1 ════════════════[‡]═
....+...10....+...20....+...30....+...40....+...50....+...60....+...70....+...▲


mm/dd/yy                          Orders by month                      Page 9■

  ──▼group Date, range=Month─────────────────────────────────────────────────

  ┌▼table─────────────────────────────────────────────────────────
  Date     Quantity   Product #  Cost              Total
  ─────    ────────   ────────   ──────────────    ──────────────
  mm/dd/yy 999999     999999     (999,999,999.99)  (999,999,999.99)
  └▲table─────────────────────────────────────────────────────────
  ─────────────────────────────────────────────────────────────────

  ──▲group Date, range=Month─────────────────────────────────────────────────

                                                                           ▼
  1:2  ◄■                                                              ■
  F1 Help ▌Group Footer for Date, range=Month                 │  Report │
```

Figure 8-11.   *Placement of the group band*

Options in the Group Menu

The options in the Group menu allow you to work with groups of records, as discussed in the previous section. The options in this menu are shown in the following illustration:

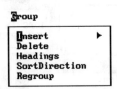

Insert   Use this option to place a group in the report. Choose **Insert/Field** to group records that have the same value in a field. Choose **Insert/R**ange to group records within a specified range, such as by date. Choose **Insert/NumberRecords** to group records according to a specified number, such as 2, 5, or 10.

Delete   Use this option to remove a group from the report. You will be asked to move the cursor to the group to be deleted, and to press ENTER. You will then get to confirm or cancel the deletion.

When you delete a group, everything in the group—including calculated fields, titles, borders, and other literals—will be deleted.

Headings This option controls printing group headers, if you have entered text for this. A group header is always printed at the beginning of each group. It is also printed on what Paradox refers to as *spillover* pages—that is, when a group cannot be printed entirely on a single page, the remainder of the group is printed on another page. If you do not want the heading to be printed on a spillover page, but only at the beginning of each group, choose **Headings/G**roup. The other option is **H**eadings/**P**age which would print the headings on the spillover page as well as at the beginning of each group. See the next section, "Entering Text in a Group Header or Footer," for further information.

SortDirection This option sorts groups of records in either ascending or descending order. The sort orders apply to number fields in numeric order, alphanumeric and memo fields in alphabetical order, and date fields from earliest to latest, which is ascending order, or from latest to earliest which is descending order. The sort order for alphanumeric fields is based on the country group that was selected during Paradox installation.

Regroup The Regroup option changes the way the group was set up. If you decide to change the field upon which the group was based, or if you want to change the range—in the example used here, you might decide to change the range of the group from months to weeks—use the **R**egroup option. Or you can use this option to change the number of records specified for a group—change from 5 to 10, for example. The procedure is basically the same as inserting a group initially. Choose **R**egroup and then choose one of the following:

- *Field* if you want to change the field that is the basis for the group

- *Range* to change the range for the group

- *NumberRecords* to change the number of records to be grouped

*You cannot use **R**egroup to change the placement of a group relative to other groups. To do this, you would have to delete the group and then insert it at another position.*

Entering Text in a Group Header or Footer

To enter text in a group header or footer, move the cursor to the group header or footer area—confirm the position in the status bar. Then type the text at the position you want. You can press ENTER to insert blank lines, but you have to be in Insert mode to do this. Figure 8-12 shows the text "Total orders for the month" and a dashed line

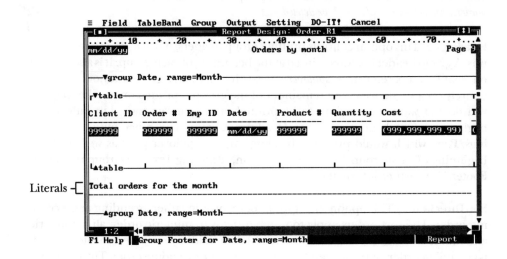

```
  ≡  Field  TableBand  Group  Output  Setting  DO-IT!  Cancel
     ┌[■]════════════════ Report Design: Order.R1 ═══════════════════[↕]┐
     ....+...10....+...20....+...30....+...40....+...50....+...60....+...70....+...▲
     mm/dd/yy                          Orders by month                      Page 9

        ┌─▼group Date, range=Month────────────────────────────────────────
        │ ┌─▼table─────────┬────────┬────────┬────────┬────────┬──────────
        │ │
        │ │Client ID  Order #  Emp ID  Date    Product #  Quantity  Cost            T
        │ │─────────  ───────  ──────  ────    ─────────  ────────  ────
        │ │999999     999999   999999  mm/dd/yy 999999    999999   (999,999,999.99)  (
        │ │
        │ │
        │ └─▲table─────────┴────────┴────────┴────────┴────────┴──────────
Literals ─┤ Total orders for the month
        │ ├──────────────────────────────────────────────────────────────
        │ └─▲group Date, range=Month────────────────────────────────────────
     └═══ 1:2 ═◄■══════════════════════════════════════════════════════════▼═┘
       F1 Help  Group Footer for Date, range=Month                Report
```

Figure 8-12.   Literals in a group band

below that have been entered with blank lines above and below. These blanks lines visually separate the groups and make the output of the report easier to read.

If you entered extra lines in any of the bands and decide later that you want to delete them, move the cursor to the leftmost column for that line and press CTRL-Y to delete the blank line.

Placing a Summary Field in a Group Band

A summary field can be entered in a group band that displays a summary of values in the group. This can be entered at any appropriate position in the group band. Figure 8-13 shows a summary field placed after the text, "Total orders for the month," in the group band. This is a new field—one that isn't in the table—that will show the total amount of sales for each month.

To place a summary field, follow these steps:

1. Choose **F**ield/**P**lace/**S**ummary from the Report Designer menu. A second menu is displayed. Choose one of the following:

   • *Regular* summarizes data from a specific field in the table. A list of fields in the table is displayed when **R**egular is chosen. Choose the field that is to be the basis for the group (Date was chosen here) and press ENTER.

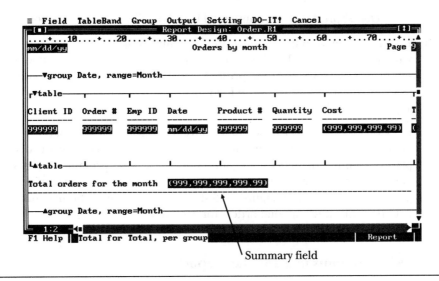

≡ Field TableBand Group Output Setting DO-IT! Cancel
═══════════════════ Report Design: Order.R1 ═══════════════[↕]═
....+...10....+...20....+...30....+...40....+...50....+...60....+...70....+...▲
mm/dd/yy   Orders by month   Page 9

───▼group Date, range=Month───

┌▼table─────────┬───────┬───────┬──────┬────────┬──────┬────────┬────────
│
│Client ID Order # Emp ID Date   Product # Quantity Cost   T
│   ────── ────── ────   ───────   ──────   ──────────────
│999999   999999   999999 mm/dd/yy 999999   999999   (999,999,999.99) (
│
│
└▲table─────────┴───────┴───────┴──────┴────────┴──────┴────────┴────────

Total orders for the month (999,999,999,999.99)
───

───▲group Date, range=Month───

  1:2 ◄■
F1 Help ┃Total for Total, per group   │   Report

'Summary field

Figure 8-13.   *Report showing a summary field in a group band*

- *Calculated* summarizes values that are calculated from other fields in the report. Calculated can be used to combine the results of a horizontal calculation as displayed in a calculated field, with the vertical calculation displayed in a summary field. An expression that will produce the summary is required. Type the expression and press ENTER.

2. A menu of summary calculations is then displayed, as shown in Figure 8-14. The menu gives you these choices:

   - *Sum* will display a total of the amount of the fields in the group.

   - *Average* will produce an average of the values of the fields in the group.

   - *Count* will count the number of values of the fields in the group.

   - *High* will display the high value of a field in the group.

   - *Low* will display the low value of a field in the group.

*You can enter the summary operators shown here in the calculated expression, if you like. For example, type **sum([total])** to display an amount that adds all the values in the total field and enters it in the new summary field.*

3. Choose the summary calculation you want. Another menu is shown, from which you choose one of the following:

- *PerGroup* will produce a subtotal based on the values in the group.

- *Overall* produces a running total based on all values in the report so far.

4. You are returned to the window, and a prompt is displayed at the top of the screen to place the field. Move the cursor to the position where you want the summary to be displayed, and press ENTER. A second prompt is displayed that lets you adjust the width of the field. If the field is a numeric field, you can adjust the number of digits.

5. Press RIGHT ARROW or LEFT ARROW to adjust the width of the field or the number of digits, and press ENTER. Another prompt is then displayed to set the decimal places. All numeric fields—N, S, and $—get the same prompt for digits and decimals. Press RIGHT ARROW or LEFT ARROW to set the number of decimal places and press ENTER. Figure 8-13 shows an example of the new summary field that will show the total orders for each month.

Working with Columns in a Tabular Report

As shown in Figure 8-15, the Report Designer defines columns by a horizontal line at the top of the table band with vertical lines below it indicating the position of each of the columns.

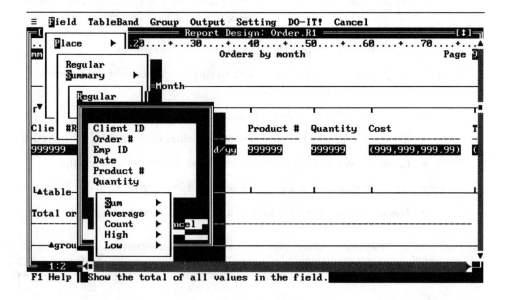

Figure 8-14.   Menus used to place a summary field

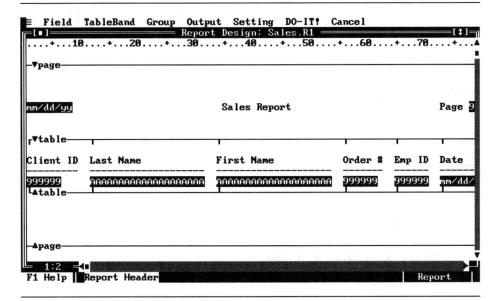

Figure 8-15.   *Vertical lines off the table band line mark the position of each column*

The columns contain the label for the field, a hyphenated line separating the label from the field mask, and the field mask below that represents the actual placement of the field. These columns can be erased, moved, copied, or resized. Additional columns can be inserted and new fields placed in them if there is enough room in the table band. If there is not enough room, you can use Setting/PageLayout to increase the page width, or you can erase or resize existing columns.

The TableBand option in the Report Designer lets you erase, move, insert, resize, or copy columns.

Fields, columns, and groups can be inserted in any order as the report is being designed. You do not necessarily have to group data before moving columns or inserting fields.

Erasing Columns

You can delete columns that are not pertinent to a particular report. You may want to do this to allow the remaining columns to be displayed on one page width.

To erase columns, follow these steps:

1. Choose **TableBand/Erase** from the Report Designer menu. A prompt is displayed to move to the column to be erased.

2. Move the cursor to the column to be erased and press ENTER. The column, including the label, hyphenation line, and field mask, is removed from the report.

Moving Columns

The TableBand/**M**ove option moves the entire column, which consists of all fields, labels, and hyphenated lines in the column.

You can use CTRL-R (Rotate) to rearrange the fields in the report, as you can in tables. Pressing CTRL-R on a field moves it to the right end of the report.

To move a column, follow these steps:

1. Choose **T**ableBand/**M**ove from the Report Designer menu. A prompt is displayed at the top of the screen to move to the column to be moved.

2. Move the cursor to the column you want to move. The cursor can be placed at any point in the column. Press ENTER when you have selected the column.

3. Another prompt, shown here, tells you how to position the column:

Now use → and ← to show the new location. then press ↵ .

4. Press RIGHT ARROW or LEFT ARROW to move to the new position, and press ENTER. The entire column, including the labels and hyphenated lines, is moved, pushing other columns, if any, to the left or to the right.

Inserting Columns

Insert is used to place a column in the report. If you create a new field—a calculated field, for example—and want to place it in the table, you must first create a column for it.

To insert a column, follow these steps:

1. Choose **T**ableBand/**I**nsert from the Report Designer menu.

2. Move the cursor to the position for the new column, and press ENTER. The new column is inserted in front of columns that are to the right of the cursor. If the cursor is following the last column in the table band, then the new column will be at the end or to the right of the other columns.

The default width of a new column is 15 characters. If there is not enough room for the column in the existing table band, use **T**ableBand/**E**rase or **T**ableBand/**R**esize to remove or reduce the size of another existing column. You can also use **S**etting/**P**ageLayout to increase the size of the page width.

Resizing a Column

Resize is used to adjust the width of a column. Do this to reduce the size of a column to make room for other columns, or to increase the size of the column if you need more room on the page to display the values.

To resize a column, follow these steps:

1. Choose **T**ableBand/**R**esize from the Report Designer menu.

2. Move the cursor to the exact location where you want to adjust the spacing, to the right of the space you want to remove, or to the left of the space to be added, and press ENTER. You cannot place the cursor within the field; doing so will cause an error.

3. You are then prompted to resize the column by pressing RIGHT ARROW to increase the size or LEFT ARROW to reduce it. When you have resized the column as you wish, press ENTER.

Reducing the size of a column requires using three different operations: Use **F**ield/**R**eformat to reduce the field mask to the size you want displayed. Use DELETE to delete the characters in the label and in the hyphenated line to reduce the size of the column. Use **T**ableBand/**R**esize to resize the column, moving the adjoining fields into the reduced space.

*A column cannot be reduced less than the field size—use **F**ield/**R**eformat for that. Also, if you are reducing the width of the column, you cannot position the cursor in the label or any other literals in the column. To reduce the label or other literals, just delete the characters using the DELETE key.*

Copying a Column

Copy is used to copy the column and its contents and place the duplicate at a new position.

To copy a column, follow these steps:

1. Choose **T**ableBand/**C**opy from the Report Designer menu.

2. Move the cursor to the column to be copied, and press ENTER. You are prompted to move to the location where you want to place the copy.

3. Move the cursor to that position, and press ENTER. Other fields will be moved automatically to the right.

As in other actions using the **TableBand** menu, if there is not enough room, you can use the **Resize** option or the **Erase** option to make room for the copied column. You can also make a new page width, if necessary.

Working with Fields

When you have a tabular report displayed in the Report Designer window, the fields from the table are automatically displayed in columns. The fields are represented by masks (discussed earlier in this chapter). The mask consists of either A's representing the number of alphanumeric characters allowed in the field, or by 9's representing numeric, short number, or currency amounts in the field. You can print the report leaving the fields as they are; however, you may want to manipulate the fields using the **Field** options.

The options in the **Field** menu are used to manipulate the size, placement, and look of fields. You can insert or place a field using **P**lace; delete a field using **E**rase; change the size or display of a field using **R**eformat; or realign data within a field with **J**ustify. Use **C**alcEdit to edit the expression for a calculated field, and use **W**ordWrap to allow longer fields to wrap around to the next line. Use the last option, **L**ookup, to retrieve data from other tables. The **Field** menu is shown here:

You can work with fields at any time in the Report Designer. There is no particular order for working with fields, columns, or groups.

Moving Fields

There is no Move option in the **Field** menu. If you want to push fields (not an entire column) to the left or right *on the same line,* press INSERT to change to Insert mode, move the cursor to the left of the field mask, and press the SPACEBAR to move the field to the right, or press BACKSPACE or DELETE (depending upon the cursor position) to move the field to the left. This is an alternate way to perform **Table Band/Resize**.

To move the field to a new position, follow these steps:

1. Choose **Field/Erase** from the Report Designer menu.

2. Move the cursor to the field to be deleted, and press ENTER.

3. Choose **F**ield/**P**lace/**R**egular, choose the field name, move the cursor to the new position, and press ENTER.

4. Adjust the width and press ENTER to place the field in a new position.

Placing a Field

Place is used to insert or place various types of fields in a report. When placing a field, select the field from the list of table field names, move the cursor to the location you want, and press ENTER. A field mask consisting of characters representing the field is automatically displayed in the field location. You then adjust the width of the field. Respond to the prompts at the top of the screen for directions, which differ depending upon the type of field you are placing. You can use **F**ield/**R**eformat later to change field size, if you like.

To place a field, choose **F**ield/**P**lace from the Report Designer menu and choose the type from the following list:

Regular   Use this option to place fields that are currently in the table used for the report. When you choose this option, a menu displaying the list of fields in the table is displayed. Choose the field you want, and then respond to the prompts at the top of the screen to place the field where you want it in the report. The two exceptions are BLOB and OTHER field types. These cannot be printed in a report.

Summary   Use this option to place a field that summarizes values in a group or column. This creates a new field, consisting of the sum, average, a count, or the maximum or minimum values of fields in a group or column. Refer to the section, "Placing a Summary Field in a Group Band."

Calculated   Use this option to place new fields that contain the results of calculated expressions. When you choose this option, a dialog box appears asking for the expression. Enter an expression like the expressions entered in other calculation fields. "Using Calculations" in Chapter 6 and "Inserting Calculated Fields" in Chapter 7 give examples of calculation expressions.

Expressions can be arithmetic; they can combine table field names enclosed in brackets—for example, [city] + [state] would combine the values in those two fields in one field. They can include constant values such as alphabetical characters, decimal numbers, or dates, or the summary operators SUM, AVERAGE, COUNT, HIGH, and LOW. Later in this chapter, the section "Creating a Report Containing Calculated and Calculated Summary Fields" will show how to place these fields and give examples of expressions that can be entered here. You can also use PAL variables and functions, and embed printer setup strings to style the report. (*Setup strings* are groups of characters sent to the printer that specify using printer options such as italic, bold, or condensed print.) This is discussed in more detail later in the section, "Changing the Printer Setup."

Calculated fields can also be used to make font changes within a report. The Report Designer is not specifically set up to support formatting changes, such as adding bold, underlining, or expanded or condensed printing. Therefore, if you want to make these types of changes, you can enter the printer control code for the type of attribute you want in the expression dialog box for a calculated field. Then place it at the beginning of the characters where you want to make the change. At the end of the area where you want to make the change, enter a calculated field containing the control code for returning to the original font. (Refer to your printer manual for the various control codes needed to produce the results you want.) The following illustration shows an example of adding bold to the title of a report if you were using an Epson LQ 1500 printer. The fields, each containing a single *A* for the field mask, are placed in front and directly following the title.

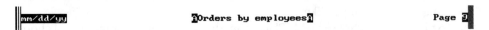

To do this, choose **Field/Place/Ca**lculated, and in the expression dialog box, type the control code for the font you want. Shown in the next illustration, the printer control code is **"\027E"** for printing in Epson Emphasized mode. The code must be enclosed in quotation marks. After typing the code, press ENTER and then follow the screen directions to move the cursor to the position where you want the code. Press ENTER, adjust the width, and press ENTER again.

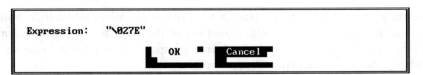

Repeat this procedure, placing another calculated field at the end of the area that is to be formatted with the attribute just entered. In the expression dialog box, type the code for returning to the original font. In this case, **"\027@"** is entered to return to the Epson Master Reset mode. The following illustration shows an example of this. Then follow the screen prompts to place and adjust the field.

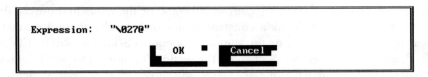

 If you want to change the font for the entire report before printing, you can enter these control codes in the Setting/Setup/Custom/Setup String dialog box. This is discussed in the section on using the Setting menu.

Date   Use this option to place the current date when the report is printed in the report. Choose **D**ate, select the format you want for the date, and respond to the prompts to place it in the report. Your system clock must be accurate for this field to enter the correct date.

Time   Use this option to place the current time when the report is printed in the report. Choose **T**ime, select the format for the time, and respond to the prompts to place it in the report. Again, the system clock must be accurate for this field to enter the correct time.

Page   Use this option to place the page number field at whatever position in the report that you want. The page number field is placed in the page header by default, but you can change this, if you like, perhaps to a page footer. You should keep the page number in a page header or page footer. If you move the page number field to a place other than in the page header or footer, you might not get page numbers printed accurately or in the position you want on each page.

#Record   Use this option to place a number for each record included in the report. When choosing this option, a second menu is displayed with the following options:

- *PerGroup* is chosen if you want to begin renumbering at the beginning of each group.

- *Overall* is chosen if you want to display the numbers consecutively throughout the report and not start renumbering at the beginning of each group.

Erasing a Field

Erase is used to remove a field from its current position. Do this when you want to make room for other fields on the page, or if the field is not needed in the report. Choose **F**ield/**E**rase, move the cursor to the field to be removed, and press ENTER.

Reformatting a Field

Reformat is used to change the way a field is displayed in the report. The changes allowed and the choices in submenus depend upon the type of field being reformatted.

Alphanumeric and Memo Fields   These can only be changed by changing the number of characters that can be displayed in the field. Choose **F**ield/**R**eformat, move the cursor to the field to be changed, press ENTER, adjust the width by pressing RIGHT ARROW to increase the width or LEFT ARROW to reduce the width, and press ENTER again.

Numeric Fields   These can be changed with the **R**eformat option in four ways: the number of digits or decimal places can be changed, the way signs are shown for negative and positive numbers can be specified, commas can be placed or not, and the U.S. convention for formatting numbers can be changed to an international convention.

Choose **F**ield/**R**eformat, move the cursor to the numeric field to be changed and press ENTER. A menu showing **D**igits, **S**ign-Convention, **C**ommas, and International will be displayed, as shown here:

Choose the option for the type of change you want to make, and respond to the menu prompts and message bar at the bottom of the screen to make changes.

- *Digits* lets you increase or decrease first the digits and then the decimal places of a number. Press the LEFT or RIGHT ARROW to reduce or increase the digits in the number and press ENTER. Then press the LEFT or RIGHT ARROW to reduce or increase the decimal places in the number, and press ENTER.

- *Sign-Convention* lets you specify the way a sign will be displayed for a positive or negative number. When you choose this option, this menu will be displayed:

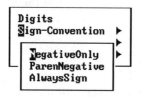

Choose **N**egativeOnly if you want a minus sign in front of negative numbers only, such as –546.72. No sign will be used for positive numbers. Choose **P**arenNegative if you want negative numbers surrounded by parentheses, such as (546.72), and no sign for positive numbers. Choose AlwaysSign if you want a sign displayed for both negative and positive numbers, such as +546.72 or –546.72.

- *Commas* lets you specify whether to display numbers with commas, such as 5,297,260.07, or without commas, such as 5297260.07.

- *International* lets you specify the U.S. convention to format numbers with comma separators and a period for decimal places, such as 6,547.36. Or you can select the InternationalConvention option, which uses periods as separators and a comma as a decimal place, such as 6.547,36.

Date Fields   These can be changed to display the values in a different format. Choose **Field/Reformat**, move the cursor to the Date field and press ENTER. A list of date formats is displayed, as shown in the following illustration:

Choose the new format and press ENTER.

Time Fields   These can also be changed to display the values in a different format. Choose **Field/Reformat**, move the cursor to the Time field and press ENTER. A choice between displaying regular and military time will be displayed, as shown here:

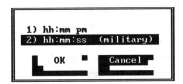

Choose the new format you want, and press ENTER.

Page and #Record Fields   These can only be changed by adjusting the width of the field. Choose **Field/Reformat**, move to the field to be changed, press ENTER, and then adjust the width, using LEFT ARROW to decrease the size and RIGHT ARROW to increase it, and press ENTER again.

Aligning Values

Justify is used to specify the alignment of values in a field. The choices are to justify characters at the left edge of the field, in the center of the field, at the right edge of the field, or use default, which returns the alignment to the default for that particular field. Alphanumeric and memo fields are justified by default at the left. Numeric fields are justified at the right and at their decimal points, if there are decimals.

Choose **Field/Justify**, move the cursor to the field you want and press ENTER. A list of alignment options will be displayed: **L**eft, **C**enter, **R**ight, and **D**efault. Choose the one you want and press ENTER.

Editing Calculations

CalcEdit is used to edit calculation expressions in a calculated field or in a calculated summary field. Choose **Field/CalcEdit**, move the cursor to the Calculation field, and press ENTER. The expression for that field will be displayed in a dialog box, as shown in the following illustration. Edit the expression and press ENTER to return to the report.

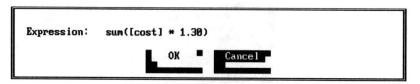

Using WordWrap

WordWrap specifies that text in an alphanumeric field can be wrapped to the next line in fields where the values don't fit on one line. WordWrap will not break words in the middle, but if a word does not fit on the first line, the entire word will be moved to the next line. When you use this option, you will be asked to enter the number of lines for the field. You can enter any number of lines up to 255 for an alphanumeric field. For a memo field, you can enter **v** for *variable*. This allows as many lines as needed for the field. If you want to prevent text from being wrapped onto a line, you can preserve a blank line by typing the reserved word **BLANKLINE** at the beginning of the line.

To use this option, choose **Field/WordWrap**, move the cursor to the field you want, and press ENTER. A dialog box will appear, as shown here, asking for the number of lines.

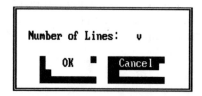

Enter the number of lines, or for a Memo field, the value **V**, and press ENTER.

Using Lookup

Lookup is used to combine information from additional tables with the data in the master table. The options in the submenu are used to link lookup tables or to unlink a table. This will be covered in more detail later in this chapter in the "Designing Tabular Reports Based on Multiple Tables" section.

Using the Setting Menu for Tabular Reports

You use the Setting menu in the Report Designer to change the format of the report. This includes changing the length and width of the page, changing the margins, setting printing options, and controlling the relationship between group and table headers. The Setting menu options for a tabular report are somewhat different than those for a free-form report. Refer to the "Designing Free-Form Reports" section later in this chapter for information about the Setting menu. The Setting menu is shown here:

Formatting Settings

The Format menu, shown in the following illustration, is used to change the display of group and table headers. The default—the TableOfGroups format—prints the table header at the top of each page, with the group headers printed under it. The other choice in this menu is GroupsOfTables, and it is just the opposite of TableOfGroups. If you choose GroupsOfTables, then the group headers are printed above the table headers.

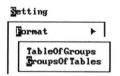

The following illustration shows the Report Designer with a group header and table header.

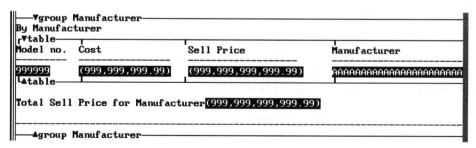

When TableOfGroups is used, as shown next, the table header (field names and hyphenated lines) are printed only once at the top of the page. The group header (which is text you can enter—here it is "By Manufacturer") is printed in every group.

```
Model no.  Cost                   Sell Price             Manufacturer
---------  --------------         --------------------   ----------------------
By Manufacturer
  17890        12,500.00                   16,250.00     Aqua Products

Total Sell Price for Manufacturer          16,250.00


By Manufacturer
  15620        15,750.00                   20,475.00     Boats Unlimited
  16901        10,000.00                   13,000.00     Boats Unlimited
  16911        14,500.00                   18,850.00     Boats Unlimited
  16916        10,000.00                   13,000.00     Boats Unlimited

Total Sell Price for Manufacturer          81,575.00
```

When **Groups**OfTables is chosen, the table header (field names and lines) is printed at the top of each group and the group header is printed above it. An example is shown here:

```
By Manufacturer
Model no.  Cost                   Sell Price             Manufacturer
---------  --------------         --------------------   ----------------------
  17890        12,500.00                   16,250.00     Aqua Products

Total Sell Price for Manufacturer          16,250.00


By Manufacturer
Model no.  Cost                   Sell Price             Manufacturer
---------  --------------         --------------------   ----------------------
  15620        15,750.00                   20,475.00     Boats Unlimited
  16901        10,000.00                   13,000.00     Boats Unlimited
  16911        14,500.00                   18,850.00     Boats Unlimited
  16916        10,000.00                   13,000.00     Boats Unlimited

Total Sell Price for Manufacturer          81,575.00
```

Repeating Group Values

You use **G**roupRepeats to specify whether or not to display repeated values that the field used to group the records. The default is **R**etain, which prints all values. The other choice is **S**uppress, which prints only the value from the field used to group in the first record—values in this field (which are always the same) are suppressed.

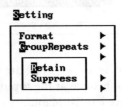

The following illustration shows a report that suppresses group values. Here the name of the boat manufacturer in each group is printed only once. It is not repeated for each record.

```
By Manufacturer
 15620          15,750.00          20,475.00      Boats Unlimited
 16901          10,000.00          13,000.00
 16911          14,500.00          18,850.00
 16916          10,000.00          13,000.00

Total Sell Price for Manufacturer       81,575.00
```

Setting PageLayouts

You use **PageLayout** to format the length and width of the page and to add or delete extra pages. **PageLayout**, shown next, gives you these options:

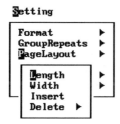

- *Length* is used to specify the number of lines in a page. The page length can be set anywhere from 2 to 2000 lines. The default is 60 lines per page. When **Length** is chosen, a dialog box is then displayed where the new page length is entered. Enter **C** for continuous to print the entire report on one long page. This is used primarily for continuous-feed labels.

- *Width* is used to either increase or decrease the width of the page. The default is 80 characters. When **Width** is chosen, a dialog box appears that lets you enter the number of characters for the page. You can enter from 10 to 2000 characters depending on your printer.

- *Insert* is used to insert another page width at the right of the existing page. This page will be the same width as the existing page.

- *Delete* is used to remove page widths that have been added to the first page width. When this is used, all fields appearing in the deleted page width are removed from the report.

Setting Margins

You use **Margin** to increase or decrease the size of the left margin. When **Margin** is chosen, a dialog box appears asking for the number of spaces you want the left margin to be. You can enter only a number representing characters—not inches, picas, and so on. The default here is 0, which prints the data beginning at the left side of the paper. Enter a new number here to format the page with a wider left margin. You can enter any number as long as that number doesn't extend the margin beyond the size of the page.

 *Enter **10** for a 1-inch left margin, if you are printing with fonts that equal 10 characters per inch.*

To create other margins (top, bottom, or right), you must modify the report itself. For example, to change a top margin, work with the blank lines in the page header; a bottom margin, the blank lines in the page footer. Right margins can be increased or decreased by changing the width of the page or the column sizes. Place the fields where you want them to be on the report.

Changing the Printer Setup

Use **Setup** to choose a printer port other than the default printer port. **Setup** can also be used to enter a string that gives specific instructions to control the printer. Generally this is not needed. Paradox is set up to work with most IBM-compatible printers. When you choose **Setup**, you have two choices as shown here:

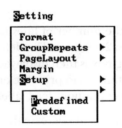

- *Predefined* shows a list of setup strings for each predefined setup as shown in the following illustration. Choose the one that meets your needs.

- *Custom* is used when you want to choose a different printer port and/or enter your own string.

When you choose **S**etup/**C**ustom, a list of printer ports is displayed. Choose the one you want. A Setup string dialog box is then displayed, as shown next. If a string had been entered previously, it will be displayed in the box. You can press ENTER to accept it, or enter a new string. The string can be up to 175 characters long. You can enter characters, or enter ASCII values that represent characters. Press ENTER to display the Reset string dialog box and enter a reset string, which is sent after printing. When a PostScript printer is being used, both a setup string and a reset string are required, as discussed next.

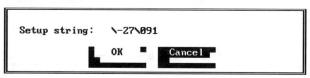

The setup string specifies how you want your report to be printed. For example, if you are using a Toshiba P351 printer and want to print in compressed mode, type \027\091 in the Setup string dialog box. To return to normal mode after printing, in the Reset string dialog box, type \027\0261. To get help in determining which string to enter, refer to Appendix C in the *Paradox 4 User's Guide*, which includes a list of printers and the codes that instruct the printer to select various modes, or perform actions that you want. If you still are not getting the results you want, consult your printer's manual for further information.

Here are some tips for entering strings:

- To enter more than one code, type one directly following another *without entering a space* between the codes.

- Type **1** for the number one, and type a lowercase **l** for the alphabet character l. Do not substitute the letter "el" for the number 1.

- Type **0** (zero) for the number 0. Type a capital **O** for the uppercase letter "oh".

- To enter a control command (a command that uses the CTRL key with another key), type \0 and the ASCII code that represents the letter. Refer to Appendix C in this book for a list of ASCII codes.

- Test several strings. You may not get the results you want with your first entry.

- If your printer is not listed in Appendix C in the *Paradox 4 User's Guide*, enter a string for a printer that is close to the one you are using.

The information pertaining to strings also applies when you choose Report/SetPrinter/Override/Setup from the Paradox Main menu. However, when a string is entered in this way, it stays in effect only for the current Paradox session or until you change the string during the current session.

You can also change the setup string from System/Utilities/Custom.

Using a PostScript Printer   Paradox supplies two printer files containing setup information for a PostScript printer—PDOXPORT.PS for portrait orientation and PDOXLAND.PS for landscape orientation. The name of the file you want is entered in the Setup string dialog box. Choose **S**etting/**S**etup/**C**ustom and select the printer port you want. A dialog box for the Setup string is displayed where you can type either **file=pdoxport.ps** to specify portrait, or **file=pdoxland.ps** to specify landscape. An example is shown here:

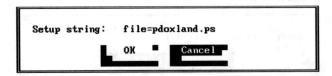

Press ENTER to display the Reset dialog box and type **\004** to enter the reset string, as in the following example. Press ENTER when done.

Portrait orientation *prints text vertically on a page—the length of the page is greater than the width.* Landscape orientation *prints text horizontally—the width of the page is greater than the length.*

Using Wait to Enter a Pause

Wait is used to enter a pause between pages to allow you to manually feed paper into the printer. Choose **N**o if you do not want the printer to pause; **Y**es if you do. This is used primarily for printing on letterhead stationery or forms that won't feed automatically through the printer.

Creating a Report Containing Calculated and Calculated Summary Fields

As described earlier in this chapter, new calculated fields can be placed that will show the result of entering an expression. Calculated summary fields can also be placed that show summaries of the calculated fields; however, you can enter a calculated summary field without necessarily having calculated fields in the report.

In the examples shown in Figure 8-16 (the report specifications) and in Figure 8-17 (the report output), records are grouped by manufacturer, and a calculated field, "Sell Price" is placed after the Cost field. The expression in this field is **[cost] * 1.30**, which will multiply the value in the Cost field by 1.30, showing a markup of 30 percent. A calculated summary field is placed in the group band that contains the expression **sum([cost] * 1.30)**. This expression calculates the sum of the values in the new calculated field in the group band.

You do not necessarily have to group records to insert calculated and calculated summary fields.

When entering expressions, enclose existing field names in brackets—**[cost]**, for example. Arithmetic operators, plus (+), minus (–), multiply (*), and divide (/) can be entered to produce the results you want. When you use the summary operators, SUM, AVERAGE, COUNT, HIGH, or LOW, they do not have to be typed in upper-case, but are shown here in uppercase to distinguish them from other text. The field name of a new calculated field is displayed in the status bar at the bottom of the screen when you move your cursor to the new field. This field name, which is the expression that was entered when the field was placed, is typed in parentheses following the summary operator when you want to include the field name in a calculated summary field—**average([cost] * 1.30)**, for example.

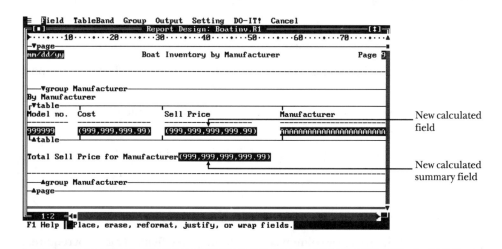

Figure 8-16. *Report Designer showing report for boat inventory containing calculated and calculated summary fields*

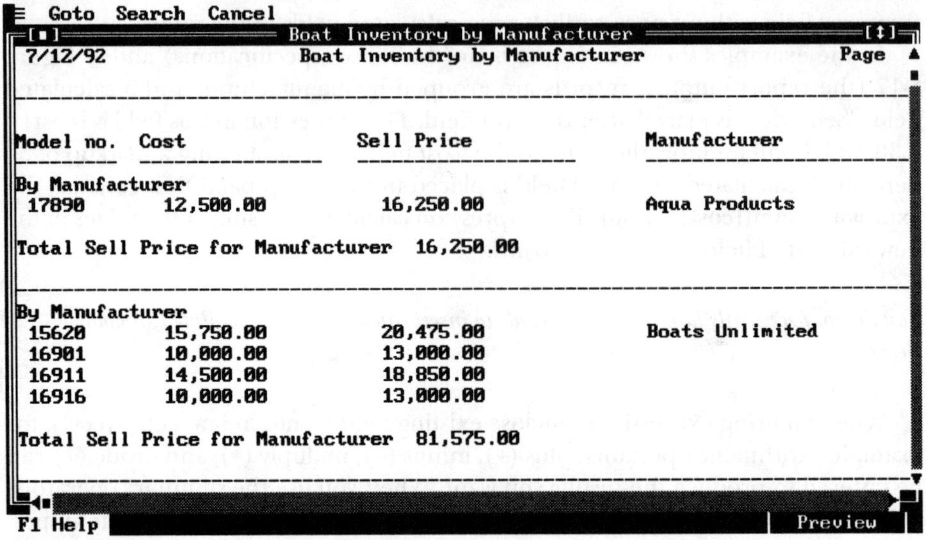

```
≡  Goto  Search  Cancel
┌[■]════════════════ Boat Inventory by Manufacturer ═══════════════[↕]┐
│  7/12/92                Boat Inventory by Manufacturer          Page  ▲
│                                                                      ■
│ ──────────────────────────────────────────────────────────────────────
│
│ Model no.  Cost               Sell Price           Manufacturer
│ ─────────  ───────────        ────────────────     ────────────────
│ By Manufacturer
│   17890        12,500.00          16,250.00         Aqua Products
│
│ Total Sell Price for Manufacturer  16,250.00
│ ──────────────────────────────────────────────────────────────────────
│
│ By Manufacturer
│   15620        15,750.00          20,475.00         Boats Unlimited
│   16901        10,000.00          13,000.00
│   16911        14,500.00          18,850.00
│   16916        10,000.00          13,000.00
│
│ Total Sell Price for Manufacturer  81,575.00
│                                                                      ▼
│ ■──────────────────────────────────────────────────────────────────→
│ ◄■                                                                    ■
│ F1 Help                                              │ Preview │
```

Figure 8-17.   *Screen output showing the report as it will be printed*

Designing the Report

First, you will need to choose the table that is the basis for the report and the type of report—tabular or free-form. Generally a tabular report will be used for reporting on this type of data; however, you can also group records and use calculated and calculated summary fields in a free-form report.

1. From the Main menu, choose **R**eport/**D**esign (or **R**eport/**C**hange if you want to change an existing report).

2. Choose the table that is to be the basis for the report and choose a report number for it.

3. Type a description of the report. This will become the title shown in the page header. Press ENTER.

4. Choose the type of report you want. Tabular was chosen in the example used here.

Inserting a New Column and the New Calculated Field

You may want to insert a new column before placing a new field. (This is not required; however, you probably would want to do this, particularly in a tabular report.) Depending upon the other fields in the report, you may have to rearrange the columns or adjust the size of other columns to make room for the new one.

Because there is no TableBand menu in a free-form report, you cannot place a column in that type of report—just place the new field.

To insert the new column, follow these steps:

1. In the Report Designer, choose **TableBand/Insert**. Move the cursor where you want the new field and press ENTER. You can use **TableBand/Resize**, if necessary, to adjust the width of the column.

2. If needed, type in a label and enter a hyphenated line to correspond to other columns in the report. In the examples shown in Figures 8-16 and 8-17, the new column is labeled "Sell Price."

To place the new calculated field, follow these steps:

1. Choose **Field/Place/Calculated** to display the dialog box for the expression.

2. Type the expression. In the example shown in the following illustration, the expression is **[cost] * 1.30**. The field name is enclosed in brackets followed by a space, the arithmetic operator, another space, and the number to multiply by. Press ENTER.

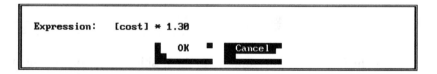

3. Follow the screen prompts to place the field and to adjust the number of digits. Press ENTER when done.

Grouping the Records

In the examples shown in Figures 8-16 and 8-17, the records are grouped by manufacturer.

To group the records, follow these steps:

1. Choose **Group/Insert** and choose the type of group you want.

2. If you choose **Field** or **Range**, then choose the field upon which to base the group. If you choose **NumberRecords**, enter a number in the dialog box for grouping the records and press ENTER.

3. Move the cursor to the position where the group band is to be placed and press ENTER. If you try to place the group within the table band, an error message will be displayed. The cursor must be outside the table band.

Entering a New Calculated Summary Field

In this example, the calculated summary field will show a total of the values in the new calculated field that has just been placed—showing the total of selling prices for all boats from each manufacturer.

To enter the new field, follow these steps:

1. Type the text you want to describe the new summary field, if any. In the example, the text is "Total Sell Price for Manufacturer." It is typed in the group footer.

2. Choose **F**ield/**P**lace/**S**ummary/**C**alculated. A dialog box for the expression will be displayed.

3. Type the expression. In the example shown here, the expression is **sum([cost] * 1.30)**. Press ENTER.

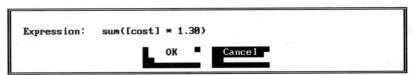

```
Expression:    sum([cost] * 1.30)
                     OK  ▪    Cancel
```

4. Follow the screen prompts to move to the position where the new field is to be placed and press ENTER. Then adjust for the number of digits and press ENTER.

It is not required that the SUM operator be entered in the expression. If you do not include an operator such as SUM, AVERAGE, COUNT, HIGH, or LOW, Paradox will automatically display a list of these operators for you, and you can choose the one you want. See an example in Figure 8-18 of entering the expression without the operator. When you press ENTER after typing the expression, the list of operators is displayed.

This also means that you do not necessarily have to place a calculated summary field here to summarize the totals in the group. If you do include the operator in the expression, you can place just a calculated field instead of a calculated summary field to summarize the values in the group.

 After placing the calculated or calculated summary field, whenever the cursor is positioned on the field, the expression for the field will be displayed in the status bar at the bottom of the screen.

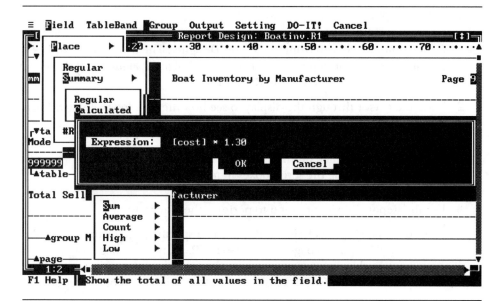

Figure 8-18.   *A calculated summary expression entered without an operator and the list of operators Paradox displays automatically*

Using the Report Previewer

After designing the report, you can use the Report Previewer to see how the actual data will look when it is printed. Then if you want to make changes before saving the design you can.

The Report Previewer mode is in effect whenever you choose to send the output of the report to the screen rather than to the printer or to a file. This allows you to see the actual data from a table, as it will be printed or saved to a file, before printing or saving. If you don't like the way the data is displayed, you can make changes in the report design. The advantage of using the Report Previewer is that you can actually see the outcome of the report design, whereas when you are in the Report Designer, you only see the format or layout of the report—not the data itself. You may find that the layout does not produce the results you want when the data is printed. If so, go back to the Report Designer, change the layout, then return to the Report Previewer to see the results of the change in layout.

You will not see font characteristics such as font type, pitch, typeface, and so on in the Report Previewer.

The image displayed in the Report Previewer is not saved. If you change the data in the associated table, the data will be changed in the image the next time you use Report Previewer. If you want to save the image, you can choose **R**eport/**O**utput or **R**eport/**R**angeOutput to save it as an ASCII file.

To use the Report Previewer, follow these steps:

1. Choose **O**utput/**S**creen from the Report Designer. The data will be displayed on the screen in the report format that you designed. Figure 8-19 shows an example of data displayed in the Report Previewer.

2. Move the cursor through the display to see how the data looks. Table 8-1 lists the keys that you can use to scroll through the window.

 To use the mouse, click on the scroll bar arrows to scroll up and down, or to the left or right. Drag the scroll boxes to move more quickly.

3. Use the Report Previewer menu to perform these actions:

   • *GoTo* gives you a choice of displaying a specific page or the end of the report. To go to a page, choose **G**oTo/**P**age, type the page number you want in the dialog box shown in the following illustration, and press ENTER. Choose **G**oTo/**E**ndOfReport to go to the end of the report.

```
 ≡  Goto  Search  Cancel
┌─[■]══════════════════════ Report Preview ════════════════════[↕]─┐
│ 4/18/92                    Orders by month                 Page ▲│
│                                                                 ▓│
│                                                                 ▓│
│Date      Quantity  Product #  Cost            Total             │
│────────  ────────  ─────────  ──────────────  ───────────────   │
│                                                                 │
│ 2/01/92      1       123            400.00          400.00      │
│ 2/12/92      2       123            400.00          800.00      │
│Total orders for the month         1,200.00                     │
│─────────────────────────────────────■──────────────────────────│
│                                                                 │
│ 3/05/92      4       156            200.00          800.00      │
│Total orders for the month           800.00                     │
│─────────────────────────────────────────────────────────────── │
│                                                                 │
│ 4/03/92      2       176            285.00          570.00      │
│ 4/05/92      1       156            200.00          200.00     ▼│
├◄■═══════════════════════════════════════════════════════════►┘ │
│F1 Help                                             Preview      │
└─────────────────────────────────────────────────────────────────┘
```

Figure 8-19.   Data displayed in the Report Previewer

Key	Movement
UP ARROW	Up one line
DOWN ARROW	Down one line
RIGHT ARROW	Right one character
LEFT ARROW	Left one character
HOME	Scroll left one window screen
END	Scroll right one window screen
PGUP	Scroll up one window screen
PGDN	Scroll down one window screen
CTRL-PGUP	Beginning of the report
CTRL-PGDN	End of the report

Table 8-1.   *Cursor Moves in the Report Previewer*

- *Search* allows you to find a specific value or to go to the next value. To find a specific value choose **S**earch/**F**ind, type the value in the dialog box shown in the following illustration, and press ENTER. Choose **S**earch/**N**ext to go to the next value that is the same as the previously entered value. If no value was previously entered, you won't be able to use this option.

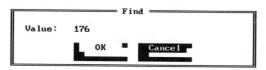

- *Cancel/Yes* returns to the Report Designer.

4. When you are finished viewing the output, choose **C**ancel/**Y**es to return to the Report Designer window. Make any adjustments you want to the report specification.

You can use the System menu in the Report Previewer the same way you use it in other Paradox windows.

Ending a Report Design Session

You can end a report design session by either saving the report specifications or by canceling or closing the Report Designer window without saving.

Saving the Report

Saving a report is similar to saving other Paradox objects. Press F2 (Do-It!) or click on **Do**-It! with the mouse. The report specifications are saved, the Report Designer session is ended, and you are returned to the Main menu.

Closing the Report Designer Without Saving

You can cancel all report specifications using either the menu or the mouse. Choose **Cancel/Yes** from the menu to end the session and return to the Main menu. If you are using a mouse, click on the Close box in the upper-left corner of the window. If you click on the Close box, a dialog box is displayed as shown in the following illustration, asking if you are sure you want to close. Choose **Yes**.

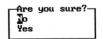

Printing the Report

You can print a report from the Main menu or from the Report Designer. The **R**eport/**O**utput option is used to send the report to the default printer from the Main menu. The **O**utput option is used to print from the Report Designer menu.

You can also specify printing only specified pages of the report, or change from the default printer to another available printer.

Printing a Report from the Main Menu

Choose **R**eport/**O**utput, choose the table that is the basis for the report, choose the number of the report specification that you want to use, and choose **P**rinter to print the report.

Other options in the Output menu shown in Figure 8-20 are **S**creen, which would send the output to the Report Previewer, or **F**ile. If you choose **F**ile, you then have to enter a filename to save the output as an ASCII file.

Printing a Report from the Report Designer

Display the report specification that you want using **R**eport/**D**esign or **R**eport/**C**hange. Then choose **O**utput/**P**rinter from the Report Designer menu. The report will be printed immediately. Use this when you are working on the report in the Report Designer window and do not want to return to the Main menu to print. Figure 8-21 shows the **O**utput menu in the Report Designer.

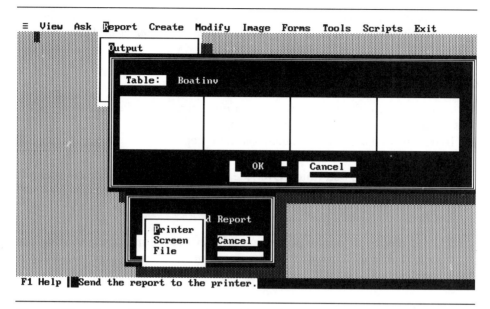

Figure 8-20. *Report/Output menu from the main menu*

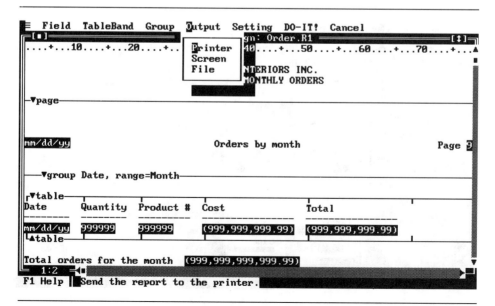

Figure 8-21. *Output menu in the Report Designer*

To print a subset of the report, use RangeOutput, discussed in this section. To print multiple pages, use the setup string discussed earlier in "Changing the Printer Setup."

Choosing a Different Printer

If you want to print the report on a printer other than the default printer, you will need to select the port for that other printer.

To do this from the Main menu, follow these steps:

1. Choose **R**eport/**S**etPrinter/**O**verride/**P**rinterPort. A list of ports is displayed as shown in Figure 8-22.

2. Choose the printer port that you want.

3. Print the report on the printer just selected. The printer port override lasts only during the current Paradox session or until you change to a different printer.

The **S**etPrinter menu includes two options, **R**egular and **O**verride. Choose **R**egular when you want to use the setup string and printer port that have been saved with the report specification for a specific table or tables. Choose **O**verride when you want to override the setup string and the printer port that have been saved with the report specification. The override is in effect for the current session only—it is not saved as

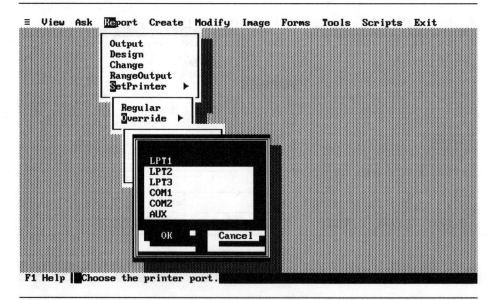

Figure 8-22.   *Menu to select a printer port*

part of the report specification. From the **Override** menu, shown in the following illustration, you can choose

- *PrinterPort* to select a different printer port

- *Setup* to enter a setup string

- *Reset* to enter a reset string

- *EndOfPage* to choose **Linefeed** to end a page or **FormFeed** to end a page. Choose **LineFeed** to use continuous feed paper, and **FormFeed** to use cut sheets.

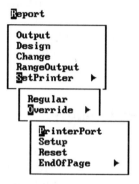

To change the printer permanently, use the Custom Configuration Program (covered in Appendix B).

You can also choose Setting/Setup/Custom from the Report Designer window to select a different printer port. Using this option was covered earlier in the section, "Changing the Printer Setup."

Using RangeOutput to Print Selected Pages

Sometimes you may want to print only specified pages from the report rather than the whole thing. You can do this easily from the **Report** menu.

Follow these steps to print only specified pages from the report:

1. Choose **Report/RangeOutput** from the Main menu.

2. Choose the table you want to be the basis for the report, and then choose the number of the report specification you want.

3. Choose **P**rinter, **S**creen, or **F**ile. A dialog box asking for the beginning page number appears, as shown here:

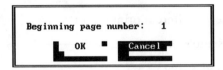

4. Type the page number for the first page you want to be printed and press ENTER.

5. A dialog box appears asking for an ending page number. Enter the page number of the last page you want printed, and press ENTER to print the range of pages. If you don't enter a number here, every page from the beginning page number through to the end of the report will be printed. If you want to print just one page, make the beginning and ending page numbers the same.

Changing the Report Design

The **R**eport/**C**hange menu is used to modify the report specifications. The changes are made in the same way you designed the report initially.

To modify report specifications, follow these steps:

1. Choose **R**eport/**C**hange from the Main menu.

2. Choose the table name that is used for the report, and then choose the report number that you want to change. Only the report numbers that have previously been used will be displayed.

3. Change the description, if you like. This will not change the page title in the report.

4. Make any changes that you like to the report.

5. Press F2 (Do-It!) or click on **D**o-It! to save the changes.

 Restructuring may change all reports if field types are changed or deleted using Modify/Restructure.

Designing Tabular Reports Based on Multiple Tables

The primary table on which a report is based is called the master table. If you want to add data from other tables to that master table you can. These added tables, called lookup tables, are linked to the master table in the report. Linked tables must have common keyed fields that can be used for the link.

Another way of combining data from several tables is to use a query based on more than one table. Then use the Answer table as the basis for the report. This is covered later in this chapter.

Other than linking lookup tables, designing a report on multiple tables is similar to designing a report on a single table. The menu in the Report Designer window is used the same as it is for a single table, and the Report Previewer can be used to show the results of the report specifications the same as it is for a single table.

Using a Master and Linked Lookup Tables

When you link a lookup table with the master table, the lookup table *must* contain keyed fields that can be linked to fields in the master table. You can link each *field* in the master table to one lookup table. Fields that link the tables must be the same data fields, but they do not necessarily have to have the same name. A maximum of five lookup tables may be used. The following examples show a report based on orders where the records are grouped by employee ID, and the Employee table that contains the employees names is linked to the master Order table by the Emp ID field. Figure 8-23 shows the report specification and Figure 8-24 shows the output of this report.

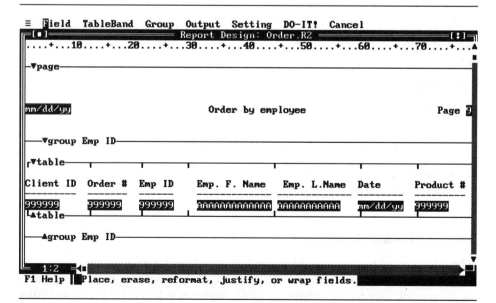

Figure 8-23.   *Order report grouped by the Emp ID field*

```
 ≡  Goto  Search  Cancel
┌─[■]══════════════════════ Orders by employees ═══════════════════[↕]─┐
│   114      2209      456   Katherine   Vanmeter    4/20/92   176    ▲ │
│   114      2214      456   Katherine   Vanmeter    4/06/92   232    ░ │
│   114      2215      456   Katherine   Vanmeter    4/06/92   156    ░ │
│   120      2213      456   Katherine   Vanmeter    5/15/92   115    ░ │
│   121      2213      456   Katherine   Vanmeter    5/05/92   200    ■ │
│   121      2222      456   Katherine   Vanmeter    5/15/92   200    ░ │
│   130      2213      456   Katherine   Vanmeter    5/05/92   200    ░ │
│                                                                      │
│                                                                      │
│   103      2201      580   Sarah       Snyder      2/01/92   123    ░ │
│   103      2203      580   Sarah       Snyder      3/05/92   156    ░ │
│   109      2207      580   Sarah       Snyder      4/06/92   115    ░ │
│   116      2216      580   Sarah       Snyder      4/25/92   231    ░ │
│                                                                      │
│                                                                      │
│   107      2205      612   William     Burns       4/03/92   123    ░ │
│                                                                      │
│                                                                      │
│   101      2202      882   Gordon      Gleason     2/12/92   123    ░ │
│   108      2208      882   Gordon      Gleason     4/10/92   124    ░ │
│   112      2211      882   Gordon      Gleason     5/01/92   157    ▼ │
└┗■┛◄■═══════════════════════════════════════════════════════════■►──┘
  F1 Help                                              │   Preview    │
```

Figure 8-24.   *Result of linking the Employee table to the master Order table and grouping by Emp ID*

To include a lookup table column in a tabular report, you must first:

- Make sure the lookup table has a keyed field and restructure it to include one if it doesn't have one.

- In the report being designed, you must identify the lookup table using the Field/Lookup/Link option.

- You must then insert a new column for each of the data fields from the lookup table.

- Then you must place the field in the column.

- After placing the item, you can reformat or resize the field as required. How to work with the report is described next.

Linking a Lookup Table

The first step is to plan which tables to link. Determine which is to be the master table and which are to be the lookup tables. If the lookup table does not contain keyed fields, you will have to restructure the table and include keyed fields that will link it to the master table.

To link a lookup table, follow these steps:

1. Choose **R**eport/**D**esign from the Main menu, choose the master table, choose
    an unused report number, type a description, choose the type—tabular or
    free-form—and press ENTER to go to the Report Designer.
    If you are providing a link in an existing report, choose **R**eport/**C**hange,
    choose the table, choose the report to be changed, replace the description
    with a different one, if you like, and then press ENTER.

2. In the Report Designer, choose Field/Lookup. A second menu showing **L**ink,
    Unlink, **R**elink is displayed, as shown here:

-   *Link* is used to choose a lookup table to link to the master table.

-   *Unlink* is used to remove a linked lookup table. When you choose this
    option, a list of linked tables is displayed and you can choose the one
    you want to unlink.

-   *Relink* is used to change the field in the master table that is used to link
    the tables. This allows you to change the link without changing fields
    including calculated fields and groupings. A menu of linked tables is
    shown when you choose **R**elink. Choose the lookup table you want, then
    choose another field from the master table to link to the keyed field in
    the lookup table. Respond to the menus if subsequent menus are shown
    (when there are multiple keyed fields in the lookup table).

3. Choose the **L**ink option, and then choose the table you want. A list of fields
    from the master table appears along with a message to select the field in the
    master table that will be used to match to the key field. Figure 8-25 shows an
    example of this.

4. Choose the field that links to the lookup table. The lookup table is now linked
    to the master table, and you can place fields from it in the report.

In the example shown in Figure 8-25, Emp ID is the field indicated in the message because
it is the only common field linking the two tables.

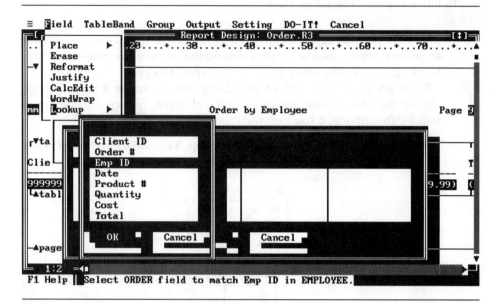

Figure 8-25. *Example of menus for linking tables*

Placing Fields from the Lookup Table

If you are linking a lookup table in a tabular report, you may want to insert new columns before placing the fields from the lookup table. To do this choose **T**ableBand/**I**nsert, move the cursor to the position where the new column is to be inserted, and press ENTER. Position the cursor on the first character in the field mask to insert a new column in front of an existing one. Figure 8-26 shows an example after inserting two blank columns.

To place the fields from the lookup table, follow these steps:

1. Choose **F**ield/**P**lace/**R**egular from the Report Designer menu. A list of field names in the master table is displayed. Press CTRL-PGDN to go to the end of the list where the lookup table name is entered in square brackets, as shown in Figure 8-27. The lookup Employee table is identified.

   You can also press DOWN ARROW to accomplish the same thing; however, using CTRL-PGDN may save keystrokes. A scroll bar may be displayed at the right of the menu to indicate that there are additional names not showing in the menu.

 A pointer is shown following the name of the table to identify it as a table rather than as a field in the master table. The pointer also indicates that when the table is selected, an additional menu of field names from the linked table appears.

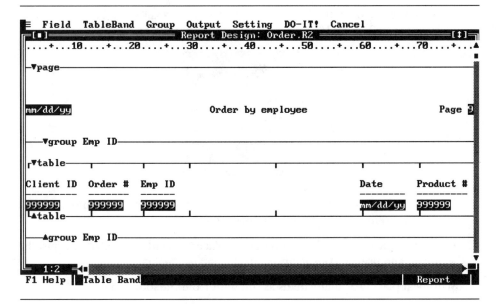

Figure 8-26.   *Report showing the inserted blank columns*

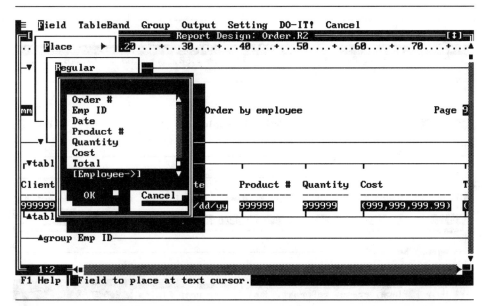

Figure 8-27.   *Field/Place/Regular menu showing the linked table name [Employee–>]*

2. Move the cursor to the lookup table name and press ENTER. The field names from the lookup table are then displayed as shown here:

3. Choose the field you want to display in the report. Press ENTER, and a prompt appears asking where you want to place the field.

4. Move to the column where you want to place the field, press ENTER, adjust the width, and press ENTER again.

5. Repeat placing as many fields as you want from the lookup table.

6. Add labels, lines, or any other literals you want in the new columns that are appropriate to the rest of the report. In the example shown in Figure 8-28, new columns for employees' first and last names from the lookup table have been inserted and labels and lines have been added.

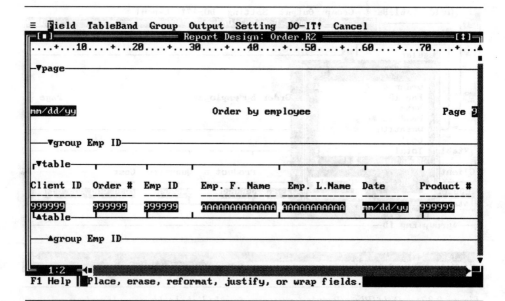

Figure 8-28. Report specifications showing linked fields

7. If you like, choose **O**utput/**S**creen to go to the Report Previewer to see how the data will look when printed. Figure 8-29 shows a partial display of the report form with records grouped by employee and including the employees' first and last names, which have been linked from the lookup table.

8. From the Report Previewer, choose **C**ancel to return to the Report Designer window.

9. Press F2 (Do-It!) or click on **D**o-It! with the mouse to save, clear the window, and return to the Main menu.

Using a Query as the Basis for a Report on Multiple Tables

There is an alternate way to produce a report based on multiple tables. You can create a query of multiple tables and then design the report based on the Answer table that results from the query.

If the report is to be used more than once, the procedure becomes more involved, so this approach is best when using a query to gather the data from multiple tables is clearer and more straightforward than specifying lookup tables in a report.

Because Paradox overwrites the current query's Answer table each time another query is run, and therefore deletes all objects (including reports) attached to the table, it is mandatory to preserve the structure of the Answer table by renaming the

```
≡  Goto   Search   Cancel
┌[■]══════════════════════ Report Preview ══════════════════════[↕]┐
│ ──────   ──────   ──────   ──────────────   ──────────────   ──────   ──────────   ────────  ▲
│   114     2204      456    Katherine        Vanmeter         4/06/92       200      ■
│   114     2209      456    Katherine        Vanmeter         4/20/92       176
│   114     2214      456    Katherine        Vanmeter         4/06/92       232
│   114     2215      456    Katherine        Vanmeter         4/06/92       156
│   120     2213      456    Katherine        Vanmeter         5/25/92       115
│   121     2213      456    Katherine        Vanmeter         5/05/92       200
│   121     2222      456    Katherine        Vanmeter         5/15/92       200
│
│   103     2201      580    Sarah            Snyder           2/01/92       123
│   103     2203      580    Sarah            Snyder           3/05/92       156
│   109     2207      580    Sarah            Snyder           4/06/92       115
│   116     2210      580    Sarah            Snyder           4/25/92       125
│   116     2216      580    Sarah            Snyder           4/25/92       231
│
│   107     2205      612    William          Burns            4/03/92       176
│                                                                                      ▼
└═◄■══════════════════════════════════════════════════════════════════■═┘
  F1 Help                                                          │ Preview │
```

Figure 8-29. *Report Previewer showing grouped records and data from a lookup table*

table. This creates a dummy table containing the structure and fields needed in the report. Then the report can be designed. Finally, when the multiple table query is rerun, the new data must be moved to the existing dummy table before an updated report can be printed. These steps are discussed next.

Creating a Dummy Table From a Query Answer Table

When you create a dummy table, you can use the word *dummy* for the table, or enter any other table name, preferably a name that has significance for the query. Follow these steps:

1. Perform the query on one or more tables. When the Answer table is on the desktop, choose **T**ools/**R**ename/**T**able.

2. Type **Answer** in the dialog box for the table to be renamed and press ENTER. Or press ENTER to display the list of table names, choose Answer, and press ENTER again.

3. In the dialog box for the new name, type a table name, and press ENTER. The renamed Answer table is displayed on the desktop.

Creating the Report Form for the Dummy Table

The process of designing a report form for this table is exactly the same as for any other table.

Follow these steps to create a report for the dummy table:

1. Choose **R**eport/**D**esign from the Main menu.

2. Choose the new table name that you created as the dummy table, choose the report number you want to use, type a description for the report, and press ENTER.

3. Choose the type of report—tabular or free-form. The report specifications are shown in the Report Designer window. The example shown in Figure 8-30 shows a report based on a query that asks for all of the clients (in this case, even those who didn't place an order), the order numbers for those who did order, and the corresponding product types for each order.

4. Go to the Report Previewer to see how the data will actually look when printed. (This step is optional.)

5. Choose **C**ancel/**Y**es from the Report Previewer.

6. Press F2 (Do-It!) or click on **D**o-It! to save the report specifications.

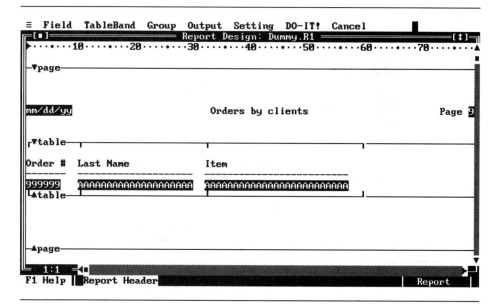

Figure 8-30. *Report specification based on new dummy table*

Moving Query Results from the Answer Table to the Dummy Table

After a dummy table has been created, you must replace the old data in it with new data each time the query is run. This is done by emptying the dummy table, thereby preserving the structure and objects, and then adding data from the Answer table to the emptied table. Here are the steps:

1. Use **T**ools/**M**ore/**E**mpty to remove the data from the dummy table stored from the preceding query.

2. Use **A**sk to query again.

3. Use **T**ools/**M**ore/**A**dd to add the records in the new Answer table to the dummy table.

Designing Free-Form Reports

Free-form reports are designed when you want to use the data from a table in a form letter or memo; to print labels; for checks, invoices, purchase orders; or any other forms that your business uses frequently. Figure 8-31 shows an example of a free-form report used to produce form letters with the Clients table as the basis for the report. The field masks show where the names and addresses will be entered in the inside

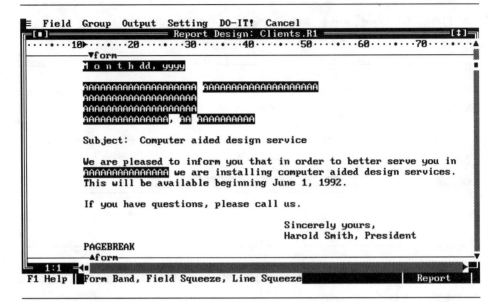

Figure 8-31.   *Example of a free-form report specification used for a form letter*

address. Also the field for the name of the city is entered twice—once in the address and again in the body of the letter. The fields are initially displayed vertically in a free-form report, rather than in columns as they are when a tabular format is chosen. The fields can then be moved to whatever position you want, in the same way fields in a tabular report are moved.

You can group and summarize records in a free-form report just as you can in a tabular report.

The Free-Form Report Designer Window

When a free-form format is chosen, a form band is displayed in the Report Designer window, rather than a table band, which is shown when a tabular format is chosen. Fields and text are entered in this form band.

If you want to group records in a free-form report, the process is similar to grouping records in a tabular report. When you position the group band, it must be outside or above the form band and below the page band. For example, you may want to group records by ZIP code when preparing a free-form report that produces mailing labels.

The status bar at the bottom of the screen again indicates the position of your cursor—naming the band or field you are in. It also indicates the settings that have been made. In Figure 8-31, the status bar shows that Field Squeeze, and Line Squeeze (discussed later in this section), have been turned on.

The Free-Form Report Designer Menu

Figure 8-32 shows an example of the free-form report and menu. Notice that the Report Designer menu is different from the menu that is used for a tabular report—this menu does not include the TableBand option. The other options here are the same as in a tabular report, with the exception of the Setting menu.

Field Menu   The Field menu, shown in the following illustration, is used to place and adjust fields in the report. You can erase fields, reformat them, set alignment for them, enter expressions in calculated fields and edit the expressions, turn on WordWrap when a field contains text that is longer than one line, and link the master table to lookup tables. The menu options here are the same as those used for tabular tables and are discussed in detail earlier in this chapter.

Group Menu   The Group menu, shown in the following illustration, allows you to group records by field, range, or number of records. You can insert a group band,

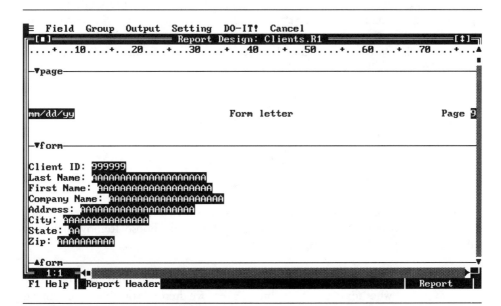

Figure 8-32.   *Free-form report specifications in the Report Designer window*

delete it, add headings to it, specify a sort direction for the records in each group, or you can change the way the group was set up by choosing **Regroup**. Again, this menu is the same as that used for tabular reports and is covered earlier in this chapter.

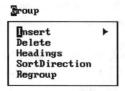

Output Menu   The **O**utput menu allows you to send the report to the printer, to the screen, and to a file. These options were covered in the section on the Report Previewer and on Print a Report. When you choose **O**utput/**S**creen, you go to the Report Previewer and use it the same way it is used for tabular reports. You can see your output and make changes before printing, if you like. The following shows an example of the Output menu.

Setting Menu   The options **R**emoveBlanks and **L**abels are included in the **S**etting menu used for a free-form report, as shown in the following illustration; they are not included for a tabular report. The **P**ageLayout, **M**argin, **S**etup, and **W**ait options are used in a free-form report the same way they are used in a tabular report. These options are discussed earlier in this chapter in the section, "Using the Setting Menu for Tabular Reports."

RemoveBlanks is chosen when you want to eliminate extra spaces between fields, or when you want to suppress blank lines. When you choose **R**emoveBlanks, a submenu gives you the following options:

- *LineSqueeze* suppresses extra lines. When you choose this option, you then have to choose whether to retain the lines or remove them. If you choose to remove them, you then have to choose either **F**ixed or **V**ariable. **F**ixed moves the blank lines to the bottom of the form. You generally use **Fixed** when working with labels, so every label has the same number of lines; however, if there is a blank field, such as a record with no company name, the blank line will be moved to the bottom of the label form. Choosing **Variable** removes the blank lines from the form entirely.

- *FieldSqueeze* eliminates extra spaces in front of and after fields that are on the same line. Choose **Yes** to eliminate any extra spaces that might be inserted between the first name and the last name, and also between the city and the state. If **FieldSqueeze** is set at **No**, these fields will be the size that is set in the table and extra spaces will be inserted when the values (numbers or characters) in the field are not as great as the size that was set in the table structure. FieldSqueeze only affects fields in the form band.

Labels is chosen to use the free-form report to print labels. In the submenu under **Labels**, choose **No** if you are going to print single-width continuous labels. Choose **Yes** if you are going to print labels that are in columns across the page. This is discussed in the later section, "Designing Labels."

Designing Form Letters

Form letters, memos, or any other type of document can be produced easily using the free-form report format. When fields and text are entered in a free-form report, they are entered in this form band, as shown in Figure 8-31.

To design a free-form report for a form letter, follow these steps:

1. Choose **Report/Design** from the Main menu, choose the table that is to be the basis for the report, and choose the number for the report.

2. Type a description, press ENTER, and choose **Free-form**. The Report Designer window now shows the fields from the table vertically.

3. Do any of the following to create the report specifications for a form letter:

   - Delete the blank lines between the page band line and the form band lines unless you want them to be inserted at the top of each page. Also delete the line containing the date and page field, and the description if one was entered, unless you want that line to be printed at the top of every page. Press CTRL-Y at the beginning of each line to do this.

   - Erase the fields that you don't want—choose **Fields/Erase** from the Report Designer menu.

   - Delete the labels for the erased fields and any text or other literals that you do not want by pressing DELETE or BACKSPACE to delete the characters.

   - Move fields to new positions—choose **Field/Erase** to remove the field from its original position, then use **Field/Place/Regular**, choose the field, and press ENTER at the new position where you want the field to be placed. You can also place the same field in more than one position in the report. In the example shown in Figure 8-31 (the report specification), the City field was placed twice in the report—once in the inside address and again in the body of the letter. In Insert mode, you can also move fields with the SPACEBAR or BACKSPACE.

- Reduce spaces between fields by choosing **Setting/Remove-Blanks/FieldSqueeze/Yes**, as shown here:

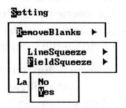

- Set a left margin by choosing **Setting/Margins**. A dialog box is displayed with 0 as the default as shown here:

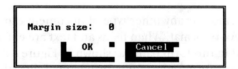

- Type **10** (if your printer prints 10 characters per inch) and press ENTER to set a one-inch left margin. The margin is immediately moved to the right in the Report Designer window, as shown in Figure 8-31. You can enter a number here to set a left margin of any width that fits on the page.

- Enter the reserved word **PAGEBREAK** to print each record on a separate page. This must be typed in all uppercase and entered in the form band, either at the top or at the bottom of the band. See Figure 8-31.

- Enter text for the body of the form letter, plus the closing, and other text as needed.

- If you like, go to the Report Previewer (**Output/Screen**) to see how the data will look when printed. Figure 8-33 shows an example of the Report Previewer screen.

4. When finished, return to the Report Designer and press F2 (Do-It!) or click on **Do**-It! to save the report specifications.

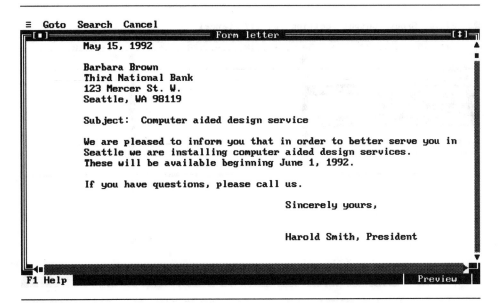

```
 ≡  Goto   Search   Cancel
┌─[■]══════════════════ Form letter ══════════════════[↕]─┐
║     May 15, 1992                                        ▲
║                                                         ■
║     Barbara Brown
║     Third National Bank
║     123 Mercer St. W.
║     Seattle, WA 98119
║
║     Subject:  Computer aided design service
║
║     We are pleased to inform you that in order to better serve you in
║     Seattle we are installing computer aided design services.
║     These will be available beginning June 1, 1992.
║
║     If you have questions, please call us.
║
║                                Sincerely yours,
║
║
║                                Harold Smith, President
║                                                         ▼
║◄■                                                        ■
 F1 Help                                      Preview
```

Figure 8-33.   *Form letter shown in the Report Previewer*

Designing Labels

Use a free-form report to design mailing labels—either single-width, continuous feed; or multiple width, sheet or continuous feed. In the Report Designer, set **Settings/Labels** at **Yes**. This tells Paradox that multiple page widths represent multiple forms across one page. Then design the report for one label, and enter the number of page widths that represent the columns of labels across one page. An example of a report design for labels is shown in Figure 8-34.

To design a report to print labels, follow these steps:

1. Choose **Report/Design** from the Main menu, choose the table name, choose the report number you want, type a description, press ENTER, and choose **Free-form**.

2. In the Report Designer window, choose **Setting/Labels/Yes**. A message appears telling you that the label status has been recorded.

3. Delete the lines between the page band line and the form band line—press CTRL-Y at the beginning of each line to do this.

4. Delete the labels and the fields that you don't want. Move the fields for the label to appropriate positions. Be sure you include the same number of lines

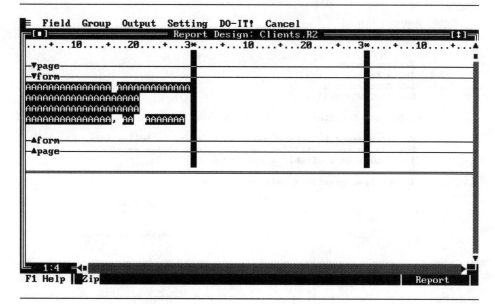

Figure 8-34.   *Report design for labels in three columns*

within the form band that are in your labels, based on the lines per inch your printer will print. If you are printing on 1-inch labels and your printer is set to print six lines per inch, you need to have six lines in your form band; if you print on 1.5-inch labels, you need nine lines, and so on.

Press CTRL-V (Vertical Ruler) to help count the lines. This toggles on and off the display of the number of lines in the form band.

5. Choose **Setting/RemoveBlanks/LineSqueeze/Yes/Fixed**. This will eliminate blank lines caused by fields with no values, but will retain the lines and move them to the bottom of the label, thus keeping every label the same length. For example, if there is no company name in a record, that blank line could be suppressed and moved to the end of the label rather than printing a blank space on the label between the name and street address.

6. Choose **Setting/RemoveBlanks/FieldSqueeze/Yes** to eliminate extra spaces between fields that are on the same line.

7. Depending upon the number of labels across, do one of the following:

   • If you are printing continuous-feed labels—either single column or multiple columns—choose **Setting/PageLayout/Length**. A dialog box for the page length is displayed. Type a **C** in the box and press ENTER, as shown here:

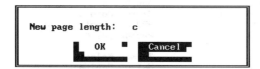

- If you are printing labels in multiple columns on cut sheets of paper—8.5 by 11-inch paper for example, leave **Length** at 60 or whatever the length is of the pages of labels you are going to be using. (The default length was previously set at 66 in Paradox 3.5; however, with so many using laser printers, the default in Paradox 4 has been changed to 60.) Then choose **S**etting/**P**ageLayout/**W**idth, type the number of characters for the width of each label, and press ENTER. If the fields do not fit the page width, you may get an error message (shown in the following illustration). If you do, erase the text and delete the fields or change the size of the fields, so they will fit the new page size. Then repeat this to enter two or more columns on the page.

- Because **S**etting/**L**abels was specified for the report, setting the page width at 30 or some comparable number will cause the labels to be printed across the page. Thick vertical lines are now shown on the screen indicating each page width, as shown in Figure 8-34.

8. Go to the Report Previewer to see how the labels look. Figure 8-35 shows an example of the output.

9. Return to the Report Designer and press F2 (Do-It!) or click on **Do-It!** to save.

Invoices, Purchase Orders, Grade Reports, or Other Forms

As mentioned previously, the Report Designer can be used to print data from tables in any format. Using the Report Designer options covered in this chapter, select a table for the report, choose free-form as the format, and position the fields at the exact position where they would be printed on one of these forms.

Enter any text, labels, or other comments that are appropriate. Use the ruler line at the top of the Report Designer window as a guide to placement of these elements. You can also link lookup tables to provide information not in the master table. Group the data according to a field, as needed, enter summary fields to enter summaries of data—for example, totals of orders or sales, or enter expressions that multiply values by sales tax.

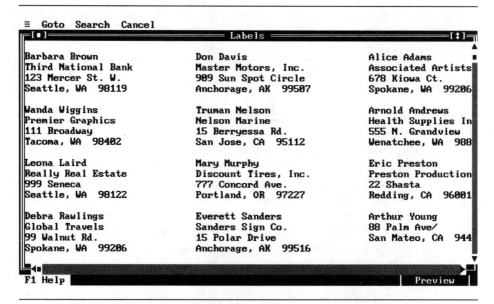

Figure 8-35.   *Labels shown in Report Previewer*

Working with Reports on a Network

As in working with many other Paradox objects, when you are working on a report on a network, a prevent full lock is placed on the table associated with the report. This allows others to access the table, if needed. A full lock is placed on the report, however, to prevent others from changing the report while you are working on it.

If the table already has a full lock on it because someone else is using it, you must wait until the full lock is removed.

The owner of the table can require a password to gain access to the table. In this case, you would have to know the password to access the table in order to create or change a report associated with it.

When a report from a table that others may be using is printed, displayed, or saved to a file, Paradox will restart the procedure if changes to the data occur while Paradox is processing the data. A message appears on the screen each time this happens. You can press CTRL-BREAK if you want to cancel these restarts. If you want to avoid these restarts entirely when you start to print, display, or save to a file the current report, choose Tools/Net/Changes/Continue. If you are printing a report containing lookup tables and Paradox starts reprocessing data, the restarts will be based only on data in the master table. Paradox will not detect the data changes in any of the lookup tables.

Chapter **9**

Working with the Image Menu and Graphs

This chapter discusses how to modify the images you see on the screen, and in the context of graphs, on a printer or disk file. Often the image on the screen is not exactly what you need to see. The Image menu allows you to change such things as the size of a table view, the size of the columns displayed, the format of the data, or the positioning of the columns. You can change both the form and table views.

The Image menu is also where you access the Graph feature within Paradox. You can create both a standard and instant graph or a custom graph. The graphs include bar and stacked bar graphs, line, pie, marker, and five other variations of graphs. Using the Crosstab feature to prepare data for graphs or for easier comprehension is also covered.

Some of the functions in the Image menu have been covered in previous chapters, but they will be reviewed briefly here.

Using the Image Menu

The Image menu is used primarily to arrange data on the screen so that the data is as easy as possible for the user to read and use. Figure 9-1 shows an example of the Image menu in table view. The Image menu is displayed whenever you work in table

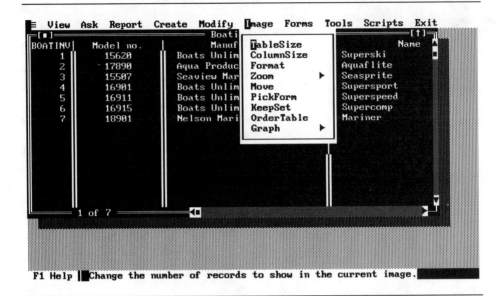

Figure 9-1. *Image menu*

view or form view. The menu is slightly different depending upon which view you are in.

The Image menu in *table view* contains the options TableSize, ColumnSize, Format, Zoom, Move, PickForm, KeepSet, OrderTable, and Graph.

The Image menu in *form view* contains the options Format, Zoom, PickForm, KeepSet, OrderTable, and Graph. TableSize, ColumnSize, and Move are not available in form view.

The Image menu, with some variations in options, is available from the Main menu, or from the Edit, CoEdit, or DataEntry menu. The DataEntry menu contains only TableSize, ColumnSize, Format, Zoom, Move, and PickForm. The Edit menu contains all of these options plus KeepSet; and the CoEdit menu contains all the options in the DataEntry Image menu plus KeepSet and OrderTable.

You can perform some of the Image menu functions from the System menu or with a mouse. You'll learn how in the upcoming sections.

Using TableSize

The TableSize option is used to change the number of records a table displays on the desktop. Having the table display full size on the screen can make editing easier. You change the size for the current session only; you cannot save size changes permanently.

The TableSize option is not available in form view.

To change the table size, follow these steps:

1. Choose **I**mage/TableSize from the Main menu, or from the **E**dit, **C**oEdit, or **D**ataEntry menu. A prompt is displayed as shown here:

   <code>Use ↑ and ↓ to change table size, then press ◄┘.</code>

2. Press UP ARROW or DOWN ARROW to change the size of the table, and press ENTER when the table is the size you want.

While in Image/TableSize, you can also press HOME to shorten the number of records displayed to only two records, or press END to increase the number of records displayed to 20. You can display as many as 45 records if you choose a video mode that supports EGA/VGA 80 X 43/50 mode.

Using the mouse to resize the table is simple. Point to the Resize corner in the lower right of the table and drag it to a new size. Release when the table is the size you want. You can use the mouse in table view and in form view.

The advantage of using the mouse is that you can resize the table both horizontally and vertically. You can also resize both horizontally and vertically when you use the System menu.

An alternate way to resize a table is to use the Size/Move option in the System menu. Press ALT-SPACEBAR to get to the System menu and choose Size/Move. Use SHIFT plus an arrow key to resize the window, or the arrow keys alone to move the window. A message at the bottom of the screen gives instructions for using the arrow keys to change the size of a window.

Using ColumnSize

You can use **C**olumnSize to reduce the width of the column in order to show additional fields that may be off to one side of the screen. This option is not available in form view since there are no columns in form view.

There are some limits on the field size: A numeric or currency field cannot be wider than 25 characters, and if the field name is shorter than 25 characters, then the column width cannot be longer than the field name; a numeric short field cannot be wider than 5 characters; a date field cannot be wider than 14 characters (unless the field name is wider); and an alphanumeric or memo field cannot be wider than its defined widths.

To change the column size, follow these steps:

1. Choose **Image/ColumnSize**. A prompt asks you to move to the column you want, as shown here:

   `Move to the column you want to resize, then press ↵...`

2. Move the cursor to the column to be resized and press ENTER. A second prompt appears, as shown here:

   `Now use → and ← to change width, then press ↵.`

3. Press LEFT ARROW or RIGHT ARROW to adjust the column width and press ENTER when done.

 While in Image/ColumnSize, press HOME *to reduce the width to one character. Press* END *to increase the width of the column to the maximum field width as specified in the table structure.*

 To change a column's width using a mouse, simply point to the right border of the column and drag it to extend or reduce the width of the column. Release the mouse button when the column is the width you want. You will not be able to increase the width more than the number of characters entered for the field in the table structure.

Using Format

You change the format in which you display dates, numbers, and currency amounts by using the Image/Format menu. This option does not apply to alphanumeric or memo fields since data in those fields is only displayed as text. The choices in the Format menu vary depending upon the type of field selected for the format change; for example, when you select a currency field to format, the formatting options will be different from those had you selected a date field.

The Format option is available in both table view and form view.

Changing the Date Format

Format gives you these four date format choices:

Date Format	Example
MM/DD/YY	9/01/92

Date Format	Example
DD-Mon-YY	1-Sep-92
DD.MM.YY	1.09.92
YY.MM.DD	92.09.1

To change the date format, follow these steps:

1. Choose Image/Format. A prompt appears asking you to move to the date field you want to reformat, as shown here:

```
Move to the field you want to reformat, then press ↵...
```

2. Move the cursor to a date field and press ENTER. A menu of date formats is displayed, as shown here:

3. Choose the date format you want and press ENTER.

Changing the Format in Numeric or Currency Fields

The options for formatting numbers in numeric or currency fields allow you to specify the number of digits and decimals to be displayed, whether or not to insert commas, or display numbers in exponential notation—that is, scientific format. The choices of formats are as follows.

General   This option displays numbers aligned at a decimal if that is appropriate. If you choose this option, you are asked to specify the number of decimals you want, but the decimals will show only when numerals containing decimals are used. Trailing zeros are dropped. Whole number separators (commas for example) are not used, and negative numbers are displayed preceded by a minus sign (–).

Fixed   This option lets you specify a fixed number of digits following a decimal. You are asked to indicate the number of decimals you want. Trailing zeros are displayed, whole number separators (commas) are not included, and negative numbers are preceded by a minus sign (–).

Comma This option displays whole numbers separated by commas inserted every third digit (thousands commas). If you are using an international format, a period will be the separator.

Scientific This option is chosen primarily when working with very large or very small numbers. Separators are not used and negative numbers are preceded by a minus sign (–). Scientific format displays numbers as a decimal number between 1 and 10 multiplied by 10. Thus, the whole number 1,234 will be displayed as 1.234e+03.

To specify a number or currency format, follow these steps:

1. Choose **Image/Format**. A prompt is displayed at the top of the screen.

2. Move the cursor to the field you want and press ENTER. A menu appears, as shown here:

3. Choose the type of numeric format you want and press ENTER. A second dialog box like the one shown in Figure 9-2 asks for the number of decimal places that you want. A message at the bottom of the screen gives information about the number of digits you can show after the decimal. Respond to the box and press ENTER.

 You can be in either table view or form view to use the Format option.

Using Zoom

Zoom is a quick way to get to a specific record, field, or value in the active table. You supply the field name, record number, or value, and Paradox finds the record. After using the Zoom option to find a value, you can use ZoomNext to repeat the search and go to the next record containing the same value. This option is available in both table view and form view.

When you choose **Image/Zoom**, a menu with three options appears:

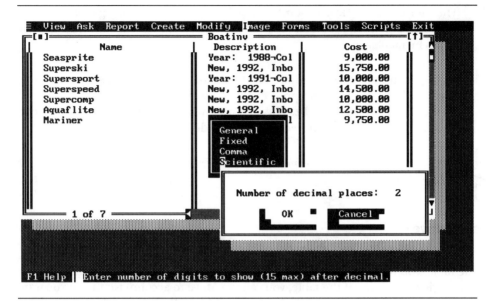

Figure 9-2.   Dialog box requesting number of decimal places

Field   This option is used to go to a specific field. If you choose this option, a second menu of the field names in the active table is shown. Choose the field you want, and press ENTER to go to it immediately.

Record   This option is used to go to a record as identified by its number. Type the number of the record you want, and press ENTER to go to it immediately. On the bottom of the window frame you'll see the record numbers, *n* of *m*. The record number you supply cannot be greater than *m*.

Value   This option is used to go quickly to a record that contains a specific value. After choosing **Value**, move the cursor to the field that contains the value you want, and press ENTER. Type the value in the dialog box shown here, and press ENTER.

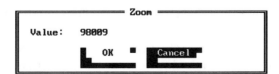

After choosing the formatting option you want, respond to the screen prompts to complete the search.

The shortcut keys CTRL-Z (Zoom), which displays the Zoom dialog box, and ALT-Z (ZoomNext), which moves you to the next value, are quick ways to locate specific values in a table.

To use Zoom, press CTRL-Z to display the dialog box for a value. Type the value you want in the dialog box, and press ENTER to go directly to it.

To use ZoomNext, press ALT-Z. The cursor moves immediately to the next occurrence of the value that was entered in the Zoom dialog box.

If the Zoom dialog box does not have a value in it, you will not be able to use ALT-Z (ZoomNext).

Using Move

You use the **M**ove option to rearrange columns in the active table. If after creating the table, you want to see the fields in a different order but do not want to change the original structure of the table, you can use **M**ove to accomplish this. If you want the new display to be permanent, you can use Image/**K**eepSet to save it. (The table structure remains as it was created.)

To move a column in the active table, follow these steps:

1. Choose Image/**M**ove. A list of field names appears, as shown here:

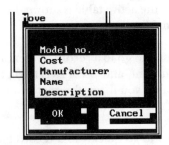

2. Choose the field you want to move. A prompt for moving the cursor is displayed at the top of the screen.

3. Move the cursor to the field that is to follow the inserted field, and press ENTER.

You can also use the shortcut key, CTRL-R, to rotate the order of fields. When you use this key, the field is moved to the end—or the far right—of the table. Move the cursor to the field you want to rotate and press CTRL-R. The current field then becomes the last field in the table view.

Using PickForm

Use **PickForm** to choose the standard F form or a custom form for the active table. Normally, if you press F7 (Form Toggle), the standard or F form for the table appears. You press F7 again to toggle the form off. After using **PickForm** to choose a custom form, F7 will toggle that form with the table view.

An active table must be on the desktop.

To choose a custom form, follow these steps:

1. Choose **Image/PickForm**. A list of available forms appears, as shown in Figure 9-3.

2. Choose the form you want to use and press ENTER. The custom form will be displayed. You can now use F7 (Form Toggle) to toggle between it and the table view.

Using KeepSet

KeepSet is used to save the current image being displayed for the active table. If you change fields and want to keep the new display, use **KeepSet**; or if you change the column width or change the format for a date field, use this option to permanently save the display changes.

KeepSet does not modify the structure of the database—only the display of the data. Use Modify/Restructure to change the database itself.

Saving the Image

When you choose **Image/KeepSet** from the menu, the current image is automatically saved, and the next time you view the table these changes will be in effect. The saved image is stored in a file ending with the extension .SET. This file can be deleted later if you decide you want to return to the original format, as explained next.

In addition to saving the format settings, you can also save a form setting. You can make any form the default by selecting the new form, and then choosing Image/KeepSet. When you press F7 (Form Toggle) you will get the new form.

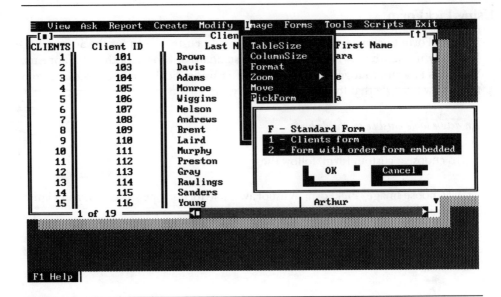

Figure 9-3.   *Image/PickForm menu*

Deleting Settings

To return the settings for a specific table to their original format, you can use **T**ools/**D**elete. To use the **T**ools/**D**elete menu to return to the original format settings, follow these steps:

1. Choose **T**ools/**D**elete/**K**eepset from the Main menu.

2. Enter the name of the table and press ENTER; or press ENTER to display the list of table names, choose the one you want, and press ENTER again. Paradox will delete any KeepSet files. The next time you view the table, the table will be displayed in its original format.

   If the table is on the desktop when you delete the .SET file, the format will not be changed. To confirm that you have returned to the original format, clear the desktop, and then view the table again.

Using OrderTable

You use **O**rderTable to temporarily view a table by a field other than the keyed field. The order is temporary and disappears as soon as you enter another mode, such as Edit. It is only a way to get a quick view using another sort sequence. You can also use **O**rderTable either to view the records on the basis of an existing secondary index or create a new secondary index. The table must be keyed to use this option—it works the same way the shortcut key ALT-S works. Secondary indexes are covered in Chapter 5.

1. Display a table on the desktop and choose **Image/O**rderTable. A prompt asks you to move to the column you want.

2. Move the cursor to the field to be sorted and press ENTER. A dialog box will show the field name, as illustrated here:

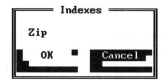

If no additional secondary indexes have previously been created, only the field name will be displayed in the dialog box, and a message at the bottom of the screen will instruct you to "Choose an index to order the table by." Press ENTER to display a menu and choose either OK to build an index on the field, or **C**ancel to not build the index.

If you have used the **O**rderTable option earlier to build an index on a field, you simply confirm the field name and press ENTER.

Working with Graphs

Graphs are used to display data in a format different from that displayed in either table view or form view. This is useful since data is often more meaningful when it is displayed in graph form. Paradox provides the ability to create bar graphs, line graphs, pie charts, and seven other graph types. An instant stacked bar graph can be displayed by moving your cursor to a numeric field and pressing CTRL-F7 (Instant Graph). Prompts guide you through specifying the parameters needed for the instant graph. You can also create custom graphs using the **Image/G**raph/**M**odify menu, which is explained further in this chapter. Then either press CTRL-F7 (Instant Graph) to see the graph in a different format or choose **Image/G**raph/**V**iewgraph to see the graph on the screen, send it to the printer, or save it to a file.

Elements in a Graph

It is important to know the terms applied to the various parts of a graph, so that when you are preparing a table for a graph, you can determine which fields should be used for the various graph elements. Paradox follows specific rules in converting the data in a table into bars, lines, pies, and so on, in a graph. In doing this, various information from the table is converted into the elements in a graph. Figure 9-4 shows a stacked bar graph with its various elements labeled.

The elements used and referenced in a graph are

- *X-axis* The horizontal line along the bottom of the graph, the x-axis charts categories or groups of data such as the categories by state, shown in Figure 9-4, or by sales persons, vendors, products, and so on. Time is often charted on the x-axis. The x-axis labels or values are found beneath the x-axis. In Figure 9-4, the x-axis labels show the names of the states where the office products are sold.

- *Y-axis* The vertical line to the left of the graph, the y-axis charts values such as quantities or dollars. The y-axis labels and values are found to the left of the graph. In Figure 9-4, the y-axis shows the dollars sold for each product.

- *Legends* These show the breakdown of the categories being grouped. *Series elements* are the various components of the categories that are being graphed. In Figure 9-4, the series elements are the types of products being sold in each state. (So the category in the x-axis is state, and the series element for each state is the dollar amount of each type of product sold.) The *legend labels* identify each series element, such as the product type.

- *Title* This is the name of the graph.

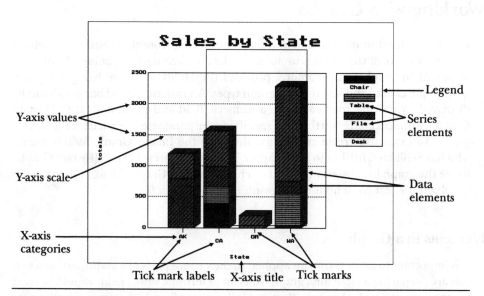

Figure 9-4. *Elements in a graph*

- *Scale* The increments measured by the x- and y-axes, scale is derived from the values in the fields being used for the x-axis and y-axis, and is used to produce the tick marks.

- *Tick marks* These are the increments assigned to the graph to show values.

How Values Are Displayed

Paradox determines how to convert data in tables into graph elements through its structure. That is, the way fields are arranged in a table determines how Paradox will build the graph. If a table is structured appropriately, the graph will be meaningful. If not, the graph may be useless. If the table you want to graph is not structured appropriately, you can either move the columns the way you want them, or perhaps more easily, you can perform a query with just the fields you want, arranged as you want them graphed. You can also create a Crosstab table (discussed later in this chapter) either on the active table or on the Answer table that results from a query. A Crosstab procedure can summarize data in a way that will produce an effective graph.

The following rules lay out the approach Paradox takes in converting table data to graphic elements:

- In an *unkeyed* table, the first field becomes the x-axis in the graph.

- In a *keyed* table, the keyed field that is *furthest to the right* will be the x-axis in the graph. If you are not sure which field that is, choose **Tools/Info/Structure** to see which fields are keyed and in what order. The last field with an asterisk in the table structure will be the field that will become the x-axis.

*If you want to change this, choose **Modify/Restructure**, and change the order of the fields or remove the asterisks. (This is the only way you can change the field that will be used for the x-axis in a keyed table.)*

- The number of categories in the x-axis is determined by the number of records in the table. The name of each category will come from the contents of the field. The name of the x-axis will be the field name. Obviously, if you have more than a few records in the table, the graph will be useless—or cluttered and ineffective at best. Consequently, a frequent first step in building a graph is to query the table for a summary of the records you want displayed. A Crosstab (discussed in this chapter) can often be used for this task as well as a query (discussed in Chapter 6).

- The series elements that are included in the graph depend upon the position of the cursor when you press CTRL-F7 (Instant Graph). The numeric field in which the cursor is located is the first series element, and the next five numeric fields are subsequent series elements. The series elements are named after the field names, and the values in the field become the y-axis values.

If your cursor is in the leftmost field in a non-keyed table when you press CTRL-F7 *(Instant Graph), the series element will be the same as the x-axis categories.*

- If the fields are not in the order you want, use CTRL-R (Rotate) to move the fields to a position that will produce the results you want.

- If data that you want to graph is located in more than one table, create an Answer table based on a query. Then create the graph from the Answer table. You can also summarize data using **C**rossTab. This will be covered later in this chapter.

Exceptions to the Rules   Pie graphs and XY graphs differ from other graph types. Pie graphs contain only one series element. XY graphs scale both the x- and y-axes. Therefore, the rules given in the previous section may not always apply when working with these two types of graphs.

The exceptions are as follows:

- Pie graphs contain only one series element. They show values for only one category in a stacked bar graph. The first nonnumeric field is used for the categories. The field in which the cursor is located supplies the quantities for the categories. This field must be a numeric field.

- XY graphs scale both the x- and y-axes (both x- and y-axes are numeric). The x-axis values are from the first numeric field in the table. The numeric field in which the cursor is located and the next five numeric fields become the y-axis series elements. The names of the fields are the legend labels.

Planning the Table for the Graph

The critical factor in creating a graph is to display the information on the desktop so that it will produce the results you want when it is graphed. The order in which the fields are positioned in the table controls how information is displayed in a graph. Not all fields will be included in a graph. For example, alphanumeric fields and memo fields generally will not be included in a graph; however, you may want to use information from these types of fields in a pie chart or for x-axis categories. If you want to use information from an alphanumeric field for an x-axis category, or for section labels in a pie chart, use CTRL-R (Rotate) to rearrange the fields so that the field you want to use for the x-axis category is the leftmost field in the table. CTRL-R (Rotate) moves the field in which the cursor is positioned to the far right.

Using the Instant Graph

Paradox 4 provides an instant graph of your data when you press CTRL-F7 (Instant Graph). The data is displayed in a stacked bar graph by default; however, you can display data differently by choosing **Image/Graph/Modify** and selecting a different graph type. All data may not be displayed—what is displayed depends upon the field types and the arrangement of the fields. A query or a crosstab can be used to control the fields that are displayed and the order in which they are displayed.

To use Instant Graph, follow these steps:

1. Display the table that is to be the basis for the graph on the desktop.

2. If you are using a nonkeyed table, be sure the first field is the one you want for the x-axis. If you are using a keyed table, the last keyed field on the right will be used for the x-axis. If the field you want is not displayed in the correct position in the table, you can change it by pressing CTRL-R (Rotate) to rearrange the fields in a nonkeyed table. If the table is keyed, use **Modify/Re**structure to change the table structure. In Figure 9-5, which shows an example of using Instant Graph, the name of the boat manufacturer is used for the x-axis.

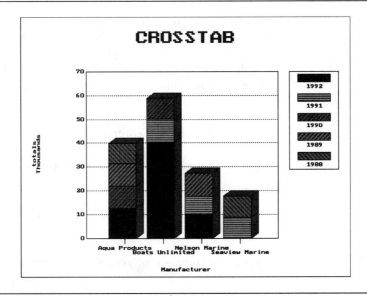

Figure 9-5.   Instant stacked bar graph

3. Move the cursor to the numeric field that you want to be the first series element. That field and the next five numeric fields to the right will be graphed as *series* values.

To produce the results displayed in Figure 9-5, a Crosstab table was created that displayed the names of the manufacturers, the model years of the boats, and the dollar value of boats for each manufacturer for each model year. Once the Crosstab table was displayed on the desktop, CTRL-F7 *(Instant Graph) was pressed to produce the graph. The name of the table becomes the title of the graph, unless you choose to change it using* **I**mage/**G**raph/**M**odify *(covered later in this chapter). In this case, Crosstab is the name of the table and, therefore, the title of the graph.*

4. Press CTRL-F7 (Instant Graph). If your cursor is not in a numeric field, an error message appears, as shown here:

```
Active field not numeric
```

5. If you got an error message, move the cursor to a numeric field and press CTRL-F7 again.

6. When finished viewing the graph, press any key to return to the desktop.

Using CrossTab

You use **I**mage/**G**raph/**C**rossTab to create temporary Crosstab tables that summarize data and make it more usable for a graph. The Crosstab table converts data into a table resembling a spreadsheet. Values are summarized into columns and intersecting rows. In addition to providing summaries, CrossTab can also be used to count the values in a field, and to display minimum and maximum values. The following choices are available from the CrossTab menu.

Sum   This is used to total values for its row and column.

Min   This is used to display a minimum or smallest value for its row and column combination.

Max   This is used to display a maximum or largest value for its row and column combination.

Count   This is used to display the number of records for a row and column combination.

The information in a Crosstab table comes from three fields. These three fields produce row labels, column labels, and values. During the process of creating the Crosstab table, you are prompted to move the cursor to the fields that are going to be used for each of these elements. The results in the Crosstab table depend upon the arrangement of the fields in the original table. If there are any fields to the left of the field that is used for the row labels, they will be included in the Crosstab table and will be in the same order as in the original table. If you do not want these fields to be in the Crosstab table, rearrange the fields using CTRL-R (Rotate) to produce the results you want.

As an example, you might use a Crosstab table to show the names of the states as row labels, the types of products sold as column labels, and the total amount of sales for each type of product as values in the grid. The three elements in a Crosstab table that would produce this result are:

- *Row labels* These are the values listed on the left side of the Crosstab table and are values from the field that you want to use as one source of information in the graph. In Figure 9-6, State is used for row labels. (In an instant graph, these values will become the x-axis.)

- *Column labels* These are the values displayed across the top of the Crosstab table and are the values from the field that is the second source of information

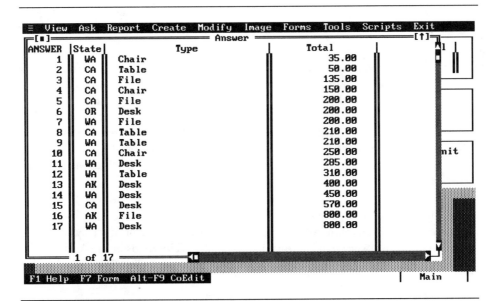

Figure 9-6.   *Answer table used for a Crosstab table*

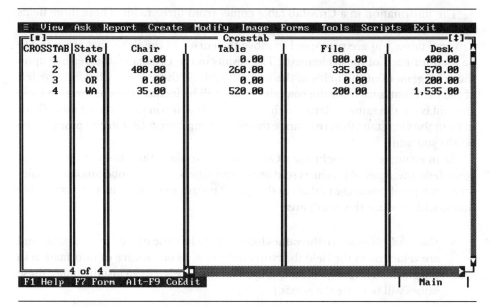

Figure 9-7.   *The types of products from the Answer table in Figure 9-6 become the column labels in this Crosstab table*

in the graph. See an example in Figure 9-7. The types of products from the Answer table shown in Figure 9-6 become the column labels in the Crosstab table shown in Figure 9-7. (In an instant graph, this will become the series elements.)

- *Values* These are the figures in the grid that are calculated on the basis of information from the fields used for the row labels and column labels. These values can be either a sum of values, a count of values, or minimum or maximum values. The totals in the grid in Figure 9-7 represent the crosstab of sales in each state, types of products sold, and total amount of sales of each type of product. The Total column shown in Figure 9-6 produces the values in the grid in the Crosstab table shown in Figure 9-7. (These values will form the bases for the y-axis in an instant graph.)

In the example here, a query, as shown in the next illustration, was first used to produce an Answer table that displays sales of each type of product by state. (An example of the Answer table is shown in Figure 9-6.) The fields in the Answer table have been rotated to produce the appropriate results when CrossTab is used.

Creating a Crosstab Table

Now that you understand the concepts behind CrossTab, you can use those concepts to create a table.

To create a Crosstab table, follow these steps:

1. Display the table that you want for the basis of the Crosstab table. This can be an Answer table resulting from a query.

2. Rearrange the fields, if necessary. The field for the row values should be at the left, the field for the column labels to its right, and the field for the values, also to the right of the row values.

3. Choose **Image/Graph/CrossTab**. A menu of four kinds of Crosstab tables appears, as shown in Figure 9-8.

4. Choose the type of Crosstab you want.

5. A prompt asks you to move to the column with the row label, as shown here:

   `Move to column containing crosstab row labels, then press ⏎...`

6. Move the cursor to the column that is to be used for the row label (the x-axis in instant graphs) and press ENTER. A second prompt asks you to move to the field containing the column labels, as shown here:

   `Move to column containing crosstab column labels then press ⏎...`

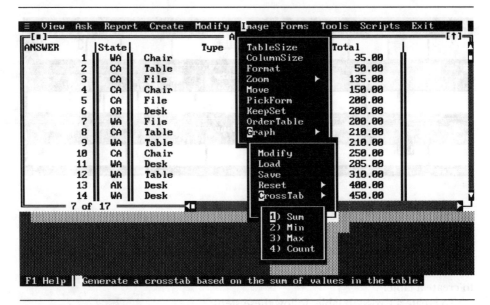

Figure 9-8. *CrossTab menu*

7. Move the cursor to the column to be used for the column label (the series elements in instant graphs) and press ENTER. A third prompt asks you to move to the field containing the values, as shown here:

```
Move to column containing crosstab values, then press ↵.
```

8. Move the cursor to the column for the Crosstab values (the y-axis in instant graphs) and press ENTER. The Crosstab table is created, as shown in Figure 9-9.

In this example, State will be the x-axis categories in the graph, the types of products which are now the column labels will be the series elements, and the Total will be used for the y-axis values.

Using the Crosstab Table for an Instant Graph

Once the temporary Crosstab table is displayed on the desktop, it is a simple matter to use CTRL-F7 (Instant Graph) to produce a graph.

As you'll recall, the field to the left is used for the x-axis, and the next field and up to five additional fields to the right are used for series elements and the y-axis values.

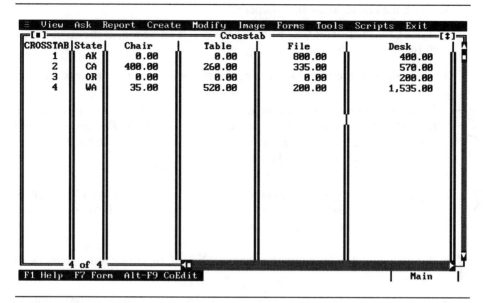

Figure 9-9. *Final Crosstab table*

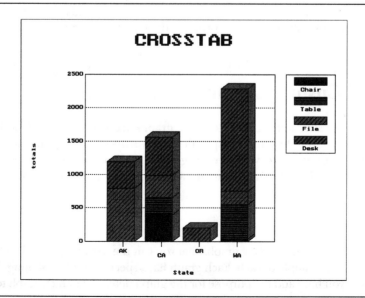

Figure 9-10. *Instant graph based on a Crosstab table*

1. Move the cursor to the first numeric field.

2. Press CTRL-F7 (Instant Graph) to see the graph on screen, as shown in Figure 9-10.

3. Press any key when finished viewing the graph to return to the desktop.

 If you want to save the Crosstab table, use Tools/Rename to give it a new name. The Crosstab table is a temporary table similar to an Answer table. The next time a cross tabulation is performed, the data in the Crosstab table will be replaced; therefore, it must be saved with a different name if you want to keep it.

 You can instantly produce a Crosstab table with the shortcut key, ALT-X (Cross-Tab). When you press ALT-X, you will not be prompted to select fields for the table. The selection will be automatic based on the following:

- Row labels will be based on the data in the field the cursor is in and all fields to the left of it.

- The data in the field that is second to last (or second from the right) will be the values in the column labels at the top of the Crosstab table.

- The data in the field at the far right will be the values that are summarized for every row and column in the Crosstab table.

This is a much faster method of producing the Crosstab table; however, be aware of the position of the columns. Use CTRL-R to rotate the fields, if necessary, before using ALT-X (CrossTab) so that you produce the results you want.

Planning Custom Graphs

You design, create, and manage custom graphs from the Image/Graph menu. However, before you dive into the specifics, it is worthwhile to consider some design implications. For example, you have ten graph types from which to choose, and the data placement within the table remains a high priority in custom graphs.

Graph Types

There are ten different styles of graphs that you can use to display data. The following figures show an example of each. Each graph has a special way of presenting data. The type of data you have and the purpose for the graph determine which graph to use.

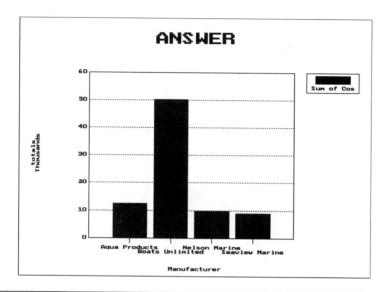

Figure 9-11.   Regular bar graph

Regular Bar Graph

In a regular bar graph, each bar represents a single element in the table, and its height represents the value as measured by the y-axis. See Figure 9-11. Bar graphs are good for showing totals and for comparing one element against another.

Stacked Bar Graph

A stacked bar graph can show up to six series elements, as shown in Figure 9-12. These show the comparison of each element to the total. The elements can be stacked on top of each other or side by side.

Rotated Bar Graph

The rotated bar graph displays the values in horizontal, rather than vertical bars, as shown in Figure 9-13. This can be particularly effective when displaying values over time, for example.

3D Bar Graph

The 3D bar graph shows shaded bars to present a three-dimensional effect, as shown in Figure 9-14. Although this loses its effect with more bars, it can be very professional looking for a few of them.

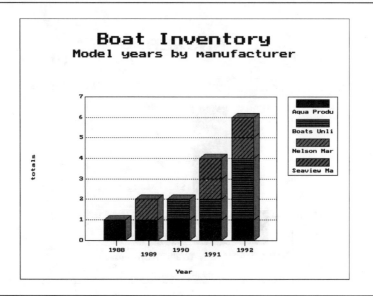

Figure 9-12.   *Stacked bar graph showing each series in relation to the total*

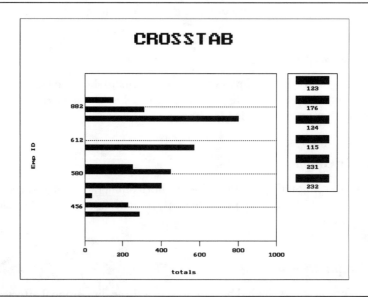

Figure 9-13.   *Rotated bar graph*

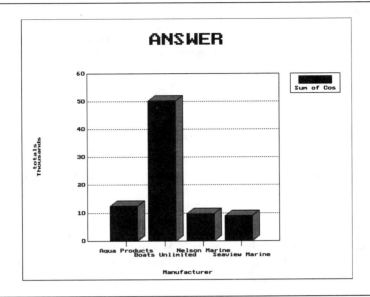

Figure 9-14.   *3D bar graph*

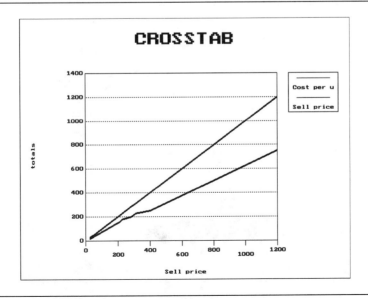

Figure 9-15.   *XY graph*

XY Graph

The XY graph displays a relationship between two sets of values in a line graph format. See Figure 9-15. For example, you might show absentee days on one axis and increased overhead expenses on the other—one value relating to another perhaps in a causative manner.

Area Graph

An area graph displays cumulative values, as shown in Figure 9-16. It is a cross between a line graph and a stacked bar graph, showing the sum of the parts in a line graph format.

Line Graph

A line graph shows values as one or more lines and is often used to display trends, as shown in Figure 9-17. Although they can be a very effective way to show trends, they can become quickly cluttered and unreadable with too many lines.

Pie Graph

The pie graph, as shown in Figure 9-18, dramatically shows the parts of a whole. These graphs are used to show the relationship of the parts. For example, how many dollars are spent by various departments, or which products bring in the most revenue.

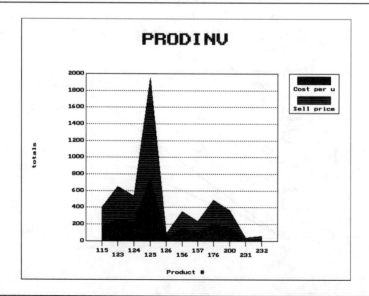

Figure 9-16.   *Area graph*

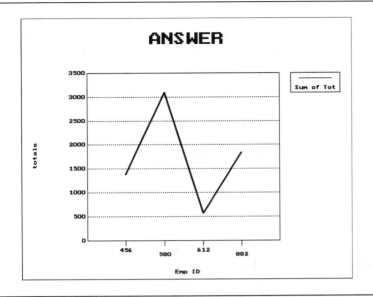

Figure 9-17.   *Line graph*

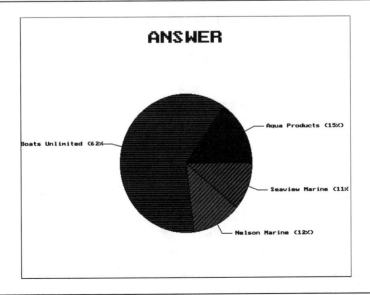

Figure 9-18.   *Pie graph*

Marker Graph

A marker graph displays or plots individual values represented by markers at specific points in the graph for each series, as shown in Figure 9-19. These can show patterns between values.

Combined Line and Marker Graph

The combined line and marker graph plots values with markers and then links them together with lines, as shown in Figure 9-20. This can show the individual patterns as well as any trends represented.

Design Concepts

The concepts and rules for planning a table for a graph have been covered earlier in this chapter. It is important that the fields are placed in the positions that produce the desired results. Briefly, the rules are that in a nonkeyed table, the first nonnumeric field is used for the x-axis in the graph. This may mean rearranging the fields. In a keyed table, the last keyed field becomes the field for the x-axis. The field that is used for the first of the series elements is the one in which the cursor is positioned when you press CTRL-F7 to create the graph, and this must be a numeric field. The next five

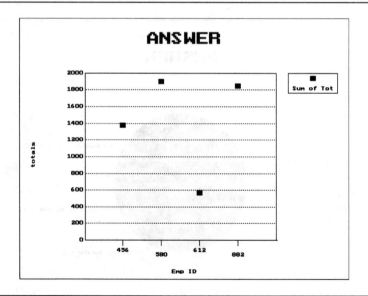

Figure 9-19.   *Marker graph*

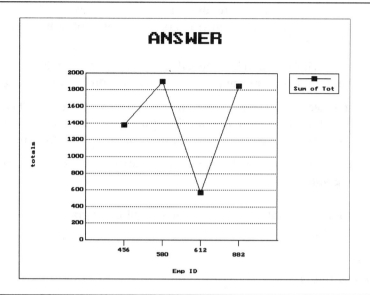

Figure 9-20. *Combined line and marker graph*

fields (if there are that many) to the right of the one the cursor is on are used as additional series elements.

Refer to "Elements in a Graph" and "How Values Are Displayed" to review how data is transformed from the table to a graph.

You may want to perform a query that produces an Answer table that can be the basis for the graph, or create a Crosstab table that summarizes the data that you want to graph.

Other Considerations

In addition to arranging the fields in the table so that data is presented in the most usable way, consider the best type of graph to use for the display.

Here are some concepts to consider:

- Bar graphs are generally used for displaying comparisons of values. For example, you could compare corporate earnings for each of the last five years.

- Stacked bar graphs show how each of the series elements contributes to a category total, for example, how different products are sold by a salesperson.

- Area graphs are good for displaying cumulative totals, for example, the cumulative sales for a product over time.

- Line graphs best display trends. For example, you could show the rate of inflation over a period of ten years, or the number of housing starts over a period of time.

- If too much information is crammed into a graph, it loses its impact. Too many dates in the x-axis, for example, make a graph cluttered and hard to read.

- Select a color that attracts attention, if that is available to you. If color is not available, think about how you can display information so that it is emphasized. You might choose a large font size for titles, or explode sections of a pie chart.

- Titles attract attention to the graph. Use a title that easily identifies the purpose of the graph.

The best idea is probably to experiment with different graph types for the same data to compare the effectiveness of each.

Handling Defaults

Within the Custom Configuration Program, permanent defaults have been set that affect the way your graphs will be produced. For example, the default graph produced with Instant Graph is set here, as well as color and fill defaults. If you want to change these permanent defaults, it must be done from the Custom Configuration Program (CCP).

However, you can change the defaults for the current session only from **Image/Graphs/Modify**. When you change this setting, your changes will be lost when Paradox is exited, unless you specifically save the modified settings with **Image/Graph/Save**, as you'll see later in the chapter.

If you want to return the changes to the default just for the duration of the current session, choose **Image/Graph/Reset**.

Using the Graph Designer with Modify

Designing a custom graph is done from the **Image/Graph** menu shown here:

It contains six options for modifying the graph settings file (the file containing graph specifications as opposed to the image of the graph), saving the settings, loading a setting file not currently in use, resetting the setting to reinstall defaults, creating a Crosstab table, and printing or saving the modified image itself.

The first option on the Graph menu is **M**odify. Choose **I**mage/**G**raph/**M**odify from the Main menu to go to the Graph Designer where custom graphs can be designed. In the Graph Designer you can make any of the following changes: choose the type of graph that will best display the data in a specific table; change the way the axes and grids display ranges of values or the intervals between marks; change the titles; change colors—either colors displayed on the screen or colors used to print; and change the margins and orientation (landscape or portrait) before printing. You can also choose whether to print the graph, view it onscreen, or save it to a file; and specify how long the graph will be displayed on the screen.

The System menu is available in the Graph Designer menu, just as it is in other Paradox functions. See Chapter 2 for details on the System menu.

Selecting a Type of Graph

The Modify option allows you to enter the Graph Designer where you can create or modify a graph. Your first task can be to change the type of graph and the type of series for a mixed-type graph. You saw the ten types of graphs displayed earlier in this chapter. Follow these steps to select one of the types:

1. Choose **I**mage/**G**raph/**M**odify. The Customize Graph Type form is displayed on the desktop, as shown in Figure 9-21. A list of graph types is displayed in the upper-right section of the form. A highlighted letter in parentheses is displayed as part of the name of each graph type.

2. The cursor is in the first field displaying the default graph type—Stacked Bar is displayed unless it was changed in the Custom Configuration Program. Type a letter representing the type of graph you want. As soon as you type the letter, the entire name of the new graph type is displayed in the field.

3. You can further customize the graph after choosing the graph type. The choices available depend upon the graph type you select.

4. When finished customizing the graph settings, press F2 (Do-It!) or click on **D**o-It! to save and return to the desktop.

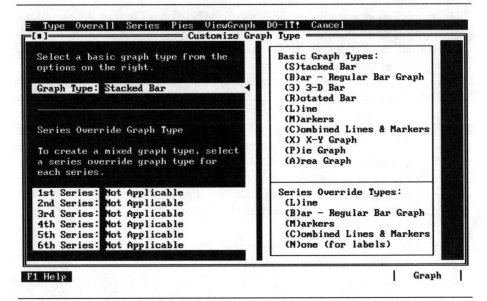

Figure 9-21.   *Customize Graph Type form*

Using Series Override

The Series Override options in the lower half of the Customize Graph Type form are used to combine two or more types of graphs in one graph. You can use this for emphasis in line, bar, marker, and combined line and marker graphs. For example, you could use a bar graph to show the sales of each product by each sales rep; and, to emphasize the sales of one of the products, show those sales as a line and marker graph overriding the bars.

The Override option can be applied to any of the series elements used in the graph. The series are represented by numbers in the lower-left corner of the Customize Graph Type form, and the choices for the override are displayed to the right.

The basic Graph Type is used for the graph as a whole. The Series Override Graph Type is used for any series that you want to emphasize by showing it as a different graph type.

Only four of the basic graph types can be used in combination with series override graph types: line, bar (not stacked bar or 3D bar), marker, and combined line and marker. An individual basic graph type can be overridden with the line, bar, marker, combined line and marker, or none (used for labels) graph type. If you choose an override that is not valid, an error message will be displayed. To correct this, choose a different override type, or return to the Graph Type field and choose a different graph type.

*If you choose **None** as the series override, no graph will be displayed for that particular series, and you can use labels in place of graph elements (such as a bar or a marker). To do this, after choosing **None** as the series override, choose Series/LegendsAndLabels to enter the labels you want.*

To use Series Override, follow these steps:

1. Choose **Image/G**raph/**M**odify to display the Customize Graph Type form.

2. In the Customize Graph Type form, press TAB to move to the Series Override section and type the letter representing the type of override you want for the first series. Repeat for the remaining series, if you like.

3. After entering the overrides, make further changes, if you like, or press F2 (Do-It!) or click on **D**o-It! to save and return to the desktop.

4. You can then create a graph that shows the changes. Figure 9-22 shows a graph with a line override. The bar graphs show the selling price of each product, and the line graph shows the cost of each unit, emphasizing the mark-up for each product.

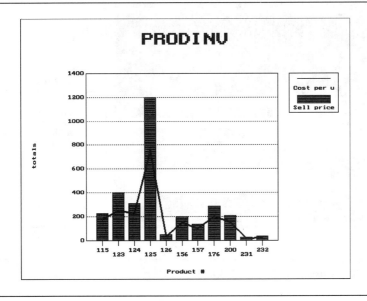

Figure 9-22.   *Graph containing a Series Override*

It is a good idea to use contrasting graph types when combining a basic graph type with a series override. A combination that is used frequently is a bar graph for the basic graph type and a line graph for a series override.

Using the Overall Menu

The **O**verall menu is used to change titles, screen and printer colors, axes and grids, margin settings before printing, portrait or landscape orientation, the output device, and to specify the time the graph is displayed on the screen.

Changing or Adding Titles

The **O**verall/**T**itles menu is used to change or add titles, and select a different font size.

To edit or add a title, follow these steps:

1. From the Customize Graph Type form, press F10 (Menu) to access the Graph Designer menu and choose **O**verall/**T**itles. A Customize Graph Titles form appears, as shown in Figure 9-23.

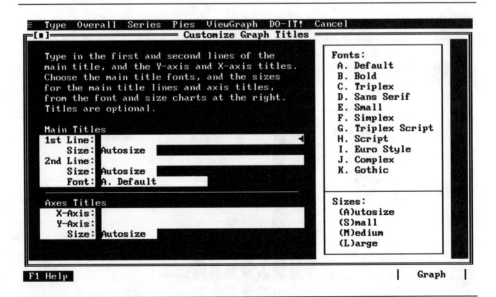

Figure 9-23.   *Customize Graph Titles form*

2. Move the cursor to the various title fields, and type a new title or edit the present title. You can enter two lines for the main title, as well as adding a title for both the x- and y-axis lines. You can enter up to 25 characters for the titles.

3. If you want to remove a title, enter a blank in the 1st Line titles box. To do this, Paradox recommends entering the blank characters produced by pressing ALT and the numbers **255** entered from the number keypad.

You may now change the size and the font. You have four sizes, listed in the lower-right corner of the form, to choose from:

- *(A)utosize* allows Paradox to choose the font.
- *(S)mall* selects a small-sized font.
- *(M)edium* selects a medium-sized font.
- *(L)arge* selects a large-sized font.

(S)mall, (M)edium, and (L)arge may depend on the availability of small, medium, or large fonts for your printer.

The fonts are listed in the upper-right of the form and also depend upon the fonts available for your printer.

To change the size, follow these steps:

1. Move the cursor to the Size field.

2. Type the letter displayed in parentheses to select the size you want.

To change the font, follow these steps:

1. Move the cursor to the Font field.

2. Type the letter representing the font you want.

3. When done, choose another option from the Graph Designer menu, or press F2 (Do-It!) or click on **D**o-It! to save and return to the desktop.

Changing Colors

You can use the **O**verall/**C**olors menu to change screen colors or the colors used to print depending upon your printer capabilities. Colors can also be changed for the screen and printer using the **S**eries menu. The process is the same as that used here in the **O**verall menu.

To change colors for pie graphs, choose Pies from the Graph Designer menu.

The **C**olors menu has the following options.

Screen   This option allows you to change the colors for your screen display. You can set different colors for each of the various parts of the graph.

Printer   This option allows you to change the colors for your printer. Make the selections the same way you select colors for the screen.

Copy   This option allows you to copy the colors you set for the screen to the colors to be used when printing (or vice versa). When you choose **C**opy, another menu is displayed with two choices:

- *ScreenToPrinter* copies the screen colors to the printer.

- *PrinterToScreen* copies the colors set for the printer to the screen.

To change colors, follow these steps:

1. Choose **O**verall/**C**olors. A second menu appears, with the **S**creen, **P**rinter, and **C**opy options, as shown here:

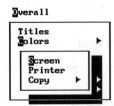

2. Choose **S**creen to change screen colors; choose **P**rinter to change the colors for printing the graph; choose **C**opy to copy the colors that have been set for the screen to the printer, or the reverse. When either **S**creen or **P**rinter are chosen, a Customize Graph Screen Colors form is displayed, as shown in Figure 9-24.

3. To change colors, move your cursor to the element you want to change and type the letter representing the color you want for it.

4. When finished, choose other options from the Graph Designer menu, or press F2 (Do-It!) or click on **D**o-It! to return to the desktop.

Changing Axes

Choose **O**verall/**A**xes to change scaling and tick mark displays. As discussed previously, there are two axes in graphs (except for pie graphs). The horizontal x-axis at

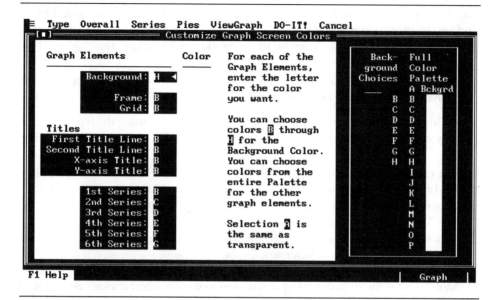

Figure 9-24.   *Customize Graph Screen Colors form*

the bottom of the graph generally displays the categories used in the graph. The vertical y-axis at the left side of the graph generally displays the values for each category. The axes display a range of values, and tick marks and labels are shown at various increments along these axes. These markers can be changed depending upon the scale you choose. *Tick mark labels* are the currency or other numerical amounts, percentages, dates, product numbers, names of sales reps, and so on, that are displayed along the x- and y-axes to identify the categories or the range of values.

You have two choices for changing scaling: (A)utomatic and (M)anual.

(A)utomatic   This is normally used, so you would select it only when changing from Manual back to Automatic. The scale starts at 0 and extends upward depending upon the values in the graph. It ends slightly higher than the largest value that is to be graphed.

(M)anual   This allows you to specify the increments. You use this option if you wanted to emphasize the differences in values between the various categories. Perhaps the differences in values between categories are fairly small. By changing the increments, you can add emphasis to the differences. When you choose Manual, you then fill in the high and low values for the axis. Be sure the values are consistent with the values that are to be graphed.

For example, to graph the cost of products that range from $9000 to $16,000, Paradox will automatically create a y-axis with a range from 0 to 18,000, and with increments of 2000. To better display the differences in costs of each product, set the scaling for the y-axis at **M**anual, set the low range at 7000, set the high range at 17,000, and set the increments at 1000.

To change the scale (the intervals of the marks), follow these steps:

1. Choose **O**verall/**A**xes from the Graph Designer menu. A Customize Graph Axes form appears, as shown in Figure 9-25.

2. In the top half of the Axes form, type the letter representing the type of scaling you want, and enter new increments if you chose Manual as the type of scaling.

You can reduce the numbers in tick mark labels by specifying a Low and High setting in the Scaling area only if you have chosen **M**anual for scaling. Then enter an increment value larger than the one Paradox uses. After that, type **Y** for Yes in the Display Axis Scaling field at the bottom of the screen.

Tick mark choices are displayed in the lower half of the Customize Graph Axes form. You have six choices of tick mark displays.

(F)ixed   This is the default setting and is used to display numbers with two decimal places.

(S)cientific   This displays numbers in scientific notation.

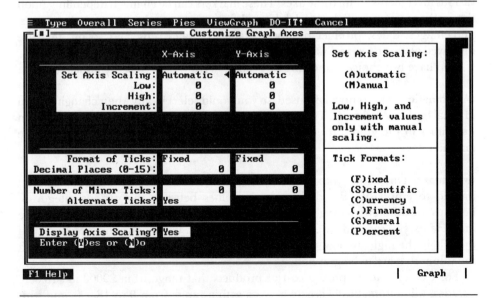

Figure 9-25.   Customize Graph Axes form

($)Currency   This displays numbers with a dollar sign.

(,)Financial   This separates digits by commas and encloses negative numbers in parentheses.

(G)eneral   This displays numbers as they appear in the table.

(P)ercent   This displays numbers as percentages.

To change the format for tick mark labels, follow these steps:

1. Move the cursor to the Format of Ticks field and type the character representing the choice you want to use.

2. After entering the type of tick format, you can further change the tick display options by following one of these steps:

   • Create minor ticks (minor ticks have no labels) by entering a value in the Number of Minor Ticks field. Enter the number of ticks appearing between major ticks—**5**, for example, will place five ticks between the major tick labels.

   • If you want tick mark labels to be displayed all on the same level, type **N** for No in the Alternate Tick Mark field. If tick mark labels are to be displayed on two levels, type **Y** for Yes. Yes is the default for tick mark labels.

3. After entering the choices you want, choose other options from the Graph Designer menu, or press F2 (Do-It!), or click on **Do**-It! to return to the desktop.

Changing Grids

You can have grid lines represent the tick marks on your graphs; this makes viewing and interpreting the graph easier. You can change the patterns and colors for these lines if you like.

To change patterns or colors of grid lines, follow these steps:

1. Choose **O**verall/**G**rid. A Customize Grids and Frames form appears, as shown in Figure 9-26.

2. If you don't want the grid lines to be displayed, set the color for the grid lines to be the same as the background color. The background color is indicated in the Color Palette at the right.

   If you have a rotated bar graph, for example, that clearly shows the values in each category, the graph may be less cluttered by not showing the grid lines.

3. Type a number representing the type of grid line and a letter for the color you want.

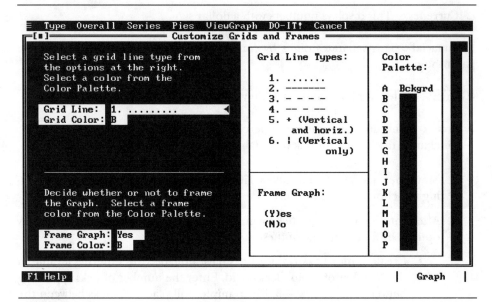

Figure 9-26.   *Customize Grids and Frames form*

4. To frame the grid lines, type **Y** for Yes at the Frame Graph field. Type **N** for No to remove the frame.

5. Type a letter representing the frame color you want.

6. When finished, choose other options from the Graph Designer menu, or press F2 (Do-It!) or click on **D**o-It! to return to the desktop.

Changing Printer Layout

You use the **O**verall menu to change printer layout for the graph. You can change margins, the height, and width of the graph, select between landscape or portrait orientation, enter page breaks, and set color plotter speeds.

To use the **O**verall menu to change layout, follow these steps:

1. Choose **O**verall/**P**rinterLayout from the Graph Designer menu. A Customize Graph Layout for Printing form is displayed, as shown in Figure 9-27.

2. Choose the measurement standard you want. Type **I** in the Units field to set the measurement in inches. Type **C** to choose centimeters.

3. To set the margins and height and width, select any of the following:

   • Measurement for the Left Margin

   • Measurement for the Top Margin

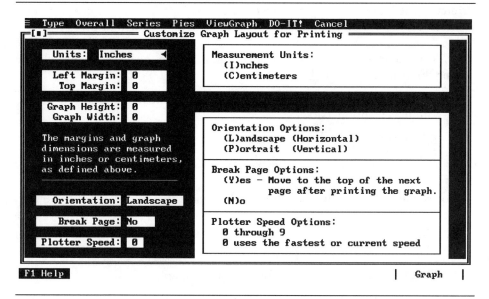

Figure 9-27. *Customize Graph Layout for Printing form*

- Measurement for the overall height of the graph

- Measurement for the overall width of the graph

4. Choose an orientation. In the Orientation field, type **P** to choose Portrait (where the page height is usually 11 inches); type **L** to choose Landscape (where the page height is usually 8.5 inches).

5. Specify page breaks by typing **Y** for Yes, if you want to begin a new page after printing the graph, or type **N** for No, if you want printing to continue below the graph on the same page.

6. Set a plotter speed between 0 and 9. The 0 is the default and is the fastest setting, and 9 is the slowest. If you are printing transparencies, 2 is recommended.

7. When finished, choose other options from the Graph Designer menu, or press F2 (Do-It!), or click on **Do**-It! to return to the desktop.

Specifying How to Print

You use the **O**verall/**D**evice menu to specify printing issues, including selecting a printer or specifying how to save the graph image to a file. Two options are available from the **D**evice menu.

Printer   This allows you to specify the printer to be used. You can choose up to four printers. Use the Custom Configuration Program to define the four printers.

File   This allows you to store the image of your graph on the disk. You then choose among three more options:

- *CurrentPrinter* saves the file as a printer output formatted for the current printer with the extension .GRF.

- *EPS* saves the file as an encapsulated postscript file with the extension .EPS.

- *PIC* saves the file as a Lotus file using the extension .PIC.

To use the **O**verall menu for printing, follow these steps:

1. Choose **O**verall/**D**evice from the Graph Designer menu, as shown in Figure 9-28.

2. Choose the options you want for the current graph.

3. When finished, choose other options, or press F2 (Do-It!), or click on **D**o-It! to return to the desktop.

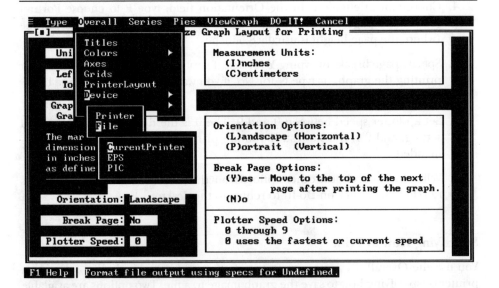

Figure 9-28.   *Overall/Device menu*

Using Wait

You use Wait on the Overall menu to specify what length of time the graph is on screen. When you choose **O**verall/**W**ait from the Graph Designer menu, you have two choices: **K**eystroke and **D**uration.

Keystroke   This allows you to specify that the graph is displayed until a key is pressed. This is the default.

Duration   This allows you to set the length of time the graph remains displayed before the screen reverts automatically to the Main menu. **D**uration can be used if you want to display a series of graphs and limit the time each is displayed on the screen. This creates a display similar to a slide presentation, except the display is on the monitor. If you have access to an overhead projector that can show the images from your monitor, **D**uration is a good way of presenting a "slide" show. Chapter 10 discusses using scripts to create and display graphs that may be chained automatically.

Using the Series Menu

The **S**eries menu in the Graph Designer is used to change markers, colors, and patterns for each of the data series elements in your graph. It is also used to customize the labels for each of the series. The **S**eries menu offers three options.

(L)egendsAndLabels   This displays a second form where you can move around and change labels as in any other Paradox form. You can type **Y** for Yes at the field asking for Legend to indicate that you want the legend to be printed. If you do not enter text for each Series legend, the field name will be used for the legend. Type **N** for No if you do not want to display the legend. At the bottom of the form you can specify the alignment of the *interior labels*, which show the values in the graph itself. The choices there are **C**enter, **A**bove, **R**ight, **B**elow, or **N**one. The alignment is in relation to the graph element. Type the letter in parentheses that represents the choice you want.

(M)arkersAndFills   This displays a second form where you can make changes to the display of markers and fill patterns for each series in the graph. *Markers* are the symbols used to represent values in a marker graph or a line and marker graph. *Fills* are the characters used to fill in areas in bar graphs or area graphs. Again, you can move around in this form, entering the letters that represent the fill patterns and marker symbols that are available as shown in the form. You enter the letter you want for each series listed at the left of the form.

(C)olors   This allows you to select colors for each series element for the screen; for the printer; or to copy color settings from screen to printer, or from printer to screen. After choosing the option you want, a second form is displayed in which you choose the colors you want for each of the series. Choose the colors the way you choose colors in **O**verall/**C**olors.

To use the **S**eries menu, follow these steps:

1. Choose **S**eries. The second menu appears, as shown here:

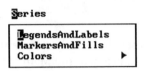

2. Select one of the three choices.

3. When finished, choose other options from the Graph Designer menu, or press F2 (Do-It!) or click on **D**o-It! to return to the desktop.

Using the Pies Option

Pie graphs have no axes and contain only one data series; therefore, they are formatted differently than other graphs. The **P**ies option allows you to change the label and explode sections of the graph. You can also change the colors or fill patterns used for the slices of the pie.

To use the Customize Pie Graph form, follow these steps:

1. Choose **P**ies from the Graph Designer menu. A second form appears, as shown in Figure 9-29.

2. Type the character representing the choice you want in the Label Format field, then select from one of these four choices:

   • *(V)alue* is the default format and shows the values as they appear in the table.

   • *(%)Percent* displays a percentage of the whole for each portion of the pie.

   • *($)Currency* displays the value for each portion in a dollar format.

   • *(N)one* displays no labels.

3. To explode a portion of the pie, type **Y** for Yes at the label for that portion that you want to explode. The portions are numbered 1 through 9 in the lower section of the Customize Pie Graph form. Type **N** for No if you want to return the portion to normal size. An example of an exploded pie graph is shown in Figure 9-30.

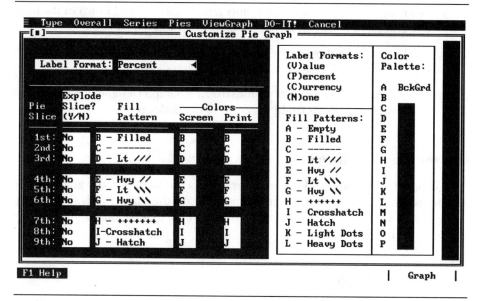

Figure 9-29. *Customize Pie Graph form*

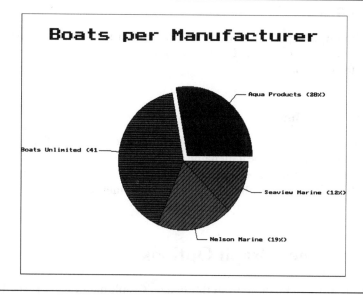

Figure 9-30. *Exploded section in a pie graph*

4. To change colors, move to the Colors section (Screen and Print) of the form and enter letters that represent the colors that you want.

5. To change fill patterns, move to that section of the form, and type the letters representing the fill patterns you want for each slice of the pie.

6. When finished, choose other options from the Graph Designer menu, or press F2 (Do-It!), or click on **D**o-It! to return to the desktop.

Using the ViewGraph Option

The **I**mage/**G**raph/**M**odify/**V**iewGraph option is used to display the graph on the screen, to print it, or to save the image as a file on the disk. This is the same as **I**mage/**G**raph/**V**iewGraph, except that you don't have to leave the Graph Designer mode to use it.

Displaying the Graph

It is helpful to first view the graph on screen before printing it, to see how it will look. You can then make any changes you want before actually printing the output.

To display the graph on screen, choose **V**iewGraph/**S**creen. This is the same as pressing CTRL-F7 (Instant Graph). When finished viewing, press any key to return to the desktop.

Printing a Graph

After designing the graph and viewing it to see that it displays information in an effective way, you can print it. To print, choose **V**iewGraph/**P**rinter. The output is sent directly to the printer.

Saving the Graph Image

The *graph image* is the way the specific graph is displayed on screen. To save this image, choose **V**iewGraph/**F**ile, type a filename, and press ENTER.

ViewGraph/**F**ile cannot be used to save changes in graph settings. To save graph settings, choose **I**mage/**G**raph/**S**ave from the Main menu.

Using the Other Graph Options

Much of the work to be done from the **I**mage/**G**raph menu is concerned with the **M**odify option. However, there are other options which are critical to effectively using a graph. These options allow you to load a setting file into memory, override the current settings in memory, save settings created wth the **Modify** option, and reset the options and restore the original defaults into memory. The **C**rossTab option is discussed earlier in the chapter, and the ViewGraph option is much the same as Image/Graph/Modify/ViewGraph, also discussed earlier.

Loading a Setting

If you have saved any custom settings using **I**mage/**G**raph/**S**ave, they can be retrieved using the **L**oad option. You might want to save settings, if you consistently produce graphs with the same settings for each month, for example. Just use the **L**oad option to bring up those settings whenever you want to produce graphs with them. Use the following steps to do this:

1. Choose **I**mage/**G**raph/**L**oad. A dialog box asking for the filename of the settings will be displayed.

2. Type the name of the settings file, or press ENTER to display a list of filenames. Choose the setting file you want and press ENTER.

If you want to confirm what the settings are, place a table on the desktop (be sure it's active) and press CTRL-F7 (Instant Graph). The new graph settings should be applied to the graph that is displayed.

Saving a Setting

The graph settings that have been used to design a specific custom graph can be saved by choosing **I**mage/**G**raph/**S**ave from the Main menu. Paradox adds the extension .G automatically to a graph filename. The saved graph is an object; however, it is not associated with a specific table family as other Paradox objects are. It can be applied to any table with data that is appropriate for the graph design. To emphasize, this saves the settings, not the graph image. When you use these saved settings to produce a graph, the result is an image, and the image is not saved.

If you want to save the image (that is, the actual graph) use Image/Graph/View- *Graph/File, give the image a filename, and press* ENTER. *The file is saved in a format that is compatible with the printer being used.*

To save a setting follow these steps:

1. Modify the graph settings to produce the type of graph you want.

2. Choose **I**mage/**G**raph/**S**ave. A dialog box will be displayed for a filename.

3. Type a filename for the new settings and press ENTER to save.

Resetting a Setting

To return graph settings to the default graph settings, use **R**eset. You might use this if you do not want to use the current settings to graph the active table; or if you have been changing the settings, don't like what you have done, and want to start over.

To return graph settings to the default, follow these steps:

1. Choose **I**mage/**G**raph/**R**eset.

2. Choose **OK** to restore the defaults, or **C**ancel to leave the current settings as is.

To change the default graph settings, use the Custom Configuration Program (CCP).

Saving or Printing the Image

Use the ViewGraph option to save the *image* (not the graph settings) to a file on disk, to display the graph image on the screen, or to print the graph. The **V**iewGraph option here is the same as the **V**iewGraph option on the Graph Designer menu.

To save a current image, follow these steps:

1. Make the table that you want to graph the active table on the desktop.

2. Choose **I**mage/**G**raph/**V**iewGraph. A menu showing **S**creen, **P**rinter, **F**ile is displayed.

3. Choose **S**creen to display the graph on screen; choose **P**rinter to send the current image to the printer or plotter; choose **F**ile to save the graph image to a printer output file on the disk. If you choose **F**ile, a dialog box for a filename will be displayed. Type the filename you want and press ENTER. Paradox will automatically add the extension .GRF, saving it in the format for the current printer. You can also save it in EPS (Encapsulated PostScript) or in PIC format. This file can be printed later, or you can bring it into a word processor and print it there, if it is in a compatible format.

To send the image to the printer or to a file, a printer must have been defined in the CCP. If it has not been defined, you will get an error message when choosing either Printer or File. To define a printer, go to the CCP and choose Graph/Printer. You can then choose SetPrinter and select a printer for the output.

You can also choose Overall/Device/Printer from the Graph Designer menu to specify a printer that is different from the default printer.

Working with Graphs on a Network

As with other Paradox objects, when you work with graphs, you must first show the table in table view, which puts a prevent full lock on the table. This allows others the maximum usage of the table while you work on it. If others on the network have a full lock on the table you want to use, you must wait until they finish their work before you can use the table.

You can use a script to create an autoregraph system that updates your graph as changes are made throughout the network. This will be covered in Chapter 10.

If you are using a Crosstab table on a network, Paradox tries to detect changes, and will restart the CrossTab if changes are made. When this happens a message will appear; you can cancel the automatic restarts by pressing CTRL-BREAK if you do not want the interruption.

Part *IV*

Scripts and Programming

Chapter **10**

Creating and Using Scripts

In this chapter you learn how to create and use scripts. A *script* is a file that stores frequently used keystrokes that perform Paradox functions or PAL commands. This chapter also teaches how to plan for a script, how to chain or combine several scripts, how to repeat one script several times, and how to use the Editor to change scripts. In addition, the Instant Script feature is covered here. The **S**cripts menu, shown in the following illustration, is used for these functions.

Scripts

Play
BeginRecord
QuerySave
ShowPlay
RepeatPlay
Editor ▶

Recording a Script

The keystrokes stored in a script can be played back at any time to reproduce Paradox functions or PAL commands. Paradox automatically adds the extension .SC to script files. When the script is played back the first time, a second related file is created with the extension .SC2. Because it is faster than the .SC file, the .SC2 file is used to play each script; however, the .SC file is the one displayed when you edit the script.

There are three ways of recording keystrokes for the script:

- Choose **Scripts/BeginRecord** from the Main menu. Enter the keystrokes you want to save. To stop recording, choose **Scripts/End-Record** from the Main menu.

- Press ALT-F3 (Instant Script Record), and enter the keystrokes you wish to save. To stop recording, press ALT-F3 again.

- Press ALT-F10 to access the PAL menu and choose **BeginRecord**, record the keystrokes, then press ALT-F10 again, and choose **End-Record** from the PAL menu.

Before recording your keystrokes, plan the results you want to produce and determine which keystrokes will accomplish these results. Suggestions for planning are discussed later in this chapter.

Using the Scripts Menu to Create a Script

The **S**cripts menu is used to save the recorded keystrokes in a scripts file. This is different from using ALT-F3 (Instant Script Record), which saves the keystrokes in a file named INSTANT.SC. The keystrokes saved in the INSTANT.SC file are only available until you next use Instant Script Record, at which time the new script replaces the old.

To record keystrokes in a script, follow these steps:

1. Choose **Scripts/BeginRecord** from the Main menu. A dialog box appears asking for the script's filename, as shown here:

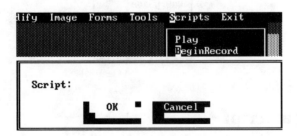

2. Type a filename using standard DOS naming conventions—eight characters or less, no spaces. Press ENTER to begin recording. An *R* displayed in the lower-right corner of the screen in the status bar indicates that you are recording keystrokes.

3. Enter the keystrokes you want to save (the keystrokes needed to perform the various Paradox functions). From this point on, all keystrokes will be saved in the script.

4. When finished, choose **S**cripts/**E**nd-Record. This stops recording, saves the keystrokes in the script file, and returns you to Main mode; you can also choose **C**ancel to stop recording without saving.

If the Main menu is not available so you can choose **S**cripts, follow these steps:

1. Press ALT-F10 (PAL Menu). A second menu is displayed, as shown here:

```
┌─PAL Menu──┐
│ ▒ancel    │
│ End-Record│
└───────────┘
```

2. Choose **E**nd-Record, or choose **C**ancel to end recording without saving.

*Sometimes the Main menu will be unavailable in order to begin recording a script. If you are designing a form or in **E**dit or **C**oEdit mode for example, you would not be able to access the **S**cripts menu. In these cases, press ALT-F10 to get to the PAL menu, which allows you to choose some of the same options that are available in the **S**cripts menu.*

Example of a Script

This example shows how to create a script that displays an order form on the desktop. This is a task that would be performed frequently; saving all the keystrokes in a script makes using the form more efficient.

To create the script, follow these steps:

1. Choose **S**cripts/**B**eginRecord, type a name for the script, and press ENTER. You'll see the letter *R* appear at the right end of the status bar.

2. Choose the table on which the form will be based.

3. Choose **I**mage/**P**ickForm, and select the form for the table. (If you want a custom form for the table, design it before creating the script.)

4. Press F9 to go to **E**dit mode.

5. Press END and PGDN to go to the next blank record.

6. Press ALT-F10 (PAL Menu), and choose **E**nd-Record to end the recording and save the script. Use the PAL menu to end recording when you are in **E**dit mode or working in a form. You should no longer see an *R* in the status bar.

Scripts Menu Options Available While Recording

While you are recording the script, all Paradox menu options and features are available, with the exception of the Report Previewer and the Scripts Editor. Also, you cannot record the keystrokes used inside another script. You can, however, do a MiniEdit, and write a script or open the script you are recording.

During the recording, use the keystrokes you normally use to perform the various Paradox functions.

The Scripts menu changes during recording, as shown here:

```
Scripts
┌─────────────┐
│ Cancel      │
│ End-Record  │
│ Play        │
│ QuerySave   │
│ RepeatPlay  │
└─────────────┘
```

These options are in effect while you are recording:

- *Cancel* stops recording, deletes the keystrokes that have been saved up to that point, and returns to the Main mode.

- *End-Record* stops recording, saves the keystrokes in the script file, and returns to the Main mode.

- *Play* runs another script within the current script that you are recording. This is used to *chain* or combine several scripts, one after the other.

- *QuerySave* saves the query that is on the desktop. This is an efficient way of storing the keystrokes that are used to display results of a frequently asked question. When the query forms are displayed on the desktop, and the checkmarks and any operators or expressions have been entered in the various fields, you can then use **Q**uerySave to save the forms. This script does not perform the query; rather it displays the query forms that are saved in the script. You can then press F2 (Do-It!) to perform the query. This command is covered in Chapter 6, and it is also discussed briefly later in this chapter.

- *RepeatPlay* repeats playing a script a specified number of times. **R**epeatPlay is convenient, for example, if you want to perform the same action on several records in a table.

Playing the Script

To run the keystrokes stored in the script, you can either use the **S**cripts/**P**lay menu, or you can use Instant Script Play if Instant Script was used to create the script. (Instant Scripts are discussed next.)

To use the **S**cripts menu to play back keystrokes that have been saved in a script file, follow these steps:

1. Choose **S**cripts/**P**lay from the Main menu. A dialog box, as shown in Figure 10-1, asks for a filename. (You can also press ALT-F10 to display the PAL menu and choose **P**lay.)

2. Type the filename of the script and press ENTER; or press ENTER to display a list of script filenames, choose the one you want, and press ENTER again to run it. The stored keystrokes are run immediately.

Figure 10-2 shows the results of playing back the script that was created in the previous example. The custom order form is displayed in **E**dit mode, and the cursor is positioned at the first field in a blank record. The accompanying table is under the form on the desktop.

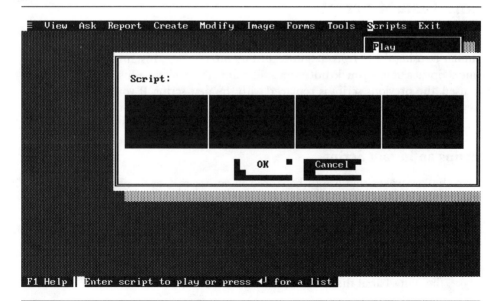

Figure 10-1.   *Scripts/Play dialog box*

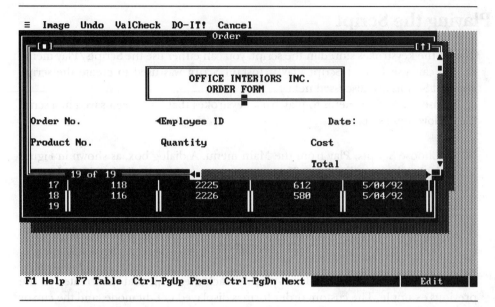

Figure 10-2.   *Results of playing back a script*

Using Instant Script

You start Instant Script by pressing ALT-F3 (Instant Script Record). The procedure is similar to using the **Scripts/BeginRecord** menu; however, Instant Script stores only one script at a time—you do not enter a filename. The next time Instant Script Record is used, the previous script is replaced with the new script. If you want to save the keystrokes stored in Instant Script, use **Tools/Rename/Script** to save it.

Creating an Instant Script

Plan the keystrokes that are to be stored in your script, as you would when using **Scripts/BeginRecord**.

To use Instant Script Record, follow these steps:

1. Press ALT-F3 (Instant Script Record). A message appears briefly on the screen telling you the recording is beginning. An *R* is displayed at the right end of the status bar at the bottom of the screen.

2. Enter the keystrokes to be stored in the Instant Script.

3. When finished, press ALT-F3 to end the recording. Another message appears briefly telling you recording has ended.

Example of Using Instant Script

The following example uses Instant Script to add the same area code in front of several telephone numbers. The keystrokes include pressing ALT-F5 to go to field view, entering the parentheses and area code numbers, ending field view, and moving the cursor to the next record.

To use Instant Script, follow these steps:

1. Display the table on the desktop. In this example, the area code (206) is added to telephone numbers in the Wash-ton table.

2. Press F9 (Edit) if you are not already in **E**dit mode.

3. Move the cursor to the end of the first telephone number.

4. Press ALT-F3 (Instant Script Record). A message tells you recording is beginning, and *R* appears at the right end of the status bar.

5. Press ALT-F5 (Field View). The cursor becomes a shaded box.

6. Move the cursor to the first digit in the telephone number.

7. Type **(206)** and press the SPACEBAR once.

8. Press ENTER to end field view, and press the DOWN ARROW to go to the next value.

9. Press ALT-F3 to end recording.

Playing the Instant Script

When Instant Script Record is used to store keystrokes temporarily, use Instant Script Play to run them by pressing ALT-F4 (Instant Script Play).

You are not able to use ALT-F4 (Instant Script Play) while you are using Instant Script to record a script. Before pressing ALT-F4 (Instant Script Play), check the status bar to see if the R indicating Recording is turned off.

Saving the Instant Script

If the keystrokes entered in Instant Script are to be used later or in other Paradox sessions, you can save them in a regular Scripts file. They are, however, stored in INSTANT.SC and will be available in the next Paradox session, unless they have been replaced with other keystrokes.

To save the keystrokes that are stored temporarily in Instant Script, follow these steps:

1. Go to the Main menu, if you are not already there, and choose **T**ools/**R**e-name/**S**cript. A dialog box prompts you for the script filename, as shown in Figure 10-3.

2. Type **Instant** and press ENTER, or choose Instant from the list of script filenames.

3. A dialog box asks for a new script filename, as shown in Figure 10-4. Type a filename using standard DOS naming conventions and press ENTER.

*To use the script, choose Scripts/**P**lay.*

Handling Script Errors

If an error occurs while the script is playing, the message "Script error" will be displayed with a menu containing the following options:

- *Cancel* stops the playing of the script and returns to whatever mode you were in when the script error occurred.

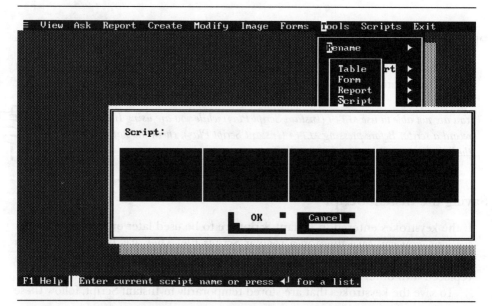

Figure 10-3. *Dialog box for Tools/Rename/Script*

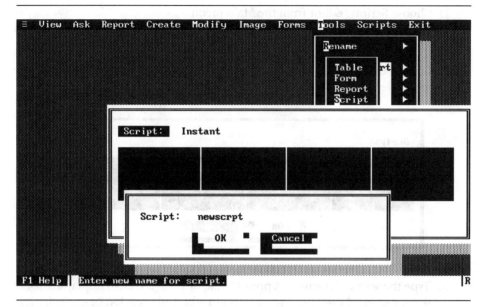

Figure 10-4.   *Dialog box asks for a new script name*

- *Debug* returns to Main mode, cancelling any **E**dit or **C**oEdit change you have made, clears the desktop, and goes to the PAL Debugger where the script can be tested and revised.

If you choose **C**ancel, you can either edit the script or record the keystrokes again, replacing the original script. Unless you have a very long script, recording the keystrokes a second time is sometimes easier than editing the script.

Editing a Script

The Scripts Editor can be used to edit the keystrokes stored in the script file, and it can also be used to print the script. Scripts can be edited using your own word processor, if you prefer. Just retrieve the script file, enter the filename and the extension .SC, edit the file, and save it. Before starting, be sure your editor is able to produce plain ASCII text without embedded control codes.

When scripts are viewed in the Scripts Editor, you can see the PAL commands and menu equivalents that were recorded when you created your script. If you are not familiar with these, refer to Chapters 12 and 13.

To edit a script, follow these steps:

1. Choose **Scripts/Editor** from the Main menu.

   As an alternate first step, you can also press ALT-E (MiniEdit). You will need to type the extension **.sc**.

2. Choose **O**pen to edit an existing script. A dialog box appears asking for the script filename, as shown here:

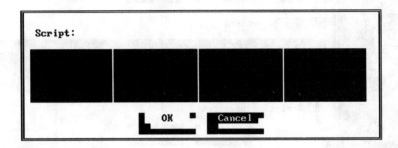

3. Type the script filename and press ENTER; or press ENTER to display the list of script names, choose the one you want to edit, and press ENTER to display it in the Editor. (See Figure 10-5.) You do not type the **.sc** here.

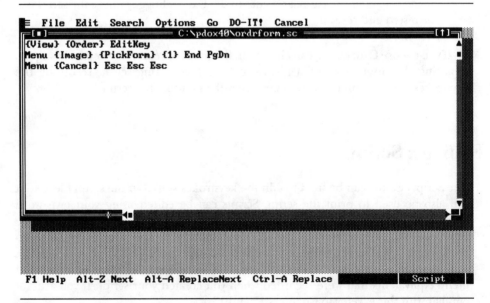

Figure 10-5.   *Scripts Editor window*

4. Edit your script. While in the Editor:

- Items shown in curly brackets are menus and options you selected.

- Items shown without brackets or quotes are key commands, variables, or array elements.

- Delete items by pressing DELETE or BACKSPACE.

- Add commands by typing the characters representing them. Enclose menu options in curly brackets.

5. To end the editing and save changes, press F2 (Do-It!) or click on **Do**-It!. To cancel editing and leave the Editor without saving, choose **Cancel** or click on the Close box.
   You can also choose **G**o from the Editor menu to leave the Editor and save the script.

*The **E**ditor menu is the same as in any other **E**ditor window except you have the **G**o option.*

Using ShowPlay

You use the **S**howPlay option in the **S**cripts menu to play back the keystrokes at a slower speed in order to see every step that has been saved. You use this to test the script, or to explain or display the script. **S**howPlay also sets Echo to fast or slow depending on the mode you choose.
   To use **S**howPlay, follow these steps:

1. Choose **S**cripts/**S**howPlay. A dialog box asks for the script filename.

2. Choose the name of the script and press ENTER.

3. A second menu appears, as shown in Figure 10-6.

4. Choose one of the following:
   - *Fast* immediately runs the script at a "fast" speed, which is slow compared to Echo normal. You can still read the keystrokes if you choose **Fast**.

   - *Slow* immediately runs the script at a speed that makes the keystrokes readable.

To stop playing the script, press CTRL-BREAK.

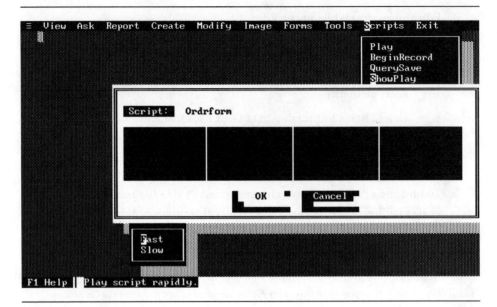

Figure 10-6.   *ShowPlay options*

Using QuerySave

The **Q**uerySave option is used to save all of the query forms that may be on the desktop at one time (it is covered in detail in Chapter 6). The query itself is not performed when the script is played later, but the query forms that have been saved in the script are displayed on the desktop automatically. You do not have to reconstruct the query forms each time you want to use them. This makes complex queries easy to use repeatedly.

To save query forms, follow these steps:

1. Display all the query forms for the query you want to perform.

2. Choose **S**cripts/**Q**uerySave.

3. Type a filename for the script, and press ENTER.

To use the script for the query, follow these steps:

1. Choose **S**cripts/**P**lay.

2. Choose the filename for the query form and press ENTER. The query forms are displayed on the desktop.

3. Press F2 (Do-It!) or click on **D**o-It! to perform the query.

Using RepeatPlay

You use the **RepeatPlay** option to repeat a script several times. **RepeatPlay** is used primarily to change values in several records in the same table. It can be used from **S**cripts in the Main menu, or from the PAL menu.

Using RepeatPlay from the Scripts Menu

1. Choose **S**cripts/**R**epeatPlay from the Main menu.

2. Choose the script you want and press ENTER. A dialog box asks for the number of times you want to repeat, as shown in Figure 10-7.

3. Type the number of times you want to repeat the script, or type **c** (for continuous) and press ENTER.

You can press CTRL-BREAK to stop playing any script. However, if a query is being played from a script, the query cannot be stopped with CTRL-BREAK.

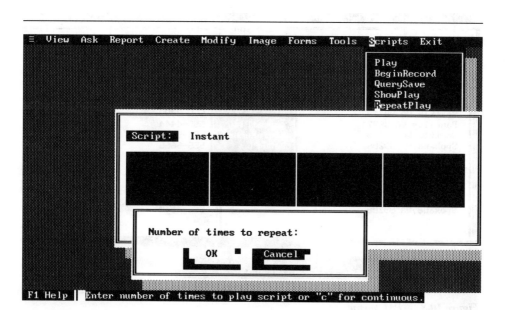

Figure 10-7. *Dialog box asks how many times to repeat*

Example of Using RepeatPlay from the PAL Menu

The following example repeats the script created previously that entered area codes in front of telephone numbers.

To use **R**epeatPlay, follow these steps:

1. Display the table on the desktop and press F9 to go to **E**dit mode. In this example, the Wash-ton table is used.

2. Move the cursor to the record where you want to begin using the script.

3. Press ALT-F10 (PAL Menu) since the **S**cripts menu is not available in **E**dit mode. The PAL menu appears, as shown in Figure 10-8.

4. Choose **R**epeatPlay.

5. Choose the script you want. Instant was the script in this example.

6. Type the number of times you want to repeat the script and press ENTER. In this example, the area code is entered 15 more times, as shown in Figure 10-9.

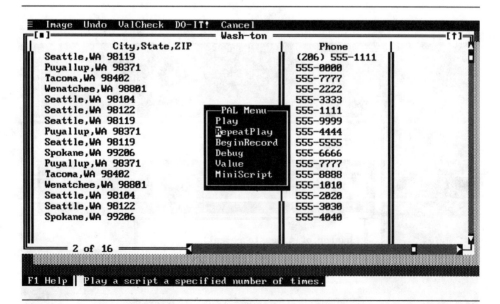

Figure 10-8. *PAL menu*

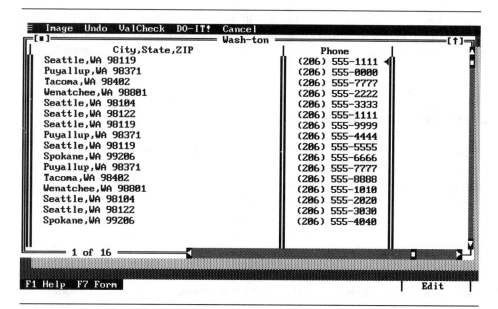

Figure 10-9.   *Area codes entered automatically as a result of repeating the Instant script*

Planning Scripts

Before recording the keystrokes, take some time to plan what belongs in the script. Here are some planning tips:

- Decide what tables, forms, queries, or graphs will be used.

- Construct any queries you want to use and save them before creating the script.

- If graphs are to be used, save the graph settings that you want before creating the script.

- Clear the desktop before recording. If a query form is on the desktop and if F2 is included in the script, when the script is played you may get some unexpected results. Clearing the desktop avoids these kinds of problems.

- If you are planning a complex script, plan to save small modules as separate scripts, then chain them in a larger script. You can rename script modules using **T**ools/**R**ename.

- Empty any temporary tables that may be used, such as Answer tables or CrossTab tables. Use **T**ools/**M**ore/**E**mpty in your script to do this.

- Use **S**cripts/**S**howPlay/**S**low to test your script.

- Use the Scripts Editor window to edit the script. However, it is often just as easy to record the keystrokes a second time if there are many changes you want to make to the script.

Using Scripts with Graphs

The Scripts feature can be used with graphs to create each graph individually; when you then combine these scripts into one large script, the graphs display sequentially. Chapter 9 gives more information on this. The Wait option in the Graph menu is used to specify the length of time the graph will be displayed on the screen.

Chaining Graph Scripts

The following is an example of creating graphs on the Prodinv table that show the sale of various products by month. Scripts that produce graphs for each month are created. Then these scripts are chained together to display the graphs on the screen for a specified length of time. The graphs that are created are shown in Figures 10-10 and 10-11.

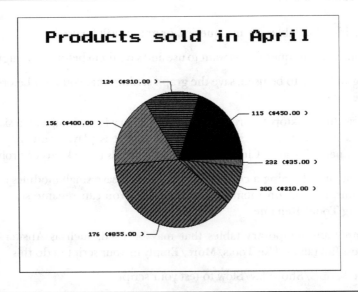

Figure 10-10.   *Graph for products sold in April*

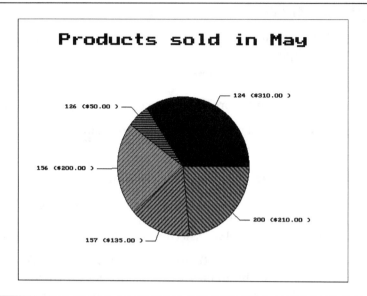

Figure 10-11. *Graph for products sold in May*

Preparing by Saving Graph Settings

In this example, you first need to save the graph settings for each graph you want to include in the script.

To save the graph settings, follow these steps:

1. Set up the graph settings in the format you want—choose **I**mage/**G**raph/**M**odify. In the Customize Graph form, make any changes you like. For the first graph in this example, the Pie format is chosen, and the title "Products sold in April" is entered in the Customize Pie Graph form.

2. While still in the Graph Designer menu, choose **O**verall/**W**ait/**D**uration, enter a time (in seconds), and press ENTER. If you choose **K**eystroke, the graph will be displayed until you press a key.

3. When finished, press F2 (Do-It!) to return to the Main menu.

4. Save the graph settings—choose **I**mage/**G**raph/**S**ave, type a name for the graph setting, and press ENTER.

5. Repeat steps 1 through 4 for each remaining graph that you want to include. In this example, only two graphs are used. In the settings for the second graph, Pie format is chosen and the title "Products sold in May" is entered. The Wait time was set again the same as in the first graph setting.

Creating Scripts That Produce Each Graph

A script is needed to produce each graph; these scripts are then chained together to display a series of graphs.

To create the script for the first graph for sales in April, follow these steps:

1. Choose **S**cripts/**B**eginRecord, type a name for the script, and press ENTER.

2. Perform the query that produces the results you want. In this example, to find the total of products sold in April, choose **A**sk/**O**rder, and place a checkmark in the Product # field. In the Total field, type **calc sum**. In the Date field, type **>=4/1/92,<=4/30/92**. Then press F2 to perform the query.

3. With the Answer table displayed on the desktop, choose **I**mage/**G**raph/**L**oad, and choose the graph setting you want. In this example, the setting with the title for the month of April was selected. You then return to the Answer table.

4. Move the cursor to the Sum of Total column, and press CTRL-F7 (Instant Graph) to display the graph. The graph will be displayed for the length of time that is entered in the Wait dialog box in the graph settings. At the end of the Wait interval, the graph will disappear from the screen and the Answer table will appear again.

5. Clear the desktop with ALT-F8 (Clear All), and choose **S**cripts/**E**nd-Record.

6. Repeat steps 1 through 5 for additional graphs.

Chaining the Scripts That Create Graphs

Once you create the scripts that produce the graphs you want (in this example, one for each month), you can combine the scripts to produce one large script that will display the graphs on the screen in order.

To chain scripts, follow these steps:

1. Clear the desktop with ALT-F8 (Clear All) before recording to avoid unexpected results from the queries.

2. Choose **S**cripts/**B**eginRecord, type a filename, and press ENTER.

3. Choose **S**cripts/**P**lay, and choose the name of the first script to be played. In this example, choose the script named Aprlgrph that creates the graph for April.

4. After that graph has been displayed and left the screen, choose **S**cripts/**P**lay, and choose the script for the next graph you want. In this example, the next script is Maygrph.

5. Repeat step 4 for additional scripts. When finished, choose **Scripts/End-Re-cord**.

Playing the Chained Scripts

Before playing the script, press ALT-F8 (Clear All) to clear the desktop if needed. Then choose **Scripts/Play**, choose the name of the script that contains the chained scripts—the name used here is Show—and press ENTER to play the script. Figure 10-10 and Figure 10-11 show examples of the graphs.

Creating an Init Script

You can create an *Init* script that plays each time Paradox is started. For example, if you always change directories, or if you always begin your Paradox session using a specific table, save the keystrokes used to change directories or to display that table in the Init script.

You create the Init script the same way you create other scripts. At the dialog box for the filename, type **init** to name the script. Enter the keystrokes to be saved, and end the recording. Each time you start up, Paradox looks for this Init script, and plays it automatically before the Main menu is displayed. On a stand-alone system, your Init script should be in the same directory as your Paradox system files. On a network, it should be in your private directory.

Scripts on a Network

Scripts are treated differently than other Paradox objects when you are on a network. Two or more users can use a script at the same time; however, while you are playing a script, others cannot edit it. Also, if you are editing a script, others cannot play it or edit it. If you try to use a script that another user is editing, the message "Can't access script" will be displayed.

Using Scripts/RepeatPlay for Autoregraph

You can create a script that will *autoregraph,* or automatically update a graph contin-uously. This is useful if you are working on a network where data is frequently

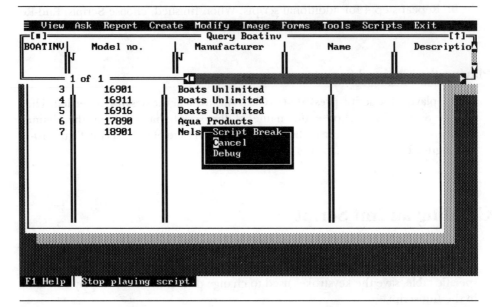

Figure 10-12.   *Script Break menu*

changing when the graph is onscreen. When autoregraph is used, you will see the changes on the screen as you view the graph.

To create a script that autoregraphs a graph, follow these steps:

1. Make the changes you want to the graph settings—choose **I**mage/ **G**raph/**M**odify.

2. Choose **S**cripts/**B**eginRecord, type a filename, and press ENTER.

3. Perform any queries or crosstabs to display the data that you want to graph.

4. Set the Wait duration at zero—to do this, choose **I**mage/**G**raph/**M**odify. In the Graph Designer menu, choose **O**verall/**W**ait/**D**uration, and type **0** in the dialog box, if it is not already there.

5. Press CTRL-F7 (Instant Graph).

6. Choose **S**cripts/**E**nd-Record to end the recording.

To play the script, follow these steps:

1. Choose **S**cripts/**R**epeatPlay (rather than **S**cripts/**P**lay), and choose the script filename for the autoregraph.

2. At the dialog box asking for the number to repeat, type **c** (for continuous), and press ENTER. This causes the graph on screen to be continuously updated.

3. To end the autoregraphing, press CTRL-BREAK. The Script Break menu is displayed, as shown in Figure 10-12. Choose Cancel.

Use autoregraph in any situation where the data in the tables changes frequently.

Chapter *11*

Using the Application Workshop

The Application Workshop is used to build an *application*—a system of menus and tasks that supports business or personal functions. For instance, an inventory system or a billing/invoicing system are examples of applications.

You might want to build a unique application using the Workshop for several reasons. You might have people using the application who do not know Paradox, for example, and who do not need to know it. Your application can lead the user through the tasks step by step, without their even knowing Paradox is at work.

Often terminology for an application is specialized and not easily duplicated in Paradox. You can customize the terminology and menu choices for each task, and you can include just those functions or tasks that the user needs to perform. It is easy to create an application in the Application Workshop even if you have no programming knowledge. Paradox operates in the background when the application is running, but the user needn't be aware of this.

You can build an application in two ways: with the Paradox Application Workshop, or by programming it yourself using PAL (Paradox Application Language). The Application Workshop is a structured approach to creating the application, which leads you through the building process using a menu system. The Workshop generates programming code automatically, storing it in a procedure library, all without the creator having to know PAL or programming. Using PAL requires programming skills. This approach is explained in Chapters 12 and 13.

This chapter covers how to prepare, create, and use the application with the Application Workshop. Creating the application includes building the menu, defining and assigning actions to the menu choices, defining Paradox objects in the application as needed, modifying the menu, and testing and running the application.

You will also learn how to manage your application, including copying, renaming, or deleting objects, and you will see documentation for cross-references and menu trees.

Planning for an Application

Planning means considering hardware requirements as well as the specifics of the application itself. Since the Paradox Application Workshop is optional software, you may not have installed it when you installed Paradox. If this is the case, refer to Appendix A to install the Application Workshop software.

Hardware Requirements for the Application Workshop

In addition to the programs for Paradox 4 and the Application Workshop, you must have at least 1MB of available space on a hard disk or a network file server. This 1MB is in addition to Paradox's requirements and is used by Paradox to store your new application programs. If you do not have this amount of available disk space, you may have to remove some files before beginning your work.

You also need 1MB of RAM (2MB is recommended) for developing the applications, and 640K of RAM for running the applications.

Planning the Application Structure

If you develop a plan detailing the structure of the application before creating the application, you save time in the long run by eliminating the need for extensive changes in the completed application. This doesn't mean you can't change the application once it's created—changes can be made fairly easily in the Application Workshop. But a good working plan can make the entire process much more efficient.

Consider these points when planning the application:

- List functions you want to include in the application. Think of the actions you want to perform, and organize them into categories. This can be the basis for your menu structure.

  For example, perhaps you want to be able to maintain an inventory file by adding new items to it, removing obsolete items, changing the item prices (sometimes for categories or items in addition to individual items), or changing other item information. You might want specialized reports, such as the orders for the month, or a comparison of orders by products or by sales reps.

Here is a sample beginning list:

Orders
–Add new orders
–Modify information about orders
–View orders

Inventory
–Look at current inventories
–Add new items
–Modify information

Reports
–Print monthly sales
–Print sales by each sales rep
–Print sales of each product—overall and by month

Clients
–Add new names
–Edit information about clients

Employees
–Add new names
–Edit information

- Consider who will be using the application. Include terminology in the menus that users will understand.

- Consider security—will passwords be needed for any tables or reports?

- Refine the tentative list into a menu structure that will include the functions listed.

- Determine which objects—tables, forms, reports, scripts, views—are needed to accomplish the tasks in the application.

- Create a separate directory for the application and name the application.

- Create the Paradox objects to be used in the application either in Paradox or in the Application Workshop. It may be easier to create them in Paradox before you create the application because objects can be tested in Paradox more easily than in the Workshop. *Recorded scripts,* which are stored records of keystrokes, cannot be created in the Workshop—they have to be recorded in Paradox. (Scripts are discussed in Chapter 10.) After creating the objects, you can then copy them to the new application directory using the Paradox **T**ools menu; or you can copy them using the **T**ools menu in the Application Workshop.

Starting the Application Workshop

You use the System/Utilities menu to access the Application Workshop, where you will create the new application. After opening the Workshop, you create a new directory for the application and copy the objects from the Paradox directory to the new application directory. Starting the application also involves naming it. To start the Workshop, follow these steps:

1. Press ALT-SPACEBAR to activate the System menu, or click on the System menu.

2. Choose Utilities/Workshop. After a short wait, the Workshop window appears, as shown in Figure 11-1. A message box advises you how to begin using the menu options. It tells you that the Application option is used for setting directories and creating or opening applications. The bottom line shows the current directory.

The choices in the menu bar are Application, ActionEdit, ParadoxEdit, Tools, Documentation, and Exit.

Application   Use Application to open or close an existing application, create a new application, or edit or remove an existing application. You can also set the default directory for the Workshop session here. The session will initially default to the

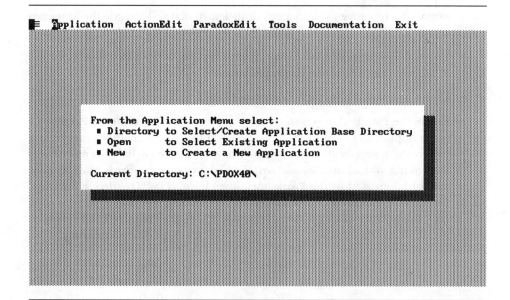

Figure 11-1.   The Workshop window

directory set in the Custom Configuration Program. Application is also used to test the application and run Finish. Finish copies all files associated with the application into the directory that contains the application (covered later in this chapter).

ActionEdit   Use ActionEdit to create, edit, and borrow action objects that can then be assigned to menu commands. *Action objects* can be edit sessions, printing a report, performing a standard query, executing a script, or performing multiple actions. For example, you can specify that when a particular menu option is chosen, Report *X* will be printed.

ParadoxEdit   Use ParadoxEdit to create Paradox objects (tables, forms, reports, or scripts) within the Workshop. You can create them or modify an existing object from this menu. These objects are then used to perform the application tasks.

Tools   Use Tools to copy, rename, delete, and otherwise manage objects and action objects in the application.

Documentation   Use Documentation to display menu trees and lists of actions and cross-references for the application being developed.

Exit   Use Exit to leave the Workshop and either return to Paradox or to DOS.

Working in the Application Workshop is similar to working in Paradox. Press F10 (Menu) to access a menu bar or click on the option you want. Press F2 (Do-It!) or click on **Do-It!** to end and save an operation. Press ESC to move back a step. Press F1 (Help) to go to the Help screen.

Setting Up a Directory for the Application

The first step in creating an application is to identify an existing directory or to create a new directory where it is to be stored. Doing this keeps an application and its objects separate from other applications.

To set up a directory follow these steps:

1. From the Workshop menu, choose **Application/Directory**. A dialog box requests the new directory name, as shown here:

2. Type the path for the new directory and press ENTER or choose OK. If the directory does not exist, a prompt asks if you want to create the directory.

3. Choose OK to confirm the new or changed directory name. The named directory is now the working directory and appears in the box in the Workshop screen.

Copying Objects to the New Directory

If you have already created some of the tables, forms, reports, or scripts for the new application, you will want to copy them into a common directory. The objects may have been created previously in Paradox or in another Workshop session. Use the **T**ools option in the Workshop menu bar to copy the objects to the new directory. (Other options in the **T**ools menu are covered later in this chapter.)

To copy objects, follow these steps:

1. Choose **T**ools from the Workshop menu bar. A menu appears.

2. Choose the objects you want to copy—ActionObjects, Tables, Forms, Reports, or Scripts.

3. A dialog box, as shown in Figure 11-2, asks for the path and name of the object (a table was chosen in this example) to be copied. Type the path and name of the object in the text box following Table, and choose **C**opy.

*To see the list of objects (tables, forms, reports, and so on) type just the path—**c:\pdox40**— and press ENTER. A list of the tables, forms, or reports will be displayed. The objects displayed depend upon the choice in step 2.*

4. Another dialog box appears, as shown here:

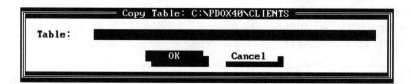

Type the new or "copy-to" name of the object and choose OK. When copying reports and forms, enter the name of the table they are associated with in this dialog box. You will then see a list of reports, forms, and so on. Select the one you want to copy to and choose OK.

*If you choose **T**ables, you can then choose **F**amily in the Tools dialog box to copy the entire family associated with a table, including the forms and reports. Scripts are not included in the family and are copied separately. The table that the family of objects will be copied to must already exist.*

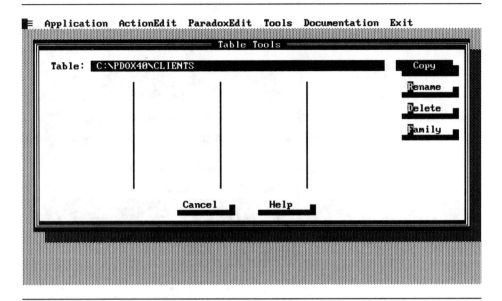

Figure 11-2.   *Dialog box for copying an object*

5. Repeat steps 1 through 4 for all other objects that you want to copy.

Defining the Application

Defining the application consists of giving it an ID (from one to eight characters) and a name. If you like, you can design a *splash screen*, which shows the title of your application. You can also create a detailed description of the application.

To define the application, follow these steps:

1. Choose Application/New. A dialog box appears asking if you want to create a new application.

2. Choose OK. The New Application dialog box appears, as shown in Figure 11-3. This dialog box is used to provide the application ID and its name, and to identify application details essential to its operation. For instance, the directory and tables containing the application menu and object information are named. Links to PAL procedures are identified here as well, so that startup procedures can be provided.

3. Type an application ID consisting of one to eight characters. The application ID will be used to execute the application when you are testing it. It is the script name of the application. Press TAB to move to the next field.

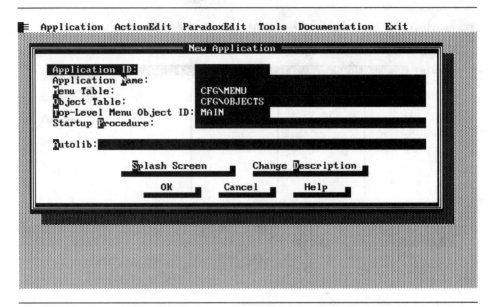

Figure 11-3.   *New Application dialog box*

4. Type an application name and press TAB to move to the next field, or choose OK to leave the New Application dialog box if you do not want to make any other changes. The application name appears in the lower-right corner of the Application Workshop window when you create or edit your application.

The next five selections in the dialog box, **M**enu Table, **O**bject Table, **T**op-Level Menu Object ID, Startup **P**rocedure, and **A**utolib, are optional. Default filenames are shown for the table that contains the application menus, the table that contains the objects used in the application, and the name of the top-level menu bar. You can enter new names that better describe the files, or if more than one application is created, enter different filenames to distinguish the files in each application. However, if your applications are located in separate directories, the default names can be used as a convenient standard; in any application the objects are found in the OBJECTS subdirectory, for example. You can also enter a startup procedure written to meet your specific needs, and you can specify in the **A**utolib field where to locate procedures that you want to use with your application.

Menu Table   This is a file that stores all the menus in the application. The default path and name is CFG\MENU. The Application Workshop automatically creates the CFG subdirectory in the new directory you create for the application and names the file MENU. If you want to enter a name that better describes the menus in the application, type a new name in the text box following **M**enu Table. When finished, press TAB to move to the next selection if you want to enter other information, or choose OK to leave the New Application dialog box.

Object Table   This is a file that stores all the objects you create for the application. The default path and name is CFG\OBJECTS. The **O**bject Table is treated the same as the **M**enu Table. The Application Workshop automatically creates the CFG subdirectory in the new directory you created and names the file OBJECTS. You can enter a new filename, if you like. Press TAB when finished to move to the next selection, or choose OK to leave the dialog box.

Top-Level Menu Object ID   The menu bar that is displayed at the top of the screen when you load the application (similar to the Paradox Main menu when you load Paradox) is the top-level menu object; the default name for this menu bar is MAIN. Here again, if you want to enter a different name that is more descriptive of the application—or if other applications are already using this name and you want a different menu name for the current application—type a new name in the text box following the label. When finished, press TAB to go to the next selection, or choose OK to leave the dialog box.

Startup Procedure   You may want to run a specific procedure whenever the application is started. A *procedure* is a script containing programming commands that perform a specific action. Using a procedure organizes and enhances the use of scripts. For example, a procedure may be used to count the number of pending orders for the day before starting the application. Refer to Chapter 12 for more information on procedures.

Enter the name of the procedure here and then press TAB to go to the next selection, or choose OK to leave the dialog box.

Autolib   This enables you to enter the name of a procedure library containing custom code, if you plan to use it in your application. A *library* is a file used to store procedures—in this case, pertaining to the application. When a custom PAL procedure is to be used in the application, Paradox will know where to find it. Type the name of the library and press TAB to move to the next selection, or choose OK to leave the dialog box.

At this point, you can either choose **S**plash Screen and **C**hange Description, as discussed next, or choose OK. If you choose OK, you will not have either a splash screen or a fuller description of the application displayed at startup time.

Using Splash Screen

Choosing **S**plash Screen, which is optional, allows you to display specified text each time you start your application. You may wish to create an interesting design that is appropriate for your application. The characters are entered in an Editor screen the same way you use the Editor screen in other Paradox actions. If you don't create your own splash screen, the application name is used.

To create a splash screen, follow these steps:

1. From the New Application dialog box, choose **S**plash Screen. An Editor window appears, as shown in Figure 11-4.

2. Enter the title or other text or characters that you want displayed every time the application is started.

3. Press F2 (Do-It!) or click on **D**o-It! when finished. If you do not want to enter text, choose **C**ancel to leave the window without making a change.

4. Choose OK to leave the New Application dialog box, or insert a description as discussed next.

To edit the splash screen, use ***Application/Edit.***

Using Change Description

Change **D**escription, also optional, allows you to enter a detailed description of the application. This description generally includes uses of the application, limits on its usage, contents of the various tables, and so on.

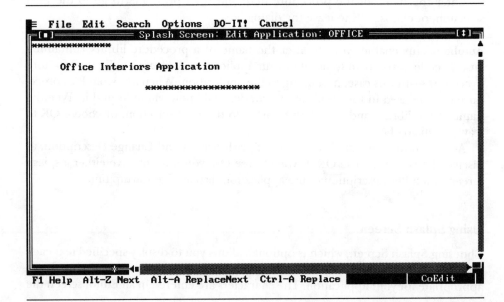

Figure 11-4.   Splash Screen

To enter a description, follow these steps:

1. From the New Application dialog box, choose Change **D**escription. An Editor window appears, as shown in Figure 11-5.

2. Type the description.

3. Press F2 (Do-It!) or click on **D**o-It! when finished.

4. Choose OK to leave the New Application dialog box. The blank application menu screen is displayed.

You can edit the description from Application/Edit.

Creating the Menu Structure

After you establish the directories for the application and name them, the blank application menu screen appears, as shown in Figure 11-6. Figure 11-7 shows an example of a completed application.

When the blank application bar appears, begin creating the application structure by entering text that identifies the options on the Main menu bar. The menu options may require other menus to be displayed in order to complete their actions, or they

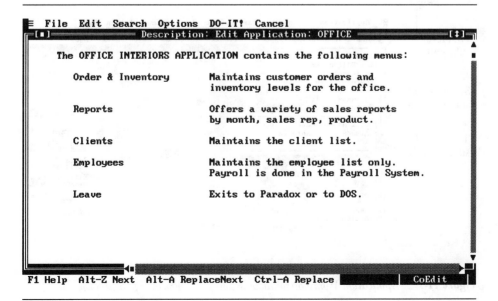

Figure 11-5. Editor window for the description

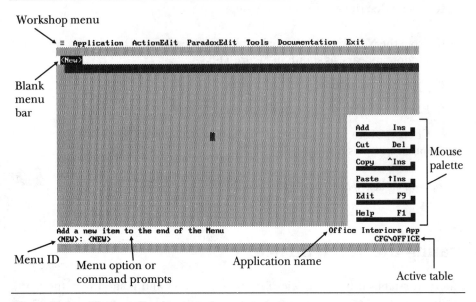

Figure 11-6. *Blank application menu bar*

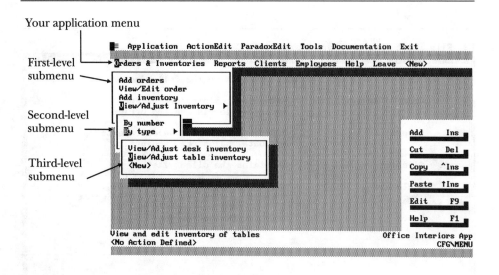

Figure 11-7. *Application Workshop window showing a completed application menu*

may be immediately executed. If the menu option has a submenu connected to it, it is referred to as a *submenu option*. In some cases, second- and third-level submenus may be needed for first-level submenu options. If the menu option is immediately executed or causes an action, it is referred to as an *action* or *command option*. An Exit command is an example of a menu command that might be placed on the menu bar.

As you create the menu structure, you specify whether the name, called a *keyword*, is intended to be a submenu or a menu command.

On the bottom two lines are the menu option prompts and the application name and active table. On the right of the screen is a mouse palette, which you can use to insert, delete, paste, copy, and edit the menu option, or get help as you develop your application.

This chapter discusses creating the menu structure before it covers defining action objects. The order is not significant. You can create the action objects and then enter the submenu and menu commands if you prefer to work in that order.

Table 11-1 shows a list of the features in the Application Workshop screen, as shown in Figures 11-6 and 11-7.

Creating the Menu Bar and Submenus

The menu bar consists of names of submenus and in some cases, menu commands. The menu bar in Figure 11-7 shows submenus that are displayed when a word is selected. In this example, when the text "Orders & Inventories" is selected, a submenu is displayed.

If your cursor is on the Workshop menu bar and you want to switch to your application menu bar, press ESC or click on the menu bar to move your cursor to it.

You create the menu by typing keywords, a description, and a help message if it's needed. Begin identifying menu keywords on the left of the menu bar and proceed to the right. Take the time to finalize the placement of your menu options before you begin. You can change them later if you need to.

To create the menu structure, follow these steps:

1. Select <New> on the application menu bar—either move the cursor to it and press ENTER, or click on it. You can also click on **Add** on the mouse palette or press INSERT. The Menu Insert menu is displayed as shown here:

```
┌Menu Insert─┐
│ SubⅢenu    │
│ Action     │
└────────────┘
```

Feature	Description
Workshop menu bar	Shows the Paradox Application Workshop submenus
Your application bar	Shows the submenus and commands you have entered for your application
Submenus	Contain the list of menu commands and other submenus. Paradox allows up to 16 levels of submenus. An arrowhead to the right of the menu keyword identifies options with submenus.
Menu commands	Names of commands you have entered in submenus. Paradox allows up to 50 menu commands in a submenu. Commands have only the keyword on the menu line.
Submenu/menu command description	Shows the description or prompt you entered when defining submenus and menu commands
Menu ID	Identifies the entry in the Name table containing this menu option
Active table	Identifies the directory and table used to store the menu items
Application name	Shows the name you entered in the Description box when you created the application
Mouse palette	Shows editing actions that are available for defining the menu options. Click on the action you want or press the key that performs that action. The keys are listed at the right, the action is listed at the left.

Table 11-1.   *Features in the Application Workshop Window*

2. To insert an option with a submenu, choose **S**ubMenu and press ENTER. The Menu Definition dialog box for entering the name of the submenu is displayed as shown here:

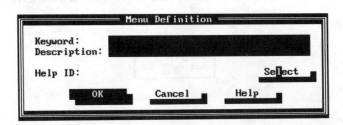

3. Type the name of the keyword in the Keyword box. The keyword can be up to 32 characters, and can contain numbers, international characters, letters, symbols, and blank spaces. In the example shown in Figure 11-7, the first keyword is Orders & Inventories.

The Workshop will automatically make the first letter of the option a hot key or shortcut key. It will be displayed in a different color or intensity, and will move the cursor to the option when the first letter is pressed. You may want to designate a different letter as the hot key, particularly if you have options beginning with the same first letter. To do this, type a tilde (~) on either side of the designated letter, like this:

By ~t~ype

4. Press TAB to move to the Description box, or click on it and type a description. The description will be displayed when the option is highlighted.

   When the application is being used, this description shows at the bottom left of the screen when the keyword is selected. The description can be up to 80 characters. You can add text for a Help screen if you choose **S**elect. This will be covered later in this chapter.

5. Choose OK when done. The name entered as the keyword is now displayed in your application menu bar.

6. Repeat steps 1 through 5 for the remaining keywords on the menu bar.

Rather than entering all names in the menu bar, you can place menu commands in each submenu as you go, if you prefer.

Placing Menu Commands

Menu commands specify the action that will be performed immediately when the command is selected. The process of placing those commands includes entering the name of the command and the description of the action that will be assigned to it. When you use the application, the description appears at the bottom of the screen when the command is selected. In Figure 11-7, **A**dd orders and **V**iew/Edit order are menu commands. **V**iew/Adjust Inventory (note the arrow on the right) is a second-level submenu with the menu command, **B**y number, and a third-level submenu, **B**y type.

You can define the actions that are to be assigned to the commands later, or you can do it as you place the menu command (whichever works best for you).

When you run the application from the application menu to test it, if you have not defined an action for a command, a message appears, telling you that no action has been assigned to that particular command.

To place a menu command, follow these steps:

1. If the command is to be placed on the Main menu bar, select <New>, select **A**dd, or press INSERT. If the command is to be on a submenu, select the keyword for the submenu in the menu bar and press ENTER. If no previous menu commands have been defined, the submenu displayed shows only <New>.

2. Select <New> and press ENTER. The Menu Insert menu is displayed as shown next. It is similar to the Menu Insert menu that was used for placing keywords in the menu bar; however, it contains an additional choice, **S**eparator.

```
┌─Menu Insert─┐
│ Action      │
│ SubMenu     │
│ Separator   │
└─────────────┘
```

3. Select **A**ction and press ENTER. The Menu Definition box appears, as shown in Figure 11-8.

4. Type the keyword in the Keyword box. This is similar to entering a keyword for a submenu. In Figure 11-7, **A**dd orders is entered as the first menu command in the **O**rders & Inventories submenu.

5. Press TAB or click on the Description box, and type a description of the command. This will be displayed when the option is highlighted or selected.

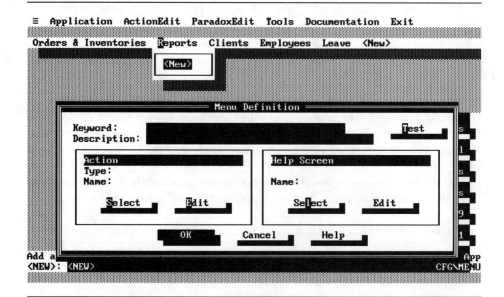

Figure 11-8.   *Menu Definition box*

At this point you can define or select either an action object or a help screen for this command, if you choose. These are covered later in the chapter.

6. Choose OK. The submenu keyword appears again, and the new menu command is shown above <New>.

7. Repeat steps 1 through 6 for all remaining menu commands in the various submenus.

Creating a Second-Level Submenu

If an option indicates a second-level submenu rather than a menu command, select Submenu rather than Action when you create it. In Figure 11-7, View/Adjust Inventory is a submenu.

To create a second-level submenu, follow these steps:

1. Move the cursor to the name on the menu bar where you want to place the second-level submenu and press ENTER. A submenu appears. If other menu commands show in the submenu, move your cursor to the position above which you want to insert the new submenu and press INSERT. If no other commands are showing, or if you want to place the submenu at the end of the list, select <New> and press ENTER.

2. For options needing lower level submenus, choose Submenu. For options that will have immediate action, choose Action and press ENTER. The Menu Definition box will be displayed.

3. In the Menu Definition box for the submenu, type a keyword and a description.

4. When finished, choose OK.

5. Continue to enter submenu and menu commands as needed. When finished, an arrow appears on the same line with the menu option, indicating that a submenu will be displayed.

You use this same process to create third-level submenus, fourth-level submenus, and so on. The level number is determined merely by its position in the overall menu structure. You may have up to 16 levels.

Inserting and Deleting Separators

Separator lines make reading the menu easier by visually grouping similar commands. To enter a separator, follow these steps:

1. Move the cursor to the command or submenu that is to be immediately below the line, and press INSERT. The Menu Insert box is displayed.

2. Choose **S**eparator to insert the line.

The separator line can be deleted by moving the cursor to the line and pressing DELETE. To insert a line at a new position, move the cursor to the new position, and repeat steps 1 and 2.

When a line is deleted, it is not deleted to the paste buffer, so it cannot be recalled using SHIFT-INSERT.

Editing Menus

You can easily add new submenus and menu commands to the menu and/or change the text displayed for existing submenus and menu commands. You can also use the Mouse palette to delete, insert, or move submenus and commands.

Inserting New Menu Commands or Submenus

To insert a new menu command or a new submenu, move the cursor to the position in the menu or submenu and press INSERT. Then enter the command or the submenu. Similarly, to add to an existing submenu, move the cursor to the keyword representing the submenu and press ENTER. You will then see the commands in the submenu, and you can insert a new command or another submenu if you like.

Deleting a Menu Command or a Submenu

Deleting a menu command is quite simple. Just move the cursor to the command or submenu and press DELETE. The command or submenu is saved in a paste buffer. If you want to reinsert it, press SHIFT INSERT.

The paste buffer is an area in RAM where a menu command or a submenu that has been deleted is stored temporarily until another command or submenu is deleted. When you press SHIFT-INSERT, the contents of the paste buffer are inserted at the cursor position.

Moving a Menu Command or Submenu

The process of moving a command or submenu involves a cut and paste procedure. First move your cursor to the keyword to be moved, then delete the command or submenu. Move the cursor to a new position and press SHIFT-INSERT to reinsert the keyword at a new place.

Editing a Menu Command or Submenu

Editing a command or submenu includes changing the keyword, changing the text in the description, and changing the action or the help text.

To edit a command or submenu, follow these steps:

1. Select the command or submenu that is to be edited and press F9 (Edit) or choose **E**dit from the mouse palette.

2. Make any changes you want in the box, and then choose OK to save the changes and return to the Workshop. To cancel the changes, press ESC or choose **C**ancel.

Defining and Assigning Action Objects

The Action**E**dit menu is used to define action objects that can then be assigned to the various menu commands in the application. *Action objects* are the instructions attached to each menu command that tell Paradox what to do when that menu command is selected.

The Action**E**dit menu is shown here:

```
ActionEdit
┌─────────────────┐
│ Edit Session    │
│ Report Print    │
│ Query           │
│ Multi Action    │
│ Help Text       │
│ Execute         │
│ OK/Cancel       │
└─────────────────┘
```

Some of the functions that are generally performed by the action objects are viewing and editing data in tables, printing reports, and performing queries. The Action**E**dit menu can also be used to define multiple action objects that can be assigned to a menu command. A *multiple action object* combines two or more action objects into one object. For example, you can create a help screen that a user can display by pressing F1, establish an executable action object (a PAL script), or create an OK/Cancel dialog box.

Additional utility action objects, such as Exit to DOS, Play a Script, and Execute a Procedure, can be created using Application/Edit or by pressing F9 when the appropriate menu command is highlighted.

You use the Menu Definition dialog box to assign the objects to menu commands. From there, the Object Type dialog box is displayed when the object to be assigned to the menu command is selected. When an object is defined, it is automatically listed under its appropriate object type and can then be assigned to a menu command.

In this chapter, assigning the object is discussed after the information on creating the object is presented; however, the action object can be assigned at any time after it has been defined.

Using ActionEdit/Edit Session

The **E**dit Session command is used to define the action objects that view, edit, or add data to the Paradox tables used in the application. These objects can then be assigned to the appropriate menu command.

Defining an action object in the **E**dit Session consists of giving it a name, adding and/or editing tables, adding forms, and specifying the mode—Edit or Read Only—for the table. Attributes that can be included in defining the object are assigning actions to various keys; specifying procedures that are to be run when an action occurs; asking for passwords; selecting the system mode—**C**oEdit, **D**ataEntry, or **E**dit—that you want; and entering prompts that will be displayed when the action is run.

Naming and Defining a New Action Object

The name of an action object can consist of 32 characters, including spaces, and must be unique for this object type. You cannot use the same name again for another **E**dit Session object; however, you can use the same name again for a report or a query.

Once you have named the object and are in the Edit Session dialog box, attributes can be assigned to the action object.

To name a new action object, follow these steps:

1. Choose Action**E**dit/**E**dit Session from the Workshop menu. You may have to press F10 (Menu) to access the Application Workshop menu if your cursor is in your own application menu bar. An Edit dialog box appears, as shown in Figure 11-9.

   If this is the first action object that is to be defined, the box will be empty. If other Edit Session action objects have been defined, a list of those objects will be displayed in the Edit dialog box. They can be edited, if you like, or you can add objects to the list by choosing **N**ew.

2. Choose **N**ew to define a new action object. Another dialog box for entering the name of the action object appears, as shown here:

```
╔══════════════ New Edit Session ══════════════╗
║  Enter New Edit Session Name:                 ║
║                                               ║
║  Name:  ████████████████████████████████████  ║
║         ┌──────────┐   ┌──────────┐  ┌──────┐ ║
║         │    OK    │   │  Cancel  │  │ Help │ ║
║         └──────────┘   └──────────┘  └──────┘ ║
╚═══════════════════════════════════════════════╝
```

3. Type a name for the object and choose OK. This name will then be attached to the menu command. In the example just given, **Add** orders is entered as the name to correspond to the first menu command in the **O**rders & Inventories submenu. The name does not have to be the same as the command name.

   Select OK to save the changes, Cancel to leave the dialog box without making any changes, and Help to access the Application Workshop Help screen. If you are not using a mouse, press TAB to move to OK, Cancel, or Help, and then press ENTER.

4. After choosing OK, the Edit Session dialog box appears, as shown in Figure 11-10, with the name of the object at the top of the box. This box is used to actually define or assign the attributes to the object.

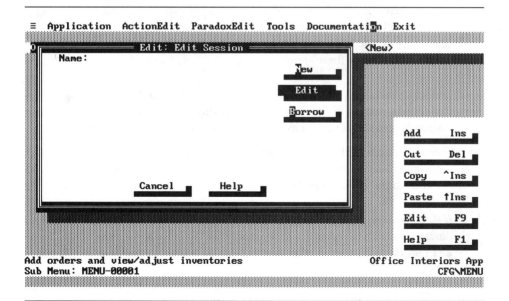

Figure 11-9. *Edit dialog box*

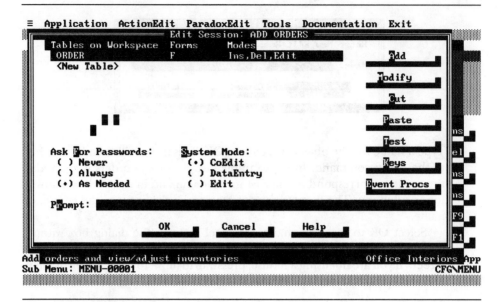

Figure 11-10.   *Edit Session dialog box*

Adding New Tables to the Application

The "Tables on Workspace" box in the Edit Session dialog box shows the names of the tables that have previously been added to the application. If no tables have been added, the list will only show <New Table>. The example displayed in Figure 11-10 shows the name of one table that has been added.

To add a table, follow these steps:

1. Select <New table> and then choose **Add** from the Edit Session dialog box. A Table Information dialog box appears, as shown in Figure 11-11. You use this dialog box to select or specify modes, views, and forms.

2. Type the name of the table you want in the Table box, or choose **T**able Select to display a list of tables in the current directory. Then select the table you want from the list and choose OK.

   *If the list is empty after choosing **T**able Select, it means there are no tables in the current directory. You may have to return to the Application Workshop menu, choose **T**ools/**T**ables and copy the tables from another directory into the directory where your application is stored.*

3. After choosing the table from a list, you will be returned to the Table Information dialog box.

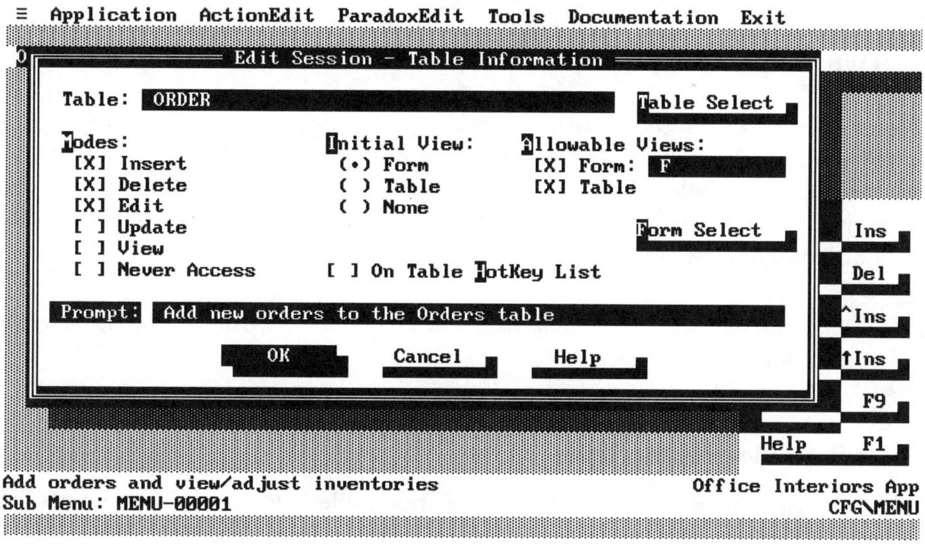

```
≡  Application  ActionEdit  ParadoxEdit  Tools  Documentation  Exit
┌─────────────────── Edit Session - Table Information ───────────────────┐
│  Table: ORDER                                          Table Select     │
│                                                                         │
│  Modes:            Initial View:     Allowable Views:                   │
│  [X] Insert        (•) Form          [X] Form: F                        │
│  [X] Delete        ( ) Table         [X] Table                          │
│  [X] Edit          ( ) None                                             │
│  [ ] Update                          Form Select           Ins          │
│  [ ] View                                                               │
│  [ ] Never Access  [ ] On Table HotKey List                Del          │
│                                                                         │
│  Prompt: Add new orders to the Orders table                ^Ins         │
│              OK          Cancel        Help                ↑Ins          │
│                                                                         │
│                                                            F9           │
│                                                                         │
│                                                    Help    F1           │
Add orders and view/adjust inventories             Office Interiors App
Sub Menu: MENU-00001                                       CFG\MENU
```

Figure 11-11.   *Table Information dialog box*

Selecting Modes

Modes refer to the type of editing that is set for the current table. The available modes are displayed at the left in the Edit Session dialog box—see Figure 11-10. The modes set in the Table Information dialog box, will override those set in the Edit Session dialog box, if they are different.

Press ALT-M to move to the **Modes** list. Press DOWN ARROW to move to each type of mode you want, and press the SPACEBAR to toggle the X on or off in the brackets; or click on the modes. You are required to set at least one type of mode. The modes will determine which editing actions a user will be able to perform on the named table when the menu option for the edit session is selected. Choices of modes are Insert, Delete, Edit, Update, View, and Never Access.

Insert Mode   Select Insert to allow users to insert records in the table.

Delete Mode   Select Delete to allow users to delete records from the table.

Edit Mode   Select Edit to allow users to edit entries and also change key fields in the table. If the Update mode is selected, you cannot select Edit.

Update Mode   Select Update to allow users to edit entries, but key fields in the table cannot be changed. If the Edit mode is selected, you cannot select Update.

View Mode   Select View to allow users only to look at the information in the table. The data cannot be edited. If Edit or Update have also been selected, users can press F9 (Edit) to make changes.

Never Access Mode   Select Never Access to prevent users from accessing the table. If you want to allow users to see the table, but not access it, select Never Access and set the appropriate allowable views. To prevent users from seeing the table and from accessing it, select Never Access, select None for Initial View, and confirm that *neither* of the allowable views is selected.

 You can remove the X in the brackets next to the options by pressing the SPACEBAR again or by clicking on the option.

Selecting a View for the Table

The choices of views for Initial View are Form, Table, and None. The choices for Allowable View are Form and Table. Choose the type of views you want. Figure 11-11 (the Table Information dialog box) shows an example.

Initial View   Use this to specify the view in which the table is displayed when the Edit Session begins. Only one option can be selected. Form is the default choice here. You can select the option (cause a dot to be entered in parentheses) by moving the cursor to the option you want. Choose None if the mode is set at Never Access and you do not want a user to see the contents of the table.

Allowable View   Use this to specify which views data can be accessed in. Both views can be used, and a user can toggle between Table and Form View. If Form was selected for Initial View, then Form must be selected for **Allowable View**. If Table was selected for Initial View, then Table must be selected for **Allowable View**. To select views, move the cursor to the view(s) you want and press the SPACEBAR to enter an X in the brackets.

Form Number   This is displayed to the right of Form under **Allowable View**. The default is F, the Standard form; however, you can type in the number of a different form, if you like. If you are not certain of the numbers for the forms, choose **F**orm Select to display a list of forms for the selected table. Then select the form you want and choose OK. Figure 11-12 shows an example of the dialog box displayed when you choose Form Select.

Assigning a Hot Key for a Table

When you select On Table HotKey List, the table is added to the list of tables that can be selected with hot keys (shortcut keys). When this option has been selected, you

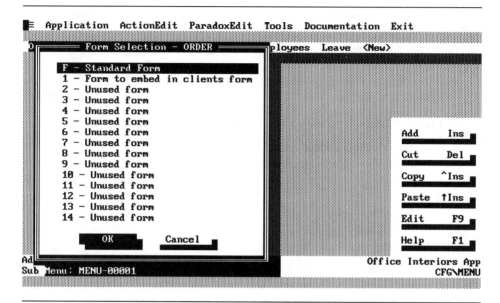

Figure 11-12. *Form Selection dialog box*

can select a table that has been added to the hot key list by pressing the hot key assigned to it. When working on multiple tables, you can press ALT-O to display the list, and then press ALT-hot key to make a table active.

Select On Table Hotkey List by pressing ALT-H or clicking on the option.

Adding a Prompt

You can add a prompt in the Table Information dialog box. This prompt will be displayed at the bottom of the screen only when the table is active. If a prompt also has been added in the Edit Session dialog box, the prompt entered here will override it when the table is active.

To add a prompt, follow these steps:

1. Select Prompt, and type a message in the Prompt box.

2. Choose OK or Cancel to return to the Edit Session dialog box. The table is now added to the list of Tables on Workspace in the Edit Session dialog box.

Modifying a Table

Select Modify when you want to change the attributes assigned to the tables as displayed in the Edit Session dialog box. The dialog box that is displayed when you choose **M**odify is similar to the Table Information dialog box that was used when you added the table.

To modify a table, follow these steps:

1. In the Edit Session dialog box, select the name of the table you want from the Tables on Workspace List.

2. Choose **M**odify to go to the Table Information dialog box.

3. Make any changes in the Table Information box the same way you did when you added the table originally. Refer to "Adding New Tables to the Application," discussed earlier. Choose OK when finished, or choose Cancel to leave the box.

Using Cut to Remove a Table

The **C**ut option allows you to remove a table from the list of Tables on **W**orkspace. Cutting a Multi-Table also removes its detail tables. When you cut a table, it is temporarily placed in a paste buffer until the **P**aste option or SHIFT-INSERT is pressed.

To remove a table, follow these steps:

1. In the Edit Session dialog box, select the table from the Tables on Workspace List.

2. Choose **C**ut or press DELETE. The table will be cut and stored temporarily in the buffer until the next action is taken. If you want to reinsert the table, choose **P**aste or press SHIFT-INSERT.

Using Paste to Reinsert or Move a Table

Use the **P**aste option if you do not want to remove a table from the application, or if you want to change the order in which the tables are displayed in the Tables on Workspace List. Paste copies the contents of the buffer to where the cursor is positioned.

To use move or reinsert, follow these steps:

1. Cut the table and store it temporarily in the buffer.

2. Move the cursor to a new position, if you want to change the order of the tables, or leave the cursor in the position from which the table was removed.

3. Choose **P**aste or press SHIFT-INSERT to insert the table.

Testing the Action Object

You can test the action object to see if it performs the way you want it to. If it doesn't produce the expected results, edit it before saving and leaving the dialog box. When you test the Edit Session action object, Paradox automatically adds a menu at the top of the screen that you can use in working with the object.

To test the action object, follow these steps:

1. Highlight the action object you want and choose **Test**. Figure 11-13 shows the form for the action object in Test mode, with the menu that has been added automatically displayed at the top of the screen.

   The menu deserves special mention since the Workshop creates it for Edit Sessions. You do not have to do anything special to get this menu bar. The menu gives you these choices.

   - *Image* can be used to Zoom to a **R**ecord, **V**alue, or **N**ext; or **T**oggle between form and table views. If you are in table view, you can then use Image to change the **T**ableSize, **C**olumnSize, or **R**otate, or to **T**oggle to form view.

   - *Undo* reverses the last change. You can also press CTRL-U to undo, just as you do in Paradox.

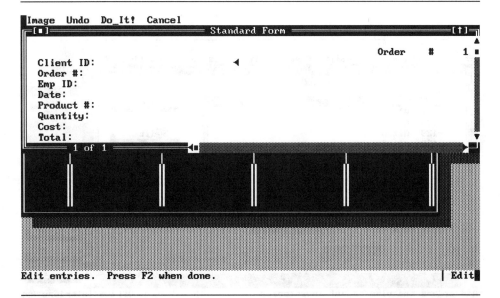

Figure 11-13.   *Action object in test mode*

- *Do-It!* saves the form. You can also press F2 here, as in Paradox.

- *Cancel* (**Yes**/**No**) leaves the form without saving.

2. When finished testing the action object, choose **C**ancel/**Y**es or click on the Close box to return to the Edit Session dialog box.

Assigning Keys

You can assign predefined actions to keys, or you can assign your own PAL procedure to keys, which will be effective during the Edit Session.

To assign keys, follow these steps:

1. From the Edit Session dialog box, choose **K**eys. A dialog box appears, as shown in Figure 11-14.

    The **C**ode/**K**ey/**P**rocedure text box displays a list of character codes and the corresponding keyboard codes. At the right of this box is a list of predefined procedures that can be assigned to a key.

2. To assign a predefined procedure, select the key from the Key list. To skip forward to a specific key, choose **Z**oom or press ALT-Z, and you will be prompted to press the key. When you do, it will be highlighted and displayed in the key list.

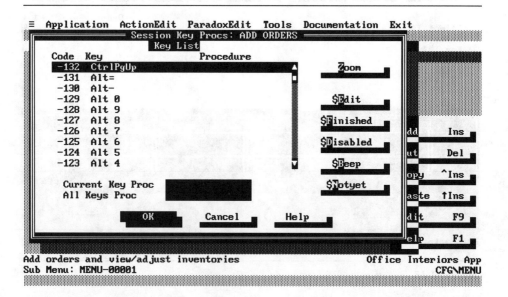

Figure 11-14.   Session Key Procs dialog box

3. If appropriate, choose the predefined procedure (listed at the right) that you want. The choice will be displayed in the Current Key Proc box. The predefined choices are

- *$Edit* assigns the Edit function to the key. The default key is F9.

- *$Finished* assigns the Finish function to the key. The default key is F2.

- *$Disabled* removes the key from being effective during the Edit Session. It is used for keys that you don't want the user to use. The default key is ALT-O.

- *$Beep* sounds a beep when the key is pressed.

- *$Notyet* displays the message, "This procedure is not yet defined," when the key is pressed. This is useful during development to assign to a menu command that has not been defined, for example.

   If, instead, you want to enter your own PAL procedure, enter its name in the Current Key Proc box. Refer to Chapter 12 for information on procedures.

4. When finished, choose OK; or choose Cancel or press ESC to leave without making any changes.

Use All Keys Proc to assign the same procedure to all keys. Type the name of the procedure in the All Keys Proc text box.

Assigning Event Procedures

As you proceed in an editing session, certain events (listed in Table 11-2) occur. These events are tied to the timing of specific actions. For example, when entering data into a table, it may be important to perform a calculation immediately upon entering one field and before moving the cursor to the next field. Or perhaps, when editing a customer's name field, it is important to double-check that the customer's ID field is correct.

   If you want a procedure to run when a specific action occurs, you can select the Event Proc option and enter the name of a procedure to be executed when the specified event occurs.

A procedure contains a set of PAL programming commands that produce a specific action. See Chapter 12 for information on procedures.

To assign event procedures, follow these steps:

1. From the Edit Session dialog box, choose Event Procs. A dialog box appears, as shown in Figure 11-15.

Event	When Procedure Executes
Startup	Before tables are loaded
Arrive Table	When the cursor moves to a table
Arrive Row	When the cursor moves onto a new record
Arrive Field	When the cursor moves onto a new field
Arrive Page	When the cursor moves to a new page when in form view
Arrive Window	When the cursor moves to a new window
Touch Row	When a new change is attempted (before the change is made)
Image Rights	When an Image Rights error happens
ValCheck	When a validity check error happens
D Entry KeyViol	When key violations occur in DataEntry mode
Shutdown	Before exiting the Edit Session
Depart Table	Just before the cursor moves from the table
Depart Row	Just before the cursor moves from a record
Depart Field	When the cursor moves from a field
Depart Page	When the cursor moves from a page in form view
Post Record	Before posting an edited record
Pass Rights	When a password error happens
Required Value	When a required value has not been entered in a field

Table 11-2.   *Events and When the Procedure Executes*

2. The dialog box displays a list of events that occur during editing sessions. Choose the event you want and type the name of the PAL procedure in the text box directly following the name of the events.

3. If you want key violation tables to be renamed, choose Rename Key Viol Tables. The Application Workshop will automatically rename key violation tables, *KV1*, *KV2*, *KV3*, and so on.

4. Choose OK when finished; or choose Cancel or press ESC to leave without making any changes.

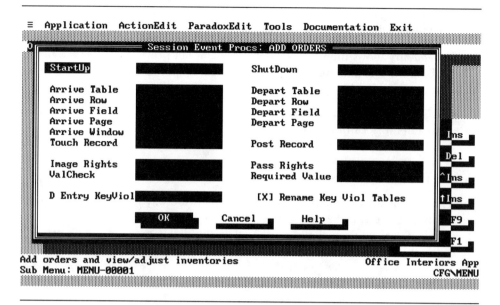

Figure 11-15.   *Session Event Procs dialog box*

Asking for Passwords

You can assign passwords that restrict access to a specific table during an editing session. Refer to Chapter 14 for information about assigning passwords to tables. You can specify conditions for asking for those passwords.

In the Edit Session dialog box, select Ask For Passwords and choose one of the following (move the cursor to the option to select it):

- *Never* aborts the Edit Session if the user tries to access a protected table.

- *Always* prompts the user for a password every time the table is accessed.

- *As Needed* prompts the user for a password only when needed. This is the default option.

Assigning a System Mode

The System mode determines the type of editing mode that will be allowed for the editing session. The default mode is CoEdit. The mode chosen in the Edit Session dialog box will be overridden by the modes that are selected in the Table Information dialog box if they are different.

To assign a mode, choose System mode and select one of the following:

- *CoEdit* edits tables in **Co**Edit mode allowing others on a network to access the table. Duplicate key fields are not allowed.

- *DataEntry* allows the user to enter new data, but previous entries will not be displayed, and therefore, cannot be edited. Duplicate key fields are entered into a Keyviol table.

- *Edit* allows the user to enter new data and also to edit existing data. Other users on a network cannot access the table.

Testing the Action Object

You can test the action object to see if it performs the way you want it to. Do this before leaving the Edit Session dialog box so you can make changes, if they are needed. However, you can always come back to this dialog box and run a test.

To test the object, follow these steps:

1. Choose **T**est in the Edit Session dialog box. The editing session is saved, and then run. You will see the effects of the editing session.

2. If errors occur, or if you want to change the way the action runs, make changes before leaving the Edit Session dialog box.

3. When you finish making corrections or changes to the object, choose OK to save the changes, or choose Cancel to leave without saving any of the changes.

Assigning the Edit Session Object to a Menu Command

The **E**dit Session objects are used to view, edit, or enter data, and are created using the Action**E**dit/**E**dit Session command. Once the object is defined, it can be attached to the appropriate menu command.

To assign objects, follow these steps:

1. Highlight the menu command that you want. A message at the bottom of the screen will tell you <No Action Defined>.

2. Press ENTER or F9 (Edit). The Menu Definition dialog box is displayed. The Keyword and Description that you entered when you created the menu structure are displayed, but the Action box is empty.

3. Choose **S**elect from the Action box. The Object Type dialog box appears, as shown in Figure 11-16. The items shown here are the names of the various types of action objects—these are either previously defined or utility objects supplied by Paradox.

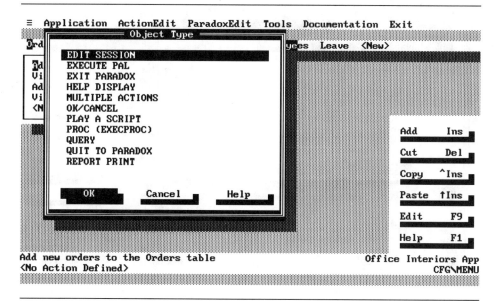

Figure 11-16.   *Object Type dialog box*

Utility action objects will be discussed later in this chapter. They are EXIT PARADOX, PLAY A SCRIPT, PROC (EXECPROC), and QUIT TO PARADOX.

4. Select EDIT SESSION as the object type and choose OK. Another dialog box appears, showing all the action objects that have been defined using the Action Edit/Edit session command, as shown in Figure 11-17. Only one action object is shown here.

5. Select the action object you want to assign to the menu command, and choose OK. You are then returned to the Menu Definition dialog box. The action object now attached to the menu command is displayed in the Action text box, as shown in Figure 11-18.

6. Choose OK to return to your application menu. The message at the bottom of the screen now shows the name of the action object assigned to the menu command.

Using ActionEdit/Report Print

The **R**eport Print option in the Action Edit menu is used to create action objects that print reports, display them on the screen, and/or write them to disk. You can design the actual report in Paradox that you want to use here or create the report in the Application Workshop with the **P**aradoxEdit menu.

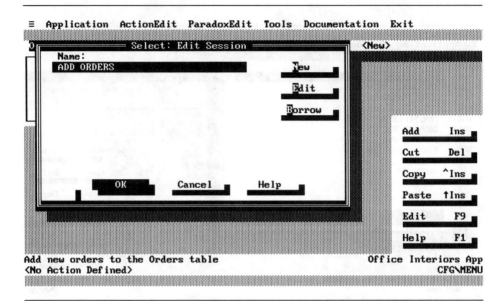

Figure 11-17. *Select: Edit Session dialog box*

 Creating reports, forms, tables, and scripts in the Application Workshop will be covered later in the section, "Creating Paradox Objects in the Workshop."

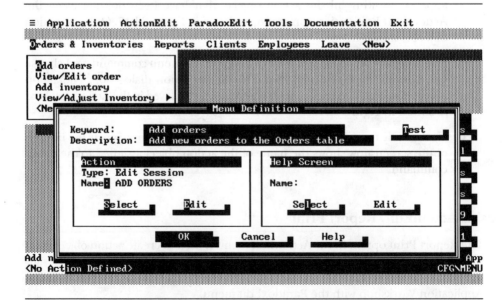

Figure 11-18. *Menu Definition dialog box showing the name of the attached action object*

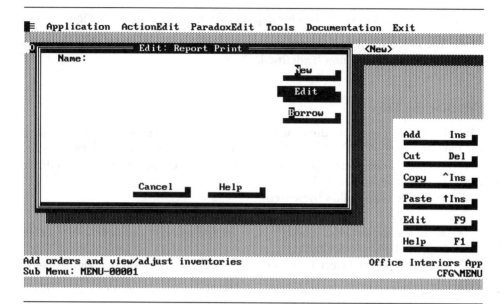

Figure 11-19. *Edit: Report Print dialog box*

The process of defining a report print object is similar to defining an action object. The following steps are appropriate whether or not the report has been designed previously. In other words, creating an action object is done separately from creating the report itself.

To begin defining the report, follow these steps:

1. From the ActionEdit menu, choose **R**eport Print. The Edit Report Print dialog box appears, as shown in Figure 11-19.

   If there are any existing reports, they are displayed under Name. At this point, you can create a new report action object or edit or borrow an existing one. Creating a new one is discussed next, followed by editing and borrowing.

2. Choose **N**ew to create a new report action object and enter the name for the object in the New dialog box shown next. The name shown here is ORDERS BY MONTH.

3. Choose OK. The dialog box for Report Print appears, as shown in Figure 11-20.

4. The object name is displayed at the top of the window and the characteristics for the object can now be defined.

Selecting the Table

The table that you select for the report may not necessarily be the table that supplies the data for the report. The Use Data From dialog box, which will be discussed later in this chapter, allows you to specify the source of data for the report; this can differ from the table that is selected here.

To select the table, follow these steps:

1. From the Report Print dialog box, enter the name of the table in the Table box, or choose **S**elect Table.

   If you choose **S**elect Table, a dialog box appears, as shown in Figure 11-21.

2. Select the table you want and choose OK. If you are not using a mouse, press TAB to move to the list of table names, press DOWN ARROW to select the table, and press ENTER. You then return to the Report Print dialog box.

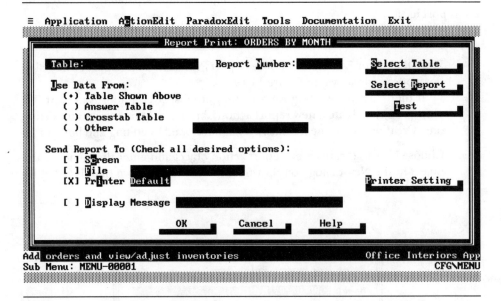

Figure 11-20.   *Report Print dialog box*

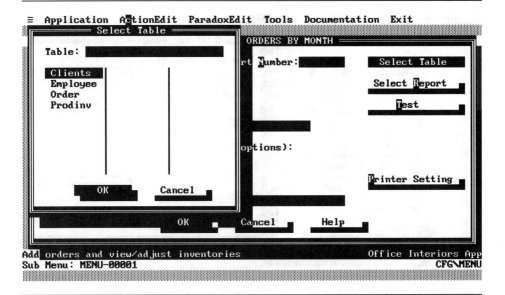

Figure 11-21.   *Select Table dialog box*

Selecting the Report

The report that you select can be the R or standard report, or it can be a customized report that you designed earlier.

To select the report, follow these steps:

1. Type the number of the report in the box following Report Number, or choose Select **R**eport. If you choose Select **R**eport, a dialog box lists available reports, as shown in Figure 11-22.

2. Select the report that you want and choose OK. The report number is displayed in the text box directly following Report **N**umber in the Report Print dialog box.

Selecting the Source of Data

As mentioned earlier, the table that is selected isn't necessarily the table that supplies the data for the report. Data can be supplied from an Answer table, from a Crosstab table, or from some other source. When a different source is chosen, the specified report is *copied* to the new data source and is printed from that table.

To select the source of data for the report, in the Report Print dialog box, select **U**se Data From and choose one of the following from the list. If you are not using a mouse, press DOWN ARROW to go to the option you want.

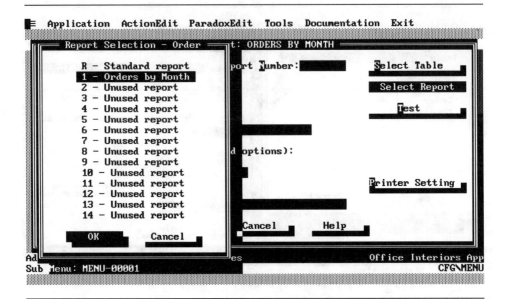

Figure 11-22. *Report Selection dialog box*

- *Table Shown Above* uses the data from the table that is named in the Table text box when the report is printed.

- *Answer Table* prints the results of queries in the report.

- *Crosstab Table* prints the results of a Crosstab in the report.

- *Other* allows you to specify a different table name in the box to the right of Other; however, the table named here must have the same structure as the table that is the basis for the report. The data in the Other table is then used when the report is printed.

Selecting the Destination

The output of the report can be sent to the printer, to the screen, to a file, or to a combination of these three choices. You can also select a different printer port or enter a setup string from within the Application Workshop.

In the Report Print dialog box, choose one, or a combination, of the following:

- *Screen* sends a copy of the report to the screen where you can view it.

- *File* sends a copy of the report to a file saved on disk. Enter the filename in the box directly to the right of *File*.

- *Printer Default* sends a copy of the report to the default printer.

Selecting a Different Printer for the Report

You can use the Report Print dialog box to select a different port or enter a setup string. (This is similar to the procedure for selecting a printer port and entering a string, which was discussed in Chapter 8.) When you do this, the change that is made applies only to the report being defined. It does not apply to all reports that may be used in the application.

To change the printer settings, select **P**rinter Setting from the Report Print dialog box, and a second dialog box appears, as shown in Figure 11-23. You may choose or change any of the settings.

Printer Port   This setting specifies the port that you want for a different printer. Default is selected. Press the arrow key to move to another port, or click on it to display a dot in parentheses.

Page Breaks   This setting allows you to choose among three methods for ending a page:

- *Default* is the option that was set in Paradox.

- *LineFeed* enters line-feed characters until the page end is reached.

- *FormFeed* sends form-feed characters to align the next page for printing.

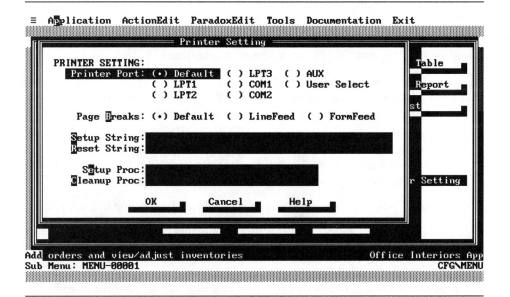

Figure 11-23.   *Printer Setting dialog box*

Setup String   This setting allows you to enter a setup string that sends commands to the printer. Type the setup string in the box to the right of Setup String. Setup strings are discussed in Chapter 8.

Reset String   This setting allows you to reset the printer after the report is printed. Type the reset string in the box directly to the right of Reset String. Again refer to Chapter 8 for a discussion of entering reset strings.

Setup Proc   This setting allows you to run a PAL procedure before the report prints. Type the name of the procedure in the box directly following Setup Proc. Refer to Chapter 12 for a discussion of procedures.

Cleanup Proc   This setting allows you to run a PAL procedure after a report is sent to the printer. Type the name of the procedure in the box directly following Cleanup Proc.

When you have finished making your selections, choose OK to return to the Report Print dialog box.

Displaying a Message

You can specify that a message appear at the bottom of the screen when the report is printing. To have a message displayed, select **D**isplay Message and type the message to be displayed when the report is printing. For example, you might type **Report is printing**. Choose OK to return to your application menu when you are finished defining the report object.

Assigning the Report Object to a Menu Command

To assign a report action object, choose the Report Print object type, and you will see the list of report objects available to be assigned to menu commands.

To assign a report object to a menu command, follow these steps:

1. Select the menu command you want. (The message at the bottom of the screen will show <No Action Defined>.) Press ENTER or F9 (Edit). The Menu Definition dialog box appears.

2. Choose **S**elect for the action object. The Object Type dialog box is displayed.

3. Select REPORT PRINT and choose OK. A dialog box showing a list of report objects appears, as shown in Figure 11-24. (Only one report object is shown here.)

4. Select the report object that you want to assign to the menu command.

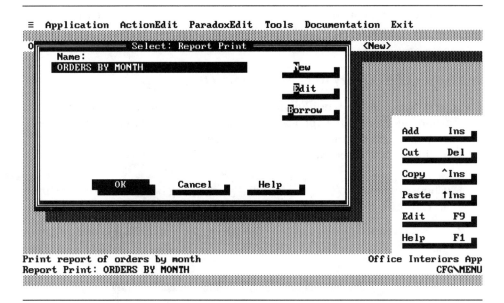

≡ Application ActionEdit ParadoxEdit Tools Documentation Exit

Figure 11-24.   *Select: Report Print dialog box*

5. Choose OK. You are returned to the Menu Definition dialog box. The Action box now shows the name of the report object.

6. Choose OK to return to your application menu. The message at the bottom of the screen shows the name of the report object that has been attached to the menu command.

Editing a Report Action Object

When you initially choose **R**eport Print from the Action**E**dit menu, a list of existing reports is displayed. Highlight the one to be changed and select Edit from the Edit: Report Print dialog box.

Once you do this, you will be shown the Report Print dialog box, as shown earlier in Figure 11-19. Use the same guidelines for **E**dit as you did for **N**ew to change the choices. When you are finished, select OK.

Borrowing a Report Action Object

You can borrow the specifications of an existing Report Action Object and use them to set up a new one. To do this, choose **R**eport Print from the Action**E**dit menu, select the name of the report action object to be borrowed, and choose **B**orrow from the Edit: Report Print dialog box. Type the name of the new report action object and choose OK.

You will then be allowed to change the specifications for the report action object the same way as for **N**ew or **E**dit of one. When finished, select OK.

Using ActionEdit/Query to Create Query Objects

The **Q**uery option in the Action**E**dit menu allows you to create objects that construct queries and run them in the application you are creating. After creating the object, you can then assign it to the appropriate menu command.

To define a query object, follow these steps:

1. Choose Action**E**dit/**Q**uery. The Edit Query dialog box is displayed, as shown in Figure 11-25.

2. Choose **N**ew and type a name for the query object in the dialog box, as shown here:

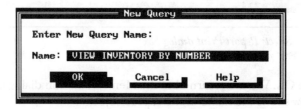

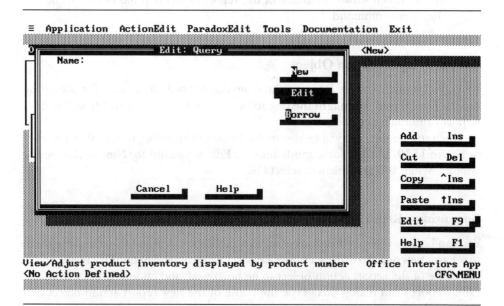

Figure 11-25.   *Edit: Query dialog box*

3. Choose OK after typing the new name for the query object. The Query By Example dialog box appears, as shown in Figure 11-26. The name of the query object is displayed at the top of the box. Various characteristics can now be assigned to the query object.

Selecting the Table(s) to Query

The names of the tables that will be queried are displayed in the box under Table(s) to Query. There may be no tables listed here—they may be displayed later during this process when you choose **Add**. The QBE button is used to add, edit, or remove query forms.

To select tables, follow these steps:

1. Choose **QBE**. The **QBE** menu appears, as shown in Figure 11-27.

   To use the **QBE** menu, press F10 (Menu) and the hot key for the option you want; or click on the option if you are using a mouse. The **Add** option is used to construct queries on tables the same way **Ask** is used in the Main menu in Paradox. **R**emove is used to remove current query forms from the workspace or to remove all query forms. **D**one saves the changes to the query images, and **C**ancel cancels the changes and returns you to the Query By Example dialog box.

```
 ≡  Application  ActionEdit  ParadoxEdit  Tools  Documentation  Exit

           ═══════════ Query By Example:VIEW INVENTORY BY TYPE ═══════════
       Table(s) to Query:
       No Table Selected      Use "QBE" to add and remove         ┌─────┐
                              query forms from the workspace,      │ QBE │
                              and to create or change the          └─────┘
                              query.

       [ ] Working Message:    ▒▒▒▒▒▒▒▒▒▒▒▒▒▒▒▒▒▒▒▒▒▒▒▒▒▒▒▒▒       ┌──────┐
       Setup Proc:                                                 │ Test │
       Query Will Generate:    (•) Answer   ( ) Deleted   ( ) None └──────┘
                               ( ) Changed  ( ) Inserted

       [ ] Display Number of Records in Results Table

       Special Actions:
       (•) No Action  ( ) Rename  ( ) Add  ( ) Empty and Add  ( ) Subtract
                                           Table Name: ▒▒▒▒▒▒▒▒▒▒▒▒▒▒▒▒▒▒

                         ┌────┐        ┌────────┐       ┌──────┐
                         │ OK │        │ Cancel │       │ Help │
                         └────┘        └────────┘       └──────┘
```

Figure 11-26.   Query By Example dialog box

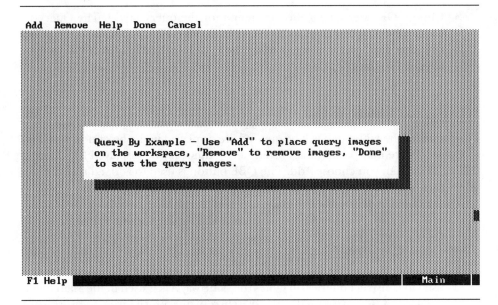

Figure 11-27. *QBE menu bar and screen prompt*

2. Choose **Add** from the QBE menu. You may have to press F10 (Menu) to go to the menu bar. A list of tables is displayed. The **Add** option works the same as the **Ask** option in the Paradox menu.

3. Choose the table that you want to query, and then choose OK. A query form for the table is displayed.

4. Define the query as you would in Paradox. Refer to Chapter 6 for information on constructing queries.

5. Choose **Add** again if you want to bring up another query form for a different table.

6. Press F2 (Do-It!) or choose **Done** to save the query and return to the Query By Example dialog box.

Removing Query Forms

You can either clear all query forms, or just the current ones from the workspace and from the Table(s) to Query list.

To remove query forms, follow these steps:

1. From the Query By Example dialog box, choose **QBE**.

2. Choose **R**emove and then either **C**urrent or **A**ll. You may have to press F10 to move the cursor to the menu bar.

- *Current* removes all active query forms. This is the same as pressing F8 or CTRL-F8 in Paradox.

- *All* removes all query forms from the workspace. This is the same as pressing ALT-F8 in Paradox.

3. Choose **D**one when you have finished. You are returned to the Query By Example dialog box.

Entering a Message

From the Query By Example dialog box, you can enter a message that will be displayed while the query is running. This message might be an explanation of the information that will be produced as a result of the query. If no message is entered, the message "Working..." will be displayed when the query is running.

To enter a message, follow these steps:

1. Select Working Message. An X should be displayed in the brackets.

2. Press TAB to go to the text box directly following **W**orking Message or click on it, and type the message.

Entering a Setup Procedure

As in other dialog boxes in the Application Workshop, you can enter a PAL procedure to perform a specific action before the query is run. Refer to Chapter 12 for information on procedures.

To enter a procedure, select Setup **P**roc and type the name of the procedure in the box directly following Setup Proc.

Specify Where to Expect Results

You can specify which temporary table will be generated by the query. The default is the Answer table. The choices are listed at the right of the Query Will Generate label. Choose one of the following:

- *Answer* is chosen when an Answer table will be generated by the query.

- *Changed* is chosen when a CHANGETO command has been entered in the query.

- *Deleted* is chosen when a DELETE command has been entered in the query.

- *Inserted* is chosen when an INSERT command has been entered in the query.

- *None* is chosen when either a CHANGETO or an INSERT command has been entered and data is not saved to a temporary table.

Displaying the Number of Records

The number of records in the temporary table as the result of the query can be displayed if an X is entered in the brackets directly in front of the message "Display Number of Records in Results Table."

To display the number of records, follow these steps:

1. Select **D**isplay Number of Records in Results Table, either by clicking on it with the mouse, pressing ALT-D, or by pressing TAB until it is selected.

2. An X should be displayed in the brackets. You can select it again to remove the X.

 *When the option to display the number of records in the Results table is turned on, the message, "Continue—OK/Cancel," appears when the query is performed. As the query is running, choose **No** to cancel any additional actions; choose **Yes** to continue.*

Assigning Special Actions

Special Actions perform certain tasks to the temporary tables as the query is being run, or after it has finished. Often queries are maintenance tasks to a table, such as selecting obsolete records or identifying duplicate records. Special Actions help maintain the tables. Choose any of the following:

- *No Action* is the default. Paradox will delete any temporary table generated by the query.

- *Rename* saves the data in the temporary table in a new table. Enter the new table name in the Table **N**ame text box located on the screen directly below the Special Actions options. This overwrites any existing table and its objects that may have the same name.

- *Add* adds the data in the temporary table to a different table. Enter the name of the *target* table in the Table **N**ame text box.

- *Empty and Add* deletes all data in a specified table and adds the data from the temporary table to the emptied table. Enter the name of the *empty* table in the Table **N**ame text box.

- *Subtract* deletes the data in the temporary table from a specified table. Enter the name of the *subtract* table in the Table **N**ame text box.

Testing the Query Object

You can test the query to see if it produces the results you want before leaving the Query By Example dialog box. Choose **T**est. The query will be performed, and the results will be displayed depending on the options and actions you selected to create the query object. If the query is not performed the way you want, you can change the options and actions using the procedures just discussed in the section "Using ActionEdit/Query to Create Action Objects."

Assigning a Query Object to a Menu Command

Assigning a query object to a menu command is similar to assigning Edit Session objects or report print objects. When a query command is selected, its query object is chosen from the Object Type dialog box.

To assign a query object, follow these steps:

1. Select the menu command you want and press ENTER or F9 (Edit). The Menu Definition dialog box appears.

2. Choose **S**elect in the Action box. The Object Type dialog box appears.

3. Select QUERY and choose OK. A list of query objects defined for the application appears in the next dialog box.

4. Select the query object that is to be attached to the menu command and choose OK. You are then returned to the Menu Definition dialog box, and the query object name is now displayed in the Action box.

5. Choose OK to return to your application menu.

Using ActionEdit/Multi Action to Combine Action Objects

The **M**ulti Action option allows you to combine two or more action objects in one object that can then be assigned to a menu command. For instance, perhaps you want one command to query a table, run a PAL procedure on the resulting Answer table, and then print a report.

You also can define new action objects from this menu if they have not already been defined; or add objects, modify them, or remove them from the list of objects in the Multi Action Type/Name list.

To define a new **M**ulti Action object that combines objects, follow these steps:

1. Choose Action**E**dit/**M**ulti Action. The Edit Multiple Actions dialog box is displayed. This is similar to other Edit dialog boxes that you have seen.

2. Choose **N**ew to display the dialog box in which you name the object.

3. Enter the object's name and choose OK. The Multi-Action dialog box appears, as shown in Figure 11-28, and the new name now appears at the top of the box. The Type/Name text box will list the types and names of each action object as they are added. You can add objects to this list, edit the objects, remove, or cut and paste the objects. You can also test the objects before leaving the dialog box.

Adding Action Objects to the Multi Action Object

After selecting Action**E**dit/**M**ulti Action, and naming a new object, you can add existing objects to the Type/Name text list in the Multi-Action dialog box. This identifies the actions that belong to the Multi Action object.

To add objects, follow these steps:

1. Choose **A**dd. A list of the object types is displayed.

2. Choose the type of object you want and choose OK.

3. A list of objects that currently exists for the type of action is displayed. If you need to create a new object or edit an existing one, choose one of the following:

   - *New* creates a new action object for the **M**ulti Action. Type a name in the dialog box, and then create the new object the same way you have created other objects.

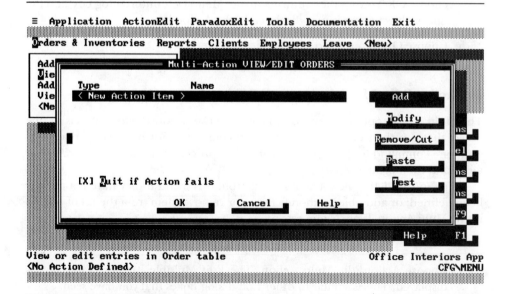

Figure 11-28.   *Multi-Action dialog box*

- *Edit* edits the attributes for an existing object. Select the name of the object and choose **E**dit. A dialog box of attributes is displayed. Edit them and choose OK.

- *Borrow* borrows the attributes of an existing object and edits it, if you like. Borrowing will be discussed later on in this chapter.

4. After creating or editing objects—or if you do not need to create a new object or edit an existing one—select the object to be included in the Multi Action object and choose OK. You are returned to the Multi-Action dialog box, and the object is added to the Type/Name list.

5. Repeat steps 1 through 4 to add other objects to the Multi Action object.

Modifying an Object

The attributes of an action object can be changed from the Multi-Action dialog box. To change attributes, follow these steps:

1. In the Multi-Action dialog box, select the action object you want to change and choose **M**odify. The dialog box for the specific action object is displayed.

2. Edit the attributes in the same way you defined the object originally and choose OK. You are returned to the Multi-Action dialog box.

Using Remove/Cut

Use **R**emove/Cut either to remove an action object from the Multi-Action Type/Name list, or to move it to a different position. When you delete the action object, it is temporarily placed in the paste buffer. When an object name is removed, it is stored in the buffer until the **M**ulti Action is saved and you leave the dialog box. Once you leave the Multi-Action dialog box, the contents of the buffer are gone.

To use **R**emove/Cut, follow these steps:

1. In the Multi-Action dialog box, select the object and choose **R**emove/Cut or press DELETE. The object name is removed from the list.

2. If you want to insert the object at a different position, move the cursor to the new position, and choose **P**aste or press SHIFT-INSERT.

When you remove the action from the list, the action object is not deleted. The name is merely removed from the Type/Name list in the Multi-Action dialog box.

Using Paste

When the name of an object is removed from the **Multi-Action Type/Name** list, it can be reinserted in the same place or in a new position by choosing **Paste** or pressing SHIFT-INSERT. This copies the contents of the paste buffer to the cursor's position.

Specifying Quit if Action Fails

If the Quit if Action fails option is selected (an X is displayed in the brackets to the left of the option), the **Multi Action** ends if an error occurs. This option is selected by default.

The Quit if Action fails option helps determine what action is taken by an OK/Cancel object. For example, if Quit if Action fails is selected and a user chooses Cancel in an OK/Cancel dialog box, all additional Multi Action objects for the selected command will be terminated.

Testing the Multi Action Object

After the action objects have been added to the Multi-Action Type/Name list, test the action to see if it performs the way you expect it to.

To test the **Multi Action** object, follow these steps:

1. From the Multi-Action dialog box, select the object to be tested, and choose **T**est.

2. As the test is proceeding, respond as you would if you were actually using the application to find out if it works the way you want it to.

3. When done, choose **C**ancel (if it is displayed at the top of the screen—this depends upon the type of action being tested). If **C**ancel is not a choice, press ESC. You then return to the Multi-Action dialog box.

4. Make any changes and choose OK to return to the Application Workshop.

Editing a Multi Action Object

You can edit the Multi Action object after using it if you decide some changes should be made. To do this, follow these steps:

1. Choose Action**E**dit/**M**ulti Action. The Edit: Multiple Actions dialog box is displayed, and the objects that you have defined are listed in it.

2. Select the name of the action object you want to change, and choose **E**dit.

3. Edit the action object the same way you created it.

4. Choose OK when finished.

Assigning a Multi Action Object to a Menu Command

Assigning a multi-action object connects the menu command with the Multi Action objects. Assigning the object is similar to assigning other types of objects to menu commands. You must identify the command and then link it to the Multi Action object.

To assign to a menu command, follow these steps:

1. Select the menu command you want and press ENTER or F9 (Edit). The Menu Definition dialog box is displayed.

2. Choose Action Select. The dialog box that appears shows a list of object types.

3. Select MULTIPLE ACTIONS and choose OK. The Select: Multiple Actions dialog box shows a list of Multi Action objects that currently exist in the application.

4. Select the Multi Action object you want to attach to the menu command and choose OK. When you return to the Menu Definition dialog box, the name of the Multi Action object is displayed in the Action box.

5. Choose OK to return to your application menu.

Using ActionEdit/Help to Add Help Text

You use the **Help** option to create objects that add text screens to aid the user. These screens tell the user what an option does, what actions to expect, or what to do next. These can be similar to the Paradox Help screens that you see when you press F1. Figure 11-29 shows an example of a Help screen.

You can make Help menus context sensitive by linking them to each command on the menu. They can either be help objects attached to a command or action objects for a command. In the first case, they are displayed when you highlight the command and press F1. In the second case, the help screens are displayed when the command is executed.

To create a help screen object, follow these steps:

1. From the ActionEdit menu, choose **Help** Text. A dialog box appears.

2. Choose **New** and enter a name for the object. Choose OK and the Help Screen dialog box is displayed, as shown in Figure 11-30. The name of the help object precedes the screen name.

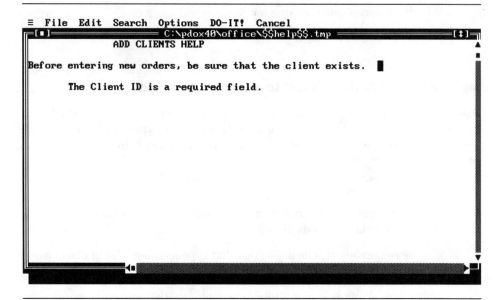

Figure 11-29.   *Example of an application help screen*

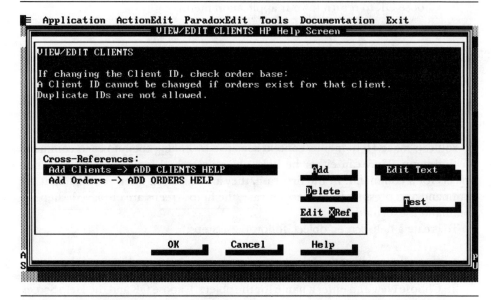

Figure 11-30.   *Help Screen dialog box*

Entering or Editing Text in the Help Screen

Enter help text explaining the menu option that the user will highlight. You could explain the use of the option—for example, why the user would want to use it; or insert warnings on the use of the option—for example, any actions which cannot be undone. You could include helpful hints on how the option could be used to greater benefit or made easier to use, and so on.

Select the **E**dit Text option to enter help text by following these steps:

1. Choose **E**dit text. A memo editor is displayed.

2. Enter text in the editor as you would in any other Paradox Editor window. (Chapter 4 covers the editor in detail.) You can generally enter about 80 lines of text. To add emphasis, you can specify different styles for the text, or portions of it. You type the characters within brackets on either side of the text, for example, **<i>Hello<n>**, prints **Hello**. The text styles and the commands you enter to determine them are as follows (characters within brackets can be either upper- or lowercase):

Intense (boldface) characters	**<I>text<N>**
Reversed characters	**<R>text<N>**
Blinking characters	**<B>text<N>**
Normal	**<N>text<N>**

3. After entering text for the Help screen, press F2 (Do-It!) to save. The Help dialog box is again displayed, and the help text is shown at the top of the dialog box.

Adding a Cross-Reference

You can cross-reference one text screen to another. For example, you may have related subjects or functions in the application where a cross-referenced help screen would give greater information to the user. Perhaps in the application you can enter information in an Orders table that relates to information in a Clients table. You could create a help screen for the Add Orders command and for the Add Clients or View/Edit Clients command and create cross-references to each other. Thereafter, if you press F1 when highlighting the View/Edit Clients command, you will see the help text for the View/Edit Clients command, and in the menu bar, a cross-reference to the Add Orders help screen. If you click on the cross-reference (as you would any menu option) the cross-reference for the Add Orders command will be displayed and the View/Edit Clients cross-reference will appear in the menu bar. Figure 11-31 shows an example.

To add a cross-reference, follow these steps:

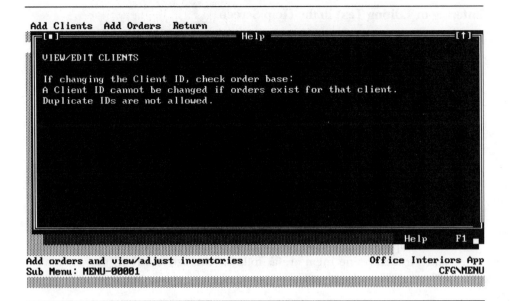

```
 Add Clients  Add Orders  Return
┌─[■]═══════════════════════════ Help ═══════════════════════════════[↑]─┐
│  VIEW/EDIT CLIENTS                                                      │
│                                                                        │
│  If changing the Client ID, check order base:                          │
│  A Client ID cannot be changed if orders exist for that client.        │
│  Duplicate IDs are not allowed.                                        │
│                                                                        │
│                                                                        │
│                                                                        │
│                                                                        │
│                                                                        │
│                                                                        │
│                                                                        │
│                                                              Help    F1 ■
 Add orders and view/adjust inventories          Office Interiors App
 Sub Menu: MENU-00001                                        CFG\MENU
```

Figure 11-31.   *Cross-referenced help menus in test mode*

1. From the Help Screen dialog box, choose **Add** located in the Cross-Reference section of the Help dialog box. An Adding Cross-References dialog box appears, as shown here:

```
┌══════════════ Adding Cross-References ══════════════┐
│                                                     │
│  Cross-Reference Title: ▐███████████████████▌       │
│                                                     │
│  Help Screen Name:      ▐███████████████████▌       │
│                                                     │
│        ▐   OK   ▌     Cancel ▌     Select ▌         │
│                                                     │
└═════════════════════════════════════════════════════┘
```

2. Enter a name in the Cross-Reference Title text box. You cannot leave this box blank. The name will appear in the menu bar above the help screen being displayed, and is the name of the screen being cross-referenced. The user will see this name.

3. Enter a name in the Help Screen Name text box. If you don't know the name, choose **S**elect to display a list of existing help screen objects in the current directory. You can then choose a name from this list, and it will be displayed in the Help Screen Name text box. This name may or may not be the same as the Cross-Reference Title. It is the actual help object name.

4. Choose OK to return to the Help screen dialog box.

*If you want to remove a Cross-Reference Help screen from the Cross-Reference text box, select the name in the text box and choose **Delete**. You cannot change the cross-reference name or title except by deleting it and adding a new one.*

5. Choose OK to save the Help object.

Use the Test option to see how the text and cross-references will appear.

Editing a Cross-Referenced Help Screen

You may find that you want to change the text for a cross-referenced help screen. For instance, as you create a help screen and add cross-references, you may need to go back to make sure text on the screens is consistent and accurate.

To edit a cross-reference, follow these steps:

1. From the Application Workshop, choose ActionEdit/**H**elp Text, to display the Edit: Help Display dialog box.

2. Select the Help object containing the cross-reference you want to edit from the list shown in the text box and choose **E**dit to go to the help screen.

3. Choose Edit **X**Ref. The Help screen dialog box for the next cross-referenced help screen is displayed.

4. Choose **E**dit Text to display the Editor. Edit the text that is displayed the same way you have edited text in other Editor screens.

5. Press F2 (Do-It!) when finished.

You can continue to choose Edit **X**Ref until all cross-referenced help screens have been displayed. This gives you a quick way to verify all cross-referenced text.

Assigning a Help Object to a Command

To assign a help object to a command, you must connect the two by using the Menu Definition dialog box.

Follow these steps to assign the help object:

1. Highlight the menu option that will have the help screen associated with it and press ENTER or F9.

2. Choose the Help Se**l**ect option to display a list of help objects.

3. Select the help object you want.

When you press ENTER the Menu Definition screen will be redisplayed with the help object selected. Now when the menu option is highlighted and the user presses F1, the selected help screen will be displayed.

The help screen also can be edited from the Menu Definition dialog box.

Using ActionEdit/Execute to Enter PAL Commands

The Execute option is used to enter a string of PAL commands in the application. You might use this to enter commands that are not necessarily available in the Application Workshop menu.

To use Execute, follow these steps:

1. Choose ActionEdit/Execute. A dialog box is displayed.

2. Choose **New**, and enter a name for the script object in the New Execute PAL dialog box. Choose OK after entering the name. An Editor screen appears.

3. Enter the PAL string in the Editor. Refer to Chapter 12 for information about PAL strings.

4. When finished, press F2 (Do-It!) to save. A dialog box asks if you want to save the code.

5. Choose **Yes** to save or **No** to cancel. The application menu bar is then displayed.

While you are in Edit mode, you can use the Go option to test your PAL strings.

You can assign the execute object to the menu in the same way you attach other objects to the menu—choose the menu command you want, press ENTER or F9 (Edit), choose Select in the Action box, select EXECUTE PAL from the list of object types, select the object you want to attach to the menu command, and choose OK in the dialog boxes to return to your application menu.

Using ActionEdit/OK/Cancel

The **OK/Cancel** command is used to create an object that confirms or cancels an action. An OK/Cancel object will often be included in a Multi Action object. For example, you can create an OK/Cancel object that asks if it is OK to print a report or run a query. Then include this object in a Multi Action object which includes another object that prints the report or performs a query. If the OK/Cancel action object is part of a Multi Action, the Quit if Action fails option on the Multi-Action dialog box must be set correctly. If the Quit if Action fails option is selected and the user chooses Cancel in the OK/Cancel dialog box, all unexecuted objects in the Multi Action will be terminated.

To use **OK**/Cancel, follow these steps:

1. Choose Action**E**dit, and then choose **OK**/Cancel. A dialog box shows the existing objects, if any.

2. Choose **N**ew to create a new object. A dialog box asks for the object name, as shown here:

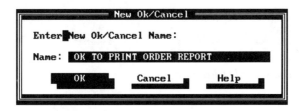

3. Type a name for the object and choose OK.

4. Type the title in the text box following Title.

5. Enter the message in the Text to Display box that you want displayed when the object runs, as shown in Figure 11-32.

6. Enter an expression in the Expression to Display text box, if you want to perform a calculation. The results of the expression will appear in the OK/Cancel dialog box beneath any text.

7. Select the OK option. An OK is displayed as the default in the text box; however, you can enter different text if you like. If you want to show Yes rather than OK, enter it in the text box. To make the *Y* a hot key, enclose it in tildes, as in, **~Y~es**.

8. Select the Cancel option. Cancel is displayed as the default response when this option is chosen. As in the OK option, you can change that to No or other text, if you like. Type **~N~o** in the text box—this changes the response to No and makes the *N* a hot key.

9. Choose **T**est if you want to see if the object works the way you want it to.

10. Choose OK when finished.

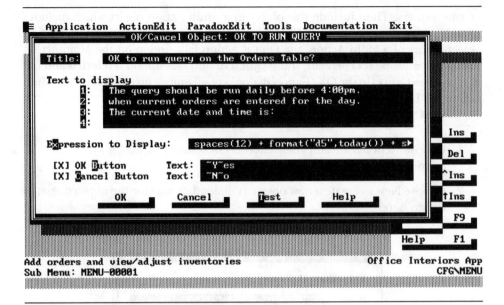

Figure 11-32.   *OK/Cancel Object dialog box*

If you are not going to include this object in a multi-action object, you can assign it to a menu command. Choose the menu command you want, press ENTER or F9 (Edit), choose Select in the Action box, select OK/CANCEL from the list of object types, select the object you want to attach to the menu command, and choose OK to return to your application menu.

Figure 11-33 shows the test of the sample OK/Cancel action object.

If your OK/CANCEL object results in errors and does not work as you intended, you may find it easier to handle if you type it into a PAL script. Then it can be attached to the command or Multi Action as an Execute PAL object.

Using Utility Actions

In addition to the categories that contain the action objects that you have created, Paradox supplies some utility object types. Two of the action objects, EXIT PAL and QUIT TO PARADOX, are predefined. Two of the objects, PROC (EXECPROC) and PLAY A SCRIPT, must be defined by you. For example, this is the only way you can implement password protection and graphs into a workshop-created application.

Figure 11-34 shows the dialog box with the list of object types.

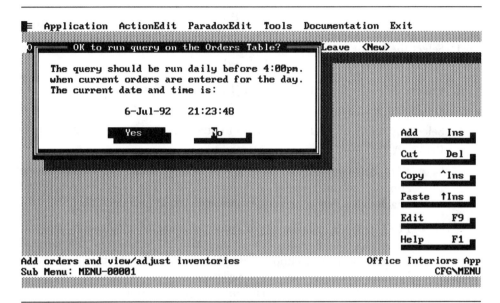

Figure 11-33.   *Test of the OK/Cancel action object*

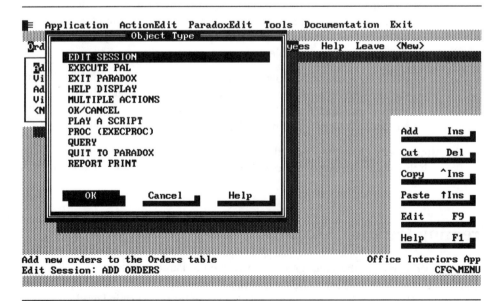

Figure 11-34.   *List of object types*

To assign a utility action, follow these steps:

1. Select the menu command that you want and press ENTER or F9 (Edit). The Menu Definition dialog box is displayed.

2. Choose **S**elect in the Action box. The list of object types appears, as shown in Figure 11-34.

3. Select the utility object type you want to attach to the menu command from the following choices.

   - *EXIT PARADOX* allows you to create a menu command that leaves the application and Paradox and goes to DOS. For example, you might attach this object to a menu command named Exit to DOS.

   - *PLAY A SCRIPT* allows you to enter the name of a PAL script that has been created in Paradox or an editor. You will be asked for the name of the script when you choose this option. Your more complex scripts may perform better if you attach procedures to the command using the PROC (EXECPROC) objects, rather than the scripts.

   - *PROC (Execproc)* contains scripts with PAL statements in them that make the script a *procedure.* By placing your scripts between PROC and END-PROC commands, you can create a procedure. With the CREATELIB and WRITELIB commands, you can write your procedures to a library. This improves both performance and security for the application. See Chapter 12 for more information. When you choose this object type you will be asked for the name of the procedure. (This is different than choosing an Execute object.)

   - *QUIT TO PARADOX* allows you to create a menu command that leaves the application and returns to Paradox. You may attach this object to a menu command, *Exit to Paradox,* that appears in the same submenu with an *Exit to DOS* menu command.

4. After selecting a utility object, the Menu Definition dialog box will be displayed with the object displayed in the Action box. Choose OK when you are finished.

Creating Paradox Objects in the Workshop

As discussed earlier in this chapter, you can create the Paradox objects—tables, forms, reports, and scripts—that are to be used in the application either in Paradox, or in the Application Workshop. It is generally a good idea to create the objects in Paradox because it is easier to test them there; however, as you develop the application, you may realize that additional objects should be created. To do this, use the **P**aradoxEdit menu.

Using ParadoxEdit to Create or Modify a Table

Use the Table Designer to create or modify a table from the Application Workshop. After entering a table name, you can choose whether to create a new table, restructure an existing table, or add or modify validity checks or image settings. Chapters 3 and 5 cover these subjects. Refer to these chapters if you need additional information.

To use the Table Designer, follow these steps:

1. Choose **P**aradoxEdit/**T**ables. A Table Designer dialog box appears, as shown in Figure 11-35.

2. Enter the name of the new table and choose **C**reate.

   You have two options available to help. You can borrow the structure of an existing table to use or modify. You can borrow several structures and delete the fields you do not want. The borrowed structure will be inserted above the cursor position. The second option, FileFormat, allows you to create a table compatible with Paradox 3.5.

3. Enter the field names and types the same as you would in Paradox.

4. When done, press F2 (Do-It!) to save and return to the Table Designer dialog box.

5. Choose **D**one, or press ESC to cancel.

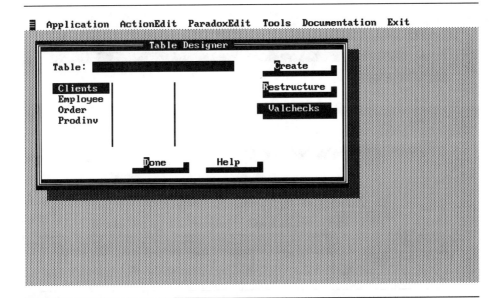

Figure 11-35.   *Table Designer dialog box*

*If you want to change the table structure, choose **ParadoxEdit/Tables**, enter the name of the table to be changed, and choose **Restructure**. Then make the changes as you would in Paradox, and press F2 (Do-It!) when finished. Choose **Done** from the Table text box. (See Chapter 5 for more information.)*

*Validity checks can be chosen in the Table text box to add or modify validity checks, or to change image settings for the various tables. After making the changes, press F2 (Do-It!) and then choose **Done** from the Table text box. You can also press ALT-F10 to access the Quick Valcheck menu and set validity checks in the current field. (See Chapter 5 for more information.)*

Using ParadoxEdit to Create or Modify a Form

Forms can be created or modified using the **ParadoxEdit/Forms** option. You may prefer to create nonstandard input forms for the application, for example, or to modify the standard form. The form can be created in Paradox or the Workshop.

Follow these steps to create a new form:

1. Choose **ParadoxEdit/Forms**. A Form Selection text box appears, as shown in Figure 11-36.

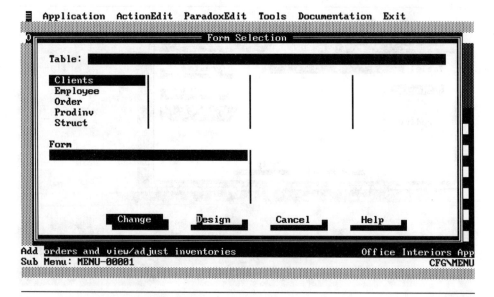

Figure 11-36. *Form Selection dialog box*

2. Select the table that is the basis for the form you are going to create and press ENTER. The list of forms is then available.

3. Select an unused form and choose **Design**. You are prompted for a title.

4. Enter the name for the form title and choose OK. The Form Designer is then displayed.

5. Design the form as if you were in Paradox. Refer to Chapter 7 if you need additional information.

6. Press F2 (Do-It!) when finished, or choose Cancel to leave the Form Selection dialog box without saving the changes. You can also click on the Close box and choose **Yes** to leave the form design window without saving the form.

To change the form, select Change from the Form selection box, and respond to the prompts. You will be given the chance to change the description or to retain the previous one, then you can change the form as you would in Paradox. When finished, press F2 (Do-It!) to save the changes.

Using ParadoxEdit to Create or Modify a Report

The **ParadoxEdit/R**eports option is used to create or modify a report within the Application Workshop. If you are modifying a report, the report could have been created in Paradox or the Workshop.

To create a report, follow these steps:

1. Choose **ParadoxEdit/R**eports. A Report Selection dialog box appears.

2. Select the table for the report and press ENTER. The list of reports is then displayed.

3. Select an unused report and choose **Design**. You are prompted for the title.

4. Enter a title and choose the type of report style—**T**abular or **F**reeform—that you want. You will be placed in the Report Designer.

5. Design the report as you would in Paradox. See Chapter 8 for additional information on how to design or modify a report.

6. Press F2 (Do-It!) when finished. Or choose **C**ancel/**Y**es, or click on the Close box and choose **Yes**, to leave the window without saving the report.

*If you want to change the report after designing it, choose **ParadoxEdit/R**eport, enter the name of the table for the report, select the report to be changed, and then choose **Change**. Make the changes as you would in Paradox, and press F2 when finished.*

Using ParadoxEdit to Create a Script

The **P**aradoxEdit/**S**cripts menu allows you to create new scripts, edit existing scripts, or play scripts. You cannot record keystrokes for scripts in the Application Workshop. That must be done in Paradox.

To create a new script from within the Application Workshop, follow these steps:

1. Choose **P**aradoxEdit/**S**cripts. A Select Script dialog box appears, as shown in Figure 11-37. It lists existing scripts.

2. Enter a new script name in the Script text box, and choose **N**ew. The Editor is displayed.

3. Create a script as you would in Paradox. Refer to Chapter 12 for information about creating scripts in Paradox.

4. When finished, press F2 (Do-It!) to save and return to the Workshop. Or choose **C**ancel/**Y**es, or click on the Close box to leave the window without saving the script.

 *To edit an existing script, choose **P**aradoxEdit/**S**cripts, select the script to be edited, and choose Open. The Editor appears; here you can change the script as you would in Paradox. Press F2 (Do-It!) when finished.*

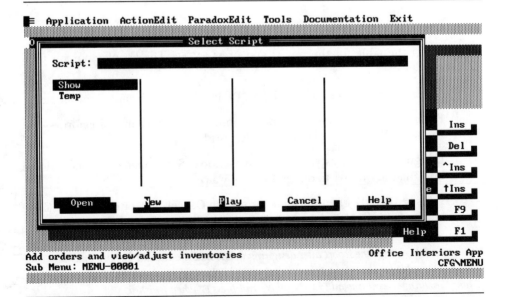

Figure 11-37.   Select Script dialog box

The Play option in the ParadoxEdit/Scripts dialog box allows you to run the script. First select the script you want to run and then choose Play. You may find yourself in the Debug mode. Refer to Chapter 12 if you have questions about the Debugger.

Changing the Application

You can easily make changes to the application after it has been created. You may want to change the title or description, you may wish to edit the menu structure or change action objects, or make changes to any other part of the application. You will learn how to change the application in this section, and about borrowing objects.

Changing the Application Title

If you find that the title displayed in the splash screen is not appropriate for the application, you can change it using the **E**dit option.

To change the title, follow these steps:

1. Choose **A**pplication/**E**dit from the Workshop menu bar. You may have to press F10 (Menu) to access the menu bar. The Application Edit dialog box appears.

2. Choose **S**plash Screen. The Splash Screen Editor window appears. Edit the text in the Splash Screen.

3. Press F2 (Do-It!) to save the changes. Or choose **C**ancel/**Y**es, or click on the Close box, to leave the window without saving the changes.

The title is the text that appears on the splash screen when you run the application. The application name is the text that appears in the lower-right corner of the Application Workshop when you are working on the application. This name can also be changed. At step 2 in the previous procedure, instead of choosing Splash Screen, move the cursor to the Application Name text box, delete the old name, and type a new one.

Changing the Application Description

The **A**pplication/**E**dit option is also used to change the description of your application.

To change the description, follow these steps:

1. Choose **A**pplication/**E**dit from the Workshop menu bar. Press F10 (Menu) if you need to access the menu bar from your application menu. A dialog box appears.

2. Choose Change **D**escription. A Description Editor window is displayed. Edit the description the same way you edit text in other Editor windows.

3. Press F2 (Do-It!) to save the changes. Or choose **C**ancel/**Y**es, or click on the Close box, to leave the window without saving the changes.

Changing the Menu Commands

The text in the menu commands can be changed, the position of the menu commands can be changed, or you can edit the menu commands in the Menu Dialog box using the same procedures you used originally. You can use the mouse palette that is displayed in the Application Workshop window to delete, copy, insert, or edit the menu commands.

Removing an Action Object from a Menu Command

You may want to remove the object attached to a menu command, yet keep the same name and attach a different object to it.

To remove an object, follow these steps:

1. Select the menu command to be changed and press F9 (Edit) or click on Edit in the mouse palette. The Menu Definition box appears.

2. In the Menu Definition box, choose **E**dit. Depending upon the type of objects assigned to the command, a dialog box showing the objects will be displayed.

3. Select the object to be removed and press DELETE or choose **C**ut or **Re-** move/**C**ut. Again, the choice here depends upon the type of object.

4. Choose OK to return to your application menu.

*To reinsert the object at the cursor position, press SHIFT-INSERT or choose **P**aste.*

Changing the Menu Name

If the name of the command does not seem suitable—perhaps it does not indicate the actions assigned to it—change it in the Menu dialog box.

To change the menu name, follow these steps:

1. Select the command you want to change.

2. Press F9 (Edit) or choose Edit. The Menu Definition dialog box appears.

3. Change the menu name in the Keyword text box.

4. Choose OK.

Changing the Order of Commands

To move a menu command to a new position, delete the command, move the cursor to a new position and insert it.

To change the order of commands, follow these steps:

1. Select the menu command that you want to move.

2. Press DELETE or choose **C**ut to move the command to the buffer.

3. Move the cursor to a new position and press SHIFT-INSERT or choose **P**aste. The command and all actions attached to it are moved.

Removing a Command

To delete a command, just move the cursor to the command and press DELETE or choose **C**ut.

Editing an Action Object

You can change the attributes given to the various action objects by following these steps:

1. Choose Action**E**dit and then choose the type of action you want to change. For example, if you want to change a query object, choose **Q**uery from the Action**E**dit menu. An Edit dialog box appears for that object type.

2. Select the object that you want to edit from the list and choose **E**dit. The dialog box that was used when you created the object is then displayed.

3. Make the changes you want in the same way you assigned the attributes when you first created the object.

4. Choose OK when finished.

Borrowing an Action Object

If one of your objects has characteristics that you want to use in a different object, you can *borrow* those characteristics and attach them to the new object.

You do not necessarily have to wait until you modify your application to borrow an object. You can borrow an object any time after it has been created.

To borrow an action object, follow these steps:

1. Choose Action**E**dit and select the type of action you want. The Edit dialog box is displayed.

2. Select the object that has the characteristics you want to borrow, and choose **B**orrow. A Borrow dialog box shows the old name. A Report Print object is borrowed in the example shown here:

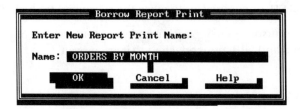

3. Type a new object name in place of the old.

4. Choose OK. The old object's characteristics are displayed in a dialog box.

5. Change the characteristics the same way you entered them originally. The procedure used here depends upon the type of action object that is borrowed.

6. Choose OK when finished.

Testing the Application

Run the application while you are still in the Application Workshop to see if it works the way you want it to. You can then make adjustments and changes before exiting the Application Workshop. Test it several times as you develop it. You do not have to wait until it is completed before testing.

To test the application, follow these steps:

1. Open the application, if it is not already open (choose **A**pplication/**O**pen, select the name of the application, and choose OK).

2. Choose **A**pplication/**T**est to run the application. The Application Workshop will disappear from the screen and your application will occupy the desktop.

3. Choose any of the application menu commands that have objects assigned to them to see if they work the way you want them to. An example is shown in Figure 11-38.

4. When done testing, press F9 to return to the Application Workshop.

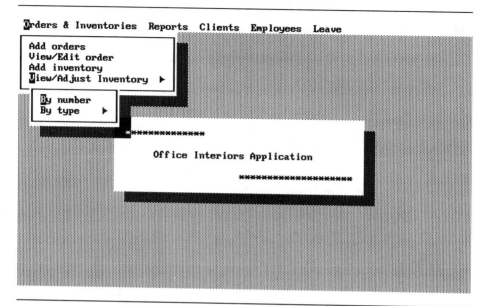

Figure 11-38.   *Testing the application*

Finishing the Application

You use the **Finish** option in the **Application** menu to copy all files associated with the application into the directory you named to contain the application. Before using Finish, two of the files used with the application are located in the Application Workshop directory, rather than in the application subdirectory. Those files are the library code and a master table. *Library code* refers to the programming code that Paradox creates to run your application. The *master table* contains the information for the action objects. A Paradox program converts the information in the tables to the action.

When you choose Finish, all application files are copied to the application subdirectory, making them able to run without the Application Workshop. All files in the subdirectory can be copied to another directory or to a floppy disk. Finish also creates a startup script that activates the application and translates the menu information now contained in table form to a PAL script.

To use **Finish**, follow these steps:

1. Choose **Application/Finish**.

2. The **Finish** procedure will start, and information about its progress will appear on the screen.

Use Finish if you plan to copy the application to disks so that it can be distributed to others.

Running the Application

In addition to running the application in the workshop using **Application/Test**, you can also run the finished application either from Paradox or from DOS; or you can use it with Paradox Runtime. Paradox Runtime, which can be obtained from Borland, is a program that allows you to run a Paradox application without having the full Paradox program. The *PAL Programmer's Guide* provides specific information for getting the Runtime package.

Running the Application from Paradox

In order to run an application from Paradox, first load Paradox, then change to the directory where the application is stored, and then use **Scripts/Play** to run the application. The startup script is created when **Application/Finish** is used to translate menu information to a script.

To change the directory, follow these steps:

1. Choose **Tools/More/Directory**. Type the directory name where the application is stored, and press ENTER.

2. To run the application, choose **Scripts/Play**. Type the application ID in the dialog box and choose OK; if you are not sure of the name, press ENTER before entering an ID to see the list of scripts. The name of the application appears there. Select the name of the application and choose OK or press ENTER. The application menu bar is then displayed.

 The application ID is shown when you choose Application/Open in the Workshop, so you can also check the exact spelling of the name there.

Running the Application from DOS

It is sometimes easier to run the application from DOS, rather than from the Paradox menu. This prevents others from accessing tables and other objects in Paradox.

First you must "finish" your application by running **Application/Finish**. Then you must place the Paradox program directory (usually PDOX40) on the DOS command path by typing it in with the DOS PATH command. Then, depending on whether the application directory is the default in the Custom Configuration Program (CCP) **S**tandard Setting dialog box, you can use one of two methods for loading the application.

If the application directory is the default, simply start the application by typing **paradox** *application-ID* from the root directory prompt. Or, if the application directory is not the default, you can follow these steps:

1. At the DOS prompt, type **cd** *application-ID*, which is where your application is stored, and press ENTER. For example, if you were to run the application *Office*, which has been discussed in this chapter, at the DOS prompt type **cd \pdox40\office**. (The directory does not have to be a subdirectory to \pdox4.)

2. At the new DOS prompt, type **paradox***application-ID* (the name that was entered in the New Application dialog box when the application was created). Then press ENTER. Again, as an example, at the DOS prompt, c:\pdox40\office>, type **paradox office** and press ENTER to run the application.

In the second step no default must be set in CCP or it will override your attempt to set the application directory path.

You can also use a batch file to start the application. Both the batch file and the Paradox program directory must be on the DOS command path. If you choose this method you type the batch file name from DOS. If you set up an AUTOEXEC.BAT file with the batch file name as the last entry, you only need to boot the computer and the application will appear on the screen.

Using Tools to Manage the Application

The **T**ools menu in the Application Workshop is used to manage the application action objects, tables, forms, reports, and scripts that are located in the application subdirectory. An example of the **T**ools menu is shown here:

```
Tools
┌─────────────────┐
│ ActionObjects   │
├─────────────────┤
│ Tables          │
│ Forms           │
│ Reports         │
│ Scripts         │
└─────────────────┘
```

Each of the options in the **T**ools menu gives you the following choices:

Copy   This option allows you to copy the selected action object, table, form, report, or script. First highlight the option you want to copy and then select **C**opy. A dialog box will be displayed with the name of the highlighted object in the text box, or it may be blank. Delete the name, type the name of the new copy (or just type a new name if the dialog box is blank), and choose OK.

Rename   This option allows you to give the selected action object, table, form, report, or script a new name. Select the object to be renamed and choose **R**ename.

When **R**ename is chosen, a dialog box is displayed showing the current name or it may be blank. Delete it, enter a new name (or just type a new name if the dialog box is blank), and choose OK.

Delete   This option allows you to remove the selected action object, table, form, report, or script from the application. Highlight the object to be deleted and choose **D**elete. When **D**elete is chosen, a dialog box is displayed where you can confirm the deletion. Choose OK to delete the object.

*The **T**ools/**T**able option also includes a choice, **Family**, that allows you to copy the forms and reports associated with the table. This will be discussed later in this chapter.*

Using Tools/ActionObject

The **A**ctionObject option is used to copy, rename, or delete the action objects that are used in the current application. To use ActionObject, follow these steps:

1. Choose **T**ools/**A**ctionObject from the Workshop menu. The Action Object Tools dialog box is displayed. An example is shown in Figure 11-39.

2. From this dialog box select the action object that you want and then choose **C**opy, **R**ename, or **D**elete.

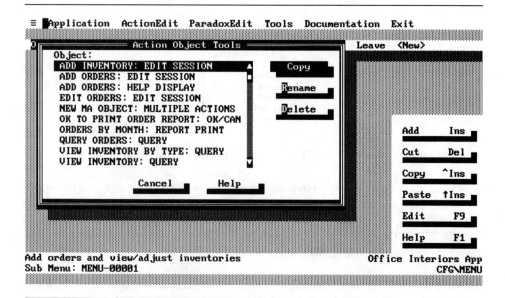

Figure 11-39.   Action Object Tools dialog box

Using Tools/Tables

The Tools/Tables option is similar to the ActionObject option in that it can be used to copy, rename, or delete tables. It also allows you to copy the table's family of reports and forms to another table. To use Tools/Tables, follow these steps:

1. Choose Tools/Tables from the Workshop menu. A dialog box showing the list of tables used in the application will be displayed.

2. Select the table you want and choose Copy, Rename, Delete, or Family (discussed below).

3. For Copy or Rename, enter the name of the copy or the new name.

Family   This option allows you to copy the forms and reports associated with the selected table to a different table *with the same structure.* Select the table you want, or type the table name, and then choose Family to display a Copy Family To: dialog box. See an example in Figure 11-40. Type the table name or select the table that you want to copy the reports and forms to and press ENTER. A dialog box is displayed prompting you that the current family members will be overwritten. Choose either Cancel or OK.

Using Tools/Forms

The Tools/Forms menu is used to copy, rename, or delete the forms used in the current application. To use Tools/Forms, follow these steps:

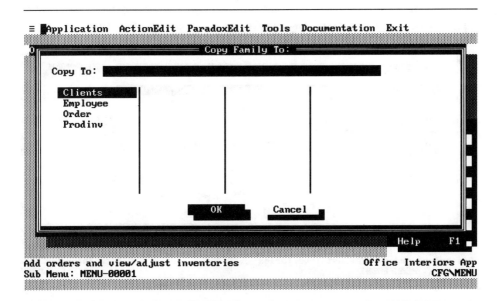

Figure 11-40.   Copy Family To dialog box

1. Choose **T**ools/**F**orms from the workshop menu and press ENTER to display a dialog box showing a list of the current tables and the forms for each. The names of the tables are listed at the left. An example is shown in Figure 11-41.

2. Select the table and the form you want and choose **C**opy, **R**ename, or **D**elete. These choices are slightly different for forms, as discussed below.

Copy   Choose **C**opy to display another dialog box showing the list of tables. Select the table that you want to copy the form to. The Form Picklist then can be accessed. Select the form to copy to and choose OK. The **S**ame option is shown in the upper-right corner of the dialog box. Choose **S**ame if you want to copy the form to the same table.

Rename   Select the table and form to be renamed and choose **R**ename. A dialog box shows a list of all the forms for that table. Select the new form number and choose OK.

Delete   Select the table and the form that you want to remove and then choose **D**elete. A dialog box for confirmation of the deletion will be displayed. Choose OK to remove the form.

Using Tools/Reports

The **R**eports option is used to copy, rename, or delete reports. To use **R**eports, follow these steps:

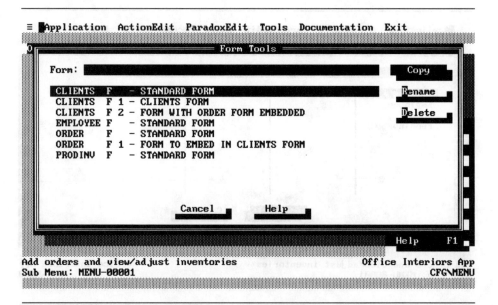

Figure 11-41.   *Form Tools dialog box*

1. Choose **T**ools/**R**eports from the Workshop menu and press ENTER. A dialog box showing the list of tables and their reports in the application will be displayed.

2. Select the table and the report that you want and then choose **C**opy, **R**ename, or **D**elete. **C**opy and **R**ename are slightly different in **T**ools/**R**eports.

Copy   This allows you to copy the selected report to either another report for the same table or to a different table. Choose **C**opy to display another dialog box containing the table names. Select the table to copy the report to—the Report Picklist can then be accessed. Select the report you want to copy to and choose OK. If you want to copy the report to the same table, choose **S**ame.

Rename   Choose **R**ename to display a dialog box showing the list of report numbers. Choose the report number you want to use as the new name (new number), and choose OK.

Using Tools/Scripts

The **S**cripts option is used to copy, rename, or delete scripts used in the application. To use **T**ools/**S**cripts, follow these steps:

1. Choose **T**ools/**S**cripts to display the dialog box showing a list of scripts used in the current application, as shown in Figure 11-42.

2. Choose the script that you want and then choose **C**opy, **R**ename, or **D**elete.

If any of the scripts in a private directory start with a dollar sign ($), they are temporary scripts and may be deleted.

Using the Documentation Menu

You use the **D**ocumentation menu to display information about your application. This information can be the menu structure of your application, a detailed list and definition of all action objects, or a cross-reference that shows a list of all action objects, their reference types and names, and their object types and names.

Using the Documentation/Menu Tree

The menu tree displays the menu structure of your application. This structure shows the options in the application menu bar, the submenus and menu commands listed

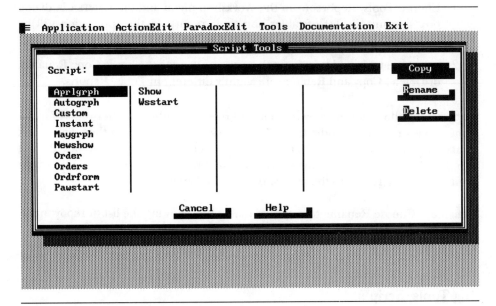

Figure 11-42. *Scripts Tools dialog box*

under each of these options, and the action objects that are assigned to each menu command. This display can be sent to the screen, printer, or to a file.

To generate a menu tree, follow these steps:

1. Choose **D**ocumentation/**M**enu Tree from the Workshop menu. A dialog box appears, as shown here:

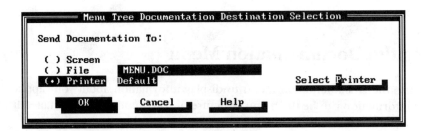

2. Select the output you want—Screen, File, or Printer. Click on the choice or press the DOWN ARROW to reach the option you want. If you select File, enter a filename in the box directly following File. The default name is MENU.DOC. If you select Printer, you can select a different printer if you like. Choose Select Printer and respond to the dialog box as in other dialog boxes for selecting printers.

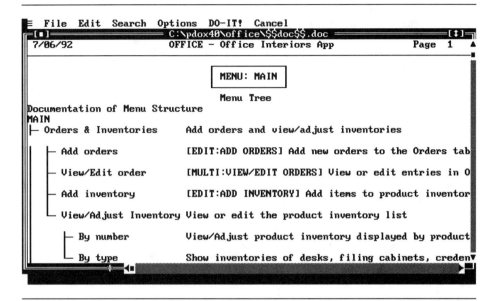

```
≣  File  Edit  Search  Options  DO-IT!  Cancel
┌─[■]════════════════ C:\pdox40\office\$$doc$$.doc ═════════════[↕]─┐
│ 7/06/92                OFFICE - Office Interiors App         Page  1  ▲
│                                                                        ░
│                    ┌─────────────────────┐                            ░
│                    │   MENU: MAIN        │                            ░
│                    └─────────────────────┘                            ░
│                         Menu Tree                                     ░
│Documentation of Menu Structure                                        ░
│MAIN                                                                    ░
│├─ Orders & Inventories     Add orders and view/adjust inventories     ░
│  │                                                                    ░
│  ├─ Add orders            [EDIT:ADD ORDERS] Add new orders to the Orders tab
│  │                                                                    ░
│  ├─ View/Edit order       [MULTI:VIEW/EDIT ORDERS] View or edit entries in O
│  │                                                                    ░
│  ├─ Add inventory         [EDIT:ADD INVENTORY] Add items to product inventor
│  │                                                                    ░
│  └─ View/Adjust Inventory View or edit the product inventory list     ░
│     │                                                                 ░
│     ├─ By number          View/Adjust product inventory displayed by product
│     │                                                                 ░
│     └─ By type            Show inventories of desks, filing cabinets, creden▼
│  ═╪═◄■ ░░░░░░░░░░░░░░░░░░░░░░░░░░░░░░░░░░░░░░░░░░░░░░░░░░░░░░░░░░░░░░►■
└────────────────────────────────────────────────────────────────────┘
```

Figure 11-43.   *Menu tree for an application*

3. When you have selected the output you want, choose OK. Figure 11-43 shows an example of a menu tree.

Using Documentation/Action Detail

Use the Action Detail option to display a detailed list of action objects and the attributes assigned to each. Figure 11-44 shows an example of an Action Detail list.

To use the Action Detail option, follow these steps:

1. Choose Documentation/Action Detail from the Workshop menu. A dialog box appears, as shown here:

```
┌══════ Detail Documentation Destination Selection ══════┐
│                                                         │
│  Send Documentation To:                                 │
│                                                         │
│   (•) Screen                                            │
│   ( ) File      ┌─────────────────┐                     │
│   ( ) Printer   │ ACTION.DOC      │                     │
│                 │ Default         │   Select Printer ▄  │
│                                                         │
│      ┌────────┐    ┌─────────┐    ┌───────┐             │
│      │  OK    │    │ Cancel ▄│    │ Help ▄│             │
│      └────────┘    └─────────┘    └───────┘             │
└─────────────────────────────────────────────────────────┘
```

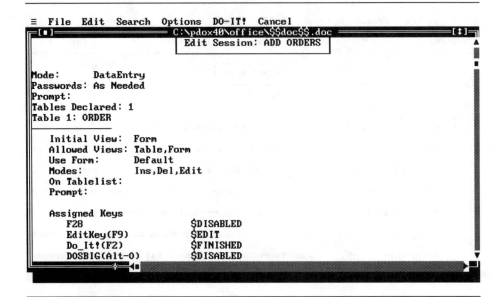

```
≡  File  Edit  Search  Options  DO-IT!  Cancel
╒═[■]══════════════ C:\pdox40\office\$$doc$$.doc ═══════════════[‡]═╕
                    ┌─────────────────────────────┐
                    │  Edit Session: ADD ORDERS   │
                    └─────────────────────────────┘

 Mode:       DataEntry
 Passwords: As Needed
 Prompt:
 Tables Declared: 1
 Table 1: ORDER
 ──────────────
    Initial View:  Form
    Allowed Views: Table,Form
    Use Form:      Default
    Modes:         Ins,Del,Edit
    On Tablelist:
    Prompt:

    Assigned Keys
      F28                   $DISABLED
      EditKey(F9)           $EDIT
      Do_It!(F2)            $FINISHED
      DOSBIG(Alt-0)         $DISABLED
```

Figure 11-44.   *Action Detail list*

```
≡  File  Edit  Search  Options  DO-IT!  Cancel
╒═[■]══════════════ C:\pdox40\office\$$doc$$.doc ═══════════════[‡]═╕
  7/06/92              OFFICE - Office Interiors App          Page ▲

                    ┌─────────────────────┐
                    │   Cross Reference   │
                    └─────────────────────┘
              Action Objects & Paradox Objects in Use

 Objects Within Application (by type):    Referenced by:

 Object Type       Object Name        Object Type       Object Name

 Edit Session      ADD INVENTORY      Menu              CFG\MENU
                                      Multiple Actions  NEW MA OBJECT
                                      Multiple Actions  NEW MA OBJECT
 Edit Session      ADD ORDERS         Menu              CFG\MENU
                                      Multiple Actions  ASD
                                      Multiple Actions  NEW MA OBJECT
 Edit Session      EDIT ORDERS        Multiple Actions  VIEW/EDIT ORDERS

 Exit Paradox                         Menu              CFG\MENU
```

Figure 11-45.   *Cross Reference list for an application*

2. Select the output you want. If you choose Printer, you can also select the printer you want by choosing Select **P**rinter. Then select a different printer port. If you choose File, also enter a filename in the text box directly following File. The default name is ACTION.DOC.

3. When you have chosen the output you want, choose OK. Figure 11-44 shows an example of the **A**ction Detail list. If you chose Screen as the output device, scroll through the screens to see all information.

Using Documentation/Cross-Reference

The **C**ross-Reference option generates a list of the object types used in the application. They are referenced by the action objects that have been used for each object type. Figure 11-45 shows an example of a cross-reference.

To use the **C**ross-Reference option, follow these steps:

1. Choose **D**ocumentation/**C**ross-Reference. A dialog box appears, as shown here:

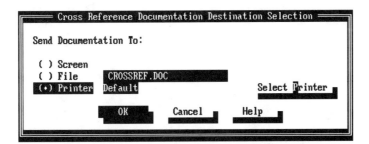

2. Choose the output you want. If you choose Printer, you can also choose Select **P**rinter and choose a different printer to use for printing the output. If you choose File, type a filename in the text box directly to the right of File. The default filename is CROSSREF.DOC.

3. After selecting the type of output you want, choose OK. Figure 11-45 shows an example. If you chose Screen as the output device, scroll through the screens to see all information.

Chapter **12**

Using PAL

Introducing PAL

This chapter examines the Paradox Application Language (PAL). The text here is not meant to replace the Borland *PAL Programmer's Guide* or the *PAL Reference.* Rather, the intent is to summarize the Borland manuals, to supply an overview and some details, thereby giving you a quick grasp of the most important (or most complex) parts of the language. The chapter emphasizes the changes made in Version 4.

In this chapter you will learn what PAL is, how to build a program using PAL, to edit it, and to debug it. You will learn the basic skills needed to create a program, such as how to build menus, use expressions, format data, trap events, work with control structures such as IF THEN ELSE and WHILE ENDWHILE, and display information on screens.

This chapter does not teach general programming techniques. It assumes that the reader has programmed before and is familiar with basic programming commands and techniques. It will orient programmers to PAL if they are new to this particular language. The commands and functions of PAL are summarized in Chapter 13.

What Is PAL?

PAL is a comprehensive programming language designed to be an integral part of Paradox. If you have used the Script Macro Record feature, you have used PAL. PAL allows you to create your own applications so that other users do not have to understand or use Paradox to use your application. The application can have its own custom menus, dialog boxes, validity checking, password-protection features—any feature that you can have with Paradox. In fact, PAL contains approximately 400 commands and functions that you can use.

You needn't use PAL to create applications, however; you can also use PAL solely to enhance the Paradox environment by creating custom tools that fit your needs. Whether you use PAL to build complex and lengthy applications or simply to customize tools for your own convenience, this chapter tells how to get the most from PAL.

Who Writes PAL Programs?

Although anyone with some programming experience can write a PAL program, those accustomed to working with C or Pascal have a strong advantage. And, since PAL is so intimately tied to Paradox, a thorough knowledge of Paradox is really necessary. The commands and functions reflect Paradox's capabilities, so without an understanding of Paradox, you will not know how to solve problems. For example, if you do not know how Paradox selects menu options, you will not be able to program a PAL application to do so. First learn Paradox. Then you can easily pick up PAL.

PAL, Scripts, and the Application Workshop

PAL is used to create scripts or programs in two ways: using the **Scripts** menu to record keystrokes (described in Chapter 10) or to write PAL scripts, or using the Application Workshop (described in Chapter 11).

When you create a script, you are creating a PAL program. You can create a script either by recording keystrokes using **Scripts/BeginRecord** or by writing the script using the **Scripts/Editor**. Once the script is saved to disk under the extension name .SC (or .SC2 if the script has actually been executed), you have a PAL program. Then, using the **Scripts/Editor**, you can enhance the script with PAL commands and functions not available by recording the script keystrokes. You can also save a query image in a script.

When you build an application using the **Workshop**, you are also creating PAL programs and procedures. You can enhance the automatically created programs by linking your own PAL procedures to the **Workshop** programs.

You will probably use all three methods—using the **Workshop**, recording keystrokes, and writing scripts—when you create a PAL application. A typical development of a PAL application might proceed this way:

1. Design (on paper) the tables you will need and the data each will contain. List the reports and what they must contain. List the entry forms needed. List relationships between the tables and the key fields linking them.

2. Build the database tables, reports, and forms using the normal Paradox menus and commands. Create queries with **Ask**, then save them with

Scripts/QuerySave. Build in the linkages and other important attributes of the tables.

3. Use the System/Utilities/Workshop to build the menu structure and consequent actions of the application using the prebuilt tables, reports, and forms.

4. Use the Scripts recording facility to record reoccurring actions. Link the scripts together as needed to create more comprehensive routines.

5. Use Scripts/Editor to develop PAL enhancements that cannot be created using the Workshop applications or recorded scripts. Make procedures out of script subroutines.

6. Tie the procedures and scripts together using Scripts/Editor. After the scripts have been tested, build application procedures and libraries.

7. If needed, add a control or top-level script driver that calls the procedure library and begins the application. You may want to build a macro that can initiate the application as well. Paradox automatically runs a script named INIT.SC before loading Paradox. This also can be used to initiate an application rather than to load Paradox.

Obviously, there are many steps connected with each of the steps in this scenario. You do not have to use the Workshop at all if you find straight PAL programming easier. However, note that using the Workshop can be a good way to familiarize yourself with PAL.

PAL Building Blocks

When you use PAL you will become thoroughly familiar with three building blocks: the PAL menu, the PAL Debugger, and the PAL commands and functions.

The PAL Menu

Although you can use Scripts/Editor to create PAL programs, the PAL menu, shown here, contains some options not available with the Scripts menu.

```
┌─PAL Menu─┐
│ Play
│ RepeatPlay
│ BeginRecord
│ Debug
│ Value
│ MiniScript
└──────────┘
```

In addition, the Scripts menu is only available from the Main menu. There are times when you will want to invoke, create, or test a routine while in another mode.

You will find that the PAL menu is always accessible and has important programming tools.

Displaying the PAL Menu

To display the PAL menu, press ALT-F10. The menu contains six options: **P**lay, **R**epeatPlay, **B**eginRecord, **D**ebug, **V**alue, and **M**iniScript.

You can display the menu almost anywhere within Paradox with two exceptions. If you press ALT-F10 while debugging a script, you'll see only the Debugger menu, described later in this chapter. If you are recording a script when you press ALT-F10, you'll see this menu:

Cancel stops the recording of the script without saving it. **E**nd-Record "finishes" the script and then saves it. Using these two options is the same as using the **C**ancel and **E**nd-Record options on the **S**cripts menu.

Using Play

Play "plays" a script, regardless of how the script was created. When you choose **P**lay, the dialog box shown in Figure 12-1 appears, asking you to type or select the name of the script to be run.

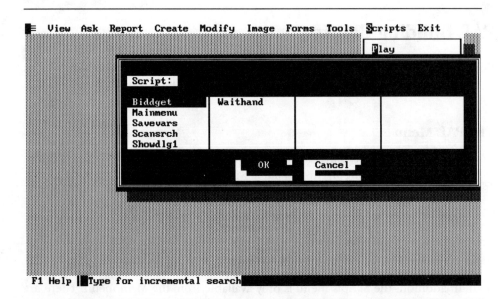

Figure 12-1.   *Dialog box that appears when Play is selected*

You can use the PAL **P**lay option within any mode in Paradox; you are not restricted to the Main menu. The PAL menu disappears when the script begins to play.

Using RepeatPlay

RepeatPlay plays a script a specific number of times. When you choose this option you will first be asked for the name of the script. When you have entered the script name, you'll be shown this dialog box asking for the number of times you want the script to repeat:

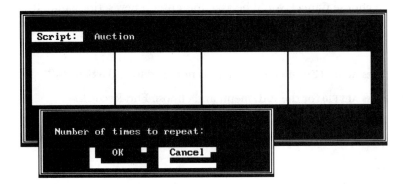

You can either enter a number or type **C**. If a number is entered, the script repeats that number of times. If you type **C**, the script repeats continuously until you press CTRL-BREAK. The PAL menu disappears from the screen when the script begins to play.

Using PAL **R**epeatPlay is identical to using **S**cripts/**R**epeatPlay except that you can use the PAL option within any mode in Paradox.

Using BeginRecord

BeginRecord initiates the recording of any keystrokes that follow. You use it the same way you use **S**cripts/**B**eginRecord except that the PAL option is available within almost any mode in Paradox. This allows you to capture keystrokes within a specific environment; you do not have to capture the keystrokes that take you from the Main menu to the specific mode you want.

When you choose this option by pressing ALT-F10 for the PAL menu and choosing **B**eginRecord, a dialog box asks for the name of the script. If the name does not already exist, it will be assigned to the recorded keystrokes. If the name already exists, you will be asked if you want to replace the existing script or cancel the request, as shown here:

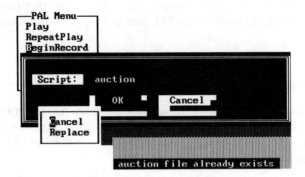

If you choose Cancel, you'll be asked to enter a new script name. If you choose **R**eplace, the recorded keystrokes will replace the existing script of the same name.

You can end the recording in one of three ways:

- Press ALT-F3 (End-Record). (This is not used to end a **Scripts/B**eginRecord.)

- Press ALT-F10 for the PAL menu and choose **E**nd-Record.

- From the Main menu choose **Scripts/E**nd-Record.

Using Debug

Choosing **D**ebug from the PAL menu lets you use the Debug tool to find errors within a script. When you choose this option, you are asked for the name of the script to be debugged. Paradox then enters the Debug mode, which is discussed later in this chapter.

Using Value

Value provides a way to quickly evaluate an expression or value. *Expressions,* which are described later in the chapter, contain operators or functions which equate to a value. The expression can consist of up to 175 characters and is named Value. Value is a temporary script that will exist for the current session only, or until it is replaced by another Value script.

When you select this option by pressing ALT-F10 for the PAL menu and then choosing Value, a dialog box asks you to type the expression, as shown here:

Type the functions or expression you want to test. The expression can include PAL variables and arrays storing data values in the script being debugged. If you make an error, use the arrow keys to move the cursor to the error and correct it. If you enter the expression past the end of the dialog box, the text box will scroll so that you can continue entering characters.

When you press ENTER, Paradox quickly evaluates the expression and displays the result in a small window in the lower-right corner of the screen. This window disappears when you press the next key.

When you press ENTER to execute the expression, Paradox creates a script named Value. After it executes, you can recall it by bringing up the PAL menu, choosing Value again, and then pressing CTRL-E. It will be displayed in the Value dialog box for you to edit.

The script is not available to you as a file, to rename or copy, for instance.

After you have evaluated an expression, you can add another expression to it. If you want to link two Value scripts together, choose Value, type in a new expression, press CTRL-E, and then press ENTER. Be sure that the expression being added is adequately linked to the first, by providing an operator to connect the two expressions, for example. Otherwise, PAL may not be able to recognize what to do with the added expression.

You can use Value scripts to perform any of these tasks:

- Determine the values of variables and arrays

- Calculate arithmetic expressions

- Execute PAL functions

Remember that Value evaluates an expression, while MiniScript executes commands.

If the Value script contains an error, you will be shown the Script Break menu, shown here:

Choose Cancel if you know what the problem is and want to abandon your effort or begin again from scratch. The script will be canceled.

Choose Debug if you are not sure what the problem is or if you want to edit the script. You'll see a message indicating where the problem is, as shown here:

```
                                     Syntax error: Unrecognized command
Line 73 of Script FIG12-4E                            Type Ctrl-Q to Quit
            CASE(MenuNow = "Edititems"):   ▶ EditItemsProc
```

The specific cause of this syntax error is the missing parentheses following the procedure name. PAL could not tell whether EditItemsProc was a procedure name or not.

Press CTRL-E to redisplay the Value script and edit the expression.

Using MiniScript

MiniScript provides a way to quickly and easily try out a short, single-line script. The script can consist of up to 175 characters and is named Mini. It is a temporary script that will exist for the current session only, or until it is replaced by another miniscript. Any canvas changes made by the miniscript will be removed when the script is finished. Changes made to the desktop will not be removed.

When you select this option by pressing ALT-F10 for the PAL menu and then choosing **MiniScript**, a dialog box will appear in which you type the script, as shown here:

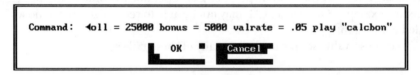

```
Command:   ◀oll = 25000 bonus = 5000 valrate = .05 play "calcbon"
                    OK  ▪  Cancel
```

Type the commands and functions you want to test. If you make an error, use the arrow keys to move the cursor to the error and correct it. As you enter commands past the end of the dialog box, the text box will scroll so that you can continue entering characters.

You cannot enter a PROC command. You cannot enter a command that does not accept any other commands on the same line, or the command will have to be the last one of the miniscript.

When you press ENTER to execute the **Miniscript**, Paradox creates a script named Mini that is the most current script on the stack. After it executes, you can recall it by bringing up the PAL menu, choosing **Miniscript** again, and then pressing CTRL-E. The miniscript appears in the **Miniscript** dialog box for you to edit.

As with Value, the Miniscript is not available to you as a file, to copy or rename, for example.

After you have executed a miniscript, you can add or link another miniscript to it. If you want to link two miniscripts together, choose **M**iniscript, type in a new script, press CTRL-E, and then press ENTER.

You can use miniscripts to perform any of these tasks:

- Test a small routine before writing it

- Test a larger script by "calling" it within the miniscript

- Test a debugging run by assigning values to a variable before running the script under the debug mode

- Learn PAL

- Set up a keyboard macro for the duration of the Paradox session, for example, to reset values during a debugging session

*Remember that **V**alue evaluates an expression, while **M**iniScript executes commands. A common mistake is to use one option when the other is what you need.*

If the miniscript contains an error, the **S**cript Break menu appears, as shown here:

```
┌Script Break┐
│Cancel      │
│Debug       │
└────────────┘
```

Choose Cancel if you know what the problem is or you want to retype the script from scratch. The script will be canceled and you can retype it correctly.

Choose **D**ebug if you are not sure what the problem is or if you want to edit the script without retyping it from scratch. You'll see a message indicating where the problem is, as shown here:

```
Line 1 of Script MINI                                    Type Ctrl-Q to Quit
  maxdoll = 25000 bonus = 5000 valrate = .05 play  ▶ "calcbon"
```

Press CTRL-E to redisplay and edit the most recent miniscript.

Leaving the PAL Menu

You can exit the PAL menu by pressing ESC. This returns you to the Paradox desktop where you were when you pressed ALT-F10 to display the PAL menu.

However, most of the options on the PAL menu automatically exit the menu as they execute.

The PAL Debugger

When programming a PAL application you'll find the Debugger is a valuable resource. With it you can find programming errors, step through the program instructions one line at a time, find the current values of variables and expressions, insert miniscripts during the execution of the programs, see at which levels an error has occurred in a nested routine, edit the script while you are actually debugging it, and more.

There are two types of programming errors. *Syntax errors* are caused when the expected format or structure of the command is not followed. This type of error occurs when PAL code is mistyped or a necessary command or part of a command is omitted. A syntax error may be due to a misspelled word, a missed comma, or an unfinished set of quotes or parentheses. Syntax errors are common, easy to find generally, and easy to correct.

The more subtle type of error, *run errors*, occur when the PAL syntax is correct, but the Paradox environment is in an incorrect state. Paradox cannot continue the run for some reason. Examples of run errors are when a specified image is not present, a variable has not been assigned a value, a command is being used in an inappropriate mode, or a function does not exist, or has the wrong number of *arguments*—that is, values required for the functions to operate. The errors can be deeply buried in a nested routine. Run errors often require careful searching and analysis, which the Debugger can help you with.

How to Invoke the Debugger

The Debugger is available to you both while scripts are executing and before executing the script. You can access the Debugger in four ways:

- Press ALT-F10 to display the PAL menu and choose **D**ebug, as shown here. After you enter the script name, the Debugger begins executing the script while debugging. This process starts at the beginning of the script.

```
┌─PAL Menu──────┐
│ Play          │
│ RepeatPlay    │
│ BeginRecord   │
│ Debug         │
│ Value         │
│ MiniScript    │
└───────────────┘
```

- Choose **D**ebug from the **S**cript Break menu. The menu is displayed when a script is being played and a syntax or run error occurs, as shown in the following illustration. In this case, the Debugger will begin processing at the site of the error that caused the **S**cript Break menu to be displayed.

- Embed a DEBUG command in a script where you want the debugging features available, and then play the script. The Debugger is active on the line containing the DEBUG statement.

- When you want to invoke the Debugger in a specific place while a script is executing, play the script and then press CTRL-BREAK to interrupt the execution. (Depending on the context, you may have to press another key, such as the key designated to end a WAIT, to break out of the script.) The Script Break menu appears, and you can choose **D**ebug. This can be turned off in the Custom Configuration Program (CCP).

The Debugger Screen

Figure 12-2 shows an example of a script containing a run error that is revealed with the Debugger. The Debugger messages appear on the bottom three to five lines of the screen.

On the first line (fifth from the bottom line on the screen) is the Error message. This is where the Debugger describes the error as best it can. It may not be able to

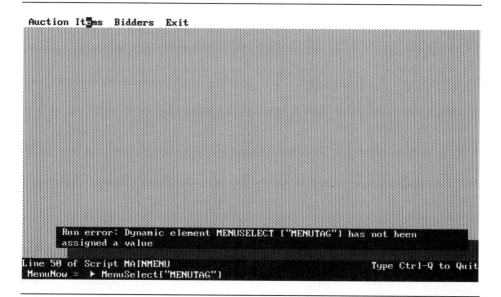

Figure 12-2. *Debugger screen*

precisely identify what caused the error; it can only describe what the problem seems to be. In Figure 12-2, the problem is that a dynamic array element was not assigned a value.

The fourth line (second from the bottom) is the Status line. This names the script being processed and displays the line number containing the error. To the right of this is the shortcut key to exit the Debugger. By pressing CTRL-Q you can return to the normal Paradox desktop.

The bottom line shows the script line containing the error. This may or may not be where the error actually occurred. This simply marks the point where Paradox could no longer continue executing the current script or procedure.

Depending on the Debugger feature being used, you will either quit when an error is displayed, edit the error in the script, reset values so the script can continue, or select another option from the Debugger menu.

The Debugger Shortcut Keys

During the Debugger session, you can use certain shortcut keys that provide immediate tools. These keys are listed here:

Key	Description
ALT-F10 (PAL menu)	Displays the **D**ebugger menu during the debug session (although the menu is labeled PAL menu, this book distinguishes it from the regular PAL menu by calling it the Debugger menu, as Borland does)
CTRL-E (Edit)	Invokes the Editor to edit the script
CTRL-G (Go)	Continues script play after a pause
CTRL-N (Next)	Executes the Next command and skips the current one
CTRL-P (Pop)	Pops up one level within a nested routine
CTRL-Q (Quit)	Quits the Debugger
CTRL-S (Step)	Steps through the script command by command
CTRL-T (Trace)	Traces through the script, including procedures
CTRL-W (Where)	Displays where the current nesting level is

These keys are only available during the Debugger session. Upon leaving the Debugger, the keys take other actions or are not used at all.

The Debugger Menu

After choosing the **D**ebug option, press ALT-F10 to display the Debugger menu, as shown here:

```
┌─PAL Menu──┐
│Value      │
│Step       │
│Trace      │
│Next       │
│Go         │
│MiniScript │
│Where?     │
│Quit       │
│Pop        │
│Editor     │
└───────────┘
```

It contains ten options: Value, Step, Trace, Next, Go, MiniScript, Where?, Quit, Pop, and Editor. These give you the full debugging capability found within PAL.

Using Value   Value, as explained earlier in the PAL menu, provides a way to quickly evaluate an expression or value. The expression can consist of 175 characters and is named Value. Value is a temporary script that will exist for the current session only, or until it is replaced by another Value script.

Select this option by choosing Value from the Debugger menu. A dialog box appears in which you define the expression by typing the functions or expression you want to test. PAL variables and arrays (described later in the chapter) can be used in an expression evaluated by Value. If you make an error, you can use the arrow keys to move the cursor to the error and correct it. As you enter commands past the end of the dialog box, the text box scrolls to allow you to continue entering characters.

When you press ENTER, Paradox quickly evaluates the expression and displays the result in a small window in the lower-right corner of the screen. This window is removed when you press the next key.

Refer to the "Using Value" section earlier in the chapter for more information.

Using Step   You use Step to move forward through a script command by command. Step is much the same as Trace except that Step does not step through procedures and PLAY, EXECUTE, or EXECPROC commands. These are executed but the Debugger does not step through them.

To select Step, display the Debugger menu and choose Step.

Remember that variables hold their values throughout a Paradox session. If the script itself does not clear or initialize these values, you may have to do it with a miniscript before using Trace or Step. Otherwise, the values in the variables may obscure the results you are trying to test.

Step cannot be used to step through commands containing syntax errors.

 The shortcut key for Step is CTRL-S.

Using Trace   **T**race, like **S**tep, is used to move through a script, command by command. **T**race will step through procedures and commands such as PLAY, EXECUTE, and EXECPROC.

While tracing through commands you can use the shortcut keys to interrogate the variables and expressions, and perform other debugging tasks.

To select **T**race display the Debugger menu and choose **T**race.

Remember that variables hold their values throughout a Paradox session. If the script itself does not clear these values, you may have to do it with a miniscript before running Trace or Step. Otherwise, the values in the variables may obscure the results you are trying to test.

As with Step, Trace cannot be used to advance through commands containing syntax errors. Errors must be corrected first.

The shortcut key for **T**race is CTRL-T.

Using Next   **N**ext is used to move over the current command and on to the next command. You can use **N**ext to skip over a routine you don't want to test and move to a command you do want to test.

Next cannot be used to avoid commands with syntax errors.

The shortcut key for Next is CTRL-N.

Go   **G**o is used to continue execution of a script. If you have been stepping through an area of a script, you can then continue normal execution once you have passed the commands you wanted to examine more closely. The script will continue to execute until it ends, is stopped by an error, or until CTRL-BREAK or another debug command is encountered.

Go cannot be used when syntax errors have caused you to enter the Debugger mode.

The shortcut key for **G**o is CTRL-G.

MiniScript   The Debugger **M**iniScript, as in the PAL menu, provides a way to quickly and easily try out a short, single-line script. Refer to the PAL "Using **M**iniScript" section earlier in this chapter for information on using it. The script can consist of 175 characters and is named Mini. It is a temporary script that exists only for the current session, or until it is replaced by another miniscript.

When you press ENTER to execute the miniscript, Paradox creates a script named Mini. Unlike the PAL menu **Mini**Script, the Debugger **Mini**Script does not immediately execute. Rather, the miniscript becomes part of the script being debugged. It is the current script and is similar to a called procedure in that it is a "level down" from the script being debugged when the miniscript was created. You can use the shortcut keys to **S**tep through the miniscript, or use **G**o, or **T**race. You cannot use **E**dit. However, you can use the **P**op option to pop up to the higher level script being executed when the miniscript was initiated. (You'll learn about the **P**op option shortly.)

In the Debugger mode, you can use miniscripts to perform these tasks:

- Fix an error that occurred in the script being tested

- Assign values to a variable before running the script under the debug mode, such as:

```
varname1=100,varname2=200,varname3="A"
```

*Remember that **V**alue evaluates an expression, while **Mini**Script executes commands. A common mistake is to use one option when the other is what you need.*

If the miniscript contains an error, you will be shown the **S**cript Break menu. Choose **C**ancel to end the miniscript and return to the previous Debugger mode. Choose **D**ebug to have the Debugger identify the problem as best it can.

*After executing a miniscript and again choosing **Mini**Script from the Debugger menu, press CTRL-E to redisplay and edit the most recent miniscript.*

Where?   **W**here? displays the currently active levels of nested programs. Figure 12-3 shows an example that has three active levels of procedures. The script containing the nested procedures is named Fig12-3.SC. The first procedure, named Level1, placed a call to the second procedure, named Level2, and so on. The third level, Level3, contained the error. The values of formal parameters and private variables, when they exist, are also displayed.

The shortcut key for **W**here? is CTRL-W.

Quit   **Q**uit cancels the execution of the program and returns to the previous Paradox workspace. All procedure definitions are released, as though the program had successfully completed. Values of variables and array remain defined for the rest of the session, unless RELEASE VARS ALL is specified.

The shortcut key for **Q**uit is CTRL-Q.

```
Proc LEVEL3 **Debugger** [Run Error]
Formals: X = 3000

  Proc LEVEL2
  Formals: X = 6000

    Proc LEVEL1
    UseVars: RETVAL = True

      Script FIG12-3.SC
```

`Press any key to continue...`

Figure 12-3.   *Where? displays the levels of nested programs currently being processed by the Debugger*

Pop   **P**op cancels the current program and "pops" you up one level to the program that issued the call. **P**op is the same as **Q**uit when the program being popped has no calling program.

The shortcut key for **P**op is CTRL-P.

Editor   To edit the script when you are in the Debugger, choose **E**ditor from the Debugger menu. You will leave the Debugger and enter Scripts/Editor. Choosing the editor will cancel the script, return you to the Main mode, and clear the desktop. The editor will be positioned at the script line causing the error.

If you have changed the editor default to one of your own choosing with the Custom Configuration Program, you will not be using the Paradox Scripts/Editor when you choose the Editor option. Also, you will not be positioned at the erroneous line unless the alternate editor accepts a line number as an input parameter.

When you are finished editing the script, test it by playing it using the **G**o option on the **S**cripts/**E**dit menu, or by bringing up the Debug menu to use one of its features.

The shortcut key for **E**dit is CTRL-E.

Leaving the Debugger

When you leave the Debugger, the screen returns to the way it was prior to the Debug mode. As with **Q**uit, leaving the Debugger causes all procedure definitions to be released, but all global values in variables and arrays to be maintained for the duration of the session or until RELEASE VARS ALL is executed.

The Debugger can be exited in several ways. You can leave it by choosing a specific command, such as **Q**uit, or pressing CTRL-Q, or you can leave the Debugger for another mode, such as the Editor. You can exit using a PAL command such as EXIT, QUIT, or RETURN, which causes the Debugger mode to be terminated (when in the topmost level program). Finally, you can select one of the Debugger menu options, such as **T**race, **S**tep, **N**ext, or **G**o, which terminate the mode when they end.

PAL Commands and Functions

Commands and functions are summarized in Chapter 13. This chapter discusses some of the more critical commands. Commands perform tasks, such as to display menus, as with SHOWMENU, or to find a record, as with LOCATE. Functions evaluate expressions and perform calculations. Examples are the financial Present Value function, PV( ), and TIME( ), which displays the time. Functions return a value, whereas commands may or may not. PAL scripts contain both commands and functions.

When you write scripts, you do not have to follow a rigid set of rules, as far as how to put commands together on a line. The format is rather flexible; you can put as many or as few commands and functions on a line as you wish, being careful not to split names across lines. However, for readability and ease of debugging, you will find that it pays to put commands on separate lines, spacing them to show in-line command paths—that is, to show which commands or options fall under the overall control of other commands or options.

In addition, commands and functions may be uppercase, lowercase, or a mixture of both. For readability, settle on some standard for entering scripts, such as entering PAL keywords in uppercase, procedure names in uppercase and lowercase, and variables in lowercase, for example.

There are three types of commands available through PAL: programming commands and functions, keypress commands, and abbreviated menu commands.

Programming Commands and Functions

Programming commands and functions are those that cannot be duplicated using Paradox's system of menus and function keys. These commands are powerful and add the ability to create menus, control the path a program may execute by using such branching commands as IF THEN ELSE statements, or to perform loops (which you'll learn about later in this chapter). The programming commands and functions consist of a keyword and perhaps one or more arguments. These commands and functions cannot be recorded into a script. They must be typed in using an editor, such as **Scripts/Editor**.

Keypress Commands

Keypress commands are those that duplicate the Paradox menu and keypress commands. These may be menu choices, shortcut keys, or queries saved with **Scripts/SaveQuery**. These types of commands may be recorded, thereby creating a script, or created using the **Scripts/Editor**. In the case of queries saved with **Scripts/SaveQuery**, a script containing text representations of the query will be saved. The script will include fields selected and any criteria defined.

Abbreviated Menu and Key Names

You can use abbreviated menu and key names instead of the longer names. For example, instead of typing this,

```
Tools/Copy/Table/Replace
```

you can type this:

```
Copy
```

You must be in the correct mode to use the shortened names, just as you must be to use the longer menu or key choices. Table 12-1 lists the abbreviated commands.

Using Comments

Comments, set apart from the script itself by a semicolon, help you understand the intent of the script. Be generous in applying comments. Paradox ignores all text following the semicolon.

Essential Programming Tasks

Certain essential tasks must be programmed when developing an application. This section explains some of the more important tasks, as well as tasks that are new with Release 4. You'll learn about creating procedures and libraries, formulating expressions, and formatting data during input and output operations. A discussion of the commands used in controlling the structure of PAL scripts also is discussed.

Abbreviations	Menu Commands
ADD	Tools/More/Add
CANCELEDIT	Cancel/Yes in Edit, Form, or Report
COEDIT	Modify/CoEdit
COPY	Tools/Copy/Table/Replace
COPYFORM	Tools/Copy/Form/Replace
COPYREPORT	Tools/Copy/Report/Replace
CREATE	Create
DELETE	Tools/Delete/Table/OK
DOS	Tools/More/ToDOS
EDIT	Modify/Edit
EDITOR FIND	Editor Menu/Search/Find
EDITOR FINDNEXT	Editor Menu/Search/Next
EDITOR GOTO	Editor Menu/Edit/GoTo
EDITOR NEW	Editor Menu/File/New
EDITOR OPEN	Editor Menu/File/Open
EDITOR READ	Editor Menu/File/InsertFile
EDITOR REPLACE	Editor Menu/Search/Replace
EDITOR WRITE	Editor Menu/File/WriteBlock
EMPTY	Tools/More/Empty/OK
EXIT	Exit/Yes
INDEX	Tools/QuerySpeed
LOCK	Tools/Net/Lock or Tools/Net/PreventLock
MOVETO	Image/Zoom/Record (Field or Value)
PICKFORM	Image/PickForm
PLAY	Scripts/Play
PROTECT	Tools/More/Protect/Password/Table
RENAME	Tools/Rename/Table/Replace
REPORT	Report/Output/Printer
SETDIR	Tools/More/Directory/OK
SETPRIVDIR	Tools/Net/SetPrivate
SETUSERNAME	Tools/Net/UserName
SORT	Modify/Sort

Table 12-1. *Abbreviated Commands and Keypresses*

Abbreviations	Menu Commands
SUBTRACT	Tools/More/Subtract
UNDO	Undo/Yes
UNLOCK	Tools/Net/Lock or Tools/Net/PreventLock
UNPASSWORD	Tools/More/Protect/ClearPassword
VIEW	View

Table 12-1. *Abbreviated Commands and Keypresses* (continued)

 For information about commands not covered in this chapter, refer to Chapter 13, which contains a summary of all PAL commands and functions.

Procedures and Libraries

Scripts are the basic program component. When you write a script it becomes a file with the extension .SC. When the file is first executed (and each time the script is changed) a new copy of the script is created and named the same name but with the extension .SC2. The .SC2 copy is preparsed and is consequently faster to run and more efficient than .SC files. Procedures are preparsed as well. *Parsing* resolves the PAL script components into values, addresses, and commands that can be executed by Paradox.

Procedures are more formalized scripts. They are subroutines that are called by scripts or other procedures to perform a specific task—for example, to retrieve a record from the database, or to perform a menu-selected option. However, in a larger sense, procedures also contain major application modules, and eventually whole applications can be called with one procedure. Procedures can provide definite benefits, such as programming power, better memory management, portability of code, and easier application maintenance.

Procedures can have arguments passed to them, and they can return a value back to the calling script or procedure. Procedures are both flexible and useful, in that they can be used repeatedly by separate calling programs to perform a common function.

Variables can be declared PRIVATE to a procedure. This ensures that manipulating the private variable will not affect a variable with the same name outside of the procedure's scope.

After a procedure is thoroughly debugged, you may want to store procedures in special procedure libraries. From libraries, the procedures can be called from scripts or other procedures without first defining them again. You may want to use libraries, particularly for larger applications, to distribute programs to other users, or for security reasons. Libraries are discussed in detail later in this chapter.

Creating Procedures

Procedures are created by writing a script, debugging it, and then embedding it between PROC and ENDPROC statements, with syntax such as this:

```
PROC [CLOSED] ProcName()
     Body of the procedure goes here
ENDPROC
```

The *header* of the procedure, the first line, must have the word PROC, optionally, the word CLOSED, the procedure name, and a list of the arguments that it needs. The parentheses after the *ProcName* are required even if no arguments are used. The body of the procedure contains the PAL commands and functions that perform the task to be done. The procedure ends with the command ENDPROC.

PROC identifies the script as a procedure, and ENDPROC ends it. CLOSED converts the procedure into a closed procedure, which is explained later in this chapter. *ProcName* is the name of the procedure (how it will be called by other scripts and procedures), and the parentheses contain any arguments that are passed to the procedure.

The parentheses are required even if no parameters are used.

All procedures should be uniquely named if you intend to call them from an Autolib library. Once a procedure is in memory, others of the same name will not be searched for.

Procedures can be nested to 55 levels, and closed procedures (discussed later in this chapter) can be nested to 255 levels.

Here is an example of a procedure:

```
PROC GetCurID(TableName,SrchVal)
   ; This procedure, passed a TableName, locates a record based
   ; on SrchVal
   ; If the search is successful, returns the record ID
VIEW TableName      ; Using the passed table name, get a record
MOVETO [OrdNo]      ; Move to the OrdNo field
LOCATE SrchVal      ; Using the passed search criteria, find a
                    ; record
    IF Retval = True    ; If the record is found
```

```
     THEN RETURN RECNO() ; Return the record ID
     ELSE RETURN 0      ; Otherwise return value 0
   ENDIF
ENDPROC ; End the procedure
```

Closed Procedures

Procedures can be defined as being CLOSED, which allows you to control the application environment more closely. CLOSED procedures are self-contained, in that they define and use what they need within the procedure, and then release it when they terminate. Because of this, all variables and arrays defined within a CLOSED procedure are private to the procedure and its called procedures. Each procedure defined or called by a CLOSED procedure is by definition a CLOSED procedure itself. CLOSED procedures can be nested to 255 levels, and each level, if defined as CLOSED, is self-contained. As each level of CLOSED procedures terminates, its variables, arrays, and called procedures are all forgotten and the memory released and made available to new routines.

You define a CLOSED procedure by declaring it CLOSED, as shown here:

```
PROC CLOSED ProcName (parameters) ; Declares a CLOSED procedure
   body of the procedure
ENDPROC                           ; Ends the procedure
```

CLOSED procedures, because of the control exercised over exactly what variables and arrays and procedures are released at any one time, are recommended over **RELEASE PROCS** and **RELEASE VARS** commands, which release all procedures or variables in memory.

You can pass variables to a CLOSED procedure and from one level of CLOSED procedure to another with the command USEVARS. USEVARS allows you to list those variables you want made available to a CLOSED procedure. The procedures will use the variables as needed, perhaps even changing values. When the procedure terminates, the USEVARS variables will be retained with the changed values, if any.

CLOSED procedures are recommended for major application modules and for top-level procedures. Use them for all major branches or modules of an application in order to use memory more efficiently.

Effects of Executing a Procedure

When a procedure is first executed, Paradox loads it into memory, parses it, and creates a .SC2 file. Thereafter, Paradox simply loads the procedure into memory. Scripts and procedures are swapped in and out of a special holding area called *cache* memory and another area of memory designated for executing the current program. This swapping in and out of areas of memory is how Paradox manages memory.

Because of this loading and swapping in memory, it's best to keep procedures fairly small. Borland recommends that you not create procedures larger than 10K.

A procedure loaded into memory stays there until all procedures end or until the RELEASE PROCS command is used to remove procedures from memory. However, if the procedure is a CLOSED procedure, it is automatically removed from memory when it finishes processing.

The procedure, when parsed, is *defined*. A defined procedure cannot be read by a programmer. It is converted to a highly memory-efficient format that is only intelligible to other Paradox scripts and procedures that use it. This is the form the program has when stored in procedure libraries in a script with the .SC2 extension. When procedures are called from a library, they are already memory efficient and ready to be executed. Libraries are explained fully later in the chapter.

Calling Procedures

A procedure can be called either by a direct call, by EXECPROC (if it has no parameters), or as an expression. It can be called by scripts or other procedures.

Here is an example of a direct call:

```
GetCurId("Auction")   ; Calls GetCurID procedure with the Auction
                      ; table name
```

Here is an example of a call using EXECPROC:

```
EXECPROC ReadRec      ; Procedure has no parameters in this
                      ; case
```

Here is an example of a call used as an expression:

```
RecID = GetCurID("Auction")   ; When executed GetCurID evaluates
                              ; to a record ID which is stored in
                              ; the variable RecID
```

Calling Procedures Within a Script   If a procedure is contained in the same script or procedure that calls it, it must be defined before it is called by the script. This simply means that the procedure has to come first in the script. The PAL statements could be arranged as follows:

```
; CallGetCurID.SC       This PAL script gets the current record
                        ; ID, etc.
PROC GetCurID(TableName,SearchVal)   ; GetCurID procedure is
                                     ; defined first
; This procedure, passed a TableName and a SearchVal to locate a
```

```
; record, gets the record ID from the found current record.
VIEW TableName             ; Using the passed table name, get a
                           ; record
MOVETO [OrdNo]             ; Move to a specific field
LOCATE SearchVal          ; Search the file for the value in
                           ; SearchVal
IF Retval = True          ; If the search is successful
    THEN RETURN RECNO()   ; Return the record ID
    ELSE RETURN 0         ; Otherwise, return 0
ENDIF
ENDPROC                    ; End the procedure
; Somewhere in the script the procedure is called, as shown here:
RecID = GetCurID("Customer", "A1020")  ; The procedure GetCurID
; is called using the "Customer" table and "A1020" as the Order
; Number value to be found. Procedure is called as an expression.
```

Executing Procedures from Libraries and Directories   Procedures can be called from a procedure library in two ways, depending on which library is used. If the procedure is stored in the Autolib variable, Paradox knows where to find it, and the procedure can simply be called by name. If the procedure is stored in another procedure library, you must specifically identify the library with the READLIB command. These are discussed more fully later in this chapter.

During development, you may find it more convenient to keep all related scripts in one application directory. This makes testing and debugging easier. Then create procedure libraries when you are ready to distribute the application.

Passing Parameters to and from Procedures

When a procedure specifies arguments, as in *ProcName* (arguments), it is dealing with *parameters*, which are a series of one or more values or expressions that are passed to the procedure so that it can complete its task. Parameters are the values that are placed inside the parentheses when calling the procedure.

Parameters can be constants, variables, one or more single entries in an array, functions, field specifiers, or a value returned as the result of a previous procedure. In all these cases, what is passed to the procedure is a value, a copy of the contents of an existing variable or array.

Parameters can also be fixed or dynamic arrays. In this case, what is passed is the pointer or reference to the array, rather than the value itself.

    Parameters may not be PAL commands.

Procedures may return values to the calling script or procedures. One way this may be done is through the RETURN command. The values returned can be those stored in a specific variable, such as this:

```
RETURN BidderID
```

When RETURN is used, a value is automatically stored in the system variable Retval. In the case of the example just given, BidderID would be stored in Retval. This means you can simply retrieve the information from that variable this way:

```
    ; A procedure is defined to get the Bidder ID and return it
    ; to calling script.
PROC GetBidID()
    Body of procedure
RETURN BidderID
ENDPROC
    ; Later in the same script, or from another script, the
    ; procedure is called.
NewBidID = GetBidID()   ; Called procedure Stores the returned
                        ; value in a variable.
```

In this example, the procedure GetBidID returns a value in the variable BidderID that is automatically stored in the system variable Retval. As soon as control returns to the calling script, the value in Retval is saved to another variable NewBidID.

It is important to immediately save a returned value to a variable other than the automatic Retval because many commands use Retval to store their return statuses. If the value is not saved before another command uses it, it will be lost.

Scopes of Variables and Arrays   Within scripts, variables are generally globally available to all procedures and scripts throughout the Paradox session, or until released by a RELEASE VARS ALL command. What this means is that a variable may be created in one script and used in another script later in the Paradox session.

This global characteristic sometimes is useful in that values may be available systemwide, without formally passing them from one script or procedure to another. However, global access has severe disadvantages as well. Variables having the same name but different uses may cause the global variable to be corrupted unintentionally. Or one script may alter the global variable, not realizing its value will again be used somewhere else.

Variables within procedures can be declared PRIVATE, which makes them known and used only within the scope of a procedure. The scope of a procedure includes the procedure itself and any procedure it calls. When a variable is declared PRIVATE, it disappears from memory when the procedure is finished. Also, it cannot change the value of a global variable that may have the same name.

Variables may be declared private in three ways:

- By being an argument in a procedure (it will be private only within the procedure)

- By specifically being declared PRIVATE

- By being contained within a CLOSED procedure

The following example identifies global and private variables:

```
; ScriptName.SC          Example of how global and private
;                         variables are identified
PROC ProcName1(VarName1) ; Private to this procedure because it
                         ; is formal parameter
VarName2 = "GHI"         ; Global variable
ProcName2()             ; Call to 2nd level procedure
ENDPROC

PROC CLOSED ProcName2()  ; CLOSED procedure
VarName3 = "JKL"         ; Private because it is in a CLOSED
                         ; procedure
ProcName3()             ; Call to third level procedure
ENDPROC

PROC ProcName3()         ; Third level procedure contained in
                         ; 2nd level CLOSED procedure
VarName4 = "MNO"         ; Private to ProcName3 and ProcName2
PRIVATE VarName4 = "MNO" ; Private to ProcName3
ENDPROC

VarName1 = "ABC"    ; Global variable in calling script
VarName2 = "DEF"    ; Global variable in calling script
ProcName1()         ; Call to ProcName1 and nested ProcName2 and
                    ; ProcName3
```

Arrays cannot be declared private in the same way. As parameters to the argument, they are pointers or references to the array rather than values. Consequently, they cannot be declared private simply by being parameters to a procedure. However, they can be made PRIVATE by being defined within procedures or by being defined in a CLOSED procedure. They must be defined *within* the procedure to be PRIVATE to it and its called procedures.

Using Libraries

Procedure libraries are used to store parsed procedures. Once procedures are stored in libraries, you can call them without defining them in your calling script or procedure; you simply issue a call to them.

Libraries give you several advantages, not the least of which is security. Because the scripts are in a parsed format, they cannot be read except by PAL. Applications are safe from being modified or changed unintentionally. Parsed scripts are equally secure, of course. However, because libraries are somewhat more cumbersome to access and maintain, they do have an added security aspect.

Libraries contribute to organizing applications. All procedures relating to a certain application or parts of a major application can be stored in the same library. This is particularly important when you are distributing Paradox applications to other users. Procedures in libraries are made available or read into memory at the same time.

Because procedures in a library are loaded into memory at one time, it is important to keep the size of procedures small, under 10K in size. Smaller sizes are also beneficial when maintenance is a priority, since updating requires all procedures to be rewritten to the newly created library. On the other hand, smaller libraries can be less efficient in terms of performance. A single library uses memory more efficiently when considering the swapping of procedures in and out of cache memory.

The command INFOLIB lists all procedures contained within a library plus an estimate of the number of bytes it requires in memory. This is useful when maintaining the library.

Creating and Writing to Procedure Libraries   To create a procedure library, use the CREATELIB command. This command will store up to 50 procedures in a library. If that is not enough, the SIZE option of the command can increase the library potential to 640 procedures. However, because approximately 4K of disk space is allocated for each procedure prior to storage, the size should not be increased until necessary.

To write the procedure to the library, use the WRITELIB command, naming the newly created library and the procedures to be stored within it.

Here is an example of the CREATELIB command:

```
CREATELIB "Auction"           ; Creates the procedure library
                              ; named "Auction".
PROC ProcName()               ; Defines the procedure to be stored
                              ; in the library.
    Body of the procedure
ENDPROC                       ; Ends procedure definition.
WRITELIB "Auction" ProcName   ; Writes the procedure to the
                              ; Auction library so as not to run
RELEASE PROCS ProcName        ; out of memory while compiling
                              ; library.
```

To create a library, you must first write the script, cause it to be written in the library, write the scripts calling or activating the procedure, and provide for the maintenance of the procedure within the library. Follow these steps in creating a library:

1. Write the script that will become a procedure and stored in the library, and debug it.

2. Put the script in a PROC ENDPROC statement. Precede the script with CREATELIB to create the library. Place WRITELIB after the procedure to write it to the library.

3. Execute the procedure causing it to be defined and stored in the library in a parsed form.

4. Create a driver script to call the procedure from the library either using the Autolib or the specific library name.

5. Store the original procedure with the CREATELIB and WRITELIB statements in a safe place, where you can find them if you need to debug the procedure or re-create the library.

The directory path and names of the procedures as they were when the library was created are stored in the library (with the procedure). Keep the WRITELIB script there so Paradox can find them if it needs them when defining other procedures that may call those stored in the library.

Using Autolib Library   The Autolib library by default is named PARADOX.LIB. When initially looking for a procedure, Paradox looks in that library, unless told to look somewhere else. This is the recommended place to store the most commonly used procedures, as it is fast and efficient.

You can designate another file to be an Autolib file by specifying its name, like this:

```
Autolib = "Auction"     ; Makes "AUCTION.LIB" an Autolib library
```

This makes AUCTION the Autolib file. AUCTION.LIB will now be searched instead of PARADOX.LIB. You can name a series of libraries that you wish to include, like this:

```
Autolib = "Auction","Bidders","Donors" ; Makes 3 files Autolib
                                        ; libraries
```

Note that there are no spaces in the list of libraries, and that they are separated by commas. The libraries will be searched in the order they appear in the list.

By declaring Autolib a PRIVATE variable within a procedure, you can make Autolib differ from the standard for one procedure only.

Procedure names should be unique, since once a procedure is in memory, others of the same name will not be searched for.

Using Non-Autolib Libraries   If you do not want to change the Autolib designation, you must identify the procedure library to be searched with the READLIB command. This command loads all of the named procedures into memory as they are referenced. You use it this way:

```
READLIB "Auction" ProcName1,ProcName2
    ; Reads ProcName1 and ProcName2 from "Auction" into memory
```

In addition, with the IMMEDIATE option you can load all of the procedures in the library into memory at one time. Loading them all can be an advantage when you want to use several procedures in one application.

```
READLIB "Auction" IMMEDIATE ProcName1,ProcName2
    ; Reads listed procedures immediately into memory
```

If you don't have enough memory to handle the procedures in memory, Paradox will issue a script error.

Updating Procedure Libraries   When you update a procedure library, you use the WRITELIB statement. When you write a procedure to the library that has the same name as one already existing in the library, the original procedure is no longer usable and the procedure still occupies the space on the library. The space cannot be recovered or reduced.

Obviously, you will want to avoid using WRITELIB this way. You must re-create the whole library to reallocate the space by using the original procedure with both the CREATELIB and WRITELIB on them. You execute all procedures on the library again, as you did initially.

Procedure libraries created prior to Release 4 must be converted before being used by Paradox 4. Use the FILEVERSION and the CONVERTLIB commands to help with this. These are summarized in Chapter 13.

When debugging procedures, you need the original nonparsed procedures as they were before being written into the library. This is true of procedures called by those being debugged as well (however, you can Step over them now using CTRL-S). The directory path and procedure names from the original procedures are recorded in the procedure library.

It is important to keep them there so that Paradox can find them when debugging. If it cannot find them, a script error will be issued. When a procedure has been debugged, you must WRITELIB it again into the library in order to update the procedure.

Using Expressions

Paradox uses expressions as arguments to functions and commands. *Expressions* provide values that allow the function or command to act. You'll see shortly how these examples of expressions work:

```
"This is a string" ; Example of an alphanumeric string
TODAY() + 30       ; Example of a function, operator (+),
                   ; and a number
[HoursWorked] * 24.56 ; Example of field specifier, operator,
                      ; and currency
```

Expressions are values. One expression may be a single value or series of elements that evaluates to a single value. In the example just given, the expressions all evaluate to a value. In the first example, the value is "This is a string." The second value will be 30 days from today, and so on. Paradox, when executing a command or function, examines its expressions, determines values, and proceeds with the task at hand.

The value of an expression can be one of eight data types. A data type is simply the type of data that can be contained within an element. In addition to the five data types discussed in Chapter 3 (alphanumeric, numeric, currency, dates, and short numbers), three other data types are available only in PAL. These are logical, fixed or dynamic arrays, and procedures (which are limited to expressions that evaluate to procedure names). Table 12-2 describes these data types.

An expression can be evaluated with the PAL menu option, Value.

Elements of expressions contain the values that you find within expressions. They are the storage units of an expression. The following elements can be used in PAL: variables, constants, arrays (fixed or dynamic), operators, other functions or user defined procedures, and field specifiers.

Variables

Variables are used to store values. The values can be of any data type and a variable can store varying data types throughout a script. For example, at one point a variable may contain numbers, at another time, dates or currency. Data types do not have to be identified for a variable to contain them. However, you can identify the data type by using the TYPE function.

Type	Abbrev.	Description
Alphanumeric	(A, M)	Strings that may be any numbers, alpha characters, or special characters up to a length of 64MB characters. Strings up to 255 characters are alphanumeric (A) and over that are Memo fields (M). The length of the string determines which data type it is.
Currency	($)	Dollar values between 10^{-307} and 10^{308}
Dates	(D)	A date value
Dynamic arrays	(DY)	Values contained in a changing-length array, wherein each value is located by a unique key or identifier associated with the value
Fixed arrays	(AY)	Values contained in a fixed-length array wherein each value can be located by its position in the array
Logical	(L)	A value evaluating to a True or False, such as Product = ABC
Numbers	(N)	Numeric values between 10^{-307} and 10^{308}
Procedures	(-)	Limited in its use as a data type to a few commands, such as RELEASE PROCS Procname
Short Numbers	(S)	Numeric values between -32767 and 32768

Table 12-2. *Data Types Available for Use in Expressions Within PAL*

To assign a value to a variable, you use the assignment command (=) or use TO to move a value to it, as in these examples:

```
HourlyWage = 15.50      ; Makes HourlyWage contain 15.50
ACCEPT "D" TO DateVar ; Moves the entered date to DateVar
FirstPrompt = "Enter the complete description of the item:"
                    ; Makes first prompt equal to the string
```

Like ACCEPT, some commands assign values to variables as part of their function, such as SHOWPULLDOWN, LOCATE.

Variables must contain a value before being included in an expression. The function ISASSIGNED can be used to determine if a value has been assigned to a variable before using it.

Variable names can be up to 132 characters long. The first character must be a letter (either uppercase or lowercase). No spaces or tabs may be used, but you can use any letters, numbers, or the following characters:

. $ _   !   .

In queries, variables must be preceded by a tilde (~).

Within PAL, variables can be accessed globally. That is, they are available to be used throughout the PAL session, from script to script. The exception to this global availability is when you are dealing with CLOSED procedures or PRIVATE variables. In these cases, the variables only exist inside a procedure or script, and disappear when it terminates.

Because of the global availability of variables, you should clear them from memory at the end of a script or application by using RELEASE VARS ALL, unless your intent is to pass values from one script or application to another.

You can use the SAVEVARS command to save the values within variables. These are saved in a special script file named SAVEVARS.SC. They can then be restored when needed.

Retval is a special variable used by Paradox to store True or False results from some command actions. For example, when you use ACCEPT to enter data into a variable, Paradox sets Retval to True or False (indicating whether or not the entry was successful). Retval may also be assigned string values, such as "Esc" or the key codes and PAL key names used to end WAIT. Some other commands that use Retval are SHOWPULLDOWN, LOCATE, RETURN, and others.

Constants

A *constant* is named appropriately since its value will not change. Throughout a PAL program, a constant's value never changes. You may have alphanumeric, numeric, date, or logical constants.

Alphanumeric constants are called *strings*. They contain upper- or lowercase letters, numbers, and some special characters. These strings are enclosed in double quotes, like this:

```
"This is some string!"  ; A simple alphanumeric string
"Enter your table name now:" ; A request to the user
```

Numbers, when enclosed in quotes, are alphanumeric strings, not numbers. Numbers contained in strings cannot be used in calculations. This is an example of a number contained in a string:

```
"10,100.50"
```

Numeric constants are numbers that can be used in calculations. They may be positive or negative and may contain decimal places. Numbers are stored as floating point numbers to an accuracy of 15 digits. Numeric constants can store numbers, currency, and short number data types. These are examples of numeric constants:

```
10,100.50        ; A simple number unnamed
Cash = 4,000     ; A constant of 4,000 is named Cash
Percent = .075   ; A constant of 7.5% is named Percent
```

You can use scientific notation in constants. These will begin with a decimal value and end with an E and a positive or negative exponent, like this:

```
BigNo = 10,100E+50  ; BigNo is equal to 10,100 X 10^{50}
```

Special characters are those that cannot be typed directly into the computer via the keyboard. You type ASCII and extended ASCII character codes to enter these characters. For example, to enter a ½, you press ALT-171 (press ALT plus the numbers on the numeric keyboard; do not use the number keys in the row at the top of the keyboard when entering ASCII codes). See the ASCII and extended ASCII character code chart in Appendix C.

You can enter a special character by preceding it with a \ (backslash). Use either the ASCII code or the character itself. For example, the following illustrates the use of special characters within constants:

```
Cents = "\155"              ; Sets Cents equal to ¢
"Enter 25" + Cents " now"   ; Prints "Enter 25¢ now"
```

You also can use ASCII codes to place some keyboard actions in a program. For example, pressing ENTER can be programmed by pressing ALT-013 into the program or typing **"\013"**. Some of these keys are so frequently used that they have special codes within Paradox. These are preceded by \ (backslash) and are strings:

Code	Resulting Keypress
\"	Quotes
\\	Backslash
\f	Formfeed

Code	Resulting Keypress
\n	Newline
\r	Carriage Return
\t	Tab

In most cases, other than these special strings, a character preceded by a backslash is to be taken literally. This means, for example, that \% in a program is read as %.

Date constants contain dates and may be in one of four formats: mm/dd/yy, dd-Mon-yyyy, dd.mm.yyyy, or yy.mm.dd. Dates cannot contain spaces. The dates may span from 1/1/100 to 12/31/9999.

Logical constants contain either "True" or "False." They can be in upper- or lowercase letters. They can be changed to On/Off or Yes/No using the FORMAT function.

Arrays

Arrays are similar to variables in that they store values of any data types. Anywhere you can use a variable, you can use an array. However, arrays contain a group of values rather than a single one. Arrays may be fixed or dynamic.

Arrays must have values assigned to them before they are used in expressions.

Fixed Arrays   These contain a fixed number of values and are created with the ARRAY command, like this:

```
ARRAY ProdType[10]   ; Creates an array ProdType of 10 elements.
```

The elements are accessed by indicating the position of the element within the array. For example, ProdType[5] refers to the fifth element in the array. The elements can contain any data type, and one element can contain a different data type than the next.

Fixed arrays can contain up to 15,000 elements. You can use an array element anywhere you use a variable.

Commands that can be used with fixed arrays are COPYTOARRAY, COPYFROMARRAY (for copying to and from records into an array), ARRAYSIZE (for determining the size of an array), and TYPE (to determine the data type of an element).

Dynamic Arrays   These are similar to fixed arrays except that you do not have to designate the size of the array; it varies. Dynamic arrays can change sizes.

Values within dynamic arrays are accessed by a unique *tag,* which is assigned to each element. For example, in the following, the values "Type", "Descrip", "Cust", and "OrdDate" are all tags. "A" is the value assigned to one element of the dynamic array.

```
DYARRAY ProdType[]
ProdType["Type"] = "A"
ProdType["Descrip"] = "Travel Brochure"
ProdType["Cust"] = "012"
ProdType["OrdDate"] = TODAY()
```

When you want to retrieve a value, you reference the array's tag like this:

```
RETURN ProdType["Type"]   ; would return "A" as its value
```

Tags must evaluate to strings. If they do not, Paradox will automatically convert "declared" tags. For example, in ProdType[89] = "Science Fiction", Paradox would convert 89 to a string.

Dynamic arrays may be created explicitly, as shown in the ProdType example. Before you can assign values to a dynamic array, it usually must be explicitly declared. However, dynamic arrays may also be created by certain commands, to be used for specific purposes. In this case, they receive their values as a function of the command and do not have to be declared first.

Some commands that create dynamic arrays as part of their function are WINDOW GETATTRIBUTES, which creates a dynamic array to store window attributes; GETCOLORS, to store colors in the color palette; SYINFO, to store system information; and GETEVENT and WAIT, to store trapped event information. Other commands used specifically for dynamic arrays are DYNARRAYSIZE, to get the number of elements in a dynamic array, and FOREACH, to loop through the elements in a dynamic array.

Field Specifiers

Field specifiers allow you to retrieve or store values within fields. Before using a field specifier, you must have the correct record available as the current record. Field specifiers can be used in query or display images. The display image can be either a form or table view.

Field specifiers are enclosed in brackets, like this:

```
[Cust ID]
```

Format	Description
[]	Empty brackets for current field where cursor is
[#]	For record number of current field—same as RECNO()
[*FieldName*]	For the value in *FieldName* of the current field
[*TableName* ->]	For the value in the current field of *TableName*
[*TableName* ->*FieldName*]	For the value in *FieldName* of *TableName*
[*TableName*(*n*)->]	For the value in the current field of the *n*th display image of *TableName* on the stack
[*TableName*(*n*)->*FieldName*]	For the value in *FieldName* of the *n*th display image of *TableName* on the stack
[*TableName*(Q)->]	For the value in the current field of the *TableName* query image
[*TableName*(Q)->*FieldName*]	For the value in *FieldName* of the *TableName* query image

Table 12-3.   *Formats Available for Use with Field Specifiers*

When the value is retrieved for a query, it will be in a string data type. When the value is retrieved for a display image, it will be the data type of the field.

Field specifiers have the formats specified in Table 12-3. (The current field is identified as the field where the cursor is positioned or was last positioned when the cursor is no longer on a field.)

Assigning Values to Fields   Assigning values to fields can be done by equating a value to a field name like this:

```
[TaxAmt] = [Paid] * .075
```

Assigning a value to a field using PAL and the field specifiers must be done in DataEntry, Edit, or CoEdit mode, just as you would change a field using Paradox menus. The value assigned must be of the same data type as the field, or of a compatible data type.

Operator	Description
Arithmetic	
+	Addition, add two numbers or a number to a date Concatenate, combine two strings
-	Subtraction, subtract two numbers or a number from a date, or two dates
*	Multiply, perform multiplication with numbers
/	Divide, perform division with numbers
Comparative	
=	Equal to, compare two elements for equality
>	Greater than, test for *A* greater than *B*
<	Less than, test for *A* less than *B*
<>	Not equal to, test for *A* not equal to *B*
<=	Less than or equal to, test for *A* less than or equal to *B*
>=	Greater than or equal to, test for *A* greater than or equal to *B*
Logical	
AND	Logical AND, test for *A* AND *B* both being True
OR	Logical OR, test for *A* OR *B* being True
NOT	Logical NOT, test the negative of a test

Table 12-4.   *Operators Used in Expressions*

You can move to a field using the MOVETO command, as shown in these examples using the Invoice table and TaxAmt field:

```
MOVETO [TaxAmt] ; Moves to TaxAmt field of current table
MOVETO FIELD "TaxAmt" ; Moves to TaxAmt field of current table
MOVETO [Invoice->TaxAmt]  ; Moves to TaxAmt field of Invoice
                          ; table
MOVETO [Invoice(Q)->TaxAmt] ; Moves to TaxAmt of query image of
                            ; Invoice
```

Operators

Paradox provides operators to include in expressions. Table 12-4 lists the operators available.

Addition   When adding using + (Add), you can add two numbers, concatenate two strings, or add a number to a date field. You cannot add dates to a number field, as shown here:

```
"The Honorable " + [FirstName] + [LastName] + ", US Senate"
    ; would result in "The Honorable John Smith, US Senate"
[Date] + [number] ; Adding a number to a date field is OK
[Number] + [Date] ; This form is not OK.
```

Subtraction   When subtracting, you may subtract two numbers, subtract a number from a date (but not the reverse), subtract two dates, or subtract a single number to reverse its sign.

Multiplication and Division   When multiplying or dividing you must use only number data types. Dividing by zero results in zero, not an error. You must program a routine to catch that situation if it is important to your results.

Testing   When testing, the result of the comparative and logical operators (in Table 12-4, this is the = operator through the NOT) is always True or False. Comparing two different data types (such as number versus string) will return a value of False, except for <> (not equal) which returns True.

When making size comparisons, such as < or >, blank values are considered less than other values and a value of False is less than True. Alphanumeric sort sequences depend on the sort order established at installation time; that is, uppercase and lowercase letters may sort together as in a dictionary, or lowercase letters may sort higher than uppercase, as in the ASCII sort sequence.

Here are some examples of comparison and logical testing:

```
[Dog] = "Brown" AND [Cat] = "Brown"
    ;True, if both fields Dog and Cat contain "Brown"
[Dog] = "Brown" OR [Cat] = "Brown"
    ;True if either field contains "Brown"
NOT [Dog] = "Brown"
    ; True if Dog is blank or not equal to "Brown"
[Dog] <> "Brown" ; True if Dog is not equal to Brown
```

    NOT and <> are different; NOT checks for the "trueness" of a single value while <> tests the equality of two values.

```
"DOG" = "dog" ; False, since upper- and lowercase letters are
              ; not equal
```

```
[Number] > "ten" ; False since data types are different
[Number] <> "ten" ; True since data types are different
5 * 2 > 10/2 ; True
```

Precedence of Evaluations   The precedence of evaluations proceeds as follows: parenthetical expressions are evaluated first, then multiplication and division, addition and subtraction, comparison operators, and finally, logical operators.

Functions

Functions are Paradox-provided formulas that perform commonly needed tasks, such as manipulating strings, calculating financial and mathematical equations, converting values from one data type to another, manipulating time and date values, retrieving or testing arrays, variables, or fields, and more. Chapter 13 includes a summary of the Paradox functions.

Formatting Data for Input and Output

PAL provides for formatting of data upon input, when a user is entering data into a table, and for output, when a PAL script prints or displays data. Input is formatted using pictures.

Using Pictures

Pictures are patterns used by PAL to define data that is being entered. They can be used to define defaults, formatting as with telephone numbers, required entry of data, definition of size, and definition of limits imposed on the entry. For example, the following is a pattern used to control the entry of a telephone number:

```
[(###)] ###-####    ; Picture of a telephone number field
```

   This example allows the entry of an optional three-digit area code that will be enclosed with parentheses, three digits followed by a hyphen, followed by four digits. If the user wants to enter an area code, the left parenthesis must first be typed, so Paradox knows that the area code is to be entered. If just a digit is entered, Paradox assumes that the area code will not be entered. Table 12-5 shows the pattern codes that can be used in a picture.

Picture Pattern Characters	Description
# (pound sign)	Specifies a digit only should be entered
##.##	Two digits, period, two digits; for example, 25.50
? (question mark)	For an upper- or lowercase letter
???	Three letters; for example, Sam
* (asterisk)	Repeat the character
*15#	For 15 digits; for example, 555555555555555
*10{1}	For 1111111111
??*?	Two letters accepted, maybe more; for example, Washington or WA (no actual number with * allows zero or more characters to be entered)
! (exclamation)	For any character, convert letters to uppercase
!*?	First uppercase, than any letters; for example, Adamson
& (ampersand)	Specifies a letter, convert to uppercase
&*?	For first uppercase, any other letter; for example, Martin
@ (at sign)	Specifies any character be accepted
@;@	Any character followed by a literal @; for example, 8@
(any character)	Any other character to be taken literally
##abc???/	Two digits, *abc*, three letters, slash; for example, 24abcddd/
; (semicolon)	Next character to be taken literally
###;,###	Accepts three digits, comma, three digits; for example, 303,309
???;;???	Three letters, semicolon, three letters; for example, cdc;ibm
[] (brackets)	Enclosed characters optional, not required
## [###]	Three digits not required (when optional parts are of the same picture type, they must often come last to be effective—see the following "Note")

Table 12-5.   *Picture Pattern Codes for Formatting Entry of Data*

Picture Pattern Characters	Description
[&]##	Capital letter followed by two digits allows option to be first. (To enter optional part, type first character: [(###)] ###-#### type "(" (left paren) to enter area code)
{} (curly brackets)	(1) Group enclosed characters into a set
*3{###}	For three groups of three digits; for example, 123123123
{} (curly brackets)	(2) Do not fill in the enclosed automatically
{23.24.25}	Inhibit fill after first letter is filled in (Paradox automatically fills in after first letter. In the above example, 23 would be automatically filled in)
, (comma)	Enter one or the other, choose an alternative
A###,B###, D###	Choose one of the three; for example, B201
{A,B,D}###	To get the same result, choose one of the three

Table 12-5. *Picture Pattern Codes for Formatting Entry of Data* (continued)

Optional choices are a little difficult. To choose an optional element, you must type the first character of it to let Paradox know that you want to use the optional element. Either the first digit must be unique, so that it cannot be confused with the patterns following (such as [(###)] ###-#### where the parenthesis is unique), or the optional pattern must be last in the sequence so that when all non-optional digits have been entered, Paradox knows that one more character indicates the option is chosen.

Picture statements can be used in such commands as ACCEPT. You can use pictures for all data types, except memo fields. Here is an example of ACCEPT:

```
ACCEPT "A4"            ; Accept entry of four alphanumeric
                       ; characters
    PICTURE "?###"     ; Pattern is 1 letter and 3 digits
TO ProdCode            ; Store the entry in variable ProdCode
```

When a picture is specified for a field, Paradox will not let you leave the entry partially complete. You can leave the field blank, unless the REQUIRED option is used. You can use the normal editing keys to correct mistakes: BACKSPACE, DELETE, *and* CTRL-BACKSPACE.

Using Paradox ValCheck

Pictures are not the only way to control user input. You can also use the Paradox Edit mode, and the ValCheck option to create pictures for fields. (Refer to Chapter 3 for a full description of this approach.) Sometimes it is easier to use the Paradox ValCheck option for defining validity checks than to use pictures in PAL scripts.

Using FORMAT Specifiers

When formatting data for printing or display, use the FORMAT command. With it you can control width and alignment, positive and negative sign displays, uppercase or lowercase displays, currency displays, date formats, and choices of logical default displays.

Width Formats   The width option has two formats: *Wn* and *Wn,m*, where *n* is characters wide, and *m* is number of decimal points. The number of decimal places cannot be greater than 15.

Here is the syntax of the width format:

```
FORMAT (Wn,string)     ;For all data types
FORMAT (Wn.m, string) ;For dollars and numbers with decimals
```

It is important to accommodate all digits that may be in a numeric display, including a decimal point. If the width isn't large enough to contain all characters, a row of asterisks is displayed instead. In the case of strings, just the number of characters that will fit will be printed. Numeric fields formatted with dollar signs and commas are considered to be strings.

Here are examples using the width format:

```
? FORMAT("W2","NOW HEAR THIS")   ;Displays "NO"
? FORMAT("W4.2",1234567)         ;Displays "****"
```

Alignment Formatting   To align a display you must specify a width as well as the alignment. If alignment is not specified, strings and logical defaults are left-aligned, and dates and numbers are right-aligned.

Here is the syntax for alignment formatting:

```
FORMAT ("Wn,AC",string)   ;Center, for all data types
FORMAT ("Wn,AL",string)   ;Left align, for all data types
FORMAT ("Wn,AR",string)   ;Right align, for all data types
```

Here are examples of alignment formatting for centering and left and right alignment:

```
FORMAT ("W10,AC","Yellow")    ; Centers "Yellow" in a 10-character
                              ; display
FORMAT ("W10,AL","12345")     ; Left aligns "12345" in a 10-
                              ; character display
FORMAT ("W10,AR","Red")       ; Right aligns "Red" in a 10-
                              ; character display
```

Sign Formatting   Sign formatting determines how signs for negative or positive numbers will be displayed. DB and CR notations are used for Debit and Credit identification in accounting.

This is the syntax for sign formatting:

```
FORMAT ("S+",number) ;Use leading plus or minus signs, for numbers,
                     ;currency, short numbers
FORMAT ("S-",number) ;Use leading minus, for numbers, currency,
                     short ;numbers
FORMAT ("SC",number) ;Print CR after negatives, for numbers,
                     currency,;short numbers
FORMAT ("SD",number) ;Print DB or CR for Debit and Credit, for
                     numbers,;currency, short numbers
FORMAT ("SP",number) ;Use Parenthesis for negatives, for numbers,
                     ;currency, short numbers
```

These examples show sign formatting:

```
FORMAT ("W9,SP",-135.67)        ;Displays (135.67)
FORMAT ("W9,SD",-135.67)        ;Displays 135.67CR
FORMAT ("W9,S+",-135.67)        ;Displays -135.67
```

Case Formatting   Case formatting ensures the proper capitalization of strings. Choices are to use uppercase, lowercase, or leading caps where the first letter only is capitalized.

This is the syntax for case formatting:

```
FORMAT ("CC",string)      ;Print in initial caps, for all data types
FORMAT ("CL",string)      ;Print in lowercase, for all data types
FORMAT ("CU",string)      ;Print in uppercase, for all data types
```

These examples show case formatting:

```
FORMAT ("CU","abc corporation, inc.")
        ;Displays "ABC CORPORATION, INC."
FORMAT ("CL","ABC CORPORATION, INC.")
        ;Displays "abc corporation, inc."
FORMAT ("CC","abc corporation, iNC.")
        ;Displays "Abc Corporation, INC."
```

In this last example, you might want to first use the "CL" format in order to set all letters to lowercase before setting the initial capitals.

Currency or Edit Formatting   You can manipulate the way numbers are displayed using the edit formatting options. When you use one of the edit formats, you must also use a width format. Options can be combined under a single E identifier, except that you can only have one of the following: *, Z or B.

This is the syntax for the currency and edit formatting:

```
FORMAT ("E$",number)      ;Float the position of the $, for numbers,
                          ;currency, short numbers
FORMAT ("E*",number)      ;Print ** for leading zeros, for numbers,
                          ;currency, short numbers
FORMAT ("EB",number)      ;Display blanks for leading zeros, for
                          ;number ;currency, short numbers
FORMAT ("EC",number)      ;Print commas every three numbers, for
                          ;numbers, ;currency, short numbers
FORMAT ("EI",number)      ;Use the international format, for numbers,
                          ;currency, short numbers
FORMAT ("ES",number)      ;Use scientific notation, for numbers,
                          ;currency,;short numbers
FORMAT ("EZ",number)      ;Display leading zeros, for numbers,
                          ;currency,;short numbers
```

The following two examples show currency and edit formatting:

```
FORMAT ("W12,2,E$C*",1234567)      ; Displays $**12,345.67
FORMAT ("W12,2,E$CZ",1234567)      ; Displays $0012,345.67
```

Date Formats   Date formatting allows you to display dates according to one of 11 formats. When using the width format, be sure that the display field is large enough for the date display.

This is the syntax for formatting of date data types:

```
FORMAT ("D1",date)    ;Formats dates as mm/dd/yy
FORMAT ("D2",date)    ;Formats dates as Month dd,yyyy
FORMAT ("D3",date)    ;Formats dates as mm/dd
FORMAT ("D4",date)    ;Formats dates as mm/yy
FORMAT ("D5",date)    ;Formats dates as dd-Mon-yy
FORMAT ("D6",date)    ;Formats dates as Mon yy
FORMAT ("D7",date)    ;Formats dates as dd-Mon-yyyy
FORMAT ("D8",date)    ;Formats dates as mm/dd/yyyy
FORMAT ("D9",date)    ;Formats dates as dd.mm.yy
FORMAT ("D10",date)   ;Formats dates as dd/mm/yy
FORMAT ("D11",date)   ;Formats dates as yy-mm-dd
FORMAT ("D12",date)   ;Formats dates as yy.mm.dd
FORMAT ("D13",date)   ;Formats dates as dd/mm/yyyy
```

Here is an example of date formatting:

```
FORMAT ("W8,D9",4/19/92)       ; Displays 19.04.92
FORMAT ("W10,D8",12/23/93)     ; Displays 12/23/1993
FORMAT ("W9,D5",4/5/93)        ; Displays 04-Apr-93
```

Logical Defaults   Logical formatting replaces Yes/No or On/Off for True/False values.

This is the syntax for logical formatting:

```
FORMAT ("LY",value) ;Print Yes/No instead of True/False, for
                    Logical; data types
FORMAT ("LO",value) ;Print On/Off instead of True/False, for
                    Logical; data types
```

Here is an example of changing a logical default from True/False to On/Off:

```
FORMAT ("LO",(Fetchit = "True"))  ;When variable Fetchit = "True,"
                                  ;displays "On"
```

Working with Control Structures

Control structures are used in programming to direct the path through a program when straight sequential processing is not possible or desirable. This chapter briefly introduces control structures. For additional information on the syntax for commands discussed in this chapter, refer to Chapter 13.

There are some situations when you may want to branch to a procedure based on some condition, as you would when handling menu choices. If one menu choice is chosen, you want to branch or switch control to one procedure. If another menu choice is made, a different branch is required.

Other control structure commands deal with *loops,* or repeatedly executing the same commands until some condition is met. An example of a loop would be for the program to repeat the same error routine until the user does something to correct the problem.

Leaving control structures involves another set of commands. Under some circumstances you might want to force control to leave a control structure without further processing. Or you might need to leave and pass a value on to the calling program.

Branching Commands

Branching commands include IF, IIF, SWITCH, and EXECPROC and dynamic array combinations. They are used in slightly different ways.

The traditional IF THEN ELSE command is used to determine between a True and False condition this way:

```
IF test condition                      ; Test for condition
    THEN perform some action           ; If True, do this
    ELSE perform some other action     ; If False, do this
ENDIF                                  ; End the IF
```

IIF is used for similar conditions. It is simply written in a different format. It can be used as an expression like this:

```
RETURN IIF (Retval = true, Var1, IsDyArray[Group5])
    ; Upon returning, if True, return value of variable,
    ; if False, return value in dynamic array.
```

A SWITCH is used to handle many possible branches, such as you might have with choosing a menu option. For each menu option, you would have a possible branch, for example:

```
SWITCH
    CASE firstmenu condition:
            FirstProc()    ; If firstmenu chosen, execute
                           ; FirstProc
    CASE secondmenu condition:
```

```
        SecondProc()    ; If secondmenu chosen, execute
                        ; SecondProc
    etc.
ENDSWITCH
```

Dynamic arrays combined with EXECPROC can be used instead of SWITCH in cases where efficiency is important. When many alternatives are possible, SWITCH may be slower than the immediate dynamic array processing. SWITCH is also often used in determining menu choices, as you will see later in this chapter.

IF THEN ELSE   An IF statement, as mentioned earlier, is used to handle simple True/False conditions. However, IF statements can be embedded to many levels, so they may not always be simple to work with.

The command reads like this: IF some condition is true, THEN execute these commands, ELSE execute these commands, ENDIF. The ELSE is optional, and if it is absent, and the condition for True is not met, control passes to the command following the ENDIF.

This is an example of a nested IF statement:

```
IF Retval = True                     ; If Retval is True prepare
    THEN                             ; for nested IF
        IF Count > 500               ; And if Count is greater than
                                     ; 500
            THEN SetCountProc() ; Then execute this procedure
            ELSE RETURN              ; If Count is not greater than
                                     ; 500, return to calling script
        ENDIF                        ; End of nested IF
    ELSE ResetCountProc()            ; If Retval is False, execute
                                     ; this
ENDIF                                ; End of first level IF
```

IIF   IIF is much the same as IF, but the syntax differs. IIF can be used as an expression and placed within commands and formulas. This is the syntax for IIF:

```
IIF (condition, true value , false value)
```

Here is an example of IIF:

```
IIF (Retval = True, SetVar = 500, SetVar = 0)
    ; If Retval equates to True, set variable to 500;
    ; otherwise, to 0
```

SWITCH ENDSWITCH   The SWITCH command handles branching with many possibilities. It is commonly used when working with menu choices. This is the syntax for SWITCH ENDSWITCH:

```
SWITCH
    CASE condition
    CASE condition
    [OTHERWISE]
ENDSWITCH
```

There are as many CASE statements as branching possibilities. The OTHERWISE is optional and handles any other conditions that may arise that are not covered by the CASE statements.

This example shows how SWITCH can be used with SHOWMENU:

```
SHOWMENU
        "Auction" : "Add and Edit Auction Items"
        "Bidders" : "Add and Edit Bidders"
        "Donors"  : "Add and Edit Cash Donors"
TO MenuItem           ; Store menu choice in variable MenuItem

SWITCH                              ; Begin the SWITCH
    CASE MenuItem = "Auction" ; If Auction is the choice,
          : PLAY "AuctPick"   ; Execute this script
    CASE MenuItem = "Bidders" ; If Bidders is the choice
          : PLAY "BiddPick"   ; Execute this script
    CASE MenuItem = "Donors"  ; If Donors is the choice
          : PLAY "DonPick"    ; Execute this script
    OTHERWISE : PLAY "GoBack"  ; If no choice, execute script
ENDSWITCH                          ; End the SWITCH
```

In this example, the user chooses one of the items in the SHOWMENU menu. Once the choice is made, it is stored in the variable MenuItem. Then, during the SWITCH, MenuItem is tested for each of the menu items. When a match is found, the appropriate script is executed. If no match is found, the GoBack routine is executed.

EXECPROC and Dynamic Arrays   Dynamic arrays can be used with EXECPROC to accomplish the same tasks as SWITCH with some performance improvements. While SWITCH is processed sequentially, the dynamic array is immediate, saving response time when it is important to do so.

Dynamic arrays, discussed earlier in this chapter, are storage areas for groups of values. Each individual group is identified by a unique tag.

This example shows how to use a dynamic array with SHOWMENU:

```
      ; First define the dynamic array, equating menu options with
      ; procedures to be executed when chosen
DYNARRAY ChooseMenu[]
      ChooseMenu ["Auction"] = "AuctProc"
      ChooseMenu ["Bidders"] = "BidProc"
      ChooseMenu ["Donors"]  = "DonProc"
; Then define the menu, with options and prompts
WHILE True
      SHOWMENU
            "Auction" : "Add and Edit Auction Items"
            "Bidders" : "Add and Edit Bidders"
            "Donors"  : "Add and Edit Cash Donors"
      TO MenuItem
                        ; Store menu choice in variable MenuItem
                        ; Next if a choice is made, execute the
                        ; procedure in the array
      IF ISASSIGNED(ChooseMenu[MenuItem])
                        ; Has a menu item been chosen?
            THEN EXECPROC ChooseMenu[MenuItem]
                        ; If yes execute the procedure
            ELSE ErrProc()
                        ; If no execute the error procedure
      ENDIF
ENDWHILE
```

Looping Commands

Looping is when a series of commands is continually and repeatedly executed until some condition is met. Looping in PAL is accomplished with the FOR, FOREACH, SCAN, and WHILE commands.

FOR Loops   FOR executes a series of commands a set number of times, based on the value in a variable. This is the syntax for the FOR command:

```
FOR VarName                 ; Variable containing the count
    [FROM Value of beginning number]
                            ; Expression yielding beginning count
    [TO Value of ending number]
                            ; Expression yielding ending count
    [STEP Value of increment]
                            ; Expression yielding number by
                            ; which count is incremented
ENDFOR
```

The following example, the results of which are shown in Figure 12-4, will execute three times, once for each of the array elements. A message will be displayed for each element and a number will be accepted from the user. That number will be added to a variable SumArray. The loop will repeat until all elements of the array have been handled. After the loop has completed, a message displaying the sum will appear.

```
ARRAY ProdCode[3]
ProdCode[1] = "A"
ProdCode[2] = "G"
ProdCode[3] = "M"
SumArray = 0
FOR CtArray FROM 1 TO ARRAYSIZE(ProdCode)
     ? "Enter the number of orders today for", " ",
        ProdCode(CtArray), "  "
     ACCEPT "N" TO NumOrd
     SumArray = SumArray + NumOrd
ENDFOR
@12,12
? "The total orders for today are"," ",SumArray
x= GETCHAR()
```

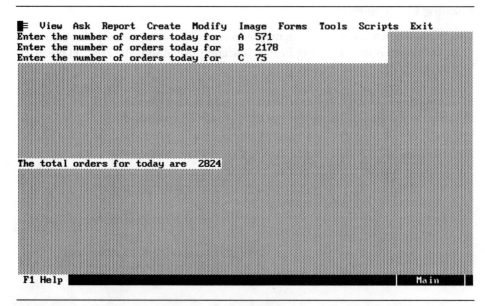

Figure 12-4.   *Results of the FOR and ARRAY sample script*

FOREACH Loops FOREACH is used as the FOR, but for dynamic arrays. (FOR cannot be used with dynamic arrays since they are not subscripted by numbers, but by unique tags.) The dynamic array elements will not be accessed in a numeric order since the tags are not numeric.

```
FOREACH VarName IN DynamicArrayName
     Commands to be executed in the loop
ENDFOREACH
```

The following example shows how these are used. It goes through the dynamic array and displays each element.

```
DYNARRAY Capitals[]
Capitals["AL"] = "Montgomery"
Capitals["AK"] = "Juneau"
Capitals["AR"] = "Little Rock"
Capitals["AZ"] = "Phoenix"
(etc)
FOREACH State IN Capitals
     ? "The Capital of", " ", State, " ", "is:", " ",
        Capitals[State]
     Retval = GETCHAR()
ENDFOREACH
```

SCAN Loops SCAN is used to search a table for records meeting certain conditions; when it finds these it executes a series of commands. SCAN is used for updating a table with the same changes, or for making the same changes to a class or category of records in the table.

This is the syntax of the SCAN command:

```
SCAN [FOR Condition] [:]
     Commands if condition is met
ENDSCAN
```

If the FOR option is not used, SCAN goes through each record in the table, executing the commands for each record. If FOR is used, only the records meeting the condition will have the commands executed against them. The : option allows you to use the FOR ENDFOR loop command. Without the : Paradox would think it is an error since FOR is also an option of SCAN.

The following example goes through a table searching for those auction items that sold for an amount greater than $1,000. When a record is found that meets the search criteria, the Bidder Number identifying the purchaser is printed. When the user presses any key, the next Bidder is displayed. At the end a message prints telling the user that no more items meet the criteria.

```
VIEW Item
SCAN FOR [Actual Paid] > 1000
     ? "Bidder No. is   ", [Bidder No]
     Retval = GETCHAR()
ENDSCAN
@12,12
? "No more items on file purchased for more than $1,000"
x = GETCHAR()
```

WHILE Loops   WHILE is used to execute commands repeatedly until some condition is met. When the condition is no longer True, the loop is terminated and control passes to the first command following the ENDWHILE. This is the syntax for WHILE:

```
WHILE Condition
     Commands executed while condition remains True
ENDWHILE
```

The test is performed each time before the commands are executed again, or before the loop is repeated.

This example of WHILE uses the example given in the SWITCH command explanation. Figure 12-5 shows the results of this script:

```
Outkey = " "
WHILE ((OutKey <> "Esc") AND (OutKey <> "F2"))
     ; Continue until Esc or F2 is pressed
SHOWMENU
     "Auction" : "Manage Auction Items",
     "Bidders" : "Add and Edit Bidders",
     "Donors"  : "Add and Edit Cash Donors"
     UNTIL "F2", "Esc" KEYTO OutKey
TO MenuPick       ; Store menu choice in variable MenuItem

SWITCH                               ; Begin the SWITCH
     CASE MenuPick = "Auction"       ; If Auction is the choice,
          : AuctProc()               ; Execute this procedure
     CASE MenuPick = "Bidders"       ; If Bidders is the choice
          : BiddProc()               ; Execute this procedure
     CASE MenuPick = "Donors"        ; If Donors is the choice
          : DonProc()                ; Execute this procedure
     OTHERWISE : OtherProc()         ; If no choice, execute
                                     ; this procedure
ENDSWITCH                            ; End the SWITCH
ENDWHILE
```

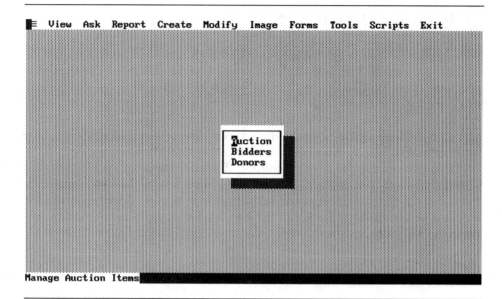

Menu bar: View Ask Report Create Modify Image Forms Tools Scripts Exit

Auction
Bidders
Donors

Manage Auction Items

Figure 12-5. *Using WHILE with SHOWMENU and SWITCH*

Ending Loops Loops can be terminated with the QUITLOOP command. QUITLOOP immediately terminates the loop and passes control to the command following the loop.

LOOP causes the loop to immediately be repeated, even if the commands in the loop have not all been executed. If the loop is a FOR, the loop counter is incremented; if a WHILE, the condition is tested once again; or if a FOREACH, the next dynamic array element is retrieved.

Exiting Commands

There are three commands that can be used to immediately return control to a calling script, to exit or abandon the script altogether: RETURN, EXIT, and QUIT.

RETURN returns control, and optionally a value or a message, to the calling script or procedure. The variable Retval is assigned the RETURN value and can be used by the calling script or procedure. A called script or procedure becomes the value of its RETURN. Consequently, the called procedure can be used in an expression for the RETURN value. When the RETURN is made to the top-level procedure, the RETURN value is displayed in the message window when interactive Paradox regains control.

QUIT ends all commands and returns to Paradox immediately.

EXIT ends all commands and returns to DOS immediately.

The Paradox User Interface

With Release 4, Paradox has changed considerably how the user interfaces with the screens and menus. The first change (mostly experienced in behind-the-scenes programming techniques) is the advent of event-driven programming. For the user, this immediately and very obviously affects how menus are selected and screens are manipulated. Defining "layers of Paradox" (which contain various Paradox objects), and then defining exactly what windows versus images versus canvases are, have further changed how users and programmers experience Paradox.

This section explores some of the considerations faced by programmers in dealing with the new way Paradox interfaces with the user: how to handle event-driven interfaces, how to create menus and work with them in an event-driven environment, and how best to view and work with the Paradox layers, and window, images, and canvases.

Event-Driven Programming

In previous versions of Paradox, a PAL application was under the control of the programmer. The user was tied to the design of the application and entered data and commands into the application under program control. With Release 4, the application can now be free from this closed and structured approach. It can be *event-driven*, which means the user, with a mouse or keyboard, controls events by entering commands and data according to the demands of the moment. This produces a more powerful and supportive application. Users do not have to follow a strict path or script; rather, each user determines what actions to take next.

From the programmer's standpoint, this requires a different way of thinking about the problems to be solved. Event-driven logic is so basic to the overall design of a program, that trying to use the PAL commands to solve problems without having the concepts firmly in mind is no better than guesswork.

An *event* is a separate action that occurs within Paradox. Typing a table name, for example, comprises several events. The typing of each letter, and pressing keys such as ENTER or a function key, are all events.

Other examples of events include typing a letter on the keyboard, pressing the mouse button, or moving from one field to another in a form (by pressing TAB or using the mouse). In PAL you can trap events and control what action occurs next.

Paradox collects events in an *event stream*. This stream is a queue of events made available to an application to be processed one at a time in the order in which they occur. Certain event-retrieval commands, such as GETEVENT, GETMENUSELECT, or WAIT, can intercept or trap these events, collecting them in a dynamic array. The events can then be examined and decisions made as to what to process, what to pass on to Paradox for processing, and what to ignore. Events not trapped flow on to Paradox to be handled normally.

The sequence of processing may proceed like this:

1. A program initiates event trapping with the GETEVENT, GETMENUSELECT, or WAIT command. Then it waits for an event.

2. An event occurs, such as a key being pressed or a mouse button being clicked.

3. Either the GETEVENT, GETMENUSELECT, or WAIT command intercepts the event and stores it in a dynamic array. There it is examined, and action taken or not. SWITCH/CASE and IF THEN ELSE with EXECPROC are examples of commands used to examine the event and act on it.

4. Typically, if the command, such as GETEVENT or WAIT, traps a specific or listed event, the application can then deal with it. If the event is not specified in the command and therefore not trapped, it passes on to Paradox for normal processing. The programmer only needs to trap those events affecting the particular application logic being handled. However, it is possible to trap all events, preventing any events from passing through to Paradox without application control. This might be necessary to force the user to select a menu option or to respond in a specific way when using the application.

Figure 12-6 shows the flow of events through a typical application. Table 12-6 describes some of the commands that are important to event-driven programming. This is not an exhaustive list, just some examples of how you might use these

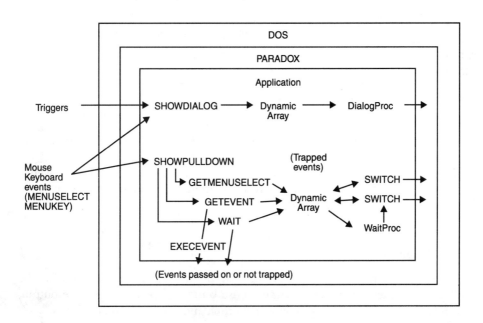

Figure 12-6. *Flow of events through an application*

Command	Description
GETEVENT	Traps specific events by collecting event information in a dynamic array. If events are not specifically trapped, they flow on to Paradox to be executed or ignored.
EXECEVENT	Passes GETEVENT trapped events on to Paradox to be executed.
WAIT	Traps specific events by collecting them in a dynamic array. Other events pass on to Paradox.
GETMENUSELECT	When used with SHOWPULLDOWN, forces user to select a menu option.
DYNARRAY	A dynamic array that GETEVENT, GETMENU-SELECT, and WAIT use to store event information.
SWITCH/CASE	Used to analyze the dynamic array information and execute procedures when a match is found.
IF THEN ELSE	Used to analyze the dynamic array information and then execute procedures, with EXECPROC, when a match is found.
SHOWPULLDOWN	Used to define menu options and procedures to execute when they are selected.
SHOWDIALOG	Used to define dialog box options and procedures to execute when they are selected.

Table 12-6.   Examples of Event Handler Commands

commands. The commands are summarized in Chapter 13 and described later in this chapter.

There are four types of events in PAL: mouse events, key events, message events, and idle events. Triggers are also a type of event that can be used with some commands.

Mouse Events

Mouse events are the result of a movement of the mouse. The mouse event can be one of four movements: releasing the mouse button, pressing the mouse button, moving the mouse from one position to another, and holding a button down.

Mouse events are external, in that they are generated by the user outside of Paradox.

Mouse events collected into a dynamic array have the following components. Refer to the earlier section, "Arrays" for information on dynamic arrays.

Tag or Index of Dynamic Array	Description or Contents of Dynamic Array
TYPE	Contains MOUSE for Mouse Event
ACTION	Contains one of the following: UP, when mouse button is released DOWN, when mouse button is pressed MOVE, when mouse button is moved AUTO, when button is pressed continually
ROW	Row number where event occurred
COL	Column number where event occurred
BUTTONS	Contains one of the following: LEFT if left button was involved RIGHT if right button was involved BOTH, if both or center button was involved NONE, if no button involved
DOUBLECLICK	Contains True for a double-click, or False for no double-click

When the mouse event is clicking on the Close box, double-clicking the title bar, or clicking the Maximize/Restore icon, a Message event is also generated.

Key Events

Key events occur when a key on the keyboard is pressed. It may be an alphanumeric key, such as *a,* or a combination of keys, such as CTRL-F2. Key events are external, in that they are produced by the user pressing a key.

Key events, similar to mouse events, may create message events when they affect a window.

Key events collected into a dynamic array have the following components. Refer to the earlier section, "Arrays" for information on dynamic arrays.

Tag or Index of Dynamic Array	Description or Contents of Dynamic Array
TYPE	Contains KEY for the event type
SCANCODE	Contains a number representing the key as it is recognized by the system BIOS
KEYCODE	Contains a number for the ASCII or IBM extended code representation of the key

You do not need both SCANCODE and KEYCODE. Only one has to be specified.

Message Events

Message events are created by the system when certain key or mouse events occur. They are the result of interactions with a menu or screen, such as when the user clicks on a field, a window, or a dialog box, or selects a menu item.

Some message events inform Paradox that they are about to occur. These "before" events can be prevented, or some other action taken before the event occurs, by using commands such as RESIZE or CLOSE. Other message events tell Paradox after they have occurred, such as MENUSELECT or MENUKEY. These "after" events cannot be prevented. In this case, only after-the-fact actions can be taken.

Message events collected into a dynamic array have the following components. Refer to the earlier section, "Arrays" for information on dynamic arrays.

Tag or Index of Dynamic Array	Description or Contents of Dynamic Array
TYPE	Contains MESSAGE for the event type
MESSAGE	Contains the message event, such as the following: CLOSE if Close is invoked MAXIMIZE if Maximize is invoked NEXT if Next is invoked MENUSELECT if a menu selection has been made MENUKEY if a key in the UNTIL list is pressed
MENUTAG	For MENUSELECT or MENUTAG messages, contains the tag associated with SHOWPULLDOWN
SCANCODE	For MENUSELECT or MENUTAG messages, contains a number representing the key as it is recognized by the system BIOS
KEYCODE	For MENUSELECT or MENUTAG messages, contains a number for the ASCII or IBM extended code representation of the key

Idle Events

An idle event is generated internally by the system. It is produced when nothing else is happening in the system. The only element idle events contain in a dynamic array is a TYPE of IDLE.

Triggers

A *trigger* is a type of event that can be trapped only with the SHOWDIALOG and WAIT commands. Trigger events are very specific keyboard or mouse movements relating to an application. For example, perhaps the user is attempting to enter or exit a field, or to arrive at a specific row on a table or form. Using the SHOWDIALOG and WAIT commands, these triggers can be trapped and the application can then control the immediate time before or after an event occurs.

Triggers can be trapped before or after an action has taken place. When the trap is before an action occurs, the action can be screened or prevented. In Table 12-7 the before triggers are stated, "About to ...", indicating the action is yet to occur. You are only informed when the trigger is trapped after an action; however, appropriate "after" actions can be taken. In Table 12-7 the after triggers are stated, "Having arrived ...". Table 12-7 lists the triggers available for a WAIT command. The number in parentheses is the relative order in which the triggers will be trapped or presented to you.

One event, or movement of a cursor, may cause several triggers. However, the order of the triggers is predictable since they are presented to you in the same relative sequence. The triggers themselves may differ, but their order in relation to each other remains the same. For example, if you move the cursor from one field in a form to another, the triggers that are trapped might be DEPART FIELD, DEPART ROW, ARRIVE ROW, and ARRIVE FIELD. You can see from the table that DEPART FIELD will always precede DEPART ROW and the ARRIVE triggers. Triggers generated as a result of a single action can be identified as belonging to a *trigger cycle*. This is simply a way to track the group of triggers belonging to a single event, such as the movement from one field to another. The cycle number, which is used by WAIT, remains the same for the trigger group.

Creating Menus

Menus are, of course, one of the primary ways in which a user communicates with an application. PAL provides two types of menus: pull-down and pop-up menus. Pull-down menus are created with SHOWPULLDOWN and feature a menu bar across the top of the screen, just as in the Paradox Main menu, from which submenus are pulled down. Pop-up menus are created with one of three menus: SHOWMENU, SHOWARRAY, and SHOWPOPUP. These menus display the menu in a box somewhere on the screen, such as the PAL menu. SHOWMENU and SHOWARRAY menus are placed in the center of the screen. You can specify the placement of SHOWPOPUP menus.

Menus can be *modal* or *non-modal*. Modal menus require the user to select an option before the application continues; the application is frozen until the menu option is completed. Pop-up menus are modal.

Non-modal menus display the menu on the screen, but it is inactive. The application continues to be active until the menu is activated, at which point the application is frozen until the menu action is completed. The Paradox Main menu is non-modal. SHOWPULLDOWN menus can be modal or non-modal.

WAIT Triggers Trigger (Order)	Description
ARRIVEFIELD (17)	Having arrived in a new field
ARRIVEPAGE (13)	Having arrived in a new form page
ARRIVEROW (16)	Having arrived in a new record
ARRIVETABLE (15)	Having arrived in a new table
ARRIVEWINDOW (14)	Having arrived in a new window
DEPARTFIELD (1)	About to leave a field
DEPARTPAGE (4)	About to leave a form page
DEPARTROW (2)	About to leave a record
DEPARTTABLE (5)	About to leave a table
DISPLAYONLY (11)	About to change a display-only form
EVENT (18)	About to invoke an event, as opposed to a trigger
IMAGERIGHTS (7)	About to change a field without proper rights
PASSRIGHTS (8)	About to violate password rights
POSTRECORD (6)	About to post a record
READONLY (12)	About to change a read-only table
REQUIREDVALUE (9)	About to leave without a required entry
TOUCHRECORD (3)	About to touch any record in Edit mode, or any previously untouched record in CoEdit mode
VALCHECK (10)	About to violate a validity check

Showdialog Triggers Trigger (Order)	Description
ACCEPT (4)	About to accept a dialog box
ARRIVE (6)	Having arrived in on a new control
CANCEL (5)	About to cancel a dialog box
CLOSE (8)	Having closed a dialog box
DEPART (2)	About to depart from a control
OPEN (7)	Having opened a dialog box, before displaying it
SELECT (3)	About to select a pick list item
UPDATE (1)	About to place the value of a control in its variable

Table 12-7. *Triggers Trapped by a WAIT Command*

SHOWPULLDOWN

SHOWPULLDOWN creates the pull-down menu bars you see at the top of the screen, for example in the Paradox Main menu. You can create submenus off of the menu bar options, as Figure 12-7 shows.

The syntax of the SHOWPULLDOWN command is as follows:

```
SHOWPULLDOWN
     MenuList
             [Option: Description:[DISABLE] Tag
             [Option: Description :[DISABLE][Tag]
                     SUBMENU
                             MenuList
                     ENDSUBMENU
                 Separator
ENDMENU [UNTIL KeycodeList]
```

- *MenuList* is a list of menu options, separated by commas. The menu list can be developed using one of three techniques, as shown in the preceding syntax.

- *Option* is a string showing the menu options that appear on the menu bar or the submenu. All but the last option in a menu section must end with a comma.

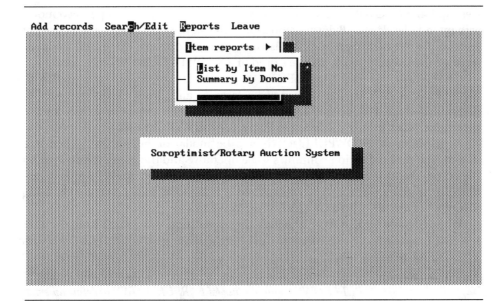

Figure 12-7. *Menu bar and submenus created by SHOWPULLDOWN*

- *Description* is the string that appears on the bottom of the screen when *Option* is highlighted.

- DISABLE makes specified options unavailable. They cannot be selected by the user. MENUENABLE and MENUDISABLE can also be used to enable and disable menu options.

- *Tag* is a value assigned to an index representing the menu item. It is the name of the MENUTAG element of a message event.

- *Separator* creates a line that separates the menu options on the pull-down menu.

- SUBMENU is used to specify submenu options. The submenu list has the same syntax and options as the SHOWPULLDOWN MenuList.

- ENDSUBMENU ends the definition of the SUBMENU options.

- ENDMENU ends the definition of the SHOWPULLDOWN menu options.

- UNTIL defines an alternate way of exiting the menu, using the keys specified in KeycodeList.

- *KeycodeList* is an optional list of Paradox key codes (or expressions that evaluate to key codes). The entries are separated by commas.

When more than one Option:Prompt line is included for a MenuList, commas must be placed at the end of each line (perhaps after Tag if there is one) on all but the last line.

Description   SHOWPULLDOWN displays a menu bar of up to 50 top-level options, with up to 16 levels of pull-down menus. Options can be selected even if they are not seen on the screen. Submenus may also have up to 50 options. Up to 2000 nodes or separate individual options may be stored in a SHOWPULLDOWN command.

GETEVENT, GETMENUSELECTION, or WAIT commands are used with SHOWPULLDOWN to trap the menu selections and other events in order to determine which PAL scripts to execute when a menu choice is made, and to determine which events to pass on to Paradox (with EXECEVENT).

As mentioned, SHOWPULLDOWN can be modal or non-modal. When it is non-modal, the application continues to be operative and the menu is displayed on the screen, but is inactive. When the menu is activated, the application becomes dormant until the menu action is completed. A non-modal menu is created by using SHOWPULLDOWN with a GETEVENT or WAIT loop.

When SHOWPULLDOWN is modal, the application is dormant until the user selects a menu choice. A modal menu can be created using SHOWPULLDOWN with a GETMENUSELECT loop.

To clear a SHOWPULLDOWN menu bar, use CLEARPULLDOWN or define an empty SHOWPULLDOWN command like this:

SHOWPULLDOWN ENDMENU

When a SHOWPULLDOWN menu is displayed, and a MESSAGE event occurs and is trapped by GETEVENT, GETMENUSELECT, or WAIT, a dynamic array is created with three elements:

- TYPE   Contains "MESSAGE" to denote the type of event (as opposed to KEY, IDLE, or MOUSE events).

- MESSAGE   Contains "MENUSELECT" to define the type of message generated, that is, a menu item was selected.

- MENUTAG   Contains the tag associated with menu option. This names the procedure that is to be executed or the action to take when an option is selected.

    When an UNTIL *key code* is pressed a similar dynamic array is created containing five elements:

- TYPE   Contains "MESSAGE" to denote the type of event.

- MESSAGE   Contains "MENUKEY" to define the type of message generated; that is, a key in the UNTIL list was pressed.

- MENUTAG   Contains the tag associated with menu option. This names the procedure or the action to take when a key has been pressed.

- SCANCODE   A number representing the BIOS scan code.

- KEYCODE   A number representing the ASCII or IBM extended code of the key pressed.

SHOWPULLDOWN cannot be used with the Compatibility mode.

Example   The following example defines a pull-down menu and traps the menu selections. A menu bar with three options, "Auction Items," "Bidders," and "Exit" is defined. A submenu of the Auction Items option provides two options to "Add Items" and "Edit Items." The "Bidder" option has a similar submenu. "Exit" clears the application menu bar from the screen.

    The GETEVENT command traps two types of events: a F2 key press and the menu selections. When an event to be trapped occurs, the dynamic array, Choosetag, is created. It contains a TYPE element of MESSAGE, and a MESSAGE element of either MENUKEY or MENUSELECT. (Refer to the discussions on dynamic arrays and event trapping for more information on the elements.) If a MENUKEY event (that is, pressing F2) occurs, a variable Endit is set to "F2". If a MENUSELECT event (that is, a menu selection) occurs, a variable *MenuNow* will be set to the MENUTAG element of the dynamic array, which contains the identifying menu item tag. The SWITCH command uses the contents of the variable to determine which procedure to execute.

```
; First set up the encompassing WHILE which ends when F2
; is pressed, or when "Exit" is selected from the menu.
; Preceding this section of code are several procedures
; referenced below.
Endit = ""
WHILE (Endit <> "F2")
     ; The menu bar and submenus is defined
SHOWPULLDOWN
"Auction Items" : "Add or Edit Auction Items" : "Items"
     SUBMENU
          "Add Items" : "Add new auction items" :
          "Additems",
          "Edit Items" : "Edit an auction item" :
          "Edititems"
     ENDSUBMENU,
"Bidders" : "Add or Edit Bidders" : "Bidders"
     SUBMENU
          "Add Bidders" : "Add New Bidders" : "Addbids",
          "Edit Bidders" : "Edit a Bidder" : "Editbids"
     ENDSUBMENU,
"Exit" : "Leave the Auction Application" : "Exit"
ENDMENU
     ; The GETEVENT traps F2 and menu selections to a
     ; dynamic array named Choosetag.
GETEVENT KEY "F2" MESSAGE "MENUSELECT" TO Choosetag
     IF Choosetag["TYPE"] = "MESSAGE"
                    ; If a menu selection is made,
                    ; place the tag into a variable.
          THEN MenuNow = Choosetag["MENUTAG"]
     ENDIF
     IF Choosetag["TYPE"] = "KEY"
                    ; If the only key listed is trapped,
                    ; get out of the WHILE loop.
          THEN QUITLOOP
     ENDIF

     ; The switch now uses the dynamic array to determine
     ; which menu choice was made. The appropriate
     ; procedures will then be executed.
SWITCH
     CASE (MenuNow = "Additems"): AddItemsProc()
     CASE (MenuNow = "Edititems"): EditItemsProc()
     CASE (MenuNow = "Addbids"):  AddBidProc()
     CASE (MenuNow = "Editbids"): EditBidProc()
     CASE (MenuNow = "Exit"):  EnditProc()
```

```
ENDSWITCH

ENDWHILE
EnditProc()
```

You can use the loops and the GETEVENT commands to achieve different results. For instance, in the example just given, only specific events are trapped with GETEVENT and then executed with SWITCH. Another possibility is to trap all events, using GETEVENT TO *DynamicArray*, and then to analyze the trapped events for the one you want to handle differently, perhaps with IF THEN ELSE, or with a qualifying WHILE. For example, look at how WHILE is used here:

```
WHILE (Choosetag["TYPE"] <> "MESSAGE")
EXECEVENT Choosetag
ENDWHILE
```

The events that you do not want to control can be passed on to Paradox with EXECEVENT.

SHOWMENU

SHOWMENU creates a pop-up menu in the center of the screen. Figure 12-8 presents an example of the type of menu created by this command.

Syntax

```
SHOWMENU MenuItemList
    [UNTIL KeycodeList [KEYTO VarName1]]
    [DEFAULT Choice]
TO VarName2
```

- *MenuItemList* is the list of options displayed on the menu and their descriptions or prompts. Each option is separated from its prompt by a colon. All but the last option line ends with a comma.

- *UNTIL* defines an alternate way of exiting the menu.

- *KeycodeList* is an optional list of Paradox keycodes (or expressions that evaluate to keycodes). The entries are separated by commas.

- *KEYTO* contains the ASCII keycode of the pressed key.

- *VarName1* contains the keycode of the key used to exit.

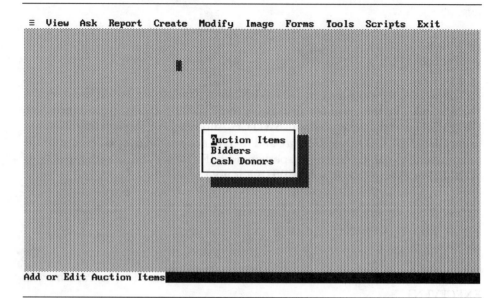

Figure 12-8. *Menu created using SHOWMENU*

- *DEFAULT* is optional and is used as the default pick list selection, which will be highlighted on the pick menu. The user will only have to press ENTER to select the default.

- *Choice* contains the default menu option, if not the first entry in the table.

- *VarName2* contains the menu choice selected by the user or the value "Esc" if it is pressed. (Notice this is the actual menu choice, not an identifying tag.)

Description   When a choice is made from the SHOWMENU menu, it is stored as a string in *VarName2* and control then returns to the next line of the script. Optionally, UNTIL provides a list of additional keys that can be recognized in addition to the selection from the table. When one of these keys is pressed, it can be stored as a string in *VarName1* using the optional KEYTO. DEFAULT provides an opportunity to assign one of the menu options as the default to be highlighted when the menu is first displayed. When the key is pressed or a menu option is selected, control is returned to the next command in the script.

Up to 50 menu options may be listed.

If no menu selection is made, and ESC is pressed, *VarName2* is set to ESC and Retval is False.

SHOWMENU is case sensitive, indicating that the string assigned to *VarName2* will contain leading caps. Therefore, CASE statements used with SHOWMENU must use leading caps as well.

Example The following example, the results of which appear in Figure 12-8, displays three items. If the user picks a menu choice, the name is entered into MenuPick. If the user presses F2 or ESC the ASCII keycode is entered into OutKey. The program can then use OutKey and MenuPick to control what happens next.

```
SHOWMENU
     "Auction Items"        : "Add or Edit Auction Items",
     "Bidders"              : "Add or Edit Bidders",
     "Cash Donors"          : "Add or Edit Cash Donors"
     UNTIL "F2" KEYTO OutKey
TO MenuPick
```

In order to act upon a menu selection once it is made, you can either use a SWITCH/CASE command to isolate the chosen menu item, or a dynamic array. For instance, the SHOWMENU and SWITCH commands can be enclosed in a WHILE loop. The SWITCH would contain the possible menu choices and the procedures or scripts to be played.

A dynamic array could be used to contain the potential menu choices to be selected and the appropriate procedures as well. See the example in the section, "EXECPROC and Dynamic Arrays," earlier in the chapter. When using a dynamic array, you must specifically declare it before the SHOWMENU command is used. Then you could use an IF THEN ELSE control structure to analyze the menu selection and execute the associated procedure in the dynamic array.

SHOWARRAY

SHOWARRAY creates a pick list menu in the middle of the screen. Figure 12-9 displays a menu created with SHOWARRAY. The script creating it is listed in the following example. You must first declare two arrays and then use the SHOWARRAY command.

```
SHOWARRAY Array1 Array2
     [UNTIL KeycodeList [KEYTO VarName1]]
     [DEFAULT Choice]
TO VarName2
```

- *Array1* is the name of an array containing items that will be the options on the menu.

- *Array2* is the name of a second array containing the prompts in the message line.

- UNTIL is used to recognize keypresses other than ESC. If you list more than one, the KEYTO option can be used to store whichever one the user presses.

- *KeycodeList* is an optional list of Paradox keycodes (or expressions that evaluate to key codes). The entries are separated by commas.

- *VarName1* contains the key code of the key used to exit.

- The optional DEFAULT is used as the default pick list selection, which will be highlighted on the menu. The user will only have to press ENTER to select the default.

- *Choice* is the name of the item in Array1 that will become the default for the menu choice.

- *VarName2* contains the array option selected by the user.

When ESC is pressed, *VarName2* is set to "Esc" (note the string value) and Retval is set to False.

SHOWARRAY is case sensitive and the value stored in VarName2 contains a leading capital letter. Consequently, all CASE statements following the SHOWARRAY should also use leading caps.

Example   The following example, illustrated in Figure 12-9, creates a pick list containing three options. The options and their prompts are created as an array

Figure 12-9.   Menu created using SHOWARRAY

immediately prior to the SHOWARRAY command. The third item is the default choice. The variable *PrintRept* contains the option picked by the user.

```
Array Options[3]
Array Prompts[3]
Options[1] = "Auction Item List"
Options[2] = "Auction Bidder List"
Options[3] = "Cash Donor List"
Prompts[1] = "Print list of auction items"
Prompts[2] = "Print list of bidders"
Prompts[3] = "Print list of cash donors"
SHOWARRAY
     Options Prompts
     DEFAULT Options[3]
TO PrintRept
```

SHOWPOPUP

SHOWPOPUP creates a pop-up menu either centered or placed at a location on the screen specified within the command. Figure 12-10 shows an example of a pop-up menu created by this command. The script used is given in the example for this section.

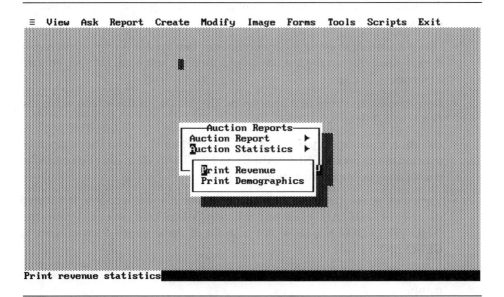

Figure 12-10. *Pop-up menu created by SHOWPOPUP*

SHOWPOPUP has considerably more power and flexibility than SHOWMENU or SHOWARRAY. With it you not only specify the menus and submenus, but you can place the menu on a screen and give it a title.

Syntax

```
SHOWPOPUP Title {CENTERED} | @Row,Column}
     MenuList
            [Option: Description:[DISABLE] Tag
            [Option: Description:[DISABLE][Tag]
                    SUBMENU
                        MenuList
                    ENDSUBMENU
             Separator
ENDMENU
     [UNTIL] KeycodeList [KEYTO VarName1]
     TO VarName2
```

- *Title* is the name of the menu. In Figure 12-10 the title is "Auction Reports."

- CENTERED places the menu in the center of the screen.

- *@Row,Column* is the row and column number of the upper-left corner of the menu.

- *MenuList* is a list of menu options, separated by commas. The menu list can be developed using one of three techniques (including *Separator*), as shown in the example.

- *Option* is a string showing the menu options that appear on the menu bar or the submenu. All but the last option of a menu or submenu list must contain a comma.

- *Description* is the string that appears on the bottom of the screen when the *Option* is highlighted.

- DISABLE makes specified options unavailable, which means they cannot be selected by the user. MENUENABLE and MENUDISABLE can also be used to enable and disable menu options.

- *Tag* is a value assigned to an index representing the menu option. It is stored in the MENUTAG element of the MESSAGE event. (See the "SHOWPULLDOWN" section for a layout of the dynamic array created by GETEVENT or WAIT.)

- *Separator* creates a line that separates the menu options on the pull-down menu.

- SUBMENU is used to specify submenu options. The submenu list has the same syntax and options as the SHOWPOPUP MenuList.

- ENDSUBMENU ends the definition of the submenu options.

- ENDMENU ends the definition of the SHOWPOPUP menu options.

- UNTIL defines an alternate way of exiting the menu.

- *KeycodeList* is an optional list of Paradox keycodes (or expressions that evaluate to keycodes) that exit the menu. The entries are separated by commas.

- KEYTO stores the key in the KeycodeList that was pressed in the named variable, VarName1.

- *VarName1* contains the code of the key pressed.

- TO names the variable that will contain tne tag of the selected menu item.

- *VarName2* stores the tag of the selected menu choice.

Description   The SHOWPOPUP command displays a menu that may be centered with the option CENTERED, or placed with the upper-left corner at a location specified by *@Row,Column.*

The SHOWPOPUP menu can display up to 50 options, with up to 16 level of submenus. Options can be selected even if they are not seen on the screen. Submenus may also have up to 50 options. Up to 2000 nodes or separate individual options may be stored in a SHOWPOPUP command.

The title is placed on the pop-up menu, or is blank when the title is defined as a blank string.

When a choice is made from the list, the tag of the menu choice (not the choice itself) is stored as a string in *VarName2* and control then returns to the next line of the script. Optionally, UNTIL provides a list of keypresses that can be recognized and used to exit the menu. When more than one keypress is listed, the key pressed can be stored as a string in *VarName1* using the optional KEYTO.

If no menu selection is made, and ESC is pressed, *VarName2* is set to "Esc" (a string value) and Retval is false.

To act upon a menu selection, you can use either a dynamic array or a SWITCH/CASE command.

SHOWPOPUP is not available in Compatibility mode.

Example   The following example displays a centered pop-up menu, the results of which are shown in Figure 12-10. It contains three menu options and two submenus. F3 is defined as a key that will exit the menu. When a menu selection is made, the variable OptionVar contains the *Tag,* which can then be used to initiate action.

```
SHOWPOPUP "Auction Reports" CENTERED
"Auction Report" : "Select Auction Reports" : "Repts"
     SUBMENU
          "List Items" : "List new auction items" :
               "Listitems",
          "List Bidders" : "List bidders" : "Listbidders"
     ENDSUBMENU,
"Auction Statistics" : "Print auction statistics" : "Stats"
     SUBMENU
          "Print Revenue" : "Print revenue statistics" :
               "Rev",
          "Print Demographics" : "Print demographics of
               items" : "Demo"
     ENDSUBMENU,
"Exit" : "Leave auction reports" : "Exit"
ENDMENU
UNTIL "F3"
TO OptionVar
```

Creating Dialog Boxes

Dialog boxes are used to get information from the user about the task being done. With them users can select a file from a list, or a table from a list, or in more complicated situations, choose one out of a number of choices, choose several out of a group of choices, type in names, or more. Creating dialog boxes can be done with SHOWDIALOG, SHOWFILES, and SHOWTABLES.

SHOWDIALOG

SHOWDIALOG is a complex command that allows you to create a dialog box. You can enter a title for the dialog box, its location on the screen, and a number of control elements. For example, pushbuttons let you simply choose an option and click or "push" it, such as you're used to with the Cancel/OK choice.

Pick lists allow you to pick a choice from a scrolling list, such as a list of files in a directory. Radio buttons let you select one option from a list, such as selecting a font for highlighted text (radio buttons are mutually exclusive—only one choice can be accepted). Other control elements include check boxes where you can choose as many options as you want from a list; type-in boxes, where you type data into a box, such as with the prompts to enter a name; and sliders, where you scroll through a list using a slider with arrows at each end and a scroll box. Figure 12-11 shows an example of some of the alternatives you may have.

In addition, you can specify canvas elements for the dialog box, such as background colors, background text, single or double lines for frames, and style and location for background text.

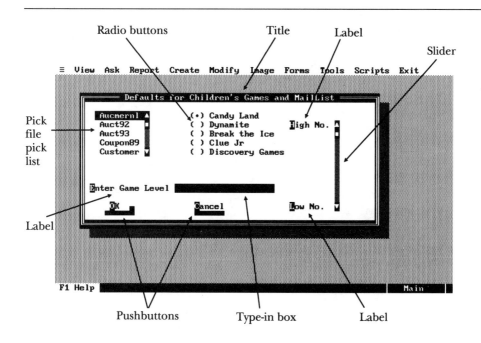

Figure 12-11. *SHOWDIALOG created this example of a dialog box containing a number of control elements*

The syntax for the SHOWDIALOG command covers several pages and you can find it in the command summary in Chapter 13. Here is the PAL code needed to produce the dialog box shown in Figure 12-11.

Example

```
SHOWDIALOG "Defaults for Children's Games and Maillist"
@3,5 HEIGHT 15 WIDTH 60
    PICKFILE
        @1,2 HEIGHT 5 WIDTH 10
        "C:\\PATEST\\*.DB"
        NOEXT
        TAG "THISPICK"
        TO FILEPICK
    PUSHBUTTON
        @11,2 WIDTH 8
        "~O~K"
        OK
        VALUE "ACCEPT"
```

```
              TAG "Yes"
              TO Yesorno
     PUSHBUTTON
              @11,20 WIDTH 8
              "~C~ancel"
              CANCEL
              VALUE "Cancel"
              TAG "No"
              TO Yesorno
     RADIOBUTTONS
              @1,20 HEIGHT 5 WIDTH 20
              "Candy Land",
              "Dynamite",
              "Break The Ice",
              "Clue Jr."
              "Discovery Games"
              TAG "Games"
              TO GameSelect
     LABEL
              @9,0
              "~E~nter Game Level"
              FOR "EnterName"
     ACCEPT
              @9,18 WIDTH 20 "A12"
              TAG "EnterName"
              TO ToName
     LABEL
              @2,40
              "~H~igh No."
              FOR "Slide"
     LABEL
              @11,40
              "~L~ow No."
              FOR "Slide"
     SLIDER
              @2,50 VERTICAL
              LENGTH 10
              MIN 0 MAX 50
              ARROWSTEP 1
              PAGESTEP 5
              TAG "SLIDE"
              TO SlideVar
 ENDDIALOG
```

SHOWFILES

SHOWFILES displays a dialog box in the center of the screen that contains all the files in a named directory. The user then selects a file by choosing it in one of the normal ways. Figure 12-12 shows a dialog box created using SHOWFILES.

The syntax of the SHOWFILES command is as follows:

```
SHOWFILES [NOEXT] DOSPath Prompt
     [UNTIL KeycodeList [KEYTO VarName1]]
TO Varname2
```

- *DOSPath* is the DOS path to the directory where the files are stored. It may contain wildcards, for example, to select files with specific extensions, such as "*.SC.

- *Prompt* is the message displayed at the bottom left of the screen.

- *KeycodeList* is an optional list of Paradox keycodes (or expressions that evaluate to keycodes). The entries are separated by commas.

- *VarName1* contains the keycode of the key used to exit.

- *VarName2* contains the file selected by the user.

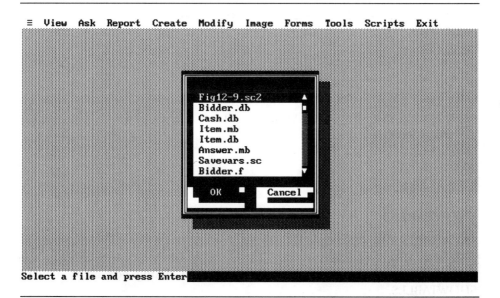

Figure 12-12. *SHOWFILES displays a list of selected (or all) files in a directory, with or without extensions*

Description   SHOWFILES displays a list in the center of the screen of the files in the named directory. Optionally, the list of files can be shown with no extensions displayed, as shown here:

```
SHOWFILES NOEXT "C:\\APPL\\*.SC"
```

This shows all script files in \APPL without the .SC extensions.

 It is useful to use the NOEXT together with the *.DB search when you are waiting to choose a file to display with VIEW, since that command does not accept extensions in the name.

When a choice is made from the list, it is stored in *VarName2* and control then returns to the next line of the script. Optionally, UNTIL provides a list of additional keys that can be used to exit from the menu. When one of these keys is pressed, it can optionally be stored in *VarName1* using KEYTO. When the key is pressed or a table is selected, control is returned to the next command in the script.

If no file is selected and ESC is pressed, *VarName2* is set to "Esc" (a string value) and Retval is False. If no files are found in the directory, VarName1 is set to "None."

Example   The following example lists the files in the defined directory, as shown in Figure 12-12. When the user selects a file, the name is stored in FileVar. Then the variable is used to view the file. In the second example, the selected file, without the extension, is used in the following VIEW command.

```
SHOWFILES "C:\\APPL\\" "Select a file and press Enter"
UNTIL "F2"
TO FileVar
```

or

```
SHOWFILES NOEXT "C:\\APPL\\*.DB" "Select a file and
   press Enter"
UNTIL "F2"
TO FileVar
VIEW FileVar
```

SHOWTABLES

SHOWTABLES displays a dialog box in the center of the screen that contains all the table files (.DB) in a named directory. The user then selects a table by choosing it in one of the normal ways. Figure 12-13 shows a dialog box created using SHOWTABLES.

The syntax of the SHOWTABLES command is as follows:

```
SHOWTABLES DOSPath Prompt
     [UNTIL KeyCodeList [KEYTO VarName1]]
TO Varname2
```

- *DOSPath* is the DOS path to the directory where the tables are stored.

- *Prompt* is the message displayed at the bottom left of the screen.

- *KeycodeList* is an optional list of Paradox keycodes (or expressions that evaluate to keycodes). The entries are separated by commas.

- *VarName1* contains the keycode of the key used to exit.

- *VarName2* contains the table selected by the user.

Description   SHOWTABLES displays a list of the tables in the named directory. When a choice is made from the list, it is stored in *VarName2* and control then returns to the next line of the script. Optionally, UNTIL provides a list of additional keys that can be recognized in addition to the selection from the table. When one of these keys is pressed, it can optionally be stored in *VarName1* using KEYTO. When the key is pressed or a table is selected, control is returned to the next command in the script.

   If no table is selected and ESC is pressed, *VarName2* is set to ESC and Retval is False. If no tables are found in the directory, *VarName1* is set to "None."

Example   The following example lists the tables in the defined directory, which is shown in Figure 12-13. F3 or F8 is used to exit the menu. If one of the two keys is pressed, its code is stored in the variable KeyVar. When a table is selected from the list, its name is stored in TableVar where it can be used as an argument in another command.

```
SHOWTABLES "C:\\APPL\\"  "Select the table and press F2"
     UNTIL "F3","F8" KEYTO KeyVar
TO TableVar
```

Working with Windows, Images, and Canvases

Special consideration must be given in dealing with displaying information on screens, such as how to manipulate and control displays, how to enter or display data, how to hide or display objects, and how to work with images versus canvases versus windows.

   Although they appear to be the same, windows, images, and canvases are different. By understanding their differences, you'll know what can be done in each.

   One related concept that is relevant and important for the PAL programmer to understand is that of layers.

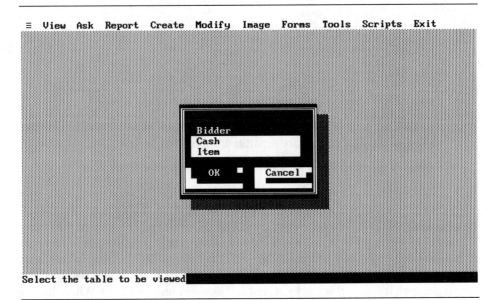

Figure 12-13.   *Dialog box created using SHOWTABLES*

Paradox Layers

The concept of layers is importance in understanding how Paradox views what occurs in the system at any one time. Paradox divides the screen into three layers. The layers can be thought of as a stack, with the first level on the bottom of the stack. The stack would run on the z-axis, as illustrated by Figure 12-14. If you can visualize a monitor, the screen can be used to illustrate the z-axis. The bottom horizontal line of the screen becomes the x-axis; the left vertical line of the screen becomes the y-axis; and the line from the inside center of the screen coming out straight at you is the z-axis.

Of course the z-axis doesn't come out of the screen, but it illustrates the stack concept of windows, images, and canvases that must be handled by the application.

The z-axis consists of three layers.

The first, or deepest, level is the desktop layer. It is where Paradox objects, such as tables, reports, and forms are located. The Paradox menu bar and status line are here. As new windows are created, they are also in the desktop layer (unless they are created to float over the echo layer with the WINDOW CREATE FLOATING command). The new windows stack up on the z-axis in the order in which they are created, the newest on top. However, when you select a desktop window, you bring it to the top, changing the order of the stack (also known as *changing the z-order*). This is why it is so important to use the window handle (with WINDOW SELECT *windowhandle*) to select a window, rather than manipulating the stack of windows.

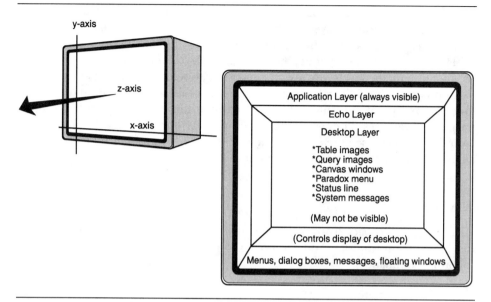

Figure 12-14. *Paradox levels are stacked along a z-axis*

The second level of the z-axis is the echo layer. It controls the display of desktop objects. It contains itself as well as the desktop layer, and can display all that the desktop layer contains. At the top of the echo layer is a full-size canvas.

The ECHO command affects this level only and determines which objects on the desktop are seen. ECHO can be global, managing the display of the whole desktop. ECHO can also be local, controlling the display of selected windows. When the echo layer is off, the desktop display is dormant. Changes may occur, but they are not seen until the echo is turned on.

Windows created with WINDOWS CREATE FLOATING are not affected by the ECHO command. As mentioned earlier, these floating windows are windows that float above the echo layer. They are always visible above the contents of the echo layer and can be used to display messages while the echo layer is frozen. Floating windows work best with ECHO OFF. When ECHO ON is used with floating windows, you see the activity occurring on the desktop as a result of application programming, but the floating windows obscure the view. Even though the floating window may be deselected, it is still visible.

Avoid selecting the desktop windows while floating windows are visible.

The third and top level in the z-axis is the application layer. This contains the canvases, menus, and dialog boxes that you create in your PAL programs. It runs "over" the echo layer, floating above the desktop and echo layers. Consequently, the application layer often hides the echo layer and the contents of the desktop. Again, the objects are still there, just hiding behind the application-generated floating displays. The application layer is not affected by the ECHO command; application-created menus and canvases float above the echo layer.

The three layers are separate, but each higher level contains the one beneath it. As you move up the levels, you are encompassing, not leaving a lower level.

In programming, it is critical that the layers be understood. You must often mask lower layers so that current application activity is not confused with background images and canvases. These masked images may also be affected by the application layer, but you can't see the results on the screen. You don't want to be performing an action on one layer when you intended it to occur on another.

Windows

Windows are the backdrops for images and canvases. Images and canvases are displayed within windows. You can create window canvases within PAL, using the following command,

```
WINDOW CREATE TO VarName
```

where *VarName* will receive the assigned handle.

Window Handles   Windows are assigned a sequential number that is called a *handle*. This is the identifying number of the window. A window's handle is very important to know and to track since you can easily program changes to the wrong window. Windows change and it can be difficult to notice the change. Always check to be sure the handle you're using is the correct one for the window you want.

Get the handle when you first open the window.

Handles are only assigned to a window once in a Paradox session. Newly created windows get unique unassigned numbers, even if prior numbered windows have been closed.

In addition to the WINDOW CREATE command, you can get handles of windows with the following four commands:

```
WINDOW HANDLE IMAGE 1 TO VarName
WINDOW HANDLE CURRENT TO VarName
```

```
VarName = GETWINDOW()
WINDOW LIST TO ArrayName
```

You can test for a handle with the **ISWINDOW(** *VarName*) function to make sure the window is the one you are expecting before changing it with your PAL script.

Window Attributes   Windows have attributes, which are listed in Table 12-8. These attributes tell Paradox what the user can do with the window and other characteristics about the window. An attribute may contain the value True if a user can change a window characteristic, or False if no change is allowed. Other attributes contain actual numbers of rows, columns, and so on, which describe the window. These attributes can be retrieved into a dynamic array, examined, and changed, giving you great flexibility in controlling screen displays.

To read the attributes into a dynamic array where they can be examined or changed, use this command:

```
WINDOW GETATTRIBUTES WindowHandle TO DynamicArrayName
```

To set the attributes for a window, first store them in the dynamic array and then use this command to update the attributes:

```
WINDOW SETATTRIBUTES WindowHandle FROM DynamicArrayName
```

In addition, the **WINDOW CREATE** command can apply changed attributes immediately to a window, like this:

```
WINDOW CREATE ATTRIBUTES DynamicArrayName TO WindowHandle
```

Chapter 13 gives more syntax information about each of these commands.

You can use the WINDOW RESIZE, WINDOW MOVE, and WINDOW MAXIMIZE commands to change windows, rather than the attributes.

Attributes Available for Windows

The following attributes contain True if a user can perform the actions or if a window contains the attribute, and contain False otherwise. Many contain physical characteristics of the window.

Array Tag	Description
CANCLOSE	User can close the window
CANMAXIMIZE	User can maximize the window
CANMOVE	User can move the window
CANRESIZE	User can resize the window
CANVAS	User can immediately display writing commands, not later (applies to canvas windows and canvases attached to image windows)
CANVASHEIGHT	Gives height of canvas buffer
CANVASWIDTH	Gives width of canvas buffer
ECHO	Echo is used to reflect window changes or not (Applies to image windows only)
FLOATING	Window floats above the echo layer or not
HASFRAME	Window is framed or not
HASSHADOW	Window has a shadow or not
HEIGHT	Number of rows, including the frame
MARGIN	Number of characters in left margin. Off if none
MAXIMIZED	Window is maximized or not
ORIGINCOL	Upper-left column number
ORIGINROW	Upper-left row number
SCROLLCOL	Horizontal scroll bar offset
SCROLLROW	Vertical scroll bar offset
STYLE	Attribute number for style of canvas text (See the color display tables in the next section for details)
TITLE	Title on top of the frame
WIDTH	Number of columns in the width, including frame

Table 12-8.   *Attributes That Can Be Modified for a Window*

Style Canvas Attribute

The Style attribute contains a number from 0 to 255 with the following meanings:

Foreground Color Displays

0	Black
1	Blue
2	Green
3	Cyan
4	Red
5	Magenta
6	Brown
7	Light Gray
8	Dark Gray
9	Light Blue
10	Light Green
11	Light Cyan
12	Light Red
13	Light Magenta
14	Yellow
15	White

Background Color Displays

0	Black
16	Blue
32	Green
48	Cyan
64	Red
80	Magenta
96	Brown
112	Light Gray

To get both background and foreground colors, add the two numbers together. For example, for a green foreground and light gray background the code would be 2 + 112 or 114.

The codes for the style attributes may also contain the following values for monochrome displays:

Monochrome Displays

0	No Display
1	Underline text
2	Normal text
9	High intensity, underlining
10	High intensity text
112	Reversed video text

For blinking text add 128 to any of the values in the "Monochrome Displays" table.

Images

Image windows contain Paradox tables (whether form or table views) or queries. When you create one of these objects, you create an image window automatically.

The *current* image is not necessarily the current window. The current window is the one on top, which has the mouse tools active (if you use a mouse). A canvas might overlay the image, and be the current window. If the image is not the window (and is not the current window), the current image is the most recent current image. Figure 12-15 shows an example.

Even though the current image is not the current window, it still can be affected by some commands that affect images and not canvases. In other words, Paradox commands not relevant to the current canvas may still affect and change the current image.

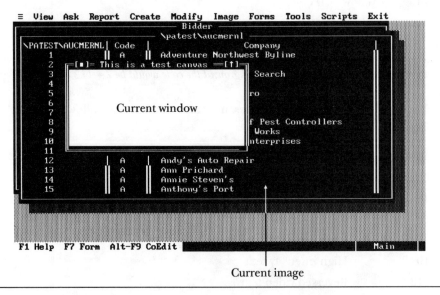

Figure 12-15.   *The image window is not the current window; the canvas is*

Canvases

Canvases are screens you see when you create a PAL application. In addition to the problem of distinguishing between the current image and the current window, you can add the current canvas. All three can be different.

There are three types of canvases:

- Canvases created by WINDOW CREATE. These canvases don't contain objects, such as tables or queries.

- Canvases that are attached to objects (such as tables) and are part of the image window. These canvases are created with SETCANVAS. You can write messages onto them concerning the objects to which they are attached.

- The full-size canvas that fills the screen and is on top of the echo layer. This canvas is used as a default when displaying output to a user, if the application does not specifically create a window.

One primary use of canvases is to display messages or text. You can use ?, ??, TEXT, or MESSAGE to output messages to a canvas.

Summary of PAL Functions and Commands

This chapter summarizes the functions and commands for PAL (Paradox Application Language) in Paradox 4. In alphabetical order, it's intended to be a quick reference for the use and syntax of PAL. For detailed information, refer to Borland's *PAL Programmer's Guide* and the *PAL Reference*.

The following conventions are used in the syntax of the commands and functions:

- Replaceable parameters appear in italics. These are items you must replace with an appropriate value or expression, for example:

```
COEDIT TableName
```

- Optional elements are enclosed in brackets, for example:

```
QUIT [ Expression ]
```

- Selection of only one choice from several listed is shown by a vertical bar between options, with the option list enclosed in braces, for example:

```
CURSOR { BAR | BOX | NORMAL | OFF }
```

- You'll see references to a variable named Retval. This is a special Paradox variable that traps certain values for later processing. See specific commands for the uses of Retval.

PAL Functions and Commands

The summary of functions and commands in alphabetic sequence follows.

=

VarName = Expression

Assigns the value of *Expression* to *VarName*, for example:

```
user_name = "Mary"
```

ArrayName[Element] = Expression

Assigns the value of *Expression* to *ArrayName[Element]*, for example:

```
months[10] = "October"
```

FieldSpec = Expression

Assigns the value of *Expression* to *FieldSpec*, for example:

```
[customer->balance] = 199.57
```

? *[ExpressionList]*

The ? command displays the values specified in *ExpressionList*, starting at the beginning of the line beneath the cursor. *ExpressionList* is a list of expressions that will be displayed.

For example, assume *NameVar* contains the value "William". The command,

```
? "Good morning ", NameVar
```

will display the phrase "Good morning William" at the beginning of the line beneath the cursor.

?? *[ExpressionList]*

The ?? command displays the values specified in *ExpressionList*, starting at the cursor position. *ExpressionList* is a list of expressions that will be displayed.

For example, assume *NameVar* contains the value "William". The command,

```
?? "Good morning ", NameVar
```

will display the phrase "Good morning William" at the cursor position.

@ *Row, Column*

The @ command moves the cursor to position *Row, Column* in the current canvas. *Row* specifies the row number within the current window. *Column* specifies the column number in *Row*. For example, the command,

```
@5,7 ?? "Good morning!"
```

will move the cursor to row 5, column 7 on the current canvas, and display the phrase "Good morning!" at that location.

ABS(*Number*)

ABS() generates the absolute value of *Number*. ABS() always generates a positive value. *Number* can be any numeric value between $+10^{-307}$ and -10^{+308}.

```
ABS(-15) = 15
```

ACCEPT

ACCEPT lets a user enter data from the keyboard.

```
ACCEPT Datatype [PICTURE Picture]
   [MIN Value1] [MAX Value2] [DEFAULT Value3]
   [LOOKUP TableName] [REQUIRED]
TO VarName
```

ACCEPT provides validity checking and lets a user edit data before continuing. The entry is stored in the variable, *VarName*. The user can press ESC to proceed without entering a value. If the user presses ESC, the Retval system variable becomes false; if the user enters a value, Retval becomes true.

Parameter	Meaning
DataType	The type of data the user can enter. This also determines the allowable size of the input.
PICTURE *Picture*	The entry format for the data. For example, a phone number might appear as PICTURE "(###) ###-####".
MIN *Value1*	The minimum allowable value.
MAX *Value2*	The maximum allowable value.
DEFAULT *Value3*	A default value, which the user can either leave as is, or change before pressing enter.
LOOKUP *TableName*	Checks that the user's entry matches one of the values in the first field of *TableName*.
REQUIRED	Indicates that the user cannot enter a blank value.
VarName	The variable used to store the accepted entry.

The following forces the user to enter a number in standard social security number format. Paradox automatically adds the hyphens. The user's entry gets stored in the memory variable, *ssn*.

```
ACCEPT "A11" PICTURE "###-##-####" REQUIRED TO ssn
```

ACCEPTDIALOG

Simulates pressing an OK button in the active dialog box, causing the program to accept the dialog.

ACOS(*Number*)

Generates the arc cosine of *Number*. The result is in radians. *Number* must have a value between –1 and +1.

```
radians = ACOS(0.5)
```

ADD *TableName1 TableName2*

Adds records from *TableName1* to *TableName2*. The table structures must be compatible. If *TableName2* is keyed, records in *TableName2* will be replaced by records from *TableName1* that would cause key violations. For example,

```
ADD "newcust" "custlist"
```

adds records from table NewCust to table CustList. If CustNum is the key field of CustList, any records from NewCust with CustNum values identical to those in CustList will replace the corresponding records in CustList.

Menu Equivalent   Menu {Tools} {More} {Add} {Update}

ALTSPACE

Activates the Paradox System menu.

Keystroke Equivalent   ALT-SPACEBAR

APPENDARRAY *ArrayList*

Copies data from each array in *ArrayList* into a new record in the current table. *ArrayList* is a comma-delimited list of arrays. Each array has an identical structure. The array elements 2, 3, ..., *n* must correspond to the sequence of fields in the table structure, regardless of the sequence showing in the current image. The array element #1 corresponds to the table name of the current record. The table must be in Coedit mode for APPENDARRAY to work. Compare this command with COPYFROMARRAY, which adds only a single record.

ARRAY *ArrayName[Number]*

Defines a fixed array named *ArrayName*, with *Number* of elements. The square brackets are required. For example, the following command defines a 12-element array named Months:

```
ARRAY Months[12]
```

ARRAYSIZE(*Array*)

Indicates the number of elements in *Array*. For example, if months is an array with 12 elements, the following command would display the number 12:

```
? ARRAYSIZE(months)
```

ASC(*Character*)

Indicates the ASCII code of *Character*.

ASIN(*Number*)

Calculates the arc sine of *Number*.

ATAN(*Number*)

Calculates the two-quadrant arc tangent of *Number*.

ATAN2(*Number*)

Calculates the four-quadrant arc tangent of *Number*.

ATFIRST()

Generates logical True if the current record is the first record available in the current image.

ATLAST()

Generates logical True if the current record is the last record available in the current image.

BACKSPACE

Moves the cursor to the left and deletes characters as it moves.

Keystroke Equivalent   BACKSPACE.

BANDINFO()

Indicates the name of the report band the cursor is currently positioned in (for example, "Page Header").

BEEP

Makes the computer speaker beep.

BLANKDATE()

Generates a blank (null) date value. For example, assume the table CustList has a date field named Member_Date. The following code populates the table with blank dates in the Member_Date field:

```
COEDIT "custlist"
SCAN
   [member_date] = BLANKDATE()
ENDSCAN
DO_IT!
```

See also, ISBLANK().

BLANKNUM()

Generates a blank (null) numeric value. For example, assume the table CustList has a currency field named Balance. The following code populates the table with blank values in the Balance field:

```
COEDIT "custlist"
SCAN
   [balance] = BLANKNUM()
ENDSCAN
DO_IT!
```

See also, ISBLANK().

BOT()

BOT() generates a value of True if a SKIP or MOVETO command tries to move to a record that would be positioned before the beginning record of the current image. If the move stays within the allowable records in the image, BOT() generates a value of False.

CALCDEBUG { ON | OFF } *String*

Toggles error messages on or off for calculated fields in forms and reports. *String* is a message that Paradox displays in place of the calculation results if the field data isn't valid.

Menu Equivalent   Menu {PAL} {CalcDebug} (in the Custom Configuration Program).

CANCELDIALOG

Simulates pressing a CANCEL button in the active dialog box, causing the program to cancel the dialog.

CANCELEDIT

Simulates the menu sequence **M**enu {**C**ancel} {**Y**es} in Edit mode, Report Designer, Form Designer, or Editor. This exits back to Main mode without saving any changes.

CANVAS { ON | OFF }

Toggles output to the canvas on or off. If on, changes will be displayed on the canvas. If off, changes will not be displayed.

CAVERAGE(*TableName, FieldName*)

Calculates the arithmetic average of nonblank values in *FieldName* of *TableName*. The following example calculates the average customer balance:

```
ave_bal = CAVERAGE("custlist", "balance")
```

CCOUNT(*TableName, FieldName*)

Calculates the number of nonblank entries in *FieldName* of *TableName*. The following example counts the number of customers who show a balance (even if the balance is zero):

```
show_bal = CCOUNT("custlist", "balance")
```

CHARWAITING()

Generates a logical True if at least one character is in the keyboard buffer. The following code displays the time of day until the user presses a key:

```
CURSOR OFF
CLEAR
WHILE True
```

```
@10,5 ?? TIME()
IF CHARWAITING() THEN
        QUITLOOP
    ENDIF
ENDWHILE
CURSOR NORMAL
```

CHECK

Places or removes a checkmark in the current column of a query form.

Keystroke Equivalent   F6

CHECKDESCENDING

Places or removes a checkdescending mark in the current column of a query form.

Keystroke Equivalent   CTRL-F6

CHECKMARKSTATUS()

Indicates the type of checkmark, if any, in the current column of a query form. Possible results are

- " " (null string—no checkmark)
- "Check"
- "CheckPlus"
- "CheckDescending"
- "GroupBy"

CHECKPLUS

Places or removes a checkplus in the current column of a query form.

Keystroke Equivalent   ALT-F6

CHR(*Number*)

Generates the character whose ASCII value is *Number*. For example, the following command displays an uppercase *A*.

```
?  CHR(65)
```

CLEAR { EOL | EOS }

CLEAR

Completely erases the current canvas.

CLEAR EOL

Erases from the cursor position to the end of the current line.

CLEAR EOS

Clears a rectangle defined by the cursor position and the lower-right corner of the current canvas.

CLEARALL

Removes all images from the desktop.

Keystroke Equivalent   ALT-F8

CLEARIMAGE

Removes the current image from the desktop.

Keystroke Equivalent   F8

CLEARPULLDOWN

Erases a menu generated by SHOWPULLDOWN.

CLIPCOPY

Copies the currently selected area from the Editor to the Clipboard. The selected area remains in the Editor.

Keystroke Equivalent   CTRL-INSERT

CLIPCUT

Moves the currently selected area from the Editor to the Clipboard. The selected area is deleted from the Editor.

Keystroke Equivalent   SHIFT-DELETE

CLIPPASTE

Copies the currently selected contents of the Clipboard into the Editor at the cursor position. The contents of the Clipboard remain untouched.

Keystroke Equivalent   SHIFT-INSERT

CLOSE PRINTER

Closes a printer that was opened with OPEN PRINTER.

CMAX(*TableName, FieldName*)

Calculates the maximum of the values in *FieldName* of *TableName*. The following code displays the largest customer balance:

```
? "The largest balance is ", CMAX("custlist", "balance")
```

CMIN(*TableName, FieldName*)

Calculates the minimum of the values in *FieldName* of *TableName*. The following code displays the smallest customer balance:

```
? "The smallest balance is ", CMIN("custlist", "balance")
```

CNPV(*TableName, FieldName, Number*)

Calculates the net present value of the nonblank values in *FieldName* of *TableName*. *Number* is a decimal number representing the discount rate per period.

COEDIT *TableName*

Activates CoEdit mode for *TableName* and all other tables that are open on the desktop.

When used as a Multiuser, COEDIT allows multiple users to change data in the same table at the same time.

When used as a Single user or Multiuser, COEDIT allows table editing (like Edit), with the following features:

- Posts changes to a table after each record is changed, rather than batch-posting when the user presses F2.

- Traps key violations as each record is posted, and lets the user fix the key violations.

While Edit lets you incrementally undo your changes before you press F2, CoEdit commits your changes after each record.

Menu Equivalent   Menu {Modify} {Coedit}

COEDITKEY

Activates CoEdit mode for all tables currently on the desktop.

Keystroke Equivalent   ALT-F9

COL()

Indicates the horizontal position of the cursor in the current canvas. The position is the offset from the left edge of the canvas.

COL() is used in the context of a canvas; COLNO() is used in the context of an image.

COLNO()

Indicates the horizontal position of the cursor. If the cursor is in a display or query image, the position is the field number in the image. If the cursor is in the Form Designer or Report Designer, the position is the offset from the left edge of the window.

COLNO() is used in the context of an image; COL() is used in the context of a canvas.

CONTROLVALUE(*TagName* [, *LabelName*])

Reports the value of the SHOWDIALOG control element identified by *TagName*. If the control element is a checkbox, you must include the *LabelName* of the checkbox item whose value to get. Use CONTROLVALUE() within a SHOWDIALOG procedure.

CONVERTLIB *OldLibraryName NewLibraryName*

Creates a Paradox 4 library file *NewLibraryName* from a Paradox 3.x library file *OldLibraryName*.

COPY *TableName1 TableName2*

Copies *TableName1* and its family of objects to *TableName2*.

Menu Equivalent   Menu {Tools} {Copy} {Table} {Replace}

COPYFORM *TableName1 FormName1 TableName2 FormName2*

Copies *FormName1* of *TableName1* to *FormName2* of *TableName2*. *TableName2* and *TableName1* can be the same table or different tables. If they're different tables, they must have compatible structures (the same field types in the same sequence).

Menu Equivalent   Menu {Tools} {Copy} {Form} {Replace}

COPYFROMARRAY *ArrayName*

Copies data from *ArrayName* to the current record. The array elements 2,3,...,*n* must correspond to the sequence of fields in the table structure, regardless of the sequence showing in the current image. The array element #1 corresponds to the table name of the current record.

See COPYTOARRAY for an example.

COPYREPORT *TableName1 ReportName1 TableName2 ReportName2*

Copies *ReportName1* of *TableName1* to *ReportName2* of *TableName2*. *TableName2* and *TableName1* can be the same table or different tables. If they're different tables, they must have compatible structures (the same field types in the same sequence).

The following code copies report 5 from the CustList table to an Answer table with the same structure. This would be used to print customer data meeting specific criteria.

```
COPYREPORT "custlist" "5" "answer" "r"
```

Menu Equivalent   Menu {Tools} {Copy} {Report} {Replace}

COPYTOARRAY *ArrayName*

Copies data from the current record to *ArrayName*. The array elements 2,3,...,n correspond to the sequence of fields in the table structure, regardless of the sequence showing in the current image. Array element #1 corresponds to the table name of the current record. You can use a combination of COPYTOARRAY and COPYFROMARRAY to copy data selectively from one table to another.

The following code copies data from the first record in NewCust to a new record in CustList:

```
VIEW "newcust"
COPYTOARRAY custrec
COEDIT "custlist"
END
DOWN
COPYFROMARRAY custrec
DO_IT!
```

See also, COPYFROMARRAY.

COS(*Number*)

Calculates the cosine of *Number*. *Number* is an angle expressed in radians.

CREATE

There are two forms of the CREATE command, described here.

CREATE *TableName FieldDefList*
Creates a new table *TableName* with the structure defined by *FieldDefList*. The following code creates a table to store product data:

```
CREATE "products"
     "Prod Num"          :      "N*",
     "Description"       :      "A20",
     "List Price"        :      "$"
```

CREATE *TableName2* **LIKE** *TableName1*

Creates a new table *TableName2* with the same structure as an existing table *TableName1*. This acts like the **B**orrow option of the Create mode. The following code creates a table to store old product data, using the table structure of the Products table:

```
CREATE "old_prod" LIKE "products"
```

Menu Equivalent   Menu {Create}

CREATELIB *LibraryName* [SIZE *Number*]

Creates a new procedure library, *LibraryName*, with a maximum of *Number* procedures. *Number* can be in the range 50 to 640.

CROSSTABKEY

Creates a temporary Crosstab table from the current table image. The following conditions apply:

- The data in all the columns to the left of and including the cursor column will become the key fields of Crosstab.

- The data in the next-to-the-last column will be used as field names for all fields after the key fields in Crosstab. Be sure the data values are suitable for use as field names.

- The data in the last column will be summed to create the values used to populate Crosstab.

- No other columns will be used to create Crosstab.

Keystroke Equivalent   ALT-X

CSTD(*TableName, FieldName*)

Calculates the standard deviation of nonblank values in *FieldName* of *TableName*.

CSUM(*TableName, FieldName*)

Calculates the sum of nonblank values in *FieldName* of *TableName*. The following example calculates the total of all customer balances:

```
tot_bal = CSUM("custlist", "balance")
```

CTRLBACKSPACE

Erases the contents of the current field.

Keystroke Equivalent   CTRL-BACKSPACE

CTRLBREAK

Interrupts the current operation and returns to the preceding mode. For example, in the middle of a table edit, CTRL-BREAK cancels the edit and returns to the Main mode. In Main mode, CTRL-BREAK behaves like CLEARALL (ALT-F8), and clears all images from the desktop.

Keystroke Equivalent   CTRL-BREAK

CTRLEND

Moves the cursor according to the following guidelines:

Mode	CTRLEND Moves Cursor To
Main/Edit/CoEdit	Last field of record
Field view	Last character in field
Form	End of cursor line on screen
Report	Last character of cursor line
Editor	No movement

Keystroke Equivalent   CTRL-END

CTRLHOME

Moves the cursor according to the following guidelines:

Mode	CTRLHOME Moves Cursor To
Main/Edit/Coedit	First field of record

Mode	CTRLHOME Moves Cursor To
Field view	First character in field
Form	Start of cursor line on screen
Report	First character of cursor line
Editor	No movement

Keystroke Equivalent   CTRL-HOME

CTRLLEFT

Moves the cursor according to the following guidelines:

Mode	CTRLLEFT Moves Cursor To
Table view	One screen to left
Form view	No movement
Field view	Left one word
Form design	No movement
Report design	One screen to left
Editor	Left one word

Keystroke Equivalent   CTRL-LEFT ARROW

CTRLPGDN

Moves the cursor according to the following guidelines:

Mode	CTRLPGDN Moves Cursor To
Form view	Same field of next record
Editor	End of file
All other modes	No movement

Keystroke Equivalent   CTRL-PGDN

CTRLPGUP

Moves the cursor according to the following guidelines:

Mode	CTRLPGUP Moves Cursor To
Form view	Same field of previous record
Editor	Start of file
All other modes	No movement

Keystroke Equivalent   CTRL-PGUP

CTRLRIGHT

Moves the cursor according to the following guidelines:

Mode	CTRLRIGHT Moves Cursor To
Table view	One screen to right
Form view	No movement
Field view	Right one word
Form design	No movement
Report design	One screen to right
Editor	Right one word

Keystroke Equivalent   CTRL-RIGHT ARROW

CURSOR { BAR | BOX | NORMAL | OFF }

Affects the appearance of the canvas cursor.

CURSOR BAR
Displays a box cursor in inverse video.

CURSOR BOX
Displays a box cursor in inverse video (same as CURSOR BAR).

CURSOR NORMAL
Displays the cursor if it was hidden. The cursor shows as a small bar unless you change it with CURSOR BAR or CURSOR BOX.

CURSOR OFF
Both modes: hides the cursor if it was visible.

The following code displays the current time. If the cursor isn't turned off, an annoying flicker occurs.

```
CURSOR OFF
CLEAR
WHILE True
    @10,5 ?? TIME()
    IF CHARWAITING() THEN
        QUITLOOP
    ENDIF
ENDWHILE
CURSOR NORMAL
```

CURSORCHAR()

Reports the character at the current position of the cursor.

CURSORLINE()

Reports the contents of the line the cursor is positioned in.

CVAR(*TableName, FieldName*)

Calculates the variance of nonblank values in *FieldName* of *TableName*.

DATEVAL(*String*)

Calculates a valid date value from a valid *String* representation of the date.

DAY(*DateValue*)

Calculates the number of the day of the month of *DateValue*.

DEBUG

Stops playing the script and calls the Debugger at the command following DEBUG.

DEL

Deletes according to the following guidelines:

Mode	Deletes
Query form	Current line
Table edit/CoEdit	Current record
Form edit/CoEdit	Current record
Field view	Current character
Form design	Current character
Report design	Current character
Editor	Current character, or highlighted selection

Keystroke Equivalent   DELETE

DELETE *TableName*

Erases a data table and its entire family of objects. This doesn't ask for confirmation, so be careful.

Menu Equivalent   Menu {Tools} {Delete} {Table} {OK}

DELETELINE

Erases text according to the following guidelines:

Mode	Deletes
Report design	From cursor to end of line
Editor	Entire current line

Keystroke Equivalent   CTRL-Y

DELETEWORD

In the Editor only, erases from the cursor position through the space preceding the next word.

Keystroke Equivalent   ALT-D

DIRECTORY()

Indicates the DOS path of the directory Paradox is currently using.

DIREXISTS(*DOSPath*)

Indicates whether or not the directory specified by *DOSPath* exists.

DITTO

Duplicates the contents of the same field from the previous record.

Keystroke Equivalent   CTRL-D

DO_IT!

Completes the current operation, saves the results, and performs the requested action, if any.

Keystroke Equivalent   F2

DOS

Shells out to DOS, while keeping Paradox suspended in memory. You can work interactively at the DOS prompt. Type **EXIT** at the DOS prompt to return to Paradox.

Keystroke Equivalent   CTRL-O

Menu Equivalent   Menu {Tools} {More} {ToDOS}

DOSBIG

Shells out to DOS with the maximum amount of memory free, while keeping Paradox suspended in memory. You can work interactively at the DOS prompt. Type **EXIT** at the DOS prompt to return to Paradox.

Keystroke Equivalent   ALT-O

DOW(*DateValue*)

Generates the first three letters of the name of the day of the week that *DateValue* falls on. *DateValue* can be any valid date expression.

For example, the following code displays "Mon":

```
vdate = 6/8/92
?? DOW(vdate)
```

DOWN

Moves the cursor down one line or field, depending on the mode.

Keystroke Equivalent   DOWN ARROW

DOWNIMAGE

Moves the cursor to the next available image.

Keystroke Equivalent   F4

DRIVESPACE(*String*)

Indicates the amount of free space, in bytes, remaining on the drive named by *String*. *String* is a single letter, without a colon. For example, the following code displays the space available on drive D:

```
? DRIVESPACE("d")
```

DRIVESTATUS(*String*)

Indicates a value of True if the drive named by *String* is ready; False if it isn't. *String* is a single letter, without a colon. For example, the following code displays True if drive A is ready; False if it's not:

```
?? DRIVESTATUS("a")
```

DYNARRAY *DynamicArrayName[ ]*

Creates a dyamic array named *DynamicArrayName*. The square brackets are required. The size of a dyamic array changes as needed—in contrast with a fixed array, whose size is fixed when you create it.

Refer to elements of a dynamic array with the syntax,

DynamicArrayName[Index]

where *Index* is any valid PAL expression.

Several PAL commands create dynamic arrays:

EDITOR INFO
ERRORINFO
GETCOLORS
GETEVENT
GETKEYBOARDSTATE
SHOWDIALOG
SYSINFO
WAIT
WINDOW GETATTRIBUTES
WINDOW GETCOLORS

See the specific commands for details.

DYNARRAYSIZE(*DynamicArrayName*)

Indicates the current number of elements in *DynamicArrayName*.

ECHO { FAST | NORMAL | OFF | SLOW }

Determines whether or not the actions of a script are visible.

ECHO FAST
Exhibits the actions of the script currently running, at a speed slower than NORMAL, but faster than SLOW.

ECHO NORMAL
Exhibits the actions of the script currently running, at their normal speed. This is usually much faster than FAST, and might be too fast to be useful in most situations.

ECHO OFF
Hides the actions of the script currently running. This is the default setting of ECHO.

ECHO SLOW
Exhibits the actions of the script currently running, at a very slow speed.

EDIT *TableName*

Lets you change the data in *TableName*. For example, the following code lets you edit data in the CustList table:

```
EDIT "custlist"
```

 COEDIT is usually a better choice, because it checks for key violations as each record is added or changed.

Menu Equivalent   Menu {Modify} {Edit}

EDITKEY

Lets you change data in the table(s) already open on the desktop. EDITKEY only works if Paradox is in Main mode.

The following code places two tables on the desktop and lets you edit both of them:

```
VIEW "orders"
VIEW "products"
EDITKEY
```

Keystroke Equivalent   F9

EDITLOG { INDEX | MARK | PERMANENT | REVERT }

Controls the use of the transaction log maintained for a table during an Edit session.

EDITLOG INDEX
Updates all indexes for the table to speed searches during the Edit session. Changes can still be undone.

EDITLOG MARK
Marks the current spot in the transaction log.

EDITLOG PERMANENT
Updates all indexes for the table and commits all changes made to this point. You can't undo those changes after this.

EDITLOG REVERT
Undoes all changes recorded in the transaction log since the most recent marker was set. If no marker has been set, undoes all changes for the current Edit session.

The following code undoes the changes you've made to the CustList table if you press ALT-U:

```
EDIT "custlist"
WAIT TABLE UNTIL -22, "F2"
IF retval = -22      ; ALT-U
    EDITLOG REVERT
ENDIF
DO_IT!
```

EDITOR EXTRACT TO *VarName*

Copies the highlighted selection in an Editor session and stores it in variable *VarName*.

EDITOR FIND *String*

Finds the first occurrence of *String* in the text currently loaded in the Editor. The search is case sensitive unless you include a wildcard (@ or ..).

Keystroke Equivalent   CTRL-Z

Menu Equivalent   Menu {Search} {Find}

EDITOR FINDNEXT

Finds the next occurrence of the search string used by EDITOR FIND *String* in the text currently loaded in the Editor.

Keystroke Equivalent   ALT-Z

Menu Equivalent   Menu {Search} {Next}

EDITOR GOTO { LINE *Number* | POSITION *CharOffset* }

Places the cursor at a specified location in the current Editor session.

EDITOR GOTO LINE *Number*
Places the cursor at line *Number* in the current Editor session.

EDITOR GOTO POSITION *CharOffset*
Places the cursor at character number *CharOffset* from the beginning of the text in the current Editor session.

EDITOR INFO [COMPLETE] TO *DynamicArrayName*

Stores information about the current editor session in the dynamic array *DynamicArrayName*. COMPLETE includes more information, but might be slow because of the calculations involved.

EDITOR INSERT *Expression*

Copies the value of *Expression* into the current Editor session at the cursor position. The value is written as a string, no matter what the data type of *Expression*.

EDITOR NEW *FileName*

Creates a text file named *FileName*, and loads that file into the text editor. If the specified file already exists, this command will overwrite it with a new file. Use caution.

Keystroke Equivalent   ALT-E

Menu Equivalent   Menu Home {Editor} {New} (You have to press the HOME key to access the System pull-down menu.) Or, use [ALT-SPACEBAR] {Editor} {New}

EDITOR OPEN *FileName*

Opens an Editor session using file *FileName*. If the file doesn't already exist, use EDITOR NEW instead.

Keystroke Equivalent   ALT-E {Open}

Menu Equivalent   Menu (HOME) {Editor} {Open} (You have to press the HOME key to access the System pull-down menu.)

EDITOR READ *FileName*

Inserts the contents of file *FileName* into the current Editor session at the cursor position.

Menu Equivalent   Menu {File} {Read}

EDITOR REPLACE *String1* *String2*

Finds all occurrences of *String1* in the text currently loaded in the Editor, and replaces them with *String2*. The search starts at the current cursor position and is case sensitive unless you include a wildcard (@ or ..).

Menu Equivalent   Menu {Search} {**R**eplace}

EDITOR SELECT *StartLoc EndLoc*

Selects a section in the current Editor session beginning with the character at position *StartLoc* and ending with the character at position *EndLoc*.

Keystroke Equivalent   SHIFT plus cursor movement keys

EDITOR WRITE *FileName*

Copies the contents of the selected area of the current Editor session into file *FileName*. This overwrites an existing file of the same name.

Menu Equivalent   Menu {**F**ile} {**W**riteblock} {**R**eplace}

EMPTY *TableName*

Removes all records from table *TableName*. EMPTY doesn't ask you to confirm the action, so be careful.

Menu Equivalent   Menu {**T**ools} {**M**ore} {**E**mpty} {**OK**}

END

Moves the cursor according to the following guidelines:

Mode	END Moves Cursor To
Main/Edit/CoEdit	Last record of image
Field view	Last character in field
Form	Last line on form
Report	Last line on report
Editor	Last character of current line

Keystroke Equivalent   END

ENTER

Has the following actions:

Mode	Action
Main/Edit/CoEdit	Advances one field
Field view	Ends field view
Forms designer	Advances to next line
	If Insert is on, splits the current line
Reports designer	Advances to next line
	If Insert is on, splits the current line
Editor	Advances to next line
	If Insert is on, splits the current line
Any mode	Selects highlighted menu item
Any mode	Completes current dialog

Keystroke Equivalent   ENTER

EOT()

EOT() generates a value of True if a SKIP or MOVETO command tries to move to a record that would be after the last record of the current image. If the move stays within the allowable records in the image, EOT() generates a value of False.

ERRORCODE()

Stores a number that indicates the type of error that most recently occurred. If no errors have occurred, ERRORCODE() contains the value 0 (zero).

ERRORINFO TO *DynamicArrayName*

Stores information about the most recent script error in the dynamic array named *DynamicArrayName*. You can examine this information for troubleshooting. The array contains the following elements:

Array Element	Description
SCRIPT	The name of the PAL script where the error occurred
LINE	The line number in the script that caused the error

Array Element	Description
POSITION	The character position in the line that caused the error
CODE	The code number of the most recent error; ERRORCODE() returns the same number
USER	The name of the user who has placed a lock on the object involved in the error; ERRORUSER() returns the same value
MESSAGE	The text of the most recent error message; ERRORMESSAGE() returns the same value
PROC	The name of the PROC currently running; blank if no procedure is running
SQLERRORMESSAGE	The text of the most recent SQL error message generated by the database server. If SQL Link is not active, or if no SQL error has occurred, this value is blank. The SQLERRORMESSAGE() function returns the same value.
SQLERRORCODE	The code number of the most recent SQL error generated by the database server. If SQL Link is not active, or if no SQL error has occurred, this value is blank. The SQLERRORCODE() function returns the same value.

ERRORMESSAGE()

Stores the message of the most recent error. If no errors have occurred, ERRORMESSAGE() contains a null string.

ERRORUSER()

Stores the name of the user who has locked a Paradox object.

ESC

Moves backward one level in a menu. If already at the top menu level, exits the menu and returns to the desktop.

Keystroke Equivalent   ESC

EXAMPLE

Lets you place an example element in the current query image.

Keystroke Equivalent   F5

EXECEVENT *DynamicArrayName*

Performs the event described in the dynamic array named *DynamicArrayName*. The event description must adhere to certain standards, which vary with the type of event. EXECEVENT is useful in situations where you've trapped an event, examined it, possibly altered it, and then want Paradox to perform the intended action.

Assume the dynamic array *SaveEvent* contains two elements for a KEY event:

```
SaveEvent["TYPE"] = "KEY"
SaveEvent["KEYCODE"] = 65
```

The following code simulates typing the letter *A*:

```
EXECEVENT SaveEvent
```

EXECPROC *ProcName*

Executes procedure *ProcName*. The procedure can't have any arguments. EXEC-PROC *ProcName* does the same thing as EXECUTE ProcName + "()", but it performs faster. If you need to call a procedure with arguments, you must use EXECUTE. EXECPROC is especially useful if you want to call a procedure whose name is stored in a table or an array. Used with dynamic arrays, EXECPROC and EXECUTE let you build very flexible program systems.

EXECUTE *Commands*

Performs a series of commands that can be generated during the processing of a script. This lets you create and execute commands on the fly. You could, for instance, let the user pick values from one or more menus, then build a command with those values and use EXECUTE to execute it. You can also use EXECUTE to perform a command that Paradox might otherwise misunderstand. For example,

```
x = "First Name"
MOVETO [x]
```

would attempt to move the cursor to the field named "X". To move to the field "First Name", the following would work:

```
x = "First Name"
EXECUTE "MOVETO [" + x + "]"
```

EXIT

Ends all processing, closes Paradox, and returns to the operating system.

EXP(*Number*)

Calculates the value that has *Number* as its natural logarithm.
In the following example, x gets assigned a value of 10.0:

```
x = EXP(2.303)
```

FAMILYRIGHTS() *TableName, String*

Indicates if you have rights to create or change the object specified by *String* for *TableName*. If you have the requested rights, FAMILYRIGHTS() has a value of True, otherwise it has a value of False. *String* can have the following values:

Value	Object Referenced
F	Form
R	Report
S	Image settings
V	Validity checks

FIELD()

Indicates the name of the currently selected field.

FIELDINFO()

Indicates the current contents of the field indicator in Form mode or Report mode. The field indicator contains the name and attributes of the currently selected field.

FIELDNO(*FieldName, TableName*)

Indicates the numeric position of field *FieldName* in table *TableName*.

FIELDRIGHTS(*TableName, FieldName, String*)

Indicates if you have rights to read or change field *FieldName* in table *TableName*. If you have the requested rights, FIELDRIGHTS() has a value of True, otherwise it has a value of False. *String* can be either "ReadOnly" or "All".

FIELDSTR()

Generates a string containing the current contents of the field at the cursor.

FIELDTYPE()

Indicates the data type of the current field.

FIELDVIEW

Lets the user edit within the contents of the current field.

Keystroke Equivalents   ALT-F5, CTRL-F

FILEREAD [BINARY] *FileName* TO *VarName*

Stores the contents of file *FileName* into variable *VarName*. If *VarName* doesn't exist, FILEREAD creates it. FILEREAD alone converts each CR/LF pair to a single LF character. The BINARY option leaves the CR/LF pairs unchanged.

FILESIZE(*FileName*)

Calculates the size of file *FileName* in bytes, rounded up to include the unused space in the last cluster occupied by the file.

FILEVERSION({ *TableName* | *LibraryName* })

Indicates the version of Paradox used to create table *TableName* or library *LibraryName*.

FILEWRITE [BINARY] [APPEND] *FileName* FROM *Expression*

Stores the contents of *Expression* into *FileName*. If *FileName* doesn't exist, FILEWRITE creates it. If *FileName* already exists, FILEWRITE will overwrite the original file, unless the command includes the APPEND option. FILEWRITE converts CR/LF pairs to a single LF character, unless you include the BINARY option. The BINARY option leaves the CR/LF pairs unchanged.

FILL(*Expression, Number*)

Generates a string of length *Number*, filled with the first character of *Expression*. *Expression* is usually a single character. The following code displays a line of 50 asterisks:

```
? FILL("*",50)
```

FIRSTSHOW()

Moves the current table image to the top of the screen, no matter how many display rows are in the image. FIRSTSHOW() works only in compatibility mode.

FOR...ENDFOR

Performs commands a specified number of times. For example,

```
FOR VarName [ FROM Value1 ] [ TO Value2 ][ STEP Number ]
    Commands
ENDFOR
```

performs a set of *Commands* the number of times indicated by the optional parameters.

Parameter	Meaning
VarName	Stores the current value of the counter controlling the loop
Value1	The starting value of the counter. If you leave out FROM *Value1*, the initial value of the counter is determined by the current value of *VarName*.
Value2	The ending value of the counter. If you leave out TO *Value2*, the loop will run forever.
Number	The value used to increment the counter. *Number* can be positive or negative. If you leave out STEP *Number*, Paradox increments the counter by 1 (one) each time through the loop.

Parameter	Meaning
Commands	The commands to execute on each pass through the loop

The following code displays the squares of the even numbers from 6 through 16:

```
FOR x FROM 6 TO 16 STEP 2
    ? x, SPACES(5), x*x
ENDFOR
```

FOREACH...ENDFOREACH

Performs commands on the elements in a dynamic array. For example,

```
FOREACH VarName IN DynamicArrayName
    Commands
ENDFOREACH
```

performs the *Commands* for each element of dynamic array *DynamicArrayName*. As FOREACH processes each element of the array, the index value of that array element gets assigned to *VarName*. The *Commands* can then process the contents of the array element whose index value is stored in *VarName*.

The following code creates a dynamic array that contains information about the current keyboard state, then displays the contents of the array:

```
GETKEYBOARDSTATE TO keyarray
FOR EACH item IN keyarray
    ? keyarray[item]
ENDFOREACH
```

FORM()

Indicates the name of the form currently in use. If a form is in use, FORM() will have a value of "F" or "1" through "14". If a table is on the desktop, but no form is active, FORM() is assigned a value of "None". If no table is on the desktop, or if the current image is not in a display mode, an error occurs.

FORMAT(*FormatSpec, Expression*)

Formats *Expression* according to the specifications of *FormatSpec*. FORMAT() gives you great control over the appearance of output. The data type of *Expression* determines the allowable values of *FormatSpec*.

FORMKEY

Toggles between displaying data in form view and table view.

Keystroke Equivalent   F7

FORMTABLES *TableName FormName ArrayName*

Creates a fixed array *ArrayName*, containing the names of the tables embedded in form *FormName* of table *TableName*. If form *FormName* has embedded tables, Paradox creates and dimensions the array, and sets Retval to True. If there are no embedded forms in *FormName*, no array is created, and Retval gets set to False.

FORMTYPE(*String*)

Indicates if the current form is of the type specified by *String*. Only one of four possible values is permitted for *String*: "MultiRecord", "Linked", "Detail", "DisplayOnly". Any given form can be various combinations of these form types, so you'll probably have to evaluate FORMTYPE() for each possible value of *String*.

FRAME [SINGLE | DOUBLE] FROM *Row1, Col1* TO *Row2, Col2*

Draws a frame on the current canvas, from position *Row1, Col1* to position *Row2, Col2* of the active window. The frame has a single-line border unless you include the keyword DOUBLE.

FV(*Payment, Rate, Periods*)

Calculates the future value of *Periods* equal payments, each of amount *Payment*, invested at an interest rate of *Rate* per period. You must express *Rate* as a decimal (for instance, express 8.5 percent as 0.085).

GETCANVAS()

Indicates the handle of the window that will be the target of commands that write to the canvas. The handle is a unique number that Paradox assigns to each window you create. If you have multiple windows open on the desktop, GETCANVAS() lets you keep track of where screen output will go.

GETCHAR()

Reports the numeric keycode value of the next character read from the keyboard. This can be an ASCII value or an extended keycode value.

The following code displays the keycode of the key pressed. When the user presses capital "Q", the loop terminates:

```
WHILE True
    keycode = GETCHAR()
    @12,20 ?? SPACES(5)
    @12,20 ?? keycode
    IF keycode = ASC("Q") THEN
            QUITLOOP
    ENDIF      ; keycode = asc("Q")
ENDWHILE
```

GETCOLORS TO *DynamicArrayName*

Stores the attributes of the current color palette into dynamic array *DynamicArrayName*. Each array element contains one attribute of the palette.

GETEVENT [*EventList*] TO *DynamicArrayName*

Traps one of the events specified in *EventList*. Information about the event is stored in the dynamic array specified by *DynamicArrayName*. You can alter the array elements or use them as is. Use the EXECEVENT command to execute the trapped event.

EventList is one or more of the following events:

- ALL

- MOUSE { ["ALL"] | ["UP" | "DOWN" | "MOVE" | "AUTO"] }

- KEY { ["ALL"] | [KeyValueList] }

- MESSAGE { ["ALL"] | [| "CLOSE" | "MAXIMIZE" | "NEXT" | "MENUSELECT" | "MENUKEY"] }

- IDLE

GETKEYBOARDSTATE TO *DynamicArrayName*

Stores information about the current state of each SHIFT, ALT, CTRL, and lock key into the dynamic array specified by *DynamicArrayName*. For each key, the array contains True if the key is on, False if it's not.

GETMENUSELECTION [KEYTO *KeyVar*] TO *MenuSelVar*

Used with a SHOWPULLDOWN command, GETMENUSELECTION stores the value of the tag of the highlighted menu option in the variable *MenuSelVar*. If the user presses the ESC key, *MenuSelVar* contains the word "Esc". If "Esc" is one of the items in the SHOWPULLDOWN keycode list, *MenuSelVar* receives the menu option tag. If the user presses one of the keys specified in the keycode list, and you use the KEYTO *KeyVar* option here, *KeyVar* receives the numeric value of the key. If the user doesn't press any of the keys in the keycode list, *KeyVar* contains the value False.

GETWINDOW()

Reports the handle of the current window. A handle is a unique number that Paradox assigns to each window.

GRAPHKEY

Creates a graph of the table currently active on the screen.

Keystroke Equivalent   CTRL-F7

GRAPHTYPE()

Identifies the type of graph that GRAPHKEY will display.

GROUPBY

Toggles the Groupby symbol in the current field in the active query image. The Groupby symbol groups records in an answer table by values in the current field in the query image, but doesn't display values from the field.

Keystroke Equivalent   SHIFT-F6

HELP

Activates the Paradox on-line Help system.

Keystroke Equivalent   F1

HELPMODE()

Indicates what type of help is being displayed, if any. HELPMODE() can return any one of the following values:

Helpmode()	Meaning
"Help"	Regular help screen
"Lookup"	TableLookup valcheck screen
"None"	No help screen active

HOME

Moves the cursor according to the following guidelines:

Mode	HOME Moves Cursor To
Main/Edit/CoEdit	First record of image
Field view	First character in field
Form	First line on form
Report	First line on report
Editor	First character of current line

Keystroke Equivalent   HOME

IF...ENDIF

Executes commands only if specified conditions are true. IF...ENDIF executes *Commands1* if *Condition* is True. If *Condition* is False, and if the ELSE option exists, it executes *Commands2* instead.

```
IF Condition THEN
     Commands1
[ ELSE
     Commands2 ]
ENDIF
```

The following code chooses between printing two letter types, depending on the customer's balance:

```
VIEW "custlist"
SCAN
     IF [balance] > "1000" THEN
```

```
        PLAY "dunn_ltr"      ; print dunning letter
ELSE
        PLAY "thnk_ltr"      ; print thanks letter
ENDIF
```

IIF(*Condition, ValueIfTrue, ValueIfFalse*)

IIF returns *ValueIfTrue* if *Condition* is True. If *Condition* is False, IIF returns *ValueIfFalse*. For example, in a report, use the following expression to print "Okay" or "Not Okay":

```
IIF([credit rating] > 3, "Okay", "Not Okay")
```

IMAGECAVERAGE()

Calculates the arithmetic average of the nonblank values in the current column in the current image. If used in a linked detail table in a multitable form, IMAGECAVER-AGE() respects the bounds of the subset of data displayed for the detail table.

IMAGECCOUNT()

Counts the number of nonblank values in the current column in the current image. If used in a linked detail table in a multitable form, IMAGECCOUNT() respects the bounds of the subset of data displayed for the detail table.

IMAGECMAX()

Determines the highest nonblank value in the current column in the current image. Gives an error if all the entries are blank. If used in a linked detail table in a multitable form, IMAGECMAX() respects the bounds of the subset of data displayed for the detail table.

IMAGECMIN()

Determines the lowest nonblank value in the current column in the current image. Gives an error if all the entries are blank. If used in a linked detail table in a multitable form, IMAGECMIN() respects the bounds of the subset of data displayed for the detail table.

IMAGECSUM()

Calculates the sum of the nonblank values in the current column in the current image. Gives an error if all the entries are blank. If used in a linked detail table in a multitable form, IMAGECSUM() respects the bounds of the subset of data displayed for the detail table.

IMAGENO()

Reports the position number (1,2,3,...) of the current image.

IMAGERIGHTS [{ UPDATE | READONLY }]

Lets you set or remove access restrictions to the current table, on a temporary basis.

IMAGERIGHTS UPDATE
Restricts the user to changing data in non-key fields. The user cannot add or delete records.

IMAGERIGHTS READONLY
Restricts the user to reading data, with no changes allowed.

IMAGERIGHTS by Itself
Removes access restrictions that were set by IMAGERIGHTS UPDATE or IMAGERIGHTS READONLY. IMAGERIGHTS cannot remove access restrictions imposed by the password system.

IMAGETYPE()

Indicates what type of image is currently active. The result is "Display", "Query", or "None".

INDEX

Builds a secondary index for a table, using one or more fields of the table. There are two forms of the index command.

Use the following form to build a secondary index on a single field.

```
INDEX [ MAINTAINED ] TableName
  [ LABEL LabelName ]
  [ CASESENSITIVE ]
ON FieldName
```

Use the following form to build a secondary index on multiple fields.

```
INDEX  [ MAINTAINED ] TableName
  LABEL LabelName
```

```
[ CASESENSITIVE ]
ON FieldNameList
```

Here are the parameters for the INDEX command:

Parameter	Meaning
TableName	The name of the table to index
MAINTAINED	Tells Paradox to update the index whenever you change data in the table
LABEL	Lets you assign a name to an index
LabelName	The name for the index. The name can be up to 25 characters long. It must be unique among all the indexes for a single table.
CASESENSITIVE	Tells Paradox to make the index case sensitive (in ASCII order rather than dictionary order)
FieldName	The name of the field to use for a single-field index
FieldNameList	A list of up to 16 field names, separated by commas

The following code creates a maintained index to use in mailing bulk-rate junk mail to our customers:

```
INDEX MAINTAINED "custlist" LABEL "BulkRate" ON "zip code",
                 "last name", "first name"
```

INFOLIB *LibraryName*

Creates a temporary table named List containing the name and size of each procedure in the library defined by *LibraryName*.

INS

INS behaves according to the following guidelines:

Mode	INS Action
Query form	Inserts a blank row
Edit	Inserts a blank record
CoEdit	Inserts a blank record
DataEntry	Inserts a blank record
Create	Inserts a blank field specification
Restructure	Inserts a blank field specification

Mode	INS Action
Field view	Toggles Insert/Overwrite
Form design	Toggles Insert/Overwrite
Report design	Toggles Insert/Overwrite
Editor	Toggles Insert/Overwrite

Keystroke Equivalent   INS

INSTANTPLAY

Plays the script named Instant.

Keystroke Equivalent   ALT-F4

INSTANTREPORT

Prints an instant report. The report produced depends on the mode, according to the following table:

Mode	Action
View	Prints report "R" for the current table
Report designer	Prints data using the current report
Editor	Prints the text file being edited

Keystroke Equivalent   ALT-F7

INT(*Number*)

Calculates the integer value of *Number*.

ISASSIGNED(*VarName*)

Tests for the existence of *VarName*. Returns a value of True or False. Returns True even if *VarName* has a blank value.

ISBLANK(*Expression*)

Returns True if *Expression* evaluates to a blank value.

ISBLANKZERO()

Indicates whether the Blank=Zero option is currently on (True) or off (False).

ISEMPTY(*TableName*)

Indicates if the table specifed by *TableName* contains any records. Returns True if the table is empty, False if it contains records.

ISENCRYPTED(*TableName*)

Returns True if the table specifed by *TableName* is encrypted (password protected); False if it's not.

ISFIELDVIEW()

Returns True if field view is currently active.

ISFILE(*String*)

Returns True if the file specifed by *String* exists.

ISFORMVIEW()

Returns True if the current image is a form view.

ISINSERTMODE()

Returns True if Insert mode is turned on, False if Overwrite mode is active.

ISLINKLOCKED()

Returns True if the current table has a link lock. A link lock is applied to each of the tables being edited through a multitable form. As long as a table is link locked, the user can change that table only through the form.

ISMASTER(*TableName, MasterPassword*)

Tests the table specified by *TableName* to see if it's password protected, and if the password specified by *MasterPassword* is the master password for the table.

ISMULTIFORM(*TableName, FormName*)

Returns a value of True if *FormName* of *TableName* is a multitable form; returns False if it's not.

ISMULTIREPORT(*TableName, ReportName*)

Returns a value of True if *ReportName* of *TableName* is a multitable report (contains linked lookup tables). It returns False if it's not.

ISRUNTIME()

Returns a value of True if Paradox Runtime is running. Returns False if regular Paradox is running.

ISSHARED(*TableName*)

Returns a value of True if table *TableName* resides in a shared network directory that is not the user's private directory. Returns False if the table resides in the user's private directory or in a local directory. Generates an error if *TableName* doesn't exist or if it resides in a private directory belonging to another user.

ISTABLE(*TableName*)

Generates a value of True if *TableName* exists. Generates False if can't find a table with the specified name.

ISVALID()

In Edit or CoEdit mode only, checks the current field to see if its contents would pass all relevant validity checks. Generates a value of True if they would, False if they wouldn't. In any mode other than Edit or CoEdit, ISVALID() always generates a value of True.

ISWINDOW(*WindowHandle*)

Checks the value of *WindowHandle* to see if it's the handle of one of the active windows. A handle is a unique number that Paradox assigns to each window. Generates a value of True if the *WindowHandle* is valid, False if it's not.

KEYLOOKUP

If a key violation occurs in CoEdit mode KEYLOOKUP finds the record that has the same key as the record you're trying to save. This lets you correct conflicts between the two records.

KEYPRESS *Keycode*

Passes to Paradox the character represented by *Keycode*. *Keycode* can be any expression that evaluates to an ASCII code, a function key name, IBM extended codes, special key names, or a single character.

LEFT

The effect of LEFT varies with the Paradox mode:

Mode	LEFT Moves Cursor
Table view	One field left. If at leftmost field, moves to last field of previous row.
Form view	One field left or up
Field view	One character left
Form designer	One character left
Report designer	One character left
Editor	One character left

Keystroke Equivalent   LEFT ARROW

LEN(*Expression*)

Calculates the length of a text representation of *Expression*.

LINKTYPE()

On a multitable form, LINKTYPE() indicates the type of relationship between the master table and the current detail table. LINKTYPE() can generate the following values:

Value	Type of Relationship
"1-1 Group"	One-to-one

Value	Type of Relationship
"1-M Group"	One-to-many
"Group"	Many-to-many
"None"	No link, or not a multitable form

LN(*Number*)

Calculates the natural logarithm of *Number*. For example, the following command assigns x a value of 2.302585....

```
x = LN(10)
```

LOCALIZEEVENT *DynamicArrayName*

Calculates the coordinates of a mouse event relative to the current window, given coordinates relative to the whole screen. *DynamicArrayName* is the name of a dynamic array created by GETEVENT, containing information about the mouse event. In particular, the array elements with indexes of "ROW" and "COL" are affected by LOCALIZEEVENT.

LOCATE

Locates a record having specified field value(s).

LOCATE [NEXT] [PATTERN] *FieldValue*
Locates a record having the specified *FieldValue* in the current field. If NEXT is used, the search starts with the current record, otherwise the search starts from the first record. PATTERN lets you include the wildcards .. and @. The search is case sensitive, unless you include the PATTERN keyword.

LOCATE [NEXT] *FieldValueList*
Locates a record that has field values that match the values in *FieldValueList*. The fields must be at the beginning of the table structure, and must match the contents of *FieldValueList* in both order and number. If NEXT is used, the search starts with the current record, otherwise the search starts from the first record. If you include NEXT, be sure to move to the next record with DOWN first. If you don't, you'll keep finding the same record.

For either form, Paradox sets Retval to True if LOCATE succeeds; False if it doesn't.

The following code displays the names of the customers who live in Seattle:

```
VIEW "custlist"
MOVETO [city]
LOCATE "Seattle"
WHILE retval
   ? [last name] + ", " + [first name]
   IF ATLAST() THEN
       QUITLOOP
   ENDIF
   DOWN
   LOCATE NEXT "Seattle"
ENDWHILE
```

LOCATE INDEXORDER

Locates records using values in secondary indexes.

LOCATE INDEXORDER [BY *LabelName*] NEXT | PREV] [PATTERN] *FieldValue*

Locates a record that has the specified *FieldValue* in the current field. If BY *LabelName* is used, the search is performed using the secondary index specified by *LabelName*. If NEXT or PREV is used, Paradox searches forward or backward, respectively, from the current record; otherwise, the search starts from the first record. PATTERN lets you include the wildcards (.. and @). The search is case sensitive, unless you include the PATTERN keyword.

LOCATE INDEXORDER [BY *LabelName*] [NEXT | PREV] *FieldValueList*

Locates a record that has field values that match the values in *FieldValueList*. If BY *LabelName* is used, the fields must occur at the beginning of the index structure. If BY *LabelName* is omitted, the fields must occur at the beginning of the table structure. In either case, the fields must match the contents of *FieldValueList* in both order and number. If NEXT or PREV is used, Paradox searches forward or backward, respectively, from the current record; otherwise the search starts from the first record.

LOCATE INDEXORDER [BY *LabelName*] BESTMATCH *FieldValue*

Locates the first record that has a value that matches or exceeds the specified *FieldValue* in the current field. If BY *LabelName* is used, the search is performed using the secondary index specified by *LabelName*.

LOCATE INDEXORDER [BY *LabelName*] BESTMATCH *FieldValueList*

Locates the first record that has field values that match or exceed the values in *FieldValueList*. If BY *LabelName* is used, the fields must occur at the beginning of the index structure. If BY *LabelName* is omitted, the fields must occur at the beginning of the table structure. In either case, the fields must match the contents of *FieldValueList* in both order and number.

LOCATE INDEXORDER [BY *LabelName*] { FIRST | LAST }

Locates either the FIRST or LAST record in the current field. If BY *LabelName* is used, the search is performed using the secondary index specified by *LabelName*. If BY *LabelName* is omitted, Paradox performs the search using a suitable secondary index for the current field. If none is available, the current record remains the same.

In all forms, Paradox assigns True to Retval if LOCATE succeeds; False if it doesn't.

For example, if CustList has an index for the last name, the following code will display the first occurrence of a person whose last name is Smith or later, alphabetically:

```
VIEW "custlist"
MOVETO [last name]
LOCATE INDEXORDER BESTMATCH "Smith"
? [last name] + "," + [first name] ":" + [balance]
```

LOCK *LockList*

Places locks on the tables specified in *LockList*. *LockList* has the form *TableName1 LockType1, TableName2 LockType2, ..., TableNameN LockTypeN*. *TableName* is any valid table name, and *LockType* is one of the following values:

LockType	Meaning
FL	Full lock
WL	Write lock
PFL	Prevent full lock
PWL	Prevent write lock

If LOCK successfully locks all the tables in *LockList*, Retval is set to True; otherwise Retval is set to False.

The following code attempts to place a write lock on the CustList table:

```
LOCK "custlist" WL
```

LOCKKEY

Locks/unlocks the current record. Works only in CoEdit mode.

Keystroke Equivalent   ALT-L

LOCKRECORD

Locks the current record. Works only in CoEdit mode.

LOCKSTATUS(*TableName, LockType*)

Reports how many times a table has been locked. *TableName* is any valid table name, and *LockType* is one of the following values:

LockType	Meaning
FL	Full lock
WL	Write lock
PFL	Prevent full lock
PWL	Prevent write lock
ANY	Any of the lock types listed

LOG(*Number*)

Calculates the base 10 logarithm of *Number*.

LOOP

Returns to the beginning of the current FOR, FOREACH, SCAN, or WHILE loop without processing commands occurring later in the loop.

The following code waits for the user to press a key. If the user types **L**, the program proceeds to the next iteration of the FOR loop. Any other key results in playing script Letters, for example:

```
FOR counter FROM 1 TO 10
    x = GETCHAR()
    IF x = ASC("L")
        LOOP
    ENDIF
    PLAY "letters"
ENDFOR
```

LOWER(*Expression*)

Converts *Expression* to lowercase characters.

MATCH(*String, PatternString [, VarNameList]*)

Searches the contents of *String* for substrings that match *PatternString*. *PatternString* can contain wildcards (.. and @). If you include a list of variables, *VarNameList*, any parts of *String* that match the wildcards will be assigned to the variables, in sequence.

The following code tests whether we stock any products whose descriptions end in the word "tape". If so it displays the type of tape.

```
VIEW "products"
SCAN
    x = MATCH([description], "..tape", tapetype)
    IF x THEN
        ? tapetype
    ENDIF
ENDSCAN
```

MAX(*Number1, Number2*)

Identifies which of two numeric expressions has the larger numeric value.

MEMLEFT()

Measures the amount of free memory left, in bytes, for PAL applications.

MENU

Displays the Paradox menu for the current mode. MENU appears first in a sequence of menu commands used to perform actions that have no counterpart in PAL.

Keystroke Equivalent   F10

MENUCHOICE()

If a Paradox menu is active, MENUCHOICE() indicates which menu item is currently highlighted. If no menu is active, MENUCHOICE() returns the word "Error".

MENUDISABLE *Tag*

Disables a menu item in a SHOWPULLDOWN menu. Each menu item is identified by its own tag, which you assign when you create the menu item. *Tag* in this command identifies which menu item to disable. A disabled menu item shows on the menu, but it's grayed out and it doesn't respond.

MENUENABLE *Tag*

Enables a menu item in a SHOWPULLDOWN menu. Each menu item is identified by its own tag, which you assign when you create the menu item. *Tag* in this command identifies which menu item to enable. An enabled menu item shows on the menu, and it responds when the user selects it.

MENUPROMPT()

Reports the prompt being displayed by the current menu dialog box. If no dialog box is displayed, MENUPROMPT() reports a value of "Error".

MESSAGE *ExpressionList*

Displays the contents of *ExpressionList* as a message. The message appears in the lower-right corner of the screen.

MIN(*Number1, Number2*)

Identifies which of two numeric expressions has the smaller numeric value.

MINIEDIT

Activates the Editor menu, to edit a text file.

Keystroke Equivalent   ALT-E

Menu Equivalents   Menu HOME {Editor} or ALT-SPACEBAR {Editor}

MOD(*Number1, Number2*)

Calculates the remainder left when *Number1* is divided by *Number2*.

MONITOR()

Indicates the current type of monitor. The result is either "Mono", "B&W", or "Color".

MONTH(*DateValue*)

Calculates the numeric value of the month of *DateValue*.

MOUSE CLICK [LEFT | RIGHT | BOTH] *Row, Column*

Simulates clicking the indicated mouse button(s) at screen location *Row, Column*. If you don't specify a mouse button, Paradox uses LEFT.

MOUSE DOUBLECLICK [LEFT | RIGHT | BOTH] *Row, Column*

Simulates double-clicking the indicated mouse button(s) at screen location *Row, Column*. If you don't specify a mouse button, Paradox uses LEFT.

MOUSE DRAG [LEFT | RIGHT | BOTH] FROM *Row1, Column1* TO *Row2, Column2*

Simulates holding down the indicated mouse button(s) at screen location *Row1, Column1*, and dragging the mouse cursor to screen location *Row2, Column2*. If you don't specify a mouse button, Paradox uses LEFT.

MOUSE HIDE

Hides the mouse cursor, deactivating the mouse. While MOUSE HIDE is in effect, Paradox ignores mouse actions and mouse simulation commands.

MOUSE SHOW

Shows the mouse cursor, activating the mouse. This reverses the effect of the MOUSE HIDE command.

MOVETO

Moves the cursor to the specified field, record, or image. There are five variations of the **MOVETO** command.

MOVETO *FieldSpec*
Moves the cursor to the specified field in either the current or another image. *FieldSpec* must be a valid field specifier.

```
MOVETO [last name]
```

MOVETO *Image*
Moves the cursor to the image indicated by *Image*. If the desktop contains more than one image for the same table, the cursor moves to the first image placed for that table.

```
MOVETO "products"
```

MOVETO *Number*
Moves the cursor to the image indicated by *Number*. The images are numbered in the order they're placed on the desktop.

```
MOVETO 4
```

MOVETO FIELD *FieldName*
Moves the cursor to the field named in the string *FieldName* in the current image.

```
vfield = "city"
MOVETO FIELD vfield
```

MOVETO RECORD *Number*
Moves the cursor to the record specified by *Number* in the current image. If the cursor is in a linked detail table in a multi-table form, the records are numbered within that detail list, not within the entire table.

```
MOVETO RECORD 16
```

MOY(*DateValue*)

Calculates the first three letters of the name of the month of *DateValue*.

NETTYPE()

Indicates the type of network that Paradox is running on, if any.

NEWDIALOGSPEC *EventList*

Activates a new event list for the current dialog procedure, to dynamically change the actions of the dialog.

NEWWAITSPEC *EventList*

Activates a new event list for the current WAIT procedure, to dynamically change the actions of the WAIT.

NFIELDS(*TableName*)

Reports the number of fields in the table specified by *TableName*.

NIMAGERECORDS()

Indicates the number of records in the current image or restricted view.

NIMAGES()

Indicates the number of images currently on the desktop. If the embedded tables in a multitable form are already on the desktop, NIMAGES() doesn't count them again.

NKEYFIELDS(*TableName*)

Indicates the number of key fields in the table specified by *TableName*.

NPAGES()

For a form, NPAGES() indicates the total number of pages in the form currently active on the desktop. Embedded forms of a multitable form always show NPAGES() = 1.

For a report, NPAGES() indicates the total number of page widths in the report specification currently showing in the Report Designer.

NRECORDS(*TableName*)

Indicates the number of records in the table specified by *TableName*.

NROWS()

In view or query mode, NROWS() indicates the number of rows in the current display or query image.

In the Report Designer, NROWS() indicates the total number of rows in the report specification currently showing.

NUMVAL(*String*)

Converts a *String* representation of a valid number into the corresponding numeric value.

OPEN PRINTER

Opens the currently selected printer port to receive output. OPEN PRINTER is useful only on a network.

Be sure to issue the CLOSE PRINTER command at the end of the print job.

ORDERTABLE

Displays a list box containing the name of the current field and the names of maintained or multi-field indexes available for the current image. If you pick one of these, the data in the image will appear in the selected order.

Keystroke Equivalent   ALT-S

PAGENO()

For a form, PAGENO() indicates the current page number in the form currently active on the desktop. Embedded forms of a multitable form always show PAGENO() = 1.

For a report, NPAGES() indicates the number of the page width the cursor is currently on.

PAGEWIDTH()

Indicates the page width, in characters, of the report currently loaded into the Report Designer.

PAINTCANVAS

Paints an area on the canvas.

```
PAINTCANVAS [ BORDER ] [ FILL String ]
{ MonoOptionList | ATTRIBUTE Number | BACKGROUND }
{ Row1, Column1, Row2, Column2 | ALL }
```

PAINTCANVAS uses the following parameters:

Parameter	Meaning
BORDER	Paints a one-character border around the area
FILL *String*	Fills the area with the contents of *String*
MonoOptionList	One or more of BLINK, INTENSE, and REVERSE
ATTRIBUTE *Number*	Use the color attribute specified by *Number*
BACKGROUND	Change only the FILL string
Row1, Column1	The top-left coordinates of the area
Row2, Column2	The bottom-right coordinates of the area
ALL	Use the entire canvas

PASSWORD *PasswordList*

Supplies the words in *PasswordList* as passwords to use in the current Paradox session, or until they're removed from use. If you attempt to use a protected table, Paradox will check to see if any word in *PasswordList* is a valid password for the table. If one of the words matches, you can use the table; if none of the words is valid, Paradox will ask you to type a valid password for the table.

PGDN

Moves the cursor according to the following guidelines:

Mode	PGDN Moves the Cursor
Table	Down one screenful of records
Multirecord form	Down one screenful of records
Single-record form	Down one record or form page
Form designer	To next page of form
Report designer	Down one-half screen
Editor	Down one window-full of lines

Keystroke Equivalent   PGDN

PGUP

Moves the cursor according to the following guidelines:

Mode	PGUP Moves the Cursor
Table	Up one screenful of records
Multi-record form	Up one screenful of records
Single-record form	Up one record or form page
Form designer	Previous page of form
Report designer	Up one-half screen
Editor	Up one window-full of lines

Keystroke Equivalent   PGUP

PI()

Supplies the value of pi (3.1415...).

PICKFORM *FormName*

Activates the form specified by *FormName* to use with the current display image. *FormName* is an expression that results in "F" or "1" through "14".

PLAY *ScriptName*

Runs the script specified by *ScriptName*.

PMT(*Amount, Rate, Term*)

Calculates the payment due in each period for a loan of *Amount*, at interest of *Rate* per period, for *Term* number of periods. The loan is assumed to be a standard amortization-type loan.

Parameter	Meaning
Amount	The amount of the loan.
Rate	The interest rate per period, expressed as a decimal value; for instance, express 1.5% as 0.015
Term	The number of payment periods in the life of the loan

POSTRECORD [*KeyViolAction* [LEAVELOCKED]]

Posts a record to a table if there is no key violation. If there is a key violation, *KeyViolaction* indicates what action is to occur.

KeyViolAction has one of the following values:

KeyViolAction	Meaning
NOPOST	Post the record only if there's no key violation
FORCEPOST	Post the record whether or not there's a key violation
KEYVIOL	If there's a key violation, don't post the record; leave the key violation active so the program can use the KEYLOOKUP command to determine whether or not to post the record

If you don't specify a value for *KeyViolAction*, Paradox assumes a value of NOPOST. LEAVELOCKED tells the program to leave the record locked after posting it.

POW(*Base, Exponent*)

Calculates the value of *Base* raised to the power of *Exponent*. If the absolute value of the result is outside the range 10^{-307} to 10^{+308}, POW() returns the value "Error".

PRINT

PRINT *ExpressionList*
Sends the contents of *ExpressionList* to the currently selected printer.

PRINT FILE *FileName, ExpressionList*
Sends the contents of *ExpressionList* to the file specified by *FileName*. If *FileName* already exists, *ExpressionList* gets appended; if *FileName* doesn't exist, PRINT FILE creates it.

PRINTER {OFF | ON }

PRINTER OFF
Directs output created with the ?, ??, or TEXT command to the screen only.

PRINTER ON
Directs output to the printer as well as the screen.

PRINTERSTATUS()

Indicates True if the printer is ready; False if it's not.

PRIVDIR()

Reports the DOS path of the current user's private directory. This is useful mostly on a network, where each user's temporary files must be stored in their own private directory. See the SETPRIVDIR command for information about how to designate a private directory.

PRIVTABLES *TableList*

Directs Paradox to store the tables named in *TableList* in the current user's private directory. See the SETPRIVDIR command for infomation about how to designate a private directory.

PROC...ENDPROC

Defines a procedure.

```
PROC [ CLOSED ] ProcName ([ ParamList ])
[ USEVARS VarNameList1 ]
[ PRIVATE VarNameList2 ]
    Commands
ENDPROC
```

PROC...ENDPROC uses the following parameters:

Parameter	Meaning
CLOSED	Designates this as a closed procedure
ProcName	The name of the procedure
ParamList	Parameters passed to the procedure
USEVARS *VarList1*	Make the global variables listed in *VarList1* available to this procedure
PRIVATE *VarList2*	Make the variables listed in *VarList2* private to this procedure; release them when the procedure ends
Commands	Execute these commands

PROMPT

PROMPT [*Prompt*]

Used in standard mode only, this displays the text of *Prompt* in the status line at the bottom of the screen. PROMPT by itself cancels the prompt defined by *Prompt.*

PROMPT [*Prompt1, Prompt2*]

Used in compatibility mode, this displays a two-line prompt at the top of the screen. In standard mode, this acts like form one, displaying only the text of *Prompt1.*

PROTECT *TableName, Password*

Encrypts table *TableName*, and assigns *Password* as its master password.

PV(*Payment, Rate, Periods*)

Calculates the present value of *Periods* equal payments, each of amount *Payment*, invested at an interest rate of *Rate* per period. You must express *Rate* as a decimal (for instance, express 8.5 percent as 0.085).

QUERY...ENDQUERY

Defines a query.

```
QUERY
     QueryImage
ENDQUERY
```

The query image represented by *QueryImage* is placed on the work surface. The easiest way to create this structure is to build the query image through the Paradox menus, then save the query as a script (using Menu {Scripts} {QuerySave}).

QUERYORDER()

Reports the order in which fields will appear in an Answer table. There are two possibile responses:

- "TableOrder" indicates the fields in an Answer table will appear in the same order as in the source table.

- "ImageOrder" indicates the fields in an Answer table will appear in the same order as in the query image.

QUIT [*Expression*]

Stops playing the script and returns to interactive Paradox. The value of the optional *Expression* is displayed in the lower-right corner of the screen.

QUITLOOP

Immediately ends the current FOR, FOREACH, SCAN, or WHILE loop without processing any other commands in the loop.

RAND()

Creates a pseudorandom number with a value between 0 and 1.

READLIB *LibraryName* [IMMEDIATE] *ProcNameList*

Reads the procedures named in *ProcNameList* from the procedure library file *LibraryName* into memory. The optional parameter IMMEDIATE tells Paradox to load the named procedures immediately, rather than wait until they're called.

RECNO()

Reports the record number of the current record in the current image. If the cursor is in a linked detail table in a multitable form, the records are numbered within that detail list, not within the entire table.

RECORDSTATUS(*String*)

Returns True or False upon testing the status of the current record for any of these four values of *String*: "New", "Locked", "Modified", or "KeyViol". RECORDSTATUS() works only in CoEdit mode. It doesn't work in multitable forms.

REFRESH

Updates the current display images. This is used on a network to see changes that other users have made to tables.

Keystroke Equivalent   ALT-R

REFRESHCONTROL *Tag*

Refreshes the SHOWDIALOG control element identified by *Tag*. The effect of REFRESHCONTROL varies with the type of control element referenced.

REFRESHDIALOG

Performs a REFRESHCONTROL for every contol element in the current SHOWDIALOG dialog box.

RELEASE

Use RELEASE to free up memory occupied by procedures and variables. There are two variations of RELEASE.

RELEASE PROCS { ALL | *ProcNameList* }

Releases from memory either ALL procedures or the procedures specifically named in *ProcNameList*, freeing up the memory occupied by those procedures.

RELEASE VARS { ALL | *VarNameList* }

Releases from memory either ALL variables, fixed arrays, dynamic arrays, and array elements, or the items specifically named in *VarNameList*, freeing up the memory occupied by those items.

RENAME *TableName1 TableName2*

Renames table *TableName1* and its family of objects to *TableName2*. The family of objects are the forms, reports, indexes, validity checks, and image settings associated with the table. If *TableName2* already exists, it and its family of objects get overwritten.

Rename your tables using the Paradox menus or commands. If you rename a table in DOS, Paradox may lose track of the relationships between the table and its family of objects.

   Caution: If you rename a table, then nonfamily objects that referenced the table will no longer work. These include objects such as multitable forms, linked reports, queries, scripts, and so on.

REPAINTDIALOG

Redraws the active SHOWDIALOG dialog box after recalculating expressions used in the dialog.

REPLACE

In the Editor, replaces the selected text with the text currently in the replace buffer.

Keystroke Equivalent   CTRL-A

REPLACEFIELDS

Replaces the contents of one or more fields with the values from expressions. The table must be in Edit or CoEdit mode.

```
REPLACEFIELDS
  FieldName1  Expression1,
  FieldName2  Expression2,
  ... ...,
  FieldNameN  ExpresssionN
```

REPLACENEXT

In the Editor, replaces the selected text with the text currently in the replace buffer, then finds the next occurrence of the search text.

REPORT *TableName ReportName*

Prints report *ReportName* of table *TableName*. *ReportName* is an expression that equals "R" , "1" through "14", or 1 through 14.

Menu Equivalent   Menu {Report} {Output} {Printer}

REPORTTABLES *TableName ReportName ArrayName*

Creates a fixed array *ArrayName*, containing the names of lookup tables linked to report *ReportName* of table *TableName*. If report *ReportName* has linked tables, Paradox creates and dimensions the array, and sets Retval to True. If there are no linked tables in *ReportName*, no array is created, and Retval gets set to False.

REQUIREDCHECK { ON | OFF }

REQUIREDCHECK OFF disables validity checking for required fields in the image currently on the desktop. This is used to get out of a field that requires a value, if your program needs to access other fields first.

REQUIREDCHECK ON re-enables validity checking that was turned off.

RESET

Restores Paradox to a clean state. RESET returns to Main mode, clears the desktop, writes changed memory blocks to disk, and removes explicit table locks. RESET is often used at the start of a top-level script to initialize the environment.

RESYNCCONTROL *Tag*

Resynchronizes the SHOWDIALOG control element identified by *Tag* so it agrees with the current value of its corresponding memory variable. The effect of RESYNCCONTROL varies with the type of control element referenced.

RESYNCDIALOG

Performs a RESYNCCONTROL for every contol element in the current SHOWDIALOG dialog box.

RESYNCKEY

Forces Paradox to match up master and detail records in a multitable form after you change the key value of the master record.

Keystroke Equivalent   CTRL-L

RETRYPERIOD()

Reports how many seconds Paradox will keep trying to access a needed resource on a network.

RETURN [*Expression*]

Returns control from the current script or procedure to the script or procedure that called it. If you include *Expression*, Paradox passes the value of *Expression* back to the calling script or procedure. If the script is the top-level script, the contents of *Expression* get displayed in the desktop message area.

REVERSETAB

In a display image, REVERSETAB moves the cursor to the previous field. In a table band in the Report Designer, REVERSETAB moves the cursor to the previous column.

Keystroke Equivalent   SHIFT-TAB

RIGHT

The effect of RIGHT varies with the Paradox mode:

Mode	RIGHT Moves Cursor
Table view	One field right
Form view	One field right or down
Field view	One character right
Form design	One character right
Report design	One character right
Editor	One character right

Keystroke Equivalent   RIGHT ARROW

RMEMLEFT()

Reports the number of bytes of free memory left in the code pool. This is a reserved memory area that Paradox uses for its own program code. It can allocate some of this area for applications, but performance degrades. RMEMLEFT() lets you monitor how much memory is left in the code pool.

ROTATE

In a table view or a query image, ROTATE moves the current field to the rightmost position in the image. All other fields to the right of the cursor shift one column to the left.

Keystroke Equivalent   CTRL-R

ROUND(*Number, Digits*)

Rounds the value of *Number* to the number of digits indicated by *Digits*. If *Digits* is positive, round *Number* to the right of the decimal point; if *Digits* is negative, round *Number* to the left of the decimal point; if *Digits* is zero, round *Number* to the nearest integer.

ROW()

Indicates the vertical position of the cursor in the current canvas. The position is the offset from the top edge of the canvas.

ROW() is used in the context of a canvas; ROWNO() is used in the context of an image.

ROWNO()

Indicates the vertical position of the cursor in the current display or query image, the Form Designer, or the Report Designer. The position is the offset from the top edge of the window.

ROWNO() is used in the context of an image; ROW() is used in the context of a canvas.

RUN

Suspends Paradox and runs a DOS command. The command must be a program external to Paradox.

```
RUN [ BIG ] [ SLEEP Number ] [ NOREFRESH ] [ NORESTORE ]
[ NOSHELL ] DOSCommand
```

RUN uses the following parameters:

Parameter	Meaning
BIG	Suspend Paradox and free up maximum amount of memory for DOS command
SLEEP *Number*	Pause for *Number* milliseconds after running DOS command; *Number* ranges from 0 to 30,000
NOREFRESH	Don't clear the PAL canvas before running the DOS command
NORESTORE	Don't restore the PAL canvas after running the DOS command

Parameter	Meaning
NOSHELL	Don't load COMMAND.COM before executing the DOS command
DOSCommand	The DOS command to run. If you use the NOSHELL option, you can't run batch files or internal DOS commands

SAVETABLES

Forces Paradox to write table buffers from memory to disk. This protects the data in case of a power failure.

SAVEVARS { ALL | *VarNameList* }

Stores the values of variables and arrays in a script named SAVEVARS.SC.

Parameter	Meaning
ALL	Store all the variables and arrays currently in memory
VarNameList	Store only the variables named in *VarNameList*

SCAN...ENDSCAN

Repeats a set of commands for each record in the current table.

```
SCAN [ FOR Condition ]   [ : ]
     Commands
ENDSCAN
```

SCAN...ENSCAN uses the following parameters:

Parameter	Meaning
FOR *Condition*	Perform the commands only on records matching the *Condition*
:	Use a colon if the next command after SCAN is a FOR loop. The colon distinguishes between the FOR *Condition* and the FOR loop.
Commands	Perform these commands for each (matching) record in the current table

Assume table CustList has a date field named Member_Date, and a three-charac-ter alphanumeric field named Member_Date_DOW. We can use the following code to populate the Member_Date_DOW field with the day of the week of each corre-sponding value in the Member_Date field.

```
COEDIT "custlist"
SCAN
    [member_date_dow] = DOW([member_date])
ENDSCAN
DO_IT!
```

SCROLLPRESS *KeyName*

Duplicates the action of pressing a cursor-movement key while SCROLL LOCK is on. *KeyName* is a word representing one of the cursor-movement keys: UP, DOWN, LEFT, RIGHT, PGUP, PGDN, HOME, END, CTRLPGUP, CTRLPGDN, CTRLLEFT, CTRLRIGHT.

SDIR()

Identifies the full DOS path name of the directory containing the script that's currently running.

SEARCH(*SubString, String*)

Locates the starting position of *SubString* within *String*. The search starts at the first position of *String*.

SEARCHFROM(*SubString, String, Position*)

Locates the starting position of *SubString* within *String*. The search starts at *Position* within *String*.

SELECT *Expression*

Lets you select a menu choice using an expression rather than a value hard-coded into menu selection braces. This lets the same program code make varying menu choices.

SELECTCONTROL *Tag*

Selects the dialog control element indicated by *Tag*. By using a variable to represent *Tag*, a program can conditionally select various control elements in a dialog box.

Tag is the TAG assigned to each dialog control element in a SHOWDIALOG command.

SETAUTOSAVE *Seconds*

Sets the number of seconds between the times that Paradox writes table buffers to disk. *Seconds* is a value between 0 and 255.

SETBATCH { ON | OFF }

Groups multiple operations to improve performance in a multiuser environment. SETBATCH ON forces Paradox to lock all the resources in the working directory, so the system doesn't have to keep checking to see which resources are available. This speeds up operations for the user executing the SETBATCH ON command, but it locks all other users out of the resources until the current user executes SETBATCH OFF. Use SETBATCH for the shortest time necessary to complete a few resource-intensive operations.

SETBW

Tells Paradox to use the black-and-white display palette.

SETCANVAS { DEFAULT | *WindowHandle* }

Tells Paradox where to send the output of canvas painting commands (@, ?, ??, TEXT).

DEFAULT is the full-screen canvas. *WindowHandle* is the unique number assigned by Paradox to each window.

SETCOLORS FROM *DynamicArrayName*

Sets the attributes of the current color palette from the dynamic array named *DynamicArrayName*. Each array element contains one attribute of the palette.

SETDIR *DOSPath*

Specifies the drive and directory where Paradox looks for data. *DOSPath* is a valid DOS PATH specification. Any backslash characters used in *DOSPath* must be doubled (\\), because the backslash is a special character to Paradox.

Menu Equivalent   Menu {Tools} {More} {Directory}

SETKEY *Keycode* [*Commands*]

Defines a set of commands that Paradox executes when you press a specified key (for instance, a keyboard macro). SETKEY *Keycode* with no commands specified resets the key to its normal meaning.

Parameter	Meaning
Keycode	A valid Paradox representation of the key to define
Commands	A sequence of commands to assign to the key

SETKEYBOARDSTATE FROM *DynamicArrayName*

Uses information stored in the dynamic array specified by *DynamicArrayName* to set the current state of the CAPS LOCK, NUM LOCK, and SCROLL LOCK keys.

SETMARGIN { OFF | *Number* }

Defines the left margin to use for text displayed with the ? or TEXT command. The setting affects only the current canvas. If you've directed screen output to the printer with a PRINTER ON command, that left margin is also changed.

Parameter	Meaning
Number	The number of spaces of margin to allow
OFF	Sets the margin back to 0

SETMAXSIZE *Number*

Sets the maximum size of tables created by Paradox. *Number* specifies the maximum size in megabytes. It must be a multiple of 64, and should be set no lower than 128. The maximum size of a table affects the size of the blocks Paradox uses to store data in the table, so it may affect storage efficiency. Once you use SETMAXSIZE on a table larger than 128MB, you should always use SETMAXSIZE in an INIT script to be sure that tables derived from the large table can themselves be large enough to hold the necessary data.

SETNEGCOLOR { CURRENCY | NUMERIC | BOTH } { ON | OFF }

Turns color ON or OFF for the display of negative numeric and/or currency values in tables. With color ON, it's easy to spot losses on your balance sheet. Color OFF is less shocking but might not give you the warning you need. The default color for negative values is red, but you can change this in the Custom Configuration Program (Menu {Video} {NegativeFields}).

SETPRINTER *String*

Selects a port for printer output. Valid values of *String* are LPT1, LPT2, LPT3, COM1, COM2, or AUX.

Menu Equivalent   Menu {Report} {SetPrinter} {Override}

SETPRIVDIR *DOSPath*

Specifies a user's private directory for the current session of Paradox. Paradox uses the private directory to store temporary tables and tables named in the PRIVTABLES command. *DOSPath* is a valid DOS PATH specification. Any backslash characters used in *DOSPath* must be doubled (\\), because the backslash is a special character to Paradox. SETPRIVDIR is useful mainly on a network.

Menu Equivalent   Menu {Tools} {Net} {SetPrivate}

SETQUERYORDER { TABLEORDER | IMAGEORDER }

Specifies the order in which fields will appear in an *Answer* table. There are two possibilities.

SETQUERYORDER TABLEORDER
Indicates the fields in an *Answer* table will appear in the same order as in the source table.

SETQUERYORDER IMAGEORDER
Indicates the fields in an *Answer* table will appear in the same order as in the query image.

SETRECORDPOSITION *RecordNumber Row*

Scrolls the data in a multitable form so the record specified by *RecordNumber* is at the form row specified by *Row*. The value of *Row* must be less than or equal to the value of *RecordNumber*.

SETRESTARTCOUNT [OFF | *Number*]

Limits the number of times Paradox will restart a report, query, or crosstab if data changes in shared tables. The default setting is SETRESTARTCOUNT OFF, so Paradox will continually restart the operation until it either completes successfully or is interrupted. SETRESTARTCOUNT *Number* limits the number of retries to the value of *Number*.

SETRESTARTCOUNT has an effect only if you use Menu {**T**ools} {**N**et} {**C**hanges} {**R**estart}. It has no effect if you use Menu {**T**ools} {**N**et} {**C**hanges} {**C**ontinue}.

SETRETRYPERIOD *Number*

Specifies how many seconds Paradox will keep trying to access a needed resource on a network. *Number* can have a value between 0 and 30,000. If *Number* is 0, Paradox won't retry at all.

SETSWAP *Number*

In Paradox versions prior to 4, specifies the smallest amount of free memory that Paradox should maintain in the central memory pool. *Number* specifies the number of bytes kept free for uses other than PAL scripts and procedures. Paradox maintains this minimum amount of free memory by swapping PAL procedures out of memory as necessary. Has no effect starting with Paradox 4.

SETUIMODE { STANDARD | COMPATIBLE }

SETMODE STANDARD tells Paradox to use the standard version 4 user interface. SETMODE COMPATIBLE tells Paradox to use the interface compatible with version 3.5.

SETUSERNAME *Name*

Specifies the user name that Paradox will display to other users if the current user locks resources needed by those other users. *Name* is a string between 1 and 14 characters long.

Menu Equivalent   Menu {Tools} {Net} {UserName}

SHIFTPRESS *KeyName*

Duplicates the action of pressing a cursor-movement key while holding down a SHIFT key. *KeyName* is a word representing one of the cursor-movement keys: UP, DOWN, LEFT, RIGHT, PGUP, PGDN, HOME, END, CTRLPGUP, CTRLPGDN, CTRLLEFT, CTRLRIGHT.

SHOWARRAY

Creates a pick list or menu from fixed arrays.

```
SHOWARRAY FixedArrayName1 FixedArrayName2
[ UNTIL KeycodeList [ KEYTO VarName1 ] ]
[ DEFAULT Choice ]
TO VarName2
```

In standard mode, SHOWARRAY uses elements from two fixed arrays to create a pick list dialog box in the middle of the screen. This is a quick way to create a pick list, but if you need more control over the dialog box, use the SHOWDIALOG command.

In compatibility mode, SHOWARRAY creates a ring menu at the top of the screen, rather than a scrolling pick list.

SHOWARRAY uses the following parameters:

Parameter	Meaning
FixedArrayName1	An array of strings to display as choices in the pick list
FixedArrayName2	An array of strings to use as prompts for the items in the pick list
KeycodeList	A list of Paradox keycodes to trap by SHOWARRAY
VarName1	Stores the value of the keycode used to exit the pick list
Choice	Specifies a menu item to be highlighted as the default menu choice
VarName2	Stores the value of the item selected from the pick list

The following code creates a menu with four choices:

```
ARRAY actions[4]
ARRAY prompts[4]
actions[1] = "Customers"
```

```
actions[2] = "Orders"
actions[3] = "Reports"
actions[4] = "Utilities"
prompts[1] = "Maintain Customer Data"
prompts[2] = "Maintain Orders Data"
prompts[3] = "Print Reports"
prompts[4] = "Run System Utilities"
SHOWARRAY
    actions prompts
    DEFAULT actions[3]
TO menuchoice
```

SHOWDIALOG

Creates a dialog box to let users interact with your program. You can create pick lists, pushbuttons, and other interactive elements in a dialog box.

```
SHOWDIALOG
TitleExpression
[ PROC DialogProc EventList ]
@ Row, Column HEIGHT Number1 WIDTH Number2
CanvasElements
ControlElements
ENDDIALOG
```

SHOWDIALOG is an extremely powerful command. The syntax appears more complex than it actually is. It's made up of discrete pieces that you can use alone or in combination.

You must provide a way to exit a dialog box. You can use an OK pushbutton or a Cancel pushbutton, or include an ACCEPTDIALOG or CANCELDIALOG command in the dialog procedure. If you don't use one of these exits, the user will get trapped in the dialog box.

The following sections describe the various components of the SHOWDIALOG command.

SHOWDIALOG Parameters—General

The following table describes the parameters listed in the SHOWDIALOG syntax. Detailed explanations of the parameters appear in the following sections.

Parameter	Description
TitleExpression	The title of the dialog box; *TitleExpression* is a string expression that displays centered in the top frame of the dialog box

Parameter	Description
DialogProc	The PAL procedure to call when a specified event occurs. (See the detailed explanation later in this section.)
EventList	A list of events that will cause the dialog to call the *DialogProc*. (See the detailed lists of events later in this section.)
@Row, Column	The coordinates of the top-left corner of the dialog box
Number1	Height of the dialog box in rows
Number2	Width of the dialog box in characters
CanvasElements	Commands that control the background elements of the dialog box (frames, colors, and so on). (See detailed descriptions of individual canvas elements later in this section.)
ControlElements	Commands that control the elements that the user interacts with in the dialog box (pick lists, for example). (See detailed descriptions of individual control elements later in this section.)

DialogProc

DialogProc specifies the procedure to call when a specified event occurs. *DialogProc* requires four arguments: *DialogProc(EventType, TagValue, EventValue, ElementValue)*.

If *DialogProc* is called by a MOUSE, KEY, MESSAGE, or IDLE event, SHOWDIALOG assigns values to the arguments as follows:

Argument	Value Assigned
EventType	The string "EVENT"
TagValue	A null value
EventValue	A dynamic array containing the event details. This array is identical to the array that GETEVENT would create for the same event.
ElementValue	A null value

If *DialogProc* is called by a TRIGGER event, SHOWDIALOG assigns values to the arguments as follows:

Argument	Value Assigned
EventType	The name of the trigger. (See the detailed list later in this section.)

Argument	Value Assigned
TagValue	The TAG value of the *ControlElement* active when the trigger occurred
EventValue	The value the *ControlElement VarName* would receive if the dialog box were accepted now
ElementValue	The *Label* text if the *ControlElement* is a CHECKBOX; otherwise, a null value

EventList Syntax

EventList specifies the events that will call the dialog procedure. Information about a trapped event is stored in a dynamic array that is passed as a parameter to the dialog procedure. The contents of this array are identical to the array created by GET-EVENT for the same event. The dialog procedure can examine and manipulate the contents of the event dynamic array.

The following list shows the categories of events you can specify in *EventList*. Detailed descriptions of the events follow the list.

- ALL

- IDLE

- KEY { ["ALL"] | [*KeyValueList*] }

- MESSAGE { ["ALL"] | ["CANCEL" | "DEFAULT" | "OK"] }

- MOUSE { ["ALL"] | ["AUTO" | "DOWN" | "MOVE" | "UP"] }

- TRIGGER { ["ALL"] | ["ACCEPT" | "ARRIVE" | "CANCEL" | "CLOSE" | "DEPART" | "OPEN" | "SELECT" | "UPDATE"] }

ALL   Responds to any event. When ALL is used in the *EventList*, all events will be trapped. Your dialog procedure must then identify the event and determine what actions, if any, to take for each event.

IDLE   IDLE causes SHOWDIALOG to continually call the dialog procedure. This is useful if your program needs to perform some repetitive action while waiting for the user to do something. For example, you can cause the program to monitor the clock and sound an alarm if the user fails to respond in a reasonable time.

KEY   KEY events occur when the user presses any key ("ALL"), or one of the keys specified by the numeric values listed in *KeyValueList*. The numeric values are either ASCII codes or extended codes, depending on the key.

MESSAGE   MESSAGE events occur when the user performs specific interactions with the dialog box. The following table lists the MESSAGE events that SHOWDIALOG can trap.

MESSAGE Event	Meaning
ALL	Any message event
OK	An OK button has been selected
CANCEL	A CANCEL button has been selected
DEFAULT	The button specified as the DEFAULT has been selected

MOUSE Events   Mouse events occur when the user performs one or more of the following mouse actions.

MOUSE Event	Caused By
ALL	Any mouse action
UP	Releasing a mouse button
DOWN	Pressing a mouse button
MOVE	Moving the mouse
AUTO	Holding down a mouse button without moving the mouse (to scroll a list, for example)

TRIGGER   TRIGGERs are special events that occur only with SHOWDIALOG and WAIT commands. The following table lists the TRIGGERs available to SHOWDIALOG:

TRIGGER Name	Caused By
ACCEPT	Trying to accept the dialog box
ALL	Any trigger event
ARRIVE	Arriving at a control element
CANCEL	Trying to cancel the dialog box
CLOSE	Closing the dialog box
DEPART	Trying to leave a control element
OPEN	Opening the dialog box, but before displaying it
SELECT	Trying to select a pick list item
UPDATE	Trying to update the *TO* variable associated with a control element

CanvasElements Syntax

CanvasElements specify the background elements of a dialog box. The syntax for the *CanvasElements* is as follows:

```
[ STYLE [ MonoOptionList ] | STYLE ATTRIBUTE Number ]
[ @ Row, Column ]
[ ? ExpressionList ]
[ ?? ExpressionList ]
[ FRAME [ SINGLE | DOUBLE ] FROM Row1, Col1 TO Row2, Col2 ]
[ CLEAR [ EOL | EOS ] ]
[ PAINTCANVAS [ BORDER ] [ FILL String ]
    { MonoOptionList | ATTRIBUTE Number | BACKGROUND }
    { Row1, Col1, Row2, Col2 | ALL } ]
```

These canvas elements are identical to their counterparts used outside dialog boxes. For details of their use, please refer to the individual elements in this chapter (STYLE, FRAME, CLEAR, PAINTCANVAS).

ControlElements Syntax

ControlElements are commands that control the elements the user interacts with in the dialog box. These elements include pick lists, pushbuttons, check boxes, sliders, radio buttons, type-in boxes, and hot keys. The following section shows the syntax of the commands that control these elements. Detailed explanations of the parameters follow the syntax listings.

PICKARRAY PICKARRAY creates a pick list made up of the values of the elements of a fixed array. The values are displayed in ascending order, and the user can pick one value. Here is the PICKARRAY syntax:

```
PICKARRAY
        @ Row, Column
        HEIGHT Number
        WIDTH Number
        [ COLUMNS Number ]
        FixedArrayName
        TAG Expression
        TO VarName
```

Parameter	Description
@Row, Column	Relative coordinates of the first line of the pick list within the dialog box

Parameter	Description
HEIGHT	Height of the pick list in rows
WIDTH	Width of the pick list in characters
COLUMNS	Number of item columns in the pick list
FixedArrayName	Name of the fixed array to use for the pick list
TAG	Name passed to the dialog procedure to identify this control element
VarName	Variable that receives the value from the highlighted item in the pick list when Paradox accepts the dialog

PICKDYNARRAY   PICKDYNARRAY creates a pick list made up of the values of the elements of a dynamic array. The values are displayed in ascending order, and the user can pick one value. Here is the PICKDYNARRAY syntax:

```
PICKDYNARRAY
     @ Row, Column
     HEIGHT Number
     WIDTH Number
     [ COLUMNS Number ]
     DynamicArrayName
     TAG Expression
     TO VarName
```

Parameter	Description
@Row, Column	Relative coordinates of the first line of the pick list within the dialog box
HEIGHT	Height of the pick list in rows
WIDTH	Width of the pick list in characters
COLUMNS	Number of item columns in the pick list
DynamicArrayName	Name of the dynamic array to use for the pick list
TAG	Name passed to the dialog procedure to identify this control element
VarName	Variable that receives the value from the highlighted item in the pick list when Paradox accepts the dialog

PICKDYNARRAYINDEX   PICKDYNARRAYINDEX creates a pick list made up of the indexes of the elements of a dynamic array. The index values are displayed in ascending order, and the user can pick one value. Here is the PICKDYN-ARRAYINDEX syntax:

```
PICKDYNARRAYINDEX
      @ Row, Column
      HEIGHT Number
      WIDTH Number
      [ COLUMNS Number ]
      DynamicArrayName
      TAG Expression
      TO VarName
```

Parameter	Description
@Row, Column	Relative coordinates of the first line of the pick list within the dialog box
HEIGHT	Height of the pick list in rows
WIDTH	Width of the pick list in characters
COLUMNS	Number of item columns in the pick list
DynamicArrayName	Name of the dynamic array to use for the pick list
TAG	Name passed to the dialog procedure to identify this control element
VarName	Variable that receives the value from the highlighted item in the pick list when Paradox accepts the dialog

PICKFILE   PICKFILE creates a pick list of the files in a directory. The filenames are displayed in ascending order, and the user can pick one value. Here is the PICKFILE syntax:

```
PICKFILE
      @ Row, Column
      HEIGHT Number
      WIDTH Number
      [ COLUMNS Number ]
      DOSPath
      [ NOEXT ]
      TAG Expression
      TO VarName
```

Parameter	Description
@Row, Column	Relative coordinates of the first line of the pick list within the dialog box
HEIGHT	Height of the pick list in rows
WIDTH	Width of the pick list in characters
COLUMNS	Number of item columns in the pick list

Parameter	Description
DOSPath	Full DOS path of the directory containing the items to show in the pick list
NOEXT	Don't show file extensions in PICKFILE
TAG	Name passed to the dialog procedure to identify this control element
VarName	Variable that receives the value from the control element when Paradox accepts the dialog

PICKTABLE   PICKTABLE creates a pick list of the tables in a directory. The table names are displayed in ascending order, and the user can pick one value. Here is the PICKTABLE syntax:

```
PICKTABLE
    @ Row, Column
    HEIGHT Number
    WIDTH Number
    [ COLUMNS Number ]
    DOSPath
    TAG Expression
    TO VarName
```

Parameter	Description
@Row, Column	Relative coordinates of the first line of the pick list within the dialog box
HEIGHT	Height of the pick list in rows
WIDTH	Width of the pick list in characters
COLUMNS	Number of item columns in the pick list
DOSPath	Full DOS path of the directory containing the items to show in the pick list
NOEXT	Don't show file extensions in PICKFILE
TAG	Name passed to the dialog procedure to identify this control element
VarName	Variable that receives the value from the control element when Paradox accepts the dialog

PUSHBUTTON   PUSHBUTTON creates a single pushbutton with a single associated value. Each pushbutton requires a separate PUSHBUTTON command.

You must provide a way to exit a dialog box. The most common way is to use an OK pushbutton or a Cancel pushbutton. You can also use an ACCEPTDIALOG or

CANCELDIALOG command in the dialog procedure. If you don't use one of these exits, the user will get trapped in the dialog box. Here is the PUSHBUTTON syntax:

```
PUSHBUTTON
      @ Row, Column
      WIDTH Number
      Label
      [ OK | CANCEL ]
      [ DEFAULT ]
      VALUE Expression
      TAG Expression
      TO VarName
```

Parameter	Description
@Row, Column	Relative coordinates of the pushbutton within the dialog box
WIDTH	Width of the pushbutton in characters
Label	The text that appears on the pushbutton
**OK	CANCEL**	Pushbutton action: OK accepts the dialog; CANCEL cancels the dialog
DEFAULT	Select this pushbutton when the user presses ENTER; available only for OK or CANCEL
VALUE	Value assigned to *VarName* when the user presses this pushbutton
TAG	Name passed to the dialog procedure to identify this control element
VarName	Variable that receives the value from the pushbutton when Paradox accepts the dialog

RADIOBUTTONS   RADIOBUTTONS creates a list of mutually exclusive choices. You present a set of allowable choices, and the user can pick just one. Here is the RADIOBUTTONS syntax:

```
RADIOBUTTONS
      @ Row, Column
      HEIGHT Number
      WIDTH Number
      Label1, Label2, ..., LabelN
      TAG Expression
      TO VarName
```

Parameter	Description
@Row, Column	Relative coordinates of the first radio button within the dialog box
HEIGHT	Height of the list of radio buttons, in rows
WIDTH	Width of the radio buttons, in characters
Label	The text that appears next to a radio button
TAG	Name passed to the dialog procedure to identify this control element
VarName	Variable that receives the value from the *Label* of the selected radio button when Paradox accepts the dialog

CHECKBOXES   CHECKBOXES creates a list of choices that are not mutually exclusive. You present a set of allowable choices, and the user picks one or more. Here is the CHECKBOXES syntax:

```
CHECKBOXES
     @ Row, Column
     HEIGHT Number
     WIDTH Number
     TAG Expression
     Label1 TO VarName1
     Label2 TO VarName2
     ...,
     LabelN TO VarNameN
```

Parameter	Description
@Row, Column	Relative coordinates of the first checkbox within the dialog box
HEIGHT	Height of the list of checkboxes in rows
WIDTH	Width of the checkboxes in characters
Label	The text that appears next to a checkbox
TAG	Name passed to the dialog procedure to identify this control element
VarName	Variable that indicates if the checkbox was selected. *VarName* becomes True if the checkbox is selected; False if it's not.

ACCEPT   ACCEPT creates a type-in box that lets the user enter text. Here is the ACCEPT syntax:

```
ACCEPT
     @ Row, Column
     WIDTH Number
     DataType
          [ PICTURE Picture ] [ MIN Value1 ] [ MAX Value2 ]
          [ LOOKUP TableName ] [ REQUIRED ] [ HIDDEN ]
     TAG Expression
     TO VarName
```

Parameter	Description
@Row, Column	Relative coordinates of the left side of the text box within the dialog box
WIDTH	Number of characters you can type before text scrolls within the text box. To prevent scrolling, make the width three spaces larger than the maximum number of characters that will be entered.
DataType	The type of data the user can enter; also determines the allowable size of the input
Picture	The entry format for the data; for example, a phone number might appear as PICTURE "(###) ###-####"
Value1	The minimum allowable value
Value2	The maximum allowable value
TableName	The name of a table containing allowable values
REQUIRED	The user cannot enter a blank value
HIDDEN	Masks the entry; useful for passwords
TAG	Name passed to the dialog procedure to identify this control element
VarName	Variable that receives the value from the text box when Paradox accepts the dialog

SLIDER   SLIDER creates a slider bar. The slider has arrows at each end, a scroll bar, and a scroll box. The user can position the slider, and your program can determine the relative position of the slider in the control element. Here is the SLIDER syntax:

```
SLIDER
     @ Row, Column
     [ VERTICAL | HORIZONTAL ]
     LENGTH Number
     MIN Value1
     MAX Value2
```

```
ARROWSTEP Value3
PAGESTEP Value4
TAG Expression
TO VarName
```

Parameter	Description
@Row, Column	Relative coordinates of the left or upper-end of the slider within the dialog box
VERTICAL | HORIZONTAL	Specifies the orientation of the slider within the dialog box
LENGTH	Length of slider in rows or columns
MIN	Minimum value on slider
MAX	Maximum value on slider
ARROWSTEP	Incremental change of slider value when user clicks on slider arrow
PAGESTEP	Incremental change of slider value when user clicks on slider bar
TAG	Name passed to the dialog procedure to identify this control element
VarName	Variable that receives the slider value when Paradox accepts the dialog

LABEL   LABEL creates a hot key for another dialog box control element. You designate a letter to use as the hot key, which the user can activate by pressing ALT plus the key (for example, ALT-C). Here is the LABEL syntax:

```
LABEL
    @ Row, Column
    LabelName
    FOR TagExpression
```

Parameter	Description
@Row, Column	Relative coordinates of the label within the dialog box
LabelName	A letter unique within this SHOWDIALOG, enclosed in tildes (~); for example, ~B~
TagExpression	Identifies the control element associated with this label

The following code creates a dialog box that lets the user enter a name to search for:

```
SHOWDIALOG
    "Enter search name"
    @10,10
    HEIGHT 12 WIDTH 50
    @ 2,5 ?? "Type a name:"
    ACCEPT @2,20 WIDTH 20 "A15"
    TAG "searchtag"
    TO searchname

    PUSHBUTTON
        @6,5 WIDTH 8
        "Cancel"
        CANCEL
        VALUE "Canceled"
        TAG "No"
        TO buttonvar

    PUSHBUTTON
        @6,20 WIDTH 8
        "Accept"
        OK
        VALUE "Accepted"
        TAG "Yes"
        TO buttonvar

ENDDIALOG
```

SHOWFILES

Creates a pick list or menu of the files in a directory.

```
SHOWFILES [ NOEXT ] DOSPath Prompt
[ UNTIL KeycodeList [ KEYTO VarName1 ] ]
TO VarName2
```

In standard mode, SHOWFILES creates a dialog box with a pick list of the files in a directory. The dialog box appears in the center of the screen. In compatibility mode, it creates a ring-style menu with a pick list of the files in a directory. The menu appears at the top of the screen.

Use the following parameters with SHOWFILES:

Parameter	Description
NOEXT	Don't show file extensions in pick list

Parameter	Description
DOSPath	Full DOS path of the directory containing the files to show in the pick list
Prompt	Text to display at the bottom of the screen
KeycodeList	A list of Paradox keycodes to trap by SHOWFILES
VarName1	Stores the value of the keycode used to exit the pick list
VarName2	Stores the value of the item selected from the pick list

SHOWMENU

Displays a menu.

```
SHOWMENU MenuItemList
[ UNTIL KeycodeList [ KEYTO VarName1 ] ]
[ DEFAULT Choice ]
TO VarName2
```

In standard mode, SHOWMENU displays a popup menu in the middle of the screen. In compatibility mode, it displays a ring-style menu at the top of the screen. Use the following parameters with SHOWMENU:

Parameter	Description
MenuItemList	A comma-separated list of menu items in the format *MenuItemName : MenuItemPrompt*. The *MenuItemName* will appear as a pick list. A *MenuItemPrompt* appears at the bottom of the screen when the user highlights the corresponding *MenuItemName*. *MenuItemList* can contain up to 50 items.
KeycodeList	A list of Paradox keycodes to trap by the SHOWMENU command
VarName1	Stores the value of the keycode used to exit the pick list
VarName2	Stores the value of the item selected from the pick list

SHOWPOPUP

Displays a pop-up menu.

```
SHOWPOPUP Title { CENTERED | @ Row, Column }
MenuList
ENDMENU
```

```
[ UNTIL KeycodeList [ KEYTO VarName1 ] ]
TO VarName2
```

Use the following parameters with SHOWPOPUP:

Parameter	Meaning
Title	A string that will appear centered in the top frame of the menu
CENTERED	Center the pop-up on the screen
@ *Row, Column*	Relative coordinates of the top-left corner of the pop-up menu
MenuList	A comma-separated list of menu items (see below for the allowable formats). *MenuList* can contain up to 50 items.
KeycodeList	A list of Paradox key codes to trap by the SHOWPOPUP command
VarName1	Stores the value of the key code used to exit the pick list
VarName2	Stores the *Tag* of the item selected from the pick list

Acceptable formats for menu items in *MenuList* are

```
Option : Description : [ DISABLE ] Tag
Option : Description : [ DISABLE ]  [ Tag ]
    SUBMENU
         MenuList
    ENDSUBMENU
Separator
```

Following are the menu item parameters:

Parameter	Meaning
Option	Text that will display in the menu
Description	Prompt that will display at the bottom of the screen
DISABLE	Display this menu item, but don't activate it
Tag	Name used to identify this menu item
SUBMENU	A submenu that will pop up if the user chooses this item. You can nest submenus 16 levels deep.
Separator	Display a horizontal line to divide the menu into groups

SHOWPULLDOWN

Displays a menu bar with pull-down menus.

```
SHOWPULLDOWN
MenuList
ENDMENU
[ UNTIL KeycodeList ]
```

Following are the SHOWPULLDOWN parameters:

Parameter	Meaning
MenuList	A comma-separated list of menu items (see below for the allowable formats). *MenuList* can contain up to 50 items.
KeycodeList	A list of Paradox keycodes to trap by the SHOW-PULLDOWN command

Acceptable formats for menu items in *MenuList* are

```
Option : Description : [ DISABLE ] Tag
Option : Description : [ DISABLE ]  [ Tag ]
     SUBMENU
            MenuList
     ENDSUBMENU
Separator
```

Following are the menu item parameters:

Parameter	Meaning
Option	The text that will display in the menu
Description	The prompt that will display at the bottom of the screen
DISABLE	Display this menu item, but don't activate it
Tag	The name used to identify this menu item. Paradox assigns this name to the MENUTAG element of the MESSAGE event generated by SHOWPULLDOWN.
SUBMENU	A submenu that will pop up if the user chooses this item. You can nest submenus 16 levels deep.
Separator	Display a horizontal line to divide the menu into groups

SHOWTABLES

Creates a pick list or menu of the tables in a directory.

```
SHOWTABLES DOSPath Prompt
[ UNTIL KeycodeList [ KEYTO VarName1 ] ]
TO VarName2
```

In standard mode, SHOWTABLES creates a dialog box with a pick list of the tables in a directory. The dialog box appears in the center of screen. In compatibility mode, it creates a ring-style menu with a pick list of the tables in a directory. The menu appears at the top of the screen.

Parameter	Description
DOSPath	Full DOS path of the directory containing the tables to show in the pick list
Prompt	Text to display at the bottom of the screen
KeycodeList	A list of Paradox keycodes to trap by SHOWTABLES
VarName1	Stores the value of the keycode used to exit the pick list
VarName2	Stores the value of the item selected from the pick list

SIN(*Number*)

Calculates the sine of *Number*. *Number* is an angle expressed in radians.

SKIP [*Number*]

Moves the cursor a specified number of records from its current position. If *Number* is positive, the cursor moves forward. If *Number* is negative, the cursor moves backward. If you don't specify a *Number*, the cursor moves forward one record.

SLEEP *Number*

Pauses the script for the number of milliseconds specified by *Number*.

SORT

Sorts a table.

```
SORT TableName1 [ ON FieldNameList [ D ] ]
[ TO TableName2 ]
```

Sorts *TableName1*. If you don't include any options, Paradox sorts the table in ascending order on each field in the table, progressing from the first field to the last, and stores the results back in the same table.

Use the following parameters with SHOWTABLES:

Parameter	Meaning
TableName1	The name of the table to sort
TableName2	The name of a table to create to store the results of the sort operation
FieldNameList	A list of fields to sort on, in the order they appear in the list
D	A letter *D* after a field name tells Paradox to sort on that field in descending order

Menu Equivalent   Menu {**M**odify} {**S**ort}

SORTORDER()

Reports the sort order set up in the Custom Configuration Program. SORTORDER() reports a value of "ascii", "intl", "nordan", or "swedfin".

SOUND *Frequency Duration*

Sounds the computer speaker at *Frequency* Hertz for *Duration* milliseconds.

SPACES(*Number*)

Generates a string value of *Number* spaces.

SQRT(*Number*)

Calculates the square root of *Number*.

STRVAL(*Expression*)   Calculates the string representation of *Expression*, no matter what data type.

Expression Type	STRVAL(*Expression*)
String < 255 char	*Expression*
String > 255 char	First 255 characters of *Expression*
Date	Current date format
Numeric	Depends on value of the number
Logical	"True" or "False"

STYLE

Defines the attributes to use on the current PAL canvas for output from the ?, ??, and TEXT commands.

Used by itself, STYLE displays subsequent canvas output with normal attrubutes. Two other variations of STYLE specify display attributes. These are described below.

STYLE *MonoOptionList*

Displays subsequent canvas output in the style specified by *MonoOptionList*. This can be one or more of BLINK, INTENSE, or REVERSE.

STYLE ATTRIBUTE *Number*

Displays subsequent canvas output with the color attribute specified by *Number*. A color attribute number is made up of both a foreground color and a background color. To specify an attribute, find the desired foreground and background colors in the lists below, then add them together. For example, for a blue background (16) and brown foreground (6), use the number 22.

Foreground Colors		Background Colors	
0	Black	0	Black
1	Blue	16	Blue
2	Green	32	Green
3	Cyan	48	Cyan
4	Red	64	Red
5	Magenta	80	Magenta
6	Brown	96	Brown
7	Light Gray	112	Light Gray
8	Dark Gray		
9	Light Blue		
10	Light Green		

Foreground Colors	Background Colors
11 Light Cyan	
12 Light Red	
13 Light Magenta	
14 Yellow	
15 White	

SUBSTR(*String, Position, Number*)

Extracts a substring from a string.

Parameter	Meaning
String	The original string expression
Position	The number of the starting position of the substring to extract
Number	The number of characters to extract

SUBTRACT *TableName1 TableName2*

Subtracts the records in *TableName1* from the records in *TableName2*. If *TableName2* is keyed, records are removed from *TableName2* if their key values exactly match the values in the corresponding fields in *TableName1*. If *TableName2* is not keyed, records are removed from *TableName2* if they completely match any records in *TableName1*.

Menu Equivalent   Menu {Tools} {More} {Subtract}

SWITCH...ENDSWITCH

Chooses between mutually exclusive sets of commands based on conditions it tests.

```
SWITCH
    CASE Condition1 : Commands1
    CASE Condition2 : Commands2
    ...
    CASE ConditionN : CommandsN
    [ OTHERWISE : Commands ]
ENDSWITCH
```

Use the following parameters with SWITCH...ENDSWITCH:

Parameter	Meaning
CASE	Introduces a *Condition* and its related *Commands*. The colon separating the *Condition* and the *Commands* is required.
ConditionN	A condition to test. The test must yield a True or False result.
CommandsN	A set of commands to execute if the condition is True
OTHERWISE *Commands*	If present, use these commands if all the conditions are False

SYNCCURSOR

Synchronizes the positions of the cursor on the current canvas and the current Paradox object.

SYSCOLOR(*Number*)

Reports the numeric value of the color attribute of the screen element identified by *Number.*

SYSINFO TO *DynamicArrayName*

Stores information about the system Paradox is running on. SYSINFO creates a dynamic array *DynamicArrayName* whose elements represent the system attributes and their current values.

SYSMODE()

Indicates the current system mode. SYSMODE() reports one of the following string values: Main, Create, DataEntry, Edit, CoEdit, Form, Graph, Password, Report, Preview, Restructure, Script, File Editor, Sort, Index, SetConn (if SQL Link is installed).

TAB

Paradox Mode	TAB Action
Any display image	Moves cursor to the next field

Paradox Mode	TAB Action
Report designer	In a table band, moves the cursor to the next column
Editor	Moves the cursor to the next tab stop (positioned every eight spaces)

Keystroke Equivalent   TAB

TABLE()

Reports the name of the table or query image currently on the desktop.

TABLERIGHTS(*TableName, String*)

Indicates if the current user has specified rights to a table. *TableName* is the name of the table to test. *String* is one of the following words: "ReadOnly", "Update", "Entry", "InsDel", "All".

TAN(*Number*)

Calculates the tangent of *Number*. *Number* is an angle expressed in radians.

TEXT

Displays text on the current PAL canvas.

```
TEXT
      Text
ENDTEXT
```

Text is the literal text to display. You can't use variables here.

TICKS()

Reports the system time as the number of milliseconds since midnight.

TIME()

Reports the system time as a string value in 24-hour format.

TODAY()

Reports the current system date.

TOGGLEPALETTE

Toggles the color palette on and off when you are coloring an area during form design.

Keystroke Equivalent   ALT-C

TOQPRO

Switches control to Quattro Pro, when Paradox and Quattro Pro are running at the same time.

Keystroke Equivalent   CTRL-F10

TYPE(*Expression*)

Indicates the Paradox data type of *Expression.* TYPE() returns one of the following values:

TYPE() Value	Meaning
A*n*	Alphanumeric, *n* characters long; *n* can have a maximum value of 255
N	Numeric
D	Date
S	Short number
$	Currency
L	Logical
AY	Fixed array
DY	Dynamic array
M	Alphanumeric longer than 255 characters

TYPEIN *Expression*

Enters the contents of *Expression* just as if it were typed at the keyboard. *Expression* is usually converted to a string, but you can force Paradox to maintain a specific data type by using the appropriate conversion function; for example, NUMVAL().

UNDO

Undoes the most recent change made during an Edit, DataEntry, or CoEdit session.

In Edit and DataEntry modes, UNDO lets you reverse changes incrementally back to the start of the session.

In CoEdit mode, UNDO can reverse changes on only the last record edited. In addition, some processes may prevent you from undoing changes in CoEdit.

In either case, you must use UNDO before you use Do_It!

Keystroke Equivalent   CTRL-U

UNLOCK { *LockList* | ALL }

Removes locks from ALL tables or just the tables specified in *LockList. LockList* has the form *TableName1 LockType1, TableName2 LockType2, ..., TableNameN LockTypeN. TableName* is any valid table name, and *LockType* is one of the following values:

LockType	Meaning
FL	Full lock
WL	Write lock
PFL	Prevent full lock
PWL	Prevent write lock

UNLOCKRECORD

Unlocks the current record. Works only in CoEdit mode.

UNPASSWORD *PasswordList*

Removes one or more passwords from use in the current work session. Any tables that were accessed using these passwords can no longer be accessed, unless you reenter the proper passwords.

UP

Moves the cursor up one line or field, depending on the mode.

Keystroke Equivalent   UP ARROW

UPIMAGE

Moves the cursor to the previous image.

Keystroke Equivalent   F3

UPPER(*Expression*)

Converts *Expression* to uppercase characters.

USDATE(*DateValue*)

Converts *DateValue* to the U.S. date format of dd-Mon-yyyy.

USERNAME()

Reports the name of the current user on a network.

VERSION()

Indicates which version of Paradox is running.

VERTRULER

Displays or hides the vertical line count ruler in the Report Designer.

Keystroke Equivalent   CTRL-V

VIEW *TableName*

Places a new display image of *TableName* on the desktop.

Menu Equivalent   Menu {View}

WAIT

Controls how the user interacts with a field, record, table, or the desktop (workspace). There are two forms of WAIT.

The first form lets your program control interaction from the keyboard only. This is the same WAIT that exists in Paradox 3.5.

```
WAIT {FIELD | RECORD | TABLE | WORKSPACE }
    [ PROMPT Expression1 ]
    [ MESSAGE Expression2 ]
UNTIL KeycodeList
```

The second form of WAIT lets you control interaction from both the keyboard and a mouse.

```
WAIT { FIELD | RECORD | TABLE | WORKSPACE }
    PROC WaitProc EventList
ENDWAIT
```

The WAIT parameters are as follows:

Parameter	Description
Expression1	The text of a prompt displayed while the WAIT is active. The prompt appears at the bottom line of the screen
Expression2	The text of a message displayed when the program first enters the WAIT. This message disappears when the user presses any key.
KeycodeList	A list of Paradox keycodes to trap by the WAIT command
WaitProc	The PAL procedure to call when a specified event occurs. *WaitProc* must return a value of 0, 1, or 2. (See below for the meaning of each value.)
EventList	A list of events that will cause the wait to call the *WaitProc*. (See the detailed list of trigger and mouse events later in this section.)

WaitProc

WaitProc specifies the procedure to call when a specified event occurs. *WaitProc* requires three arguments: *WaitProc(EventType, EventRecord, CycleNumber)*.

If *WaitProc* is called by a MOUSE, KEY, MESSAGE, or IDLE event, WAIT assigns values to the arguments as follows:

Argument	Value Assigned
EventType	The string "EVENT"
EventRecord	A dynamic array containing the event details. This array is identical to the array that GETEVENT would create for the same event.
CycleNumber	A unique number for any given trigger cycle

If *WaitProc* is called by a TRIGGER event, WAIT assigns values to the arguments as follows:

Argument	Value Assigned
EventType	The name of the trigger. (See the detailed list later in this section.)
EventRecord	A dynamic array containing the event details. This array is identical to the array that GETEVENT would create for the same event.
CycleNumber	A unique number for any given trigger cycle

WAIT Procedure Return Values

WaitProc must return a value of 0, 1, or 2 back to the WAIT command, to tell Paradox how to handle the event. The return values are as follows:

Return Value	Meaning
0	Paradox processes the current event, then goes on to the next event in the same trigger cycle.
1	Paradox discards the current event and exits from the trigger cycle but stays in the WAIT.
2	Paradox discards the current event and exits from both the trigger cycle and the WAIT.

EventList Syntax

EventList specifies the events that will call the WAIT procedure. Information about a trapped event is stored in a dynamic array that is passed as a parameter to the dialog procedure. The contents of this array are identical to the array created by GETEVENT for the same event. The WAIT procedure can examine and manipulate the contents of the event dynamic array.

The following list shows the categories of events you can specify in EventList. Detailed descriptions of the events follow the list.

- ALL

- IDLE

- KEY { ["ALL"] | [*KeyValueList*] }

- MESSAGE   { ["ALL"] | ["CLOSE" | "MAXIMIZE" | "MENUKEY" | "MENUSELECT" | "NEXT"] }

- MOUSE { ["ALL"] | ["AUTO" | "DOWN" | "MOVE" | "UP"] }

- TRIGGER { ["ALL"] | ["ARRIVEFIELD" | "ARRIVEPAGE" | "ARRIVEROW"
  | "DEPARTFIELD" | "DEPARTPAGE" | "DEPARTROW" | "DEPARTTABLE" |
  "DISPLAYONLY" | "EVENT" | "IMAGERIGHTS" | "PASSRIGHTS" |
  "POSTRECORD" | "READONLY" | "REQUIREDVALUE", | "TOUCHROW" |
  "VALCHECK"] }

ALL   Responds to any event. When *ALL* is used in the *EventList*, all events will be trapped. Your WAIT procedure must then identify the event and determine what actions, if any, to take for each event.

IDLE   IDLE causes WAIT to continually call the WAIT procedure. This is useful if your program needs to perform some repetitive action while waiting for the user to do something. For example, you can cause the program to monitor the clock and sound an alarm if the user fails to respond in a reasonable time.

KEY   KEY events occur when the user presses any key ("ALL"), or one of the keys specified by the numeric values listed in *KeyValueList*. The numeric values are either ASCII codes or extended codes, depending on the key.

MESSAGE   MESSAGE events occur when the user performs specific interactions with the current window. The following table lists the MESSAGE events that WAIT can trap.

MESSAGE Event	Meaning
ALL	Any message event
CLOSE	User has closed the window
MAXIMIZE	User has maximized or restored the window
NEXT	User has selected the next window on the desktop
MENUSELECT	User has selected a menu item in a SHOW-PULLDOWN menu
MENUKEY	User has pressed a key in the UNTIL list of a SHOWPULLDOWN menu

MOUSE   MOUSE events occur when the user performs one or more of the following mouse actions.

MOUSE Event	Caused By
ALL	Any mouse action
UP	Releasing a mouse button
DOWN	Pressing a mouse button
MOVE	Moving the mouse
AUTO	Holding down a mouse button without moving the mouse (for example, to scroll a list)

TRIGGER   TRIGGERs are special events that occur only with SHOWDIALOG and WAIT commands. The following table lists the TRIGGERs available to WAIT:

TRIGGER	Caused By
ALL	Any trigger event
EVENT	Any mouse or keyboard interaction listed in the *EventList*
ARRIVEFIELD	Arriving at a field
DEPARTFIELD	Trying to leave a field
ARRIVEROW	Arriving at a record
DEPARTROW	Trying to leave a record
TOUCHROW	Edit mode: touching any record CoEdit mode: touching a record that hasn't been touched before
ARRIVEPAGE	Arriving at a new form page
DEPARTPAGE	Trying to leave a form page
ARRIVETABLE	Arriving in a new table
DEPARTTABLE	Trying to leave a table
ARRIVEWINDOW	Arriving in a new window
POSTRECORD	Trying to post a record
IMAGERIGHTS	Trying to modify a field without modify rights
PASSRIGHTS	Trying an action in a password-protected field without rights to do so
REQUIREDVALUE	Trying to leave a field without supplying a required value
VALCHECK	Trying an action that causes a valcheck violation
DISPLAYONLY	Trying to modify a display-only image
READONLY	Trying to modify a read-only image

IDLE events are events generated internally by the computer system when no external events have occurred for a while.

WHILE...ENDWHILE

Repeatedly executes one or more commands.

```
WHILE
     [ Commands ]
ENDWHILE
```

Repeatedly executes *Commands* while *Condition* is True. For example, the following code displays the numbers 1 through 100:

```
x = 0
WHILE x < 100
    x = x + 1
    ? x
ENDWHILE
```

WINCLOSE

Closes the current window only if the value of the CANCLOSE attribute is True for this window. WINCLOSE asks for confirmation, if appropriate.

Keystroke Equivalent   CTRL-F8

WINDOW()

Reports the contents of the Paradox message window. WINDOW() traps system-generated messages so your script can test them and respond appropriately.

WINDOW CLOSE

Closes the current window no matter what the value of the CANCLOSE attribute for this window. WINDOW CLOSE doesn't ask for confirmation before closing the window.

WINDOW CREATE

Creates a canvas window.

```
WINDOW CREATE [ FLOATING ]
@ Row, Column
HEIGHT Number
WIDTH Number
ATTRIBUTES DynamicArrayName
TO WindowHandle
```

Use the following parameters with WINDOW CREATE:

Parameter	Meaning
FLOATING	Create the canvas window above the echo layer

Parameter	Meaning
@Row, Column	Coordinates of the upper-left corner of the window
HEIGHT	Height of the window, in lines
WIDTH	Width of the window in characters
ATTRIBUTES	Set the initial window attributes to those specified in *DynamicArrayName*
WindowHandle	Stores the value of the handle assigned to this window

WINDOW ECHO *WindowHandle LogicalExpression*

Turns echoing on or off for the specified window.

Parameter	Meaning
WindowHandle	The handle assigned by Paradox to identify a specific window
LogicalExpression	True for echo on, False for echo off

WINDOW GETATTRIBUTES *WindowHandle* TO *DynamicArrayName*

Builds a dynamic array whose elements contain information about the attributes of a window.

Parameter	Meaning
WindowHandle	The handle assigned by Paradox to identify a specific window
DynamicArrayName	The name of the dynamic array to hold information about the window attributes

The dynamic array will contain information about the following window attributes:

Attribute	Meaning
CANCLOSE	True if user can close
CANMAXIMIZE	True if user can maximize and restore
CANMOVE	True if user can move
CANRESIZE	True if user can resize
CANVAS	True if canvas display commands show immediately in the window

Attribute	Meaning
CANVASHEIGHT	Height of the canvas
CANVASWIDTH	Width of the canvas
ECHO	True if WINDOW ECHO is True
FLOATING	True if window is above echo layer
HASFRAME	True if window is framed
HASSHADOW	True if window has a shadow
HEIGHT	Height in rows, including frame
MARGIN	Left margin setting, or "OFF" for none
MAXIMIZED	True if maximized
ORIGINCOL	Column number of upper-left corner
ORIGINROW	Row number of upper-left corner
SCROLLCOL	Horizontal offset location of the window
SCROLLROW	Vertical offset location of the window
STYLE	Style attribute for canvas text
TITLE	Title centered in the top frame line
WIDTH	Width in characters, including frame

WINDOW HANDLE

Reports the value of the handle for a window.

```
WINDOW HANDLE { IMAGE Number | FORM [ DESIGN ] |
REPORT [ DESIGN ] | CURRENT }
TO WindowHandle
```

Use the following parameters with WINDOW HANDLE:

Parameter	Meaning
IMAGE *Number*	Get a handle for the specified image
FORM	Get a handle for the current form
[DESIGN]	Get a handle for the current form designer window
REPORT	Get a handle for the current report
[DESIGN]	Get a handle for the current report designer window
CURRENT	Get a handle for the current window
WindowHandle	Variable in which to store the value of the window handle

WINDOW LIST TO *FixedArrayName*

Builds a fixed array, *FixedArrayName*, whose elements contain the window handles of all the windows currently on the desktop. The window handles appear in "z-order". If the windows on the desktop were arranged in a single stack, the handle of the window at the top of the stack would appear first in the array, and the handle of the window at the bottom of the stack would appear last.

WINDOW MAXIMIZE *WindowHandle*

Maximizes or restores the window identified by *WindowHandle*, no matter what the value of the CANMAXIMIZE attribute for this window.

WINDOW MOVE *WindowHandle* TO *Row, Column*

Moves the window identified by *WindowHandle* so that its upper-left corner is at the screen coordinates specified by *Row, Column*. WINDOW MOVE works no matter what the value of the CANMOVE attribute for this window. *Row* and *Column* can each have values between –10,000 and +10,000.

WINDOW RESIZE *WindowHandle* TO *Height, Width*

Resizes the window identified by *WindowHandle* to the height and width specified by *Height* and *Width*, respectively. WINDOW RESIZE works no matter what the value of the CANRESIZE attribute for this window.

WINDOW SCROLL

Scrolls the contents of a window to a specified location.

```
WINDOW SCROLL WindowHandle TO Row, Col
```

WINDOW SCROLL scrolls the contents of the window specified by *WindowHandle* so that the offset specified by *Row, Col* is placed at the top-left corner of the window. (Location 0,0 is the top-left corner of the contents of the window.)

WINDOW SELECT *WindowHandle*

Makes the window identified by *WindowHandle* the current window.

WINDOW SETATTRIBUTES *WindowHandle* FROM *DynamicArrayName*

Assigns attributes to window identified by *WindowHandle* according to values stored in the dynamic array identified by *DynamicArrayName*.

The dynamic array can contain information about any or all of the following window attributes:

Attribute	Meaning
CANCLOSE	True if user can close
CANMAXIMIZE	True if user can maximize and restore
CANMOVE	True if user can move
CANRESIZE	True if user can resize
CANVAS	True if canvas display commands show immediately in the window
CANVASHEIGHT	Height of the canvas
CANVASWIDTH	Width of the canvas
ECHO	True if WINDOW ECHO is True
FLOATING	True if window is above echo layer
HASFRAME	True if window is framed
HASSHADOW	True if window has a shadow
HEIGHT	Height in rows, including frame
MARGIN	Left margin setting, or "OFF" for none
MAXIMIZED	True if maximized
ORIGINCOL	Column number of upper-left corner
ORIGINROW	Row number of upper-left corner
STYLE	Style attribute for canvas text
TITLE	Title centered in the top frame line
WIDTH	Width in characters, including frame

WINDOWAT(*Row, Column*)

Reports the handle of uppermost window containing the screen coordinates specified by *Row, Column*. If the windows on the desktop were arranged in a single stack, the uppermost window would be at the top of the stack.

WINMAX

Maximizes or restores the current window only if the value of the CANMAXIMIZE attribute for this window is True.

Keystroke Equivalent   SHIFT-F5

WINNEXT

Moves the lowest window in the window stack to the top of the stack, making it the current window.

Keystroke Equivalent   CTRL-F4

WINRESIZE

Lets the user move the current window with the arrow keys, and resize the window with the SHIFT-arrow keys.

WINRESIZE works only if the value of the CANRESIZE attribute for this window is True.

Keystroke Equivalent   CTRL-F5

WRITELIB *LibraryName ProcNameList*

Stores the procedures listed in *ProcNameList* in the procedure library named in *LibraryName*. You must first create the procedure library with the CREATELIB command. You must use the PROC command to define the procedures and load them into memory before executing WRITELIB.

YEAR(*DateValue*)

Calculates the year of the date represented by *DateValue*.

ZOOM

Lets the user enter a value to search for in the current field of the current image, or in the Editor. If you want the script to enter the value, use ZOOM SELECT *value*.

Keystroke Equivalent   CTRL-Z

Menu Equivalent   Menu {Image} {Zoom} {Value}

ZOOMNEXT

Searches for the next occurrence of the value entered with the ZOOM command.

Keystroke Equivalent   ALT-Z

Functions and Commands by Category

This section lists the PAL functions and commands by task-type category. Use this list to identify the command or function you need, then look up the details of the command or function in the alphabetical listing earlier in this chapter.

Date and Time

BLANKDATE()	MOY()
DATEVAL()	TICKS()
DAY()	TIME()
DOW()	TODAY()
FORMAT()	USDATE()
MONTH()	YEAR()

Desktop Manipulation and Canvas Status

ATFIRST()	FIELDNO()
ATLAST()	FIELDSTR()
BANDINFO()	FIELDTYPE()
BOT()	FIRSTSHOW
CHECK	FORM
CHECKDESCENDING	FORMTYPE()
CHECKMARKSTATUS()	GROUPBY
CHECKPLUS	IMAGENO()
CLEARALL	IMAGETYPE()
CLEARIMAGE	INDEX
COL()	ISFIELDVIEW()
COLNO()	ISFORMVIEW()
CURSORCHAR()	ISINSERTMODE()
CURSORLINE()	ISLINKLOCKED()
DITTO	ISMULTIFORM()
DOWNIMAGE	ISMULTIREPORT()
EOT()	LINKTYPE()
EXAMPLE	LOCATE
FIELD()	LOCATE INDEXORDER
FIELDINFO()	LOCKSTATUS()

Desktop Manipulation and Canvas Status

MENUCHOICE()	ROTATE
MENUPROMPT()	ROW()
MOVETO	ROWNO()
NFIELDS()	SELECT
NIMAGERECORDS()	SETBW
NIMAGES()	SETNEGCOLOR
NKEYFIELDS()	SETQUERYORDER
NPAGES()	SETRECORDPOSITION
NRECORDS()	SKIP
NROWS()	SYNCCURSOR
PAGENO()	SYSMODE()
PAGEWIDTH()	TABLE()
PASSWORD	TYPEIN
PRIVTABLES	UNPASSWORD
RECNO()	UPIMAGE
RECORDSTATUS()	WINDOW()
REQUIREDCHECK	

Dialog Control

ACCEPTDIALOG	REPAINTDIALOG
CANCELDIALOG	RESYNCCONTROL
CONTROLVALUE()	RESYNCDIALOG
NEWDIALOGSPEC	SELECTCONTROL
REFRESHCONTROL	SHOWDIALOG
REFRESHDIALOG	

Editor Control

EDITOR EXTRACT	EDITOR OPEN
EDITOR FIND	EDITOR READ
EDITOR FINDNEXT	EDITOR REPLACE
EDITOR GOTO	EDITOR SELECT
EDITOR INFO	EDITOR WRITE
EDITOR INSERT	SHIFTPRESS
EDITOR NEW	

Financial

CNPV()

FV()

PMT()

PV()

Input/Output

?	MOUSE HIDE
??	MOUSE SHOW
@	NEWDIALOGSPEC
ACCEPT	NEWWAITSPEC
BEEP	OPEN PRINTER
CANVAS	PAINTCANVAS
CHARWAITING()	PRINT
CLEAR	PRINTER
CLEARPULLDOWN	PROMPT
CLOSE PRINTER	SCROLLPRESS
CURSOR	SETKEYBOARDSTATE
ECHO	SETMARGIN
EXECEVENT	SETPRINTER
FRAME	SHIFTPRESS
GETCHAR()	SHOWARRAY
GETEVENT	SHOWFILES
GETKEYBOARDSTATE	SHOWMENU
GETMENUSELECTION	SHOWPOPUP
KEYPRESS	SHOWPULLDOWN
LOCALIZEEVENT	SHOWTABLES
MENUDISABLE	SOUND
MENUENABLE	STYLE
MESSAGE	TEXT
MOUSE CLICK	TYPEIN
MOUSE DOUBLECLICK	WAIT
MOUSE DRAG	

Key Equivalents

ALTSPACE	ENTER
BACKSPACE	ESC
CHECK	EXAMPLE
CHECKDESCENDING	FIELDVIEW
CHECKPLUS	FORMKEY
CLEARALL	GRAPHKEY
CLEARIMAGE	GROUPBY
CLIPCOPY	HELP
CLIPCUT	HOME
CLIPPASTE	INS
COEDITKEY	INSTANTPLAY
CROSSTABKEY	INSTANTREPORT
CTRLBACKSPACE	KEYLOOKUP
CTRLBREAK	LEFT
CTRLEND	LOCKKEY
CTRLHOME	MENU
CTRLLEFT	MINIEDIT
CTRLPGDN	ORDERTABLE
CTRLPGUP	PGDN
CTRLRIGHT	PGUP
DEL	REFRESH
DELETELINE	REPLACE
DELETEWORD	REPLACENEXT
DITTO	RESYNCKEY
DO_IT!	REVERSETAB
DOS	RIGHT
DOSBIG	ROTATE
DOWN	SCROLLPRESS
DOWNIMAGE	SHIFTPRESS
EDITKEY	TAB
END	TOGGLEPALETTE

Key Equivalents (*continued*)

TOQPRO	WINMAX
UNDO	WINNEXT
UP	WINRESIZE
UPIMAGE	ZOOM
VERTRULER	ZOOMNEXT
WINCLOSE	

Mathematical

ABS()	LN()
ACOS()	LOG()
ASIN()	MOD()
ATAN()	PI()
ATAN2()	POW()
BLANKNUM()	RAND()
COS()	ROUND()
FORMAT()	SIN()
EXP()	SQRT()
INT()	TAN()

Menu Equivalents

ADD	EDITOR FINDTEXT
CALCDEBUG	EDITOR GOTO
CANCELEDIT	EDITOR NEW
COEDIT	EDITOR OPEN
COPY	EDITOR READ
COPYFORM	EDITOR REPLACE
COPYREPORT	EDITOR WRITE
CREATE	EMPTY
DELETE	EXIT
EDIT	LOCK
EDITOR FIND	PICKFORM

Menu Equivalents (*continued*)

PLAY	SETPRIVDIR
PROTECT	SETUSERNAME
QUERY	SORT
RENAME	SUBTRACT
REPORT	UNLOCK
SETDIR	VIEW
SETPRINTER	

Multiuser (Concurrency Control)

APPENDARRAY	REPLACEFIELDS
IMAGERIGHTS	SETBATCH
LOCK	SETPRIVDIR
LOCKKEY	SETRESTARTCOUNT
LOCKRECORD	SETRETRYPERIOD
POSTRECORD	SETUSERNAME
PRIVTABLES	UNLOCK
REFRESH	UNLOCKRECORD

Paradox Environment

DEBUG	SETBW
EDITLOG	SETKEY
EXECUTE	SETMAXSIZE
RESET	SETUIMODE
RUN	SLEEP
SAVETABLES	SYSINFO
SETAUTOSAVE	

Paradox Information

ARRAYSIZE()	EOT()
BOT()	ERRORCODE()
CHECKMARKSTATUS()	ERRORINFO()
DIREXISTS()	ERRORMESSAGE()
DYNARRAYSIZE()	ERRORUSER()

Paradox Information (*continued*)

FAMILYRIGHTS()	ISENCRYPTED()
FIELDRIGHTS()	ISFILE()
FILESIZE()	ISMASTER()
FILEVERSION()	ISSHARED()
FORMTYPE()	ISTABLE()
GETCHAR()	ISVALID()
HELPMODE()	ISWINDOW()
IIF()	RECORDSTATUS()
ISASSIGNED()	SYSINFO
ISBLANK()	TABLERIGHTS()
ISEMPTY()	TYPE()

Procedures and Procedure Libraries

CONVERTLIB	PROC
CREATELIB	READLIB
EXECPROC	RELEASE
FILEVERSION()	SETSWAP
INFOLIB	WRITELIB

Program Control

FOR	QUIT
FOREACH	QUITLOOP
IF	RETURN
IIF	SCAN
LOOP	SWITCH
PROC	WHILE

Statistical Functions

CAVERAGE()	CNPV()
CCOUNT()	CSTD()
CMAX()	CSUM()
CMIN()	CVAR()

Statistical Functions (*continued*)

IMAGECAVERAGE()	IMAGECSUM()
IMAGECCOUNT()	MAX()
IMAGECMAX()	MIN()
IMAGECMIN()	

String Manipulation

ASC()	MATCH()
CHR()	NUMVAL()
DATEVAL()	SEARCH()
FIELDSTR()	SEARCHFROM()
FILL()	SPACES()
FORMAT()	STRVAL()
LEN()	SUBSTR()
LOWER()	UPPER()

System Status

DIRECTORY()	PRIVDIR()
DRIVESPACE()	QUERYORDER()
DRIVESTATUS()	RETRYPERIOD()
GRAPHTYPE()	RMEMLEFT()
ISBLANKZERO()	SDIR()
ISRUNTIME()	SORTORDER()
MEMLEFT()	SYSCOLOR()
MONITOR()	SYSMODE()
NETTYPE()	USERNAME()
PRINTERSTATUS()	VERSION()

Variable and Array Control

=	FILEWRITE
APPENDARRAY	FORMTABLES
ARRAY	RELEASE
COPYFROMARRAY	REPLACEFIELDS
COPYTOARRAY	REPORTTABLES
DYNARRAY	SAVEVARS
FILEREAD	

Window Control

GETCANVAS()	WINDOW HANDLE
GETCOLORS	WINDOW LIST
GETWINDOW()	WINDOW MAXIMIZE
ISWINDOW()	WINDOW MOVE
LOCALIZEEVENT	WINDOW RESIZE
SETCANVAS	WINDOW SCROLL
SETCOLORS	WINDOW SELECT
WINDOW CLOSE	WINDOW SETATTRIBUTES
WINDOW CREATE	WINDOW SETCOLORS
WINDOW ECHO	WINDOWAT()
WINDOW GETATTRIBUTES	
WINDOW GETCOLORS	

Part V

Tools and Networking

Chapter 14

Using Paradox Tools

You use the **Tools** options to manage information in your database. Some of these options—**R**ename, **C**opy, **D**elete, **M**ore/**D**irectory, and **M**ore/**T**oDOS—are discussed in Chapter 2. The other **Tools** options are covered here. These options include using **Q**uerySpeed to speed up the processing of queries, using **E**xportImport to transfer files between Paradox and other programs, using **I**nfo to display information in tables and associated objects, and using **N**et to manage data on a network. This chapter also discusses the **M**ore options **A**dd, **M**ultiAdd, **F**ormAdd, **S**ubtract, and **E**mpty, which work with records in tables, and the **M**ore/**P**rotect option, which prevents data from being changed accidentally.

The **Tools** menu is shown here:

Using QuerySpeed

You use **Q**uerySpeed to speed up the rate at which complex, frequently used queries are performed. **Q**uerySpeed also affects the rate at which **Z**oom is processed.

The **QuerySpeed** option creates a secondary index on every non-key field that has been selected in the query. Paradox examines the query that is created, and if it determines that a secondary index would not speed up the query, gives you the message "No speedup possible".

Creating additional indexes does require more disk space. In some cases, particularly in small tables, speeding up a query may not be advisable, because the increased speed may not justify the disk space required for the index. If, after using **QuerySpeed**, you decide that you don't want it or need it, use **Tools/Delete/Index** to remove one or all secondary indexes from the table.

Be careful when removing secondary indexes not to delete indexes that you want to keep.

To use **QuerySpeed**, follow these steps:

1. Perform the query, and, if you like, save it using **Scripts/QuerySave**.

2. While the query is on the desktop, choose **Tools/QuerySpeed**.

From that point on, when that query is performed, it will be processed faster.

Using ExportImport

Choose the ExportImport option to transfer files between Paradox and other software programs. The ExportImport menu is shown here:

Exporting Files

The process of exporting a table *copies* the data from a Paradox table to a file in a different program. The existing table in Paradox remains as it is. When you choose **Export**, Paradox converts the files you want to export to the format for the program that you have selected.

Data can only be exported into *new* data files. You cannot export data into existing files. If you enter the name of an existing file, you will be asked to confirm that the existing data will be replaced, or you can cancel the operation.

Graphs, forms, reports, or other objects cannot be exported or imported.

You can export to the following formats:

Program	Format
Quattro Pro	.WKQ or .WQ1
1-2-3	.WKS or WK1
Symphony	.WRK or WK1
dBASE II, III, III PLUS, IV	.DBF
PFS or IBM Filing Assistant	.PFS
Reflex, version 1.0 or 1.1	.RXD
Reflex, version 2.0	.R2D
VisiCalc	.DIF
ASCII	.TXT

To export files, follow these steps:

1. Choose **T**ools/**E**xportImport. Another menu appears, with the options **E**xport and **I**mport.

2. Choose **E**xport. You get a list of programs, as shown here:

3. Choose the program you want. Depending upon the program chosen, select the version you want.

4. A dialog box asks for the name of the table to be exported.

5. Type the table name and press ENTER, or press ENTER to display the list of table names, choose the one you want, and press ENTER again.

6. Another dialog box appears, asking for the name of the new file. Type the new filename and press ENTER. If you are saving to a different directory, type the path name before the filename. You do not need to enter the extension; it will be added automatically depending upon the format you selected. As the table is converted, messages onscreen report the status of the conversion.

Exporting to an ASCII File

To convert your data to an ASCII.TXT file, follow these steps:

1. Choose **Tools/ExportImport/Export**. The list of programs is displayed.

2. Choose ASCII from the list. A second menu appears, as shown here:

3. Choose from **D**elimited or **T**ext on the menu.

   - *Delimited* converts the data to a file where fields are *delimited* (surrounded) by a character, usually quotes, and separated by another character, usually a comma. Each record ends with a carriage return/linefeed. The default delimiters and separators can be changed to almost any character using the Custom Configuration Program.

   - *Text* converts a table that contains a single alphanumeric field.

4. After choosing the type of ASCII file, you are prompted to choose a table. Type the name of the table that you want to export, or choose the table name from a list. A dialog box requests a filename, as shown in Figure 14-1.

5. Type the filename and press ENTER.

The Delimited option is often used to convert data to a file for use in a word processor's merge function. Separating the fields by commas and ending the records with a carriage return/linefeed makes it convenient to use the information from the table in a data document used in a merge function. If you plan to use the information in a regular document, use Report/Output/File, rather than Tools/ExportImport/Export/ASCII.

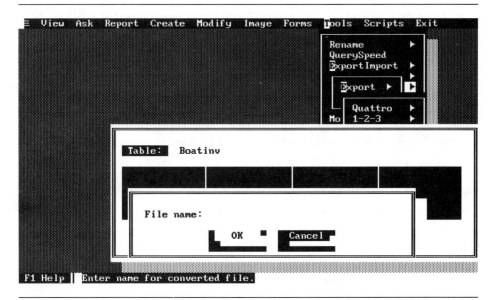

Figure 14-1.   *Dialog box for the ASCII filename*

Importing Files

When you choose Import, you specify the format you are importing from. These format choices are the same as the choices for exporting files.

Graphs, forms, reports, or other objects cannot be imported. Except for ASCII AppendDelimited files, when data is imported, Paradox automatically creates a *new* table for the data. You can use **Tools/More/Add** later to add these records to an existing table, if the structure in the two tables is compatible.

To import a file, follow these steps:

1. Choose **Tools/ExportImport/Import** from the Main menu. A list of the same programs that you saw in the **Export** menu is displayed.

2. Choose the program you want. You may have to specify a version of the program from which you are importing the file. A dialog box appears, asking for a filename.

3. Type the name of the file to be imported and press ENTER, or choose the filename from a list and press ENTER again. A second dialog box appears, asking for a new table name.

4. Type a name for the new table and press ENTER. As the file is imported, messages tell you the status of the conversion process. When complete, the new table is displayed on the screen.

How Paradox converts the data depends upon the individual formats. In general, Paradox tries to convert fields into numeric, currency, or date fields, rather than alphanumeric or memo fields, because alphanumeric and memo fields are more restrictive. If there are problems during the conversion, any records that do not fit in the new table are displayed in a temporary Problems table. You can then use **M**odify/**R**estructure to change the fields in either the Problems table or in the table created during the conversion process. If you change the structure of the Problems table, use **T**ools/**R**ename to rename it, or choose **T**ools/**M**ore/**A**dd and add the records that are in the Problems table to the new table.

Importing ASCII Files

Use **I**mport/**A**SCII to import, for example, data files that have been used in merge functions in a word processing program. These files must be saved in ASCII format—that is, the records must be separated by carriage return/linefeed characters. When you choose this option, a second menu appears with further options, **D**elimited, **A**ppendDelimited, and **T**ext, as shown here:

Delimited   This option imports a data file with fields separated by commas, and ending with carriage return/linefeed characters. Paradox imports these files into a new table and automatically creates fields based on the fields in the imported file. (The commas, which are default separators, can be changed using the Custom Configuration Program.)

AppendDelimited   This option imports an *ASCII file containing commas as separators into an existing table.* (The commas, which are default separators, can be changed using the Custom Configuration Program.) This is much quicker than if a new table has to be created. If the table into which the data is imported is *keyed,* then another menu with the following choices is displayed:

- *NewEntries* imports the records without changing the existing records. If an imported record has the same key as an existing record, the imported record is placed in a Keyviol table, which can then be edited so that the record can be added to the table.

- *Update* merges the new records into the table in key-field order. If a record in the existing table has the same key as an imported record, the existing record is placed in a Changed table. The existing record is replaced in the table by the imported record.

If some of the imported records that are to be *appended* contain fields that cannot find a match in the existing table, these records are stored temporarily in a Problems table. They can be edited to correct the problem and then added to the table.

Text This option imports ASCII files that do not contain separators. When you choose this option, Paradox creates a new table consisting of one alphanumeric field. Each line in the imported file becomes one record in the Paradox table. If any record has more characters than 132, Paradox wraps those excess characters into the next record. If Paradox has problems converting records, it places those records in the temporary Problems table, where records may be edited and then added to the existing table.

To import ASCII files, follow these steps:

1. Choose **T**ools/**E**xportImport/**I**mport/**A**SCII. A menu appears, listing types of ASCII files.

2. Choose from **D**elimited, **A**ppendDelimited, and **T**ext.

3. Enter in the dialog box the name of the file to be imported. You can also enter a path name here to display .TXT files in a different directory. Or press ENTER, as prompted in the status bar, and select the filename from a list. The dialog box in Figure 14-2 shows a path name and the text files that result.

4. In the next dialog box that appears, enter the name of the table and press ENTER. A message reports the status of the conversion. When finished, the new table is displayed on the screen.

Using the Info Option

The Info option provides information about the structure of tables, the names of the tables, scripts, and files in a specific directory or drive, what objects are in a database, and the indexes on a specific table. If you are on a network, this option can be used to show the names of users who are currently working on the network, and it can also be used to show any locks currently placed on a table and its family.

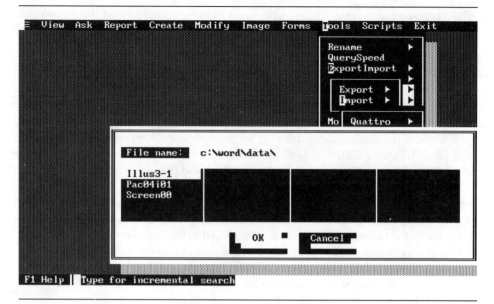

Figure 14-2.   *Prompt for a filename*

The Tools/Info menu is shown here:

Info/Structure

The **S**tructure option displays the current structure of a table. This is useful when you want to know the field types that have been assigned, which are key fields, and the size of a field.

To use **S**tructure, follow these steps:

1. Choose **T**ools/**I**nfo/**S**tructure. A dialog box appears, asking for a table name.

2. Type the table name and press ENTER, or press ENTER to display a list of table names, choose the one you want, and press ENTER again. A temporary Struct

table appears, as shown in Figure 14-3. At the bottom of the window a message tells you the number of records currently stored in the table.

3. Press ALT-F8 (Clear All) to clear the desktop.

Info/Inventory

The Inventory option is used to see the tables, scripts, or files in a drive or directory. When you choose Tools/Info/Inventory, another menu asks which type of file you want to view, as shown here:

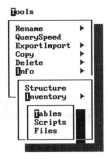

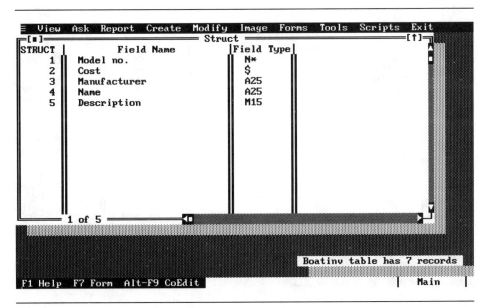

Figure 14-3.   *Struct table showing information about an existing table*

Tables   This option shows the names of the table in the drive or directory that you specified.

Scripts   This option shows the names of the scripts in the drive or directory that you specified.

Files   This option allows you to specify a pattern for the files you want to see. When you choose Files, a second dialog box appears. Enter the pattern the same as you would if you were using a DOS DIR command. You can enter a path name and a pattern such as ***.txt** to see the text files in the drive or directory that you specified.

If you choose Tables or Scripts, a dialog box appears, asking for the directory. Type the name of the directory if you know it; if you don't, leave this dialog box blank, and press ENTER. The tables or scripts in the current directory will be displayed.

If you choose Files, a dialog box for a pattern is displayed as shown here:

After choosing the option you want and responding to the prompts, a list of files appears in a temporary List table, as shown in Figure 14-4. This list shows the filenames and the dates when each file was modified. You would enter **Boatinv.*** to produce the list in this example, which displays all files named Boatinv.

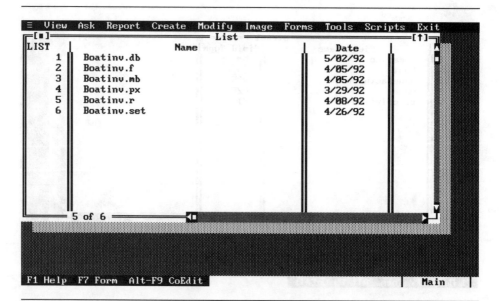

Figure 14-4.   *List table showing files*

Info/Family

The Family option displays the list of forms, reports, and other objects associated with a specific table. To use Family, follow these steps:

1. Choose **Tools/Info/Family**. A dialog box appears, asking for the table name.

2. Choose the table you want—either type the table name, or choose from the list of table names.

The list displayed next contains the names of the objects associated with the table and the dates when each was last modified, as shown in Figure 14-5. Boatinv was the table chosen in this example. Compare the Family table here with the List table that displays all files for the Boatinv table, as shown in Figure 14-4.

The Family table shows the *objects* associated with the Boatinv table. They are the table, an image setting (the result of using **Image/KeepSet**), a form, and a report. The List table shows the *files* stored in the current directory that are associated with the Boatinv table. The following extensions indicate the files that have been created for the table:

.db	Database table
.f	Form associated with the table
.mb	Memos in the table

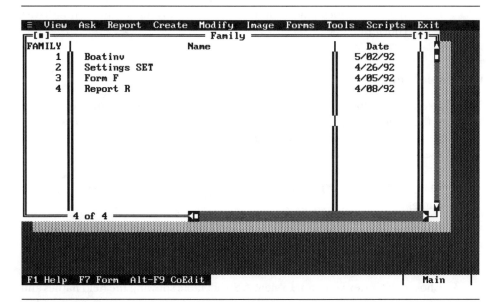

Figure 14-5. *List of objects associated with the table*

.px	Primary index on the table
.r	Report on the table
.set	Image setting for the table

Info/Who

You use the **Who** option to see a list of current users on a network. The information comes directly from the network or from information entered using the **Tools/Net/UserName** command. The information is displayed in a List table that may then be saved using **Tools/Rename**. If you are not on a network, no names will be displayed.

Info/Lock

The **Lock** option is used on a network to display a list of current locks and the names of users who placed them. All locks are listed except those placed by a PAL application.

To use **Lock**, follow these steps:

1. Choose **Tools/Info/Lock**. A dialog box appears, asking for the table whose locks you want to see.

2. Choose the table by either typing the table name or choosing from a list. A temporary List table is then displayed, showing the names of users who locked it and the type of lock placed on the table. This List table can then be saved using **Tools/Rename**.

Info/TableIndex

The **TableIndex** option displays a list of indexes that have been created for a table. You can then choose a specific index that you want to view. A Struct table will then show the names and types of fields that are in the index you selected.

To use **TableIndex**, follow these steps:

1. Choose **Tools/Info/TableIndex**. A dialog box appears, asking for a table name.

2. Type the name of the table, or choose the table from the list of table names. A list of secondary indexes for that table is then displayed, as shown in Figure 14-6.

3. Choose the index you want to view. A Struct table showing the field names and types included in the index appears on the desktop, as shown in Figure 14-7.

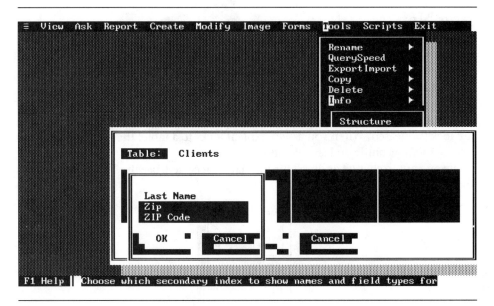

Figure 14-6. *List of secondary indexes for a table*

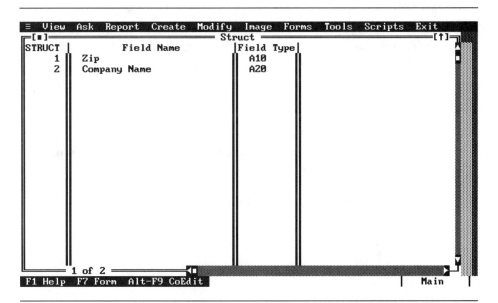

Figure 14-7. *Struct table showing the field names and types in a secondary index*

Using Net

You use the **Net** option to specifically control how other people access shared data. As mentioned in other chapters, Paradox usually controls the access to data automatically when you work on a network, which means you work on a network the same way you would work on a stand-alone computer. When an automatic lock is placed on a table, it remains in effect until the situation requiring the lock changes. Then the lock is released. When you assign explicit locks to a table, they remain until you release them or until you leave Paradox.

If you want to change or direct the way data is accessed, use the **Tools/Net** options shown here:

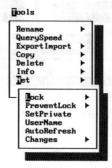

Using Net/Lock

The **Lock** option allows you to specifically establish a lock or release a lock on the table or tables on which you are working, or to place a lock on a directory to which you have full access.

Placing or Removing a Lock on a Table

You can place a lock on a table that prevents any access to the table, or you can place a lock that allows users to see the data in the table, but not change it. To place or remove a lock on a table, follow these steps:

1. Choose **Tools/Net/Lock**. A second menu appears, as shown here:

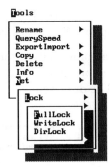

2. Choose one of the following to either place the lock or to release it:

   - *FullLock* prevents others from accessing the tables or their objects for any reason. This option takes precedence over all other locks and prevents concurrent access to the table.

   - *WriteLock* allows others to access the tables or objects, but the structure or the contents of the tables cannot be changed by others.

3. A dialog box asking for the table you want is displayed. Enter the name of the table, or choose from the list of tables. After selecting a table, another menu containing the options **Set** and **Clear** is shown.

   - *Set* places the choice of lock on the table.

   - *Clear* releases the lock that has been placed on the table.

Placing or Removing a Lock on a Directory

You can place a read-only lock on a directory to which you have full access rights; however, you cannot lock the current working directory. Nor can you lock a private directory of anyone currently using Paradox, or a directory to which you do not have full access rights, or a local drive on a nonshareable stand-alone system. To place or remove a lock on a directory, follow these steps:

1. Choose Tools/Net/Lock.

2. Choose **D**irLock from the menu that is displayed. You are then prompted for a directory name. The current directory is displayed in the dialog box.

3. Type a new path for a directory to which you have full access rights, and press ENTER. A menu with the options **S**et and **C**lear is displayed.

4. Choose **S**et to place a read-only lock on the directory, or choose **C**lear to remove a lock that has been placed on the directory. If you cannot set a lock, the following message will be displayed:

```
Directory can't be locked/unlocked because it is a working or private
directory, directory doesn't exist, you have insufficient access
rights to this directory, or directory is on a non-shared disk
```

5. If you want to set a lock on a different directory, repeat steps 1 through 4, entering a different directory name.

Net/PreventLock

You use the **P**reventLock option to restrict the locks that other users can place on tables. To use **P**reventLock, follow these steps:

1. Choose **T**ools/**N**et/**P**reventLock. A second menu appears, as shown here:

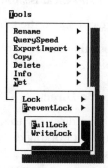

2. Choose one of the following to either place or release a **P**reventLock on the table:

   - *FullLock* prevents others from placing a full lock on a table and its objects (but other users can still place write locks or prevent write locks on the table). FullLock allows the maximum level of concurrent use on the table.

   - *WriteLock* prevents others from placing either a full lock or a write lock on the table and its objects. This ensures that you can edit data in the table, if you like.

3. After choosing the type of **P**reventLock you want, a dialog box asks for a table name. Enter the name of the table, or choose from the list of tables. After selecting a table, another menu containing **S**et and **C**lear is shown.

4. Choose **S**et to place the choice of lock on the table. Choose **C**lear to release the lock that has been placed on the table.

Net/SetPrivate

Paradox uses a private directory for storing temporary objects, and also to store non-temporary objects that you do not want others to have access to. On a network, most users share a working directory; however, each user on a network must have a private directory where temporary objects are stored. Most often a network administrator establishes the private directories for users. This can be done in the Custom Configuration Program, where a private directory can be designated as the default directory. Or use **N**et/**S**etPrivate to designate the private directory for each Paradox session.

If you don't specify a private directory, Paradox automatically tries to make the directory from which you started your private directory. If Paradox cannot lock this directory for any reason, you won't be able to start Paradox. On a network, it is recommended that you specify a private directory explicitly to avoid this problem.

To designate a private directory for the current session, follow these steps:

1. Choose **T**ools/**N**et/**S**etPrivate. A dialog box appears, requesting a directory name, as shown here:

2. Enter the full path name of the directory you want. If another user has specified the same directory, you will not be able to designate it as a private directory. When you change your private directory, all objects on the desktop will be cleared and all temporary objects will be deleted.

3. Because temporary objects can be deleted when you do this, you can either choose **C**ancel, which will leave the desktop and temporary objects as is, or choose OK to make the change.

Net/UserName

Choose UserName to designate a name during the current Paradox session. If your network supports user names, you won't need to do this, unless you want to change your user name.

If you want to designate a default user name, use the Custom Configuration Program.

To designate a user name, follow these steps:

1. Choose **Tools**/Net/UserName. You are prompted to enter a user name, as shown here:

   If you already have a user name and want to change it, the current user name will be displayed.

2. Type a new user name. It may consist of 1 to 14 characters and does not have to be your network login name.

3. Choose OK to enter a new name or to make the change. Choose **C**ancel if you decide you do not want to change the name.

Net/AutoRefresh

Paradox checks data on the network to see if changes have been made. If they have been made, then the screen is automatically refreshed. If you find the changes are too frequent and become distracting, this interval can be changed using the **Au**-toRefresh option.

Press ALT-R at any time to manually refresh the screen image.

To change the AutoRefresh interval, follow these steps:

1. Choose **Tools**/Net/**A**utoRefresh. You are prompted to enter the number of seconds for the interval, as shown in Figure 14-8. Notice the prompt in the status bar with instructions for the entry.

2. Type the number of seconds you want. You can enter intervals from 1 up to 3600, which is one hour, or you can leave the box blank to disable the automatic refresh.

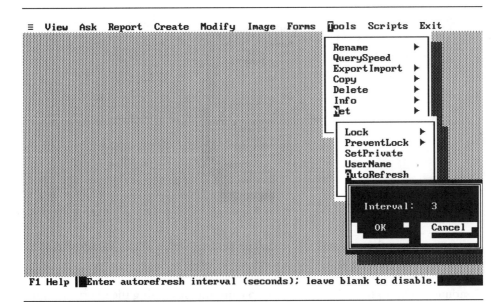

Figure 14-8.   *AutoRefresh prompt*

3. Press ENTER to save the setting, which means it is in effect for the current Paradox session.

To set a default AutoRefresh interval, use the Custom Configuration Program; however, using the Net/AutoRefresh option overrides the default for the current session.

Net/Changes

The Changes option allows you to process queries and reports that may be delayed because of automatic restarts that are the result of changes others are making to the tables on which you are working. Because you generally want the latest information, whenever Paradox detects a change, the query or report is restarted automatically to reflect the most recent data. However, there are situations in which you may not want to wait for restarts. You can cancel entirely the automatic restarts and the query or report on which you are working by pressing CTRL-BREAK; however, if you want to use a recent update, but don't want to wait for restarts, then use the Change option.

To control the changes, choose Tools/Net/Changes. A second menu appears, with two options, Restart and Continue, as shown here:

Restart   This option returns to the default setting, which allows Paradox to automatically restart queries and reports when data changes.

Continue   This option directs Paradox to continue processing the query or report even if changes are detected in the tables being used. Continue is in effect until the session ends, or until you choose **R**estart.

*The default setting, **R**estart, can be changed to **C**ontinue using the Custom Configuration Program.*

Using More

The **T**ools/**M**ore menu contains the options used to add or remove records in tables as well as the option used to protect tables and scripts. These options are shown here:

This section discusses all the options listed except for **D**irectory and **T**oDOS, which are covered in Chapter 2.

More/Add

The **A**dd option allows you to add records from one table to another. The field types in the two tables must be compatible—although not necessarily identical—and they must be in the same order. Any numeric fields can be added to other numeric fields. Alphanumeric fields can be added to other alphanumeric fields of any length. Memo and Date fields can only be added to other Memo and Date fields. The records added remain in the source table. They have actually been copied from the source table to the target table.

To add records to a table, follow these steps:

1. Choose **T**ools/**M**ore/**A**dd. A dialog box asking for the source table appears, as shown in Figure 14-9.

2. Type the name of the source table and press ENTER, or choose the table name from a list. A second dialog box requests a target table name, as shown in Figure 14-10.

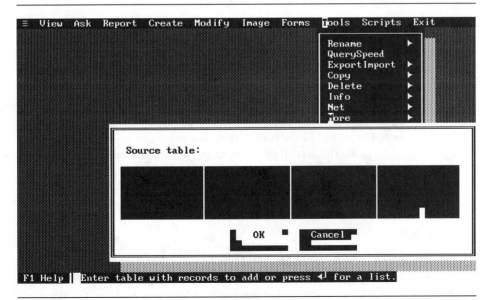

Figure 14-9. *Source table for the More/Add option*

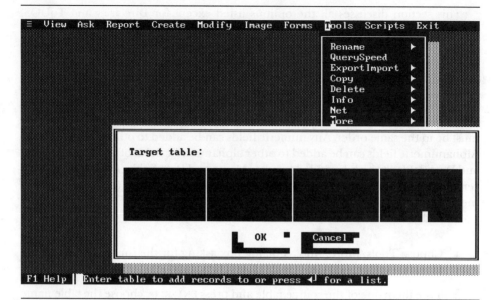

Figure 14-10.   *Target table for the More/Add option*

3. Type the name of the target table and press ENTER, or choose the table name from a list. If the target table is *not keyed,* the records are added. If the target table is *keyed,* additional options are displayed.

4. Choose one of the following:

   - *NewEntries* adds the new records without changing the existing records. If a record in the source table has the same key as a record in the target table, the record is placed in the temporary Keyviol table. This table can be edited to remove the violation and then added to the target table.

   - *Update* adds the new records to the target table in the order of the key field. If a record in the source table has the same key as a record in the target table, the record from the target table is placed in the temporary Changed table. The record is replaced in the target table by the record from the source table.

More/MultiAdd

The MultiAdd option is similar to Modify/MultiEntry in that it is used to add records from one table to the records in two or more tables. A map that tells Paradox which fields in the target table correspond to the fields in the source table is required.

A map is actually a Paradox table containing three fields. The first field contains the *names of fields in the source table, the second field contains the names of corresponding fields in the target table, and the third field contains the names of the target tables.*

When you use **MultiAdd** you can replace records in target tables with the records from the source table; whereas **Modify/MultiEntry** is used only for data entry. Before using **MultiAdd**, create a map from a query using **Modify/MultiEntry/Setup**. If you need information on creating a map, refer to Chapter 6.

To use **MultiAdd**, follow these steps:

1. Choose **Tools/More/MultiAdd**. The dialog box that appears asks for the source table name.

2. Type the name of the table, or choose it from the list. It must have a corresponding map table. A second dialog box appears, asking for the map table.

3. Type the name of the map, or choose it from the list. A menu with the choices **NewEntries** and **Update** appears, as shown in Figure 14-11.

4. Choose **NewEntries** or **Update**.

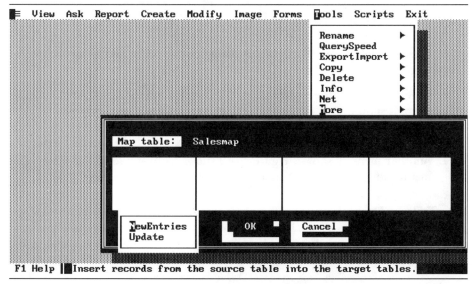

Figure 14-11.   More/MultiAdd dialog box for a map table and menu

NewEntries   This option adds records from the source table without changing the existing records. If there are key values that are the same in both the source table and a target table, but the remaining non-key fields are not the same, a key violation occurs, and the entire record from the source table is placed in a Keyviol table. You can edit the record in the Keyviol table, and then use Tools/More/MultiAdd to add it to the target tables.

 If the entire record in the source table exactly duplicates an entire record in the target tables, the record is "absorbed" in the target tables—that is, it is neither added to the table nor is it placed in a Keyviol table.

Update   This option does one of the following:

- New records are added at the end of target tables if the target table is not keyed.

- New records are inserted in key field order in the target table if the target table is keyed.

- If both the source and the target tables are keyed, and if there are duplicate keys, but the non-keyed fields are different, the non-key values from the record in the source table will update the non-key values in records in the target tables.

More/FormAdd

FormAdd is similar to MultiAdd in that it can be used to add records to multiple tables; however, you do not need a map for this option. To use FormAdd, follow these steps:

1. Choose Tools/More/FormAdd. A dialog box appears, asking for the master target table.

2. Type the name of the master table or choose it from the list. A list of available forms is shown.

3. Choose the form you want to use.

4. Another menu is shown. Figure 14-12 shows an example of the subsequent menus when using FormAdd. Choose from EntryTables or AnyTables.

EntryTables   This option adds new records that are in current Entry tables to target tables using the form as a map. If any key violations occur, the records will be placed in a Keyviol table where they may be edited and then added to the table using Tools/More/Add.

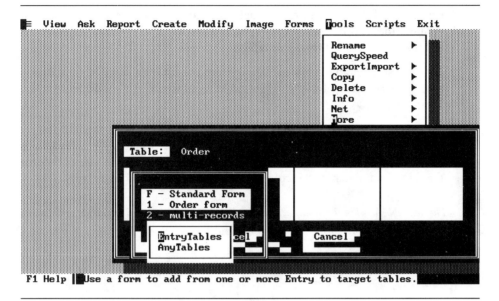

Figure 14-12. *FormAdd dialog box and menus*

AnyTables This option adds records from any table with the same structure as the master table. If you choose **AnyTables**, specify the source table. Another menu is displayed where you can choose from the following:

- *Entries* adds records without changing the existing records. (See the discussion of **NewEntries** in the "More/MultiAdd" section.)

- *Update* adds records that update existing records. (See the discussion of **Update** in the "More/MultiAdd" section.)

More/Subtract

You use **Subtract** to remove records from one table that also exist in another table. For example, in earlier chapters in this book, a new table for clients was created that contained only the names of those who lived in Washington. These records had been entered originally in the Clients table, which contained records of clients who lived in several states. Once you create the new Wash-ton table and add the clients living in Washington, you can use **Subtract** to remove those records from the Clients table.

To use **Subtract**, follow these steps:

1. Choose **T**ools/**M**ore/**S**ubtract. A dialog box appears, asking for the table that contains the records that are to be subtracted from another table. (The records will not be subtracted from this table.)

2. Type the source table name or choose from the list of tables. A second dialog box appears, asking for the target table from which the records are to be subtracted.

3. Type the table name or choose from the list of tables. At this point, if the target table is *keyed,* all records with key fields that are exact matches with key fields in the source table will be removed. If the target table is *not keyed,* all records that are exact matches to records in the source table will be removed.

The two tables used in the Subtract command must have identical fields except for numeric and currency fields, which are interchangeable.

More/Empty

Empty deletes all records from a table. You use **E**mpty if you want to preserve the table structure, but have no further use for the records in it. You also can use **E**mpty to remove records that have been entered in tables as a result of queries.

To use **E**mpty, follow these steps:

1. Choose **T**ools/**M**ore/**E**mpty. A dialog box appears, asking for the table name.

2. Type the name of table you want, or choose it from the list.

3. A menu asks if you want to cancel or proceed with the functions. Choose **C**ancel to quit and leave the records in the table; choose OK to remove the records.

More/Protect

You use the **P**rotect option to enter passwords that restrict access to your tables or scripts, to remove passwords, or to set a write-protect on files. When you choose **P**rotect from the **M**ore menu, you see a second menu, as shown here:

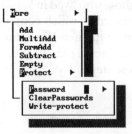

Assigning a Password for a Table

The **P**assword option allows you to set passwords for access to either tables or to scripts. The password can be removed using this same menu; however, you will have to enter the password to remove it.

1. Choose **T**ools/**M**ore/**P**rotect/**P**assword. A second menu displays the choices **T**able or **S**cript, as shown here:

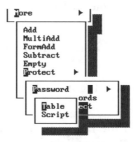

2. Choose **T**able. A dialog box asks for the table name.

3. Type the table name or choose from the list of tables. Another dialog box requests the password, as shown in Figure 14-13.

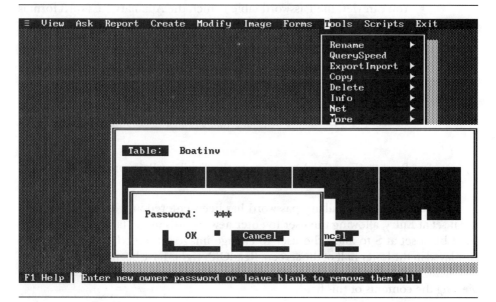

Figure 14-13.   Password dialog box

4. Type the password and press ENTER. The password can consist of up to 15 characters, including spaces, and it is case-sensitive. When you type the password, asterisks appear onscreen instead of the letters you're typing so that nobody can get your password by looking over your shoulder. It is a good idea to write down exactly how you typed the password because there is no way to access the table later without entering the correct password.

5. A second password dialog box appears. Type the password again to confirm it, and press ENTER. An Auxiliary Password form is then displayed, as shown in Figure 14-14. Refer to Table 14-1 for descriptions of the Auxiliary Password form.

6. Enter additional password instructions if you like (they are not required). Do any of the following:

- Type a user password of up to 15 characters following "Auxiliary password."

- To enter one of the five levels of access for Table Rights, move your cursor to Table Rights and type the first letter of the level you want.

- To choose the type of object the user is given access to, move the cursor to Family Rights and type the letter in parentheses for the object.

- To enter rights to specific fields in the table, move the cursor to the field name and type **R** for ReadOnly, **N** for None—if the user is not allowed to view or change the field—or leave the field blank if the user has full access to the field.

- You can view the Password table (which the Auxiliary Password form is based on) by pressing F7 (FormKey). The auxiliary passwords and access rights to specific fields are displayed there. For example:

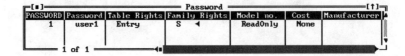

- Press F7 (FormKey) to return to the Auxiliary Password form.

In Figure 14-14 an auxiliary password has been entered and Table Rights have been set at Entry, allowing the user to enter new records in the table. Family Rights have been set at S to allow the user to change image settings. The list of fields is displayed in the lower half of the screen. ReadOnly rights have been set for the Model No. field, and None has been set for the Cost field, which prevents the user from viewing the contents of this field.

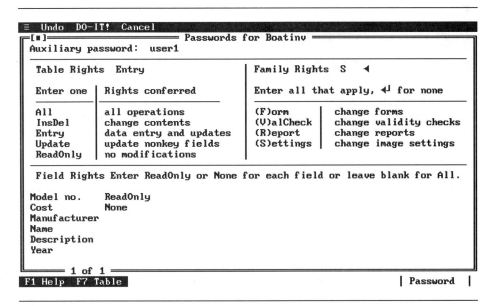

```
≡  Undo  DO-IT!  Cancel
┌[■]═════════════════════ Passwords for Boatinv ═══════════
│ Auxiliary password:   user1
│ ─────────────────────────────────────────────────────────
│  Table Rights  Entry            Family Rights  S  ◄
│
│  Enter one │ Rights conferred    Enter all that apply, ↵ for none
│  ──────────┼──────────────────   ──────────────────────────────────
│  All       │ all operations      (F)orm     │ change forms
│  InsDel    │ change contents      (V)alCheck │ change validity checks
│  Entry     │ data entry and updates (R)eport │ change reports
│  Update    │ update nonkey fields (S)ettings │ change image settings
│  ReadOnly  │ no modifications
│  ─────────────────────────────────────────────────────────────────
│  Field Rights Enter ReadOnly or None for each field or leave blank for All.
│
│  Model no.    ReadOnly
│  Cost         None
│  Manufacturer
│  Name
│  Description
│  Year
│
│  ══════ 1 of 1 ══════
╞═══════════════════════════════════════════════════════════
│ F1 Help  F7 Table                              │ Password │
```

Figure 14-14.   Auxiliary Password form

7. When done, press F2 (Do-It!) or click on **Do-It!**. You can also use CTRL-U to undo the last change, or choose **C**ancel to leave the form without making any changes.

The Auxiliary Password Form is used primarily to give other users limited (or full) access to a table. If you are the only user and you are not on a network, the owner password is all that is needed for you to restrict access to the table. Just press F2 (Do-It!) to bypass the Auxiliary Password form.

Removing or Changing a Password for a Table

The process of removing or changing the password is similar to assigning the password. Follow these steps:

1. Choose **T**ools/**M**ore/**P**rotect/**P**assword.

2. Choose **T**able from the menu displayed.

3. Choose the table that has the password assigned to it.

4. Enter the password that is assigned to the table. Another menu appears, asking if you want to change or remove the existing master password or if you want to change or remove only auxiliary passwords that were entered in the Auxiliary Password form. Figure 14-15 shows an example.

Rights	Description
Password	Type an auxiliary password, consisting of up to 15 characters.
Table rights	Enter the level of access by typing the first letter of the level you want.
ReadOnly	Allows the user to view the table but not edit or make any changes.
Update	Allows the user to view the table and change only non-key fields. Keyed fields cannot be changed.
Entry	Allows the user to use **M**odify/**D**ataEntry to enter new records.
InsDel	Allows the user to edit all fields, insert and/or delete records, and empty the table.
All	Allows the user complete access to the table. Any changes needed can be made, including restructuring the table and changing the data. This allows users to access certain tables without revealing the password for it.
Family rights	Family rights apply to the objects associated with a table. Type the letter for each object that you want to allow rights to. If none are selected, then users cannot access any of the objects. You can select All, None, or Any, in any order. If rights are not specified for an object, users can still use them, but can make no changes.
F:	Allows the user access to forms and lets them design, change, or delete them.
R:	Allows the user access to reports and lets them design, change, or delete them.
V:	Allows the user access to validity checks and lets them set them, change, or delete them.
S:	Allows the user access to image settings and lets them set them, change, or delete them.
Field rights	Three rights are available that can be assigned to each of the fields that are displayed:
ReadOnly	Allows the user to view the contents of the field but not make any changes.
None	Prevents the user from either seeing the contents of the field or making any changes.
Leave blank	Allows the user to access the field to view and to make changes.

Table 14-1.   *Auxiliary Password Form*

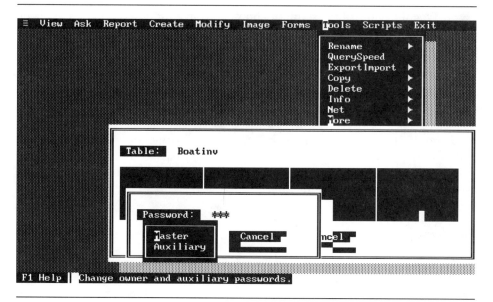

Figure 14-15.   *Menu options for removing or changing passwords*

5. Choose to either change or remove the password, by following one of these steps:

   • To remove or change the password, choose **M**aster. When prompted for the password, just press ENTER or choose OK to remove it. If you want to change your password, simply type in a new one, press ENTER or choose OK.

   • To remove auxiliary passwords, choose **A**uxiliary. In the Auxiliary Password form, press DELETE in the fields where you want to remove records from the form and press F2 (Do-It!) when done.

Assigning or Removing a Password for a Script

The procedure to assign or remove a password for a script is similar to assigning and removing passwords for a table except no Auxiliary Password form is used. When a password is assigned to a script, it can still be used by anyone; however, no one can edit the script without entering the password.

To assign a password for a script, follow these steps:

1. Choose **T**ools/**M**ore/**P**rotect/**P**assword.

2. Choose **S**cript from the menu that is displayed.

3. Type the name of the script or choose it from a list of script names. A dialog box asks for the password.

4. Type the password—you may enter up to 15 characters including spaces—and press ENTER. The password is case-sensitive. You will have to enter it a second time to make sure it is correct. It is a good idea to write it down, so you remember exactly how it was entered.

To remove the password from a script, follow the steps just given. You have to enter the existing password. When prompted for the new password, just press ENTER or choose OK to remove it. If you want to change the password at this point, type a new password in place of the existing one.

Using ClearPassword

When you present a password to gain access to tables and scripts, the password remains in memory, and they (the tables and scripts) are accessible without entering the password again during the current Paradox session. This means that if someone else uses your computer, they also can access those tables and scripts even when they are not on the desktop. This can be a problem especially on a network. ClearPassword removes all passwords from memory during the current session, thereby protecting your tables and scripts from use by others.

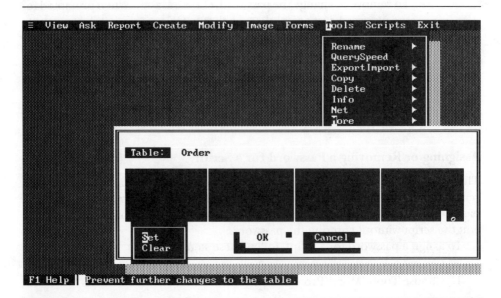

Figure 14-16.   *Write-Protect menu*

To use **C**learPassword, follow these steps:

1. Choose **T**ools/**M**ore/**P**rotect/**C**learPassword.

2. Choose OK to clear the password and clear the desktop of all tables, or choose **C**ancel to leave the password intact and leave the desktop as is. A message tells you that all passwords have been cleared.

Using Write-Protect

Write-Protect allows access to tables, but prevents data from being edited or records from being removed accidentally. To use **W**rite-Protect, follow these steps:

1. Choose **T**ools/**M**ore/**P**rotect.

2. Choose **W**rite-Protect from the menu displayed.

3. A dialog box asks for the table name. Type the table name, or choose it from the list. The menu shown in Figure 14-16, with the options **S**et and **C**lear, is displayed.

4. Choose **S**et to assign a write-protect for the table. Choose **C**lear to remove the write-protect from the table.

Chapter 15

Using Paradox SQL Link

Paradox is all the database you need for working in a PC environment, but a lot of the world's data resides on computers other than local PCs. Paradox SQL Link is an add-in product that gives Paradox the ability to interact with database programs running on remote computers. With SQL Link, you can query and manipulate data on those remote computers.

In Chapter 15 you'll learn about client-server architecture and Structured Query Language, and you'll learn how to install SQL Link, and how to connect to a database server. This chapter also gives an overview of Paradox menu selections that are added or changed by SQL Link, PAL commands and functions specifically used with SQL Link, and overviews of two utilities: the SQL Setup Program (SSP) and UseSQL, the SQL Command Editor.

Client-Server Architecture

SQL Link works in a *client-server architecture*. In this architecture, one computer acts as the *database server*, while the others act as *clients*. The server and the clients may be part of the same local area network (LAN), or they may be separated geographically, and connected through a *gateway* (hardware and software designed for linking remote computers and networks). The data resides on the server, as does the software needed to manipulate the data. This special software is called the *database engine* (the term *server* sometimes refers to just the database engine). The complete database software system consists of two parts: a front end and a back end. The *front end* runs at the client workstation; the *back end* is the database engine. Paradox SQL Link is a specific brand of front end software. Figure 15-1 shows a typical client-server architecture with both local and distant database servers. Figure 15-2 shows details of a client and a server.

In a client-server system, the user enters a query at a client workstation. The client workstation sends the query to the server, which locates the required data and sends just the results back to the client. For example, if you perform a query that finds just 25 records out of a table containing 1 million records, the records are tested at the server, and only the 25 found records get sent from the server to the client.

Contrast this with a typical PC database running on a network. Shared data on the network resides on a file server (not database server). The *file server* is a hard disk shared by everyone on the network. When a workstation loads Paradox, the entire database program runs at the workstation, even if Paradox is stored on the file server. In order to find the 25 records mentioned in the previous example, all 1 million records must travel from the file server to the workstation so they can be tested by Paradox. This results in a great deal of traffic on the network, which can slow the system during peak usage times.

Structured Query Language

For a client-server system to work, the client and the server must understand a common language. The programs that SQL Link works with all understand SQL. SQL is an acronym for Structured Query Language. It's pronounced either "S Q L"

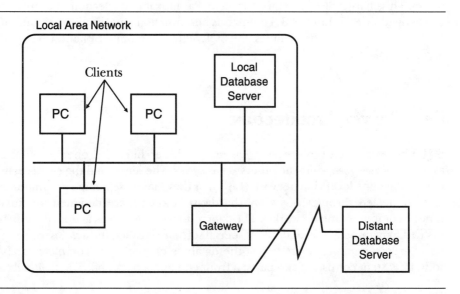

Figure 15-1.   *Typical client-server architecture*

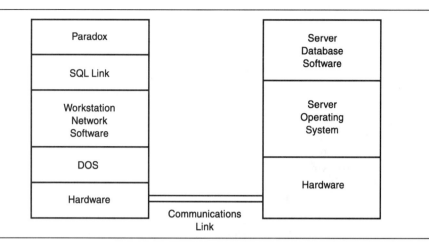

Figure 15-2.   *Client and server details*

or "sequel." SQL and query-by-example (QBE) were both developed at IBM in the mid 1970s. Because both let you manipulate data in a relational database, a Paradox QBE image can be translated into a SQL statement.

SQL lets you perform the following database functions:

- Define database structure

- Retrieve data (*query* the database)

- Manipulate data (add, remove, or change it)

- Control access to data

- Define rules that help assure the integrity of data

- Let multiple users access data simultaneously

SQL is the closest thing there is to a standardized database language. Although there is an ANSI standard SQL, each server product uses a slightly different dialect of SQL. Because of this, and because different servers use different communications protocols, there are several different versions of SQL Link. You must install the version that works with your specific database server. SQL Link then translates Paradox queries and menu choices into the proper SQL dialect for that server. You can also enter SQL commands yourself if you know the SQL dialect that your server understands.

These database servers can be accessed with Paradox SQL Link:

- Microsoft SQL Server 1.0 or later

- SYBASE SQL Server 4.0 or later

- Novell NetWare SQL server

- Oracle Server 6.0

- MDI Database Gateway for DB2 version 1.01

- IBM OS/2 Extended Edition Database Manager

- DEC Rdb/VMS

There are two categories of SQL commands. You enter *interactive* SQL commands in the SQL Editor window or use the Paradox menus. The system processes these immediately and displays the results as soon as processing finishes. *Embedded* SQL commands get stored in a PAL script and are executed when the script is run.

In this chapter, you'll see examples of some simple SQL commands. A complete discussion of SQL is beyond the scope of this book. A good general reference book on SQL is *Using SQL* by James Groff and Paul Weinberg (Berkeley, CA: Osborne/McGraw-Hill, 1990). For information about the dialect of SQL for your server, see the documentation for the server.

You do not have to know SQL in order to use SQL Link. You do have to know how to use Paradox. SQL Link translates Paradox menu selections and query images into the correct SQL dialect for the database server you're connected to.

In order to manipulate data on a server, SQL Link must know how the data is stored on the server. A *replica* table is a local table that contains the information SQL Link needs to interact with a corresponding *remote* table on a database server. Replica tables show up with regular local tables whenever Paradox presents a table list. When you highlight the name of a replica table, Paradox displays a message at the bottom of the screen telling you the name of the database server where the remote table is located. In Figure 15-3, States is a replica for a remote table located on a Novell Netware SQL server.

When you create a remote table in Paradox, SQL Link automatically creates a corresponding replica table. If you want to work with a remote table that was created with a program other than Paradox, you must first use the SQL Setup program to create a replica table. Using the SQL Setup program is covered later in this chapter.

Installing SQL Link

While installing SQL Link is a simple procedure, generally the database administrator does it. Check with your database administrator before following these instructions.

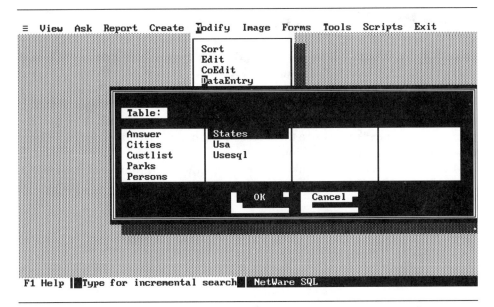

Figure 15-3.   *Tables list showing the replica table highlighted*

Upon installing SQL Link, a SQL submenu is added to the **Tools** menu. In addition, two options—SQLSetup and UseSQL—are added to Utilities in the System menu. You can also activate UseSQL by playing the UseSQL script.

To install SQL Link, follow these steps:

1. Insert Disk 1 of the Paradox SQL link in either drive A or B.

2. At the DOS prompt, type **a:install** or **b:install** and press ENTER to begin the installation process.

3. After reading the first screen, press ENTER. You'll see a screen that gives you information about the installation process.

4. Press ENTER again and follow the prompts. You can press ESC at any point in the process to cancel the installation.

5. If you want to install the SQL sample application, choose the Sample Application option. This copies the required files to your hard disk. To install the sample application on your server, start Paradox and run the script named SQLINST. You must have CREATE TABLE and CREATE INDEX rights on your server for the installation procedure to work.

Starting Paradox With or Without SQL

Once SQL link is installed, you can start a Paradox session the same way you usually start Paradox; SQL Link is started automatically. If you do not intend to use SQL Link during a Paradox session, you can start Paradox without starting SQL Link.

Before starting Paradox with SQL Link, be sure the server is started and is running the program it needs to communicate with your workstation. Be prepared with the parameters you need to log on to the server (the parameters required for each brand of server appear in the next section).

To start Paradox with SQL Link, type **paradox** at the DOS prompt and press ENTER.

To start Paradox without starting SQL Link, type **paradox -sql off** at the DOS prompt and press ENTER.

Selecting a Server Connection

Once the appropriate SQL link is installed, you need to establish a connection to the server whenever Paradox is started. This will enable you to access new remote tables that you have created in Paradox, enter data in them, query them, or delete them. You can also select a server connection from the SQL Editor window and from the Setup window (you'll see how later in this chapter).

To select a server connection, follow these steps:

1. Choose **T**ools/**SQL** from the Main menu. The following menu appears:

2. Choose **C**onnection/**S**elect. A window lists the server connections available to you, as shown in Figure 15-4. A message at the bottom of the window gives instructions for selecting the server.

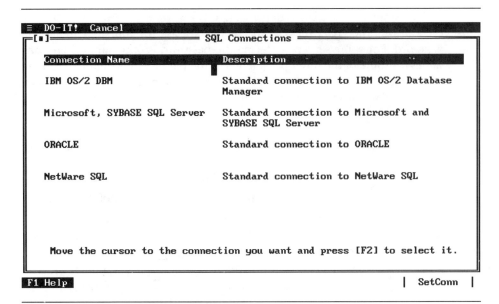

Figure 15-4. *SQL Connections list*

3. Move the cursor to the server you want and press F2 (Do-It!) or click on Do-It!.
    If needed, a second window appears, in which you enter parameters for the
    connection. See the example in Figure 15-5.

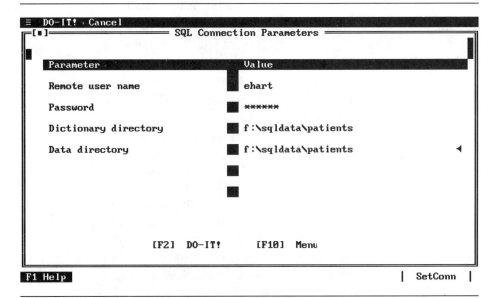

Figure 15-5. *SQL Connection Parameters window*

4. Which parameters are listed depends upon the server that was chosen; however, all windows, regardless of the server, will ask for your user name and password. For some servers, entering the password is optional as is entering values for some of the other parameters. If the parameter is optional, you can leave it blank. Table 15-1 tells you which parameters are appropriate for various servers and when a parameter is optional.

Server	Parameter	Description of Value to Be Entered
IBM OS/2	Server	Enter the workstation name of the server
	Database	Enter the location where tables will be created
	Local library	Enter the drive and directory for the location of the local catalog; if you specify just a drive (e.g., C), the directory defaults to \SQLDBDIR
MDI Database Gateways	Gateway	Enter the name of the machine running the Gateway or leave blank
	Database	Optional or enter the database name where the tables are created
	Tablespace	Optional or enter the name of the table where the table is created (the database will be the default database)
Oracle	Host	Enter the name of the server, using the proper Oracle notation
NetWare SQL	Dictionary directory	Enter the path that contains the dictionary you want to log in to
	Data directory	Enter the path that contains the data files
Microsoft and SYBASE SQL	Server	Enter the workstation name
	Database	Optional or enter the name of the database where the tables will be created; if you leave this blank, you will connect to the default database
DEC Rdb/VMS	Remote Nodename	Enter the name of the VAX computer running the server software
	Schema Name	Enter the name of the database schema (the data dictionary)

Table 15-1. *Connection Parameters for Various Servers*

5. After entering the parameters, press F2 (Do-It!) or click on Do-It!; or press F10 (Menu) to go to the menu and choose Cancel to leave the window without saving the changes.

If the entries you made are not accurate, or if you left a blank where a value should be entered, a message, "Connection parameter value is required," will be displayed at the bottom of the screen.

Working with Remote Tables

Anyone who has proper access to the server can access data in a table on the database server. Users can query the remote table with any suitable client software (remember, SQL Link is only one brand of client software). In contrast, data in a local table is accessible only to Paradox users connected to your local area network.

Naming Remote Tables

While using Paradox to create a remote table on the database server is similar to creating a local Paradox table, the rules for specifying table names, field names, and field types are different for remote tables than for local Paradox tables. Follow these guidelines when naming remote tables:

- Remote table names can usually be longer than local Paradox table names. The exact length depends on the type of server. Replica table names cannot contain more than eight characters. When you enter the table name, Paradox automatically abbreviates the replica table name to eight characters if the table name contains more than eight characters.

- Spaces and unusual characters such as hyphens are generally not allowed in field names on database servers. Refer to the documentation for your server for specific restrictions for table and field names.

- Do not use reserved words for field names. Reserved words are words such as SELECT, KEY, DATE, DESC, or NUMBER. Again refer to the documentation for your server for a list of reserved words.

- You can create an index on a field the same as you do for local Paradox tables. The server automatically maintains the index if others change the data in the table.

- You cannot assign Memo or Binary as a field type in a remote table. Other field types—Numeric, Date, Currency, Alphanumeric, Short—can be used. If your server does not support the exact field type you have defined, Paradox assigns the field type that is closest to the one you want.

- If any of the field types or names are disallowed, you will get an error message when you try to save the table structure.

Creating a Remote Table

When you create a remote table in Paradox, Paradox SQL Link automatically creates a corresponding local replica. The replica doesn't contain data; it contains instructions that tell Paradox how to interact with the corresponding remote table.

To create a remote Paradox table, follow these steps:

1. If you have not already done so, select a connection to a database server, and then choose **C**reate from the Main menu. A dialog box appears, giving you the choices **L**ocal and **R**emote. If **R**emote is not displayed, it means a connection has not been selected to a database server. Return to the Main menu and choose **T**ools/**S**QL/**C**onnection/**Se**lect to select a database server. Then choose **C**reate/**R**emote.

The name of the database server that is selected is displayed in the message bar at the bottom of the screen.

2. A dialog box appears in which you type the table name. Press ENTER. If the table name is valid—that is, if it conforms to all Paradox rules and server rules for naming tables—then the Paradox structure image will be displayed.

3. Enter the field names and types as you would for a Paradox table.

4. When finished, press F2 (Do-It!) to save the table structure. Paradox creates the remote table and the replica for it. Replicas are necessary for the Paradox SQL Link to access data from a remote table, and are discussed later in this chapter.

You cannot change the structure of a remote table using Modify/Restructure. Paradox does not support this function on a remote table. To change the structure of a remote table, create a new table with the structure you want, then use an INSERT query to add data to the new table.

Entering Data in a Remote Table

Use **M**odify/**D**ataEntry to add data to a remote table. Because you cannot directly view or edit a remote table, you cannot use **M**odify/**E**dit or **C**oEdit. You can use a form, if you like, by pressing F7 (Form Toggle) when the Entry table is on the desktop.

To add data to a remote table, follow these steps:

1. If you have not already done so, select a connection to a database server and then choose **M**odify/**D**ataEntry from the Main menu.

2. Enter the name of the remote table or choose it from the list (press ENTER to display the list).

3. An Entry table appears just as it does when you perform data entry for local tables. Enter the data using the same procedure you use for local tables.

4. When finished, press F2 (Do-It!) to store the new entries in the remote table.

If key violations occur, Paradox places duplicate records in a local Keyviol table. You can then edit the records in the Keyviol table and use **T**ools/**M**ore/**A**dd to add the records from the local Keyviol table to the remote table.

If a null value is entered in a remote table that is not allowed to contain null values, a local Problems table will be created where the records containing the null values are stored.

If, during data entry, the connection to the database server is broken, save the records in a local Paradox table by pressing F10 from the Entry table to access the menu, and then choose **K**eepEntry from the DataEntry menu.

Querying a Remote Table

You must have a connection to the database server before you can access the remote table and query data stored in it. SQL Link automatically translates a Paradox query to a SQL statement. You can save the statement as a PAL SQL...ENDSQL statement with SQLSave, or as a PAL query statement with QuerySave. Either way you get a PAL script that you can play back later. For a discussion of SQLSave versus QuerySave, see the section "Using SQL/SQLSave" later in this chapter.

Query Restrictions

There are restrictions on the types of queries you can perform on a database server:

- The SET operation is not supported.

- The FIND operation is not supported.

- The inclusive operator (!) is not supported.

- The LIKE operator is not supported.

- Multiline CHANGETO queries are not supported. (Single-line CHANGETO queries are allowed.)

- DELETE and CHANGETO queries can work with only one table at a time.

- SUM, COUNT, MIN, MAX, or AVERAGE (aggregated calculations) cannot be used as part of query selection criteria. You can use CALC COUNT and CALC SUM to compute values, but not to search for data.

- Wildcard operators (.., @) are valid only in alphanumeric fields.

- Multitable queries must use tables from the same connection. You cannot mix remote tables and local tables in a multitable query.

Performing the Query

Performing a query on a remote table is the same as performing queries on local tables.

To query a remote table, follow these steps:

1. If you have not already done so, select a connection to a database server, and then choose **Ask** from the Main menu.

2. Enter the name of the remote table, or choose it from a list (press ENTER to display the list of table names).

3. Fill in the query form the same way you fill in query forms for local tables. Refer to Chapter 6 for details on querying tables.

4. When finished, press F2 (Do-It!) to run the query. A local Answer table gives you the results of the query. You can then work with this Answer table the same way you work with other Answer tables.

Displaying the SQL Translation of the Query

SQL Link automatically translates the query to a SQL statement, which you can display on the screen. This might be useful for troubleshooting a query, or as an aid in learning SQL.

To display the SQL translation, follow these steps:

1. With the query form displayed on the desktop, press ALT-F2 (ShowSQL). The SQL Query box displayed contains the SQL commands that represent the criteria entered in the query form. Figure 15-6 shows an example of a query and its corresponding SQL statement window.

2. When you have finished viewing the SQL statement, press any key to clear it from the desktop.

Figure 15-6.   Paradox Query Form and its corresponding SQL query

Saving the Query as a SQL Translation

After creating the query for a remote table, you can save the resulting SQL statement in a PAL script. You can run the script later using **S**cripts/**P**lay if you want to repeat the query. Also, you can embed the script in a PAL program.

To save the SQL translation, follow these steps:

1. With the SQL query statement displayed on the desktop, press F10 (Menu) to access the Main menu.

2. Choose **T**ools/**S**QL/**S**QLSave.

3. Type a name for the script and press ENTER to save. This is similar to using **S**cripts/**Q**uerySave.

Displaying Reports on Data in Remote Tables

You can use **R**eport from the Main menu to produce a standard report or a custom designed report on data obtained from a remote table. You cannot, however, design a multitable report on remote tables. To report on data from more than one table, use a query to produce Answer tables for each remote table, add the data from the Answer tables to local tables, and then produce the multitable report from those local tables.

The **R**eport options are used the same way on remote tables as on local tables, with the exception of creating multitable reports. Refer to Chapter 8 for details about the **R**eport menu.

To use the **R**eport options, follow these steps:

1. If you have not already done so, select a connection to a database server, and choose **R**eport from the Main menu.

2. Choose any of the following and use them the same way you would use them for a local table:

Output   This option sends the report of data in a remote table to the screen, the printer, or to a file.

Design   This option allows you to create a custom report for a remote table.

Change   This option allows you to change the design of a custom report.

RangeOutput   This option allows you to specify the pages that you want to print.

SetPrinter   This option allows you to specify the printer port you want to use and to enter a Setup string and a Reset string if necessary.

Using Tools/SQL

Installing SQL Link adds SQL to **T**ools in the Main menu. **T**ools/**S**QL allows you to: select commands concerning the connection to the server; select commands concerning transactions between tables; perform operations—rename, copy, delete—on replicas of remote tables; save a query of a remote table as a SQL command; and change settings that affect remote tables, such as whether or not Paradox automatically saves changes, or how CTRL-BREAK affects the current SQL operation.

Using SQL/Connection

Earlier in this chapter, in the "Selecting a Server Connection" section, you saw how to select a connection between Paradox and a server using **T**ools/**S**QL/**C**onnection/**S**elect. This section covers the remaining options of the Connection menu: **S**elect, **M**ake, **B**reak, and **C**lear, as shown here:

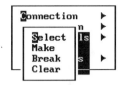

Making a Connection

Once you establish a connection to a server, you don't have to select it again during the current session unless you *clear* the connection. If you *break* the connection, SQL Link remembers the connection parameters. This lets you break a connection to perform tasks that don't require the server; you can then use **M**ake to reestablish the connection without having to select the server and reenter connection parameters. (See the following two sections for more information about breaking versus clearing a connection.)

To make a connection, choose **T**ools/**S**QL/**C**onnection/**M**ake.

Breaking the Server Connection

Breaking the connection disconnects your workstation from the server. This frees up server resources, making them available to other users. Breaking the connection leaves the current server parameters in memory so you can **M**ake the connection again without reentering the parameters. You can break the server connection in any of the following ways:

- Choose **T**ools/**S**QL/**C**onnection/**B**reak.

- Select a different server.

- Press CTRL-BREAK during a remote procedure.

- Press ALT-O (DOS Big) to perform an operation in DOS.

- Execute the PAL command DOSBIG or RUN BIG.

- Exit Paradox.

If **A**utoCommit is set to **N**o when you break a connection, the server rolls back (cancels) changes made during the current transaction.

Clearing the Connection

Clearing the connection disconnects from the server and clears the connection parameters from memory. If you clear the connection, you have to *select* the server again and enter the connection parameters (as discussed earlier in this chapter in the "Selecting a Server Connection" section) to reestablish the connection.

To clear the connection, choose **T**ools/**SQL**/**C**onnection/**C**lear.

SQL/Transaction Menu

A *transaction* is a sequence of database operations that work together as a logical unit. All the operations in a transaction must be successfully completed, or none of the operations are accepted. This is necessary to ensure the integrity of the database. For example, processing an order requires several separate but interdependent steps:

1. Post the order to the Orders table.

2. Update the account balance for the customer.

3. Update the inventory information for the items ordered.

If processing stops before all three steps are successfully completed, the database will have incorrect data. The three steps together make up a single transaction. There is no set number of steps that defines a transaction. It depends entirely on the operation being performed.

A transaction must be *started* before the first database operation occurs. Some database servers require you to manually start a transaction, while others start transactions automatically. Check the manuals for your database server to see what it requires.

At the end of the last step of a transaction, changes to the database are either *committed* (saved) or *rolled back* (canceled). If **SQL**/**P**references/**A**utoCommit is set to **Yes**, Paradox automatically commits changes. If a problem occurs (for example, the connection to the server gets broken), any incomplete transaction is automatically rolled back.

 As an aside, database engineers sometimes refer to the ACID properties of transactions. A valid transaction is ACID—that is, Atomic (an indivisible unit), Consistent (the same transaction steps always produce the same results), Isolated (unaffected by other events in the database), and Durable (a committed transaction stays committed).

The **SQL**/**T**ransaction menu, shown here, lets you explicitly start a new transaction and specify whether the current transaction should be committed or rolled back. If your server automatically starts transactions, choosing **S**tart has no effect.

```
Transaction
┌──────────┐
│ Commit   │
│ RollBack │
│ Start    │
└──────────┘
```

*Paradox automatically starts and commits transactions when you use **Tools/Copy** and **Tools/Delete** on remote tables, or when you create a new remote table. You cannot roll back these transactions.*

Using Commit to Save Changes

Use **C**ommit to save changes to remote tables when **SQL/P**references/**A**utoCommit is set to **N**o. If AutoCommit is set to **Y**es, changes to remote tables are saved automatically, and you don't need to use **Transaction/Commit**.

Commit works only with remote tables. If your server doesn't automatically start transactions, you must explicitly **S**tart a transaction if you want to be able to use **C**ommit.

*If you press CTRL-BREAK during a session involving remote tables, **Commit** will not be successful (the transaction will be rolled back).*

To choose **C**ommit, choose **T**ools/**SQL**/**T**ransaction/**C**ommit.

Using Rollback to Cancel Changes

Use **R**ollback to cancel changes to remote tables and return the data to its original status in those tables. If a condition occurs that threatens the validity of the current database operations, use **R**ollback to undo the changes.

Rollback works only with remote tables. If your server doesn't automatically start transactions, you must explicitly **S**tart a transaction if you want to be able to use **R**ollback.

To choose **R**ollback, choose **T**ools/**SQL**/**T**ransaction/**R**ollback

Using Start

When you're connected to a server that doesn't automatically start transactions, you must explicitly use **S**tart before the first operation of the transaction if you want to be able to commit or roll back the results of operations used in the transaction.

To choose **S**tart, choose **T**ools/**SQL**/**T**ransaction/**S**tart.

Once you Start a transaction, the resources it requires won't be available to other users until you either commit or roll back the transaction. Keep the transaction as short as you can.

Using SQL/ReplicaTools

You use **R**eplicaTools to copy, rename, or delete only the replicas of remote tables—not the actual remote tables. Paradox uses replicas to access remote tables. Replicas contain the information needed to connect to the remote tables; however, when you work with replicas, it is essentially the same as working with regular Paradox tables.

Paradox automatically creates replicas when remote tables are created in Paradox; however, in order to access remote tables created outside of Paradox, you must create replicas of those tables in Paradox. The SQL Setup program is used to create replicas and is discussed later in this chapter.

The **R**eplicaTools menu contains three options: **R**ename, **C**opy, and **D**elete, as shown here. The following sections explain the use of each option.

Using Rename

Use **R**ename to change the name of a replica table. You might do this if the first eight letters of the remote table name don't make a very good table name by themselves.

To rename a replica, follow these steps:

1. Choose **T**ools/**SQL**/**R**eplicaTools/**R**ename. A dialog box asks for the replica you want to rename.

2. Enter the name of the replica and press ENTER; or press ENTER to display a list of replica names, choose the one you want, and press ENTER. A dialog box asks for a new name.

3. Type the new name using standard DOS naming conventions, and press ENTER.

 While remote tables can have names consisting of more than eight characters, replica names cannot contain more than eight characters.

Using Copy

Use **C**opy to make a copy of a replica and its family of objects. One reason you might want to do this is for ease of access. You can allow others to access the data in a remote table by placing a copy of its replica in a shared directory (they can't use the replica while it is in your private directory).

To copy a replica, follow these steps:

1. Choose **T**ools/**S**QL/**R**eplicaTools/**C**opy. A dialog box asks for the name of the replica you want to copy.

2. Enter the replica's name and press ENTER; or press ENTER to display the list of names, choose the one you want, and press ENTER. A dialog box appears in which you enter a new name.

3. Type the new name using standard DOS naming conventions, and press ENTER. Enter a path name, as well as the filename, if you want to place the copy in a different directory. The replica and all associated objects are copied.

To copy a local table to a server, use **T**ools/**C**opy.

Using Delete

Use **T**ools/**S**QL/**R**eplicaTools/**D**elete to delete only the replica of a remote table— not the remote table itself. The replica's family of objects also will be deleted.

To delete both the remote table and the replica, choose **T**ools/**D**elete.

To delete a replica, follow these steps:

1. Choose **T**ools/**S**QL/**R**eplicaTools/**D**elete. A dialog box asks for the replica you want to delete.

2. Enter the name of the replica to be deleted and press ENTER; or press ENTER to display the list of replica names, choose the one you want, and press ENTER.

3. Confirm the deletion by choosing OK, or cancel the deletion by choosing Cancel.

Using SQL/SQLSave

SQLSave saves a query to a PAL script. The criteria specified in the query are translated to a SQL statement embedded in a PAL SQL...ENDSQL command. (See the discussion of the SQL...ENDSQL command structure later in this chapter.)

To use SQLSave, follow these steps:

1. Use **A**sk from the Main menu and fill in the query form(s) as you would for any other query.

2. Choose **T**ools/**SQL**/**SQL**Save. The query is automatically saved in a script as a SQL...ENDSQL statement in the SQL dialect of the current connection. Paradox saves the script in the current work directory.

The saved query can then be run using Scripts/Play, or it can be embedded in a PAL application and run from there.

You can also use Scripts/QuerySave to save the query as a PAL query image. There's an important difference between SQLSave and QuerySave: SQLSave stores the SQL state-ment for the query in the SQL dialect of the connection that exists when you execute SQLSave. If you play back the resulting script when you're connected to a different server, the query will probably fail. QuerySave saves the Paradox QBE image. When you play back this script, SQL Link translates the query into the SQL dialect of the server you're connected to at the time. This makes QuerySave more flexible for stand-alone queries. If you're developing a custom script for a specific server connection, SQLSave gives you a SQL statement that you can modify.

Using SQL/Preferences

The **P**references menu controls the default settings for AutoCommit and SetInterrupt. AutoCommit sets the default for automatically committing transactions on the server. SetInterrupt determines whether you can interrupt a SQL operation with CTRL-BREAK.

Using AutoCommit

AutoCommit controls whether or not changes made to remote tables are saved automatically. AutoCommit does not affect local Paradox operations—Paradox au-tomatically saves those as you work. Nor does AutoCommit affect PAL scripts that include embedded SQL statements. You must use SQLCOMMIT or SQLROLLBACK commands in the PAL script to save or reverse changes when a PAL script is used. To control AutoCommit, choose **Tools/SQL/Preferences/AutoCommit**. A dialog box appears with the choices **Yes** and **No**. Choose **Yes** to tell Paradox to automatically save changes made to data in remote tables. Choose **No** to tell Paradox not to automatically save changes to remote tables.

As discussed earlier in this chapter, if AutoCommit is set to No, then to save changes to a remote table, you must choose Transaction/Commit at the end of the transaction.

Using SetInterrupt

Use **SetInterrupt** to determine how CTRL-BREAK affects your work on remote tables. When **SetInterrupt** is set to **Yes**, CTRL-BREAK interrupts remote operations in scripts and breaks the current server connection. When **SetInterrupt** is set to **No**, CTRL-BREAK doesn't interrupt remote operations or break the server connection, but it still terminates the current Paradox script. **SetInterrupt** does not affect normal Paradox response to CTRL-BREAK.

To use **SetInterrupt**, choose **Tools/SQL/Preferences/SetInterrupt**. A dialog box appears with the choices **Yes** and **No**. Choose **Yes** to have CTRL-BREAK end a remote operation, roll back the transaction, and break the connection to the server. If you choose **No**, CTRL-BREAK will not affect the remote operation and the connection to the server will not be broken.

Using Tools/More

The **Tools/More** submenu contains three options you can use with remote tables: **Add**, **Empty**, and **Protect**. **Add** inserts records from one table into another. **Empty** deletes all the records from a table. **Protect** controls access to tables.

Use these options the same way for remote tables as you do for local tables. You must be connected to a database server in order to access the remote tables.

Refer to Chapter 14 for information on using the Tools menu.

Using Tools/More/Add

Use the **Add** option to add records from one table to another. You can add records from a local table to another local table, from a local table to a remote table, from a remote table to a local table, or from one remote table to another remote table.

To add records from one table to another, follow these steps:

1. Select a connection to a database server, and choose **T**ools/**M**ore/**A**dd from the Main menu. A dialog box asks for the source table name.

2. Enter the name of the source table, or choose it from a list. (Press ENTER to display the list of tables.)

3. A second dialog box asks for the target table name. Enter the name of the target table, or choose a table name from the list. Press ENTER.

4. The Changed table that appears shows the records from the source table that have been added to the target table. If key violations occur during the Add process, a Keyviol table will be displayed; if other problems occur a Problems table will be displayed. You can edit or otherwise adjust the records in either one of these two tables just as you would when working only with local tables. Then add the records to the target table. Changed, Keyviol, and Problems are all local tables.

 If a connection fails during an Add operation involving a remote table, the transaction will be rolled back, the records will not be added to the target table, and Changed, Keyviol, and Problems tables will not be created.

Using Tools/More/Empty

If you want to keep a specific table structure and its family of objects, but no longer have need for the data stored in the table, you can delete the records without removing the table or its family.

To empty a table, follow these steps:

1. Select a connection to a database server, and choose **T**ools/**M**ore/**E**mpty from the Main menu.

2. Enter the name of the table, or choose it from a list.

3. Choose OK to confirm the removal of the records, or Cancel to retain the records in the table. If you confirm the process, all records in the table will be deleted with no further warnings.

Using Tools/More/Protect

Use the **P**rotect option with remote tables to control access to the tables. You can enter master and auxiliary passwords, and remove existing passwords. The procedure for setting and removing passwords for remote tables is the same as for local tables; however, you must be connected to a database server.

In addition to the security offered by the **P**rotect option of Paradox, the server probably has its own SQL security system. Look in your server manuals for information about the SQL GRANT and REVOKE commands.

*Refer to Chapter 14 for details about using the **P**rotect option.*

Using the SQL Command Editor

You use **U**sesql, on the System/**U**tilities menu, to access the SQL Command Editor, which is similar to the regular Paradox editor. You can enter and edit SQL statements in the Command Editor using many of the same features used in other Editor windows.

Refer to Chapter 4 for a complete discussion of using the Paradox Editor.

SQL commands entered in the Editor can be executed immediately to produce the results you want. This is a convenient way to test SQL commands before including them in a PAL program. You can press F2 (Do-It!) to execute the SQL statement, or save the SQL statement in a PAL script by choosing **F**ile/**C**opyTo from the **E**ditor menu.

The SQL Editor window is referred to as a *card*. Only one SQL statement can be entered in a card. When you choose **F**ile/**S**ave, the statement entered in the current card is saved. You can use new cards for additional SQL statements. Cards are stacked in sequence by number. You can use as many new cards, or open as many existing cards as you like. You see only one card at a time; however, you can display other cards by doing one of the following:

- Press CTRL-PGUP to go to the previous card.

- Press CTRL-PGDN to go to the next card.

- Press CTRL-HOME to go to the first card.

- Press CTRL-END to go to the last card.

To use the SQL Command Editor, follow these steps:

1. Choose **U**tilities/**U**sesql from the System menu or choose **S**cripts/**P**lay from the Main menu, press ENTER to display the list of scripts, and choose **U**sesql from the list. The SQL Editor window is then displayed.

2. Enter a SQL command in the window, as shown in Figure 15-7. Use any of the options in the Editor menu to save, edit, search, or print the SQL statement.

 You can use the mouse to resize or move the window the same way you use it in other Paradox Editor windows: Point to the title bar and drag the window to a new position; point to the Resize corner and drag it to change the size of the window; click on the Maximize icon in the upper-right corner to make the window full screen size; click on the Restore icon to restore the window to its original size; or click on the arrows or drag the scroll box in the Horizontal and Vertical scroll bars to move to a different position.

The commands and submenus in the Editor menu are discussed next.

 The System menu only displays a dialog box showing the script name currently in use. Other System menu options are not available in this window.

Using the SQL Editor File Options

The File options in the SQL Editor let you manage SQL statement cards. You can create a statement in a new card, open an existing card, save the statement as a card

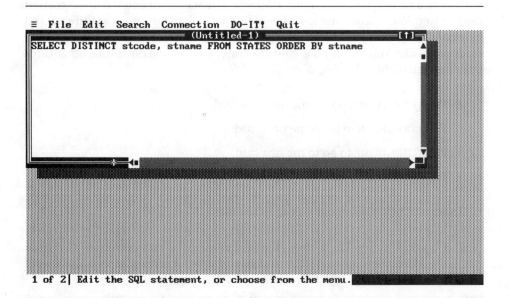

Figure 15-7. *SQL Editor window*

or as a PAL script, insert a file, write a selected block of text to a file, and print the SQL statement. Here is the File options menu:

To use the **File** commands, follow these steps:

1. Press F10 (Menu) to go to the **Editor** menu and choose **File**.

2. Select one of these options from the **File** menu: **New**, **O**pen, **S**ave, **C**opyTo, **I**nsertFile, **W**riteBlock, or **P**rint.

New   This option allows you to create a SQL statement in a new card. Choose **New** to display a blank card where you can enter the statement. Whenever a new statement is created, SQL Link automatically attaches the following information: the name of the user who created it; the date it was created; the date it was last run; and the name of the connection. This information is displayed when you choose **O**pen and select the card the next time.

Open   This option allows you to open a card containing an existing SQL statement. When you choose **O**pen, a dialog box appears as shown in the illustration. The names of existing statements are listed. Select the one you want and choose OK. You can open as many cards as you want, and they will be stacked according to number. After you open a card, you can edit it as needed.

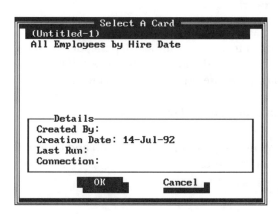

Save   This option allows you to save the statement and continue editing.

CopyTo   This option saves the statement as a script or as a PAL script. When you choose **C**opyTo, a dialog box appears as shown in the illustration. Enter the name for the script, and/or choose **S**ave as PAL Script, if you like. If you choose to save the statement as a PAL script, the statement will be automatically enclosed in a SQL....ENDSQL command. Choose OK to create the file, or choose Cancel to skip creating the file.

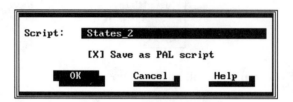

If you are not using a mouse to choose options in this dialog box, press TAB *to move from one option to another. Press the* SPACEBAR *to toggle the X on or off in the brackets at* **S***ave As PAL Script.*

InsertFile   This option allows you to insert a file in the **E**ditor window at the cursor position. Choose **I**nsertFile to display a dialog box. Enter the name of the file to be inserted and press ENTER or choose OK.

WriteBlock   This option writes a selected block to a file. Select the text to be saved and choose **W**riteBlock. Enter a filename and press ENTER or choose OK.

Print   This option prints the current SQL statement.

Using Edit Commands

The **E**dit menu contains commands similar to those in other Paradox Editor windows. You can cut a block of text to the Clipboard, paste, delete, show the contents of the Clipboard, show the line and column number position of the cursor, and go to a specific line. You can also use this option to change the title of the SQL card or to delete the card.

To use the **E**dit commands, follow these steps:

1. Press F10 (Menu) to go to the **E**ditor menu and choose **E**dit. The **E**dit menu appears, as shown here:

```
Edit
┌─────────────────────┐
│ XCut                │
│ Copy                │
│ Paste               │
│ Erase               │
├─────────────────────┤
│ Goto                │
│ Location            │
├─────────────────────┤
│ ShowClipboard       │
├─────────────────────┤
│ RenameCard          │
│ DeleteCard          │
└─────────────────────┘
```

2. Choose one of the following: **X**Cut, **C**opy, **P**aste, **E**rase, **G**oTo, Location, **S**howClipboard, **R**enameCard, or **D**eleteCard.

XCut   This option deletes a selected block of text and moves it to the Clipboard. Select the block, then choose **E**dit/**X**Cut or press SHIFT-DELETE.

Copy   This option copies a selected block of text and places it in the Clipboard. The text remains in the current card. Select the block, then choose **E**dit/**C**opy or press CTRL-INSERT.

*The contents of the Clipboard are automatically selected (highlighted) when you cut or copy a block of text. When the next block of text is cut or copied to the Clipboard, it replaces the selected block. If you open the Clipboard window (with **Edit/ShowClipboard**), then deselect the block (by moving the cursor), the next block that you cut or copy to the Clipboard will be inserted at the current cursor position without replacing the original block.*

Paste   This option inserts a selected block of text from the Clipboard to the current cursor position. Move the cursor to the position where you want to insert the block of text and choose **E**dit/**P**aste or press SHIFT-INSERT.

Erase   This option deletes a selected block of text from the Editor window, and that text is *not* moved to the Clipboard. Select the block of text and choose **E**dit/**E**rase or press DELETE.

GoTo   This option allows you to move the cursor immediately to a specific line number. Choose **E**dit/**G**oTo. A dialog box is displayed for the line number. Enter the number of the line to which you want to move, and press ENTER or choose OK.

Location   This option displays the line and column number of the current cursor position at the bottom of the Editor window. Choose **Edit/Location**. A line and column number are displayed automatically at the bottom of the window. When you move the cursor to a different position, the numbers will be removed from the window.

ShowClipboard   This option displays the current contents of the Clipboard.

RenameCard   This option allows you to change the title of the current card. Choose **Edit/R**enameCard. A dialog box displays the name of the current SQL card (window), as shown here. Enter a new name, then press ENTER or choose OK.

DeleteCard   This option deletes the current card. Choose **Edit/D**elete. A dialog box appears, as shown here. Choose OK to delete the SQL statement.

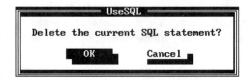

Using Search Commands

The **S**earch menu contains commands similar to those in other Paradox windows. You can locate values, repeat locating matching values, replace values, and replace all values to the end of the text in the Editor window.

To use the **S**earch commands, follow these steps:

1. Press F10 (Menu) to go to the **E**ditor menu and choose **S**earch, as shown here. These options are the same that you use in other Editor windows.

2. Choose one of the following: **F**ind, **N**ext, **R**eplace, or **C**hangeToEnd.

Find   This option locates a text string in the current **E**dit window. Type the text string in the dialog box and press ENTER to locate it.

Next   This option locates the next occurrence of the text string that matches the text string most recently entered in the Find dialog box.

 Replace   This option replaces one text string with another. Enter the text string to be replaced in the dialog box and press ENTER; enter the new text string in the next dialog box, and press ENTER.

ChangeToEnd   This option replaces all occurrences of a text string to the end of the text in the **E**ditor window.

Using Edit Connection Commands

The **C**onnection menu contains commands used to select a connection to a server, to make or break connections to a server, or to show the status of the server connection. The procedures for selecting, making, or breaking connections are the same as when you use **T**ools/**SQL**/**C**onnection. The **C**onnection menu is here as a convenience, so you can manage server connections without leaving the Editor.

To use the **C**onnection commands, follow these steps:

1. Press F10 (Menu) to go to the **E**ditor menu and choose **C**onnection, as shown here:

After you pick a server, you may have to enter parameters required for the connection (as shown in Figure 15-5). Enter the appropriate parameters, then press F2 *(Do-It!) to make the connection. Refer to the earlier section in this chapter "Selecting a Server Connection" for a table that gives information about parameters for specific servers.*

2. Choose one of the following: **S**elect, **M**ake, **B**reak, or **S**tatus.

Select   Use this option to establish a connection with a server. When you choose **S**elect, the list of available servers appears.

Make   Use this option to reestablish the connection if it has been broken as a result of choosing **B**reak, pressing CTRL-BREAK during a remote operation, or using the PAL command DOSBIG or RUN BIG. **M**ake will not reestablish a connection that has been cleared. In that case, you must use **S**elect.

Break   Use this option to close the remote files, roll back any uncommitted transaction, and disconnect from the server. You can also break the connections by pressing CTRL-BREAK during a remote procedure or using the PAL DOSBIG or RUN BIG command. You can reestablish the connection by using **M**ake.

Status   Use this option to show the current status of the connection to a server. You will see one of the following messages:

- *Connected to (servername)* shows the name of the server to which you are currently connected. Here's an example of this type of message:

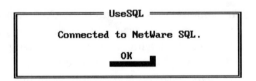

- *Connection set to (servername)* shows the name of the server that you have selected; however, you are not currently connected to it.

- *Not connected to a server* shows that you have not selected a connection.

After viewing the dialog box showing the status, choose OK to return to the Editor.

Sending the SQL Statement to the Server

You can execute the SQL statement by sending it directly to the server. If the statement is a query, UseSQL places the results of the query in an Answer table and displays it.

If you are not currently connected to a server, you can select a connection from the Editor before running the statement.

To send the statement to the server, follow these steps:

1. Connect to a server by using **C**onnection/**S**elect, selecting a connection from the list, and supplying any required parameters. (This step is optional.)

2. If you have not already done so, press F2 (Do-It!) or click on **D**o-It! with the mouse.

3. If the SQL statement is a query, an Answer table is displayed. The results in the Answer table can be saved to a different filename using **F**ile/**C**opyTo. The Answer table is temporary, so you must copy the results to another table if you want to keep them.

4. If the SQL statement is not a query (for example, GRANT or REVOKE), UseSQL will display a message acknowledging the results of the operation.

5. If the SQL statement produces an error, you'll see an appropriate error message. If the message comes from the server, you may have to refer to the manuals for the server to figure out what the message means.

Ending the SQL Edit Session

When you have finished entering and editing SQL statements, you can quit the session and return to Paradox. To do this, press F10 and choose **Q**uit from the Editor menu.

Using SQL Setup

SQL Setup is used to customize the SQL connection list to meet your specific needs, to print reports of the current connections, and to create replicas of remote views and remote tables created by programs other than Paradox.

To use **S**QL Setup, you can choose **U**tility/**S**QLSetup from the System menu or choose **S**cripts/**P**lay from the Main menu, press ENTER to display the list of scripts and choose **SQL**Setup from the list. The Paradox SQL Setup Program opening screen (Figure 15-8) will be displayed briefly, then the **S**etup menu will be displayed at the top of the screen as shown here:

Connection MakeReplicas Help Exit

Using the Connection Menu

The SQL Setup Connection menu contains three of the options found in **T**ools/**SQL**/**C**onnection, plus two new options.

From this menu, you can select, make, or break a connection to a server, check on the status of the curent connection, and customize the connection list.

To use the **C**onnection commands, choose any of the following: **S**elect, **M**ake, **B**reak, **S**tatus, or **C**ustomize.

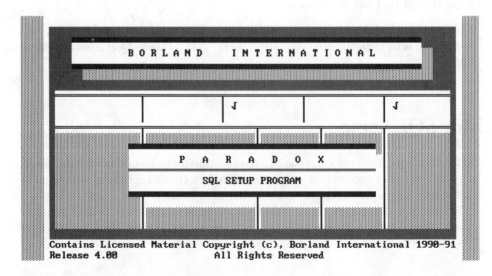

Figure 15-8. *SQL Setup Program opening screen*

Select   Use this option to establish a connection with a server. When you choose **S**elect, the list of available servers appears (as shown in Figure 15-4). After you pick a server, you may have to enter parameters required for the connection (as shown in Figure 15-5). Enter the appropriate parameters, then press F2 (Do-It!) to make the connection. Refer to the earlier section in this chapter "Selecting a Server Connection" for a table that gives information about parameters for specific servers.

Make   Use this option to reestablish the connection if it has been broken as a result of choosing **B**reak, pressing CTRL-BREAK during a remote operation, or using the PAL command DOSBIG or RUN BIG. It will not reestablish a connection that has been cleared. In that case, you must use **S**elect.

Break   Use this option to close the remote files, roll back any uncommitted transaction, and disconnect from the server. You can also break the connection by pressing CTRL-BREAK during a remote procedure or using the PAL DOSBIG or RUN BIG command. You can reestablish the connection by using **M**ake.

Status   Use this option to show the current status of the connection to a server. You will see one of the following messages:

- *Connected to (servername)* shows the name of the server to which you are currently connected.

- *Connection set to (servername)* shows the name of the server that you have selected; however, you are not currently connected to it.

- *Not connected to a server* shows that you have not selected a connection.

    After viewing the dialog box showing the status, choose OK to return to the SQL Setup menu.

Customize   Use this option to customize the connection list that appears when you choose **S**elect from a **C**onnection menu.

Customizing the Connection List

When you install SQL Link for a specific server product (for example, VAX Rdb/VMS), the install program enters default values for the connection name and description into the connection list. You can edit the names and descriptions in this list. You might want to do this so an end-user sees a connection named "CENTRAL ACCOUNTING" instead of the more cryptic "VAX RDB/VMS".

    You can enter default connection parameters for each entry on the list and you can have more than one connection for a given server. For instance, the same VAX computer might hold a Central Accounting database, a Marketing database, and a Warehouse Scheduling database. You can add additional connections for the VAX, and customize each connection to access a different database on the same VAX server. This ability to customize the connections gives you more control over access to remote databases, and helps shield end-users from needless complexity.

In this section, you'll see how to change, add, and remove information in the connections list, and produce reports to document the connection information.

Data for the connection list is stored in the file PARADOX.DSQ. SQL Link searches for PARADOX.DSQ in several locations, in this order: the current directory; the Paradox system files directory; the directories listed in the DOS path. SQL Link uses the first PARADOX.DSQ file it finds. Each user can have their own customized connection list, stored in a PARADOX.DSQ file in their own private directory. Users without a private copy of PARADOX.DSQ access a public copy in the Paradox system directory.

The database administrator should manage the connection list. PARADOX.DSQ should be password-protected so only authorized users can change the list. (See the section "Setting and Removing Passwords," later in this chapter.)

To customize the connection list, follow these steps:

1. Press F10 (Menu) and choose **C**onnections/**C**ustomize. The connection list appears, as shown in Figure 15-9.

2. You can then do any of the following:

   - *Edit the connection name* A name can be up to 28 characters long. The connection name entered here is what you'll see in SQL messages, and is the connection name displayed when you highlight a replica name in a list of tables. (See Figure 15-3.)

   - *Edit the connection description* The description can be up to 80 characters long.

   - *Edit the Parameters* Press F4 to go the **P**arameters screen and enter values that will be the defaults (Figure 15-10). If all the parameters are filled in, the users won't see the **P**arameters screen when they choose this connection. If you leave any values blank, the user will have to supply those values in order to complete the connection. Press F3 to save the changes in the **P**arameters screen and return to the **C**onnections screen.

Compare Figures 15-4 and 15-9. The connection identified in Figure 15-4 as "NetWare SQL—Standard connection to NetWare SQL" has been edited so it appears in Figure 15-9 as "Patients—Medical Histories of all Patients".

Compare Figures 15-5 and 15-10. The parameters in Figure 15-5 are good for the current session only. If the user exits from Paradox, the parameters are lost. The parameters in Figure 15-10 will be saved as default values for the connection named Patients. When a user selects Patients from the connection list, these parameters will be used automatically.

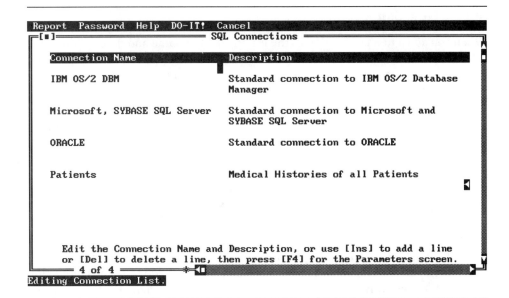

Figure 15-9. *Customize connection names and descriptions window*

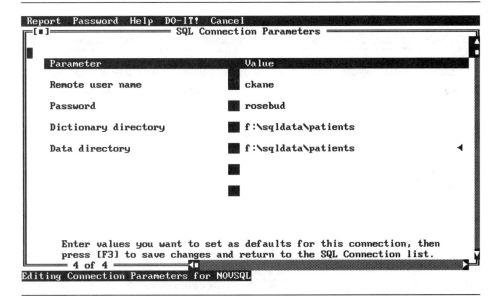

Figure 15-10. *Customize connection default parameters window*

Adding a New Connection

When you add a new connection to the list, the default name and description of the selected product appear in the list. You can then edit the name, description, and parameters to customize this connection, as described in the previous section.

To add a new connection, follow these steps:

1. With the cursor in the list of available connections, press INSERT to display a list of the available servers, as shown here:

2. Highlight the name of the product you want to add to the connection list, then press ENTER. The default name and description get added to the connection list, as shown in Figure 15-11. Now you can edit the name and description. Each connection name and description in the list must be unique.

3. If you want to have default parameters for this connection, press F4 to go to the **P**arameters screen and enter them.

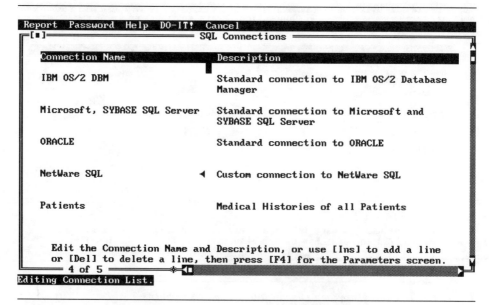

Figure 15-11. *New connection name in the list of SQL connections*

The parameters you enter here distinguish between different databases on a single server.

4. When you have finished entering values in the **P**arameters screen, press F3 to save the parameter changes and return to the connection list.

5. When you have finished editing the list or adding a new name, press F2 (Do-It!) to save the revised list. A dialog box asks where to save PARADOX.DSQ, as shown in the following illustration:

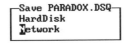

6. Choose either **H**ard Disk or **N**etwork.

Hard Disk   This option saves PARADOX.DSQ in the Paradox directory along with the Paradox system files.

Network   This option saves it to a different directory. When you choose **N**etwork, a dialog box appears, as shown in the following illustration. Type a valid directory name—either on your hard disk or on a network drive—and press ENTER.

Deleting a Connection

To delete a connection from the connection list, display the connection list, move the cursor to the row containing the name and description, and press the DELETE key. A dialog box requests that you either confirm or refuse the deletion, as shown here:

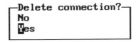

- **Y**es erases all information about the connection from PARADOX.DSQ.

- **N**o cancels the delete operation.

Reporting on the Connection List

You can generate reports of the contents of the connection list. These reports become part of the documentation of your database system. You can send the report to a printer, to the screen, or to a file. In addition, you can store a copy of the connections list in a table.

To generate a report on the connection list, follow these steps:

1. Press F10 (Menu) and choose **R**eport. A dialog box appears, as shown here:

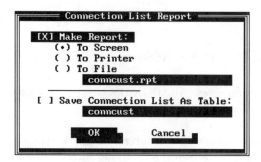

2. Choose either **M**ake Report or **S**ave Connection List As Table:

Make Report   Press the SPACEBAR or click on the option to toggle the X in the brackets on or off. If **M**ake Report is turned on, then choose one of the following:

- *To Screen*   Press TAB to move to the list of options under **M**ake Report, or click on **T**o Screen to select this option. A dot will appear in the parentheses. Choose OK to display the report on the screen, as shown in Figure 15-12. After viewing the report on the screen, press CTRL-F8 or click on the close box to close the report and return to the SQL Setup screen.

- *To Printer*   Move the cursor to this option, or click on **T**o Printer to select it. A dot will appear in the parentheses. Choose OK to send the report to the default printer.

- *To File*   Move the cursor to this option, or click on **T**o File to select it. A dot will appear in the parentheses. Change the report name if you wish (default is CONNCUST.RPT), then press ENTER or choose OK. The report will be written to the specified file.

Save Connection List As Table   You can save the connection list to a Paradox table. Press TAB and the SPACEBAR or click on the option to display an X in the brackets, and choose OK. The cursor will move to the text box below the option where the default table name, CONNCUST, is displayed. Type a new table name if needed, and

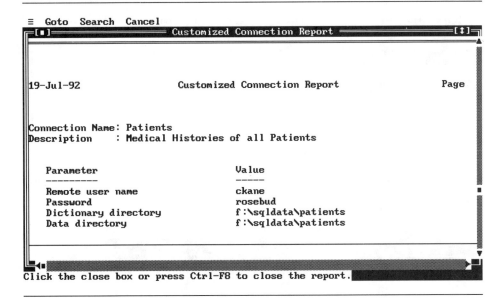

```
 ≡  Goto  Search  Cancel
┌─[■]════════════════ Customized Connection Report ═══════════[↕]─┐
│                                                                ▲│
│                                                                 │
│19-Jul-92              Customized Connection Report        Page  │
│                                                                 │
│                                                                 │
│Connection Name: Patients                                       │
│Description    : Medical Histories of all Patients              │
│                                                                 │
│                                                                 │
│   Parameter                         Value                      │
│   ─────────                         ─────                    ■ │
│   Remote user name                  ckane                      │
│   Password                          rosebud                    │
│   Dictionary directory              f:\sqldata\patients        │
│   Data directory                    f:\sqldata\patients        │
│                                                                ▼│
│■◄■▁▁▁▁▁▁▁▁▁▁▁▁▁▁▁▁▁▁▁▁▁▁▁▁▁▁▁▁▁▁▁▁▁▁▁▁▁▁▁▁▁▁▁▁▁▁▁▁▁▁►■  │
Click the close box or press Ctrl-F8 to close the report.
```

Figure 15-12.   *Customized connection report*

press ENTER or choose OK. To see the table, when you return to the Paradox Main menu choose **View** and select the new table name. You can create your own custom forms and reports for this table. Figure 15-13 shows an example.

3. When finished, choose OK to process the actions chosen, or choose Cancel to leave the screen without processing the actions.

Setting and Removing Passwords

PARADOX.DSQ should be password-protected so only authorized users can change the connection information. You can assign two different passwords to PARA-DOX.DSQ. The *administrator password* lets you read and change the connection information. The *user password* lets you read the connection information, but not change it. You must assign an administrator password before you can assign a user password.

Be sure you record the passwords in a safe place, where unauthorized users can't find them. If you forget the passwords for your copy of PARADOX.DSQ, you'll have to create a new connection list from scratch.

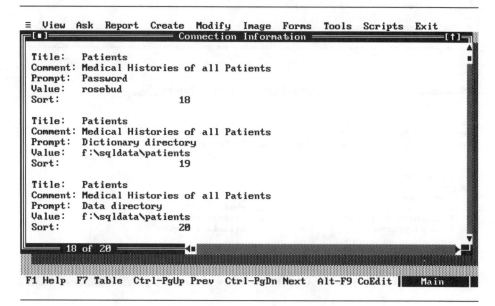

Figure 15-13.   *Customized form for viewing connection information*

To set a password, follow these steps:

1. Press F10 (Menu) and choose **P**assword from the connection list.

2. Choose either **S**etAdmin or **S**etUser.

SetAdmin   This option sets the password for the users who may read and change the connection list. A dialog box appears. In it you type the password—it will be shown only with asterisks—and press ENTER or choose OK. A second dialog box appears, as shown here. Type the password again to confirm it, and press ENTER or choose OK.

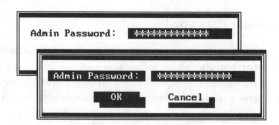

SetUser   This option sets the password for users who have *read-only rights* to the connection list. Type the password and press ENTER or choose OK. Type the password again in the confirmation dialog box, then again press ENTER or choose OK.

To remove a password, follow these steps:

1. Press F10 (Menu) and choose **P**assword from the connection list.

2. Choose **R**emove from the Password menu.

SQL Setup will not *ask you to confirm your selection before it removes the passwords.*

When you're finished customizing the connection, press F2 (Do-It!) or click on Do-It! to save the changes and return to the Paradox Main menu. Choose Cancel to leave the screen without saving the changes.

Creating Replica Tables

As discussed earlier in this chapter, in order to access a remote database that has been created with a program other than Paradox, you need to create replicas of the remote tables stored in that database. A replica doesn't contain data; it contains information that SQL Link needs to interact with the remote table represented by the replica.

To create a replica, follow these steps:

1. Choose **U**tilities/**S**QLSetup, and select a connection to the database server you are going to be using, if you haven't already done so. A connection is required in order to create replicas.

2. Choose **M**akeReplica from the Setup menu.

The Table Selection screen is then displayed, and the server to which you are connected is displayed in the lower-right corner of the screen.

3. From the Table Selection screen, specify a search by selecting one of the following: All User Tables, All User and System Tables, or Only These User or System Tables.

All User Tables   Choosing this will retrieve the names of all the user tables from your database server.

All User and System Tables   Choosing this will retrieve the names of all the user tables and system tables from the database server to which you are connected. System tables contain information about the database structure. If you want to query the structure information, create replicas of the system tables.

Only These User or System Tables   Choosing this allows you to enter criteria for selecting only specified tables. When you select this option, you can then enter a user name in the text box for "Where Owner Name is," and enter a table name in the text box for "and Table Name is." The ".." and "@" characters can be used to enter Owner and Table names. The "@" character represents one character in a string, the ".." represents any number of characters. For example, if you type **P..** all tables starting with P would be retrieved—this might locate Prodinv, Prodsale, Prodord, and so on.

4. When you have specified the tables to be retrieved, choose OK to begin searching for the tables.

A SQL Setup screen is then displayed as the program is searching for the tables. A message, "Running SQL command on server..." appears at the lower-right corner of the screen, and a check mark appears in the box indicating what is currently being processed.

When all tables have been found that match the specifications you entered in the Table Selection box, the table names are then displayed in the Remote Tables Found list of the Select Tables dialog box. From this list you can select the tables you want to replicate.

5. Select the tables you want to replicate from the Remote Tables Found list. For each table, move the cursor to the table name and press INSERT or SPACEBAR, or double-click on the name. This action copies the table name to the Tables To Replicate list.

6. Choose one of the following:

   - *All* copies all table names from the Remote Tables Found dialog box to the Tables to Replicate dialog box.

   - *None* removes all of the table names in the Tables to Replicate dialog box.

   - You can also remove a name from the Tables to Replicate dialog box by moving the cursor to it and pressing DELETE or SPACEBAR, or double-clicking on it.

7. When you are finished selecting the tables to be replicated, press F2 (Do-It!) or click on Do-It! to begin the process of creating the replicas. If you want to leave the screen without saving, choose Cancel from the Setup menu.

As the replicas are being created, the SQL Setup program automatically converts field types from the tables created on the database server to compatible field types in Paradox. If the database server you are using doesn't support a currency type field, a Type Convert window will appear in which you can specify whether or not each of these field types should be converted to currency fields. If the Type Convert window is displayed, move your cursor to the field type you want to convert, and press the SPACEBAR to toggle between N and $, or double-click on the field type.

8. Press F2 (Do-It!) to save, or if you don't want to save the changes you made in this window, press F10 (Menu) and choose Cancel.

If any conflict between names of existing tables and the replicas is detected, Setup will automatically rename the replicas with a number. After the process is completed, a list of the renamed replicas is displayed in a SQLprobs table. You can then rename, delete, or copy the replica names using **T**ools/**SQL**/**R**eplicaTools. .

When all the replicas have been created, a SQL Setup message box shows the number of replicas that have been created. From this box, you can generate a report of the tables that have been created, as you'll see in the next section.

Generating a Report on Replicas

You can generate a report on the replicas created in the current session. You can send the report to a printer, to the screen, or to a file. You can also create a Paradox table containing information about the replicas. You can view this table and generate your own custom reports about the replicas.

To generate a report on replicas, follow these steps:

1. Choose Details... from the SQL Setup message box. (This should still be on the screen from the steps in the previous section.) The SQL Setup Details screen that appears is similar to the Connections List Report dialog box shown earlier in this chapter.

2. Choose either **M**ake Report or **S**ave Replica List as Table:

Make Report   Display an X in the brackets and then choose one of the following:

- *To Screen* sends the report to the screen.

- *To Printer* prints a hard copy of the report.

- *To File* sends the report to a file. Type a filename in the box following the **T**o File option.

Save Replica List as Table   Display the information in a table that can then be viewed in Paradox by choosing **V**iew and selecting the table name. Display an X in the brackets, and type a table name in the box following the option.

3. After choosing the type of report you want, choose OK from the SQL Setup Details screen to generate the report. Choose Cancel to leave the screen without displaying or printing a report.

4. Once the report is generated you will return to the Setup menu. Choose **Exit/Yes** to return to Paradox.

Using Paradox SQL Commands

There are two ways you can use SQL Link to manipulate data on a database server: 1) You can use Paradox menus and QBE. SQL Link generates SQL code in the proper dialect for the server you're connected to. 2) You can type your own commands. Although this puts the burden on you to understand the SQL dialect for your database server, it gives you more control over how the data is used. If you're managing a distributed database, you really should learn to control the remote data using the proper dialect of SQL, as well as the special PAL SQL commands described in this section.

Here, we'll look at commands you can use to manipulate the data directly. This is not intended to be a comprehensive explanation of each command. For detailed information, refer to the Paradox SQL Link manuals.

The commands we'll look at fall broadly into three categories:

- *Regular PAL commands and functions*   These are commands that work pretty much the same whether you're manipulating data locally or on a server. The syntax of some of these commands varies slightly if you're interacting with remote data. We describe these variations later in this chapter.

- *PAL SQL commands and functions*   These are special PAL commands that work only with SQL Link, and only if you're connected to a database server.

- *Native SQL commands*   These are commands written in the SQL dialect for your database server. For information about standard SQL, you may want to check out *Using SQL*, the book by James Groff and Paul Weinberg mentioned earlier in this chapter. Please refer to the SQL manuals for your database server to learn the correct SQL dialect for your system.

There are two ways to send native SQL commands to the server. You can write the commands with UseSQL, the SQL Link command editor, or you can embed the SQL commands in a Paradox script with the SQL...ENDSQL command structure. Since each server uses a slightly different dialect of SQL (perceived as an "enhancement" or a "nuisance" depending on your viewpoint), this chapter uses only general examples. You'll probably have to modify the syntax to work with your server.

Conventions Used in This Chapter

The following conventions are used in the syntax of the commands and functions.

- Replaceable parameters appear in italics. These are items you must replace with an appropriate value or expression, as in:

```
EMPTY TableName
```

- Optional elements are enclosed in brackets, like this:

```
CREATE [ REMOTE ] TableName FieldDefList
```

- Selection of only one choice from several listed is shown by a vertical bar between options, with the option list enclosed in braces, like this:

```
SQLAUTOCOMMIT { Yes | No }
```

- You'll see references to a variable named Retval. This is a special Paradox variable that traps certain values for later processing. See specific commands for the uses of Retval.

Let's look at the Paradox SQL commands.

Regular PAL Commands and Functions

PAL commands that deal with program control rather than data manipulation will work normally with SQL Link. IF...ENDIF and WHILE...ENDWHILE are examples of commands that control program flow.

Only some PAL commands and functions that manipulate data will work with SQL Link. In general, PAL commands and functions that must deal directly with the data in a remote table won't work, while commands and functions that deal with the structure defined in a replica will work. The following PAL commands will work with SQL Link, but behave differently than they do without SQL Link. Please note that the syntax of some of these commands is different with SQL Link than it is with regular Paradox.

ADD *TableName1 TableName2*

Use this to add records from *TableName1* to *TableName2*. The table structures must be compatible. If *TableName2* is keyed, records in *TableName2* will be replaced by records from *TableName1* that have the same key values. The original contents of the changed records from *TableName2* are written to a local Changed table. If errors occur, Paradox creates a local Problems table.

If SQLAUTOCOMMIT is set to **Yes**, and the records are added as part of a transaction, Paradox automatically commits the transaction after the records are added. If an error occurs, Paradox automatically rolls back the transaction. If SQLAUTOCOMMIT is set to **No**, you'll need to use SQLCOMMIT to manually commit the transaction. See the sections on "SQLAUTOCOMMIT {Yes | No }" and "SQLCOMMIT," later in this chapter.

COPY *TableName1* [REMOTE] *TableName2*

Use this to copy *TableName1* and its family of objects to *TableName2*. Either table can be a local table or a remote table. If *TableName2* is a remote table, observe the following guidelines:

- Preface the name with the REMOTE keyword.
- Be sure the resulting table structure is valid on the database server.
- Select a connection before you use the COPY command.

If *TableName2* is remote, Paradox commits any pending transactions before starting the COPY, then commits the COPY transaction automatically when it's done. You cannot roll back a COPY command.

If you're not able to use COPY because of data type restrictions on the database server, create an empty table on the server and ADD records from *TableName1* to *TableName2*. Any records that are invalid on the server will be placed in a Problems table, where you can massage the data to get it to transfer to the server table.

CREATE

Use CREATE to make a new local or remote table.

When you create a remote table, Paradox commits any pending transactions before starting the CREATE, then commits the CREATE transaction automatically when it's finished. You cannot roll back a CREATE, but since you're creating an empty table structure, you can just delete it if necessary.

Make sure you're connected to a database server before you attempt to create a remote table.

There are two variations of CREATE. The first uses *FieldDefList* and the second uses LIKE. Here's the first variation:

CREATE [REMOTE] *TableName FieldDefList*

This version creates a new table *TableName* with the structure defined by *FieldDefList*. *FieldDefList* consists of a comma-delimited series of field definitions of the format *FieldName:FieldType*.

Example One   The following code creates a remote table to store product data. If you compare this with the CREATE example in Chapter 13, you'll notice that spaces have been removed from field names for this example, because field names of remote tables cannot contain spaces.

```
CREATE REMOTE "products"
     "ProdNum"          :          "N*",
     "Description"      :          "A20",
     "ListPrice"        :          "$"
```

Here's the second variation of CREATE:

CREATE [REMOTE] *TableName2* LIKE *TableName1*

This variation creates a new table *TableName2* with the same structure as an existing table *TableName1*. This acts like the **B**orrow option of the Create mode. The structure of *TableName1* must be valid according to the requirements of the database server. If it's not, the CREATE operation will fail.

Example Two   The following code creates a table to store old product data, using the table structure of the Products table:

```
CREATE REMOTE "oldprod" LIKE "products"
```

DELETE *TableName*

This erases a data table and its entire family of objects. DELETE doesn't ask for confirmation, so be careful. The database server should control security of its own data, so you might not be able to delete data on the server if you don't have the proper security clearance. When you delete a remote table, Paradox also deletes the replica.

When you DELETE a remote table, Paradox commits any pending transactions before starting the DELETE, then commits the DELETE transaction automatically when it's done.

You cannot roll back a DELETE!

Menu Equivalent   Menu {**Tools**} {**Delete**} {**Table**}. *TableName* {**OK**}

EMPTY *TableName*

This removes all records from table *TableName*. *TableName* can be either a local or a remote table.

If SQLAUTOCOMMIT is set to **Yes**, Paradox will automatically commit the transaction after the records are removed. If an error occurs, Paradox will automatically roll back the transaction. If SQLAUTOCOMMIT is set to **No**, you'll need to use SQLCOMMIT to manually commit the transaction. See the sections "SQLAUTOCOMMIT {Yes | No }" and "SQLCOMMIT," later in this chapter.

Menu Equivalent   Menu {Tools} {More} {Empty}. *TableName* {OK}

ERRORCODE()

ERRORCODE() produces a number that indicates the type of error that most recently occurred. If no errors have occurred, ERRORCODE() contains the value 0 (zero). All error codes related to SQL operations have a value of 1000 or greater. You should also check the values returned by SQLERRORCODE() and SQLERRORMESSAGE() to see specific information generated by the database server. Check the manuals for your database server to learn what error messages and codes it generates.

Here are the values Paradox returns for SQL errors:

ERRORCODE()	ERRORMESSAGE()
1000	General SQL error—check SQLERRORMESSAGE() to return the server error message
1001	Network error
1002	Deadlock on server
1003	User aborted (CTRL-BREAK)
1004	Not enough memory to complete operation
1005	Communication error
1006	Connection failed
1007	Insufficient access privileges or incompatible locks
1008	Object already exists
1009	Object name invalid
1010	General create error
1011	Database or disk full
1012	Object does not exist

ERRORCODE()	ERRORMESSAGE()
1013	Column type or usage invalid
1014	Remote key violations (SQL...ENDSQL only)
1015	Syntax error (SQL...ENDSQL only)
1016	Copy failed
1017	Number of authorized users exceeded
1018	Replica inconsistent with remote table
1019	A replica named *ReplicaName* already exists

ERRORINFO TO *DynamicArrayName*

ERRORINFO TO stores information about the most recent script error in the dynamic array named *DynamicArrayName*. You can examine this information for troubleshooting. The array contains the following elements:

Array Element	Description
SCRIPT	The name of the PAL script where the error occurred
LINE	The line number in the script that caused the error
POSITION	The character position in the line that caused the error
CODE	The code number of the most recent error; The ERRORCODE() function returns the same number
USER	The name of the user who has placed a lock on the object involved in the error; the ERRORUSER() function returns the same value
MESSAGE	The text of the most recent error message; The ERRORMESSAGE() function returns the same value
PROC	The name of the PROC currently running; this is blank if no procedure is running
SQLERROR-MESSAGE	The text of the most recent SQL error message generated by the database server. If SQL Link is not active, or if no SQL error has occurred, this value is blank. The SQLERRORMESSAGE() function returns the same value
SQLERRORCODE	The code number of the most recent SQL error generated by the database server. If SQL Link is not active, or if no SQL error has occurred, this value is blank. The SQLERRORCODE() function returns the same value

ERRORMESSAGE()

ERRORMESSAGE() returns the text of the most recent error message. This is the same message that Paradox displays to the user when an error occurs. If no errors have occurred, ERRORMESSAGE() contains a null string.

PROTECT *TableName, Password*

If *TableName* is a local table, PROTECT encrypts the table and assigns Password as its Admin (Owner) password. If *TableName* is a remote table, PROTECT encrypts the corresponding replica and assigns *Password* as its Admin password. To protect or unprotect the remote table itself, use the SQL commands GRANT and REVOKE. See your server manuals for information about these two commands.

Menu Equivalent   Menu (System) {Utilities} {SQLSetup} {Connection} {Customize} {Password} {SetAdmin}

QUERY

QUERY places the query image represented by *QueryImage* on the work surface. The easiest way to create this structure is to build a query image through the Paradox menus, then save the query as a script (using Menu {Scripts} {QuerySave}). You can use a query to perform some operations that you can't otherwise perform on a remote table. For example, you can't use CCOUNT() on a remote table, but you can use CALC COUNT in a query to accomplish the desired result. The complete syntax for the command is shown here:

```
QUERY
QueryImage
ENDQUERY
```

REPORT *TableName ReportName*

REPORT prints report *ReportName* of table *TableName*. *ReportName* is an expression that equals "R", "1" through "14", or 1 through 14. A report can't draw data from multiple remote tables at the same time. If you need to include several remote tables in a report, use queries to create local tables, then print a report using those local tables.

Menu Equivalent   Menu {Report} {Output} {Printer}

Commands and Functions That Don't Work with SQL Link

The following are some PAL commands and functions that will *not* work with SQL Link, because they must deal directly with the data in a table. This isn't an exhaustive list, but it illustrates the types of commands that won't work with remote tables:

```
CAVERAGE()
CCOUNT()
COEDIT
CSUM()
EDIT
ISEMPTY()
NRECORDS()
VIEW
```

If you're not sure if a command will work, create a simple script and test it.

PAL SQL Commands and Functions

PAL SQL commands and functions work only when your workstation is connected to a database server with Paradox SQL Link. They were developed to give Paradox programmers a way to interact directly with remote databases.

ISSQL()

ISSQL() indicates whether SQL Link is available. If SQL Link is installed, ISSQL() returns a value of True. If SQL link is not installed, or if you start Paradox with the command line option -sql off, ISSQL() returns a value of False. A value of True doesn't mean that you're connected to a database server, although you might be.

SHOWSQL()

SHOWSQL() displays the SQL statement created for the query on the workspace. When you create a query image, Paradox SQL Link generates an equivalent SQL statement that will be sent to the database server. SHOWSQL() lets you look at the SQL statement. You can use this as a way to learn SQL, or to check the statement for validity if you already know SQL.

Keystroke Equivalent   ALT-F2

SQL

SQL sends native SQL statements directly to the database server. This is sometimes called *passthrough* SQL, because Paradox doesn't modify or interpret the statements. You can include a valid PAL expression by enclosing it between two tildes (~). Paradox evaluates the expression, then translates it and includes it as part of the SQL statement. The complete syntax for the command is shown here:

```
SQL [ NOFETCH ]
{ SQLText | ~Expression~ }
ENDSQL
```

If a SQL statement is a query (that is, if it returns values), the PAL system variable Retval is set to True, even if the query results in an empty set. For all other SQL statements, Retval is set to False.

If the SQL statement is a query, and you do *not* use the NOFETCH keyword, Paradox creates a local Answer table from the results of the query. If you want to save this table, be sure to rename it.

If you use the NOFETCH keyword, Paradox doesn't create an Answer table. You can then use the SQLFETCH command to process the results on a row-by-row basis. When you're through with the query, use the SQLRELEASE command to release it.

If you want to treat the SQL...ENDSQL commands as a transaction, either be sure that your server automatically starts transactions, or use SQLSTARTTRANS before SQL...ENDSQL.

Paradox doesn't automatically commit remote changes produced by SQL...END-SQL commands, even if SQLAUTOCOMMIT is set to **Yes**. You must use SQLCOMMIT to commit the changes, or SQLROLLBACK to cancel them.

If a SQL...ENDSQL command results in an error at the database server, the SQLERRORCODE() and SQLERRORMESSAGE() functions give you information about the error.

In the following example, the program asks the user to enter the name of a remote table. The variable containing the name of the table is then used in a SQL SELECT statement to display data from the table.

```
CLEAR
@ 5,10
?? "Please enter the name of a remote table: "
ACCEPT "A8" TO vtable
SQL
     SELECT * FROM ~vtable~
ENDSQL
```

SQLAUTOCOMMIT { Yes | No }

SQLAUTOCOMMIT tells Paradox whether or not to commit changes after each successful remote operation. If SQLAUTOCOMMIT is set to **Yes**, Paradox automatically commits changes. If SQLAUTOCOMMIT is set to **No**, changes accumulate until you either commit the changes with SQLCOMMIT or roll them back with SQLROLLBACK. The effect of SQLAUTOCOMMIT **Yes** is to make each single operation a complete transaction.

If SQLAUTOCOMMIT is set to **No**, you must commit changes before you break the current server connection or exit Paradox. If you don't commit the changes, the database server will automatically roll back your changes when you break the connection. Any of the actions listed here will break the current server connection:

- Execute the PAL SQLBREAKCONNECT command.

- Select a different server connection.

- Press CTRL-BREAK.

- Execute the PAL DOSBIG command.

- Execute the PAL RUN BIG command.

- Press ALT-O (DOS Big).

- Exit Paradox.

Even if SQLAUTOCOMMIT is set to Yes, changes made with SQL...ENDSQL must be saved manually (for example, with SQLCOMMIT).

Menu Equivalent   Menu {Tools} {SQL} {Preferences} {AutoCommit}

SQLBREAKCONNECT

SQLBREAKCONNECT rolls back any uncommitted transactions and disconnects your workstation from the database server. If SQLAUTOCOMMIT is set to **No** and you want to commit pending transactions, you must deliberately commit them before breaking the connection. Use SQLCOMMIT for this. SQLBREAKCONNECT preserves the current connection parameters, so you can reconnect to the server without having to respecify the connection parameters.

SQLBREAKCONNECT is useful if you need to work only with local tables, and you want to free the database server resources while you do so. When you're ready to work with the same remote tables again, use SQLMAKECONNECT to reconnect to the same server using the same connection parameters as before.

Menu Equivalent   Menu {Tools} {SQL} {Connection} {Break}

SQLCLEARCONNECT

SQLCLEARCONNECT clears the current connection parameters from memory, but stays connected to the server. SQLCLEARCONNECT by itself doesn't commit or roll back pending transactions, but if you break the connection before you reconnect and commit the transaction, Paradox will roll back any uncommitted changes. After you issue SQLCLEARCONNECT, all commands work only with local tables. If you connect to a new server, or reconnect to the same server, you must enter valid connection parameters.

SQLCLEARCONNECT is useful if you want to stay connected to the database server, but you don't want your connection parameters left in memory. For example, assume that getting access to the database server is difficult, so you try to stay connected for as long as possible when you finally get on. If you need to leave your workstation for a short time, rather than disconnect from the server, you can use SQLCLEARCONNECT to clear your connection parameters from memory. This keeps your workstation attached to the server, but nobody can access the server from your workstation until they enter a valid set of connection parameters.

Menu Equivalent   Menu {Tools} {SQL} {Connection} {Clear}

*Although **SQLCLEARCONNECT** by itself doesn't roll back an open transaction, someone can still disconnect your workstation from the server, and cause your transaction to be canceled. Of course, this implies that you've left your workstation unattended with an open transaction. Since an open transaction ties up resources on the server, you should either commit or roll back a transaction before you take a break.*

SQLCOMMIT

SQLCOMMIT commits all pending transactions on the database server. If SQLAUTOCOMMIT is set to **No**, or if changes result from a passthrough command sent with SQL...ENDSQL, you must use SQLCOMMIT to explicitly save the changes before you break the server connection. If you don't commit the changes, the server will roll back the changes when you break the connection. If the commit succeeds, Retval is set to True; otherwise Retval is set to False.

Menu Equivalent   Menu {Tools} {SQL} {Transaction} {Commit}

SQLCONNECTINFO(*OptionName* [, *ReplicaName*])

SQLCONNECTINFO() returns connection information about the current connection, or about a specific remote table.

OptionName must be one of the names given in the following table. The quotes are required. You can type the word in any combination of lowercase and uppercase letters.

OptionName	Meaning
"TITLE"	Returns the connection title. This is the same title displayed in the connection list when you attempt to connect to a server.
"DESCRIPTION"	Returns the connection description. This is the same description displayed in the connection list when you attempt to connect to a server.
"PRODUCT"	Returns the code name of the database server product. See the Paradox reference manual for your server.
"DIALECT"	Returns the code name of the SQL dialect used by the database server. See the Paradox reference manual for your server.

ReplicaName is the name of a local replica for a remote table. If you use the *ReplicaName* parameter, SQLCONNECTINFO() indicates the requested connection information for that remote table. If you omit the *ReplicaName* parameter, SQLCONNECTINFO() indicates the requested connection information for the current connection.

If the name you specify for ReplicaName isn't a replica, or if you don't specify a name and your workstation isn't connected to a server, then SQLCONNECTINFO() returns a null string ("").

For example, suppose your workstation has access to both a Novell NewWare SQL server and an Oracle server. You've customized the connection list to identify the NetWare connection as Title: "Warehouse", Description: "Inventory Control", and the Oracle connection as Title: "Collections", Description: "Accounts Receivable". You have two replica tables ("Products" and "Vendors") for the Novell connection, and one replica table ("CustList") for the Oracle connection. If you're connected to the Novell database, SQLCONNECTINFO() will return the following values:

Expression	Returns
SQLCONNECTINFO("TITLE")	"Warehouse"
SQLCONNECTINFO("TITLE","PRODUCTS")	"Warehouse"
SQLCONNECTINFO("TITLE","CUSTLIST")	"Collections"
SQLCONNECTINFO("DIALECT")	"NOVSQL"
SQLCONNECTINFO("DIALECT","CUSTLIST")	"ORACLE"

SQLERRORCODE()

SQLERRORCODE() returns the code number of the most recent SQL error generated by the database server. If SQL Link is not active, or if no SQL error has occurred, this value is blank. The value returned by SQLERRORCODE() varies from one database server product to another. For a list of the error codes for your server, please see the appropriate Paradox SQL Link reference manual.

SQLERRORMESSAGE()

SQLERRORMESSAGE() returns the text of the most recent SQL error message generated by the database server. If SQL Link is not active, or if no SQL error has occurred, this value is blank. The value returned by SQLERRORMESSAGE() varies from one database server product to another. For a list of the error messages for your server, please see the appropriate Paradox SQL Link reference manual.

SQLFETCH *ArrayName*

SQLFETCH fetches one record from the database server and places the field values in a fixed array. To use SQLFETCH, you must first issue a SQL SELECT statement (a query) enclosed in the SQL NOFETCH...ENDSQL command structure. The NOFETCH keyword tells Paradox not to create an Answer table from the results of the SELECT statement, but instead to create a SQL *cursor*, which is a buffer area for retrieving data one row at a time. SQLFETCH retrieves the next record from the SQL cursor, and copies the field values to *ArrayName*. The array elements 2,3,...,n correspond to the sequence of fields listed in the SELECT statement. Array element #1 isn't used, and contains a null string (""). Retrieve the data from the array by referencing the array element numbers. When you're through with SQLFETCH, use SQLRELEASE to free the SQL cursor.

SQLISCONNECT()

SQLISCONNECT() indicates whether Paradox is connected to a server. If your workstation is currently connected to a database server, SQLISCONNECT() returns a value of True; if not, it has a value of False.

SQLISREPLICA (*TableName*)

SQLISREPLICA() indicates if *TableName* is a replica or a local table. *TableName* is a valid Paradox table name. If *TableName* is a replica, SQLISREPLICA() returns a value of True; it returns a value of False if *TableName* is a local table.

SQLMAKECONNECT

SQLMAKECONNECT tries to reconnect your workstation to the database server using the connection parameters currently stored in memory. SQLMAKECONNECT won't work if the connection parameters have been cleared from memory. You can break the connection using any of the following actions:

- Execute the PAL SQLBREAKCONNECT command.

- Use Menu {Tools} {SQL} {Connection} {Break}.

- Select a different server connection.

- Press CTRL-BREAK during a remote operation.

- Execute the PAL DOSBIG command.

- Execute the PAL RUN BIG command.

- Press ALT-O (DOS Big).

- Exit Paradox.

If the connection succeeds, Retval is set to True; otherwise it's set to False. If you don't use SQLMAKECONNECT, Paradox tries to reconnect if any of the following occurs:

- A PAL command or menu accesses a replica table

- A SQL...ENDSQL command structure occurs

- A SQLSTARTTRANS command occurs

Menu Equivalent   Menu {Tools} {SQL} {Connection} {Make}

SQLMAPINFO(*OptionName, ReplicaName* [, *ColumnNumber*])

SQLMAPINFO() produces information about the structure of a remote table. You can use this information to directly manipulate the table with the SQL...ENDSQL command structure.

OptionName must be one of the names given in the following table. The quotes are required. You can type the word in any combination of lowercase and uppercase letters.

OptionName	Meaning
"TABLENAME"	Indicates the name of the remote table
"COLUMNNAME"	Indicates the name of the remote column specified by *ColumnNumber*
"COLUMNTYPE"	Indicates the type of the remote column specified by *ColumnNumber*

ReplicaName is the name of a local replica of a remote table.

ColumnNumber is the position number of the column in the remote table referenced by *ReplicaName*. You must specify a *ColumnNumber* if you use "COLUMNNAME" or "COLUMNTYPE" for *OptionName*.

SQLMAPINFO() is useful if you want to type your own SQL commands to manipulate a remote table.

This example will display data from the third column of the table represented by the replica named "Books":

```
vtable = SQLMAPINFO("Tablename","Books")
vcolumn = SQLMAPINFO("Columnname","Books",3)
SQL
     SELECT ~vcolumn~ FROM ~vtable~
ENDSQL
```

SQLMAPINFO() produces an error if any of the following are true:

- *ReplicaName* is an invalid table name

- *ReplicaName* is actually the name of a local table instead of a local replica of a remote table

- *ColumnNumber* is out of range for the remote table

SQLRELEASE

SQLRELEASE releases an active query created with SQL NOFETCH...ENDSQL. The NOFETCH option of SQL...ENDSQL creates a buffer area for retrieving remote data one row at a time. SQLRELEASE frees this buffer area. If you try to start another query without releasing the active query, you'll get a error.

SQLRESTORECONNECT

SQLRESTORECONNECT clears the current connection parameters from memory, replaces them with the parameters stored with the most recent use of SQLSAVECONNECT, and reconnects to the server specified by those parameters. It then releases the saved parameters from memory (they remain as the current parameters). If you want to save the new connection parameters to use again, use SQLSAVECONNECT. If there are no stored parameters, SQLRESTORECONNECT clears the current parameters (it replaces the current parameters with null values). This is equivalent to using SQLCLEARCONNECT.

SQLROLLBACK

SQLROLLBACK cancels changes made during a transaction on the database server. If SQLAUTOCOMMIT is set to **No**, or if the changes resulted from SQL commands issued with SQL...ENDSQL, you must deliberately either roll back or commit the changes. If SQLAUTOCOMMIT is set to **Yes**, and you didn't use SQL...ENDSQL to create the changes, Paradox automatically commits the changes on the server. In this case, you can't roll back the changes.

If SQLROLLBACK succeeds, Retval is set to True; if not, Retval is set to False.

Menu Equivalent   Menu {Tools} {SQL} {Transaction} {**R**ollback}

SQLSAVECONNECT

SQLSAVECONNECT saves the current connection parameters in memory. If you disconnect from this server (for example, to work with another server), you can later use SQLRESTORECONNECT to reestablish the connection defined by the saved parameters. You can save information about only one connection. If you're not connected to a server, Paradox ignores SQLSAVECONNECT.

These steps guide you through an example of using SQLSAVECONNECT and SQLRESTORECONNECT:

1. Connect to server A (you must supply the correct connection parameters).

2. Work on A.

3. Execute SQLSAVECONNECT to save the connection parameters.

4. Connect to server B (you must supply the correct connection parameters).

5. Work on B.

6. Execute SQLRESTORECONNECT to reconnect to server A (you don't need to enter the connection parameters this time).

SQLSELECTCONNECT

SQLSELECTCONNECT establishes a server connection. SQLSELECTCONNECT by itself displays the Set Connections screen, lets the user choose one of the available connections, and asks the user to enter any required parameters. If the user chooses a connection, Retval is set to True; if not, Retval is set to False. The complete syntax for the command is shown here:

```
SQLSELECTCONNECT [ { PRODUCT CodeName | TITLE Title }
VALUES ParameterList ]
```

Either PRODUCT *CodeName* or TITLE *Title* lets you specify which connection to establish. You can find the correct value for *CodeName* in the Paradox SQL Link reference manual for your server. *Title* is the connection name as it appears on the SQL Connections screen.

ParameterList specifies the connection parameters for the requested connection. Enter the parameters in the same order they appear in the SQL Connection Parameters screen. Each parameter must be a valid string expression, and must be separated from the previous parameter with a comma. The parameters required vary from one server product to another. Check the Paradox SQL Link reference manual for your server.

Menu Equivalent   Menu {Tools} {SQL} {Connection} {Select}

SQLSETINTERRUPT { YES | NO }

SQLSETINTERRUPT enables or disables the ability to interrupt a remote operation with CTRL-BREAK. The default setting is **Yes**. The effects of CTRL-BREAK depend on the setting of SQLSETINTERRUPT:

- With SQLSETINTERRUPT set to **Yes**, when you press CTRL-BREAK, Paradox immediately halts the remote operation, rolls back any open transactions, breaks the connection with the database server, and returns error 1003 ("User aborted").

- With SQLSETINTERRUPT set to **No**, when you press CTRL-BREAK, Paradox lets the remote operation run to completion, then stops playing the script. The server connection remains intact.

By using SQLSETINTERRUPT, you can control when the user can and cannot interrupt remote operations.

Menu Equivalent   Menu {Tools} {SQL} {Preferences} {SetInterrupt}

SQLSTARTTRANS

SQLSTARTTRANS begins a transaction on the remote database server. All operations occurring after SQLSTARTTRANS and before a commit or roll back operation constitute a single transaction.

Some database servers automatically start a new transaction after you commit or roll back the current transaction. Other servers must be told explicitly to start a new transaction.

If SQLSTARTTRANS is able to start the transaction, Retval is set to True; if not, Retval is set to False.

If a server automatically starts a new transaction, SQLSTARTTRANS has no effect, so it's a good idea to include the SQLSTARTTRANS command in your script in case you connect to a server that requires it.

Menu Equivalent   Menu {Tools} {SQL} {Transaction} {Start}

SQLVAL(*Expression*)

SQLVAL creates a valid SQL expression from a PAL expression. Use this to create a SQL...ENDSQL statement containing embedded PAL expressions.

SQLVAL() translates PAL expressions according to the following guidelines:

- If *Expression* generates a blank value, SQLVAL(*Expression*) generates the SQL keyword NULL.

- If *Expression* generates an alphanumeric value, SQLVAL(*Expression*) generates a string of the form '*alphanumeric value*'. Note that SQL uses single quotes to delimit strings.

- If *Expression* generates an alphanumeric value with embedded single quotes, SQLVAL(*Expression*) generates a string with the single quotes correctly delimited.

- If *Expression* generates a numeric value, SQLVAL(*Expression*) generates the same numeric value.

- If *Expression* generates a date value, SQLVAL(*Expression*) generates a date expression in the correct form for the dialect of SQL used by the current database server connection.

Part VI

Appendixes

Appendix *A*

Installing Paradox 4

This appendix covers the procedure for installing Paradox 4 and gives the hardware requirements and configurations necessary for running the program.

System Requirements

Following are the requirements for both a stand-alone unit and a network. This section also lists optional hardware and software.

Requirements for a Stand-alone System

These are the hardware requirements for a stand-alone unit:

- A 286, 386, or 486 microprocessor with a hard disk and a floppy disk drive

- DOS 3.0 or higher, or OS/2 2.0

- A minimum of 2MB of RAM (more recommended)

- A minimum of 5MB of space available on the hard disk without optional software. An additional .5MB if all optional software is installed

- MDA, MCGA, CGA, EGA, or VGA monitor with adapter

- MCGA, CGA, EGA, VGA, 8514, 3270, Hercules, ATT, or Tandy T1000 (necessary only if you want to view graphs)

Requirements for a Network

The first list gives requirements for a workstation and the second gives requirements for a server.

These are the hardware requirements for the network workstation:

- 286, 386, or 486 microprocessor with a hard disk and a floppy drive

- A minimum of 640K of RAM and 384K extended memory

- DOS 3.1 or higher, or OS/2 2.0

- MDA, MCGA, CGA, EGA, or VGA monitor with adapter

- MCGA, CGA, EGA, VGA, 8514, 3270, Hercules, ATT, or Tandy T1000 (necessary only if you want to view graphs)

One of the following is needed for the network server:

- 3Com 3+ 1.5.1 or higher

- AT&T StarGROUP DOS software 3.1 or higher

- Banyan VINES 4.0 or higher

- DEC Pathworks 1.0 or higher

- IBM Token Ring or PC Network with IBM PC LAN program 1.31 or higher

- Microsoft LANMAN 2.0 or higher

- Novell Advanced NetWare 2.15C or higher

- Any network that is compatible with one on this list and also 100 percent compatible with DOS 3.1

Optional Hardware or Software

Paradox 4 supports these mice:

- IBM PS/2 mouse

- Logitech bus or serial mouse

- Microsoft bus or serial mouse

- Any other mouse that is 100 percent compatible with one of those just listed

With Paradox 4, you can also use the software or equipment listed here:

- Printers that are capable of printing ASCII files, either laser, dot matrix, or letter quality

- PostScript-compatible printers

- Microsoft Windows 3.0 or higher

- 80X87 math coprocessor

Installing Paradox 4 on a Stand-alone Unit

When you install Paradox, the screen prompts you for various responses. Among the choices you can make during the installation process are choosing the country group; choosing the sort order; and choosing which additional features used in Paradox you want to install, such as the samples, the Application Workshop, and so on.

To install Paradox, follow these steps:

1. Insert Disk 1 in drive A or B.

2. At the DOS prompt C:\>, type **a:install** or **b:install** depending upon the drive in which you inserted Disk 1.

3. Press ENTER to show the beginning screen, which contains copyright information and comments about the information you will need to enter in subsequent screens. After reading the information that is displayed, press ENTER to continue.

You can press ESC at any time to quit or to return to the previous screen10

The next dialog box shows the Source drive where Disk 1 is located and from which Paradox will be installed.

4. If you have changed drives, type the new drive name here. Press ENTER to continue.

You are now asked to specify whether the installation is on a stand-alone unit or on a network, or—if Paradox is already installed—if you want to install optional hardware.

5. Move the cursor to the type of installation you want and press F2 (Do-It!).

A box displayed near the bottom of the screen shows a description of each choice as you move the cursor from one choice to the next.

The next dialog box asks for your name, your company name, and the serial number on your Paradox Disk 1. A description of each entry is displayed near the bottom of the screen. You will not be able to proceed with the installation process until each of these is entered.

6. With the cursor on the Name field, press ENTER to display a dialog box in the center of the screen for your name. Type your name (up to 30 characters) and press ENTER. Repeat for company name, and for the serial number.

7. The default Country Group is U.S., however, you can select a different group if you like by moving your cursor to Country Group and pressing ENTER.

A menu appears, as shown in Figure A-1. Table A-1 lists the country choices available and their date and number formats and the sort order for each. Whenever you choose one of the country groups, the accompanying date and number formats become the default formats. You can override these temporarily in specific tables in Paradox using **Image/Format**, as discussed in Chapter 9; or change them permanently using the Custom Configuration Program.

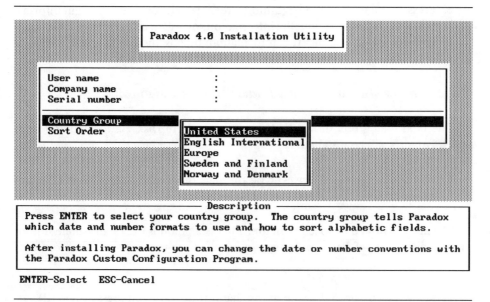

Figure A-1.   *Country Group menu*

Country	Sort Order	Date Format	Number Format
U.S.	ASCII	mm/dd/yy	1,234.56
English Int'l	Intl	dd.mm.yy	1,234.56
European	Intl	dd.mm.yy	1.234,56
Norwegian/Danish	NorDan	dd.mm.yy	1.234,56
Swedish/Finnish	SwedFin	dd.mm.yy	1.234,56

Table A-1.   *Characteristics of Country Groups*

These are the sort orders for the various country groups:

- *ASCII* sorts accented characters before characters that are unaccented and sorts uppercase letters before lowercase letters.

- *Intl* sorts characters in alphabetical order regardless of case or special accented characters.

- *NorDan* sorts characters in alphabetical order and places special characters used specifically in Norway and Denmark in their appropriate positions in the sort order.

- *SwedFin* sorts characters in alphabetical order; however, it places accented characters used specifically in Sweden and Finland at the end of the sort order.

8. Choose the country group you want and press ENTER.

9. To select a different sort order, move the cursor to Sort Order and choose one of the following:

    - *ASCII* sort order overrides the sort order for a country group if you choose a country group other than U.S.

    - *Dictionary* sets the sort order that is characteristic of the country group you have chosen.

        ASCII is the default; however, to choose Dictionary, press ENTER. The sort order is then changed to Dictionary, as shown in Figure A-2. Press ENTER again if you want to return to ASCII sort order.

10. When finished, press F2 (Do-It!).

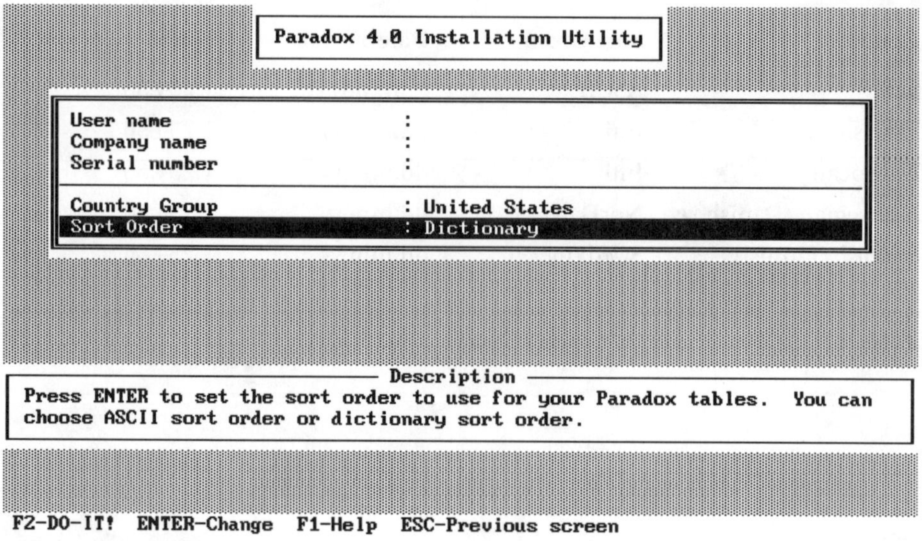

```
┌─────────────────────────────────────────────┐
│       Paradox 4.0 Installation Utility        │
└─────────────────────────────────────────────┘

  ┌──────────────────────────────────────────────────────────┐
  │ User name                  :                              │
  │ Company name               :                              │
  │ Serial number              :                              │
  │                                                            │
  │ Country Group              : United States                │
  │ Sort Order                 : Dictionary                   │
  └──────────────────────────────────────────────────────────┘

  ┌─────────────────────── Description ──────────────────────┐
  │ Press ENTER to set the sort order to use for your Paradox tables.  You can │
  │ choose ASCII sort order or dictionary sort order.        │
  └──────────────────────────────────────────────────────────┘


 F2-DO-IT!   ENTER-Change   F1-Help   ESC-Previous screen
```

Figure A-2.   *Sort Order menu*

The next screen allows you to enter a different directory name and to choose which features of Paradox 4 you want to install, as shown in the example in Figure A-3.

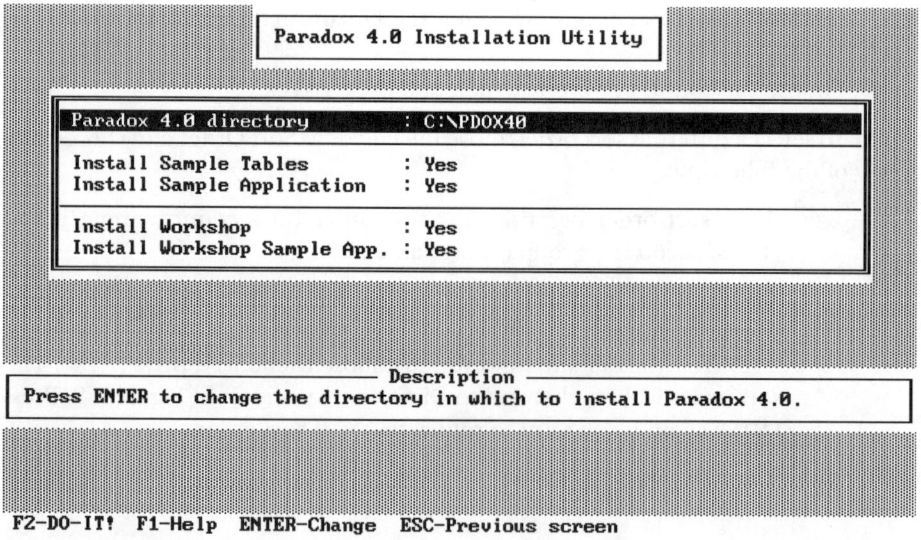

```
┌─────────────────────────────────────────────┐
│       Paradox 4.0 Installation Utility        │
└─────────────────────────────────────────────┘

  ┌──────────────────────────────────────────────────────────┐
  │ Paradox 4.0 directory        : C:\PDOX40                  │
  │                                                            │
  │ Install Sample Tables        : Yes                        │
  │ Install Sample Application    : Yes                        │
  │                                                            │
  │ Install Workshop              : Yes                        │
  │ Install Workshop Sample App.  : Yes                        │
  └──────────────────────────────────────────────────────────┘

  ┌─────────────────────── Description ──────────────────────┐
  │ Press ENTER to change the directory in which to install Paradox 4.0. │
  └──────────────────────────────────────────────────────────┘


 F2-DO-IT!   F1-Help   ENTER-Change   ESC-Previous screen
```

Figure A-3.   *Screen showing installation choices*

11. If you like, you can specify a directory name other than the directory name, C:\PDOX40, that Paradox will create for you.

    You can also choose whether to install any of the following: Sample Table, Sample Application, Application Workshop, and the Workshop Sample Application. As you move your cursor from one to the other, a description of each appears near the bottom of the screen.

To not *install a feature, move the cursor to the item that you do not want and press* ENTER. *The Yes changes to No.*

12. When finished, press F2 (Do-It!). Paradox displays the filenames as they are read and written to the new directory.

13. A dialog box appears in the center of the screen telling you when to change the disks. Respond to the prompt, inserting the appropriate disk as instructed, and press any key to continue.

14. When the installation is complete, a message tells you that Paradox is installed. Press any key to return to the DOS prompt.

If you chose to have the CONFIG.SYS file created or changed, you will need to restart your computer (press CTRL-ALT-DELETE*), so the new values in the file will be in effect. If your CONFIG.SYS file has been created previously and does not require changing, you will not see this choice.*

Installing Paradox 4 on a Network

Installing Paradox on a network may vary from one network to another. This section gives you the basic steps. Before installing Paradox, create directories for both the system files and the data files. You also may want to print the information (available on Disk 1) about installation on the type of network you are using.

Creating Directories

Before installing Paradox on a network, create a directory where the system files will be stored—\pdox40—for example. Also create a shared network directory for the data—\pdoxdata—for example. These directories must be created on the network file server.

Printing Information About Your Network

To read specific information about your network, Paradox has included text files on Disk 1 that pertain to several different networks. To print this information, follow these steps:

1. Change to the drive that contains Disk 1.

2. At the DOS prompt, type **dir *.** to see a list of text files.

3. Locate the file for your network, and at the DOS prompt type **print** *filename* (use the filename for your network).

4. Press ENTER to print.

Installing the Program

After creating the directories, you are ready to install Paradox. To run the install program, follow these steps:

1. Change to the directory for the Paradox system files.

2. Insert Disk 1 in drive A.

3. At the prompt, type **a:install** and press ENTER. A dialog box gives you choices for the type of installation.

4. Select Network Installation and press ENTER. A new screen is displayed.

5. Choose the Country Group you want. The selections here are the same as for a stand-alone installation (as discussed earlier in this chapter).

6. Choose the Sort Order you want. (Again the selections here are the same as discussed earlier in this chapter.)

7. In the User Count screen, enter the serial number or numbers of your Paradox product. When you type the serial number(s), the user count is displayed.

8. Type the directory name where the network control file, PDOXUSRS.NET, is to be stored—for convenience, this is the same directory where the shared data is to be stored. This must be a network server directory.

When the installation is complete, a message states that Paradox is installed successfully.

 If the installation was not successful because of insufficient disk space, you may have to remove some of the existing files that you do not need. You need at least 5MB of space on the server to install Paradox without the optional software. An additional 1MB is required to install this software.

Printing the Readme Document

The Readme document contains information that may be helpful, particularly if you are an experienced Paradox user. It will list new features in Paradox 4, give information about installation requirements, notes on PAL, and on the Application Workshop, to name a few. The Readme document will also contain descriptions of any last minute changes that did not make it into the official documentation.

You will need to change to the Paradox directory before printing the document. Follow these steps:

1. Type **cd pdox40** at the DOS prompt C:\> and press ENTER to change to the Paradox directory.

2. Type **print readme** at the DOS prompt C:\PDOX40\> and press ENTER to print the document. At the name of the list device to print, press ENTER; or enter a port specifier such as **LPT1** and press ENTER.

Running Paradox 4

To run Paradox either on a stand-alone unit or a network, follow these steps:

1. Change to the directory where Paradox is located by typing **cd pdox40** at the DOS prompt and pressing ENTER.

2. To run Paradox, at the prompt showing the directory name, type **paradox** and press ENTER.

If you add the Paradox 4 directory name (c:\pdox40) to the PATH statement in the AUTOEXEC.BAT, you can then start Paradox from any directory on the hard disk by just typing **paradox** and pressing ENTER.

To add the Paradox directory to the AUTOEXEC.BAT file, use any text editor, including the Paradox Editor. When you bring the file into the text editor, import it as an ASCII file. In the path statement, type **;c:\pdox40** following any existing directory names. For example, if the path is PATH C:\DOS;C:\WORD, you can change it to PATH C:\DOS;C:\WORD;C:\PDOX40. (Or you can enter the path statement in front of existing directory names—if you do that, do not type the semicolon as shown.)

Do not include spaces, except directly after the word PATH, and use a semicolon to separate directory names. When saving the edited AUTOEXEC.BAT file, be sure you save it in ASCII format. If you are using Microsoft Word to edit the file, save it in Text Only w/Break format; if you are using WordPerfect, use Text In/Out to save it.

Installing the Application Workshop

During the process of installing Paradox, you have a choice of whether or not to install additional software. The Application Workshop and the sample applications are two of these choices. If you did not install them previously, they can be installed whenever you want to use the Application Workshop. You do not necessarily have to install the sample application; however, it is helpful to be able to use it as a reference when you are creating your own application, particularly if you are not familiar with creating applications.

System Requirements for the Application Workshop

The Application Workshop requires the following:

- At least 2MB of RAM is required—between 4 and 8MB is recommended

- At least 1MB of space in addition to that needed for Paradox

- Paradox 4 must be installed

Installing the Program

If Paradox has been installed previously, you already have the directory structure that is necessary for using the Application Workshop; therefore, you will not have to make any changes there.

To install the Application Workshop:

1. Change to the directory where you want the Application Workshop to be installed—C:\PDOX40 probably.

2. Insert the Installation Disk for Paradox in either drive A or drive B.

3. At the DOS prompt, type either **a:install** or **b:install** (depending upon the drive in which you have inserted the disk), and press ENTER.

4. Follow the screen prompts for installing Paradox until a menu is displayed that shows Optional Software Installation. See an example in Figure A-4.

5. Move the cursor to select Optional Software Installation and press F2 (Do-It!).

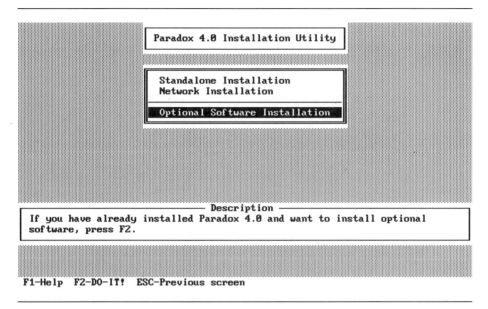

Figure A-4.   *Menu of installation choices*

6. In the menu that is displayed, move the cursor to Application Workshop and press ENTER to change No to Yes (if necessary—it may already display Yes).

7. If you want to install the Workshop Sample Application, move the cursor to it and press ENTER to display a Yes there. (Again, do this only if a Yes is not displayed.)

8. After you choose the additional software you want installed, press F2 (Do-It!). The installation process creates a directory, \PDOX40\WORKSHOP, where the Application Workshop files will be stored. If you chose to install the sample application, a second directory, \PDOX40\VIDEO, will be created to contain the sample application files.

9. When the installation is complete you can press any key to exit.

Appendix *B*

Customizing Paradox

This appendix shows you how to use the Custom Configuration Program (CCP) to change the Paradox default settings. You can change the settings affecting reports and graphs, the type of monitor or the display of colors, and the default directory and automatic save. You can also change PAL and network features and the various ASCII settings.

Starting CCP

The files used to run CCP are CUSTOM.SC, CUSTOM.LIB, and COLORS.LIB. These files are copied automatically to your Paradox directory when Paradox is installed. On a network, they are located in the directory containing the Paradox system files. If the files needed to run CCP are not in the appropriate directory, you may have trouble running the program. If they are missing, copy them from the original installation disks to the correct directory.

You can start CCP from DOS or from within Paradox. If you are starting it from within Paradox, you may either use the Custom script or run it from the System menu.

Starting CCP from DOS

To run CCP from DOS without first going to Paradox, follow these steps:

1. Change to the directory where the Paradox system files are located.

2. At the DOS prompt, type **paradox custom** and press ENTER. The Custom Configuration Program menu will appear, as shown in Figure B-1.

Starting CCP from Paradox

To run CCP from Paradox, start Paradox and display the Main menu. You can then either choose **S**cript from the Main menu and play the Custom script, or you can choose **U**tilities/**C**ustom from the System menu.

To use the Custom script, follow these steps:

1. Choose **S**cripts/**P**lay from the Main menu and press ENTER to see a list of the available scripts.

2. Select Custom and press ENTER to begin running CCP. A dialog box asks if you are using a color monitor or a black-and-white monitor, as shown in Figure B-2.

3. Choose the appropriate monitor type. The CCP menu will then appear, as shown in Figure B-1.

To use the System menu, follow these steps:

1. Press ALT-SPACEBAR or click on the System menu.

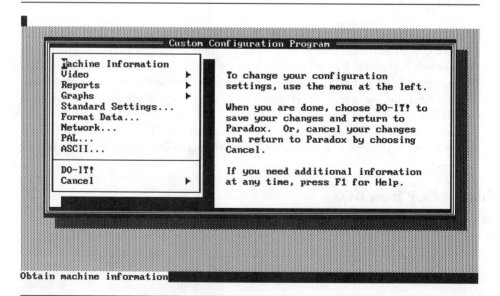

Figure B-1.   *CCP menu*

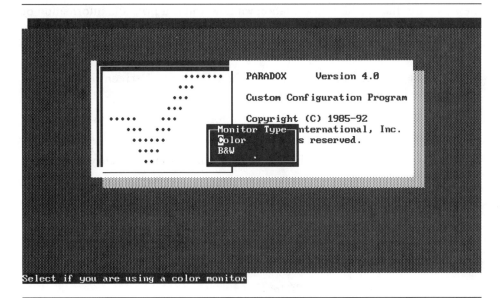

Figure B-2. *Dialog box asking for the monitor type*

2. Choose **Utilities/Custom**. A dialog box asks for the monitor type.

3. Choose the appropriate monitor type. The CCP menu will appear.

You can press F1 (Help) from any screen, window, or menu in CCP to access the Help screen pertaining to the window or menu you are using.

Leaving the Custom Configuration Program

When finished making changes, press F2 (Do-It!) to save your edits and leave the program, or choose **Cancel/Yes** to leave the program without saving the changes. If you choose **Cancel/No** you are returned to the CCP where you can continue to make changes.

Displaying Machine Information

When you choose Machine Information from the CCP menu, a message indicating that the machine is being analyzed will appear, followed by a screen showing information about the DOS version being used, the CPU type, the amount of memory available, and the type of monitor being used. Information about the disk drives also will be displayed, as well as the contents of the CONFIG.SYS and AUTOEXEC.BAT files. When in the Machine Information window, you can print the information or save it to a file.

To display machine information, follow these steps:

1. Choose **M**achine Information from the CCP menu. A screen similar to that shown in Figure B-3 will be displayed.

2. Scroll through the screen to read the information pertaining to your specific system.

3. Press F10 (Menu) to go to the Machine Information menu where you can make further selections.

From the Machine Information menu you can choose **F**ile, **S**earch, or **C**ancel.

File This selection allows you to send the information to a file or to the printer. The **F**ile menu is shown here:

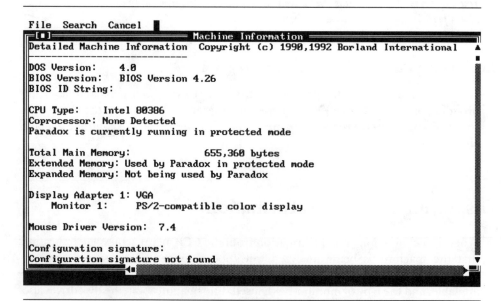

Figure B-3.   *Example of the Machine Information window*

- *CopyToFile* allows you to save the file to disk. Type a filename using standard DOS naming conventions. The file can be displayed in a text editor, including the Paradox Editor, and can be edited the same way you edit any other text file. These changes do not, however, affect the actual machine information. The next time you view the Machine Information screen, the display will show the actual information—not the edited text file.

- *Print* allows you to print the information displayed on the screen.

Search   This selection is similar to the Search commands used in Paradox. **S**earch gives you the **F**ind and **N**ext options, as shown here:

- *Find* locates a value. Enter the value you want to locate and press ENTER. You can also use CTRL-Z (Zoom) for this command.

- *Next* goes to the next occurrence of the value to be located. You can also use ALT-Z (ZoomNext) for this command.

Cancel   This selection is used to leave the window and return to the CCP menu.

Changing the Video and Color Settings

You use the **V**ideo option to change video settings such as naming the monitor type, allowing or preventing snow, specifying whether to display the Color Palette, and indicating whether negative numbers should be displayed differently than positive numbers. The Video option is also used to change the colors for specific Paradox features.

Changing Video Settings

To change video settings, choose **V**ideo from the CCP menu. A menu shows the choices **V**ideo Settings and **C**olor Settings. From the Video Settings menu (shown in Figure B-4), you can change the Monitor Type, Video "snow", Form Designer Color Palette, and Negative Colors. Instructions for moving around in the window and for making selections are displayed at the bottom of the screen. You can also move to the option you want by pressing ALT and the hot key shown in the option label.

```
┌─────────────────── Video Settings ───────────────────┐
│                                                       │
│   Monitor Type:    ( ) Autodetect  (•) Color          │
│                    ( ) Monochrome  ( ) B&W            │
│                                                       │
│   Video "snow":    (•) Allow   ( ) Prevent            │
│                                                       │
│   Form Designer                                       │
│   Color Palette:   ( ) Hide   (•) Show                │
│                                                       │
│   Negative Colors: [X] Numbers  [X] Currency          │
│                                                       │
│              OK             Cancel                    │
│                                                       │
└───────────────────────────────────────────────────────┘

[TAB] to move, [ENTER] to push buttons, [ESC] to cancel
↑ ↓ → ← for radio buttons, ↑ ↓ → ← then [SPACE] for check boxes
```

Figure B-4.   *Video Settings dialog box*

Monitor Type   Paradox automatically displays the type of monitor it thinks is being used. If you want to change that, select one of the following: Autodetect, which allows Paradox to automatically determine the monitor type; Monochrome to tell Paradox you are using a monochrome monitor with a monochrome adapter; Color to tell Paradox you are using a color monitor with a CGA, EGA, or VGA adapter; or B&W to tell Paradox you are using a black-and-white monitor (or a monochrome monitor) with a CGA or EGA adapter. Move the cursor or click on the selection you want.

Video Snow   You may specify whether or not to prevent snow from showing on the screen. In some cases, preventing snow may slow down some of your operations. Press ALT-V or TAB to choose Video "snow", and then move the cursor or click on the selection you want.

Form Designer Color Palette   If you choose to hide the Color Palette, it can be displayed in the Form Designer by pressing ALT-C (ColorPalette). When the Color Palette is displayed in the Form Designer window, it can hide part of the form; therefore, you may wish to hide it and only display it when you want it. Press ALT-C or TAB to choose Form Designer Color Palette, and then move the cursor or click on the selection you want.

Negative Colors   The default display for negative numbers is red text on a white background. If you do not want to display negative numbers differently from other numbers, move to Numbers or Currency and press the SPACEBAR or click on the option to select or deselect. An X is displayed when the option is selected. To change the colors for displaying negative numbers, choose Color Settings and make the changes you want. (The Color Settings option is discussed in the next section.) Press ALT-N or TAB to move to **N**egative Color, then move the cursor or click on the selection you want. Press the SPACEBAR to select or deselect the option. An X is displayed in the brackets when the option is turned on.

Make the changes you want to your video settings and choose OK to save, or choose **C**ancel to leave the window without making changes. If you are not using a mouse, press TAB to move to OK or **C**ancel and then press ENTER.

Using the Color Settings Menu

You can change the default color settings for any of the following: Paradox objects, PAL features, compatible user interface features, desktop components (menu bars, pull-down menus, and so forth), Help messages, or dialog box frames, contents, and so on. The color changes for the various screen elements are saved in a *color setting.* You can also change the name of existing color settings, copy color settings, assign a new setting to be used in Paradox, or delete a color setting.

If you have a monochrome monitor, the Color Palette is used to specify normal, reverse, high-intensity, or reverse high-intensity for the various features that can be changed.

To use the **C**olor Settings menu, choose **V**ideo/**C**olor Settings from the CCP. The choices available in this dialog box are listed next. Figure B-5 shows an example. Instructions for moving around in the dialog box and making selections appear at the bottom of the screen. Or press ALT and the hot key displayed in the options label to move to a specific option.

Assign   You may assign a new setting (collection of color changes) to be used in Paradox. The following illustration shows an example of this dialog box. Press ALT-A to choose **A**ssign and then specify the User Interface mode (either Standard, for Paradox 4, or Compatible, for Paradox 3.5) and choose the video mode that is appropriate.

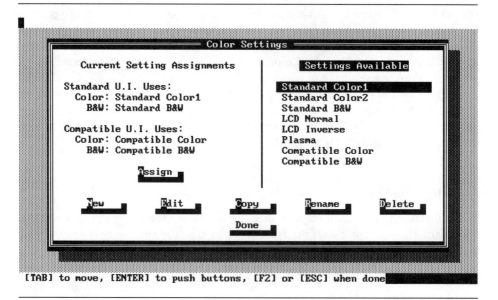

Figure B-5.   *Color Settings dialog box*

New   When you choose this option, type a new setting name and press ENTER. You are then in a window where you can change the colors for Paradox objects, as shown in Figure B-6. (Specific directions for changing colors are given in the following section "Changing the Colors.")

Edit   Select the name of the color setting you want, then choose **E**dit. Make the changes you want in the Color Settings window (as discussed in the following section "Changing the Colors") and press F2 (Do-It!) when finished, or choose **C**ancel/**Y**es to leave the window without saving the changes.

Copy   Enter a new name for the setting to copy the settings from an existing setting to the new one. When finished choose OK to save, or choose **C**ancel.

Rename   Select the name of the setting and choose **R**ename. Type a new name for the setting and press ENTER or choose OK to save, or choose **C**ancel to leave without saving the change.

Delete   Select the name of the setting you want to delete and choose **D**elete. Then you will be asked to confirm the deletion by choosing OK, or choose **C**ancel to not delete.

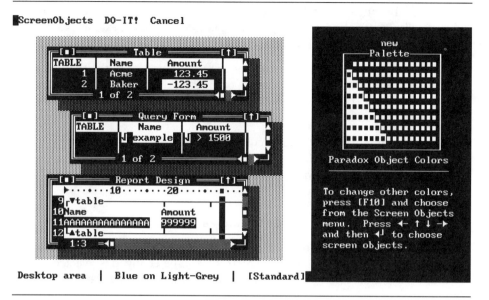

Figure B-6.   *Paradox Objects screen*

Changing the Colors

From the menu at the top of the Color Settings screen, you can change the colors for various Paradox features—Paradox objects, PAL, compatible user interface features, desktop components, help system messages, and dialog box features.

Changing Colors in Paradox Objects

Paradox objects are tables, reports, and query tables. The colors that are displayed in each of these can be changed. Follow these steps:

1. Choose **V**ideo/**C**olor Settings from the CCP menu.

2. Choose **N**ew, type a name for a new setting, and press ENTER; or select an existing setting name and choose **E**dit. You are then in the Paradox Objects screen shown in Figure B-6. The example shows Paradox objects and displays the colors that are currently used for these objects. As you move around in the screen, the message at the bottom of the screen indicates the area in which your cursor is positioned and names the colors assigned to that area.

3. To change the colors in a specific area, move your cursor to the area, or click on it to select the area, or press TAB to move to each changeable object on the screen. To use the Palette at the right, press ENTER to move the cursor to it, or click on it.

4. Move the cursor or click on the color combination you want. As you do this, the display of colors will change in the selected area in the examples at the left so you can see the effects of the changes.

5. To change colors in another area, press ENTER to return to the examples and move the cursor to a different area, or click on the area you want to change. Then press ENTER to return to the Palette, or click on the Palette and choose the colors you want.

6. When finished, you can change colors for other Paradox features (as described next), or press F2 (Do-It!) to save the changes, or choose Cancel/Yes to leave the window without saving the changes.

Changing Colors in Other Paradox Features

The process of changing colors in other Paradox features is basically the same as changing colors for Paradox objects. The feature to be changed is selected from a list that is displayed when you choose ScreenObjects from the Paradox Objects screen.

To change colors in other Paradox features, follow these steps:

1. From the Paradox Objects screen (or from any other color setting screen), press F10 (Menu) and choose ScreenObjects. A menu displays additional Paradox features, as shown here:

```
ScreenObjects

 ┌─────────────────┐
 │ Paradox Objects │
 │ PAL             │
 │ Desktop         │
 │ Help            │
 │ Dialog Box      │
 │ Compatible UI   │
 └─────────────────┘
```

2. Choose from PAL, Desktop, Help, Dialog Box, and Compatible UI. The color setting screen for that feature is then displayed. (This is similar to the color setting screen just discussed for changing the colors for Paradox objects.) The message at the bottom of the screen describes the area your cursor is in as you move from one example to another.

3. Change the colors the same way you changed colors for Paradox objects. You can press ENTER to move between the ScreenObject area and the Palette, or you can click on the area that you want. The options for each feature are described next.

4. When finished, press F2 (Do-It!) or choose **C**ancel/**Y**es to leave the color setting screen without making any changes. You return to the Color Settings dialog box.

5. Press F2 (Do-It!) to save the changes and return to the CCP menu, or press ESC to cancel the changes and return to the CCP menu.

PAL Color Settings   You can change the colors for the desktop, for the message window, for the PAL debugger status line, and for the PAL debugger line. Figure B-7 shows an example of the screen used for changing PAL color settings.

Desktop Color Settings   You can change colors for the menu bar, windows—active, inactive, and dragging—workspace areas, frame icons, status bar and message bar, menu commands, form area to be moved, and scroll bars in the active window. Figure B-8 shows an example of the screen used for changing desktop color settings.

Help System Color Settings   You can change colors for the Help menu and the Index menu. Figure B-9 shows an example.

Dialog Box Color Settings   You can change colors for inactive, active, and dragging window frames, active and inactive labels, hot keys for labels, pick list, radio button or check box items, push button labels, and hot keys and text for push button labels. Figure B-10 shows an example.

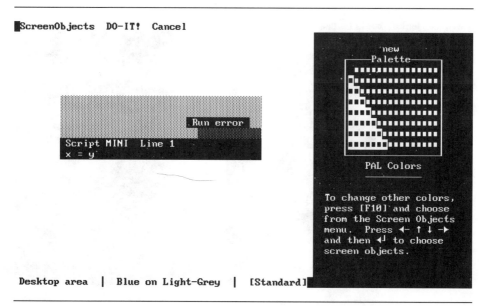

Figure B-7.   *PAL screen*

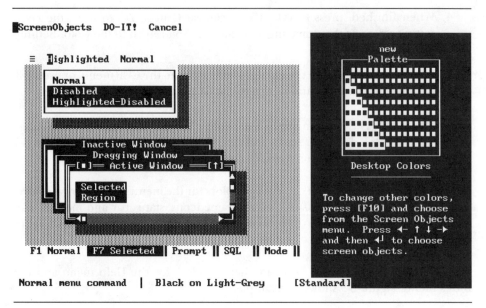

Figure B-8.   *Desktop screen*

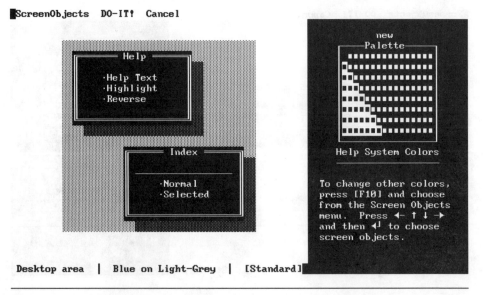

Figure B-9.   *Help System screen*

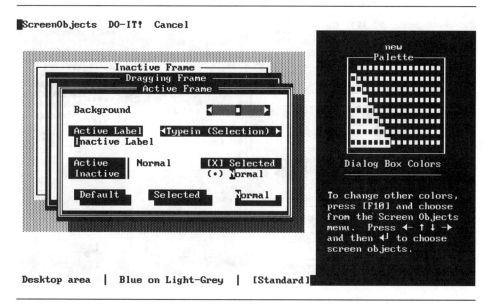

Figure B-10. *Dialog Box screen*

Compatible UI Color Settings You can change color settings for compatible user interface features—menus and workspace areas, form features, report features, and Help and Index menus. Figure B-11 shows an example of this screen.

Changing Reports

The default report settings affect the format and printing of reports. Existing reports are not affected by the changes made here. The Reports menu in CCP includes Report Settings and Printer Settings. Figure B-12 shows an example of this menu.

Changing Report Settings

The formatting changes made here can affect the page width, the page length, and the left margin. Also you can specify whether the printer will pause between pages when printing the report, select the type of paper feed necessary for your printer, and choose whether to print repeated values in a group or to suppress group repeats and print only the repeated values in the first record.

To change report settings, follow these steps:

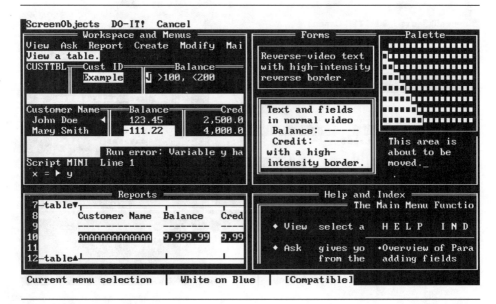

Figure B-11. *Compatible UI screen*

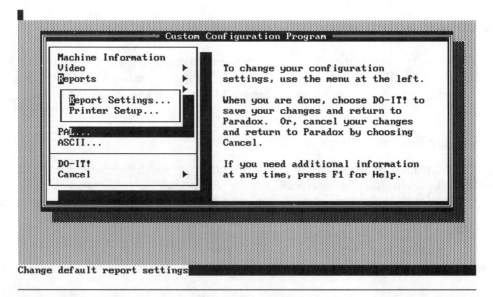

Figure B-12. *Reports menu in CCP*

1. Choose **R**eports/**R**eport Settings from the CCP menu. A Report Setting dialog box appears, as shown in Figure B-13. Instructions for moving around in the dialog box are displayed at the bottom of the screen.

2. Choose any of the following to change the default settings for reports:

   - *Page Width* allows you to enter the number of characters that can be entered on the page. The number depends upon the printer that you are using and whether you print in condensed type. You can enter between 10 and 2000 characters.

   - *Left Margin* allows you to change the left margin of the *first page width* of your report. You can enter a value from 0 up to the current page width. Left margins in subsequent page widths are not affected by this.

   - *Length* allows you to change the number of lines that are printed on a page. The default value is 60; however, if you are using a dot matrix printer you might want to change this to 66. Enter **C** for continuous.

   - *Pause Between Pages* allows you to direct the printer to pause after printing each page. This is particularly useful if you are printing on forms and inserting a new sheet for each page. Move the cursor or click on the option you want—either Yes or No.

   - *Eject Page With* allows you to specify how your printer ejects pages. Move the cursor or click on the option you want—either LineFeeds, which is

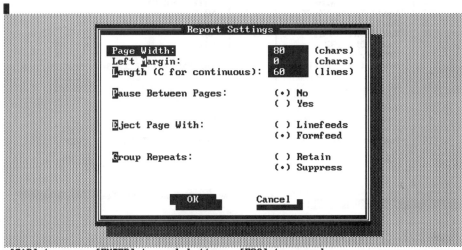

Figure B-13. *Report Settings dialog box*

generally used to begin printing at the top of the next page, or FormFeeds which is often used with some laser printers.

- *Group Repeats* allows you to suppress the printing of repeated group values. If you choose Suppress, then only the repeated group value for the first record will be printed. Choose Retain to print all group values.

3. When finished, choose OK to save the changes, or choose Cancel to leave the window without saving changes.

Changing the Printer Setup

Changing the default settings for the printer setup is similar to the way you changed settings in the **R**eport/**S**etPrinter menu discussed in Chapter 8. If you change the printer setup from the Report menu in Paradox, those changes will override the default changes set here in CCP.

To change the printer setup, follow these steps:

1. Choose **R**eports/**P**rinter Setup in CCP menu. Figure B-14 shows an example of the Printer Setup window.

```
DO-IT!   Cancel
========================== Printer Setup ========================[‡]=
PRINTER         Name            Port      Setup String        Reset String
    1     StandardPrinter*      LPT1
    2     Small-IBMgraphics     LPT1    \027W\000\015
    3     Reg-IBMgraphics       LPT1    \027W\000\018
    4     Small-Epson-MX/FX     LPT1    \015                  \0270
    5     Small-Oki-92/93       LPT1    \015
    6     Small-Oki-82/83       LPT1    \029
    7     Small-Oki-192         LPT1    \029
    8     HPLaserJet            LPT1    \027E\027&l0o6d3e60    \027E
    9     HP-Portrait-66lines   LPT1    \027E\027&l0o7.27c3    \027E
   10     HP-Landscape-Normal   LPT1    \027E\027&l1o6d3e45    \027E
   11     HP-Compressed         LPT1    \027E\027&l0o6d3e60    \027E
   12     HP-LandscpCompressed  LPT1    \027E\027&l1o6d3e45    \027E
   13     Intl-IBMcompatible    LPT1    \027\054
   14     Intl-IBMcondensed     LPT1    \027\054\015
   15     Postscript-Portrait   LPT1    FILE=PDOXPORT.PS       \004
   16     Postscript-Landscape  LPT1    FILE=PDOXLAND.PS       \004

========= 1 of 16 ===========◄■
Editing Printer Setup table
```

Figure B-14.   *Printer Setup window*

2. The window contains four columns where you can make changes. The first column, Printer, numbers the records in the table—it can't be edited. The changes can be made as follows:

- *Name* shows the name that identifies the setup string. You can enter any name, up to 22 characters with no spaces. These names appear in the Report Designer when you choose Printer Setup. The first time you see this window, Standard is the first name shown, and an asterisk (*) follows the name indicating that Standard is the default setup string. You can make any other setup string the default by typing an asterisk following the name. Only one name can be made the default.

- *Port* specifies the port used for printing the reports. Port names that can be entered here are LPT1, LPT2, LPT3, COM1, COM2, PRN, and AUX.

- *Setup String* is the column where you can enter a setup string that specifies printing characteristics for your printer. Refer to Chapter 8 for more information on setup and reset strings. For example, setup strings can be entered that will direct your printer to print in compressed mode, or italic, or bold. This can also be a filename for PostScript support, as shown in records 15 and 16 in Figure B-14.

- *Reset String* allows you to enter the reset string that returns your printer to normal mode. Again refer to Chapter 8 for information on reset strings.

3. When finished, press F2 (Do-It!) to save the changes, or choose **C**ancel/**Y**es to leave the window without saving the changes.

Changing Graphs

The Graphs option in CCP allows you to change the default graph settings. This is very similar to changing the graph settings for individual graphs from the Paradox menu. You can also change the printer settings for graphs, and choose the video adapter and mode to be used to display graphs. Figure B-15 shows an example of the Graphs menu.

Changing Graph Settings

The graph settings refer to the default choices for types of graphs, titles, X- and Y-axis settings, scales, tick marks, and other graph displays.

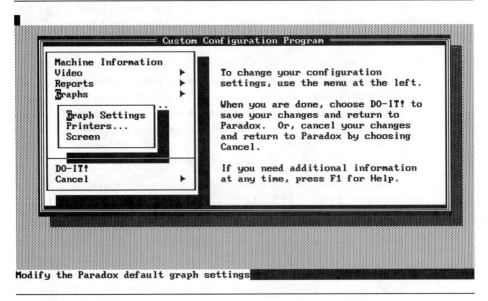

Figure B-15.   *Graphs menu in CCP*

To change graph settings, follow these steps:

1. From the CCP menu, choose **G**raph/**G**raph Settings. The Customize Graph Type window is displayed (it is identical to the Customize Graph Type window used to change settings for individual graphs). Refer to Chapter 9 for specific information about the various choices shown here. When changes are made for a specific graph using **I**mage/**G**raph/**M**odify from the Paradox Main menu, those changes override any changes made to the default graph settings done in the CCP.

2. When finished changing the default settings, press F2 (Do-It!) to save the changes, or choose **C**ancel/**Y**es to leave the window without saving the changes.

Changing Graph Printer Settings

You can choose the printer for printing graphs, and also specify the printer type, enter pauses, and set options only if you are using a serial printer. These will then be the defaults for printing graphs. You can change the print settings from the Paradox menu for individual graphs and those changes will override the defaults set in the CCP.

To change printer settings, follow these steps:

1. Choose **G**raphs/**P**rinters from the CCP menu. A Graph Printer Settings dialog box appears, as shown in Figure B-16. Instructions displayed at the bottom of the screen tell you how to move around in the window and make selections.

2. Change any of the following by moving to the field or clicking on the choice to display a dot (.) in parentheses:

   • *Choose Printer* allows you to choose the printer you want to define. You can then make the following adjustments.

   • *SetPrinterType* allows you to specify the manufacturer. When you do this, the corresponding models and modes will be displayed when you choose **Mo**del or **Mo**de. You can select both the model and the mode that you want. Figure B-17 shows an example of the Select Graph Printer dialog box. When finished, choose OK to save, or choose Cancel to leave without saving.

   • *Device* allows you to choose the printer port you want to use as the default.

   • *SetOptions* is only available if you choose a setting for a serial printer—Serial 1 or Serial 2. The options that may be changed are **B**aud rate, which sets the communications speed; **P**arity, which can be set at None, Leave As Is, Even, or Odd; and **S**top Bits, which can be set at Leave As Is, 1, or 2 to specify the bits to delimit each byte. Figure B-18 shows an example of the Serial Printer menu.

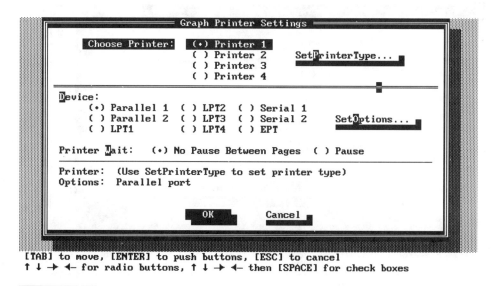

Figure B-16.   *Graph Printer Settings dialog box*

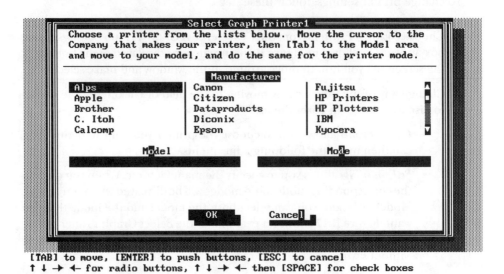

Figure B-17.   *Select Graph Printer1 dialog box*

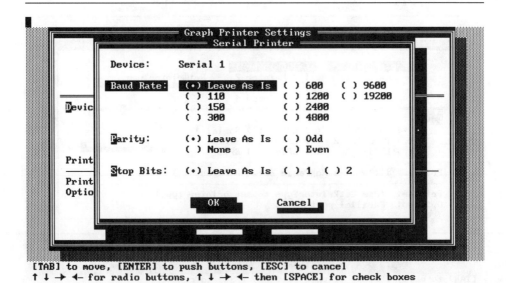

Figure B-18.   *Serial Printer menu*

- *Printer Wait* lets you instruct the printer to pause between printing pages of the graph. Select either Pause or No Pause Between Pages. The default is No Pause Between Pages.

3. When finished, choose OK to save the changes, or choose **C**ancel to leave the window without saving the changes.

Changing Screens

Using the Screen option, you can change the type of video adapter used to display graphs and the resolution.

To use the Screen option, follow these steps:

1. Choose **G**raphs/**S**creen from the CCP menu. The Graphics Screen menu appears.

2. Select the type of adapter you want to use and press ENTER. A list of resolutions that are available for the video type you selected will be displayed. Figure B-19 shows an example of resolutions available for a CGA video adapter.

3. Select the resolution you want.

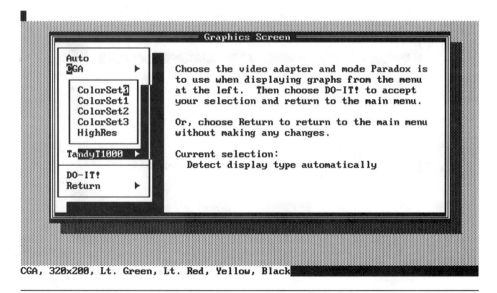

Figure B-19. *Graphics Screen menu*

If you are not sure of the video type or resolution that is available to you, choose Auto from the Graphics Screen menu. Paradox will then determine the type and resolution automatically. Auto is the default choice.

4. When finished, press F2 (Do-It!) or choose **Return/Yes** to leave without saving.

Changing Standard Settings

Standard settings include specifying the Working Directory, setting the Interface Mode, specifying whether a mouse is used, setting Disable Break on or off, selecting the Query Order, choosing the results of a blank, setting Autosave on or off, selecting the File Format, and specifying whether indexes will be automatically maintained.

To change standard settings, follow these steps:

1. Choose Standard Settings from the CCP menu. The Standard Settings dialog box appears, as shown in Figure B-20. Instructions at the bottom of the screen tell you how to move around in the dialog box.

2. Change any of the following by moving to the field or clicking on the choice to display a dot (.) in parentheses, and/or enter text in the box directly

Figure B-20. *Standard Settings dialog box*

following Working Directory. You can also press TAB to move from one choice to the next.

- *Working Directory* allows you to enter the name of the directory that you want to be in automatically when you start Paradox. This probably would be a directory where your data is stored.

- *Interface Mode* allows you to choose either Standard or Compatible. Standard mode is the way Paradox 4 displays images on the desktop, pull-down and pop-up menus, dialog boxes and prompts, etc. Compatible mode displays Paradox functions as they are displayed in Paradox 3.5. Choose Compatible if you work with applications developed in Paradox 3.5 or earlier versions.

- *Mouse Use* allows you to specify whether a mouse is used, or if it is left-handed.

- *Disable Break* allows you to prevent a break when CTRL-BREAK is pressed. The default is set at off, to prevent a possible loss of data that may happen, particularly if you are using a driver that may produce a break during some key sequences. If you are sure that this does not happen, you can turn on **D**isable Break here. Setting **D**isable Break does not disable the CTRL-BREAK key (to protect scripts, and such). It is used to control unwarranted breaks being interpreted by certain international keyboard drivers.

- *Query Order* allows you to choose whether the Answer tables that result from queries be displayed in the same order as the tables, or displayed in the same order that is displayed on the desktop if you used Image or pressed CTRL-R (Rotate) to change the field order. Choose Image Order to display the results in the same order as the order displayed on the desktop. Choose Table order to display the results in the order of the fields in the table.

- *Blank = Zero* allows you to specify whether a blank value in a field equals zero. This is particularly useful when you use fields in calculations. If a blank equals zero, then the value in the field will be calculated on the basis of the value being zero. If a blank does not equal zero, then Paradox does not calculate the value.

- *AutoSave* allows you to turn the automatic save off or on. Paradox always saves data periodically as you work, but setting AutoSave at Yes increases the frequency of the automatic saves.

- *File Format* allows you to choose either Standard format, which is the default and includes using memo fields in a table, or Compatible format, which does not allow memo fields and is compatible with Paradox 3.5 or earlier versions. The Standard format is not recognized by Paradox 3.5.

- *Maintain Indexes* tells Paradox whether to treat indexes created by Tools/Queryspeed as maintained or nonmaintained. It has no effect on indexes created in other ways—by ALT-S (OrderTable), for example. When this option is turned on, Paradox will update the index whenever data in the table to which the secondary index belongs is changed. Refer to Chapter 5 for information on secondary indexes.

3. When finished, choose OK to save, or choose Cancel to leave the window without saving the changes.

Changing Data Formats

Data formats refer to the format in which numbers and dates are displayed on the screen and in reports. The default formats are determined by the Country Group selected when Paradox is installed. Refer to Appendix A for information about format characteristics of Country Groups. You can also direct Paradox to accept ISO (International Standards Organization) dates using this option.

To change data formats, follow these steps:

1. Choose Format Data from the CCP menu. A Format Data dialog box appears, as shown in Figure B-21. Instructions at the bottom of the screen tell you how to move around in the window.

2. Change any of the following by moving to the field or clicking on your choice to display a dot (.) in parentheses:

   - *Number format* allows you to choose whether to use the U.S. number format, which is the default and displays numbers as 1,234.56, or the International format, which displays numbers as 1.234,56.

   - *Date format* allows you to choose the format in which dates will be displayed. The default is mm/dd/yy. Other choices are dd.mm.yy, dd-Mon-yy, or yy.mm.dd.

   - *Accept ISO Dates* allows you to specify whether Paradox will recognize ISO dates.

3. Choose OK when finished to save the changes, or choose Cancel to leave without saving.

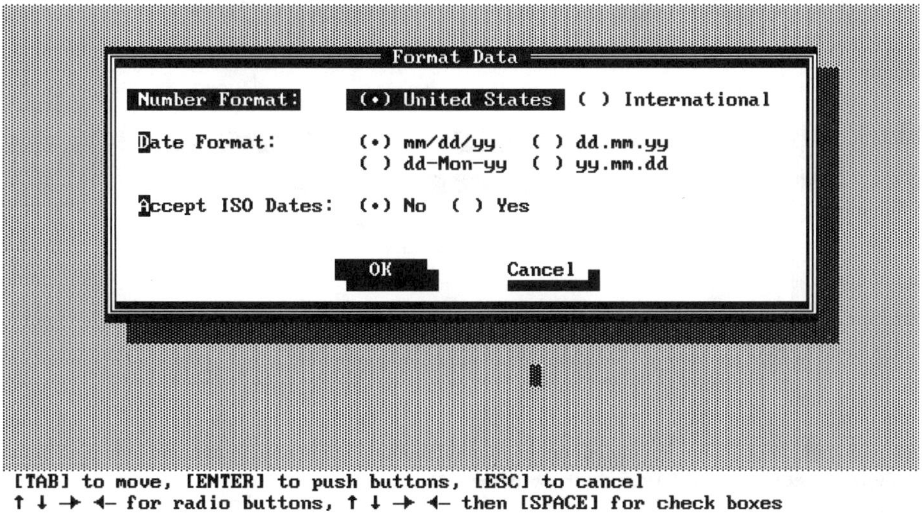

```
╔══════════════════ Format Data ══════════════════╗
║                                                  ║
║  Number Format:   (•) United States  ( ) International  ║
║                                                  ║
║  Date Format:     (•) mm/dd/yy   ( ) dd.mm.yy    ║
║                   ( ) dd-Mon-yy  ( ) yy.mm.dd    ║
║                                                  ║
║  Accept ISO Dates: (•) No  ( ) Yes               ║
║                                                  ║
║                                                  ║
║               OK          Cancel                 ║
║                                                  ║
╚══════════════════════════════════════════════════╝
```

[TAB] to move, [ENTER] to push buttons, [ESC] to cancel
↑ ↓ → ← for radio buttons, ↑ ↓ → ← then [SPACE] for check boxes

Figure B-21.   *Format Data dialog box*

Changing Network Features

The default changes that can be made on a network include changing the user name, changing the private directory, setting a new refresh interval, and specifying whether the restart option is turned on or off for restarting queries and reports when Paradox determines that changes have been made to data.

To change network defaults, follow these steps:

1. Choose **N**etwork from the CCP menu. A Network Settings window appears, as shown in Figure B-22. Instructions at the bottom of the screen tell you how to move around in the window.

2. Change any of the following:

    • *User Name* allows you to enter a user name that identifies you to other users. If your network supports user names, you do not necessarily have to enter a user name here, unless you want to change your user name. Your network name will be displayed here, and you can press CTRL-BACK-SPACE to delete it and enter a new name. If you enter a new name here, it overrides your network user name. If your network does not support user names, you can enter a name here that will be in effect whenever you start Paradox.

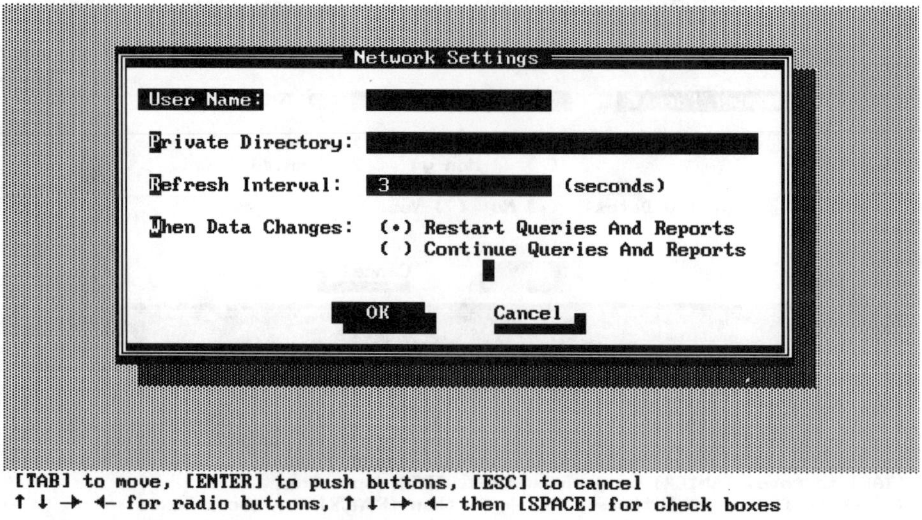

Figure B-22.   *Network Settings dialog box*

- *Private Directory* allows you to change your private directory. Refer to Chapter 14 for additional information about private directories. Each user on a network must have a private directory where temporary tables, such as Answer and Crosstab, are stored. In the text box following **P**rivate Directory, press CTRL-BACKSPACE to delete the current name, and type the path and directory name of your private directory.

- *Refresh Interval* allows you to set the amount of time between each time Paradox updates your display of shared data. The default is 3 seconds. Press CTRL-BACKSPACE to delete the current entry and enter a new time. You can enter any interval between 1 and 3600, which is one hour.

- *When Data Changes* allows you to specify whether queries and reports will be restarted when Paradox detects data changes. The default is Restart Queries and Reports. You can choose Continue Queries and Reports to eliminate the process of restarting when changes in data are detected.

3. When finished, choose OK to save the changes, or choose Cancel to leave without saving the changes.

Changing PAL Features

The PAL features that can be changed include showing Calc field errors, entering an error string that will be displayed when there is an error in a calculated field, linking the Script Editor to your own text editor, and linking the Blob Editor to your own Blob editor.

To change these features, follow these steps:

1. Choose **PAL** from the CCP menu. A PAL dialog box appears, as shown in Figure B-23.

2. Change the following by moving to the field or clicking on the choice to display a dot (.) in parentheses; or enter the appropriate information in the text box following the field:

    - *Show Calc Field Errors* allows you to specify that Paradox display an error message when an error occurs in a calculated field. The default is to not display an error message.

    - *Error String* allows you to enter the characters that will be displayed in a calculated field whenever an error occurs. Set Show Calc Field Errors at Yes when you enter characters here. If you set Show Calc Field Errors at No, you won't see your error string. If you don't enter an error string,

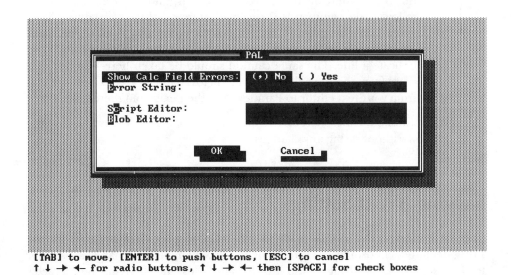

Figure B-23.   *PAL dialog box*

you will get the string error if Show Calc Field Errors is on and an error occurs.

- *Script Editor* allows you to enter the name of a text editor that you want to use to edit scripts. This would replace the Paradox Editor, and access a different text editor automatically whenever you want to edit a script. This text editor would also be used when you press CTRL-E to access the Editor window during a PAL debugging session. You would not be able to use this text editor for text files or for editing memo fields. Enter the DOS command used to start your text editor in the box directly following the prompt. If your editor can accept a DOS command that brings up a text file, this command should be followed by an asterisk (*). For example, enter **wp *** to link to WordPerfect, and to bring up the script that is current or that is currently being debugged. For example, type **wp * **** to make the current script line available in the text editor. You can get maximum memory if you add an exclamation point in front of the command like this: **!wp * ****. This will not only make the maximum amount of memory available, but will also bring up the current script line in the text editor.

Because Paradox is suspended when you go to your editor, you risk losing data if you do not return to Paradox. However, there should not be any problem as long as you quit your editor in the usual way. Quitting automatically returns you to Paradox.

- *Blob Editor* allows you to enter a command to access your own text editor (similar to using your text editor to edit scripts as discussed earlier). Type the DOS command that starts your editor, and enter an asterisk (*) following the command to bring up the binary field you are editing. Type an exclamation point (!) in front of the command to make the maximum amount of memory available. Do not use two asterisks (**) to indicate a line. The same caution should be taken here—do not shut down from the text editor—you might lose data in Paradox. Instead, exit from your text editor to Paradox, and then exit from there.

3. When finished, choose OK to save the changes, or choose Cancel to leave the window without saving any changes.

Changing ASCII Settings

The ASCII changes that can be made include changing the character used for the string delimiter, choosing what is to be delimited, changing the character used for the field separator, specifying how to export blank fields, and changing the character used for a decimal point.

To make these changes, follow these steps:

1. Choose **ASCII** from the CCP menu. An ASCII Export/Import Settings dialog box appears, as shown in Figure B-24.

2. Change any of the following:

   - *String Delimiter* allows you to specify a character other than the default character, which is the double quotation ("). Move to the box following the prompt and type the character you want to be used for the delimiter. You cannot leave the field blank, nor can you enter a space. When Paradox imports a file, it recognizes either the double quotation mark (") or the single quotation mark ('). If a different delimiter is to be used, you need to make that character the default here.

   - *Delimit* allows you to specify what is to be delimited—Strings Only or All Fields. Press ALT-D or TAB and then move to the field you want or click on the field to enter a dot (.) in the parentheses.

   - *Field Separator* allows you to specify the character that is to be used to separate fields in ASCII files. The default is the comma (,). You can enter any character except tabs; however, you cannot leave a blank space. Press ALT-F or TAB to select **Field Separator**.

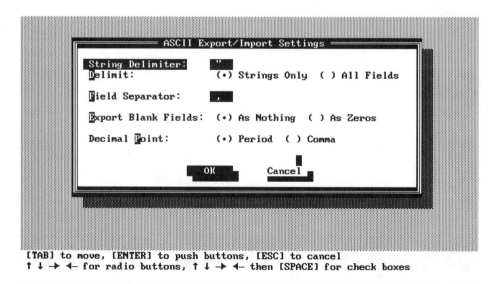

[TAB] to move, [ENTER] to push buttons, [ESC] to cancel
↑ ↓ → ← for radio buttons, ↑ ↓ → ← then [SPACE] for check boxes

Figure B-24. *ASCII Export/Import Settings dialog box*

- *Export Blank Fields* allows you to choose between exporting blank fields filled with zeros, or exporting blank fields with nothing in them. Some programs require values in fields—they do not allow you to leave them blank. Press ALT-E or TAB, and move to the field you want, or click on it to display a dot (.) in parentheses.

- *Decimal Point* allows you to change the character used for a decimal point. The default is a period (.). Your other choice here is a comma (,). Press ALT-P or TAB, and then click on the field or press an arrow key to move to the field and show a dot (.) in parentheses to choose it. Some programs that export data use a non-U.S. convention, which calls for a comma in place of a decimal point. If you are importing from such a program, you will need to specify a comma in this field.

3. When finished, choose OK to save the changes, or choose Cancel to leave the window without saving the changes.

Appendix **C**

ASCII and Extended ASCII Character Sets

Dec	Hex	ASCII Symbol	Control Code	Ctrl Key	Dec	Hex	ASCII Symbol	Control Code	Ctrl Key
0	00		NUL	^@	16	10	▶	DLE	^P
1	01	☺	SOH	^A	17	11	◀	DC1	^Q
2	02	☻	STX	^B	18	12	↕	DC2	^R
3	03	♥	ETX	^C	19	13	‼	DC3	^S
4	04	♦	EOT	^D	20	14	¶	DC4	^T
5	05	♣	ENQ	^E	21	15	§	NAK	^U
6	06	♠	ACK	^F	22	16	▬	SYN	^V
7	07	•	BEL	^G	23	17	↨	ETB	^W
8	08	◘	BS	^H	24	18	↑	CAN	^X
9	09	○	HT	^I	25	19	↓	EM	^Y
10	0A	◙	LF	^J	26	1A	→	SUB	^Z
11	0B	♂	VT	^K	27	1B	←	ESC	^[
12	0C	♀	FF	^L	28	1C	∟	FS	^\
13	0D	♪	CR	^M	29	1D	↔	GS	^]
14	0E	♫	SO	^N	30	1E	▲	RS	^ ^
15	0F	☼	SI	^O	31	1F	▼	US	^_

Dec	Hex	ASCII Symbol	Dec	Hex	ASCII Symbol
32	20		71	47	G
33	21	!	72	48	H
34	22	"	73	49	I
35	23	#	74	4A	J
36	24	$	75	4B	K
37	25	%	76	4C	L
38	26	&	77	4D	M
39	27	'	78	4E	N
40	28	(	79	4F	O
41	29	)	80	50	P
42	2A	*	81	51	Q
43	2B	+	82	52	R
44	2C	,	83	53	S
45	2D	-	84	54	T
46	2E	.	85	55	U
47	2F	/	86	56	V
48	30	0	87	57	W
49	31	1	88	58	X
50	32	2	89	59	Y
51	33	3	90	5A	Z
52	34	4	91	5B	[
53	35	5	92	5C	\
54	36	6	93	5D	]
55	37	7	94	5E	^
56	38	8	95	5F	_
57	39	9	96	60	`
58	3A	:	97	61	a
59	3B	;	98	62	b
60	3C	<	99	63	c
61	3D	=	100	64	d
62	3E	>	101	65	e
63	3F	?	102	66	f
64	40	@	103	67	g
65	41	A	104	68	h
66	42	B	105	69	i
67	43	C	106	6A	j
68	44	D	107	6B	k
69	45	E	108	6C	l
70	46	F	109	6D	m

Dec	Hex	ASCII Symbol
110	6E	n
111	6F	o
112	70	p
113	71	q
114	72	r
115	73	s
116	74	t
117	75	u
118	76	v
119	77	w
120	78	x
121	79	y
122	7A	z
123	7B	{
124	7C	|
125	7D	}
126	7E	~
127	7F	⌂
128	80	Ç
129	81	ü
130	82	é
131	83	â
132	84	ä
133	85	à
134	86	å
135	87	ç
136	88	ê
137	89	ë
138	8A	è
139	8B	ï
140	8C	î
141	8D	ì
142	8E	Ä
143	8F	Å
144	90	É
145	91	æ
146	92	Æ
147	93	ô
148	94	ö
149	95	ò
150	96	û
151	97	ù
152	98	ÿ
153	99	Ö
154	9A	Ü
155	9B	¢
156	9C	£
157	9D	¥
158	9E	Pt
159	9F	*f*
160	A0	á
161	A1	í
162	A2	ó
163	A3	ú
164	A4	ñ
165	A5	Ñ
166	A6	ª
167	A7	º
168	A8	¿
169	A9	⌐
170	AA	¬
171	AB	½
172	AC	¼
173	AD	¡
174	AE	<<
175	AF	>>
176	B0	░
177	B1	▒
178	B2	▓
179	B3	│
180	B4	┤
181	B5	╡
182	B6	╢
183	B7	╖
184	B8	╕
185	B9	╣
186	BA	║
187	BB	╗

Dec	Hex	ASCII Symbol	Dec	Hex	ASCII Symbol
188	BC	╝	222	DE	▐
189	BD	╜	223	DF	▀
190	BE	╛	224	E0	α
191	BF	┐	225	E1	β
192	C0	└	226	E2	Γ
193	C1	┴	227	E3	π
194	C2	┬	228	E4	Σ
195	C3	├	229	E5	σ
196	C4	─	230	E6	μ
197	C5	┼	231	E7	τ
198	C6	╞	232	E8	φ
199	C7	╟	233	E9	θ
200	C8	╚	234	EA	Ω
201	C9	╔	235	EB	δ
202	CA	╩	236	EC	∞
203	CB	╦	237	ED	∅
204	CC	╠	238	EE	∈
205	CD	═	239	EF	∩
206	CE	╬	240	F0	≡
207	CF	╧	241	F1	±
208	D0	╨	242	F2	≥
209	D1	╤	243	F3	≤
210	D2	╥	244	F4	⌠
211	D3	╙	245	F5	⌡
212	D4	╘	246	F6	÷
213	D5	╒	247	F7	≈
214	D6	╓	248	F8	°
215	D7	╫	249	F9	•
216	D8	╪	250	FA	·
217	D9	┘	251	FB	√
218	DA	┌	252	FC	η
219	DB	█	253	FD	^{2}
220	DC	▄	254	FE	■
221	DD	▌	255	FF	

Appendix D

Command Index

FUNCTION/DESCRIPTION	MENU PATH/SHORTCUT KEY	REFER TO
3.5 to 4.0 Compatibility		
Switch from 4 to 3.5 mode	System/Interface	Chapter 2
Choose file format default	System/Utilities/Custom/ Standard Settings, File Format	Appendix B
Choose system default	System/Utilities/Custom/ Standard Settings, Interface	Appendix B
About Paradox		
Copyright, release information	System/About	Chapter 2
Add New Records		
Add new records to a table	Modify/DataEntry	Chapter 5
Add records while editing	Modify/Edit or CoEdit, INSERT	Chapter 5
Records to multiple tables	Modify/MultiEntry	Chapter 6
ASCII Settings		
Set delimiter, separators	System/Utilities/Custom/ASCII	Appendix B
Ask a Question		
Seek information in tables	Ask	Chapter 6
Insert example element	F5 (Query Form only)	Chapter 6

FUNCTION/DESCRIPTION	MENU PATH/SHORTCUT KEY	REFER TO
Ask a Question (*cont.*)		
Select field/Insert checkmarks	F6 (Query Form only)	Chapter 6
GroupBy field, do not display it	SHIFT-F6 (Query Form only)	Chapter 6
Select field & show duplicates	ALT-F6 (Query Form only, CheckPlus)	Chapter 6
Select field & sort descending	CTRL-F6 (Query Form only, CheckDescending)	Chapter 6
Cancel	*See* Empty	
Cascade Windows	*See* Windows	
Clear		
Clear active window	F8 or CTRL-F8	Chapter 3
Clear desktop	ALT-F8	Chapter 3
Close Window		
Cancel and close	System/**C**lose or CTRL-F8 or CTRL-BREAK	Chapter 2
Copy		
Copy objects	**T**ools/**C**opy	Chapter 2
Crosstabs	*See* Graphs	
CTRL-BREAK Settings		
Enable/Disable CTRL-BREAK key	System/**U**tilities/**C**ustom/**S**tandard Settings/**D**isable break	Appendix B
Custom Configuration Program		
Change Paradox with CCP	System/**U**tilities/**C**ustom	Appendix B
Use CCP with script	**S**cripts/**P**lay, type **custom**	Appendix B
Data Entry		
Enter data in Edit/CoEdit	**M**odify/**E**dit or **C**oEdit or F9 or ALT-F9	Chapter 3
Enter data not in Edit/CoEdit	**M**odify/**D**ataEntry	Chapter 3
Enter data in multiple tables	**M**odify/**M**ultiEntry	Chapter 6

FUNCTION/DESCRIPTION	MENU PATH/SHORTCUT KEY	REFER TO
Data Entry (*cont.*)		
Use a form for data entry	**I**mage/**P**ickForm for custom form or F7 for standard form	Chapter 7
Date, Number Format Standards		
Set date, number formatting	System/**U**tilities/**C**ustom /**F**ormat Data	Appendix B
Change date format in table	**I**mage/**F**ormat	Chapter 9
Delete		
Delete objects	**T**ools/**D**elete	Chapter 2
Delete another table's records	*See* Tables	
Delete all records from a table	*See* Empty	
Delete one record	Press DELETE	Chapter 3
Delete line from cursor on	CTRL-Y (in Report Designer)	Chapter 8
Delete whole line	CTRL-Y (in Editor)	Chapter 4
Delete from cursor to end of word	ALT-D (in Editor)	Chapter 4
Directory		
Set permanently	System/**U**tilities/**C**ustom/ **S**tandard Settings	Chapter 2
Set temporarily	**T**ools/**M**ore/**D**irectory	Chapters 1, 2
DOS		
Use DOS within Paradox	**T**ools/**M**ore/**T**oDOS or	Chapter 2
	CTRL-O or ALT-O (DOSBIG, for more memory)	Chapter 1
Edit Records		
Edit, one or more users	**M**odify/**C**oEdit or ALT-F9	Chapter 3
Edit, replace key violations	**M**odify/**E**dit or F9	Chapter 3
Edit, save key violations	**M**odify/**C**oEdit	Chapter 3
Edit memo fields	CTRL-F or ALT-F5	Chapter 4

FUNCTION/DESCRIPTION	MENU PATH/SHORTCUT KEY	REFER TO
Editor		
Invoke text editor	System/**E**ditor	Chapter 4
Invoke script editor	**S**cripts/**E**ditor	Chapters 10, 12
Invoke Editor	ALT-E	Chapters 4, 12
Create new text file	System/**E**ditor/**N**ew	Chapter 4
Edit existing file	System/**E**ditor/**O**pen	Chapter 4
Invoke Field View/Edit	CTRL-F or ALT-F5	Chapter 2
Empty		
Cancel, close windows	System/**D**esktop/**E**mpty	Chapter 2
Close a window	System/**C**lose	Chapter 1
Close all images	ALT-F8	Chapters 2, 3
Close any window	CTRL-F8	Chapters 2, 3
Empty a table of records	**T**ools/**M**ore/**E**mpty	Chapter 14
Exit		
Leave Paradox	**E**xit/**Y**es	Chapter 2
Export		
Export a file	**T**ools/**E**xportImport/**E**xport	Chapter 14
Fields		
Alter field size, type, position	Modify/**R**estructure	Chapter 5
Delete a field from a table	**M**odify/**R**estructure, DELETE	Chapter 5
Add a new field to a table	**M**odify/**R**estructure, INSERT	Chapter 5
Change key fields	**M**odify/**R**estructure	Chapter 5
Change field format	**I**mage/**F**ormat	Chapter 9
Rotate fields to the right	CTRL-R (Rotate)	Chapter 9
Repeat prior field value	CTRL-D (Ditto)	Chapter 3
Move fields in an image	**I**mage/**M**ove	Chapter 9
Edit	F9	Chapter 3
CoEdit	ALT-F9	Chapter 3
Find/Search	*See* Zoom	
Forms		
Display the standard form	F7	Chapter 7

FUNCTION/DESCRIPTION	MENU PATH/SHORTCUT KEY	REFER TO

Forms (*cont.*)

Choose custom form for display	**Image/PickForm**	Chapter 9
Design a form	**Forms/Design**	Chapter 7
Modify a form	**Forms/Change**	Chapter 7
Display/Hide color palette	ALT-C (in Form Designer, Style/Color)	

Graphs

Change default graph settings	**System/Utilities/Custom/ Graphs**	Chapter 9
Produce an instant graph	CTRL-F7	Chapter 9
Alter graph settings	**Image/Graph/Modify** (temporary without Save)	Chapter 9
Save graph settings(in .G)	**Image/Graph/Save**	Chapter 9
Save graph image	**Image/Graph/ViewGraph/ File**	Chapter 9
Retrieve graph setting (.G file)	**Image/Graph/Load**	Chapter 9
Display graph onscreen	**Image/Graph/ViewGraph/ Screen**	Chapter 9
Print graph	**Image/Graph/ViewGraph/ Printer**	Chapter 9
Restore graph default settings	**Image/Graph/Reset**	Chapter 9
Convert table to crosstab table	**Image/Graph/Crosstab** or ALT-X	Chapter 9

Help

Context-sensitive help	F1	Chapter 2
Index of subjects	F1, F1	Chapter 2

Images

Change screen image	**Image**	Chapter 9
Toggle form, table views	F7	Chapter 7
Resize any window	**System/Size/Move** or use mouse on Resize corner or use CTRL-F5 and SHIFT-Arrow keys	Chapter 2

FUNCTION/DESCRIPTION	MENU PATH/SHORTCUT KEY	REFER TO
Images (*cont.*)		
Maximize/Restore a window	System/**M**aximize/Restore or use SHIFT-F5 or use mouse (double-click on frame, click on icon)	Chapter 2
Resize a table view window	Image/**T**ableSize	Chapter 9
Resize while editing tables	**M**odify/**E**dit or **C**oEdit/**I**mage	Chapter 5
Alter column size in table view	Image/**C**olumnSize	Chapter 9
Change field format	Image/**F**ormat	Chapters 5, 9
Move fields temporarily	Image/**M**ove or CTRL-R and use arrow keys	Chapter 9
Move fields permanently	**M**odify/**R**estructure	Chapter 5
Rotate field to the right	CTRL-R	Chapter 9
Import		
Import a file	**T**ools/**E**xportImport/**I**mport	Chapter 14
Indexes		
List secondary indexes	*See* Info	
Create secondary index	**M**odify/**I**ndex or Image/**O**rderTable or **T**ools/**Q**uerySpeed or cursor on field, ALT-S	Chapter 5 Chapter 9 Chapter 14 Chapter 5
Change key fields	**M**odify/**R**estructure	Chapter 5
Info		
List structure of table (Struct)	**T**ools/**I**nfo/**S**tructure	Chapter 14
List files, tables, or scripts	**T**ools/**I**nfo/**I**nventory	Chapter 14
List table's family	**T**ools/**I**nfo/**F**amily	Chapter 14
List network users	**T**ools/**I**nfo/**W**ho	Chapter 14
List all network locks in use	**T**ools/**I**nfo/**L**ock	Chapter 14
List secondary indexes	**T**ools/**I**nfo/**T**ableIndex	Chapter 14

FUNCTION/DESCRIPTION	MENU PATH/SHORTCUT KEY	REFER TO
Interface Standards		
Set defaults for 3.5 or 4	System/**U**tilities/**C**ustom/ **S**tandard Settings/**I**nterface	Appendix B
Keep Stuff		
Save image settings in .SET	**I**mage/**K**eepSet	Chapters 5, 9
Save Entry table in DataEntry	**K**eepEntry	Chapter 3
Key Fields		
Change key fields	**M**odify/**R**estructure	Chapter 5
View records with key violations	ALT-K	Chapter 3
Resynch records after key change	CTRL-L	Chapter 3
List Users/Info	*See* Info	
Machine Information		
List hardware info	System/**U**tilities/**C**ustom/ **M**achine Info	Appendix B
Macros	*See* Scripts	
Maximize Window		
Full size window	System/**M**aximize/**R**estore or SHIFT-F5	Chapter 2
Menus		
Display Main menu	F10	Chapter 1
Display PAL menu	ALT-F10	Chapter 12
Display System menu	ALT-SPACEBAR	Chapter 1
Merge		
Merge one or more tables	**T**ools/**M**ore/**A**dd	Chapter 14
Merge records to two or more tables	**T**ools/**M**ore/**M**ultiAdd or use current multitable forms **T**ools/**M**ore/**F**ormAdd	Chapter 14
Mouse Settings		
Set mouse default settings	System/**U**tilities/**C**ustom/ **S**tandard Settings/**M**ouse	Appendix B

FUNCTION/DESCRIPTION	MENU PATH/SHORTCUT KEY	REFER TO
Move		
Move window	System/**S**ize/**M**ove	Chapter 2
Move fields temporarily	**I**mage/**M**ove (CTRL-R to rotate)	Chapter 9
Move fields permanently	**M**odify/**R**estructure	Chapter 5
Network		
Set network defaults	System/**U**tilities/**C**ustom/**N**etwork	Appendix B
List network users	*See* Info	
Refresh screen with net changes	ALT-R	Chapter 14
Lock or unlock a table	**T**ools/**N**et/**L**ock	Chapter 14
Lock a record	ALT-L	Chapter 3
Prevent or unprevent a lock	**T**ools/**N**et/**P**reventLock	Chapter 14
Set temporary private directory or permanent directory	**T**ools/**N**et/**P**rivateSet or System/**U**tilities/**C**ustom/**N**etwork	Chapter 14 Appendix B
Set temporary user name or permanent name default	**T**ools/**N**et/**U**serName or System/**U**tilities/**C**ustom/**N**etwork	Chapter 14 Appendix B
Set screen refresh frequency or permanent default	**T**ools/**N**et/**A**utoRefresh or System/**U**tilities/**C**ustom/**N**etwork	Chapter 14 Appendix B
Restart queries if user changes	**T**ools/**N**et/**C**hanges/**R**estart	Chapter 14
Continue queries with changes	**T**ools/**N**et/**C**hanges/**C**ontinue	Chapter 14
PAL Settings		
Set PAL standards	System/**U**tilities/**C**ustom/**P**AL	Appendix B
Paradox Application Workshop (previously Personal Programmer)		
Workshop programming tools	System/**U**tilities/**W**orkshop	Chapter 11

FUNCTION/DESCRIPTION	MENU PATH/SHORTCUT KEY	REFER TO
Paradox Standard Defaults (overall system settings)		
Change default settings	System/**U**tilities/**C**ustom/ **S**tandard Settings	Chapter 1, Appendix B
Paradox Version, Copyright Info		
View current Paradox status	System/**A**bout	Chapter 1
Password	*See* Protect	
Printer Default Settings		
Set port, setup string, and so on	Report/**S**etPrinter	Chapter 8
Override default settings	**R**eport/**S**etPrinter/**O**verride	Chapter 8
Protect		
Set a password on a table	**T**ools/**M**ore/**P**rotect/**P**assword	Chapter 14
Remove all passwords from a table	**T**ools/**M**ore/**P**rotect/ **C**lear-Passwords	Chapter 14
Remove one password from a table	**T**ools/**M**ore/**P**rotect/**P**assword (enter old password, repeat, leave password blank)	Chapter 14
Write-protect a table	**T**ools/**M**ore/**P**rotect/ **W**riteProtect	Chapter 14
Query		
Query a table or tables	**A**sk	Chapter 6
Redraw Window		
Redraw or refresh window	System/**D**esktop/**R**edraw	Chapter 2
Refresh network changes	ALT-R	Chapter 14
Rename		
Rename objects	**T**ools/**R**ename	Chapter 2
Rename fields	**M**odify/**R**estructure	Chapter 5
Repeat Find/Search	*See* **Z**oomNext	
Reporting		
Print a report to the screen	**R**eport/**O**utput/**S**creen	Chapter 8

FUNCTION/DESCRIPTION	MENU PATH/SHORTCUT KEY	REFER TO
Reporting (*cont.*)		
Print a report to a printer	**R**eport/**O**utput/**P**rinter	Chapter 8
Print a report to disk	**R**eport/**O**utput/**F**ile	Chapter 8
Produce instant report	ALT-F7	Chapter 8
Create a crosstab	ALT-X	Chapter 9
Design a report	**R**eport/**D**esign	Chapter 8
Display/Hide vertical ruler	CTRL-V	Chapter 8
Modify a report spec	**R**eport/**C**hange	Chapter 8
Preview a report	**R**eport/**R**angeOutput or **R**eport/**O**utput/**S**creen	Chapter 8
Print selected pages	**R**eport/**R**angeOutput	Chapter 8
Printer default setting	**R**eport/**S**etPrinter	Chapter 8
Report Designer Settings		
Change default settings	System/**U**tilities/**C**ustom/**R**eports	Appendix B
Resize Window		
Resize a window	System/**S**ize/Move or CTRL-F5, resize with SHIFT and ARROW keys	Chapter 2
Resize a table view window	Image/**T**ableSize	Chapter 9
Resize while editing tables	**M**odify/**E**dit or **C**oEdit/**I**mage	Chapter 5
Restructure a Table		
Change the table structure	**M**odify/**R**estructure	Chapter 5
Make structure as another	**M**odify/**R**estructure/**B**orrow	Chapter 5
Update table objects	**M**odify/**R**estructure/**J**ustFamily	Chapter 5
Reformat 3.5 or 4	**M**odify/**R**estructure/**F**ileFormat	Chapter 5
Retrieve a Table		
Retrieve and view tables	**V**iew	Chapter 3
Run second script while recording	**S**cripts/**B**eginRecord menu, **P**lay	Chapter 10
Save		
Save entries	F2 (Do-It!)	Chapter 3

FUNCTION/DESCRIPTION	MENU PATH/SHORTCUT KEY	REFER TO
Save (*cont.*)		
Save a newly recorded script	**S**cripts/**B**eginRecord menu, EndRecord	Chapter 10
Set frequency for disk save	**S**ystem/**U**tilities/**C**ustom/ **S**tandard Settings/**A**utosave	Chapter 2, Appendix B
Save data entry table	**M**odify/**D**ataEntry/**K**eepEntry	Chapter 3
Save image settings in .SET	**I**mage/**K**eepSet	Chapter 9
Scripts		
Edit a script	**S**cripts/**E**ditor	Chapter 10
Print a script	Editor menu/**F**ile/**P**rint	
Run or play a script	**S**cripts/**P**lay	Chapter 10
Run an instant script	ALT-F4	Chapter 10
Repeat running a script	**S**cripts/**R**epeatPlay	Chapter 10
Show execution while running	**S**cripts/**S**howPlay	Chapter 10
Create or record a script	**S**cripts/**B**eginRecord or ALT-F3 (Begin/End toggle for instant script)	Chapter 10
Stop recording a script	**S**cripts/**E**ndRecord	Chapter 10
Search/Find	*See* Zoom	
Secondary Index	*See* Indexes	
Sort Records		
Sort records in a table	**M**odify/**S**ort	Chapter 5
or for temporary sort	**I**mage/**O**rderTable (needs secondary index)	Chapter 9
Sort on secondary index	ALT-S	Chapter 5
Speedup Queries		
Speedup query searches	**T**ools/**Q**uerySpeed	Chapter 14
SurfaceQueries		
Bring query window to top	**S**ystem/**D**esktop/ **S**urfaceQueries	Chapter 2
Switch Forms		
Change forms	**I**mage/**P**ickForm	Chapter 9

FUNCTION/DESCRIPTION	MENU PATH/SHORTCUT KEY	REFER TO
Switch Windows		
Move between windows	System/**W**indow or	Chapter 2
	CTRL-F4 or	Chapter 2
	use mouse, click on window frames	Chapter 2
System Menu	*See* Menus	
Tables		
Create a new table	**C**reate	Chapter 3
Create a similar structure	**C**reate/**B**orrow	Chapter 3
Create 3.5 or 4 format	**C**reate/**F**ileFormat	Chapter 3
Restructure a table	**M**odify/**R**estructure	Chapter 5
List info about table and objects	**T**ools/**I**nfo (*see also* Info)	Chapter 14
Remove another table's records	**T**ools/**M**ore/**S**ubtract	Chapter 14
Empty a table of records	*See* Empty	
Tile Windows	*See* Windows	
Undo		
Undo an action	/**U**ndo or CTRL-U	Chapter 3
Validity Checks		
Set validity checks	**M**odify/**D**ataEntry/**V**alCheck	Chapter 3
Set validity checks in Edit	**M**odify/**E**dit/**V**alCheck	Chapter 3
Video Settings		
Set video type, settings	System/**U**tilities/**C**ustom/**V**ideo	Appendix B
Change or set settings, color	System/**U**tilities/**C**ustom/**V**ideo	Appendix B
View One or More Tables		
Retrieve and view tables	**V**iew	Chapter 3
Windows		
Switch to bottom window	System/**N**ext	Chapter 2
Show previous image on stack	F3	Chapter 3
Show next image on stack	F4	Chapter 3

FUNCTION/DESCRIPTION	MENU PATH/SHORTCUT KEY	REFER TO
Windows (*cont.*)		
Show next window	CTRL-F4	
Arrange cascaded windows	System/**D**esktop/**C**ascade	Chapter 2
Arrange tiled windows	System/**D**esktop/**T**ile	Chapter 2
Close, clear window	*See* Clear	
Other window options, tasks	*See* Image	
Zoom		
Find record number in table	**I**mage/**Z**oom/**R**ecord	Chapter 9
Find field in current record	**I**mage/**Z**oom/**F**ield	Chapter 9
Find field value in a table	**I**mage/**Z**oom/**V**alue or CTRL-Z	Chapter 9
Find field value faster	**T**ools/**Q**uerySpeed	Chapter 14
ZoomNext		
Repeat **I**mage/**Z**oom/**V**alue	ALT-Z	Chapter 9

Index

COMMAND CARD

Key	In Menu	In Table (View, Edit/CoEdit)	In Field (View, Edit)	In Form (View, Edit/CoEdit)	In Form Design	In Report Design	In Report Previewer	In Editor	In Query Form
F1	Help	Help	Help	Help	Help	Help	Help	Help	Help
F2	Do-It!	Do-It!	Do-It!	Do-It!	Do-It!	Do-It!	Do-It!	Do-It!	Do-It!
F3		Previous Image	Previous Image	Previous Image				Previous Image	Previous Image
F4	Next Image	Next Image	Next Image	Next Image				Next Image	Next Image
F5									Example element
F6									Checkmark
F7	Form toggle (when table is on desktop)	Form toggle	Form toggle	Form toggle					
F8	Clear active window	Clear active window		Clear active window					Clear active window
F9		Edit	Edit	Edit					
F10	Menu	Menu	Menu	Menu	Menu	Menu	Menu	Menu	Menu
Alt-F3	Record instant script	Record instant script	Record instant script	Record instant script	Record instant script	Record instant script	Record instant script	Record instant script	Record instant script
Alt-F4	Run instant script	Run instant script	Run instant script	Run instant script	Run instant script	Run instant script	Run instant script	Run instant script	Run instant script
Alt-F5	Field view (in Memo field Editor is used)	Field view (in Memo field Editor is used)	Field view (in Memo field Editor is used)	Field view (in Memo field Editor is used)				In Memo field returns to table	In Memo field returns to table
Alt-F6	Run instant script	Run instant script	Run instant script	Run instant script	Run instant script	Run instant script	Run instant script	Run instant script	Run instant script
Alt-F7	Record instant script	Record instant script	Record instant script	Record instant script	Record instant script	Record instant script	Record instant script	Record instant script	Record instant script
Alt-F8	Close active window	Close active window							
Alt-F9		CoEdit	CoEdit	CoEdit					CoEdit
Ctrl-F6	Instant report (print)	Instant report (print)	Instant report (print)	Instant report (print)		Print report	Print report		CheckPlus
Ctrl-F7	Close All image windows	Close All image windows	Close All image windows	Close All image windows				Close All windows (except Editor)	Close All windows
Ctrl-F8									CheckDescending
Shift-F5	Move/Size window	Move/Size window	Move/Size window	Move/Size window	Move/Size window	Move/Size window	Move/Size window	Move/Size window	Move/Size window
Shift-F6	Maximize/Restore window	Maximize/Restore window	Maximize/Restore window	Maximize/Restore window	Maximize/Restore window	Maximize/Restore window	Maximize/Restore window	Maximize/Restore window	Maximize/Restore window
(Close window)	Close window	Close window	Close window	Close window	Close window	Close window	Close window	Close window	Close window
Alt-Spacebar	System menu	System menu	System menu	System menu	System menu	System menu	System menu	System menu	System menu
Alt-C	Instant graph	Instant graph	Instant graph	Instant graph	Toggle color palette				
Alt-D								Delete word right	GroupBy
Alt-E	Invoke Editor	Invoke Editor	Invoke Editor	Invoke Editor	Invoke Editor	Invoke Editor	Invoke Editor	Invoke Editor	Invoke Editor
Alt-K		View Keyviol records (in Edit)	View Keyviol records (in Edit)	View Keyviol records (not in Edit)					
Alt-L	Lock toggle (not in Edit)	Lock toggle (not in Edit)		Lock toggle (not in Edit)					
Alt-O	DOSBIG	DOSBIG	DOSBIG	DOSBIG	DOSBIG	DOSBIG	DOSBIG	DOSBIG	DOSBIG
Alt-R	Refresh screen with network changes	Refresh screen with network changes	Refresh screen with network changes	Refresh screen with network changes					Refresh screen with network changes
Alt-S	Create, sort on secondary index (in Main mode)	Create, sort on secondary index (in Main mode)	Create, sort on secondary index (in Main mode)						Create, sort on secondary index (in Main mode)
Alt-X	Create crosstab (in Main mode)	Create crosstab (in Main mode)	Create crosstab (in Main mode)						Create crosstab (in Main mode)
Alt-Z	Zoom Next	Zoom Next	Zoom Next	Zoom Next				Zoom Next	Zoom Next
Ctrl-D	Ditto (repeat value)	Ditto (repeat value)	Ditto (repeat value)	Ditto (repeat value)				Ditto (repeat value)	Ditto (repeat value)
Ctrl-F	Field view (in Memo field goes to Editor)	Field view (in Memo field goes to Editor)	Field view (in Memo field goes to Editor)	Field view (in Memo field goes to Editor)				In Memo field returns to table	In Memo field returns to table
Ctrl-L	Resynch detail records	Resynch detail records	Resynch detail records	Resynch detail records					Resynch detail records

© Martin S. Matthews and Carole Boggs Matthews

COMMAND CARD

Key	In Menu	In Table View Edit/CoEdit	In Field View Edit	In Form View Edit/CoEdit	In Form Design	In Report Design	In Report Previewer	In Editor	In Query Form
Ctrl-O	Go to DOS	Go to DOS	Go to DOS	Go to DOS	Go to DOS	Go to DOS	Go to DOS	Go to DOS	Go to DOS
Ctrl-R		Rotate field							Rotate field
Ctrl-U		Undo		Undo					
Ctrl-V						Toggle vertical ruler			
Ctrl-Y						Delete from cursor to end of line		Delete line	
Ctrl-Z	Zoom	Zoom		Zoom				Zoom	
Home		First record	Beginning of field	First record	First line	First line	Scroll left	First character of line	
End		Last record	End of field	Last record	Last line	Last line	Scroll right	Last character of line	
↑	One command up in pull-down menu	One record up	One line up in wrapped field	Previous field	One line up	One line up	Scroll up one line	One line up	One line up
→	One command down in pull-down menu	One record down	One line down in wrapped field	Next field	One line down	One line down	Scroll down one line	One line down	One line down
←	One command left	Previous field	Previous character in field	Previous field (up)	One character left	One character left	Scroll left one character	One character left	Previous field
↑	One command right	Next field	Next character in field	Next field down	One character right	One character right	Scroll right one character	One character right	Next field
Pg Up		One screen up		Previous page/record	One screen up	One screen up	Scroll one screen up	One screen up	One screen left
Pg Dn		One screen down		Next page/record	One screen down	One screen down	Scroll down one screen	One screen down	One screen right
Ctrl-Home		First field		First field	Beginning of line	Beginning of line	Beginning of report	First character in text	First field
Ctrl-End		Last field		Last field	End of line	End of line	End of report	Last character in text	Last field
Ctrl-←		One screen left	One word left in field		One screen left	One screen left		One word left	One screen left
Ctrl-→		One screen right	One word right in field		One screen right		One word right	One screen right
Ctrl-Pg Up				Same field, previous record			Beginning of report	First character in text	
Ctrl-Pg Dn				Same field, next record			End of report	Last character in text	
Ctrl-Break		Clear desktop and cancel task		Cancel	Cancel	Cancel	Cancel	Cancel	Clear desktop and cancel task
Shift-← or →								Select one row up or down	
Shift-← or ↑								Select one character to left or right	
Backspace	Delete text	Delete last character	Delete character to left	Delete last character	Delete character	Delete character		Delete character left	Delete character left
Delete		Delete record	Delete character	Delete record	Delete character	Delete character		Delete character	Delete character
Ins		New record	Toggle Overwrite/Insert	New record	Toggle Overwrite/Insert	Toggle Overwrite/Insert	Toggle Overwrite/Insert	Toggle Overwrite/Insert	
Ctrl-Backspace	Delete text	Delete field	Delete field	Delete field					Delete field's entry
Ctrl-Ins								Copy selected block to Clipboard	
Shift-Ins								Insert contents of Clipboard	
Shift-Delete								Delete selected block to Clipboard	
Enter	Choose command	Move to next field	End field view	Move to next field	Move to next line	Insert line		Insert line	Move to next field
Tab	Next field	Next field		Next field				Indent one tab stop	Next field
Shift-Tab	Previous field	Previous field		Previous field					Previous field
Esc	Return to previous menu/dialog box								

© Martin S. Matthews and Carole Boggs Matthews

Paradox 4: The Complete Reference